MULTISPECIES ARCHAEOLOGY

Multispecies Archaeology explores the issue of ecological and cultural novelty in the archaeological record from a multispecies perspective. Encompassing more than just our relationships with animals, the book considers what we can learn about the human past without humans as the focus of the question. The volume digs deep into our understanding of interaction with plants, fungi, microbes, and even the fundamental building blocks of life, DNA. *Multispecies Archaeology* examines what it means to be human—and non-human—from a variety of perspectives providing a new lens through which to view the past.

Suzanne E. Pilaar Birch is an Assistant Professor at the University of Georgia with a joint appointment in the departments of Anthropology and Geography. She combines zooarchaeology and biogeochemistry to investigate changes in diet, environment, mobility, and settlement systems spanning the late Pleistocene and early Holocene.

ARCHAEOLOGICAL ORIENTATIONS

Series Editors:
Gavin Lucas, *University of Iceland, Iceland*
Christopher Witmore, *Texas Tech University, USA*

An interdisciplinary series that engages our ongoing, yet ever-changing, fascination with the archaeological, *Archaeological Orientations* investigates the myriad ways material pasts are entangled with communities, animals, ecologies and technologies, past, present, or future. From urgent contemporary concerns, including politics, violence, sustainability, ecology, and technology, to long-standing topics of interest, including time, space, materiality, memory and agency, *Archaeological Orientations* promotes bold thinking and the taking of risks in pressing trans-disciplinary matters of concern.

Published volumes:

Ruin Memories: Materialities, Aesthetics and the Archaeology of the Recent Past
Ed. Bjørnar Olsen, Þóra Pétursdóttir

Elements of Architecture: Assembling Archaeology, Atmosphere and the Performance of Building Spaces
Ed. Mikkel Bille, Tim Flohr Sorensen

Reclaiming Archaeology: Beyond the Tropes of Modernity
Ed. Alfredo González-Ruibal

For more information on this series please visit:
https://www.routledge.com/Archaeological-Orientations/book-series/ARCHOR

MULTISPECIES ARCHAEOLOGY

Edited by Suzanne E. Pilaar Birch

LONDON AND NEW YORK

First published 2018
by Routledge
2 Park Square, Milton Park, Abingdon, Oxon OX14 4RN

and by Routledge
711 Third Avenue, New York, NY 10017

Routledge is an imprint of the Taylor & Francis Group, an informa business

© 2018 selection and editorial matter, Suzanne E. Pilaar Birch; individual chapters, the contributors

The right of Suzanne E. Pilaar Birch to be identified as the author of the editorial material, and of the authors for their individual chapters, has been asserted in accordance with sections 77 and 78 of the Copyright, Designs and Patents Act 1988.

All rights reserved. No part of this book may be reprinted or reproduced or utilised in any form or by any electronic, mechanical, or other means, now known or hereafter invented, including photocopying and recording, or in any information storage or retrieval system, without permission in writing from the publishers.

Trademark notice: Product or corporate names may be trademarks or registered trademarks, and are used only for identification and explanation without intent to infringe.

British Library Cataloguing-in-Publication Data
A catalogue record for this book is available from the British Library

Library of Congress Cataloging-in-Publication Data
A catalog record has been requested for this book

ISBN: 978-1-138-89898-1 (hbk)
ISBN: 978-1-315-70770-9 (ebk)

Typeset in Bembo
by Swales & Willis Ltd, Exeter, Devon, UK

CONTENTS

List of illustrations	*viii*
Notes on contributors	*xii*
Acknowledgements	*xiv*

Introduction	1
Suzanne E. Pilaar Birch	

PART I
Living in the Anthropocene   **9**

1	Calabrian hounds and roasted ivory (or, swerving from anthropocentrism) *Noah Heringman*	11
2	The end of the 'Neolithic'? At the emergence of the Anthropocene *Christopher Witmore*	26
3	Rehearsing the Anthropocene in microcosm: the palaeoenvironmental impacts of the Pacific rat (*Rattus exulans*) and other non-human species during island Neolithization *Thomas P. Leppard*	47
4	Trans-Holocene human impacts on California mussels (*Mytilus californianus*): historical ecological management implications from the Northern Channel Islands *Breana Campbell, Todd J. Braje, and Stephen G. Whitaker*	65
5	Drift *Þóra Pétursdóttir*	85

Contents

PART II
Multispecies ecology of the built environment 103

6 Symbiotic architectures 105
  Gavin Lucas

7 The eco-ecumene and multispecies history: the case of
  abandoned Protestant cemeteries in Poland 118
  Ewa Domanska

8 Ecologies of rock and art in northern New Mexico 133
  Benjamin Alberti and Severin Fowles

9 Oysters and mound-islands of Crystal River along the
  Central Gulf Coast of Florida 154
  Victor D. Thompson and Thomas J. Pluckhahn

10 Multispecies dynamics and the ecology of urban spaces
   in Roman antiquity 170
   Michael MacKinnon

11 Mammalian community assembly in ancient villages and
   towns in the Jordan Valley of Israel 183
   Nimrod Marom and Lior Weissbrod

PART III
Agrarian commitments: towards an archaeology of symbiosis 199

12 Animals and the Neolithic: cui bono? 201
   Terry O'Connor

13 Making space from the position of duty of care: Early Bronze
   Age human-sheep entanglements in Norway 214
   Kristin Armstrong Oma

14 The history of the human microbiome: insights from archaeology
   and ancient DNA 230
   Laura S. Weyrich

15 An archaeological telling of multispecies co-inhabitation:
   comments on the origins of agriculture and domestication
   narrative in Southwest Asia 251
   Brian Boyd

vi

PART IV
The ecology of movement — 271

16 Legs, feet *and* hooves: the seasonal roundup in Iceland — 273
Oscar Aldred

17 The rhythm of life: exploring the role of daily and seasonal rhythms in the development of human–nonhuman relationships in the British Early Mesolithic — 295
Nick J. Overton

18 Seasonal mobility and multispecies interactions in the Mesolithic northeastern Adriatic — 310
Suzanne E. Pilaar Birch

19 The role of ostrich in shaping the landscape use patterns of humans and hyenas on the southern coast of South Africa during the late Pleistocene — 333
Jamie Hodgkins, Petrus le Roux, Curtis W. Marean, Kirsty Penkman, Molly Crisp, Erich Fisher, and Julia Lee-Thorp

20 Prey species movements and migrations in ecocultural landscapes: reconstructing late Pleistocene herbivore seasonal spatial behaviours — 347
Kate Britton

Index — *368*

ILLUSTRATIONS

Figures

1.1	Pietro Fabris, "Excavation of the Temple of Isis at Pompeii" (1776)	14
1.2	Buffon 1780: 2.235 [Plate One]	17
1.3	Allan McCollum, *The Dog From Pompeii*, 1991. Cast glass-fiber-reinforced Hydrocal. Approximately 21 × 21 × 21 inches each. Replicas made from a mold taken from the famous original "chained dog" plaster cast of a dog smothered in ash from the explosion of Mount Vesuvius, in ancient Pompeii, in 79 AD	23
2.1	The upper portion Argive plain and its western mountains, seen from Mycenae	30
2.2	The canopied plain in 2014	32
2.3	Borehole irrigation pump located just west of Neo Ireo (Chronika), 2012	32
2.4	Cattle City, from the top of the feed mill, 2013	35
2.5	Cattle crowd the bunk to consume feed, 2013	36
3.1	Map of the Pacific Ocean showing most islands, island groups, and toponyms mentioned in the text	48
3.2	The Pacific or Polynesian rat (or *kiore*), *Rattus exulans*	53
3.3	The pollen diagram from Ordy Pond, 'Ewa Plain, O'ahu, from data first published in Athens *et al*. 2002, demonstrating profound floral change after ~ 950 cal BP	55
4.1	Watercolor of a *Mytilus californianus* shell with labels of several of the physiological features mentioned in the text	69
4.2	Map of the Northern Channel Islands showing the locations of archaeological sites and NPS monitoring localities where size data of California mussel shells were collected	71

Illustrations

4.3	Breana Campbell (right) and San Diego State graduate student Stephanie Duncan collecting size data at an archaeological shell midden on the west coast of Santa Cruz Island, January 2015	71
4.4	Trans-Holocene changes in mean California mussel shell length measurements for 16 Channel Island archaeological components compared to broad scale Holocene SST changes from the Santa Barbara Basin for the Early (10,000–7500 cal BP), Middle (7500–3500 cal BP), and Late Holocene (3500 cal BP–AD 1542)	76
6.1	Skálholt under excavation in 2004	107
6.2	*Epauloecus unicolor*	110
6.3	Species inter-relation diagram	111
6.4	Room ecology/anatomy	113
7.1	Evangelical cemetery in Trzciel, Poland	122
7.2	Evangelical cemetery in Trzciel, Poland	127
8.1	Map of the study area. The Rio Grande Gorge is indicated in dark gray	135
8.2	A temporary waterfall erupts from the "Kissing Fish" site (LA 102345) as a warm day in early spring melts the remaining snow	137
8.3	A boulder in the Rio Grande Gorge covered with pecked crosses	138
8.4	Names and dates in the Rio Grande Gorge at LA 102345	139
8.5	An Archaic panel (A) reinterpreted by a late pre-colonial artist on an adjacent Pueblo panel (B) at Site LA 75747	140
8.6	A boulder (A) hosting an Archaic panel (B) that was reinterpreted by a late pre-colonial Pueblo artist (C) at LA 102342	140
8.7	A boulder (A) hosting Archaic panel (B) reinterpreted by an eighteenth-century Comanche artist (C) at LA 102345	141
8.8	Deer and human prints jumbled together on a water-worn boulder in the gorge	144
8.9	Small dot-like hoof prints emerge from a game trail, curving around to define the shape of a human foot or sandal	146
8.10	A hunt reenacted. Lines of dots follow a boulder's ridges before resolving into a chaos of deer tracks at LA 55948	146
8.11	Sculpted basalt boulder, the result of the action of water and humble pebbles	148
8.12	Rock plays host to vibrant lichen bodies	150
8.13	Anthropomorph with a lichen mask at LA 102345	151
9.1	Location of Crystal River and Roberts Island in Florida, USA	155
9.2	Topographic map of the Crystal River site	157
9.3	Topographic map of Roberts Island	158
9.4	Photography of the excavation trench along the back of Mound A at Roberts Island	160
11.1	The study region with key sites	184

Illustrations

11.2	Alpha diversity (Shannon Evenness) and Beta diversity (Euclidean distance) of the different assemblages from the study region, with standard deviations. N = Neolithic cluster; EBA, MB-LB, and CLA = Bronze Age/Classical cluster; IA = Iron Age cluster	189
11.3	Relative frequencies of caprines, cattle, pigs and wild game in the study region through time	190
13.1	Austbø house 1 (top) and house 2	222
15.1	Map of Epipalaeolithic and Pre-Pottery Neolithic sites in Southwest Asia mentioned in the text	257
16.1	Study area, showing main erosion front (the area in which Skútustaðir is placed in is the area with most vegetation; the other area is greatly denuded)	276
16.2	The 46 different types of earmarks used to identify ownership of sheep	278
16.3	Hypothetical gathering paths reconstructed from Sigurjónsson (1950) and several ethnographic accounts	281
16.4	All sorting folds in the study area that have been surveyed (except rétt í Gæsdalur – see Figure 16.6)	287
16.5	Three networks (1) Spatial, (2) Temporal, (3) Social	289
16.6	Operational chain of Icelandic sheep farming practice (specific to the discussion in this chapter) with reference to the experiential difference between sheep (above) and farmers (below)	289
17.1	Map of Great Britain and Ireland, showing the location of the sites of Thatcham and Faraday Road in the Lower Kennet Valley	298
18.1	Map showing the locations of the three case study sites, Nugljanska, Pupićina, and Vela Špilja on the island of Lošinj	311
19.1	Graph indicating that elevated temperatures in PP5-6 samples did not affect their original isotopic signature	340
19.2	Graph showing isotope stages and the distance of Pinnacle Point site from the coast over the last 430,000 years	341
19.3	A $^{87}Sr/^{86}Sr$ isoscape map generated by sampling the $^{87}Sr/^{86}Sr$ values in modern vegetation growing on all known geological units surrounding PP	341
19.4	The y-axis represents $^{87}Sr/^{86}Sr$ values for modern vegetation samples , OES samples from PP5-6, and OES samples from PP30. The x-axis represents the distance from the coast	342
19.5	$^{87}Sr/^{86}Sr$ values for OES samples from PP5-6 and OES samples from PP30 plotted against time before the present	342
20.1	A pictorial representation of a caribou engraved onto caribou antler from the precontact Yup'ik site of Nunalleq, western Alaska	350
20.2	Population fluctuations in six caribou populations from western Greenland, from c. 1730 until 1985	354
20.3	Late Pleistocene reindeer lower third molar (M3) with broken roots, sequentially-sampled ahead of strontium isotope analysis	358
20.4	Sequential $^{87}Sr/^{86}Sr$ data from Rangifer and Bison/Bos enamel from Quina (Level 22) and Denticulate (Level 8) phases of Jonzac	359

Illustrations

Tables

4.1	Umbo-width and umbo-thickness method analysis	73
4.2	Summary data for archaeological samples of California mussel	73
4.3	Modern California mussel shell length data	74
4.4	Mean calculated shell length for California mussels	74
4.5	Games-Howell post hoc test results for archaeological and modern data of average California mussel size changes from San Miguel, Santa Rosa, and Santa Cruz Islands	75
6.1	List of insect species found in Building 1680 at Skálholt	108
11.1	Frequencies of large mammal taxonomic groups in the study region, in NISP	186
16.1	Grazing areas within Skútustaðahreppur, collective grazing area, and historical connections	277
16.2	Sheep numbers derived from documentary sources	279
16.3	Gathering paths taken by Skútustaðahreppur with other communities which are listed	280
16.4	Proportions of farms, herds, sheep and gatherers for Skútustaðahreppur's gathering in 1902	283
16.5	Sorting and holding folds related to Skútustaðahreppur; distance from closest farm	285
17.1	Relative frequency of species at Thatcham sites I–III and Faraday Road, presented as number of identified specimens (NISP) and the minimum number of individuals (MNI)	299
17.2	Seasonal indicators in the faunal assemblages from Thatcham sites I–III and Faraday Road	306
18.1	Radiocarbon dates for the case study sites	318
18.2	Season of collection of molluscs from the case study sites	324
18.3	Combined estimations of season of procurement for terrestrial faunal remains and marine molluscs during the Mesolithic	325
19.1	$^{87}Sr/^{86}Sr$ results of ostrich egg shell fragments from PP5-6	338
19.2	$^{87}Sr/^{86}Sr$ results of ostrich egg shell fragments from PP-30	339

CONTRIBUTORS

Benjamin Alberti, Department of Sociology, Framingham State University

Oscar Aldred, McCord Centre for Landscape, School of History, Classics and Archaeology, Newcastle University

Brian Boyd, Department of Anthropology, Columbia University

Todd J. Braje, Department of Anthropology, San Diego State University

Kate Britton, 1. Department of Archaeology, University of Aberdeen and 2. Department of Human Evolution, Max Planck Institute for Evolutionary Anthropology

Breana Campbell, Rincon Consultants, Inc., Carlsbad, CA, USA

Molly Crisp, Department of Chemistry, University of York

Ewa Domanska, 1. Department of History, Adam Mickiewicz University and 2. Department of Anthropology, Stanford University

Erich Fisher, 1. Institute of Human Origins, School of Human Evolution and Social Change, Arizona State University and 2. Centre for Coastal Palaeoscience, Nelson Mandela Metropolitan University

Severin Fowles, Department of Anthropology, Barnard College, Columbia University

Noah Heringman, Department of English, University of Missouri

Jamie Hodgkins, Department of Anthropology, University of Colorado Denver

Julia Lee-Thorp, Research Laboratory for Archaeology and the History of Art, University of Oxford

Thomas P. Leppard, McDonald Institute for Archaeological Research, University of Cambridge

Petrus le Roux, Department of Geological Sciences, University of Cape Town

Gavin Lucas, Department of Archaeology, University of Iceland

Michael MacKinnon, Department of Classics, University of Winnipeg

Contributors

Curtis W. Marean, 1. Institute of Human Origins, School of Human Evolution and Social Change, Arizona State University and 2. Centre for Coastal Palaeoscience, Nelson Mandela Metropolitan University

Nimrod Marom, Zinman Institute of Archaeology, University of Haifa

Terry O'Connor, Centre for Human Palaeoecology & Evolutionary Origins, University of York

Kristin Armstrong Oma, Museum of Archaeology, University of Stavanger

Nick J. Overton, Department of Archaeology, University of Manchester

Kirsty Penkman, Department of Chemistry, University of York

Þóra Pétursdóttir, Department of Archaeology and Social Anthropology, University of Tromsø

Suzanne E. Pilaar Birch, 1. Department of Anthropology, University of Georgia and 2. Department of Geography, University of Georgia

Thomas J. Pluckhahn, Department of Anthropology, University of South Florida, Tampa, Florida

Victor D. Thompson, Department of Anthropology, University of Georgia, Athens

Lior Weissbrod, Zinman Institute of Archaeology, University of Haifa

Laura S. Weyrich, Australian Center for Ancient DNA, University of Adelaide

Stephen G. Whitaker, Channel Islands National Park, Ventura, CA

Christopher Witmore, Department of Classical and Modern Languages and Literatures, Texas Tech University

ACKNOWLEDGEMENTS

I would like to thank the series editors, Chris Witmore and Gavin Lucas, for their guidance in the preparation of this edited volume. I would also like to thank the authors for their participation and willingness to contribute to a volume that brings together many disparate perspectives. Thanks also to my editorial assistants at Taylor & Francis, Lola Harre and Molly Marler, for their patience and help.

INTRODUCTION

Suzanne E. Pilaar Birch

The time is ripe to address the issue of ecological novelty in the archaeological record from a multispecies perspective. Pivotal research topics in archaeology have long simplified ecological novelty—or at least centered it on the human—by framing that novelty as one of many "major transitions" emphasizing the uniqueness of our species rather than viewing novelty as a collective shift shared amongst multiple species and their habitats. For example, a focus on the origins of art, language, and culture, spread out over tens of thousands of years, are often bundled together as the "human revolution", a phrase still popular in paleoanthropology today. Childe's (1936) "Neolithic Revolution" and "Urban Revolution" in Old World archaeology still loom large, implicitly if not explicitly, as major research foci, as if there is something essential to understanding ourselves emergent in what are regarded as major periods of transition.

In fact, these phenomena—of agricultural lifestyles and urbanism—have had lasting impact on human society but also ecological networks and environmental systems, visible in our globalized world today, and not just at "origin points" but throughout history. It is perhaps less common for archaeology as a discipline to look forward, but some are beginning to consider yet another "revolution": the large-scale human manipulation of terrestrial (and extra-terrestrial) systems, in the form of the Anthropocene, though the legitimacy of the period as a geological epoch and indeed its date of origin are still up for debate (e.g., Barnosky 2013; Ellis et al. 2013; Smith and Zeder 2013; Zalasiewicz et al. 2015).

Human exceptionalism and our place in nature have long been topics of academic consideration from earliest conceptualizations of the "Great Chain of Being". The dissolution of the barriers between human and nonhuman, and natural and cultural, has been a critical area within postmodernist thinking (e.g., Haraway 2008; Hartigan 2015; Latour 1993, 2013), but this paradigm has not quite found its place in archaeology, which has long been synonymous with the human past, to the detriment of gaining a more nuanced understanding of one that is shared. In the parallel—but in practice, often separate—fields of paleobiology and paleoecology, scientists have worked to understand a "natural" past, often to the point of excluding the role of the human, or viewing it as a disruptive element. Here, I argue for a multispecies archaeology that seeks to draw together these disparate foci, which create and reinforce an artificial boundary between humans and the natural world of which they are an integral part.

Though views have somewhat evolved in the last few decades from completely anthropocentric perspectives in archaeology, natural history, and related fields in the nineteenth century, there is still a pervasive sense of progressivism when we center our points of inquiry on human originality (e.g., Domanska 2010). Even in biological anthropology, many primatology studies revolve around what makes the great apes more like us rather than themselves (King, in Mullin 2002). To some extent, the very debate surrounding the creation of the "Anthropocene" belies a paradigm wherein humanity is gaining importance as a central object of inquiry in the geosciences (cf. Ellis and Ramankutty 2008; Ellis et al. 2013; Latour 2014).

It is useful here to consider the current multispecies movement in anthropology before turning to the discussion of a multispecies *archaeology*. The topic of "multispecies ethnography" was broached at the 2010 American Anthropological Association Meetings, a reprisal of a "Multispecies Salon" that also took place at the 2006 and 2008 meetings, which sought to approach the topic from anthropological and artistic perspectives. In the proceedings volume, Kirksey and Helmreich (2010) define multispecies ethnography as something that brings to the foreground what was previously taking place at the "margins of anthropology"; that is, our interactions with other species as food, parts of the landscape (environment), and symbols. They also considered the recognition of other species as integral, not subsidiary to what it means to be human—and indeed, what it means to exist. Though this growing movement in anthropology appears to have gained ground in the last decade, the start of it may be identified in an earlier movement towards understanding human-animal relationships in cultural anthropology and archaeology more broadly, when sessions at the AAA in 2000 and 2001 brought human-animal relationships to the fore (Mullin 2002).

Anthropology is far from the only discipline to recognize the importance of a multispecies perspective, and contributions from the biological and geological sciences have a longer history in this area. For example, Lynn Margulis's groundbreaking body of work in biology, first in establishing the theory of endosymbiosis, and later championing symbiosis as a driving force in evolution, broaches the idea of microbial agency and cooperation at a fundamental level (Margulis 1998). Shapiro (2007, 2013) advocates moving away from a focus on the study of "matter" in microbiology, arguing instead for studies that center on understanding information exchange and process in bacterial cooperation. The diverse contributions to this volume grounded in archaeology attest to not only theoretical conception of a pan-species agency rooted in cultural anthropology as a lens for understanding the processes that have shaped our collective past, but one that is empirically based as well.

Studying the interactions between entities in the biological, chemical, and physical realms form the basis of our scientific understanding of the world as we know it today, but the ephemeral nature of these relationships—their lack of a material trace that forms that basis of archaeological inquiry—proves a challenge in cultivating a multispecies knowledge of the past, one that requires interdisciplinary collaboration and discussion in its resolution. So, although a "multispecies ethnography" and human-animal studies offer many useful insights, they are not enough. It is essential to take as inspiration a much broader compass from the earth and life sciences that challenge our notions of evolution and life on earth.

Multispecies archaeology does not just encompass human relationships with animals or with other living organisms; nor should it be taken to mean the study of other species to better understand ourselves per se. Rather, what can we learn about the past without humans as the focus of the question? What can we learn if we frame ourselves as one actor among others in the long march of time? Archaeologists must dig deeper into considerations of life; into a wider ecology of interactions with plants, fungi, microbes, and even the fundamental building blocks of life, DNA.

Indeed, even as Kirksey and Helmreich (2010) ask what role multispecies ethnography might play in anthropology, this volume seeks to question what a wider consideration of life might play within archaeology. How might situating humans within a wider ecology serve to extend or alter our knowledge of the past? Whether interested in the emergence of the genus *Homo*, early art, language, and culture, or the later spread of domesticated species and agricultural systems to early urban trade networks—it's important as archaeologists to not only consider the interconnections between people and things but also between living beings. Viewing ecological novelty and multispecies interactions within the structure of feedback loops and in the context of niche construction theory is therefore helpful.

Behavioral ecology looms large in model building for prehistoric archaeology, and in fact optimal foraging theory, "borrowed" from ecologists, is often a first choice for explaining human interactions with other species: for example, the hunter-gatherer will choose to pursue the organism that provides the highest net gain for energy expended. In contrast, niche construction theory presents a challenge to creating archaeologically testable models because of its dependence on feedback loops and multiple variables, but at the same time may provide a better framework for an approach that is likely closer to the complexity of reality than simple one-to-one relationships (e.g. Laland and O'Brien 2010; Kendal et al. 2011; Smith 2012; Smith 2015; Zeder 2012; see also Riede 2011). We might also talk here of interspecific niche construction (borrowing a term in Candea 2010; cf. Fuentes 2010).

Multispecies archaeology in practice

The subject of human-animal interaction has recently become a hot topic in anthropology, but has always been the focus of the branch of archaeology known as zooarchaeology (or in Europe, archaeozoology). As nascent science in the 1950s, a large body of research has been produced in the last seven decades that combines aspects of zoology, biology, and ecology with archaeology. This field may still be overlooked as specialist by many archaeologists, but has wide applicability for multispecies approaches in archaeology and anthropology (e.g. Overton and Hamilakis 2013). Though not limited to human-animal interactions of the warm and fuzzy kind, less charismatic creatures such as fish, shellfish, birds, rodents, and insects are not always considered in individual studies. And while there has been a growing tendency to consider animal-animal interactions (see Speth 2013 for an excellent example of herd dynamics), there is need for more approaches that consider animals as agents in animal-human interactions. At the time of writing, the exploration of these topics in archaeology is still somewhat marginal; the recent volume "Archaeology and Human-Animal Studies" was notably published as a special issue of a philosophy journal, *Society and Animals*, rather than in a mainstream archaeology journal (Oma and Birke 2013). As the quintessential "other", animals define humanity, and our interactions with animals in the archaeological record are often considered through a lens of dominance over animals (whether from an economic, behavioral, ecological, or socio-cultural perspective). We "use" them—as sustenance, objects, symbols, and material culture. Yet, from a symbiotic point of view, this relationship can and should be seen as one of exchange. Certainly in the case of domesticated species, this partnership with humans has been an evolutionary boon, while for some wild species it has spelled disaster—the long-term consequences of which we are not yet aware.

In addition to zooarchaeology, paleoethnobotany or archaeobotany has relevance for a multispecies approach within the field of archaeology. For some archaeologists, the role of plants and vegetation may be easy to overlook as we talk about hunting and meat yields, or how food production systems might affect the overall functioning of urban societies and social hierarchy. But plants too are incredibly important determinants: for mobile hunter-gatherers, they might dictate a seasonal move; for sedentary agriculturalists, the reliability of your crop yields means the difference between survival and starvation. During the maximum extent of the last ice age, the die-off of vegetation caused the eradication of whole ecosystems, spurring mass migrations of people and animals that necessitated technological transformations, dietary shifts, and cultural exchange as well as novelties within ecosystems in refugial areas. Fungi and microbes may also be given short shrift in archaeology because they are more difficult to study; what we really have in archaeology is an ichnology of these things, perhaps only able to detect their physical traces on a bit of preserved wood or fabric or in the signs of pathology on a skeleton. Yet they are huge determining factors that cannot be overlooked. So too we might include proteins and DNA in our summary of what might be defined as multispecies archaeology. Their analysis is made possible by ever more sophisticated technology, and gene flow and symbiotic exchange play an indispensable role in the story of life (Margulis 1998). In particular, methods of stable isotope analysis and DNA analysis make it possible, from a practical standpoint, to assess these microscopic interactions through an archaeological lens.

Multispecies archaeology can really be viewed as archaeo-ecology, as an archaeology of life which understands the past through networks and interactions rather than stochastic events and places. The sections in this volume focus on pivotal areas of research within which a multispecies archaeology may bear fruitful outcomes by questioning what it means to know other living things archaeologically without recourse to humans as the subject of the inquiry, or as a controlling force.

Living in the "Anthropocene"

By its very nature, the Anthropocene suggests a split between humans and nature of the kind multispecies anthropology might seek to disrupt. There has been ample debate about the nature and existence of the Anthropocene in the earth sciences. Though they may have been a little late to join the party, archaeologists have also begun to weigh in on the topic en masse. To some extent, research in this area should include discussion of the establishment of the Anthropocene at the start of the Holocene (i.e. coinciding with ecological upheaval wrought by the onset of agricultural environments) versus the establishment of a historical date coinciding with the "Industrial Revolution" at the turn of the last century. It might also, however, consider multispecies archaeology within this modern period as an ecological setting that is radically different from anything that has come before, shedding light on the contributions of applied archaeology to issues including climate change, wildlife and habitat conservation, and the integration of natural and cultural heritage management. In this section, Heringman explores the natural historical context of anthropocentrism, considering its early conceptual role in the beginnings of archaeology and the study of the past. Witmore frames the Anthropocene as a disruption, as he considers long-term relationships with landscapes and animals in two disparate case studies in Greece and the US. Chapters by Leppard and by Campbell and colleagues consider the playing out of the Anthropocene in island environments from the Pacific to the Channel Islands, serving as models for the concept at larger scales. A photoessay by Pétursdóttir rounds out the section, musing on the role of things—and ephemerality—in this new anthropocentric epoch.

The multispecies ecology of the built environment

Cities are spaces ripe for the development of novel ecological relationships—in their genesis, continuity, and decline. The evolution and disintegration processes of urban environments and exchanges from both within and outside of built spaces, viewed from a multispecies perspective, opens up a range of opportunities for consideration of coeval relationships, whether

Introduction

centered on the earliest urbanization processes or later developments and expansion. Within this remit, we can manipulate that space between living and non-living things, entities, and/or objects. For instance, what types of new symbiotic interactions arise with the creation of new material environments, including different types of productive urban spaces and the introduction of new technologies?

How does the internal environment—inside a room, inside a building—differ from that of the outside (on the microscale), and what about relationships between city center, boundaries, and hinterland (on the macroscale)? The contributions in this section vary from those on built spaces—Lucas's consideration of symbiotic architectures in the case of old turf buildings in Iceland and Thompson and Pluckhahn's discussion of oyster mound-islands in Florida; to those focused on altered places—Domanska's chapter on the multispecies interactions occurring at abandoned cemeteries in Poland and Alberti and Fowles' contribution on rock art in New Mexico; and finally, the city—from ancient Rome (MacKinnon) to early urban centers in the Levant (Marom and Weissbrod).

Agrarian commitments: towards an archaeology of symbiosis

Currently a major research area, the origins and initial spread of agriculture worldwide offer a number of themes to be explored through multispecies archaeology. But the later emergence, movement, and adoption of agriculture, horticulture, husbandry, and pastoralism through time cannot and should not be dismissed for an emphasis on the "earliest". Relationships in agrarian environments/lifestyles/networks can be viewed as symbiotic ones, and so are crucial to development of an archaeology of symbiosis. Of interest are transitions from systems of scarcity to ones of wastefulness, as well as the specialization or narrowing of niches in response to pressures introduced by the ecological novelty of agricultural and pastoral structures. Animal and plant agency in the domestication process and the role of agriculture in the development and spread of microbial consortia are also nascent areas for research. Chapters by both O'Connor and Boyd thoroughly review these questions of agency and early domestication in the Neolithic and in southwest Asia, respectively, while Oma deals with some of the same concepts in her case study in Bronze Age Norway. Weyrich provides a rich overview of the role of these co-evolutionary relationships, developed and sustained through agrarian practices, on our microbiome.

The ecology of movement

Large-scale movement and mobility serve as another focal point for multispecies archaeology, including research questions delving into the introduction of humans into different biomes for the first time and environmental influences on different technological and cultural developments. A multispecies approach to the ecology of large-scale movement is especially needed, as many of the questions driving research in this area are human-centric, even if interdisciplinary methods are used (e.g., coring and pollen analysis for environmental reconstruction); there is lack of integration and consideration of what other factors contributed to the dispersal of individual or groups of species, for example, such as movement or regional extirpation of certain game species due to the introduction of new predators, human or otherwise. Likewise, the nuance of seasonal movements governed much of our shared human/nonhuman history. Seasonality is explored in the context of herding in Iceland (Aldred), late Pleistocene hunter-gatherers and reindeer in France (Britton), and regional settlement in Mesolithic Croatia (Pilaar Birch). Overton goes so far as to consider the role of daily movements in shaping multispecies relationships in Mesolithic

Britain, while Hodgkins and colleagues slide the scale to consider landscape use by foragers, hyenas, and ostriches in Pleistocene South Africa over thousands of years.

Conclusion

As outlined here, multispecies studies is a new, evolving area of scholarly interest which has only recently emerged in anthropology and has not been considered in detail by archaeologists. In addition to the Oma and Birke volume, a number of papers on "social zooarchaeology" in the December 2013 issue of the journal *Archaeological Dialogues* moves in this direction. Likewise, the November 2013 issue of the journal *Archaeological Review from Cambridge*, "Humans and Animals", included both more traditional zooarchaeological papers on subsistence as well as more exploratory articles on long-term human-animal relationships. These journal volumes provide evidence of interest in the topic, though no one collection of writing has successfully demonstrated a truly integrated multispecies perspective, which can only be achieved by drawing together authors with expertise in diverse areas, including archaeology, human-animal studies, biology, ecology, evolutionary theory, and philosophy for a comprehensive consideration of the topics discussed herein.

Multispecies ethnography as a form of anthropology appears to have taken hold as a formal movement in sociocultural anthropology, and multispecies perspectives have existed longer still in the biological sciences. It is necessary to assess viewpoints from archaeology and other disciplines together in order to consider perhaps the most essential linchpin in the study of the past: the multi-specific nature of major transformational periods in an inclusive, shared history of life. Research should be based not so much around these transitional periods as around the ecological novelties that underlie these concentrated areas of research foci in archaeology.

Indeed, the current disciplinary and institutional matrices seem to channel us along familiar routes, even if we want to break out of them. In this respect, it will be difficult to avoid revisiting central themes that have a strong pull in archaeological research today; this can be seen as both an asset and a challenge. While exploring some of these conventional frameworks for understanding transition, it is essential to engage with the idea that ecological novelties should not be viewed as a synonym for "origin points" or as precedent for what will come next; rather, the changing relationships and networks between organisms in disparate place and time are of primary interest. Ultimately, it is not only the subject or object of archaeology, but also broader disciplinary identities, that will be challenged by this field of research, which in addition will lead away from the reinforcing of the trope of "revolution" by approaching key changes in life with which humans are enmeshed and question what it means to be human—and nonhuman—from a variety of perspectives. To paraphrase Kirksey and Helmreich in their 2010 volume, we have at least "never only been human".

References

Barnosky, A.D. 2013. Palaeontological evidence for defining the Anthropocene. *Geological Society, London, Special Publications* 395: 149–165.

Candea, M. 2010. "I Fell in Love with Carlos the Meerkat": Engagement and detachment in human-animal relations. *American Ethnologist* 37(2): 241–258.

Childe, V.G. 1936. *Man Makes Himself*. London: Watts.

Domanska, E. 2010. Beyond anthropocentrism in historical studies. *Historein. A Review of the Past and Other Stories* 10: 118–130.

Ellis, E. and N. Ramankutty. 2008. Putting people in the map: Anthropogenic biomes of the world. *Frontiers in Ecology and the Environment* 6(8): 439–447.

Introduction

Ellis, E., D.Q. Fuller, J.O. Kaplan, and W.G. Lutters. 2013. Dating the Anthropocene: Towards an empirical global history of human transformation of the terrestrial biosphere. *Elementa: Science of the Anthropocene* 1: 000018.

Fuentes, A. 2010. Naturalcultural encounters in Bali: Monkeys, temples, tourists, and ethnoprimatology. *Cultural Anthropology* 25(4): 600–624.

Haraway, D.J. 2008. *When Species Meet.* Minneapolis: University of Minnesota Press.

Hartigan, J. 2015. *Aesop's Anthropology: A Multispecies Approach.* Minneapolis: University of Minnesota Press.

Kendal, J., J.J. Tehrani and J. Odling-Smee. 2011. Human niche construction in interdisciplinary focus. *Philosophical Transactions of the Royal Society* B 366: 785–792.

Kirksey, S. and S. Helmreich. 2010. The emergence of multispecies ethnography. *Cultural Anthropology* 25(4): 545–576.

Laland, K.N. and M.J. O'Brien. 2010. Niche construction theory and archaeology. *Journal of Archaeological Method and Theory* 17(4): 303–322.

Latour, B. 1993. *We Have Never Been Modern.* Cambridge, MA: Harvard University Press.

Latour, B. 2013. *An Inquiry into Modes of Existence: An Anthropology of the Moderns.* Cambridge, MA: Harvard University Press.

Latour, B. 2014. Anthropology at the time of the Anthropocene: A personal view of what is to be studied. Paper presented at the 113th Annual American Anthropological Association meeting, Washington, DC, 3–7 December 2014.

Margulis, L. 1998. *Symbiotic Planet: A New Look at Evolution.* New York: Basic Books.

Mullin, M. 2002. Animals and anthropology. *Society and Animals* 10(4): 387–394.

Oma, K.A. and L. Birke. 2013. Archaeology and human–animal studies. *Society and Animals* 21(2): 113–119.

Overton, N. and Y. Hamilakis. 2013. A manifesto for a social zooarchaeology: Swans and other beings in the Mesolithic. *Archaeological Dialogues* 20(2): 111–136.

Riede, F. 2011. Adaptation and niche construction in human prehistory: A case study from the southern Scandinavia Late Glacial. *Philosophical Transactions of the Royal Society* B 366: 793–808.

Shapiro, J.A. 2007. Bacteria are small but not stupid: Cognition, natural genetic engineering and socio-bacteriology. *Studies in History and Philosophy of Biological and Biomedical Science* 38: 807–819.

Shapiro, J.A. 2013. *Evolution: A View from the 21st Century.* Upper Saddle River, NJ: FT Press Science.

Smith, B.D. 2012. A cultural niche construction theory of initial domestication. *Biological Theory* 6(3): 260–271.

Smith, B.D. 2015. A comparison of niche construction theory and diet breadth models as explanatory frameworks for the initial domestication of plants and animals. *Journal of Archaeological Research.* DOI 10.1007/s10814-015-9081-4.

Smith, B.D. and M.A. Zeder. 2013. The onset of the Anthropocene. *Anthropocene* 4: 8–13.

Speth, J.D. 2013. Thoughts about hunting: Some things we know and some things we don't know. *Quaternary International* 297: 176–185.

Zalasiewicz, J., C.N. Waters, M. Williams, A.D. Barnosky, A. Cearreta, P. Crutzen, E. Ellis, M.A. Ellis, I.J. Fairchild, J. Grinevald, and P.K. Haff. 2015. When did the Anthropocene begin? A mid-twentieth century boundary level is stratigraphically optimal. *Quaternary International* 383: 196–203.

Zeder, M.A. 2012. The broad spectrum revolution at 40: Resource diversity, intensification, and an alternative to optimal foraging explanations. *Journal of Anthropological Archaeology* 31(3): 241–264.

PART I

Living in the Anthropocene

1

CALABRIAN HOUNDS AND ROASTED IVORY (OR, SWERVING FROM ANTHROPOCENTRISM)

Noah Heringman

Epochs, humans, and other species

In a review of *The Epochs of Nature* by Georges-Louis Leclerc, Comte de Buffon, the German naturalist and antiquary Johann Reinhold Forster took issue with Buffon's radical notion that human beings were a late arrival on the scene of antiquity. More like a writer of romances than a naturalist, in Forster's view, Buffon defines the limits of the primeval ocean, produces now-extinct megafauna, and then causes the continents to separate before allowing humans to exist. Forster comments disapprovingly: "At last human beings too become inhabitants of this earth" (Forster 1780: 148). Zealous to prove that human antiquity is the only antiquity accessible to science, Forster disregards the uncertainty concerning human origins that is built into Buffon's account.

The uncertainty is part of the point, however, and Buffon reflects explicitly on the instability produced by situating human origins in a diachronic history of species. *Epochs of Nature* is one of the first geochronologies to insist on a comparatively long prehuman past, and Buffon anticipates some of his contemporaries' objections by establishing a human epoch, a seventh and final age "in which Man assisted the operations of Nature." In this chapter, he locates the first advanced civilization precisely at the date of 7000 BCE. But in discussing the earlier epochs, such as the fifth, in which "the elephants [i.e., mammoths], and other animals of the south, inhabited the northern regions" (Buffon 1785: 306), Buffon raises the possibility of an earlier human presence, of beings roughly corresponding to what we now term "early hominins." The interspecies nexus designated by Buffon's term for fossilized mammoth tusks—"roasted ivory"—marks a point of archaeological curiosity in the late Enlightenment, a sub-epoch that some scholars are now calling "the early Anthropocene" (Menely 2015b: 3). Following the advent of modern geology in the nineteenth century, archaeologists located "men" more firmly "among the mammoths" (Van Riper 1993). This chapter is concerned with Buffon and his interlocutors in the 1770s and 1780s; although their conjectures on fossils and prehistory predate the discipline of archaeology (Schnapp 1997), I use the term anachronistically in the interest of a conceptual history (Koselleck 2002). Enlightenment naturalist-antiquaries such as Buffon began this conversation by expanding the area of uncertainty surrounding human antiquity, designating a domain in which fossil bones or knapped flint might count as evidence. For Buffon, then, the "archives of nature" (Buffon 1780: 1) include an archaeological record that encompasses other animal species as well as artifacts unattested in the written record.

A similar uncertainty attends the history of the Anthropocene, which some scholars backdate as far as the era of knapped flint and megafauna extinction, while others favor an industrial or postindustrial date, which correlates to Buffon's epoch of "advanced civilization" (cf. Waters 2016).[1] As Kieran Suckling points out, one of the problems with the term "Anthropocene" is the absence of a biological criterion for dating the epoch. All other epochs (e.g., Miocene, Pliocene) are "named for the condition of the Earth's plants and animals in that epoch. Epochs and epoch names are biocentric," meaning that they describe ecological conditions rather than geological "drivers" or (in this case) a single species (humans) identified as a geological driver via climate change (Suckling 2015). This break with paleontological criteria feeds into a more widely noted problem with the idea of the Anthropocene, namely the encroachment of a ubiquitous human actor on the stage of geohistory. If Buffon's seventh epoch anticipates these problematic aspects of the Anthropocene, then his earlier epochs de-center the human perspective, promoting the radical separation of history from geochronology that enabled geological reckoning in the first place. Although (pace Forster) he raises the possibility of a human presence before the separation of the continents in the sixth epoch, this is nevertheless the time of the mammoths and the question of human presence is peripheral to it. The recent recommendation by the Anthropocene Working Group to locate this epoch in the mid-twentieth century (Waters 2016; cf. Steffen et al. 2016) deliberately foregrounds human agency, but most attempts to define an "age of man" since Buffon have reached more deeply into the history of our species and others. This recommendation changes the terms of the debate, but does not diminish its relevance.

Buffon's "Age of Man" implies earlier ages in which humans are not the main actors. If, then, archaeology has become "synonymous with an exclusively human past," this may not be solely the result of its failure to depart sufficiently from the "completely anthropocentric perspectives in archaeology, natural history, and related fields in the nineteenth century" (Pilaar Birch 2018: 1). Multispecies archaeologists might, in fact, productively reach farther back to their precursors, the antiquary-naturalists, who entertained a version of the question of "how to know other living things archaeologically without recourse to humans as the subject of the inquiry, or as a controlling force" (4), before anthropocentrism became dominant in this form. The difference between Forster and Buffon illustrates the wide range of possibilities in natural history, which accommodated both Forster's insistence that all antiquity was human and Buffon's decentered engagement with geochronology, in which human time is almost an afterthought. The instability of the discourse and Buffon's particular iteration of it are both useful for contesting the modern sense of scientific terms such as "anthropology" and "paleontology," as this volume sets out to do. The project of redefining archaeology in multispecies terms calls for new origin stories, in which the boundary between archaeology and precursor sciences might be drawn differently—hence my occasionally anachronistic use of the term "archaeology" in this chapter.

The antiquity of other species

Although Buffon seeks to establish criteria for ecological novelty independent of any human-made record, he also mines the literature of antiquarianism to establish geochronological markers for his later epochs, especially the loosely defined transitional period during which "primitive" and then the first civilized societies might have established themselves. Other species play a part in these interactions, and geological conditions are even more fundamental, especially because (so Buffon claims) modern humans have a sort of evolutionary memory of the "convulsive motions of the [still-cooling] earth" that terrified their earliest ancestors (Buffon 1785: 381).

For eighteenth-century antiquaries concerned with the excavation of cities buried by the eruption of Vesuvius in 79 CE, observations of the mountain's current behavior played a somewhat similar part—though admittedly on a smaller temporal scale—in helping to establish what the experience of the ancient inhabitants of Pompeii and Herculaneum might have been. The volcanic inundation from Vesuvius was recognized as the "driver" of at least this local environmental history, and a bit later, in 1812, Cuvier used analogy to extrapolate the global force of geological catastrophe by describing the fossil record in toto as "the ruins of the great Herculaneum overwhelmed by the ocean" (Cuvier 1822: i).

The archaeological evidence from these sites, which made the daily life of the ancients so vividly present, disrupted historical temporality itself in profound ways. In addition to the volcano's continued activity, other species—dogs in particular—were among the ecological constants that suggested a deeper, unrecorded human past underlying the ruins of 79 CE. Pierre Hugues d'Hancarville, glossing a scene on a famous black-figure vase found near Naples (the Hunt Krater), insists that the species of hunting dog depicted on the vase, originally from Epirus in Greece, survives in modern-day Calabria, south of Naples (D'Hancarville 1767: 3.206). The scene itself, d'Hancarville argues, depicts an actual event so ancient as to have survived in classical Greece only as a myth (the myth of the Calydonian boar hunt). The continuity of the nonhuman species is therefore important as a kind of source material on human antiquity that predates the historical record—what we would now call prehistory. D'Hancarville, espousing a euhemerist reading of mythology indebted to Giambattista Vico's *New Science*, indicates that the boar in the vase painting is "of a monstrous size" (3.205) appropriate to the age of "heroes" in which it lived (3.207).

Buffon gives other reasons for the monumental size of the fossil bones and teeth of mammoths and other megafauna found in parts of Siberia as well as at celebrated New World sites, such as Big Bone Lick on the Ohio, remarking that "Nature was then in her primitive vigor" (Buffon 1785: 303). Buffon's version of prehistoric gigantism makes the record of nonhuman species into something more than source material for human antiquity, but in both versions nonhuman species mark a locus of continuity in the archaeological record as it was understood in the late eighteenth century. As opposed to the "unknown animal" whose molars were found in conjunction with more familiar teeth and bones, the latter could be clearly attributed to "elephants" and "hippopotami" like those of the present day in all but size. The natural histories of Vesuvius and of Big Bone Lick, though on somewhat different scales, both concerned themselves with the continuity of species (boars, dogs, "elephants") as well as their discontinuity ("the unknown animal"), unhindered by the distinction between paleontology and archaeology.

The history of Pompeii, and antiquarianism more broadly, also inspire scenarios in which humans are not the main actors. When Giuseppe Fiorelli perfected his technique of pouring plaster into the hollows that surrounded skeletons engulfed by volcanic ash and rubble—thus revealing the exact shape of the bodies of Vesuvius's victims at the time of their deaths—his second subject was the entombed body of a watchdog, who thus became "perhaps Pompeii's best-known victim": "the cast of the dog with his slender legs seeming to flail in midair has never failed to evoke pity in those who see it" (Dwyer 2010: 87–88). Taken together with the famous mosaic of a dog bearing the legend "Cave Canem," also found at Pompeii, this sympathetic identification suggests a way of decentering the human perspective in archaeology. Considering these canines, or the mammoths who take center stage in Buffon's fifth epoch, as agents in an archaeological context might be seen as promoting a goal set by Donna Haraway in *When Species Meet*, the goal of "positive knowledge of and with animals" (Haraway 2008: 21). In the case of dogs in particular—who dominate Haraway's inquiry—considering animal agency in this way might also express a kind of co-evolutionary nostalgia, harking back to a time in which hunter-hominins and their wolf-things roamed the savanna. Haraway herself rightly challenges such nostalgia (36), but acknowledges that the "temporalities" of companion species "include the heterogeneous scales of evolutionary time" (25). Cary Wolfe further extends this figurative sense of symbiogenesis, arguing that human faculties such as language derive from "ahuman evolutionary processes" and "recursive co-ontogenies" (Wolfe 2010: xxii).[2]

In one of Buffon's variations on the story of human origins, the last survivors of a giant hominin "nation" migrate across what is now the Bering Strait at roughly the same time as the "elephants"; while the elephants ultimately perish in North America because they are unable to cross the mountains, the human giants press on all the way to Patagonia (Buffon 1988: 193). The appeal for sympathy here is more muted, but this story of the New World elephants' demise arguably makes the survival of the Old World elephants more poignant. It also opens a distant prospect of the early history of domestication. In a more antiquarian register, Pietro Fabris illustrates the survival of an interspecies relation in his 1775 etching of the excavation of the Temple of Isis in Pompeii, which shows the antiquarian spectators accompanied by a hunting dog (Figure 1.1).

By asking in what sense these nonhuman creatures might have a "voice," or inscribe themselves into the "archives of nature," we are asking a question that has ethical roots in the Enlightenment. Tobias Menely offers a useful theoretical paradigm for recentering animal agency by describing Enlightenment arguments for the "creaturely voice" of animals—a term linked etymologically to "vote"—that arose as a rebuttal of Descartes' animal-machine thesis and culminated in the poetry of sensibility (which Menely credits with inspiring the first animal welfare laws). On this basis, Menely re-imagines community as literally premised on communication, as "open" to the "prelinguistic semiosis humans share with other animals" (Menely 2015a: 1). In different ways, both Buffon's multispecies history of the earth and the early archaeology of Vesuvius promote an ecological view of the past by focusing on human/nonhuman relationships. From Menely's point of view, the situation of animal rights in the late industrial era is fundamentally different because of the scale of animal exploitation. Buffon promoted the multiplication of "men and animals" as a way of generating heat to slow the approach of an ultimate ice age (Buffon 1785: 399). In the Anthropocene, the scale of Confined Animal

Figure 1.1 Pietro Fabris, "Excavation of the Temple of Isis at Pompeii" (1776). By permission of Staatsbibliothek zu Berlin—Preußischer Kulturbesitz, Abteilung Historische Drucke.

Feeding Operations (CAFO) is doubly of concern because of their production of greenhouse gases. The future past of the Anthropocene, too, looks grim from the point of view of creaturely inscription: if the assumptions of Anthropocene science are borne out, the epoch's creatures will register in the fossil record as mass extinction. Zoe Crossland helpfully frames the archaeology of the Anthropocene as a project of turning "our gaze away from [this] projected dystopia . . . to the present and past conditions that underwrite its potential unfurling" (2014: 127).

In this chapter, I am advocating for the openness and uncertainty of Enlightenment archaeological thought, for the moments when it swerves from anthropocentrism and considers other species as drivers in the history of life. As much as they differ on these points, though, the accounts by Forster, Buffon, d'Hancarville, and their contemporaries never depart entirely from a shared teleology of domestication. It remains an open question whether a future archaeologist excavating a former CAFO site would be guided by "present and past conditions" of domestication or would have a new paradigm from which to operate. Therefore it is essential to look within the history of anthropocentric (or nominally anthropocentric) thought to unravel those moments when it swerves from its ostensible teleology, such as the discourse of human animality that Buffon adopts from New World and Pacific voyage narratives.

Mammoth protagonists

The mammoth is arguably the main actor of Buffon's *Epochs of Nature*, even though the work covers the whole history of life as Buffon understood it. I have adopted the poetic phrase "roasted ivory" from William Smellie's 1785 translation because it captures the uncertain status of the mammoth as a mediator.[3] (Buffon himself does not use "mammoth" to describe the megafauna associated with find spots in Siberia and North America, but rather "unknown animal," "hippopotamus," and especially "elephant," which sometimes serves as a metonymy for all three.) "Elephant" in the specific sense of "Siberian mammoth" is used in conjunction with the substance that Buffon refers to both as *ivoire fossile* and *ivoire cuit*, with the latter being credited explicitly to the ivory merchants he consulted in Paris. Smellie's translation is admittedly eccentric; Claudine Cohen's modern rendering, "baked ivory" (2002: 98), more accurately captures the probable association with fired earthenware, and "cured ivory" might have better etymological support. Precisely as an eccentric translation, "roasted ivory" also designates an "area of uncertainty" in the sense developed by Bruno Latour in *Reassembling the Social*. Defining the "agency" of objects as one of the areas of uncertainty that disclose networks in action, Latour uses fossils to illustrate the way in which distance in time can highlight the object's role as mediator: "Even the humblest and most ancient stone tools from the Olduvai Gorge in Tanzania have been turned by paleontologists into the very mediators that triggered the evolution of 'modern man'" (Latour 2005: 80). Cohen argues that the uncertainty surrounding fossil ivory inspired *Epochs of Nature* itself: "it is not too much to claim that the question of the Siberian mammoth and the 'unknown Ohio animal' is the keystone—maybe the key—of this masterwork" (Cohen 2002: 96).

Buffon calls "elephants" into service just a few pages into his "Preliminary Discourse" to support his main hypothesis of global cooling, but in the process he also gives them their own rich history. Their remains first appear as one of five "monuments" that "prove" Buffon's account of the earth's major rock types and their formation (Buffon 1988: 11–12). Because they are found in the northern parts of both the Old and the New Worlds, he argues, the fossil tusks and bones of giant elephants and other megafauna support his thesis of the separation of the continents. The wealth of available evidence enables Buffon to construct a major portion of his narrative, the fifth epoch referred to at the outset of this chapter ("when the elephants, and other animals of the south, inhabited the northern regions"). Their history unfolds in the course of the chapter-length narrative devoted to this epoch and in parts of the following epoch as well, but Buffon provides a surprising amount of detail on these animals even at the outset, when he is simply outlining his history of the earth. The established trade in "roasted" ivory from Siberia and Tartary, together with recent discoveries in North America that had been widely debated in London and communicated to Buffon, along with specimens, in the late 1760s, increased both the visibility of the mammoth and its contemporaries and the uncertainties surrounding them. He harnesses this visibility to illustrate the magnitude of the geological transformations that would have needed to occur for large land animals to appear.

Buffon monumentalizes their remains in a more literal sense, too, in the form of engravings that dramatize their scale while at the same time collapsing the categories of natural and civil history, fulfilling a promise made in the first sentence of this work. The idea of fossils as "the antiquities of the earth" was not new, but Buffon escalated the analogy to posit geological "revolutions" of incomparably larger magnitude than civil ones (cf. Buffon 1785: 305). He gave the "elephants" and other fossil fauna tens of thousands of years to emerge and to flourish, focusing especially on giant specimens of everything from ammonites to hippos that seemed to him to corroborate formerly higher global temperatures. This long independent history is the main point of a very long excursus note on elephants—one of thirty-six essay-like *notes justificatives* that accompany the more philosophical narrative ("romance," to its critics) of the *Epochs* and were chosen by Smellie, almost to the exclusion of the main text, as the basis of his translation— that follows the initial discussion of the fourth "monument," their fossil remains. Unlike most of the other volumes of Buffon's forty-nine volume *Histoire naturelle*, which are richly illustrated, *Epochs of Nature* has only five engravings, and all five were made to accompany this one note. The first of these (Figure 1.2), like three of the others, shows the pointed molars of the "unknown animal" (mastodon) to demonstrate the scale of life in earlier epochs and support the controversial idea that these animals and others had become extinct as global climate changed. These fossil teeth and the engravings function as monuments or mediators in both the material space of print and the conceptual space of natural history, where they enact the declension from a gigantic past into modernity.

The long note (n. 9) quotes extensively from correspondence Buffon received from around the world in his position as director of the Royal Botanical Garden in Paris. On the authority of these observations and specimens from Russia and what was then New France, Buffon argued that megafauna "species had formerly existed and flourished there, in the same manner as they now exist and multiply in the southern latitudes" (Buffon 1785: 283). By insisting on an independent history for these species, Buffon is not only substantiating his new geological time scale, but also rebutting historical and catastrophist explanations of this seeming biogeographic anomaly. Prevailing theories held that the animals had been driven there by humans or by a mega-flood in the Indian Ocean, but according to Buffon, the extent of the remains precluded the idea that only "some individuals" had migrated. On the contrary, the ancient elephants lived in the North "in a state of nature and entirely at liberty" (Buffon 1988: 14). These elephants and kindred species established themselves and flourished over hundreds of generations in the locations where their remains were found, before migrating southward (and, in at least one case, becoming extinct). Hence "more ivory, perhaps, has already been brought from the north than all the elephants of India now existing could furnish," and a great deal more remains to be discovered (Buffon 1785: 278). Moreover, a substantial length of time was required for this fossil ivory to "roast." The ivory merchants, Buffon reports, distinguish fossilized tusks by the quality of their matrix, and the length of time they remained buried in it, saying that in most cases "very

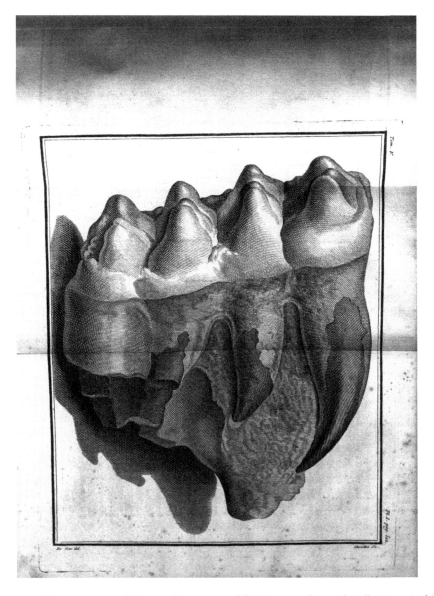

Figure 1.2 Buffon 1780: 2.235 [Plate One]. Courtesy of the Division of Special Collections, Archives, and Rare Books, University of Missouri.

fine works may be made of them" (280). This lapse of time gives him room to maneuver in his narrative of these animals' subsequent fate, including his account of their attempt to pass the Isthmus of Panama during the sixth epoch. In spite of the size difference and the lapse of time, the merchants still recognize fossil ivory as identical in structure with modern ivory: apart from size, these elephants were elephants, so their habitats must have derived their warmth from the interior of a younger, more vigorous globe (287).

Giant species and human origins

Since the earth could only have cooled very gradually (as verified by Buffon's experiments on iron), these super-heated conditions persisted for long enough to infuse the very first living creatures, followed by a whole succession of giant flora and fauna, and perhaps even—this is Buffon's most radical suggestion—a giant race of early humans. The conundrum of the "elephants" prompts his first analysis of these conditions, and they make such apt protagonists because they lend support to a larger narrative arc extending from the gigantic fossil shells of the third epoch all the way to the first humans of the sixth. The animals were larger during the "long tract of time" it took for the earth to cool (Buffon 1785: 286) because "Nature was then in her primitive vigor. The internal heat of the earth bestowed on its productions all the vigor and magnitude of which they were susceptible. The first ages produced giants of every kind" (303). Smellie is not to be faulted for rendering the singular "premier âge" (Buffon 1988: 17) as "first ages" here, as the original is full of slippages between plural and singular forms such as "age of giants" and "primitive times" (17–18, cf. 77–78). Buffon himself concedes that the epochs of nature, unlike those of civil history, are relative and not clearly demarcated (Buffon 1785: 305), but the cool temperatures of recorded history seem to have arrived only recently. In the main body of the narrative, versions of the same argument—residual internal heat producing gigantism—occur as early as the third epoch (Buffon 1988: 78) and as late as the sixth, which contains a third long excursus note (n. 30) developing the issues raised in the initial account of "elephants." This narrative strategy lends a certain coherence to the long prehuman past that Buffon proposes. The multispecies "archive of nature" displaces the human record (and with it sacred history), while also establishing geocentric and ecocentric criteria for locating human origins among those of other species.

Buffon conscientiously takes up the discourse of gigantism elaborated by scientifically minded conjectural historians from Lucretius to Vico (a discourse also manifested in d'Hancarville's mythographic thesis of boars "of a monstrous size"). He gains a critical purchase on it by introducing a much longer time scale, including the notion of extinction, and by distinguishing more sharply between descriptions of fossil bones of humans or hominids and those of other species. Pursuing an Enlightenment program inspired by his contemporary Jean-Étienne Guettard (Buffon 1988: 291n.16), Buffon singles out certain descriptions from the so-called *Gigantologie espagnole*, arguing that some of the bones described in this text must be of the same species as the "unknown animal" from the Ohio River (237). Although sacred history and "superstition" are displaced by this approach, they are not evacuated entirely. On a psychological level, the nostalgia for nature's "primitive vigor" and its gigantic forms suggests desire fueled by a trauma associated with "convulsions of nature." Not only the natural theology of the Deluge but even more secular accounts, such as that of Nicolas-Antoine Boulanger, explained human history as the effect of an original, traumatic flood.

Though he is circumspect, Buffon does not rule out the possibility of human giants, and the manuscript of *Epochs of Nature* reveals that he entertained the possibility of human beings contemporary with giant northern elephants but then suppressed it in the printed text. Buffon concludes his discussion of the fossil evidence of giant tropical animals and plants in the North with an abrupt turn to the human species, asking if the earth could have been populated with "men" at the same time that it was populated with these plants and animals, before the separation of the continents (Buffon 1988: 159). In the printed text Buffon strategically placed this question in the mouth of an imaginary interlocutor and answered in the negative, citing a separate act of creation and firmly deferring the discussion of human origins to its proper epoch (161–62). In the manuscript, both the rhetorical tactics and the long pious interpolation are absent; instead, the narrator raises this question in his own voice and answers nearly in the affirmative, citing the uniformity of the laws of nature and the worldwide distribution of human populations as premises for this conclusion:

> Without wishing to affirm it we therefore presume, according to our hypothesis, that the human species is as ancient as the elephant; that, being able to sustain the same degree of heat and perhaps an even higher degree, man will have penetrated the southern lands before the animals; but that his first long sojourn was in the northern lands.
>
> *Buffon 1988: 161n.*

The manuscript proceeds to introduce Buffon's thesis that this first civilization was established on the high plateaux of central Asia, though even at this stage he planned to defer the details and the "proofs" to the discussion of his last epoch (162n.). By deleting this material and revising the quoted passage, Buffon does much to create the impression that God deferred man's arrival till the earth was "worthy of his empire" (161).

It is striking that even this rhetorical pose of anthropocentrism was not enough to satisfy Buffon's contemporaries, including Forster and, more impressively, the Sorbonne, which condemned parts of the seventh epoch (Buffon 1988: 306n.1). The deletion of manuscript material alone provides adequate evidence for questioning the "sincerity" of the published version, as Jacques Roger pointed out in 1962 to caution those who would "accuse Buffon of anthropocentrism" (302n.29). And even though he consolidated his thinking on human origins into the seventh epoch, written last, significant material referring to human or semi-human giants was allowed to stand in the sixth epoch and the excursus notes—further suggesting human proximity to other species. In the printed text, Buffon retracted his claim that "monuments and even traditions" attest that "the human species has followed the same course and dates from the same period as other species," rendering it purely a matter of "analogy" (159n.). Several of these monuments and traditions are reported, all the same, in the material on giants that was not deleted. As Buffon puts it in one of the deleted passages, all these indications give us strong reason to presume that gigantic humans, too, existed in "these primitive times close to the origins of animated nature and on the same terrain as the first elephants and other animals" (162n.). In light of theological objections to the published work, it is thoroughly ironic that he tried to be *more* orthodox by *post*-dating the species in his revisions.

The most salient episode to have escaped these revisions is the migration of the giant species, including humans, prior to the separation of the continents. The primary evidence for such a migration, once again, is the presence of fossil remains of the same megafauna in both northern Eurasia and North America. As Roger points out, this is essentially the same body of evidence as that put forward by Alfred Wegener in the twentieth century in support of the supercontinent Gondwanaland (Buffon 1988: 275n.56). In the sixth epoch Buffon proposes that "some giants, as well as the elephants, passed from Asia into America" via the same overland route, finding there "the liberty and the tranquility" they required to "propagate their gigantic race" at a time when lowland South America was still entirely covered by the primeval ocean (193–94). Buffon points to the Patagonian giants, whose existence had been corroborated as recently as 1767 by John Byron on HMS *Dolphin*, as the last vestiges of this race. The Asiatic parent stem died out much earlier with Goliath, according to the excursus note accompanying this passage (Buffon 1785: 332). Buffon cites scripture infrequently, but in this instance it bears out his general claim in the manuscript that written tradition conserved the memory of giants; in conjunction with the Patagonians, he uses the stories of Goliath, the sons of Anak, and others to posit "permanent and successive races of giants" (341). The original account of human origins, partially overwritten by the seventh epoch, is thus a synchronic one, in which "the origins of animated nature" describes an indefinitely long process that leaves traces, such as gigantism, in most species. In *Epochs of Nature*, gigantism provides a secular vocabulary for the proximity of species as well as their collective proximity to origins. The corresponding vocabulary of domestication, though it has a biblical warrant in Genesis, now appears to connote the belatedness of modern civilization in relation to the deep gigantic past.

Species memory and the fossil archive

The memories recorded in ancient texts pass through several stages between the epochs marked by fossil "monuments" and their later preservation in writing. These stages may be traced more indistinctly in oral tradition and in a kind of race memory, or what might today be termed evolutionary memory. These other forms of memory are crucial because they substantiate the apparent agreement between the monuments and the earliest recorded traditions, such as the Old Testament stories of giants. Buffon added a substantial excursus note after the rest of *Epochs of Nature* had passed through the proof stage to report on an Arctic travel narrative delivered to him by the Russian minister Schouvaloff in autumn 1777. This narrative (based on first-hand accounts by the navigator Aphanassei Otcheredin) includes material from oral tradition among the Chukchi people on the Asian side of the Bering Strait as well as observations on the current state of their trade with people on the American side. Buffon concludes that since the Chukchi have carried on this commerce "since time immemorial" (Buffon 1988: 253), it could be regarded as a survival of the traffic occurring during the separation of the continents. More general human memory of "races of giants," having been preserved at least until the time of the earliest writings, confirms the hypothesis of gigantism in similar fashion. The high antiquity and gigantic size attributed to the first men by tradition corroborate the idea that they "received" great size and strength "from nature" during the same extended "primitive" moment in which the first elephants acquired their "prodigious" tusks (162n.). Buffon also takes the testimony of ancient geographers such as Strabo concerning the uninhabitability of the "torrid zone" as a kind of species memory of the fifth or even earlier epochs (139).

This type of geological memory "preserved by tradition" operates most powerfully at the beginning of the seventh epoch. This bleak narrative of human origins declares that "the first men were witnesses of the convulsive motions of the earth, which were then frequent and terrible" (Buffon 1785: 381). Reminiscent of the state of humanity in Plato's *Protagoras* before the intervention of Prometheus, these early humans or giants were "naked in mind as well as in body, exposed to the injuries of every element, victims to the rapacity of ferocious animals, which they were unable to combat, [and] penetrated with the common sentiment of terror." Small wonder, then, that even the first nations remained "deeply affected by the miseries of their original state"; "having still before their eyes the ravages" of flooding, earthquakes, and volcanoes on a giant scale, "these men . . . have preserved a durable, and almost eternal, remembrance of the calamities the world has suffered" (383). The secular convictions underlying this bleak narrative of human origins must have been readily apparent to the Sorbonne, and Roger has shown how deeply it is influenced by the freethinker Nicolas-Antoine Boulanger, who takes a similar approach to human origins and the origin of superstition in particular, in *Anecdotes of Nature* as well as in other works. The narrative arc of "giant race[s]" enjoying "liberty and tranquility" before declining into a cooler modern world, the onset of which is loosely marked by a "convulsion" or series of catastrophes, bears some general resemblance to an idea that Boulanger shared in common with other, more orthodox antiquaries: that laws, religion, and other institutions originated from, and commemorated, a traumatic dispersal of humanity associated with the Biblical Deluge (see further de Luca 1991: 180–87).

Boulanger's influence did not entirely change the course of the work, however, as Roger suggests; on the contrary, Boulanger's skepticism allowed Buffon to preserve a deep ambivalence about human hegemony at the beginning of the very chapter that concludes by celebrating human domestication of nature in the most strident tones. The idea of species memory, in particular, goes against the grain of some of Buffon's late theodical revisions. Using the same word, *témoin*, to designate human witnessing of larger planetary processes, Buffon's manuscript expresses a kind of relief that human beings came too late to witness the planetary upheaval of the fourth epoch, "when the volcanoes began to act." A late revision appearing from recently discovered manuscript material has these "petrifying and terrible scenes" of volcanism "heralding the birth of intelligent and sensible Nature" (Buffon 1776: 28).[4] The opening of the seventh epoch suggests that "the first men" did remember, on some level, the great eruptions of the fourth epoch, or at least their aftermath. Throughout the work, then, a synchronic, multispecies narrative that decenters human hegemony infiltrates and complicates the stock Enlightenment narrative of nature subdued.

This Enlightenment narrative prevails at the end of the final epoch, but the triumph of domestication is nonetheless instructive as an aversive reaction against the half-unwilling discovery of human animality. When he abuses "barbarians" of various eras (prehistoric, Germanic, Native American) as "animals with human faces" (Buffon 1785: 394), Buffon is, in part, exorcising a kind of newly discovered terror inherited by the entire species from its deep, turbulent past. The same goes for his extravagant claim that the twenty or so species entirely domesticated by humans are "more useful to the earth than all the others" (403), which on some level contradicts the work's preoccupation with ancient megafauna. The earlier, more nuanced account of domestication, though still teleological, depicts its history as embedded in the collective history of species and dependent on a long prehistory of sedentism (Buffon 1988: 161n.).

Perhaps the strongest support for a multispecies approach to Buffon's *Epochs of Nature* lies in the justification that he offers for his extended time scale. We can only begin to grasp the scope of geological time, he argues—an expanse that for him is ten times larger than the period generally accepted in Europe until the mid-nineteenth century, though still short by modern standards—by putting the history of our own species in relation to that of others. In a remarkable passage added to the end of the first epoch during the process of revision, Buffon enjoins his readers to envision a 6,000-foot hill of slate (as at Caen in Normandy) surmounted by a stratum of limestone (Buffon 1988: 42). Supposing that the original sediment accumulates at a rate of five inches per year, it will have been 14,000 years before shells begin to be transported to this site, and these in turn must accumulate and be turned to limestone before the sea level drops and the hill can assume its final form. Reflecting on the formation of this topography in a manner that anticipates James Hutton and Charles Darwin, Buffon enters on a philosophical digression, much of it deleted in revision, that problematizes temporal apperception on this scale. He defends his proposed chronology as already "abridged" from a scale forty times larger that would have been philosophically more adequate (40n.) This "little" scale is needed, he explains to preserve the clarity of the idea, for the "human mind," Buffon reflects, "loses itself in the expanse of duration much more readily than in that of space or number" (40). "Our too brief existence" constrains us to minute analysis of the "numerous centuries required to produce the mollusks with which the earth is filled; [and of] the even greater number of centuries that have passed since their shells were transported and deposited," and so on through the processes of petrifaction and desiccation illustrated in the example of the Norman coast (41). Scaling up or down seemingly at will, Buffon makes the point that the history of other species is indispensable for arriving at a conception of geological time that is at least commensurate with "the limited power of our intelligence" (40n.)—but may still be far short of its true extent.

Forster's rebuttal, in the review quoted at the beginning of this chapter, depends on his reading of ancient geographers, who provide him with adequate evidence for every kind of geological upheaval within the confines of the written record. In levying this criticism, Forster capitalizes on the ambivalence displayed in Buffon's handling of memory and tradition. It is unclear, in the end, how much geological upheaval the "first men" witnessed, or how far back their origin may be traced. Buffon calculates that after 60,000 years, the planet reached the state of "repose" necessary to "its most noble productions," the land animals (202). But he acknowledges that "this repose was not absolute," since the separation of the continents, and other "great changes," were still to come. Forster marshals evidence from ancient geographers to support the notion that a megaflood originating in the Black Sea basin produced the Mediterranean Sea, offering recorded (or at least remembered) "great changes" of this kind as adequate to the task of explaining the earth's present landforms. Although he does not refer to it explicitly, Forster's Pacific voyage may have conditioned his defense of a young earth model, since he had learned to identify atolls and recent volcanic islands in the course of the voyage.

The eruption of Vesuvius in 79 CE, well within the scope of the written record, captured the imagination of eighteenth-century audiences in part because it suggested that natural and social revolutions were commensurable in a certain sense. (Or, to put it another way, it might have seemed to affirm the recentering of human antiquity that Forster also was promoting.) When Fiorelli prepared his cast of the watchdog in its death throes in the 1860s, the response was conditioned by over a century of sublime pathos, and by the more recent sentimentalism of works such as Bulwer-Lytton's *The Last Days of Pompeii*. The entrance onto the scene of this one nonhuman specimen, even if it became "Pompeii's best-known victim," cannot be said to have initiated a multispecies turn in the archaeology of Vesuvius.

It does, however, evoke the evolutionary past (an appropriate term for the 1860s) in at least two ways. First, the dog as a companion animal recalls the co-evolution that underlies and complicates domestication, as Haraway observes, and as Darcy Morey further explains (Morey 2010). Since this is a watchdog specifically, like the animal labeled with the legend "Cave Canem" in the mosaic, its aggression may be seen as a carefully cultivated survival from its evolutionary past. The threat of rapid reversion in dogs is dramatized forcefully in contemporary post-apocalyptic narratives such as Octavia Butler's *Parable of the Sower*, but this specimen had no opportunity to revert to its wild type. The catastrophe came too fast. Second, this Pompeiian watchdog functions as a metonymy for the agon of extinction. The mammoth co-evolved with Pleistocene humans, and perhaps with their wolf-things, as a prey animal. At some find spots, such as the Manis Mastodon site in Washington, the accumulation of fossil bones and tusks appears with clear evidence of hunting by humans, which is sometimes held to have hastened the Pleistocene megafauna extinctions. (Science fiction again offers an analogy in the form of the "megodonts" in Paolo Bacigalupi's *The Wind-Up Girl*, mammoth clones that are carefully engineered but half-wild all the same.) In Buffon's time, it was already clear that large numbers of animals had died at some locations, including Big Bone Lick, and the sheer quantity of remains gave a certain symbolic weight to the thesis of their extinction long before it was generally accepted. The sculptor Allan McCollum, in his 1990 remediation of the cast from Pompeii (Figure 1.3), converts the agony of the individual dog, calculated to provoke sympathetic identification, to a proliferation of agonies evoking mass extinction, while commenting at the same time on the mechanical reproduction associated with the ideology of neoclassicism.

In these two very different scenarios of human-animal interaction—Fiorelli's and Buffon's—evolutionary memory is activated as a medium for recalling a more distant past, preclassical in the

Figure 1.3 Allan McCollum, *The Dog From Pompeii*, 1991. Cast glass-fiber-reinforced Hydrocal. Approximately 21 × 21 × 21 inches each. Replicas made from a mold taken from the famous original "chained dog" plaster cast of a dog smothered in ash from the explosion of Mount Vesuvius, in ancient Pompeii, in 79 AD. Produced in collaboration with the Museo Vesuviano and the Pompeii Tourist Board, Pompeii, Italy, and Studio Trisorio, Naples, Italy. Installation: Sprengel Museum, Hannover, Germany, 1995. Reproduced by permission of the artist.

former case and prehuman in the latter. In both cases, other species—the dog in Fiorelli's case and a variety of megafauna in Buffon's—mark continuities in the archaeological record, linking the human past and the human present. But at the same time, they decenter human beings as protagonists by foregrounding humans' evolutionary proximity to other species, as well as larger patterns of ecological succession. Buffon does not refer to Vesuvius, but does use travelers' accounts of Etna to illustrate the larger volcanic transformations that dominate his fourth epoch. Forster rejected Buffon's relative post-dating of human origins to maintain the possibility of a unified creation that remained indispensable to natural theological paradigms until Darwin's time and beyond. Although Buffon was unambiguous in his Eurocentrism and his commitment to the domestication of nature, he was more ambivalent than his contemporaries on the subject of anthropocentrism. By deferring human origins to a later stage in the history of life, he not only promoted a generative uncertainty but also created a unique perspective on the expanse of prehuman time required for the earth to have its own history. In this way, the study of natural history and antiquities together, not only in Buffon but throughout the early modern period, incorporates multispecies archaeology as a basic part of its intellectual framework. This legacy is essential for multispecies archaeology in the Anthropocene, this new/old epoch with its widely varying start dates and its claims on other species that range from early hunting to farming to industrial-scale exploitation to what may already be the next mass extinction.

Notes

1 In referring to the Enlightenment as the "early Anthropocene," therefore, Menely and other scholars are deliberately deviating from the very different, more famous "early Anthropocene" hypothesis of William Ruddiman, which locates this moment much earlier, in the early Holocene. The recent announcement by the Anthropocene Working Group (Waters 2016) resets the terms of this discussion without rendering it wholly moot.
2 The watchfulness of Pompeii's watchdogs invokes the long history of domestication but also the vestigial ferocity signaled, in spite of its pathos, by the studded collar clearly visible on the cast.
3 Smellie's translation is greatly abridged, but I cite it (Buffon 1785) when referring to the parts of *Epochs of Nature* that he included in vol. 9 of his translation of the *Natural History* (second edition). For all other passages, including those from manuscript portions available before 1962, I refer to Jacques Roger's critical edition of that year, *Les Epoques de la Nature* (Buffon 1988). A new translation, the first modern English version of *Epochs of Nature*, is currently being prepared by Jan Zalasiewicz of the Anthropocene Working Group together with Jacques Grinevald, Libby Robin, and Sverker Solin (forthcoming 2018 from University of Chicago Press).
4 The manuscript entitled "Quatrième époque" was acquired by the Musée national d'histoire naturelle in 2000 and integrated with MS 883. The last page of this section reads, in part: "Nous remercierons le Créateur de n'avoir pas rendu l'homme témoin de ces désastres." In print, "ces désastres" becomes "ces scènes effrayantes et terribles, qui ont précédé, et pour ainsi dire annoncé la naissance de la Nature intelligente & sensible" (28).

References

Buffon, Comte de [George-Louis Leclerc]. 1776. "Quatrième époque" [acquired 2000]. MS 883. Musée national d'histoire naturelle, Paris. Manuscript.
Buffon, Comte de [George-Louis Leclerc]. 1780. *Epoques de la Nature*, 2nd ed. Paris: Imprimerie du Roi.
Buffon, Comte de [George-Louis Leclerc]. 1785. *Natural History, General and Particular*, trans. William Smellie. London: Cadell.
Buffon, Comte de [George-Louis Leclerc]. 1988 [1962]. *Les Époques de la Nature: Édition critique* [1962], ed. Jacques Roger. Paris: Éditions du Muséum.
Cohen, Claudine. 2002 [1994]. *The Fate of the Mammoth: Fossils, Myth, and History*, trans. William Rodarmor. Chicago, IL: University of Chicago Press.
Crossland, Zoe. 2014. Anthropocene: Imagining Agency, Locating the Future. *Journal of Contemporary Archaeology* 1.1: 123–28.
Cuvier, Georges. 1822 [1812]. *Essay on the Theory of the Earth*, ed. and trans. Robert Jameson. 4th ed. Edinburgh: Blackwood.
De Luca, Vincent A. 1991. *Words of Eternity: Blake and the Poetics of the Sublime*. Toronto: University of Toronto Press.
Dwyer, Eugene. 2010. *Pompeii's Living Statues: Ancient Roman Lives Stolen from Death*. Ann Arbor, MI: University of Michigan Press.
Forster, John Reinhold. 1780. "Dr. Forster an Prof. Lichtenberg." *Göttingisches Magazin der Wissenschaft und Litteratur* 1: 140–57.
Hancarville, Pierre d' [P.F. Hugues]. 1767. *Collection of Etruscan, Greek, and Roman Antiquities from the Cabinet of Sir William Hamilton*. 4 vols. Naples: F. Morelli.
Haraway, Donna J. 2008. *When Species Meet*. Minneapolis, MN: University of Minnesota Press.
Koselleck, Reinhart. 2002. *The Practice of Conceptual History: Timing History, Spacing Concepts*, trans. Todd Samuel Presner et al. Stanford, CA: Stanford University Press.
Latour, Bruno. 2005. *Reassembling the Social: An Introduction to Actor-Network Theory*. Oxford: Oxford University Press.

Menely, Tobias. 2015a. *The Animal Claim: Sensibility and the Creaturely Voice*. Chicago, IL: University of Chicago Press.

Menely, Tobias. 2015b. "The Rise of Coal and the Dissolution of Form." Unpublished talk.

Morey, Darcy. 2010. *Dogs: Domestication and the Development of a Social Bond*. Cambridge: Cambridge University Press.

Pilaar Birch, Suzanne E. 2018. Introduction. *Multispecies Archaeology*, ed. Suzanne E. Pilaar Birch. New York: Routledge.

Schnapp, Alain. 1997. *The Discovery of the Past: The Origins of Archaeology*. New York: Harry N. Abrams.

Steffen, Will, et al. 2016. "Stratigraphic and Earth System Approaches to Defining the Anthropocene." *Earth's Future* 4: 1–22. doi:10.1002/2016EF000379.

Suckling, Kieran. 2015. Comment on T.J. Demos, "Against the Anthropocene." http://blog.fotomuseum.ch/2015/05/iii-against-the-anthropocene/.

Van Riper, Bowdoin. 1993. *Men Among the Mammoths: Victorian Science and the Discovery of Human Prehistory*. Chicago, IL: University of Chicago Press.

Waters, Colin N. 2016. "Exploring Formal Recognition of the Anthropocene." *Eos: A Publication of the American Geophysical Union*. https://eos.org/editors-vox/exploring-formal-recognition-of-the-anthropocene.

Wolfe, Cary. 2010. *What Is Posthumanism?* Minneapolis, MN: University of Minnesota Press.

2

THE END OF THE 'NEOLITHIC'?

At the emergence of the Anthropocene

Christopher Witmore

The close of an agrarian era?

The Neolithic is commonly understood as the earliest stage of agrarian society coming between nomadic forgers and configured societies (civilization). Among its features are a settled existence, living together in villages, agriculture—breaking earth on behalf of plants, sowing seed, encouraging crops, waiting for vegetal provisions to mature, bringing in the harvest, and protecting that investment—and a way of living with select animals, termed 'domestication,' specifically as partners in agriculture (co-workers, producers of fertilizer), as companions, as assets of wealth (livestock) and sustenance (milk, meat, warmth), for both agrarians and herders. If *Neolithic revolution* was the phrase used by V. Gordon Childe to herald the beginning of this period,[1] then *urban revolution* was the expression that signaled its end. For Childe, the appearance of cities coincided with a radical reorganization of society—the rise of civilization brought about the cessation of a purportedly 'simpler' mode of existence prevalent throughout the Neolithic. Among the features of this urban revolution enumerated by Childe were a rise in population, a concentration of capital, full-time craft specialization, 'truly' monumental building, ruling classes free from the toils of production, utilitarian science, scripts, long-distance trade, and a psycho-political commitment to communal solidarity (1950).

Ever since John Lubbock introduced the term to signal a taxonomic distinction from earlier 'Palaeolithic' remains (1865, 2–3), the Neolithic has been seen as a particular historic phase, as a transitory period cut from the end of the first block in the three-age system of prehistory (see Daniel 1943, 25). In Greece, for example, this temporal compartment encloses a swath of agrarian existence stretching just over four millennia, from approximately 7000 to around 3200 BCE (Bintliff 2012, 46–82; Halstead 1999). Here, the Neolithic is separated from those of us living today by the intermittent ages of Bronze and Iron, Classical Antiquity, the spread of monotheism, the Enlightenment, and an Industrial Revolution or two, each cordoned off with their own supposed breaks (Olsen et al. 2012, 136–56). However, situating the Neolithic as a link long passed within the chain of successions is not without its glitches.

Emphasis on technologies, socio-political organization, differences of economy, long-distance travel, and the management of surplus as features with which humanity supposedly took leave of a Neolithic mode of existence elevates the miniscule minority and their ways of living as the motor of history (consider Earle 2002; also Kristiansen and Larsson 2007).

The end of the 'Neolithic'?

Technocratic narratives feed into capitalist delusions of 'progress,' for the evolutionist stress conferred on 'increasing complexity' continues to exert a profound influence. The succession of replacements has always been centered on hubristic metamorphoses within human societies, rather than on a more modest and far-reaching ecology of relationships with and between other species.

As for urban living, cities such as Uruk, Babylon, Zhengzhou, Amarna, Alexandria, Rome, Constantinople, London, or New York were the exception until the middle of the last century when massive rural exoduses fueled metropolitan population growth and a metabolic regime of fossil fuels came to undergird the radical segregation of former commensals. Though Childe regarded cities as signaling radical change, though they are now seen as an exclusive domain of we humans-among-ourselves, none of these past urban ensembles was all that distant from their agrarian roots (Storey 2006); their urban populations were of more than bipedal composition (Cronon 1991; also see MacKinnon this volume). Among other animals, horses, goats, cows, swine, and oxen were common inhabitants. In twelfth-century Constantinople, the Byzantine scholar John Tzetzes lived beneath a priest who kept pigs in his apartment and above a room in which a farmer stored fodder (Harris 2007, 130). New York would not evict its population of free-roaming, offal-scavenging hogs, a ubiquitous aspect of city life, till the 1860s (Mizelle 2012, 57). For Childe, our fellow animals, whether as goods or objects of art, seem to have been little more than an afterthought.

Against long-established archaeological convention, both Robert Pogue Harrison (2003, 31, 34) and Michel Serres (2014, 3) have named a different end for the 'Neolithic.' Having never participated in history, apart from being drawn into the battles of kings or the servitude of other parasitic powerbrokers, the vast majority of humanity and their companion-partner species remained committed to, irrespective of its pervasive diversity, a farming and/or herding livelihood. Living on the land, burying their dead in worked ground, cultivating plants and/or breeding livestock, the agrarian majority went on with modes of living inaugurated at the dawning of the Neolithic, while being touched to varying degrees by different forms of kleptocracy—both in terms of taxation and those long-term fluctuations in the ownership and tenure of land (see Hanson 1997)—and their purportedly emancipatory inventions. More succinctly, this 'voiceless' majority's decisions, its morals, and its technologies followed upon living with land and humus, crops and/or wandering herds; this excessively diverse majority lived with different metabolic relations. If we situate the 'Neolithic' less as a taxonomic period within a line of successions oriented around top-down societal organization or severed by technological novelties (both of which undergird the story of human progress) and more as a style of living involving a bewilderingly variegated, yet, on some level, consistent array of rapports, then it was only in the last century, after more than one hundred years with an expanding metabolic regime of fossil fuels, that one could actually make the case that the age of the 'Neolithic,' as Harrison and Serres suggest, had drawn fully to a close.

Indeed, the transitions that marked Childe's early urban revolution pale in comparison to the loss of agriculturalists in Northern Europe and America in the twentieth century (González-Ruibal 2013). Between 1900 and 2000, the percentage of humanity that made its living from agriculture plummeted from around one half to less than one fiftieth.[2] For Serres, "[t]he greatest event of the twentieth century incontestably remains the disappearance of agricultural activity at the helm of human life in general and of individual cultures" (1995, 28; French original 1990).[3] Within the space of the last sixty years, hardly three generations, a farmer with a team of mules in North Carolina went from plowing 40 acres among hundreds of other agrarians with their labors' companions in a single county, to tending 3,400 acres with several air-conditioned tractors among eight other full-time farmers.[4] More than a generation has now passed since the last temporary cooperative of herdsmen (*tselingaton*) and their herds followed the old drover's road, unknown to history, from the slopes of Ortholithi in the Southern Argolid to those of Ziria in Arcadia (Koster 1976). For farmers who relinquish the farms, for herders who take to the roads, this process of humanity ceding its humus continues globally, with the number of incentives and career options multiplying exponentially, perhaps in equal proportion to the number of financial and ecological failures (consider González-Ruibal 2014). But life is even messier than this.

It is undemanding to speak of freely exercised choices among former agrarians. These are not pastoral dramas. Inequities were pervasive. Discrepancies were persistent. Not everyone had an equal share in the decision to move on. And poverty has continued to expand within cities. Moreover, it does not trivialize the suffering and trauma experienced by those who, forcibly uprooted from their agrarian grounds, were dispossessed, to state that the victims of these rural exoduses were not only human. Other animals, those intertwined companions, who in rendering their own survival somewhat less improbable,[5] for better and for worse, radically modified human existence, were caught up in this vast changeover to non-agrarian livelihoods. In the wake of 'Neolithic' styles of living, our former labors' companions and livestock were not let out to greener pastures. Mules and oxen were laid off. Goats and sheep that once moved on the hoof became passengers on the road. Select ruminants and domestic fowl underwent a forced diaspora from farm to factory (Imhoff 2010). Meanwhile, old agricultural lands were either transformed by a new agronomy, destroyed under the onslaught of expanding suburbs and shopping malls, or left to unguided germination (see Redman and Foster 2008; also González-Ruibal 2005; Olivier 2013a, 2013b). While the vast wealth of relations that had underwritten the long-term survival of the greater majority of humanity was relinquished, there are now few who live and work in close proximity to earth, with guided plants, and other animals. These severed relations are indicative of a species of neglect that pervades these cultures at the moment that global humanity acts as a planetary agent and the planet acts back (Serres 1995).

The 'Neolithic' was conceived and given emphasis in the late nineteenth century when every change was regarded as widening the gap between 'man' and the other animals. An artifact of the three-age system with an original fidelity to the organization of archaeological materials (stone, bronze, iron), 'Neolithic,' literally the 'new stone age,' is now a term of convention; lacking broad descriptive utility, it was never a great fit for agrarian livelihoods; especially given its former evolutionist connotations, it is certainly a less-than-apposite label for an enduring form of agrarian ecology. When apprehended in terms of ecology, to be sure, the 'Neolithic' runs deeper than the conditions of production (Thomas 2015), for it involved the intertwined relations with other species, with soil, weather, and land, with a bewilderingly diverse roster of actual entities and their rapports. By extending this name to encompass a longer-term agrarian diversity, both Harrison and Serres underscore the fundamental importance of this stretch of time, which, in turn, is suggestive of the magnitude of the transformations that signal its end. Beyond its political, practical, and rhetorical utility, the name has power and the expanded spatiotemporal scope given to 'Neolithic' by Harrison and Serres calls for consideration. Whatever we make of such use of this thoroughly archaeological term, however inadequate it may be, we as archaeologists should nonetheless take their suggestion for a recent close to the Neolithic seriously.

Emphatically, the catastrophes we now face shock us out of archaeological business as usual. A reconsideration of agrarian ecologies, which took on a completely different shape in the mid-to-late twentieth century, follows among myriad other unsettling demands of our calamitous times after the emergence of what is increasingly called the 'Anthropocene.' Of course, it follows these demands not because it feeds into the technocratic trajectory of linear, homogeneous succession at the end of which looms a humanity which shapes a new geological epoch (see Hartley 2015); on the contrary, it follows because it must struggle against it.

This chapter explores metamorphoses on both sides of the end of the 'Neolithic' and strives to tease out some of their implications. Through two case studies, one from Greece, one from Texas, it presents the changing styles of living among guided flora and farmers, herds and herders. It casts a light on the loss of long-lived rapports, without fully ignoring concomitant gains and the accidents that surface in their absence. On the Argive Plain, we see a transformation to citrus monoculture, which, having pushed the region to the edge of an ecological catastrophe, is now sustained by a technical solution harboring its own unique dangers. With the case of Cattle City, Texas, we encounter an overweight meat-industrial complex around which brews an ongoing struggle for a workable agropastoralism. Finally, more will be said concerning the tectonic shift in human rapports with our fellow species and, by way of conclusion, the role of archaeology in understanding such changes in an era when humanity has become a geobiological agent. In lieu of a more appropriate placeholder, the 'Neolithic' is maintained throughout this chapter for both the scope and feeling that the term calls forth.[6] As to the question of its end, this chapter resists succumbing fully to the 'epitaphic impulse' to inscribe a death once and for all. Old ways have their manner of returning,[7] agrarian modes of existence persist as the only option for the poor in areas outside urban zones of comfort (González-Ruibal 2014; Purdy 2015), and yet with the planetary-scale catastrophes before us, these do not exist in the way they formerly did.

In Heideggerian terms, the diverse, yet consistent, modes of living with the land and other species become conspicuous through their disruption. However, to ponder the uprooting of human intertwined species from the humic foundations of a deep agrarian ecology in the mid-twentieth century is neither to pander to that old Arcadian delusion of timelessness nor an idealized agrarian myth, nor the long-standing image of enduring constraints (Braudel 1975).[8] Agrarian communities never lacked excessive variety (Halstead 1987). Whether in terms of subsistence practices or the meanings they gave to their endeavors, the idiosyncrasies of human groups, both rational and ecstatic, were beyond legion. Whatever their ample differences—indeed, there was never a standardized pattern of mixed farming common to European Neolithic societies in the usual sense (see Thomas 2015)—these collectives, by and large, were underwritten by a diversity of rapports with soil and moisture, weather and plants, labor's companions, whether as animals or instruments, and laborers. What has become of these old things and their relations? Moreover, after the work of philosophers and microbiologists, from Merezhkovsky to Margulis, the notion that animals can be rendered exclusively as insular entities cannot be sustained. Living in close proximity, humans and other animals exchanged microbes on a daily basis, and our mutual co-habitation modified the genomic memory of our cells (Shapiro 2011, 2015). Fellow symbionts, now former commensals, we were all integrated organisms sharing in symbiotic and genetic co-development (Margulis 1998). Such a perspective, whether we label it multispecies or symbiotism (Westbroek 2015), challenges us to think (and live) beyond the level of human-among-themselves with respect to radical challenges before us. Such is an additional aspiration of this chapter.

The Argive Plain, Greece: flora and their farmers

Apart from a few scattered olive groves and vineyards, open was the Argive plain at the dawn of the twentieth century. Plate I.I in Herbert Lehmann's *Argolis: Landeskunde der Ebene von Argos und ihrer Randgebiete* (1937) captured this flat expanse as seen from Mycenae (Figure 2.1). Spreading out towards distant limestone slopes whose bare surfaces were stripped of their deciduous oak forests of nearly 5,000 years earlier (Jahns 1993), a delicate embroidery of cereal fields, some harvested, some freshly cut, and fallow pastures, speckled with horses and livestock, lay unobstructed over the whole of their dull contours, save for the extended garland of whitewashed houses in the village of Koutsopodi. Across this plain, everyone saw the toils of everyone else. Everyone saw the fruits of everyone else's labors. Every boundary, every isolated tree, every open plot, every stand of cereals, every plowed surface suggested workmanship and achievement—indeed, this region was ancient in its radical, agrarian modification by the time the walls of Mycenae were raised.

The outcome of shared and sustained work by farmers, herders, and their companion animals, a visually unencumbered plain seems to have been the norm in all previous antiquarian accounts that had bothered with mention, however meager, or illustration, however incidental (compare Gell 1810; Chateaubriand 1814; Pouqeville 1827). Among the many 'enlightened' Northern Europeans to observe the encouraged flora of the plain were two Englishmen, Edward Dodwell and William Martin Leake. On December 11, 1805, Dodwell, travelling along the road from Mycenae to Nauplia, witnessed plowing and sowing on the "perfectly flat plain," which had few trees beyond "the foot of the hills behind the ruins of Tiryns, where there is a thick and extensive grove of olives" (1819, 245).[9] Three months later, Leake described the drier parts as covered in cereals, areas with more moisture, in cotton and vines, and the marshy patches near the sea, in rice and *kalambokki* (maize) (1830, 348). For both Englishmen, the questions of what to observe and how to observe it were conditioned by a knowledge economy centered in London (Witmore and Buttrey 2008). An artilleryman with a Classical education, Leake, for example, approached this plain from the angle of making outputs known, should resources be necessary for deploying British troops to the region, should Classical scholars have interest in

Figure 2.1 The upper portion Argive plain and its western mountains, seen from Mycenae. Plate I.I from Lehmann 1937.

what has become of Greco-Roman antiquity. Yet, who would really *see* agrarian relations on the plain? Who would truly understand the antiquity of the practices witnessed from the saddle?

When Lehmann studied the plain in 1911, the moisture content of the soil continued to determine which plants were to be grown. An effect of soil and water saturation, specialization in different crops tended to fall to different villages. Around Chronika, a village about five kilometers south of where Lehmann took his photograph, tobacco and cereals were predominant. There, over the following decades—up to 1928—agrarians would increasingly turn to the cultivation of melons and tomatoes in clay-rich, red-brown soils. While the plain was self-sufficient—that is, it maintained a diversified production—it also targeted an export market with specialized cultivation in currants and tobacco.[10] Vegetable gardens were maintained near the houses, usually just out back, where, in close proximity to wells, under the close scrutiny of residents, one could care for more demanding, more valued flora—broad beans, garlic, basil, mulberry, pomegranate, and fig (Lehmann 1937, 127–28).

Set to rhythms not of human making, agrarian existence was full of delays. Waiting for rains to arrive or depart; waiting for the right soil conditions for tillage; waiting for crops to sprout, to mature—patience was requisite with every entity, every rapport. Oriented by growing plants, life was slow. In the Argive plain, in all Mediterranean lands, labor fell into an annual cycle of plowing, sowing, watching plants develop, weeding, harvest, storage, and organized consumption. Mild and wet Mediterranean winters and hot and dry summers exerted their influence. Tillage and sowing winter grains, wheat and barley, occurred from October through December, just as it did when Dodwell rode from Mycenae to Nauplia, just as it had throughout antiquity. Harvest followed in late April and May, later in surrounding hill country, and, at higher elevations, in June (ibid., 66–7).

These labors were shared with companion animals. On the plain, Lehmann noted more horses than any other area of the Argolid. Towing carriages or carts, conveying riders, and pulling plows; thus was the trifold utility of purpose for so many horses (also see Halstead 2014, 22). While iron plows were used to break ground on these flatlands, in the surrounding hills, with its rockier soils, ard plows, what Lehmann referred to the "hesiodische Hakenpflug," were still in use (1937, 118).

Abundant are the fine-grained details missing from early accounts of the plain. Did Argive farmers sow in ten-meter wide strips? Did they counsel quick work in covering the area with overlapping furrows before geese could rob the seed? Did they grow a ribbon of rye on the edge to be used for binding sheaves of barley?[11] Nothing in the plain is written.

At the dusk of the twentieth century, the plain was canopied (Figure 2.2). Where an open plain once insured everyone knew of everyone else's lot amid shared drudgery, a continuous covering of well-watered orange trees now shields the farmer's labors. Prior to 1950, citrus crops—mandarins, oranges, and lemons—were charming supplements enjoyed in the comforts of enclosed domestic gardens. Mudbrick walls or a line of cypress staved off both frost and wayward eyes. Wells in close proximity kept them supplied with the copious amounts of water they demanded. Marginal crops, Lehmann calculated that these citrus trees covered just 0.3% of the total cultivated area of the plain (1937, 130). By 1990 one crop, oranges, accounted for over 40% of an even larger cultivated area (van der Leeuw 1998, 286).

The proliferation of orange groves in the 1950s and 1960s placed new water demands on the region. Borehole irrigation, encouraged at the level of individual farmers (Lemon and Blatsou 1999, 122; also see Hector 1973), was introduced and rapidly expanded (Figure 2.3). Between 1945 and 2007, the number of hectares irrigated in the Argolid rose nearly fivefold, from 5,500 to 25,430. Between 1964 and 2004, the number of water pumps more than tripled, from 2,953 to 10,044, and the number of sprinklers surged from 3 to 10,635.[12] In 1990, citrus trees

Figure 2.2 The canopied plain in 2014. Photo: C. Witmore.

Figure 2.3 Borehole irrigation pump located just west of Neo Ireo (Chronika), 2012. Photo: C. Witmore.

accounted for over 63% of the area under irrigation on the plain. Pervasive canopies transformed the ambient temperature at ground level, thus air mixers and sprinklers, which distribute yet more water when it is least needed, are enrolled to regulate temperatures in winter.

The end of the 'Neolithic'?

With boreholes, farmers gained in self-sufficiency—labor would no longer be siphoned into digging irrigation channels from community wells to the common edge of the fields; effort would no longer be required to harness the mule to the long arm of the well pump. With a steady supply of water, farmers gained in consistency—interannual variability in rainfall would not translate into volatility in yields; the moisture content of the soil would no longer factor in which crops are grown. And yet, with the exponential increase in boreholes and their use came a radical decrease in aquifer levels. Rapidly depleted water tables opened the way for seawater intrusion into the upper aquifer. Through irrigation, saline waters were distributed and evapotranspiration on the surface led to the salinization of the soils (Balabanis 1999, 68). Agrarians responded by drilling deeper and deeper. For eight to nine millennia, this plain was father, mother, and nurse to managed species and not one drew upon waters from a depth greater than 15 meters. Whereas the average water table in the vicinity of Chronika was at 11 meters before 1950, it would eventually fall to around 100 meters (compare Lehmann 1937, 57 and 126 with Lemon and Blatsou 1999). On the periphery of the plain it would recede to far greater depths—as much as 420 meters. With waters untapped by those living here prior to the mid-twentieth century, the aquifers were drained to support the orange crop. Poised on the brink of disaster, the expansion of the Anavolos canal system—a technical fix—has allowed orange farmers to continue to behave as they did before. Now, despite fluctuations in the 1990s, the area covered in orange trees continues to expand.

What is more, the cumulative effects of salination and pollution, from fertilizers and pesticides, appropriate waters from all—residents on the plain can no longer drink the water from below their feet. By 1999, nitrate concentrations had increased to 172 milligrams/liter, well over three times the accepted limit for adults and nearly nine times what is allowed for children (Galanis and Nikitas 2000). Is there a link between these high carcinogenic-nitrate levels and the high rates of cancer in the area? Other toxins enter the soil and cling to the fruit through pesticide use. A recent testing program under the European Food and Safety Authority, coordinated by the Ministry of Rural Development and Food, found Dimethomorph on oranges from Spiliotakis and Thiabendazole on mandarins from Lefkakia (Georgios 2012).

The canopied plain is undergirded by the globally ubiquitous metabolic regime of fossil fuels.[13] Electricity, whether for the borehole pumps, air mixers, or the Anavolos system (also for juice production, refrigeration, and storage), is partially supplied by the coal- and lignite-burning power plant in Megalopolis. Between 1964 and 2004, the number of headless oxen, tractors, in the Argolid rose from 691 to 4,136.[14] Merlin and Valencia oranges, exported to the former Soviet Union prior to 1991, are now destined for markets throughout the European Union. Food-miles, the distance from the plain to where the oranges are consumed, add more fossil fuels. This long reach is based upon the logic of division and specialization. Cold storage in concentrate and shipping favors a single species, rather than diverse species with staggered harvest dates. This regime both follows and breaks with a deep agrarian logic. What is more, on a plain ruled for millennia by scarcity where there was little waste, overabundance now reigns. Indeed, with subsidies provided for overproduction, surplus oranges were routinely dumped in large quantities.[15]

Taking leave of those supposedly common drudgeries and seemingly shared miserablisms that came with being tethered to the land, the numbers of agrarians have dwindled upon this plain. Over the first decade of 2000, the population of Neo Ireo, known to Lehmann as Chronika, declined from 585 to 493.[16] Between 1981 and 2011, the population of Ira, a village at the very heart of the plain, fell from 455 to 374 (NSSG 2011). Yet, the meaning that such numbers once carried for largely agrarian societies has all but disappeared. When Lehmann wrote about demographic trends in the villages of the plain, he could trust that those numbers were representative of farmers. When roads and automobility connect the residents of these villages to Argos and Nafplion with ease, a home on the plain no longer translates into work on the plain. Village demography, admittedly, gives us an indirect sense of a problem better understood with broad statistics. The 2011 census revealed that the rural population of Greece had fallen to 23.4%.[17] Orange trees, moreover, do not demand a full-time commitment on the part of those who tend them (Lawrence 2007, 95–6). For the majority of citrus farmers who cultivate the groves on either side of the county road that links Neo Ireo with Ira, the orange crop provides supplemental income. Café owners, civil servants, lorry drivers, most producers are either part-time agrarians or retirees. Indeed, most of the registered orange growers in plain are elderly, above 65.[18] It is not always difficult to identify their passing—in many places, their progeny have severed the agrarian commitment altogether, choosing to sell the land, develop it with new houses, or harvest sun with solar farms.

The current regime of orange trees does not require other animal partners in agriculture. In 1934, there were 8,000 horses in the prefecture of Argolis-Korinth and most, Lehmann surmised, were located in the plain. In 2009, only 350 animals—not just horses, this figure is inclusive of all equidae (horses, donkeys, mules)—were to be counted in the whole of the Argolid and Corinthia. I do not speak for the surrounding hill country, but on the flat plain, there are no more yoked companions, no more animal-pulled plows. In over a decade of visiting the plain, I have rarely seen a fallow field used for pasturage, apart from the dry riverbed of the Panitza, the ancient Inachos.[19] A century ago, Lehmann observed two patterns of transhumance in the Argive Plain: one pattern involved extensive transhumance with droves and flocks in the limestone uplands, which followed a seasonal round between villages and mountain meadows; the second pertained to more integrated grazing focused on the plain. With the former, goats, hearty, were present in larger proportions; with the latter, sheep were kept in greater numbers and flocks and droves were turned out on annual fallow or recently harvested land at the end of May (1937, 134). Even at that time, Lehmann noted how the increasing intensification of agriculture was depriving livestock of more and more pasture. Less land was left fallow. Formerly vacant patches were tilled. Marshlands, previously avoided because of malaria, were drained. Church lands were redistributed. In the interval between 1911 and 1930, herd numbers on the plain had dwindled by one fifth. Today, if the numbers are faithful, then the populations of flocks and droves, former *compagnons de route*, continue to decline.[20] Few are now to be seen on the plain. While this plain has witnessed half a dozen fluctuations between agrarians and herders over the course of the last three millennia, has this erstwhile agrarian world been relegated to the realms of archaeology and history?

Cattle City, Texas: urban herds

More than 300 steel-pipe enclosures, ordered alphabetically and separated by feed roads and drover's alleys, a cattle-sorting facility, a hospital, an office building near a port of entry, hills of silage, large warehouses full of corn, a feed mill, a fifty-acre field for the collection of solid waste in consecutive linear mounds, a sewage system, and a retention pond for liquid waste, high in nitrogen, phosphorus, and potassium; these components, laid out over a square mile of flat Texas Panhandle, constitute the contrived urban envelope sustaining a fluctuating population of up to 65,000 beef cattle (Figure 2.4).[21] This is Cattle City, what the 'industry' regards as a Concentrated Animal Feeding Operation, or CAFO (see Imhoff 2010). Let us consider this giant object through the constituents of this acronym, CAFO, in terms of concentration, animals, feed, and operation.

Figure 2.4 Cattle City, from the top of the feed mill, 2013. Photo: C. Witmore.

Concentration takes on one meaning in terms of the square footage of residential space allotted to each animal, which varies by season—14 square meters in summer, 12.5 square meters in winter. Concentration follows on the logic of multiplied enclosures. In order for these containers to accommodate life, both fodder and water must be brought to livestock. Thus, ruminants are maintained within a controlled space, rather than being left to follow their appetite on the graze, to socialize without constant oversight on the hoof (see Aldred, this volume). Though there are no byres, no shady areas, no patches of buffalo, mesquite, or grama grass, there is also no duress—stress is minimized in an effort to maintain calm herds. Animal concentration is new in neither concept nor execution—indeed, its history, however sparse, is ancient. What is new relates to its pervasiveness, its reach and requirements, and its efficacy (Witmore 2015). Concentration translates into high-density, urban living conditions for beef cattle. Indeed, given its proportions, perhaps it is more appropriate to speak of this CAFO as a city. 'Feedlots' or 'industrial farms' are labels ill equipped to name an urban expanse accommodating up to 65,000 cattle. In residence for up to a year, in Cattle City, herds take on the characteristics of an urban populace. Yet in the midst of irrigated cotton fields stretching out to the horizon in all directions, their lot is one of mutual seclusion.

Animals: Beef cattle raised on pastures arrive from California, Florida, and everywhere in between. Most animals are young Angus crosses, selected not because of their suitability for grazing the high plains, but because of the quality of their flesh understood as beef, their ability to add muscle, their lack of horns, and their frame, the size of which is optimal for cattle infrastructures (swing gates, sorting holds, and ultimately the slaughterhouse). Beyond the lack of biodiversity that comes with an industry largely oriented to a single breed (Wuerthner 2010), in most cases, these animals are no more than a year old. The social life of cattle is oriented to the herd, yet in the course of a daily round between feed trough, raised mound, water tub, and fence line where socializing with other animals occurs, not a bellow is to be heard. Calm is maintained through the drug-induced suppression of the estrous cycle and the removal of aggressive or sick animals. Handlers on horseback or in observation towers keep Cattle City residents under constant surveillance. Cattle provide neither labor nor traction, neither milk nor companionship. Known by numbers, not names, they exist in a state of being-toward-slaughter. Here, the age-old somatic kinship between humans and other animals as co-mortals, subject to death, is in short supply, for when factored as proto-meat, the death of a heifer or steer is lessened to but a step along a disassembly line in a 'packing plant' (see Conover 2013; Witmore 2015, 236).

Feed is distributed by truck into thirteen kilometers of concrete trough at the rate of 1.7 million pounds daily. In addition, the residents of Cattle City gulp down over half a million gallons of water within 24 hours. Every day, each heifer or steer consumes 25 to 30 pounds of feed (Figure 2.5). Bovine diets, formulated in order to generate muscle and fat, vary depending on an animal's length of residency and their overall weight. From starter through to finish rations, four different feed combinations, designed by veterinary nutritionists, are provided. A slow shift from a high-roughage diet to a highly concentrated one aimed at adding weight is necessary to control acidosis (here we encounter a second meaning for *concentration*). Silage (fodder from corn stalks or cotton burs), flaked corn (corn heated by steam and compressed in a roller mill), corn-gluten feed (a by-product from the manufacture of cornstarch and corn syrup, this provides a kind of medium-level protein), and tallow (rendered animal fat)—the relative amounts of these constituents are ultimately determined by market price.[22] With the addition of an ionophore, which suppresses the appetite in the animal but improves their 'efficiency' (in the sense of achieving the same rate of gain with less feed), Tylan 100, an antibiotic used to reduce liver abscesses that result from a highly concentrated diet, MGA 500, an estrous suppressant, and a probiotic, feed is not so much adapted to the ruminant as the ruminant is adapted to the feed.

Operation: Operating costs are spread over the rate of production, which is to say expenditures are distributed across each resident for each day of their occupancy; this adds up to between 21 and 22 million head days per year. An effect of packaged meat, Cattle City aims to add the maximum amount of flesh within the minimum span of residency. Such orientations give rise not only to the expansion of capacity through the multiplication of animal enclosures, but also to the synthetic manipulation of bovine endocrinological and immunological systems. Since the first enclosures were constructed in 1969, Cattle City has expanded its capacity twice over and increased the finishing weight of animals by upwards of 25%—whereas in 1976 a heifer 'finished' at 975 pounds and a steer at 1,200, today they 'finish' at between 1,250 to 1,300 and around 1,400 respectively. The addition of trenbolone-acetate hormone implants and ionophore feed additives increases the rate of weight gain while transforming metabolic cycles. While the collateral damage of a highly concentrated diet, destructive to a ruminant digestive

Figure 2.5 Cattle crowd the bunk to consume feed, 2013. Photo: C. Witmore.

system, is managed with antibiotics, which are also enrolled to treat common ailments such as diphtheria and pneumonia, antibiotic use escalates the pace of microbial evolution within the gut of resident ruminants and potentially leads to the development of cross-resistance to other antibiotics within their class.

While morals and appetites, as it has been pointed out, parted ways early in human relations with animals (Sloterdijk 2012; Hanson 1995), the mode of husbandry present in Cattle City would seem to bear little resemblance to that practiced by herders on the XIT Ranch, which once encompassed a substantial portion of the Texas Panhandle more than a century ago; or, indeed, to what Lehmann observed in the Argive Plain. Here, to be sure, long-lived rapports have succumbed to a technical way of life, which endangers our former Neolithic partners and an appreciation of their living being. Here, we encounter a perversion of more than ten millennia of iterative practices and accumulated wisdoms. Thus, it is hardly surprising that increasing discontent surrounds CAFOs, which play a major role in sustaining a massive global population of 1.5 billion methane-belching cattle.

Let us in passing expose some of the ground for this mistrust. Living within ruminants (cattle, buffalo, sheep, goats, and camelids) or waterlogged soils, methanogenic bacteria generate bountiful quantities of methane from fermentation of hydrolyzed carbohydrates. Depending on the composition of their diet, each Cattle City resident belches out upwards of 50 kilograms of methane annually. A greenhouse gas up to 21 times more potent than CO_2, additional methane is produced from the breakdown of animal fertilizers and manure (see Reay et al. 2010; also Steinfeld 2006). Cattle City also generates more than its fair share of nitrous oxide, ammonia, and carbon dioxide. Fossil fuels undergird every stage in this urban-industrial complex: fertilizers in Iowa fields, fuel needed to grow fodder, the diesel used in the transportation of cattle, feed constituents, manure, and meat products, the plastics used in packaging meat. By the time 500 grams of Cattle City beef hits the freezer aisle, according to one estimate, it will have required three liters of oil to get there (Appenzeller 2004). Industrial agriculture, by other estimates, demands ten times more energy than those lighter, local alternatives that characterized the 'Neolithic' and perhaps ten times more energy than what is derived from the food that is eventually produced (von Weizsäcker et al. 1997, 50). To greenhouse gases and the overuse of fossil fuels one can add: high water consumption, not counting the water used to grow the food or spray down the dust; contamination with concentrated nitrates in groundwater or secreted antibiotics and hormones in animal waste—toxicology and residue chemistry research has yet to make explicit the adverse effects of antibiotics and hormones on bacteria and earthworms in the soil or, indeed, upon edible muscle (see Burkholder et al. 2007; Conover 2013); fear of the next pandemic emerging from the gut incubators of cattle, and detachment—for what are the unforeseen consequences of parting ways after 10,000 years of living in close proximity as fellow symbionts?

When herds have expanded into urban populations, pastoral imagery no longer makes sense. In this urban model of agronomy, grazing lands have been abandoned, and herders, known as 'handlers,' have been sidelined. While care is not altogether absent, too few of the 45 employees of Cattle City now work outside in close proximity with its 'residents.' Too few experience cattle as living animals. The majority of those who are responsible for making decisions regarding animal lives only know them as images of muscle on computer screens, as tabulations of weight in labs, as quarterly profits in offices (Witmore 2015, 241–47). Streamlined into synthetic operations, cattle are managed at a distance within a network of cattle or cow cities within a giant corporate industry of food production. Here, one encounters a form of reductionism that regards living animals as little more than proto-meat, that routinizes their selective manipulation, their exploitation, and their suffering from a comfortable distance. Little wonder comparisons of CAFOs to concentration camps are pervasive—warnings that these enclosures harbor portents

A deep rupture?

One can measure, as Serres points out, the importance of the event by the duration of the era it concludes (2014, 16). Let us here rehearse some of the features that mark the supposed end of the 'Neolithic' in light of the foregoing examples. Whatever form plant cultivation took, it was the case that the long-lived rapports with seed and stores, cereals and pulses, seasonal variations in moisture and soil, clots of earth and hoes, eventually, but not necessarily for all, olive trees and vines, traction animals and plows, fields and furrows, were constitutive of an ecology of practices for the vast majority of residents of the Argive Plain up until the middle of the last century. Now, air-conditioned and irrigated canopies of citrus, a formerly marginal crop, are pervasive through the work of an increasingly smaller minority; the alteration of the earth has extended hundreds of meters into the subsurface, first by rapidly draining an aquifer, then by recharging it with waters coopted from saline springs fed by the agrochemical infused runoff of higher agricultural plains (see Morfis and Zojer 1986); as seed stores have disappeared, so too have genetic diversities diminished; few fields under cereals and pulses are to be found; the formerly horse-bearing plain no longer bears horses.

Though the genealogy of feedlots runs deep (Witmore 2015), CAFOs, like Cattle City, proliferated in the wake of World War II, in the midst of the agrarian exodus. Long-lived, mutually symbiotic rapports with animals on the hoof, whether in fenced pastures or on the paths of transhumance, have been severed for humanity's majority. In the 'Neolithic,' the management of stock was tied to close observation of behavior, of bovine bodies known in life from the perspective of externality. Growth once followed a consistent pattern tied to the seasonal round. Now an industrial assemblage of urban infrastructures, machinic manipulators, pharmaceutical companies, and a knowledge economy that divides up the undividable regulates millions of cattle and their physiological processes. Bovine biological functions are managed with more control, the formation of tissue is controlled with more management, and the old corrals extend into the bovine microbiome walling off pathogens at the expense of commensals (probiotics are a relatively recent addition to cattle feed).

Former companions—cows, cattle, and yoked oxen, among others—have been transformed into strangers through a segregated urbanism. Unhooking ourselves from our companion animals after 10,000 years of living in close proximity has not been without its accidents, it is not without its looming dangers. The consequences of living apart for microbial exchange, for both the bovine and human microbiome, are tremendous (also see Weyrich, this volume). Allergies are on the rise for humans walled off in their microbe-impoverished, air-conditioned interiors (Schuijs et al. 2015); sensory deprivation in children follows on a lack of being outdoors (Hanscom 2016); and what of the bovine masses that also once benefited immunologically?

In the space of just over sixty years, the exceedingly rich biodiversity of guided flora and fauna developed and maintained across hundreds of generations has been squandered. In Greece, rapid and pervasive genetic erosion has occurred in local varieties of cultivated cereals—recent estimates suggest that local cereal varieties account for only 1% of the cultivated acreage today (MEECC 2014, 31; Stavropoulos 1996, 13–14)—a process only partially countered through archival practices with Gene Banking. Since 1950, in Greece, three of the five native breeds of cattle have ceased to exist and the remaining two only account for 0.64% of the cattle population; all six indigenous horse breeds are threatened with extinction, as is the one breed of buffalo (MEECC 2014, 31).

With both the Argive orange groves and Cattle City, we witness a shift from a world of scarcity to a world of blithe wastefulness, both in terms of overproduction and overconsumption (Sloterdijk 2013, 223–32). New values are shaped no longer by shortage staved off through work, but by overabundance made routine. In key zones of comfort (ibid.), pervasive seasonality succumbs to pervasiveness without seasonality. Moreover, what was known to most yesterday is known to few today. The abandoned implements of an erstwhile agrarian existence—ploughshares, whippletrees, neck yokes—hang in rotting barns, on walls in antique shops, deteriorate as rustic yard decoration, or pile up in museums. Whereas most of those Argive generations over the course of millennia would have had some measure of a mutual understanding as to their utility, few now know what they are, much less how to use them. The former ordinary is the contemporary extraordinary.

Serres ventures to posit that these are indications of how the same cultures that experienced the loss of agriculturalists, little by little, no longer took the world, as they formerly knew it, into account (2014, 41). For Harrison, the uprooting of humanity from the humus severs the connection between a patch of ground and the self in the way of our agrarian forebears and "draws a veil over the earth we live on" (2003, 32). Too few now live outdoors with the weather, or in close proximity to soil and animals. Too few now watch plants grow or accompany animals in search of green. Animals and plants are encountered now as either prepackaged cuts or boxed produce in the grocery store. At the same time that global warming becomes an explicit concern, we wall ourselves off with synthetic worlds within air-conditioned interiors; indoors is where the majority of human urbanites now spend the majority of their time. Meanwhile, we do not trust what we eat, the soil it grows in, or the waters deep below in the way that so many formerly did (though, this is not to imply that distrust is new; see, for example, Thommen 2012). If and when the majority now returns to the outdoors, they cast eyes upon, as Serres points out, an estranged world of Arcadian nature, vacations, and tourism (1995, 28).

It is of course the case that, by taking each of these examples on their own, archaeologists and historians of ecology will find antecedent situations (see examples in Balter 2013; also Edgeworth et al. 2014). One can trace much deeper genealogies for the components of Cattle City (Witmore 2015). One can find numerous examples for the broad manipulation of land with forest clearing or pervasive alteration through agriculture (Redman 1999). These situations, however, never attained the combination of mass, density, and speed, that is now underwritten by billions of living humans with trillions of other things (on land use, for example, see Foley et. al. 2005; Hooke and Martín-Duque 2012). A fundamental difference is that humans are no longer biological agents solely; they are, as it is now regularly pointed out, geological ones also (Chakrabarty 2009; Morton 2013); we now confront both a radically modified understanding of human action both spatially and temporally, and an earth that will no longer be relegated to the role of silent backdrop (Latour 2015, 154).

Possessing a collective agency comparable to that of oceans, volcanoes, or tectonic plates (Serres 1995), this humanity beyond Leviathan has become a geological force whose memories, most geologists now agree, will stand out in the 4.5 billion-year archive of Earth history. The term 'Anthropocene' was introduced to signal this uncanny transformation in what it is to be human. Increasingly, the consensus is to drive the golden spike into the sediment horizon correlating to the mid-twentieth century (Steffen et al. 2011; Waters et al. 2016; although see Edgeworth et al. 2015), fittingly enshrined as BP, or Before Present by both archaeologists and geologists.[23] All totaled, these bewildering transformations amount to a rupture that extends far deeper than history in any conventional sense.

Whether these coincidental changes were taken as indicative of modernity or tradition, progress or anachronism, accessing them in terms of a quarrel between two sides began with a bifurcation, a contrast, an oversimplification. This is not about that old obsession of telling what time we are in—first hunter-gatherers, then agrarians, now urban dwellers with unequal access to select vegetable provisions and packaged meat 'produced' at any distance. This has nothing to do with that modernist path of emancipation for we are even more entangled in the tendrils of the earth—call it the 'intrusion' of Gaia (Stengers 2015). Succinctly, the long view of an agrarian humanity stands as a counter to the technocratic march of civilization described by Childe. All these modes of life (hunter-gatherer, agrarian, urban) coexist in the present—some have even returned after a hiatus associated with modernizing failures (see González-Ruibal 2006, 113–14)—nonetheless, their overall proportions have shifted tremendously. Though maintained under different social configurations to be sure, the very long-term agrarian rapports that characterized the 'Neolithic' were always conditioned by relations that did not rely on humans, that operated with or without us. Most agrarians understood this and conditioned their practices accordingly. Now, geo-engineered systems and fossil fuels underwrite contrived monocultures; controlled growth and manipulated microbiomes facilitate the steady supply of packaged meat; entangled within this routinized artificiality is our collective humanity, which cannot persist without it, or, at least, that is what we are led to believe (Stengers 2015). Humans have emerged as geobiological agents precisely at a moment when there has been profound depletion of those who lived in close proximity to land, who lived in accordance with the rhythms of season and weather, and with other species. Should we archaeologists posit here a close to ten millennia of agrarian styles of living for both humans and their fellow animals? Did we witness the end of the Neolithic in the mid-twentieth century?

Archaeology unbound?

For hundreds of millions of years, life has shaped its environment and vice versa (Margulis and Sagan 1997). When set against the temporal horizon necessary for trillions of marine organisms to play a more formidable role in shaping the Argive Plain and the surrounding mountains, those few millennia over which agrarians and their companions modified their environment seems so very trivial. It is, however, not from the angle of duration that we archaeologists have been so overly, so narrowly, focused on human-centered agencies (Olsen et al. 2012; Witmore 2014). For over eight millennia on the Argive Plain, and for varying durations in other locales, entities were coupled together in remarkably diverse yet consistent ways, and, all totaled, this was a particular geobiological configuration involving the majority of agrarians, humans and their partners in agriculture and husbandry. The diverse forms of intertwined entities, which underwrote an agrarian mode of existence, were finally overturned in the last century. And now those processes have entered a radical acceleration, which poses incredible dangers for many, by no means all, forms of life (Margulis 1998, 119).

It has been argued that, given the profound and pervasive catastrophes we face, the past has not equipped us for what lies ahead (Sloterdijk 2016, 627–50). In other words, we confront an autodidactic situation where the past cannot act as a guide. No doubt, with a planet under protest, humanity will have to maneuver very differently from how it has over the last ten millennia. Here what has become of the past is not so much a guide, but a component of how we learn and interact. When there is no space left to learn from one's mistakes or misfortune, an archive of failures and successes, alternatives and counterexamples—whether as instances of past land use, environmental degradation, or biologically diverse alternatives for how we might live—becomes more necessary than ever (Redman 1999; also van der Leeuw and Redman 2002). There are no guarantees that the nuances of the very long term, what I have maintained under the insufficient rubric of the 'Neolithic,' or any archaeological counterexamples, will inform this learning which can no longer afford to wait for misfortune to strike. Necessary for how we understand and anticipate in accordance with the rhythms and scope of the planet, this long-term archive is now being steadily filled by archaeology and other fields. If, however, it is left as a matter of curation by the estranged—those who view it solely from computer screens indoors—then we might as well embrace absolutism and posit an end.

Contemporary realities are crushing material memories 10,000 years in the making (González-Ruibal 2008; Olivier 2013a, 122–26; also 2013b). Those archives of our 'Neolithic' existence that survive this destruction are not to be found in libraries—having never participated in written history, agrarian ecologies always operated under its radar—but beneath canopies of orange, below the accumulated infrastructures, in the earth, in the form of entire landscapes. Here, these archives persist and their importance is not secondary to what we maintain within comfortable interiors. Broken memories held by humus, by crumbling terraces, by overgrown fields, by forgotten lanes, by derelict mills, by fragmented berms and drainage ditches, by old things with which we no longer engage are fundamental, for they speak to what has become of modes of living where the backdrop was not always understood in terms of resource. These agrarian ruins hold lessons, even hint at viable alternatives, concerning other ways to live. We cannot allow them to be obliterated by the coming changes.

At the emergence of the so-called 'Anthropocene' there are new objects of archaeological concern: microplastics in the sea, ghost nets and garbage islands floating in the oceans, exhausted or polluted aquifers, submerged cities, and even the atmosphere—as pockets of breathable air become an increasing concern. While the agrarian poor outside zones of comfort are more susceptible than others in the near term (Purdy 2015)—consider the water crisis and drought that led to the dispossession of Syrian farmers prior to the revolution (Wendle 2016)—zones protected by wealth will eventually lose their comfort. With sea levels projected to rise between 20 and 200 centimeters by the end of the century, Dhaka and the lowlands of Bangladesh will become part of the Bay of Bengal; southern Florida will lie under the Gulf of Mexico. New York will become New Venice. So much will be relegated to oblivion, and thus our sole recourse will become archaeology and history. A fundamental question here: how can archaeologists understand change, pervasive on a planetary scale, which appears to exceed locality? The coupling of the earth and life sciences and the humanities—a unique feature of archaeology—has never been more necessary.

With a planet under protest, the distinction between natural history and human history, as Dipesh Chakrabarty has pointed out (2009, 201), collapses. This is certainly no less the case for archaeology. Curated by the estranged, archaeology joins other sciences in the void agrarians left as representatives of soil (we should not underestimate how our own dirty labors as archaeologists connect us to those soils formerly tilled, hoed, turned clogs of earth, an abandoned Neolithic existence, and the long view). Archaeologists need not all become ecologists, but that does not mean that we should be insensitive to our own entanglements or ignore the biopolitical—will we speak for those who cannot? Will archaeologists embrace a future-oriented understanding of what the past can be (Dawdy 2009; Domanska 2014)? Will we begin to anticipate the demands our collective futures will make; and, in so doing, will we make any substantive difference before it is too late?

Acknowledgments

This article has benefited from conversations with Bruce Clarke, Ewa Domanska, Alfredo González-Ruibal, Bjørnar Olsen, Laurent Olivier, Þóra Pétursdóttir, and Michael Shanks. I am grateful to John Beusterien, Bruce Clarke, Alfredo González-Ruibal, Tom Hawkins, Gavin Lucas, Laurent Olivier, and Suzie Pilaar Birch for their comments on various iterations of the text.

Notes

1 'Révolution néolithique' was first used by Edouard Le Roy in *Les Origins humaines et l'évolution d'intelligence* (1928, 293).

2 Whereas 41% of the US population worked in agriculture in 1900, by 2000 that percentage fell to 1.9 (Dimitri, Effland, and Conklin 2005, 2). This figure is also cited by Serres 2014, 2. Percentages of agriculturalists vary by country in the case of Europe, the numbers for which are available through Eurostat (http://ec.europa.eu/eurostat). Importantly, these changes were underway much earlier in England (see Laslett 2004).

3 Four years after *Le Contrat Naturel* (1990), Eric Hobsbawn would also regard the loss of agrarians as one of the most profound transformations in human history, truly deserving of the misattributed notion 'the end of history' (1994, 8–9; also noted by González-Ruibal 2013, 42).

4 J.P. Locklear, personal communication; on the transformation of American agriculture in the twentieth century, see Conkin 2008.

5 Here, I am paraphrasing Bruno Latour (2013).

6 Terms such as the 'Agrarian Age' or 'Agrarianism' neither have the same potency, nor do they signal the same radical changes, as many still live agrarian livelihoods.

7 Consider, for example, how seemingly 'archaic' agrarian practices have usurped 'futuristic' ones in Ethiopia, as so well discussed by Alfredo González-Ruibal (2006). Of course, these temporal eddies can occur anywhere; for instance see: M.L Johnson, Some Farmers Trade Tractors for Animals, *Washington Post*, Sunday, June 18, 2006: http://www.washingtonpost.com/wp-dyn/content/article/2006/06/18/AR2006061801074.html.

8 The 'uprooting' of 'man' from earth was Heidegger's way of conceiving of the radical changes associated with the loss of place (see Harrison 2003, 33). For Harrison, this uprooting not only posits the end of the "Neolithic era but of the human epoch as such" (ibid., 34). If humanity, as Harrison holds, "is a connection with the humus," then this is also the end "of a mode of being on the earth that rests on humic foundations" (ibid.).

9 Dodwell traced out his view of this grove, and the open plain beyond, in a camera obscura and published the illustration as *General View of Tiryns and the Plain of Argos*, 1834.

10 The global economic crisis of 1929 led to the collapse of the tobacco market and currants were slowly phased out due to phylloxera infestation (Dimaki 2008).

11 These details are described by Paul Halstead in what should be regarded as a treasure of a book, *Two Oxen Ahead* (2014, 11–12, and 96; also see Forbes 1976).

12 These numbers are derived from the Greek National Statistics Service and are also published in Green and Lemon 1996, 191. Numbers specific to the Argive Plain were supplied by the Agricultural University of Athens as part of the Archaeomedes Project.

13 In a comparable study, David Pimentel estimates 1 kcal in orange energy is generated for every 1 kcal of fossil fuel energy invested in Florida orange production (2006, 14).

14 1964 figures are provided in Green and Lemon 1996, 191, while 2004 numbers come from the National Statistical Service of Greece.

15 On overproduction, price supports and dumping, see Lemon and Blatsou 1999, 115; also Lawrence 2007, 29; on this inversion of value see Sloterdijk 2013, 227–28.

16 In 1991, the population of Neo Ireo was 547 (NSSG 1994); for 2011 census data see "De facto population census 2011(revised)."

17 This percentage is based on revised calculations by the Hellenic Statistical Authority using a methodology compatible with other EU countries. Out of a resident population of 10,815,197, 8,284,210 lived in urban areas and 2,530,987 in rural areas according to the 2011 census (ELSTAT 2013, 12). The revised numbers differ from earlier census calculations of 61.4% urban and 38.6% rural.

18 National numbers are available through the National Statistics Service of Greece; also see Lawrence 2007, 34–57. Importantly, this is also tied to inheritance, which is the main avenue to the acquisition of land.

19 Here, it is worth noting how attempts to introduce a cattle farm to the Argive Plain in the early years of liberated Greece failed due to the lack of suitable pastures (Lehmann 1937, 136).

20 In 1911, there were 99,000 goats, 117,000 sheep in the districts of Argos and Nauplia alone. The 2009 livestock census put the number of goats at just under 87,000 and sheep at 94,700 in the whole Argolid (numbers are available through the Hellenic Statistical Authority).

21 In order to protect the identity of my Cattle City guide, I will neither reveal the exact location of Cattle City nor the company that operates it.

22 This transformation of herbivores into carnivores is not without its critics, but it is also not without its history: feeding cows animal fat is not new. Norwegians, for example, are known to have collected fish scraps and boiled them into a 'nutritious mass,' which helped sustain their handful of cows through the winter. But, in the far north, locality plays a major role in how humans live with animals. Unlike the rendered by-products of Norwegian fish, Cattle City tallow is a by-product of cattle 'processing.' For discussion of the Norwegian use of fish tallow see Berglund 2010, 61. For criticism in the case of CAFOs, see Shiva 2000.

23 This last sixty years has been dubbed the 'Great Acceleration' (Steffen et al. 2015)

References

Appenzeller, T. 2004. The End of Cheap Oil. *National Geographic* (June), 80–109.

Balabanis, P. 1999. Water in Europe: Research Achievements and Future Perspectives within the Framework of European Research Activities in the Field of Environment. *Afers Internacionals*, 46–47, 59–78.

Balter, M. 2013. Archaeologists say the 'Anthropocene' is here—but it began long ago. *Science*, 340, 261–62.

Berglund, J. 2010. Did Medieval Norse Society in Greenland Really Fail? In P.A. McAnany and N. Yoffee (eds.), *Questioning Collapse: Human Resilience, Ecological Vulnerability, and the Aftermath of Empire*, 45–70. Cambridge: Cambridge University Press.

Bintliff, J.L. 2012. *The Complete Archaeology of Greece: From hunter-gatherers to the 20th century AD*. Chichester: Wiley-Blackwell.

Braudel, F. 1975. *The Mediterranean and the Mediterranean World in the Age of Philip II*. New York: Harper & Row.

Burkholder, J., B. Libra, P. Weyer, S. Heathcote, D. Kolpin, P.S. Thorne, and M. Wichman. 2007. Impacts of Waste from Concentrated Animal Feeding Operations on Water Quality. *Environmental Health Perspectives*, 115(2), 308–12.

Chakrabarty, D. 2009. The Climate of History. Four theses. *Critical Inquiry*, 35(2), 197–222.

Charbis, G. 2012. Checks for Pesticide Residues in Agricultural Products (Élenchoi gia ypoleímmata fyto-farmákon sta georgiká proïónta). Blog post. May 3, 2012, available at: http://tro-ma-ktiko.blogspot.com/2012/05/blog-post_4105.html (accessed December 18, 2014).

Chateaubriand, F.-R. 1814. *Travels in Greece, Palestine, Egypt, and Barbary, During the Years 1806 and 1807*. New York: Van Winkle and Wiley.

Childe, V.G. 1950. The Urban Revolution. *The Town Planning Review*, 21(1), 3–17.

Conkin, P.K. 2008. *A Revolution Down on the Farm: The transformation of American agriculture since 1929*. Lexington: The University Press of Kentucky.

Conover, T. 2013. The Way of All Flesh. *Harper's Magazine* (May), 31–49.

Cronon, W. 1991. *Nature's Metropolis: Chicago and the Great West*. New York: Norton.

Daniel, G.E. 1943. *The Three Ages: An essay on archaeological method*. Cambridge: Cambridge University Press.

Dawdy, S.L. 2009. Millennial Archaeology: Locating the discipline in the age of insecurity. *Archaeological Dialogues*, 16(2), 131–42.

Dimaki, G. 2008. Union of Argolid Agricultural Cooperatives (Énosi Agrotikón Synetairismón Argolídas). Available at: https://argolikivivliothiki.gr/2012/01/11/argolida/ (accessed: March 6, 2016).

Dimitri, C., A. Effland, and N. Conklin. 2005. *The 20th Century Transformation of U.S. Agriculture and Farm Policy*. USDA Economic Information Bulletin Number 3.

Dodwell, E. 1819. *A Classical and Topographical Tour through Greece During the Years 1801, 1805, and 1806*. Volume II. London: Rodwell & Martin.

Dodwell, E. 1834. *Views and Descriptions of Cyclopian, or, Pelasgic Remains, in Greece and Italy; With constructions of a later period*. London: A. Richter.

Domanska, E. 2014. The *New Age* of the Anthropocene. *Journal of Contemporary Archaeology*, 1(1), 98–103.

Earle, T. 2002. *Bronze Age Economics: The beginnings of political economies*. Boulder, CO: Westview Press.

Edgeworth, M., J. Benjamin, B. Clarke, Z. Crossland, E. Domanska, A.C. Gorman, P. Graves-Brown, E.C. Harris, M.J. Hudson, J.M. Kelly, V.J. Paz, M.A. Salerno, C. Witmore, and A. Zarankin. 2014. Archaeology of the Anthropocene. *Journal of Contemporary Archaeology*, 1(1), 73–132.

Edgeworth, M., D. DeB Richter, C.N. Waters, P. Haff, C. Neal, and S.J. Price. 2015. Diachronous Beginnings of the Anthropocene: The lower bounding surface of anthropogenic deposits. *The Anthropocene Review*, 2(1), 33–58.

ELSTAT 2013. *Living Conditions in Greece* (in Greek). Athens: Hellenic Statistical Authority.

Foley, J.A., R. DeFries, G.P. Asner, C. Barford, G. Bonan, S.R. Carpenter, F.S. Chapin, M.T. Coe, G.C. Daily, H.K. Gibbs, J.H. Helkowski, T. Holloway, E.A. Howard, C.J. Kucharik, C. Monfreda, J.A. Patz, I.C. Prentice, N. Ramankutty, and P.K. Snyder. 2005. Global Consequences of Land Use. *Science*, 309, 570–74.

Forbes, H. 1976. The "Thrice-ploughed Field": Cultivation Techniques in Ancient and Modern Greece. *Expedition*, 19(1), 5–11.

Galanis, D. and K. Nikitas. 2000. How the Argolid Was Filled with Nitrates (Pós i Argolída gémise nitriká). TO BHMA, 01/23/2000, http://www.tovima.gr/relatedarticles/article/?aid=118482 (accessed August 19, 2016).

Gell, W. 1810. *The Itinerary of Greece, With a Commentary on Pausanias and Strabo and an Account of the Monuments of Antiquity at Present Existing in that Country; Compiled in the years 1801–06.* London: Printed for T. Payne.

Georgios, C. 2014. Checks for Pesticide Residues in Agricultural Products (Élenchoi gia ypoleímmata fytofarmákon sta georgiká proïónta). Blog post May 3, 2012, available at: http://tro-ma-ktiko.blogspot.com/2012/05/blog-post_4105.html (accessed March 7, 2016).

González-Ruibal, A. 2005. The Need for a Decaying Past: An archaeology of oblivion in contemporary Galicia (NW Spain). *Home Cultures*, 2(2), 129–52.

González-Ruibal, A. 2006. The Past Is Tomorrow: Towards an archaeology of the vanishing present. *Norwegian Archaeological Review*, 39(2), 110–25.

González-Ruibal, A. 2008. Time to Destroy: An archaeology of supermodernity. *Current Anthropology*, 49(2), 247–79.

González-Ruibal, A. 2013. Embracing Destruction. In J. Driessen (ed.), *Destruction; Archaeological, Philological and Historical Perspectives,* 37–51. Louvain-la-Neuve: Presses Universitaires de Louvain.

González-Ruibal, A. 2014. *An Archaeology of Resistance: Materiality and time in an African borderland.* Lanham, MD: Rowman & Littlefield.

Green, S. and M. Lemon. 1996. Perceptual Landscapes in Agrarian Systems: Degradation processes in northwestern Epirus and the Argolid Valley, Greece. *Cultural Geographies*, 3(2), 181–99.

Halstead, P. 1987. Traditional and Ancient Rural Economy in Mediterranean Europe: Plus ça change? *Journal of Hellenic Studies*, 107, 77–87.

Halstead, P. (ed.) 1999. *Neolithic Society in Greece.* Sheffield Studies in Aegean Archaeology 2. Sheffield, UK: Sheffield Academic Press.

Halstead, P. 2014. *Two Oxen Ahead: Pre-mechanized farming in the Mediterranean.* Chichester: Wiley Blackwell.

Hanscom, A.J. 2016. *Balanced and Barefoot: How unrestricted outdoor play makes for strong, confident, and capable children.* Oakland, CA: Raincoast Books.

Hanson, V.D. 1995. *The Other Greeks: The family farm and the agrarian roots of Western Civilization.* New York: Free Press.

Hanson, V.D. 1997. *Fields without Dreams: Defending the agrarian idea.* New York: Free Press.

Harris, J. 2007. *Constantinople: Capital of Byzantium.* London: Hambledon Continuum.

Harrison, R.P. 2003. *The Dominion of the Dead.* Chicago, IL: University of Chicago Press.

Hartley, D. 2015. Against the Anthropocene. *Savage.* Available at: http://salvage.zone/in-print/against the-anthropocene/ (accessed August 19, 2016).

Hector, J. 1973. La plaine d'Argos, répercussions socio-économiques d'une spécialisation agricole. *Méditerranée*, deuxième série, tome 13(2), 1–17.

Hobsbawm, E.J. 1994. *The Age of Extremes: A history of the world, 1914–1991.* New York: Pantheon Books.

Hooke, R.LeB. and J.F. Martín-Duque. 2012. Land Transformation by Humans: A review. *GSA Today*, 22, 4–10.

Imhoff, D. 2010. *The CAFO Reader: The tragedy of industrial animal factories.* Healdsburg, CA: Watershed Media.

Jahns, S. 1993. On the Holocene Vegetation History of the Argive Plain (Peloponnese, southern Greece). *Vegetation History and Archaeobotany*, 2, 187–203.

Koster, H. 1976. The Thousand-Year Road. *Expedition*, 19(1), 19–28.

Kristiansen, K. and T.B. Larsson. 2007. *The Rise of Bronze Age Society: Travels, transformations and transformations.* Cambridge: Cambridge University Press.

Laslett, P. 2004. *The World We Have Lost: Further explored.* Fourth Edition. London: Routledge.

Latour, B. 2013. *Facing Gaia: Six lectures on the political theology of nature* (Gifford Lectures on Natural Religion, version 10-3-13) URL (March 2016). Available at: macaulay.cuny.edu/eportfolios/wakefield15/files/2015/01/LATOUR-GIFFORD-SIX-LECTURES_1.pdf (accessed August 19, 2016).

Latour, B. 2015. Telling Friends from Foes in the Time of the Anthropocene. In C. Hamilton, C. Bonneuil and F. Gemenne (eds.), *The Anthropocene and the Global Environmental Crisis: Rethinking modernity in a new epoch*, 145–55. Abingdon: Routledge.

Lawrence, C.M. 2007. *Blood and Oranges: European markets and immigrant labor in rural Greece*. New York: Berghahn Books.

Leake, W.M. 1830. *Travels in the Morea: With a map and plans*. Volume II. London: J. Murray.

Lehmann, H. 1937. *Argolis: Landeskunde der Ebene von Argos und ihrer Randgebiete*. Athens: Deutsches Archäologisches Institut.

Lemon, M. and N. Blatsou. 1999. Background to Agriculture and Degradation in the Argolid Valley. In M. Lemon (ed.), *Exploring Environmental Change Using an Integrative Method*. Amsterdam: Gordon and Breach Science Publishers.

LeRoy, É. 1928. *Les Origines humaines et l'évolution de l'intelligence*. Paris: Boivin.

Lubbock, J. 1865. *Pre-historic Times, as Illustrated by Ancient Remains, and the Manners and Customs of Modern Savages*. London: Williams and Norgate.

Margulis, L. 1998. *Symbiotic Planet: A new look at evolution*. New York: Basic Books.

Margulis, L. and D. Sagan. 1997. *Microcosmos: Four billion years of evolution from our microbial ancestors*. Berkeley: University of California Press.

MEECC (Ministry of Environment, Energy & Climate Change). 2014. *National Biodiversity Strategy & Action Plan*. Athens: MEECC. Available at: https://www.cbd.int/doc/world/gr/gr-nbsap-01-en.pdf (accessed 17 March 17, 2016).

Mizelle, B. 2012. *Pig*. London: Reaktion Books.

Morfis, A. and H. Zojer. 1986. *Karst Hydrogeology of the Central and Eastern Peloponnesus*. Venice: Springer Verlag.

Morton, T. 2013. *Hyperobjects: Philosophy and ecology after the end of the world*. Minneapolis: University of Minnesota Press.

NSSG (National Statistical Service of Greece). 1994. Actual Population of Greece by the Census of 17 March 1991 (Pragmatikós Plithysmós tis Elládos katá tin Apografí tis 17is Martíou 1991). Athens: National Statistical Service of Greece.

Olivier, L. 2013a. The Business of Archaeology Is the Present. In A. González Ruibal (ed.), *Reclaiming Archaeology: Beyond the tropes of modernity,* 117–45. Abingdon: Routledge.

Olivier, L. 2013b. Nous sommes à l'âge de la devastation. In J. Driessen (ed.), *Destruction; Archaeological, Philological and Historical Perspectives*, 21–9. Louvain-la-Neuve: Presses Universitaires de Louvain.

Olsen, B., M. Shanks, T. Webmoor, and C. Witmore. 2012. *Archaeology the Discipline of Things*. Berkeley: University of California Press.

Pimentel, D. 2006. *Impacts of Organic Farming on the Efficiency of Energy Use in Agriculture*. An Organic Center State of Science Review. August 2006. Available at: https://www.organic-center.org/reportfiles/ENERGY_SSR.pdf (accessed August 19, 2016).

Pouqueville, F.C.H.L. 1827. *Voyage de la Grèce*, Volume V. Paris: Firmin Didot.

Purdy, J. 2015. *After Nature: A politics for the Anthropocene*. Cambridge, MA: Harvard University Press.

Reay, D., P. Smith, and A. van Amstel. 2010. *Methane and Climate Change*. London: Earthscan.

Redman, C.L. 1999. *Human Impact on Ancient Environments*. Tucson: University of Arizona Press.

Redman, C.L. and D.R. Foster. 2008. *Agrarian Landscapes in Transition: Comparisons of long-term ecological and cultural change*. Oxford: Oxford University Press.

Schuijs, M.J., M.A. Willart, K. Vergote, D. Gras, K. Deswarte, M.J. Ege, F.B. Madeira, R. Beyaert, G. van Loo, F. Bracher, E. von Mutius, P. Chanez, B.N. Lambrecht, and H. Hammad. 2015. Farm Dust and Endotoxin Protect against Allergy through A20 Induction in Lung Epithelial Cells. *Science*, 349 (6252), 1106–1110.

Serres, M. 1990. *Le Contrat Naturel*. Paris: Editions François Bourin.

Serres, M. 1995. *The Natural Contract*. Ann Arbor: University of Michigan Press.

Serres, M. 2014. *Times of Crisis: What the financial crisis revealed and how to reinvent our lives and future*. New York: Bloomsbury Academic.

Shapiro, J.A. 2011. *Evolution: A view from the 21st century*. Upper Saddle River, NJ: FT Press Science.

Shapiro, J.A. 2015. Bringing Cell Action into Evolution. In B. Clarke (ed.), *Earth, Life & System. Interdisciplinary essays on environment and evolution*, 175–202. New York: Fordham University Press.

Shiva, V. 2000. *Stolen Harvest: The hijacking of the global food supply*. Cambridge, MA: South End Press.

Sloterdijk, P. 2016. *Spheres, Volume 3: Foams, Plural Spherology*. South Pasadena, CA: Semiotext(e).

Sloterdijk, P. 2012. Voices for Animals: A fantasy on animal representation. In G.R. Smulewicz-Zucker (ed.), *Strangers to Nature: Animal lives and humans ethics*, 263–69. Lanham, MD: Lexington Books.

Sloterdijk, P. 2013. *In the World Interior of Capital: For a philosophical theory of globalization.* Cambridge: Polity Press.

Stavropoulos, N. 1996. *Greece: Country Report to the FAO International Technical Conference on Plant Genetic Resources.* Leipzig. Available at: http://www.fao.org/fileadmin/templates/agphome/documents/PGR/SoW1/Europe/GREECE.PDF (accessed March 17, 2016).

Steffen, W., J. Grinevald, P. Crutzen, and J. McNeill, 2011. The Anthropocene: Conceptual and historical perspectives. *Philosophical Transactions of the Royal Society A*, 369, 842–67.

Steffen, W., W. Broadgate, L. Deutsch, O. Gaffney, and C. Ludwig. 2015. The Trajectory of the Anthropocene: The Great Acceleration. *The Anthropocene Review*, 2(1), 81–98.

Steinfeld, H. 2006. *Livestock's Long Shadow: Environmental issues and options.* Rome: Food and Agriculture Organization of the United Nations.

Stengers, I. 2015. *In Catastrophic Times: Resisting the coming barbarism.* London: The Open Humanities Press.

Storey, G.R. (ed.). 2006. *Urbanism in the Preindustrial World: Cross-cultural approaches.* Tuscaloosa: University of Alabama Press.

Thomas, J. 2015. What Do We Mean by 'Neolithic Societies'? In C. Fowler and D. Hofmann (eds.), *The Oxford Handbook of Neolithic Europe*, 1073–92. Oxford: Oxford University Press.

Thommen, L. 2012. *An Environmental History of Ancient Greece and Rome.* Cambridge: Cambridge University Press.

van der Leeuw, S.E. 1998. *The Archæomedes Project: Understanding the natural and anthropogenic causes of land degradation and desertification in the Mediterranean basin.* Luxembourg: Office for Official Publications of the European Communities.

van der Leeuw, S. and C.L. Redman. 2002. Placing Archaeology at the Center of Socio-Natural Studies. *American Antiquity*, 67, 597–606.

Waters, C.N., J. Zalasiewicz, C. Summerhayes, A.D. Barnosky, C. Poirier, A. Galuszka, A. Cearreta, A. Cearreta, M. Edgeworth, E.C. Ellis, M. Ellis, C. Jeandel, R. Leinfelder, J.R. McNeill, D. deB. Richter, W. Steffen, J. Syvitski, D. Vidas, M. Wagreich, M. Williams, A. Zhisheng, J. Grinevald, E. Odada, N. Oreskes, and A.P. Wolfe. 2016. The Anthropocene Is Functionally and Stratigraphically Distinct from the Holocene. *Science*, 351(6269), 137.

von Weizsäcker, E. Ulrich, A. Lovins, and H. Lovins. 1997. *Factor Four: Doubling wealth, having resource use.* London: Earthscan.

Wendle, J. 2016. Syria's Climate Refugees. *Scientific American*, 314(3), 50–5.

Westbroek, P. 2015. Symbiotism: Earth and the greening of civilization. In B. Clarke (ed.), *Earth, Life & System: Interdisciplinary essays on environment and evolution,* 250–68. New York: Fordham University Press.

Witmore, C. 2014. Archaeology and the New Materialisms. *The Journal of Contemporary Archaeology*, 1(2), 203–24.

Witmore, C. 2015. Bovine Urbanism: The ecological corpulence of *Bos Urbanus.* In B. Clarke (ed.), *Earth, Life & System: Interdisciplinary essays on environment and evolution,* 225–49. New York: Fordham University Press.

Witmore, C. and T.V. Buttrey. 2008. William Martin Leake: A contemporary of P.O. Brøndsted, in Greece and in London. In B.B. Rasmussen, J.S. Jenson, J. Lund, and M. Märcher (eds.), *P.O. Brøndsted (1780–1842) – A Danish Classicist in his European Context,* 15–34. Copenhagen: The Royal Danish Academy.

Wolfe, C. 2013. *Before the Law: Humans and other animals in a biopolitical frame.* Chicago, IL: University of Chicago Press.

Wuerthner, G. 2010. Assault on Nature. CAFOs and biodiversity loss. In D. Imhoff (ed.), *CAFO: The tragedy of industrial animal factories.* Healdsburg, CA: Watershed Media.

3

REHEARSING THE ANTHROPOCENE IN MICROCOSM

The palaeoenvironmental impacts of the Pacific rat (*Rattus exulans*) and other non-human species during island Neolithization

Thomas P. Leppard

Introduction: Anthropocene as present singular or past plural?

The Paris Agreement on climate change—signed on 22nd April 2016 by over 170 states and other entities—binds, in section 2(a), its ratifying parties to '*pursue efforts to limit the temperature increase to 1.5°C above pre-industrial levels*' (already perhaps a vain hope; Huntingford and Mercado 2016). Yet, at the time of writing, only 22 countries have ratified the Agreement. Many of these ratifying parties are Pacific and Indian Ocean island nations facing existential threat in the face of climate change-induced sea level rise. The plight of low-lying islands exemplifies and underscores the massive changes being wrought to the physical systems of the planet by the series of processes implied by the term 'Anthropocene' (Crutzen and Stoermer 2000). The relationship between islands, their environments, and the capacity of our species to radically alter the physical organization of the planet's surface, peculiarly exemplary as it may be in the present, might, however, have a deeper antiquity. This chapter will consider what nuances a perspective offered by island archaeology may bring to our understanding of the Anthropocene. It also argues that—because of their singular environmental organization—islands have, throughout the late Quaternary, been unusually exposed to anthropogenic biophysical change in a manner which has salutary effects for a broader understanding of human ecodynamics.

The intention is not to critique the notion that our species is having effects on the organization of the planet that are unprecedented in scale or rapidity; this much is well documented (e.g., Barnosky *et al.* 2011; Corlett 2015; Helmus *et al.* 2014; Lewis and Maslin 2015; Waters *et al.* 2014, 2016; Young *et al.* 2016). Rather, two claims are made. First, that the Anthropocene should be understood not as a process driven solely by modern humans, but as a project in which many species working—unintentionally—in concert are implicated. Second, that, following Braje (2015, 2016; Braje and Erlandson 2013a, 2013b), the Anthropocene is not fully unprecedented (also Ruddiman 2013). Rather, it comprises a series of related processes that have been rehearsed in microcosm across the world's islands throughout the later Quaternary, rehearsals which may have been local but, collectively, represent the anthropogenic construction of island ecosystems on a global scale.

The Anthropocene is the subject of competing definitions, as scholars variously view the object of study through lenses provided by biology, atmospheric chemistry, geology, and so on (Braje 2015). Averaging these definitions, we could loosely characterize the Anthropocene as that period in which humans have affected not only their immediate biological environments but broader biophysical and physical systems, up to and including the organization of the geosphere (i.e., the combined lithosphere, pedosphere, hydrosphere, and atmosphere) alongside the biosphere (e.g., Waters *et al.* 2016; Young *et al.* 2016). Implicit in this approach is the assumption that prior Late Quaternary human interactions were (a) largely limited to direct biotic impacts (introduction/extinction) and (b) that these impacts did not pattern consequentially at a global scale. This fails to reflect both how transformative anthropic ecosystems can be (especially those ecologies which were assembled during Holocene processes of domestication; cf. Smith 2012; Zeder 2015 arguments), and how these transformations can affect the nature of not only biotic systems, but also the biophysical interface between these and physical systems.

To illustrate this series of biotic and biophysical transformations, the spread of the Near Oceanian Neolithic 'package' throughout Remote Oceania (Figure 3.1)—from a range of possible examples (Diamond and Bellwood 2003)—is considered, focusing to the point of exclusivity (as a means of highlighting the specifics of much broader processes) on the effects of the invasive Pacific Rat, *Rattus exulans* (Figure 3.2). While humans imposed trauma directly and indirectly on remote islands, so did co-traveler species such as *R. exulans*; the full range of impacts of humanity's Neolithic co-conspirators has only rarely, however, been fully considered. The trauma associated with invasive and introduced Neolithic taxa was not limited

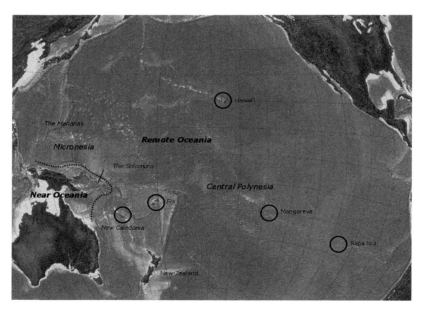

Figure 3.1 Map of the Pacific Ocean showing most islands, island groups, and toponyms mentioned in the text.

to biota but, mediated via biotic impacts, reverberated throughout biophysical systems (in particular pedological and hydrological organization) in a manner which parallels, on a reduced spatial scale, Anthropocene-type dynamics. The aim is to show that the difference between the Anthropocene and the Holocene is one best comprehended in terms of scale, rather than type, and that Anthropocene dynamics have been enacted in miniature as growing anthropic ecosystems collided with endemic types of organization during the Holocene. It is also underscored that the anthropic ecosystems which now dominate the planet are emergent outcomes of multi-species efforts.

Neolithic packages as multi-component ecosystems

Before turning to the data on how and in what terms bundles of species (intentionally or unintentionally corralled by humans) can drive biophysical change, it is important to be quite clear what these bundles—what Neolithic packages—*are*. We need to focus, not so much on their composition, but rather on how the interrelationships of their constituents have made these Holocene multi-species alliances such potent forces for change when arriving in new environments.

Co-evolutionary trajectories in Neolithic packages

It has become relatively commonplace to speak of Neolithic 'packages'—bundles of functionally related species that, from centers of incipient domestication, were carried or transmitted across the planet (Çilingiroğlu 2005). Frequently, these multi-species agglomerations are conceived only in terms of those taxa which most consistently held the attention of human agropastoralists; species used as food, or for 'secondary products' (Sherratt 1981). Neolithic packages should be thought of more broadly, however, as sets of domesticates, commensals, parasites, and even diseases which traveled together and between which ecological webs formed (Boivin *et al.* 2016).

The co-opting of these diverse sets of species into anthropogenic ecologies—'domestication'— implies a series of complex and interrelated processes, including artificial selection by humans for desirable traits in those species in which they have maintained keen interest (Zeder 2012, 2015; Fuller *et al.* 2010). Such selection, of course, has pleiotropic effects (e.g., paedomorphic traits in dogs; Morey 2010), but there are other unintentional or emergent aspects to domestication. We can assume that natural selection is also implicated in trajectories from 'wild' to 'domesticated' species; i.e., not all gene flow can be or is regulated artificially. (In general, we might imagine a spectrum occupied by those species more or less explicitly involved with trajectories of domestication; at one extreme, for those taxa in which humans have maintained intense interest in terms of morphology and behavior (e.g., *Bos*), artificial selection is the prime determinant of gene-flow; on the other extreme, for taxa in which humans have no such interest (e.g., *Mus*), natural selection the major determinant; and for species in between (e.g., *Felis catus*), both types of selection are important.) Other niches have been intentionally and inadvertently created in the construction of anthropic ecologies (Laland and O'Brien 2010, 2011; Rowley-Conwy and Layton 2011; Smith 2007, 2012), niches which have been occupied by taxa placed under peculiarly anthropogenic selective pressure which is nonetheless not artificial *sensu stricto*; most obviously commensal species, but also parasites, pests, and diseases, recognizing that these categories elide into one another at their fringes.

In the transition to domesticated ecosystems, the structure of these ecosystems (and of their interstitial forms) has exerted profound evolutionary pressure on passenger taxa. Throughout the Holocene, the emergence of agropastoral lifestyles across the planet has been a process of co-evolution, involving degrees of both artificial and natural selection within the adaptive landscapes formed by emergent Neolithic societies. How have these evolutionary trajectories been constrained by and within these landscapes? Are there macro-evolutionary trends, moving these species in general or parallel adaptive directions within evolutionary space (McGhee 2007: 6–30)?

Humans are rapacious generalists. The history of the incrementally greater range of *Homo* across the planet can be understood in part as a function of changes in cognitive architecture allowing for greater behavioral plasticity, opening vistas onto diverse and mutable adaptations (Gamble 2013; Grove 2015; Rowley-Conwy and Layton 2011). These adaptations have allowed hominins to cross latitudinal or biogeographic barriers, culminating in the capacity of modern humans to reach (if not to colonize) the most isolated habitats on the planet. For the vast majority of the history of the genus, however, hominins existed within naturally assembled trophic structures. Such hunter-gatherer lifestyles are subject to spatial restrictions, especially in higher, seasonal latitudes, exposed to the unavoidable trophic logic of carrying capacity.

The feedback dynamics of domestication in the aftermath of the Last Glacial Maximum—reliance breeding reliance—drove the emergence of subsistence systems which have certain advantages over hunter-gatherer lifestyles in terms of reliably supporting large, sedentary populations in confined spaces. The essential element is multi-component generalism, allowing a plasticity in precisely how subsistence strategies are constructed which is hard to rival. The ability to tailor agropastoral subsistence to suit the demands of a given niche—to develop bespoke anthropic ecologies—has facilitated the expansion of agropastoralists into some of the least promising environments on the planet. The co-evolution of non-human domesticates and commensals alongside humans, then, as components of Neolithic 'packages', might be understood as overall selection towards increased or exacerbated generalism in these species. Ecological generalism in this sense is simply an increased capacity to tolerate variability—in temperature, seasonality, or prey-abundance—or other types of heterogeneity in environmental organization. Selection towards greater tolerance of variability is of course evident in those species exploited primarily for nutrition; for example, *Hordeum vulgare* or *Capra hircus* in the Old World, or *Zea mays* in the New World (recognizing of course that the association with humans of some of these species is pre-Neolithic; Morey 2010). We can assume that other taxonomic elements of Neolithic packages have also experienced selective pressure towards generalism, however, from companion and commensal species (e.g., *Canis familiaris*, *Mus musculus*) to pests and pathogens.

The repeated construction by humans of Neolithic niches to which these species are pre-adapted, and their ability to tolerate wide variability in these and other, less anthropogenic types of ecosystem, render these sets of companion species especially competitive. Previously insulated environments—and, in particular, remote islands—when exposed to these dynamic, interrelated, and anthropic ecological systems have suffered appalling consequences. To understand why and in what terms, we first need to consider the nature of isolated (specifically insular) biotas.[1]

Fragility in island ecosystems

A key issue in resolving degree of impact of these bundles of species involves extent of ecological insulation. Main centers of domestication in both the Old and New Worlds were continental, or, in the case of the gradual assembly of the Near Oceanian Neolithic package, were located on large quasi-continental islands.[2] Parts of the planet with substantial ecogeographic barriers separating them from these centers were insulated from the new Neolithic[3] ecosystems and from the selective pressures they exerted. This isolation rendered islands peculiarly exposed to rapid and extensive ecological transformation in the wake of Neolithic colonization.

Rehearsing the Anthropocene in microcosm

It is productive, in both archaeological and ecogeographic terms, to think of islands less as intrinsically isolated and more as fragments of habitat surrounded by radically, qualitatively different habitat (Terrell 1999). Insular dynamics can be found across the planet (e.g., forest fragments, or taiga fading into tundra; MacArthur and Wilson 1967; now Losos and Ricklefs 2010), but 'true' islands have the distinction that they are distributed across an intervening habitat type which is uniquely, aggressively hostile to most terrestrial taxa. Variables which structure ecological dynamics on islands include the size and organization of these habitat patches, and the degree to which they are separated from similar patches by intervening sea, as well as latitude, geology, and corresponding pedology and hydrology. These factors conspire to make island biotas remarkable in several respects.

Intervening inhospitable patches of habitat act as a filter for invasive species, and the greater the distance between terrestrial fragments, the more efficacious the filter, all other factors being equal (see Losos and Ricklefs 2010; Whittaker and Fernández-Palacios 2007). Essentially, ocean gaps limit gene flow; both preventing initial colonization by taxa, and then—after colonization—limiting gene flow between colonists and ancestral populations. The former effect results in highly skewed, disequilibrial island biotas, with taxa better adapted for overwater dispersal better represented at the expense of less well-adapted taxa. What makes a taxon a good overwater adapter varies (capacity for flight, low metabolic needs, and tolerance of brine all stand out), but in general this results in islands tending to be depauperate of mammals, of taxa with high energetic demands, of K-selected taxa, and so on (recognizing that these categories, for good reason, often overlap one another). The second effect means that even if a colonist is successful, gene flow between it and its source population is likely to be circumscribed. This can operate on extant founder-effects as an engine of allopatric speciation, driving insular endemism.

It is not only distance between habitat fragments that imposes structure on island biotas (and interlocked biophysical systems). There is a relationship between habitat size, degree of qualitative difference of surrounding habitat, and complexity of trophic structure; the positive correlation between size and trophic complexity is especially relevant to the current discussion (Brose *et al.* 2004). Islands, as habitats which tend to be small and highly distinct from neighboring patches, accordingly have reduced foodweb complexity; i.e., possess fewer trophic levels. Islands are, in short, hostile to higher-tier taxa, the very taxa which struggle most—because of morphology and energetic requirements—to colonize in the first instance.

The effects combine to produce island biotas that tend to be skewed in contrast to 'mainland' equivalents. Most famously, islands tend to be highly endemic and species-poor; that is, comparatively rich in endemic taxa, but comparatively poor in total taxa. Exaggerated endemism often subsequently drives increased overall levels of specialization and the emergence of rare localized niches. Specialization, and the paucity of higher-tier taxa, means that many anti-predator adaptations are lost. The odd gravitation of smaller taxa towards gigantism, and bigger taxa towards dwarfism/nanism, may in part be explained by this, but the phenomenon of anti-predator adaptation loss is evident more broadly at the behavioral level (insular ecological naïvete). This renders island biotas relatively fragile. Various aspects of the physical organization of environments are dependent on biotas, most notably soil composition and dynamics (in terms of nutrient cycling or slope stability) as well as hydrology. Accordingly, these biophysical systems—kept stable in part by their biological components—are, on islands, intrinsically more fragile than their continental equivalents.

What are the implications for the arrival of Neolithic packages in previously insulated ecologies? We can explore this in detail with respect to a given element of a given package multiple times over, but the overall implications are clear. The arrival of continental species—species which are the outcomes of overt selection towards generalism and tolerance of variability—should be enormously disruptive. Island ecologies structured around endemics should be dangerously exposed to out-competition of their endemics by invasive Neolithic species, which should have concomitant effects on trophic neighbors. Precisely how pervasive these impacts might be, however, as well as their qualitative variety, are hard to grasp in the absence of specifics. More generally, it is not clear whether these impacts should be limited to the biosphere, or include the organization of systems which interface between the biosphere and the geosphere (i.e., the pedosphere and the hydrosphere); if the latter, are there implications for how we understand the qualitatively distinct aspect of current human impacts on biophysical systems? Consequently, it is instructive to consider now in detail one particular example of inadvertent introduction of an invasive species as part of a wider multi-species package; in this case, the prehistoric introduction of the Pacific Rat, *Rattus exulans*, to Remote Oceania.

Palaeoenvironmental transformations in the Pacific Islands

'In your case,' said O'Brien, 'the worst thing in the world happens to be rats.'
George Orwell, Nineteen Eighty-Four *(1949)*

The Pacific Rat (Rattus exulans) *and human colonization*

Beginning at around 3000 BP, Austronesian-speaking groups living in the eastern extremities of Near Oceania spread into the wider Pacific in episodic, long-distance bursts, first into the Marianas and large central Pacific groups of Vanuatu, New Caledonia, Fiji, and Sāmoa, then into central Polynesia, and finally reaching Hawai'i, Rapa Nui/Easter Island, and Aotearoa/New Zealand during the first millennium BP (Sheppard *et al.* 2015; Wilmshurst *et al.* 2011). These colonists brought a suite of Southeast Asian domesticates to previously uninhabited islands, notably taro (*Colocasia esculenta*), breadfruit (*Artocarpus altilis*), coconut (*Cocos nucifera*), banana (*Musa* spp.), and yam (*Dioscorea* spp.). The introduction of these species and the development of polycropping, combined with deliberate landscape modification by human colonists, transformed the biological organization of Remote Oceania (e.g., Kirch 2002). It would be inaccurate, however, to understand these transformations as solely mediated by humans.

The sheer scale of the human achievement that is the colonization of the Pacific is intrinsically impressive. Perhaps more impressive is that the journey from the Solomon Islands to Rapa Nui—a distance of some 9,000 km—was also completed by the Pacific or Polynesian Rat, *Rattus exulans* (Figure 3.2) (Anderson 2009). Smaller than *R. rattus* or *norvegicus*, the Pacific Rat (or *kiore* in Māori) nonetheless occupies a parallel niche as an omnivorous generalist, polyestrous, nocturnal, with short gestation and weaning cycles. Various types of data (including recent genetic work; Mattisoo-Smith and Robbins 2009) indicate that *R. exulans*, having originated in Southeast Asia, accompanied human colonists throughout Remote Oceania (Barnes *et al.* 2006). It is disputed as to whether the rat was introduced accidentally as an unwilling stowaway, or as a food source (see Allen 2015; Mattisoo-Smith *et al.* 1998). What is clear is that it spread to the most isolated corners of the Polynesian triangle coincident with their colonization by humans, and in so doing drove exaggerated and rapid environmental change. Our immediate concern here, then, is establishing through what pathways rats drove this change. These pathways range from the direct and unsurprising (predation) to more esoteric means of impact.

Figure 3.2 The Pacific or Polynesian rat (or *kiore*), *Rattus exulans*.

The Pacific rat: direct impacts on fauna

The most immediate context in which *R. exulans* is implicated in rapid environmental change associated with human colonization is in the extirpation and extinction of various species endemic to Remote Oceania. These extinctions span a wide range of taxa.

The best-known example is the eradication of large swathes of the Pacific endemic avifauna during colonization, with some 2,000 species of bird being lost (Steadman 1995). Steadman and Martin (2003) emphasize both the scale of this loss and also the various factors that conspired to drive it; introduced mammalian carnivores, however, are implicated in predation on ground-nesting avifauna, especially on eggs and juveniles (Atkinson 1985; Medway 2001). In the absence of evolved anti-predator defenses, ground-nesting endemics would have provided an initial calorific glut for invasive rats, driving up numbers and thereby exerting even greater pressure on avifauna. Combined with human predation, such pressure meant localized extirpation was swift (e.g., Kirch 2007), probably following at a decadal scale post-colonization. The capacity of *Rattus* spp. to drive local extirpations is underscored when considering instances in which rat predation has not been accompanied by human predation, or has been actively resisted via extermination programs.

Direct predation on native faunas was not limited to avifauna. It is challenging to bridge the evidential gap between the disappearance of taxa from the stratigraphic/sub-fossil records of islands and the introduction of rats, but modern proxies can illuminate the sort of ancient behaviors which would have driven such extinctions. Hadfield and Saufler (2009; see also Hadfield *et al.* 1993) record substantial modern predation on the endemic Hawai'ian land snail *Partulina redfieldi* by *Rattus* spp., with this predation indicated by characteristic shell trauma. The association with *R. exulans* as opposed to *R. rattus* is not in this case demonstrated, but similar patterns of trauma are also evident in the archaeological record of New Zealand. Discounting erroneously old radiocarbon dates, younger dates reported in association with more persuasive evidence for rat predation on another snail, *Placostylus ambagiosus* (Brook 2000) are coincident with newer, more robust dates for the colonization horizon which are themselves associated with rat-gnawed seeds (Wilmshurst *et al.* 2008). This suggests parallel prey selection in the constituent species of *Rattus*, and that types of population depression (i.e., severe depression caused by rats taking both juveniles and adults; Hadfield *et al.* 1993: 616–618) caused by modern rat predation may have occurred during *R. exulans* colonization events. To land snails (and invertebrates more broadly; St Clair 2011) we can also add vertebrate fauna. The relationship between presence/absence of *kiore* and variability in lizard populations has been demonstrated (Towns 1991), and there is reliable evidence for direct predation (rather than competition) on lizards, although not on the *tuatara* (Newman and McFadden 1990). This ecological relationship can also be retrojected to colonization by *R. exulans*.

The Pacific rat: direct impacts on flora

Rattus exulans is omnivorous, and its direct impacts upon arrival were felt by flora as well as fauna. In a landmark study, Athens *et al.* (2002) suggested a correlation between the appearance of Pacific rat in the 'Ewa plain of western O'ahu (as evidenced by radiometrically dated *R. exulans* bones) and the disappearance of endemic Hawai'ian lowland forest, dominated by *Pritchardia* spp. Crucially, the retreat of endemic flora occurs prior to radiometrically visible human presence in the area, suggesting no direct anthropic impact, yet is contemporaneous with the apparent localized extirpation of endemic avifauna (Athens 2009) (Figure 3.3). Athens interprets these data as suggestive with regard to the relationship between arrival of the Pacific rat and the collapse of native lowland forest (indeed, as Athens points out [2009: 1498], the only remnant stands of *Pritchardia* in Hawai'i in which that genus dominates come from Huelo and Nihoa, both of which remain free of *R. exulans*).

Further compelling evidence of the capacity of invasive rats to drive deforestation comes from Rapa Nui. Hunt (2007) notes that the island—which is presently deforested—was, according to the palynological and anthracological data, covered by *Jubaea* palm forest prior to human colonization at ~750 BP (Wilmshurst *et al.* 2011). The process of deforestation has often (and especially in the popular literature) been attributed to anthropogenic degradation, most conspicuously by Diamond (2005). Yet the presence in the archaeological record of *Jubaea* endocarps which have signs of rat-gnawing, the retreat of *Jubaea* forest prior to evidence for localized burning, and the substantial amount of *R. exulans* skeletal material found in post-colonization deposits all suggest an explosive rat population preying on endemic taxa at the most vulnerable point in the reproductive cycle of those taxa (Hunt 2007). Wilmshurst *et al.* (2008) present similar evidence for rat-gnawing of endemic flora in New Zealand, again tightly correlated in radiocarbon terms with retreat (although not mass extinction) of this flora. Kirch (2007) highlights that broadly parallel types of process occurred with variation across Remote Oceania.

Summing the data, there is broad evidence that the extirpation of endemic flora—and in particular palm species—was not unique to the corners of the Polynesian triangle, but rather was the norm (Prebble and Dowe 2008). Meyer and Butaud (2009) query whether *Rattus* can drive localized extinction in the absence of other factors, but research on modern rat populations and their relationship with endemic palms suggests that predation can substantially disrupt recruitment to the extent that conservation can only be guaranteed by controlling rat numbers (Auld *et al.* 2010; Campbell and Atkinson 2002). Campbell and Atkinson (2002) in particular highlight

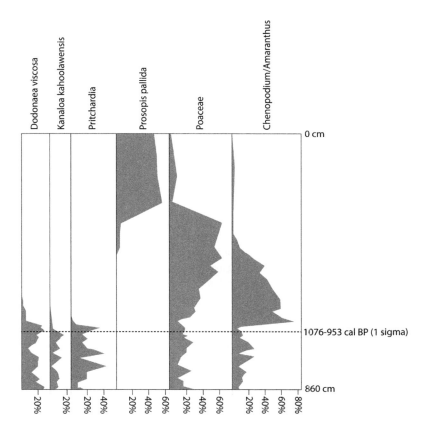

Figure 3.3 The pollen diagram from Ordy Pond, 'Ewa Plain, O'ahu, from data first published in Athens *et al.* 2002, demonstrating profound floral change after ~ 950 cal BP. Two pollen sums were used in calculating percentages for the curves; for all types except the sedges, the curves are based on a sum excluding sedge pollen from the total, while the sedge curve (not depicted here) is based on total pollen and spores (Athens 2009: fig. 2a–b). *Prosopis pallida* is a late, Euro-American introduction. Note that, in the interests of clarity, not all taxa from the original diagram are here reproduced. Modified after Athens 2009: fig. 2a–b; reproduced by permission.

the varied ways in which *kiore* predation can affect floral life-cycles, not only via endocarp consumption but also via eating flowers and saplings.

In short, there is compelling evidence from a series of proxies (archaeological, zooarchaeological, and palynological) that the arrival of *R. exulans* in Remote Oceania was closely associated in both time and space with the local or complete eradication of endemic flora and fauna, often prior to evidence for significant human occupation of a given environment and with suggestive signs of direct effects (such as endocarp gnawing). Modern data track how rats (both *R. exulans* as well as *R. rattus* and *norvegicus*) can drive these processes of eradication, achieving very high population densities by exploiting a range of food sources and thereby causing demographic collapses in native biotas (Russell *et al.* 2009). These effects move beyond these biotas, however, and drive changes in the abiotic systems with which they are interlinked.

The Pacific rat: indirect impacts

Introductions of non-native taxa, followed by the extirpation or extinction of native taxa, are recognized as common outcomes of the collision of Neolithic lifeways with previously insulated ecosystems. These collisions, however, have effects beyond driving down overall biodiversity; they promote changes in the structure of ecologies and in the organization of interwoven biophysical systems. Tracking these changes in Remote Oceania involves understanding the pathways by which deforestation occurs. Again, the Pacific rat is exemplary (Drake and Hunt 2009).

In the 'Ewa Plain, Athens (2009) charted a radiometric lag between eradication of the *Pritchardia* ecosystem and the subsequent establishment of introduced species. Conversely, in Rapa Nui, the degradation of native forest was followed by grassland succession (rather than the establishment of complex, multi-storey agroforest as on, e.g., Tikopia; Kirch 2007). The eradication of endemic lowland forest and its replacement by introduced species (e.g., *Cocos nucifera*, *Artocarpus altilis*, *Musa* spp.) in a regime of mixed arboriculture, dryland horticulture, or wetland horticulture resulted in physical reorganization. Along what pathways did these related types of process occur? Recent work from the Mangareva/Gambier Islands (Kirch *et al.* 2015) highlights the complex nature of the relevant ecological interactions, with both direct impacts (via predation on endemic flora) but also indirect (predation on native birds disrupting nutrient cycling) likely combining to impact native forest. In this as in other examples across Remote Oceania, arrival of *R. exulans* and deforestation seem to be associated; direct predation no doubt played a vital role, but rat impacts on forest organization should be conceived of more broadly. Kirch (2007), in reviewing the noted strong correlation between human colonization, the radiometrically dated Pacific rat, and deforestation, suggests that the eradication of endemic avifauna and consequent nutrient poverty should be understood as a driving factor in forest destruction. Because of the temporal distance, the ecological specificities of rat invasion, seabird extirpation, and deforestation are hard to grasp. Research on modern ecologies subject to rat invasion, however, is instructive, especially in terms of the types of change that rat invasion promotes in the pedosphere and the effects of these changes for community dynamics.

We can proceed from the reasonable assumption that *R. exulans* played a substantial role in eradicating endemic avifauna, and seabirds in particular (Steadman and Martin 2003). Seabirds play a key ecological role in their transfer of marine nutrients to terrestrial environments, driving up island nutrient levels (especially of phosphorous and nitrogen) and consequently the capacity of islands to sustain more biomass than might be expected based on raw area and latitude (Sanchez-Pinero and Polis 2000). Their extirpation should, then, theoretically alter island soil chemistries. This is borne out by recent studies which indicate that presence of *kiore* on small islands off New Zealand's North Island radically disrupts nutrient flow. Mulder *et al.* (2009) observed changes in soil chemistry as a function of depression of seabird numbers; in particular, islands with fewer seabird burrows (because of rat predation) experienced reduction in overall phosphorous and nitrogen levels, as well as their soil pH being affected. Parallel disequilibria in leaf chemistry (with lower percentages of nitrogen on invaded islands than rat-free islands, with the inverse for potassium) reflect the imbalanced soil chemistry via processes of nutrient uptake. In general, Mulder *et al.* suggest, seabird presence/absence is a strong predictor of soil pH and nitrogen content. This is especially relevant when considering that Polynesian arboriculture and horticulture may have patterned spatially to take advantage of variably organized nutrient distribution; the apparent relationship between phosphorous values and intensive cultivation in the Kohala field system on the Big Island of Hawai'i is a good example (Vitousek *et al.* 2004), and there are hints of parallel patterning on a smaller scale on Rapa Nui (Ladefoged *et al.* 2010), where intensive garden management might be interpreted as an attempt to drive up overall (impoverished) phosphorous values (Ladefoged *et al.* 2005).

Impacts are not only limited to the direct input and vegetative uptake of nutrients from seabird guano, but also include intermediaries. Fukami *et al.* (2006) demonstrate variability between the soil microfaunas of rat-free versus rat-invaded islands, as well as variability in rate of litter decomposition and overall moisture content. The role of rats as not only seed consumers but also—depending on seed morphology—seed dispersers can drive heterogeneity in soils at a larger scale (Shiels 2011 and Shiels and Drake 2011; also Traveset and Richardson 2006 on mutualism disruption). While the relevant ecological relationships are complex, in general (a) there is a relationship between rat invasion and dynamic changes in soil chemistry and also biology, and (b) this has implications for plant biomass. Again, operating on the gross assumption that higher autotroph biomass permits bigger populations of heterotrophs, from the perspective of soil biochemistry rat invasions should push tropical insular carrying capacity down, notwithstanding the calorific potential of the rats themselves.

As a function of both direct predation but also post-colonization changes in soil chemistry, the retreat of native forest drove changes in macro-scale soil organization. Destruction of primary forest—whether succeeded by secondary forest or not—leads to radical changes in soil organization, not only in consequent nutrient cycling but also in overall cohesion. In the absence of root-bonding, soil horizons can become very dynamic when exposed to waterflow, experiencing sheet erosion and gullying and exposing the regolith to weathering (see Mieth *et al.* 2002 for these processes on Rapa Nui). These processes have a number of consequences, the most conspicuous of which is the transfer of sediment and its accumulation downslope (exemplified in Mangareva). Sediment transport in turn drives downslope changes, depending on degree of consolidation (i.e., A-horizon formation), including alluviation and silting, altered frequency and severity of flooding events, and disruption of inshore—especially lagoonal, in the lower latitudes—environments (and their biota) via silting. Dynamism of this sort also renders soils exposed to further changes in nutrient composition by rendering them more susceptible to rainwater leeching. These large-scale changes in pedology ultimate affect neighboring physical systems. Hydrological organization is in part dependent on moisture retention within soils and the deposition of sediment in stream beds. In terms of lithology, erosion of the regolith ultimately exposes underlying bedrock to weathering processes, with this weathering driving geochemical changes in local soils and sediments.

To continue to list the wave of changes deriving from biotic impacts would be to labor the point; panning out from our tight geographic focus, what are the broader lessons implied? Invasive fauna are understood to have effects on islands such that they stimulate trophic cascades. Reviewing the impacts of the Pacific rat during its colonization of Remote Oceania, it is evident that its effects are best conceived of as achieved through multiple pathways and as driving biophysical cascades. Not only were island biotas reorganized, but the systems that interface with these biotas, including local soils and local hydrologies. Rats, moreover, were only one component of a Neolithic package which contained several species likely to have had as severe impacts for local biotas as rats (particularly pigs and dogs, even if these proved easier for human populations to control and eradicate in the face of trophic crunches; Kirch 2007). Do other instances of island colonization by bundles of taxa associated with Neolithic life ways parallel the types of biophysical scenarios witnessed in Remote Oceania?

Rehearsing the Anthropocene: a drama for several players

While Remote Oceania is probably exemplary in terms of sheer degree of disruption driven by the arrival of an alien Neolithic, this process—with similar and dissimilar species involved—has occurred repeatedly; in the Mediterranean and Caribbean during the early to middle Holocene, and in the more remote islands of the world's oceans (especially in the higher latitudes) during Euro-Asian expansion in the late Holocene.

We have already encountered rats in the form of *Rattus exulans*, but it is unsurprising that *R. norvegicus* and *R. rattus* have also had catastrophic effects on insular biota elsewhere. Striking examples of the impacts of these and of other murids come from remote Indian and Southern Ocean islands which remained isolated from the Euro-Asian agropastoral lifestyle the longest (Angel *et al.* 2009; Bolton *et al.* 2014). Even island environments with a long exposure to murids—and continued co-presence of rats and endemic birdlife—witness the continuing capacity of *Rattus* spp. to exert predation pressure which drives ecological organization (Ruffino *et al.* 2009). While murids are well understood to have promoted large-scale environmental change (Harris 2009; Simberloff 2009), this should nonetheless not be taken to suggest that only commensals drive generally deleterious changes. The introduction of the domestic goat (*Capra hircus*) to first the Mediterranean islands, and then subsequently islands worldwide, has had catastrophic impacts, primarily regarding goat browsing behaviors and their capacity to out-compete endemic herbivores (e.g., Leppard and Pilaar Birch 2016). In particular, the ability of goats to tolerate plant morphologies and biochemistries which make them unattractive to other herbivores (e.g., Hernández-Orduno *et al.* 2012) has had catastrophic effects for endemic floras, with by now predictable cascade-type outcomes (Chynoweth *et al.* 2015; Hata *et al.* 2014). Examples could be multiplied, including domestic rabbits, *Oryctolagus cuniculus* (e.g., Chapuis *et al.* 1994) and cats, *Felis catus* (e.g., Bonnaud *et al.* 2011). This is before turning to the direct and indirect impacts of humans themselves, clearly significant but beyond the purview of this chapter.

What do these examples have in common? In each instance, human colonization and introduction of a Neolithic *modus vivendi* equates, in ecological terms, to the invasion of a suite of co-adapted generalist species occupying a variety of trophic positions. These species exerted direct and indirect pressure on disequilibrial, specialized, and predator naïve taxa which—tending to be insular endemics—lacked the security of a broad metapopulation. This pressure was brought to bear while human colonists, as well as their accompanying species, built Neolithic niches to which these invasive species were already adapted. Through a combination of processes (being eaten; being out-competed; having mutualisms disrupted; pathogen introduction), populations of endemics underwent overall degradation (i.e., population decline) and spatially specific degradation (i.e., range fragmentation). In doing so, they became more exposed to the stochastic effects which bear more heavily on smaller populations, resulting in extirpation or extinction. Localized or generalized extinction had concomitant effects on systems predicated on endemic stability; for example, the chemical composition of soils and, by extension, plant biomass dependent on certain chemical configurations in these soils. These changes cascaded through environments, not only in biotic terms but driving broader biophysical change, change observable in a number of palaeoenvironmental proxies.

How can we characterize these changes, and what do they have to do with the Anthropocene? Recognizing that in each case the ecological specifics were unique, we can nonetheless identify significant trends. First, the outcome of these colonization events is catastrophic localized losses in biodiversity (i.e., in genetic variability), and reduction in sum global biodiversity. Moreover, biases in how this diversity is lost make the process semi-predictable. Second, as total environments provide the context for natural selection to operate on phenotypes, so radical changes in the organization of these environments can disrupt evolutionary trends. Surviving pre-colonization taxa should evolve under conditions of anthropogenic selective landscapes. Because the organization of these landscapes will often be similar, we might assume that parallelism in the resulting evolutionary trends should promote convergence. Third, as should be evident from the foregoing, these predictable effects are not limited to biotic organization, but extend to aspects of pedological and hydrological organization. There are broader implications here for the subaerial life histories of oceanic islands; if the trajectories of these histories are broadly knowable (Whittaker and Fernández-Palacios 2007), to what degree does destruction of primary forest and resulting sediment transport accelerate erosion (in the oceanic tropics, from 'high' islands to atolls) in predictable and non-local ways? Finally, these changes have been (a) global and (b) occurring throughout the Holocene. These effects are not area limited, nor restricted to the later Holocene.

These are Anthropocene dynamics—physical as well as biological, global not local, predictable not specific—enacted in miniature as growing anthropic ecosystems collided with endemic types of environmental organization. These anthropic ecosystems, corralled by humans both intentionally and unintentionally, were multi-species conglomerates comprising bundles of taxa which had been under selective pressure towards adaptability and tolerance of variation during the ongoing process of 'domestication'. Changes in island biophysical systems deriving from the introduction of these species were not affected by any single member (although clearly human direct impacts were exaggerated); rather, multiple species—humans, domesticates, and commensals—exerted pressure on endemic biota from different angles and along different ecological pathways. The result was, from the first expansion of Old and New World Neolithic packages to insulated environments, miniaturized biophysical transformations that foreshadow the various aspects of the Anthropocene.

Conclusions: the islands of the day before

The purpose of this chapter is not to suggest that there is nothing new under the sun. Certain types of biophysical impact—ocean acidification, for example, affecting the chemical pathways of organisms which rely on calcium carbonate, or atmospheric warming on a global scale—are almost certainly uniquely outcomes of industrial and post-industrial types of human social organization. Yet if we adopt a broader definition of the Anthropocene, one that involves humans driving a variety of complex processes that affect the biotic and abiotic organization of the planet, then we will have to be willing to admit that these processes have been driven not only by our, but by other, associated species which have benefited from the spread and multiplication of modern humans. This has been the case not only in deep time, but into the present. The annual CH_4 production of cattle, for example—the vast majority of which claiming descent from the ancestral domesticated population of *Bos primigenius* in Southwest Asia (Bollongino *et al.* 2012)—is a major contributor to sum atmospheric greenhouse gas totals (Ripple *et al.* 2014). While unwitting villains, our Neolithic co-species are perhaps guilty by association in the Anthropocene plot (cf. Ruddiman 2013).

In nuancing our approach to take into account data of greater antiquity, we will also be forced to recognize that understanding the Anthropocene, in part, involves understanding encroachment and isolation—the breakdown of biogeographic barriers, and the implicit reduction in genetic diversity. It is surely instructive that, as agropastoral modes of living have expanded, the environmental outcomes for islands have been broadly similar; we might then best understand human (Neolithic) niche-construction as an intrinsically homogenizing process. This almost certainly has implications, not only for scholars concerned with impending socioecological scenarios, but also for those of us interested in the ecological and subsistence parameters which have constrained and directed the evolution of human societies, arguably towards structural convergence, since the Last Glacial Maximum.[4] This view of the

Anthropocene also necessitates framing it in terms of accelerating incremental intensification throughout the Holocene, rather than looking for its genesis at a series of distinct horizons; that is, considering whether we can extend the tail of the 'great acceleration' back into the deep Holocene (Steffen *et al.* 2015).

Finally, and bleakly, an archaeological and intrinsically *longue durée* perspective on human eco-dynamics on islands offers a parable for future directions within and beyond the Anthropocene. Modern humans, excelling at maximizing return and benefit at evolutionarily relevant time-scales and genetic distances, have repeatedly disrupted previously isolated biophysical systems in a manner which is hard to characterize as other than deleterious. Despite our species' capacity to model long-term dynamics and—crucially—to act to mitigate negative effects (contra Diamond 2005), the emergent outcomes of our anthropic ecosystems have by definition driven unpredictable effects. The indigenous population of Rapa Nui was resilient, and demonstrably survived the eradication of the *Jubaea* forest. From the perspective of the intrinsic value of genetic diversity, however, we should insist on noting that the fate of the forest was sealed, not by the felling of the last palm, but by the consumption of its relatives and its own seeds by seemingly harmless Neolithic co-travelers. Whether or not the policy and will exist to mitigate present and future change in the planet's systems, our historic willingness to spread apparently innocuous anthropic ecologies has created emergent ecological, physical, and evolutionary scenarios which will be difficult to model as we progress further into the Anthropocene.

Acknowledgments

I would like to thank the volume editor, Suzie Pilaar Birch, as well as the series editor, Chris Witmore, for persuading me to write this chapter, for their patience, and for their comments on an earlier draft. Thanks to Steve Athens for kind permission to reproduce images. I am grateful to Todd Braje and Christina Giovas for valued feedback; and to Elizabeth Murphy, both for her critical reading of the text and for convincing me that 'goats' needed a sequel. This research was supported by a postdoctoral fellowship (2015–16) at Rutgers' Center for Cultural Analysis, support for which I am thankful and duly acknowledge.

Notes

1 Examples of modern humans crossing biogeographic barriers and driving profound environmental change at the continental scale come from the later Pleistocene; most notably, the colonization of Sahul/Australia at ~47 kya and the Americas at ~15 kya. Clearly, these were hunter-gatherer colonization events, thereby involving only limited suites of commensal species, yet the effects on environmental organization were nonetheless substantial (direct impacts in the form of the extinction of endemic faunas are the most conspicuous). The subsequent, catastrophic late Holocene introduction of Afro-Eurasian biota during European colonization from 500 BP is indicative of how invasion by bundles of species associated with agropastoral regimes can further transform already radically altered anthropic environments.
2 In general, it is an unhelpful yet established distinction to think in terms of continental versus insular. The Americas and Afro-Eurasia are as much islands—bodies of land surrounded by water—as are Pitcairn or Iceland. Interest lies in spatial scales of contiguous, qualitatively comparable habitat-space; as Terrell recognized (1999: 240–241) when he emphasized that 'island archaeology' is the archaeology of a certain type of environmental patchiness.
3 'Neolithic' is used throughout broadly and indulgently to connote pre-industrial communities with an agropastoral means of subsistence, rather than connoting more refined temporal specificities or cultural affiliations.
4 In general, the relationship between social organization, convergence, and directed change requires substantial further attention, but this is neither the time nor the place.

References

Allen, M.S. 2015. Dietary opportunities and constraints on islands: a multi-proxy approach to diet in the Southern Cook Islands. In *The Oxford Handbook of the Archaeology of Diet*, edited by J. Lee-Thorp and M.A. Katzenberg. Oxford: Oxford University Press. DOI: 10.1093/oxfordhb/9780199694013.013.2.

Anderson, A. 2009. The rat and the octopus: initial human colonization and the prehistoric introduction of domestic animals to Remote Oceania. *Biological Invasions* 11: 1503–1519.

Angel, A., R.M. Wanless, and J. Cooper. 2009. Review of impacts of the introduced house mouse on islands in the Southern Ocean: are mice equivalent to rats? *Biological Invasions* 11: 1743–1754.

Athens, J.S. 2009. *Rattus exulans* and the catastrophic disappearance of Hawai'i's native lowland forest. *Biological Invasions* 11: 1489–1501.

Athens, J.S., H.D. Tuggle, J.V. Ward, and D.J. Welch. 2002. Avifaunal extinctions, vegetation change, and Polynesian impacts in prehistoric Hawai'i. *Archaeology in Oceania* 37: 57–78.

Atkinson, I.A.E. 1985. The spread of commensal species of *Rattus* to oceanic islands, and their effects on island avifaunas. In *Conservation of Island Birds*, edited by P.J. Moors. ICBP Technical Publication, No. 3, Cambridge.

Auld, T.D., I. Hutton, M.K.J. Ooi, and A.J. Denham. 2010. Disruption of recruitment in two endemic palms on Lord Howe Island by invasive rats. *Biological Invasions* 12: 3351–3361.

Barnes, S.S., E. Mattisoo-Smith, and T.L. Hunt. 2006. Ancient DNA of the Pacific Rat (*Rattus exulans*) from Rapa Nui (Easter Island). *Journal of Archaeological Science* 33: 1536–1540.

Barnosky, A., N. Matzke, S. Tomiya, G. Wogan, B. Swartz, T. Quental, C. Marshall, J. McGuire, E. Lindsey, K. Maguire, B. Mersey, and E. Ferrer. 2011. Has the Earth's sixth mass extinction already arrived? *Nature* 471: 51–57.

Boivin, N.L., M.A. Zeder, D.Q. Fuller, A. Crowther, G. Larson, J.M. Erlandson, T. Denham, and M.D. Petraglia. 2016. Ecological consequences of human niche construction: examining long-term anthropogenic shaping of global species distributions. *Proceedings of the National Academy of Sciences* 113: 6388–6396.

Bollongino, R., J. Burger, A. Powell, M. Mashkour, J.-D. Vigne, and M.G. Thomas. 2012. Modern taurine cattle descended from small number of Near-Eastern founders. *Molecular Biology and Evolution* 29: 2101–2104.

Bolton, M., A. Stanbury, A.M.M. Baylis, and R. Cuthbert. 2014. Impact of introduced house mice (*Mus musculus*) on burrowing seabirds on Steeple Jason and Grand Jason Islands, Falklands, South Atlantic. *Polar Biology* 37: 1659–1668.

Bonnaud, E., F.M. Medina, E. Vidal, M. Nogales, B. Tershy, E. Zavaleta, C.J. Donlan, B. Keitt, M. Le Corre, and S.V. Horwath. 2011. The diet of feral cats on islands: a review and a call for more studies. *Biological Invasions* 13: 581–603.

Braje, T. 2015. Earth systems, human agency, and the Anthropocene: Planet Earth in the Human Age. *Journal of Archaeological Research* 23: 369–396.

Braje, T. 2016. Evaluating the Anthropocene: is there something useful about a geological epoch of humans? *Antiquity* 90: 505–512.

Braje, T., and J. Erlandson. 2013a. Human acceleration of animal and plant extinctions: a late Pleistocene, Holocene, and Anthropocene continuum. *Anthropocene* 4: 14–23.

Braje, T., and J. Erlandson. 2013b. Looking forward, looking back: humans, anthropogenic change, and the Anthropocene. *Anthropocene* 4: 116–121.

Brook, F.J. 2000. Prehistoric predation of the landsnail *Placostylus ambagiosus* Suter (Stylommatophora: Bulimulidae), and evidence for the timing of establishment of rats in northernmost New Zealand. *Journal of the Royal Society of New Zealand* 30: 227–241.

Brose, U., A. Ostling, K. Harrison, and N.D. Martinez. 2004. Unified spatial scaling of species and their trophic interactions. *Nature* 428: 167–171.

Campbell, D.J., and I.A.E. Atkinson. 2002. Depression of tree recruitment by the Pacific rat (*Rattus exulans Peale*) on New Zealand's northern offshore islands. *Biological Conservation* 107: 19–35.

Chapuis, J.-L., G. Barnaud, and P. Boussès. 1994. Alien mammals, impact and management in the French subantarctic islands. *Biological Conservation* 67: 97–104.

Chynoweth, M.W., C.A. Lepczyk, C.M. Litton, S.C. Hess, J.R. Kellner, and S. Cordell. 2015. Home range use and movement patterns of non-native feral goats in a tropical island montane dry landscape. *PLoS One*. DOI:10.1371/journal/pone.0119231.

Çilingiroğlu, Ç. 2005. The concept of 'Neolithic package': considering its meaning and applicability. *Documenta Praehistorica* 32: 1–13.

Corlett, R.T. 2015. The Anthropocene concept in ecology and conservation. *Trends in Ecology and Evolution* 30: 36–41.

Crutzen, P., and E. Stormer. 2000. The 'Anthropocene'. *Global Change Newsletter* 41: 17–18.

Diamond, J. 2005. *Collapse: How Societies Choose to Fail or Succeed.* New York: Viking.

Diamond, J., and P. Bellwood. 2003. Farmers and their languages: the first expansions. *Science* 300: 597–603.

Drake, D.R., and T.L. Hunt. 2009. Invasive rodents on islands: integrating historical and contemporary ecology. *Biological Invasions* 11: 1483–1487.

Fukami, T., D.A. Wardle, P.J. Bellingham, C.P.H. Mulder, D.R. Towns, G.W. Yeates, K.I. Bonner, M.S. Durrett, M.N. Grant-Hoffman, and W.M. Williamson. 2006. Above- and below-ground impacts of introduced predators in seabird-dominated island ecosystems. *Ecology Letters* 9: 1299–1307.

Fuller, D.Q., R.G. Allaby, and C. Stevens. 2010. Domestication as innovation: the entanglement of techniques, technology and chance in the domestication of cereal crops. *World Archaeology* 42: 13–28.

Gamble, C. 2013. *Settling the Earth: The Archaeology of Deep Human History.* Cambridge: Cambridge University Press.

Grove, M. 2015. Palaeoclimates, plasticity, and the early dispersal of Homo sapiens. *Quaternary International* 369: 17–37.

Hadfield, M.G., S.E. Miller, and A.H. Carwile. 1993. The decimation of endemic Hawai'ian tree snails by alien predators. *American Zoologist* 33: 610–622.

Hadfield, M.G., and J.E. Saufler. 2009. The demographics of destruction: isolated populations of arboreal snails and sustained predation by rats on the island of Moloka'i 1982–2006. *Biological Invasions* 11: 1595–1609.

Harris, D.B. 2009. Review of negative effects of introduced rodents on small mammals on islands. *Biological Invasions* 11: 1611–1630.

Hata, K., M. Kohri, S. Morita, S., Hiradate, and N. Kachi. 2014. Complex interrelationships among above ground biomass, soil chemical properties, and events caused by feral goats and their eradication in a grassland ecosystem of an island. *Ecosystems* 17: 1082–1094.

Helmus, M.R., D.L. Mahler, and J.B. Losos. 2014. Island biogeography of the Anthropocene. *Nature* 513: 543–546.

Hernández-Orduño, G., J.F.J. Torres-Acosta, C.A. Sandoval-Castro, A.J. Aguilar-Caballero, C.M., Capetillo-Leal, and M.A. Alonso-Díaz. 2012. In cafeteria trials with tannin rich plants, tannins do not modify foliage preference of goats with browsing experience. *Ethology, Ecology, and Evolution* 24: 332–343.

Hunt, T.L. 2007. Rethinking Easter Island's ecological catastrophe. *Journal of Archaeological Science* 34: 485–502.

Huntingford, C., and L.M. Mercado. 2016. High chance that current atmospheric greenhouse concentrations commit to warmings greater than 1.5 C over land. *Scientific Reports*. DOI: 10.1038/srep30294.

Kirch, P.V. 2002. *On the Road of the Winds: An Archaeological History of the Pacific Islands before European Contact.* Berkeley: University of California Press.

Kirch, P.V. 2007. Three islands and an archipelago: reciprocal interactions between humans and island ecosystems in Polynesia. *Earth and Environmental Science Transactions of the Royal Society of Edinburgh* 98: 85–99.

Kirch, P.V., G. Molle, C. Nickelsen, P. Mills, E. Dotte-Sarout, J. Swift, A. Wolfe, and M. Horrocks. 2015. Human ecodynamics in the Mangareva islands: a stratified sequences from Nenega-Iti Rock Shelter (site AGA-3, Agakauitai Island). *Archaeology in Oceania* 50: 23–42.

Ladefoged, T.N., C.M. Stevenson, P.M. Vitousek, and O.A. Chadwick. 2005. Soil nutrient depletion and the collapse of Rapa Nui society. *Rapa Nui Journal* 19: 100–105.

Ladefoged, T.N., C.M. Stevenson, S. Haoa, M. Mulrooney, C. Puleston, P.M. Vitousek, and O.A. Chadwick. 2010. Soil nutrient analysis of Rapa Nui gardening. *Archaeology in Oceania* 45: 80–85.

Laland, K.N., and M.J. O'Brien. 2010. Niche construction theory and archaeology. *Journal of Archaeological Method and Theory* 17: 303–322.

Laland, K.N., and M.J. O'Brien. 2011. Cultural niche construction: an introduction. *Biological Theory* 6: 191–202.

Leppard, T.P., and S.E. Pilaar Birch. 2016. The insular ecology and palaeoenvironmental impacts of the domestic goat (*Capra hircus*) in Mediterranean Neolithization. In *Géoarchéologie des îles de la Méditerranée*, edited by M. Ghilardi, S. Fachard, L. Lespez, F. Leandri and C. Bressy-Leandri. Paris: CNRS Editions Alpha, 47–56.

Lewis, S.L., and M.A. Maslin. 2015. Defining the Anthropocene. *Nature* 519: 171–180.

Losos, J.B., and R.E. Ricklefs. 2010. *The Theory of Island Biogeography Revisited*. Princeton, NJ: Princeton University Press.

MacArthur, R.H., and E.O. Wilson. 1967. *The Theory of Island Biogeography*. Princeton, NJ: Princeton University Press.

Matisoo-Smith, L., R.M. Roberts, G.J. Irwin, J.S. Allen, D. Penny, and D.M. Lambert. 1998. Patterns of prehistoric human mobility in Polynesia indicated by mtDNA from the Pacific rat. *Proceedings of the National Academy of Sciences* 95: 15145–15150.

Mattisoo-Smith, L., and J. Robbins. 2009. Mitochondrial DNA evidence for the spread of Pacific Rats through Oceania. *Biological Invasions* 11: 1521–1527.

McGhee, G.R. 2007. *The Geometry of Evolution: Adaptive Landscapes and Theoretical Morphospaces*. Cambridge: Cambridge University Press.

Medway, D.G. 2001. Causes of the demise of a breeding population of *titi* on Mangaia, Cook Islands. *Notornis* 48: 137–144.

Meyer, J.-Y., and J.-F. Butaud. 2009. The impacts of rats on the endangered native flora of French Polynesia (Pacific Islands): Drivers of plant extinction or *coup de grâce* species? *Biological Invasions* 11: 1569–1585.

Mieth, A., H.-R. Bork, and I. Feeser. 2002. Prehistoric and recent land use effects on Poike Peninsula, Easter Island (Rapa Nui). *Rapa Nui Journal* 16: 89–95.

Morey, D.F. 2010. *Dogs: Domestication and the Development of a Social Bond*. Cambridge: Cambridge University Press.

Mulder, C.P.H., M.N. Grant-Hoffman, D.R. Towns, P.J. Bellingham, D.A. Wardle, M.S. Durrett, T. Fukami, and K.I. Bonner. 2009. Direct and indirect effects of rats: does rat eradication restore ecosystem functioning of New Zealand seabird islands? *Biological Invasions* 11: 1671–1688.

Newman, D.G., and I. McFadden. 1990. Seasonal fluctuations of numbers, breeding, and food of kiore (*Rattus exulans*) on Lady Alice Island (Hen and Chickens group), with a consideration of kiore: tuatara (*Sphenodon punctatus*) relationships in New Zealand. *New Zealand Journal of Zoology* 17: 55–63.

Prebble, M., and J.D. Dowe. 2008. The late Quaternary decline and extinction of palms on oceanic Pacific islands. *Quaternary Science Reviews* 27: 2546–2567.

Prebble, M., and J.M. Wilmshurst. 2009. Detecting the initial impact of humans and introduced species on island environments in Remote Oceania using palaeoecology. *Biological Invasions* 11: 1529–1556.

Ripple, W.J., P. Smith, H. Haberl, S.A. Montzka, C. McAlpine, and D.H. Boucher. 2014. Ruminants, climate change and climate policy. *Nature Climate Change* 4: 2–5.

Rowley-Conwy, P., and R. Layton. 2011. Foraging and farming as niche construction: stable and unstable adaptations. *Philosophical Transactions of the Royal Society B* 366: 849–862.

Ruddiman, W.F. 2013. The Anthropocene. *Annual Review of Earth and Planetary Sciences* 41: 45–68.

Ruffino, L., K. Bourgeois, E. Vidal, C. Duhem, M. Paracuellos, F. Escribano, P. Sposimo, N. Baccetti, M. Pascal, and D. Oro. 2009. Invasive rats and seabirds after 2,000 years of an unwanted coexistence on Mediterranean islands. *Biological Invasions* 11: 1631–1651.

Russell, J.C., J. Abdelkrim, and R.M. Fewster. 2009. Early colonisation population structure of a Norway rat island invasion. *Biological Invasions* 11: 1557–1567.

Sanchez-Pinero, F., and G.A. Polis. 2000. Bottom-up dynamics of allochthonous input: direct and indirect effects of seabirds on islands. *Ecology* 81: 3117.

Sheppard, P.J., S. Chu, and R. Walter. 2015. Re-dating Lapita movement into Remote Oceania. *Journal of Pacific Archaeology* 6: 26–36.

Sherratt, A. 1981. Plough and pastoralism: aspects of the secondary products revolution. In *Pattern of the Past: Studies in Honour of David Clarke*, edited by I. Hodder, G. Isaac, and N. Hammond. Cambridge: Cambridge University Press, 261–305.

Shiels, A.B. 2011. Frugivory by introduced black rats (*Rattus rattus*) promotes dispersal of invasive plant seeds. *Biological Invasions* 13: 781–792.

Shiels, A.B., and D.R. Drake. 2011. Are introduced rats (*Rattus rattus*) both seed predators and dispersers in Hawaii? *Biological Invasions* 13: 883–894.

Simberloff, D. 2009. Rats are not the only introduced rodents producing ecosystem impacts on islands. *Biological Invasions* 11: 1735–1742.

Smith, B.D. 2007. Niche construction and the behavioral context of plant and animal domestication. *Evolutionary Anthropology* 16: 188–199.

Smith, B.D. 2012. A cultural niche construction theory of initial domestication. *Biological Theory* 6: 260–271.

St Clair, J.J.H. 2011. The impacts of invasive rodents on island invertebrates. *Biological Conservation* 144: 68–81.

Steadman, D.W. 1995. Prehistoric extinctions of Pacific island birds: biodiversity meets zooarchaeology. *Science* 267: 1123–1131.

Steadman, D.W. and P.S. Martin. 2003. The late Quaternary extinction and future resurrection of birds on Pacific island. *Earth-Science Reviews* 61: 133–147.

Steffen, W., W. Broadgate, L. Deutsch, O. Gaffney and C. Ludwig. 2015. The trajectory of the Anthropocene: the great acceleration. *The Anthropocene Review* 2: 81–98.

Terrell, J.E. 1999. Comment on Paul Rainbird, 'Islands out of time: Towards a critique of island archaeology'. *Journal of Mediterranean Archaeology* 12: 240–245.

Towns, D.R. 1991. Response of lizard assemblages in the Mercury Islands, New Zealand, to removal of an introduced rodent: the *kiore (Rattus exulans). Journal of the Royal Society of New Zealand* 21: 119–136.

Traveset, A. and D.M. Richardson. 2006. Biological invasions as disruptors of plant reproductive mutualisms. *Trends in Ecology and Evolution* 21: 208–216.

Vitousek, P.M., T.L. Ladefoged, P.V. Kirch, A.S. Hartshorn, M.W. Graves, S.C. Hotchkiss, S. Tuljapurkar, and O.A. Chadwick. 2004. Agriculture, soils, and society in precontact Hawai'i. *Science* 304: 1665–1669.

Waters, C., J. Zalasiewicz, M. Williams, M. Ellis, and A. Snelling (eds.). 2014. *A Stratigraphical Basis for the Anthropocene* (Geological Society Special Publications 395). London: Geological Society.

Waters, C.N., J. Zalasiewicz, C. Summerhayes, A.D. Barnosky, C. Poirier, A. Gałuszka, A. Cearreta, M. Edgeworth, E.C. Ellis, M. Ellis, C. Jeandel, R. Leinfelder, J.R. McNeill, D. deB. Richter, W. Steffen, J. Syvitski, D. Vidas, M. Wagreich, M. Williams, A. Zhisheng, J. Grinevald, E. Odada, N. Oreskes, and A.P. Wolfe. 2016. The Anthropocene is functionally and stratigraphically distinct from the Holocene. *Science* 351: DOI:10.1126/science.aad2622.

Whittaker, R.J., and J.M. Fernández-Palacios. 2007. *Island Biogeography: Ecology, Evolution, and Conservation.* Oxford: Oxford University Press.

Wilmshurst, J.M., A.J. Anderson, T.F.G. Higham, and T.H. Worthy. 2008. Dating the late prehistoric dispersal of Polynesians to New Zealand using the commensal Pacific rat. *Proceedings of the National Academy of Sciences* 105: 7676–7680.

Wilmshurst, J.M., T.L. Hunt, and A.J. Anderson. 2011. High-precision radiocarbon dating shows recent and rapid initial human colonization of East Polynesia. *Proceedings of the National Academy of Sciences* 108: 1815–1820.

Young, H.S., D.J. McCauley, M. Galetti, and R. Dirzo. 2016. *Patterns, Causes, and Consequences of Anthropocene Defaunation Annual Review of Ecology, Evolution and Systematics,* 47.

Zeder, M.A. 2012. The domestication of animals. *Journal of Anthropological Research* 68: 161–190.

Zeder, M.A. 2015. Core questions in domestication research. *Proceedings of the National Academy of Sciences* 112: 3191–3198.

4

TRANS-HOLOCENE HUMAN IMPACTS ON CALIFORNIA MUSSELS (*MYTILUS CALIFORNIANUS*)

Historical ecological management implications from the Northern Channel Islands

Breana Campbell, Todd J. Braje, and Stephen G. Whitaker

Introduction

Global fisheries and marine ecosystems have been heavily exploited and altered by the actions of humans, resulting in calls to rethink how we manage aquatic resources (e.g., U.S. Commission on Ocean Policy 2004). Decades of overfishing, degradation of marine ecosystems, and declines in marine biodiversity have spurred scientists, resource managers, and conservationists to explore new methods and interdisciplinary approaches to inform marine management policy and conservation agendas (e.g., Jackson et al. 2001; Kittinger et al. 2015; Myers and Worm 2003; Pauly et al. 1998; U.S. Commission on Ocean Policy 2004). One of the most significant challenges in conservation and restoration biology efforts has been the "shifting baseline syndrome" (Pauly 1995), where restoration efforts have relied on baseline data collected after marine ecosystems have already been degraded by human actions and overexploitation. In 1995, Pauly defined the shifting baselines syndrome and discussed the inherent flaws associated with using relatively modern data for establishing marine restoration targets. Pauly (1995) argued that every new generation of fisheries scientists tend to use catch, size, and abundance data from their early careers to measure the success of modern conservation efforts and the health of marine systems. This has resulted in the gradual degradation of marine ecosystems and global fisheries and a slow-moving ecological disaster, despite our best efforts at conservation and management. One solution for mitigating the shifting baselines syndrome is to extend the time depth of our management practices by using perspectives from archaeology, paleobiology, and history. This approach, known as marine historical ecology, can offer crucial insights into the changing seascapes of nearshore ecosystems and fisheries and help establish baselines that predate the modern collapse of the world's oceans (Crumley 1994; Erlandson and Rick 2010; Rick and Lockwood 2013; Rick and Erlandson 2008).

It has only been relatively recently, however, that archaeologists have come to recognize and appreciate the deep antiquity of human use of marine resources (Bailey 2004; Claassen 1998; Erlandson 2001; Marean et al. 2007; Stewart 1994). Although the quantity of evidence supporting the use of aquatic resources prior to 130,000 years ago is scant, coastal archaeological records probably have been heavily affected by erosion, fluctuations in eustatic sea levels, and other taphonomic processes (Steele and Álvarez-Fernández 2011). Archaeological evidence suggests that anatomically modern humans and their ancestors engaged in the harvesting of marine resources for nearly two million years (Braun et al. 2010). The earliest evidence for the incorporation of fish proteins in hominin diets is found at an archaeological site in East Turkana, Kenya, dated to 1.95 million years, where the *in situ* butchered remains of fish, turtle, and crocodile were discovered (Braun et al. 2010). Evidence for the use of shellfish as part of the hominin diet extends over 700,000 years with the recovery of freshwater oyster shells in Kao Pah Nam Cave in Thailand (Pope 1989). Despite the deep antiquity of fishing and shellfishing by humans and their hominin ancestors, the impact of these activities on marine ecosystems is not well documented prior to the Holocene. Several studies of Holocene-age shell middens have demonstrated that increased predation pressure by humans had negative impacts on aquatic resources; most notably, reducing the average size and abundances of these resources and transforming local seascapes (e.g., Bailey and Milner 2008; Braje et al. 2007, 2009, 2012a, 2012b; Braje and Rick 2011; Broughton 1999, 2002; Codding et al. 2014; Colonese et al. 2014; Erlandson et al. 2011a, 2015a; Faulkner 2009; Griffiths and Branch 1997; Jazwa et al. 2012; Jerardino 1997; Morrison and Hunt 2007; Rick 2007; Rick et al. 2015; Roy et al. 2003). These studies support the assertion that human activities have influenced earth ecosyems for millennia, contributing to widespread anthropogenic changes in biodiversity of flora and fauna communities.

A variety of studies demonstrate that humans have had significant impacts on local and regional ecosystems for millennia, influencing climate, water systems, and terrestrial land and seascapes (Alroy 2001; Crutzen 2002; Crutzen and Steffen 2003; Erlandson and Rick 2010; Foley et al. 2013; Goudie 2000; Kirch 2005; Kirch and Hunt 1997; Martin 1973; Martin and Steadman 1999; Redman 1999; Redman et al. 2004; Rick and Erlandson 2008; Steadman 2006; Steffen et al. 2011; Vitousek et al. 1997). These studies support the idea that we are now living in the Anthropocene, a geological timescale marked specifically by human-induced changes in the environment, but that the Anthropocene has been forming for thousands of years. While considerable debate continues as to where the temporal boundary between the Holocene and Anthropocene should be drawn (see Braje 2016), Braje (2015; Braje and Erlandson 2013) argued that a twentieth-century boundary marker undermines the important role of deep history in interpreting and managing modern ecosystems and discounts critical archaeological data for understanding how and when humans came to dominate the planet.

Excellent examples of why deep history matters in the Anthropocene come from California's Northern Channel Islands, which have produced some of the earliest evidence for fishing, shellfishing, seafaring, and maritime adaptations in the New World. A variety of historical ecological case studies demonstrate that increased predation pressure over thousands of years on marine resources by the Chumash and their ancestors led to a reduction in the average size of several marine species (see Braje et al. 2007; Braje et al. 2012a, 2012b; Erlandson et al. 2011a; Raab 1992). Using allometric approaches common in zooarchaeological studies, researchers have collected size measurements from archaeological specimens and used average size through time as a proxy for the health and stability of important prey species. Declines in overall size not attributed to fluctuations in climate (e.g., sea surface temperature and marine productivity) or localized foraging behaviors (see Thakar et al. 2015) are ascribed to human overharvesting. The archaeological remains of several species including California mussels (*Mytilus californianus*), red and black abalone (*Haliotis rufescens* and *H. cracherodii*), owl limpets (*Lottia gigantea*), and rockfish (*Sebastes* spp.) have been used for such studies (Braje et al. 2007, 2012a, 2012b, 2015; Erlandson et al. 2008, 2011a, 2015; Jazwa et al. 2012).

California mussels have received significant attention due to their ubiquity in island shell middens. Nearly every one of the thousands of shell middens, ranging from Paleocoastal (> 10,000 cal BP) to Historic Period (post-AD 1542) sites, on the Northern Channel Islands contains California mussel shells. Preservation and stratigraphic integrity of these sites are generally exceptional, due largely to the lack of burrowing animals, the calcareous nature of dunes and soils, and limited historical development. In many cases, however, sample sizes of whole mussel shell length measurements are limited due to taphonomic and cultural processes that cause shell fragmentation. Trampling by domesticated and wild animals introduced during the nineteenth- and twentieth-century ranching period was particularly destructive, as cattle, deer, and elk would often bed down in shell midden soils. Some studies have relied on intensive surface collections from eroding shell midden strata and subsurface excavations to recover whole shells from radiocarbon dated archaeological deposits to establish average size proxies through time (Braje 2010; Erlandson et al. 2008). Others have employed a template that estimates to within one centimeter (cm) the size of a California mussel shell based on the breadth of the hinge fragment (Braje et al. 2007; Jazwa et al. 2012; White 1989). Experimental work by Bell (2009), however, demonstrated that this template can produce unreliable results that are statistically inaccurate and not replicable between multiple zooarchaeologists. In an effort to build methods for estimating total shell length of California mussels from hinge fragments, Campbell and Braje (2015) used an allometric approach to produce three statistically reliable regression formulas that use measurements collected from the commonly recovered hinge portion to estimate total shell length (for related discussion see Glassow 2016; Glassow et al. 2016; McKechnie et al. 2015; Singh and McKechnie 2015).

Here, we use archaeological mussel shell length measurements collected using the umbo-width regression formula recommended by Campbell and Braje (2015) to extrapolate shell length data from fragmented California mussel shells. These data were collected from 16 prehistoric sites located on San Miguel, Santa Rosa, and Santa Cruz islands that were previously radiocarbon dated to the Early (10,000–7500 cal BP), Middle (7500–3500 cal BP), and Late Holocene (3500 cal BP-AD 1542). Our data were compared to paleo sea surface temperature (SST) and marine productivity records from the Santa Barbara Channel region to tease out whether declines in mussel shell length through time were the result of anthropogenic impacts or climate variability. Results were compared to shell length data for modern California mussel populations collected by Channel Islands National Park Service (NPS) biologists as part of the Rocky Intertidal Ecological Monitoring Program in spring 2014. These combined archaeological and modern datasets were used as a proxy to help assess the current health of California mussel populations. Our conclusions echo the sentiments of many historical ecologists who argue that, in order to better understand the state of modern ecosystems, it is important to extend our management baselines and perspectives into the deep past (Crumley 1994; Jackson et al. 2001; Rick and Lockwood 2013).

Environmental and cultural background

California's Northern Channel Islands are situated between 20 and 42 km off the California coast. These islands are an extension of the Santa Monica Mountain Range and include, from east to west, Anacapa, Santa Cruz, Santa Rosa, and San Miguel islands. The islands range in size from 2.9 to 249 km² and boast diverse topography including mountains, sand dunes, tablelands, marine terraces, and extensive canyons (Schoenherr et al. 1999). The bathymetry surrounding the islands suggests that during the Last Glacial Maximum (LGM), when eustatic sea levels were on average 120 m lower globally, the northern islands comprised a single island, Santarosae (Kennett 2005; Porcasi et al. 1999; Reeder-Myers et al. 2015). The steady rise of sea levels beginning ca. 18,000 years ago resulted in the inundation of low-lying portions of Santarosae, reducing the land mass by nearly 75 percent, and the fragmentation of Santarosae into the four smaller islands that exist today.

In contrast to the relatively limited land-based resources, the island marine ecosystems surrounding the Channel Islands are incredibly diverse and highly productive. These became the cornerstone of Channel Islander protein subsistence economies. Kelp forests, sandy beaches, and rocky intertidal habitats sustain hundreds of species of fish, birds, sea mammals, and shellfish. The Santa Barbara Channel marine environment benefits from localized nutrient-rich upwelling and the intersection of warm southerly and cold northerly water currents that promote a diverse and productive ecosystem. Over 900 species of fish inhabit the Santa Barbara Channel (Love 1996), dozens of which were exploited in prehistory. Six different species of pinnipeds visit the area annually and zooarchaeological evidence attests to their presence in the past. Shellfish species found in the intertidal, subtidal, sandy beach, and estuarine habitats were incredibly abundant and diverse throughout the Holocene. California mussels, red and black abalone, owl limpets, sea urchins (*Strongylocentrotus* spp.), and black turban snails (*Tegula funebralis*) are common constituents in island shell middens and were important sources of protein and raw material for tool production and ornamental artifacts, including fishhooks, beads, and pendants (Hudson and Blackburn 1985; King 1990).

Archaeological evidence suggests that for over 13,000 years humans visited, occupied, and exploited Northern Channel Island resources (Erlandson et al. 2007, 2008, 2011b; Johnson et al. 2002; Kennett et al. 2008). The Island Chumash, maritime hunter-gatherers known for their sophisticated technologies and sociopolitical complexity, heavily relied on local marine resources, supplemented by cross-channel exchange networks with mainland peoples (Arnold 2001; Kennett 2005; Rick 2007) to sustain growing populations. At most terminal Pleistocene and Early Holocene sites for which quantified faunal data are available, shellfish dominate islander protein diets (Erlandson et al. 2004, Kennett 2005; Rick et al. 2005a), although the recovery of lithic hunting tools at many early sites suggests that sea mammal hunting and fishing may have been more important to island economies than zooarchaeological analyses imply (Erlandson et al. 2011b). Throughout the Holocene, shellfish remained a central subsistence and culturally significant resource, with plant foods and increasing amounts of fish, marine mammals, and birds added to Channel Islander diets through time (Braje 2010; Braje et al. 2012a; Rick et al. 2005a).

As part of a historical ecological study of human impacts on island intertidal ecosystems, Braje and colleagues (2007) ranked the ten most important prey shellfish species on the Northern Channel Islands. Based largely on size, ease of collection, and availability, Braje et al. (2007) established a human behavioral ecology framework for understanding how island fishers would target shellfish resources. Due to their extensive distribution, ease of collection and processing, and availability in dense clusters, California mussels ranked as the top shellfish resource (Braje et al. 2007: 739). In a related meta-analysis of shellfish exploitation on the Northern Channel Islands, Braje et al. (2012a) determined that archaeological shell middens dated to the terminal Pleistocene and the Early, Middle, and Late Holocene tend to be dominated by California mussels, which account, on average, for over 50 percent of the shellfish assemblage. These findings confirm the importance of California mussels to islander diets throughout the Holocene and point to the tremendous human predation pressure exerted on this resource.

California mussel ecology

California mussels (Figure 4.1) are filter-feeding pelecypods (bivalves) found along rocky intertidal zones from the Aleutian Islands in the north to the Socorro Islands, Mexico, in the south (Jones and Richman 1995). Restricted by their narrow ecological niche, they are found attached to exposed and semi-exposed rocks in rocky intertidal and subtidal habitats via byssal threads, easily accessible to humans, and often found exposed during low tides. Although commonly predated upon by humans in ancient times, most modern California mussel communities are not threatened by human subsistence harvesting. Current anthropogenic risks to their populations include the adverse effects of human recreational activities such as trampling and collecting for use as fishing bait (Roy et al. 2003). Additionally, anthropogenic climate change including rising sea surface temperatures and ocean acidification have been linked to declining populations and reductions in average shell length (Smith et al. 2008). These environmental conditions pose a significant threat to the health and stability of mussel communities, reinforcing the need to understand the factors that affect the resiliency of this keystone species.

California mussels often dominate intertidal communities, living in dense clusters of up to 1,000 individuals per square meter within their habitat range (Jones and Richman 1995). They are distinguishable from other mussel species by their coarser, sturdier shell and prominent radiating ridges (Gosling 1992; Jones and Richman 1995). The largest California mussel on record was recorded by Suchanek (1985) at 266 mm; however, California mussels rarely exceed 180 mm in length (Jones and Richman 1995). They are common prey for many predators including

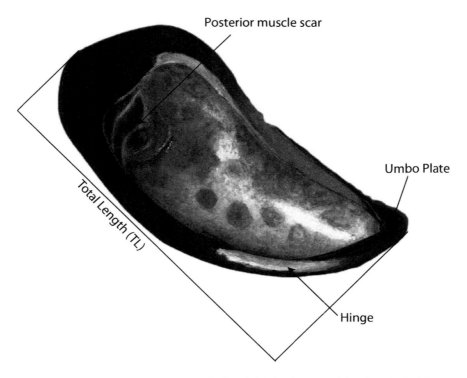

Figure 4.1 Watercolor of a *Mytilus californianus* shell with labels of several of the physiological features mentioned in the text.

shorebirds such as gulls (*Larus* spp.) and black oystercatchers (*Haematopus bachmani*); sea otters (*Enhydra lutris*), lobsters (*Panulirus interruptus*), whelks such as *Ceratostoma nuttali*, *Nucella* spp., and *Maxwellia gemma* (Sowerby); carnivorous fishes such as rock wrasse (*Halichoeres semisinctus*), señorita (*Oxyjulis californica*), and California sheephead (*Semicossyphus pulcher*); and ochre sea stars (*Pisaster ochraceus*). Sea stars are particularly voracious mussel predators, consuming up to 80 mussels per year, preferring individuals less than 100 mm in length (Feder 1970). Storm events have also contributed to high mortality instances for mussel species (Suchanek 1985). When a mussel bed is cleared, either as the result of natural factors or predation, it takes at minimum two-and-a-half years for the regeneration process to begin (Jones and Richman 1995). As mussels begin to repopulate the area, it can take between eight and 35 years for the area to return to pre-disturbance coverage. For example, in 1979 mussel harvesters removed 20 m of mussel habitat in South Yachats State Park on the central coast of Oregon. It was not until 1988 that mussel beds once again became established in the area (Yamada and Peters 1988). When environmental conditions are less than ideal, this process can take up to 100 years (Suchanek 1979). If left relatively undisturbed by heavy predation pressure or natural disasters (i.e., storms), a population can survive in an area for 50 to 100 years (Suchanek 1981).

California mussel growth rates are highly dependent on environmental conditions (Coe and Fox 1942). Factors such as tidal height, food availability, water and air temperature, wave action, sex, and age influence growth rates (Zippay and Helmuth 2012). Growth continues throughout the life cycle of a California mussel; however, rates are most rapid during the first year with individuals reaching, on average, 51 mm (Coe and Fox 1942). Growth rate remains high for the next two years with average size increases of 30 to 40 mm, and, after three years, growth rates slow considerably. Ideally, studies of the effects of human predation on the population structure of California mussels should include an analysis of the average age of death (Bailey and Milner 2008); however, methods for accurate estimates of archaeological samples are problematic. In addition, there are no comparable modern datasets from the Northern Channel Islands of mussel age structure. Our study, therefore, relies on average shell length.

Methods and materials

In 2014, Channel Islands National Park (NPS) marine biologists first began collecting size data for California mussels at several intertidal monitoring locations across the Northern Channel Islands (Figure 4.2). In addition to monitoring the percent cover of California mussels using fixed-plots (an approach that has been in place since 1982), biologists collected size data of individual California mussel shells from replicate plots (50 x 75 cm) as a proxy for mean mussel shell length for these discrete locations. Measurements were estimated to the nearest centimeter and offer the first measure of average California mussel shell length comparable to archaeological sizes for the Northern Channel Islands. To help control for geographic variation, 16 archaeological sites (five from San Miguel, seven from Santa Rosa, and four from Santa Cruz) located near NPS monitoring locations were identified. Archaeological sites were selected based on two criteria: (1) the deposit's age had to be established via radiocarbon dating of marine shell or charcoal samples with all dates calibrated to calendar years; and (2) sites had to contain abundant whole California mussel shells and/or hinge fragments (for approximate locations of these sites, see Figure 4.2).

Our sampling strategy involved the identification of 1.0 x 1.0 meter linear areas where large concentrations of California mussels were visible in embedded soils, often from sea cliff or arroyo exposures. We carefully sampled the full range of shell sizes represented by scouring the site surface for whole shells and hinge fragments of all sizes and by screening (1/16th-inch mesh) some eroded deposits (Figure 4.3). Due to U.S. Navy and NPS access restrictions,

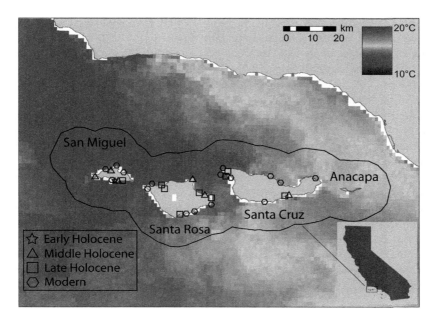

Figure 4.2 Map of the Northern Channel Islands showing the locations of archaeological sites and NPS monitoring localities where size data of California mussel shells were collected. The locations of archaeological sites are approximate due to confidentiality concerns and the protection of cultural resources within Channel Islands National Park. Sea surface temperature (SST) gradient represents mean SST for a 10-year period from June 2006 to June 2016. (Base map courtesy of L. Reeder-Myers.)

Figure 4.3 Breana Campbell (right) and San Diego State graduate student Stephanie Duncan collecting size data at an archaeological shell midden on the west coast of Santa Cruz Island, January 2015. Photo: H. Haas.

archaeological sites on San Miguel Island were selected employing the same criteria from archaeological shell midden samples temporarily housed at San Diego State University's Environmental Anthropology and Archaeology Laboratory. Whole California mussel shells and hinge fragments from San Miguel Island, as well as two samples from Santa Rosa Island (CA-SRI-2 and CA-SRI-163) curated at the Santa Barbara Natural History Museum, were measured in the laboratory.

Two similar methods for estimating the total shell length of a California mussel from hinge fragments have been recently proposed (see Campbell and Braje 2015; Singh and McKechnie 2015). To determine which method was best suited for this study, we used a sample of mussels ($n = 50$) from an archaeological site on San Miguel Island, CA-SMI-232, to test the predictive power of the umbo-width method (Campbell and Braje 2015) and the umbo-thickness method (Singh and McKechnie 2015). These data were compared using a Games-Howell post hoc test in SPSS to identify if either method produced a statistically significant difference of the mean when compared to the known mean shell length.

Based on the results of the regression formula strength analysis, California mussel hinges were measured, either in the laboratory or the field, using the umbo-width method following umbo-width measurement methods detailed by Campbell and Braje (2015). Mean shell length was calculated from these measurements and applied to the following formula:

$$y = 8.2026x + 1.5967, \text{ where } y = \text{total mussel shell length and } x = \text{umbo-width}$$

Values were inserted into the above equation and estimated total shell length was calculated. When whole mussels shells were available, umbo-width measurements were compared to whole shell measurements and used to confirm the reliability of our methodology.

In addition to new size measurements compiled for this study, we also mined published sources for additional California mussel shell length measurements (e.g., Braje 2010; Braje et al. 2007; Erlandson et al. 2008). To test the statistical significance of trans-Holocene size changes by island and to conduct cross-island comparisons during the Late Holocene and modern period, samples were pooled into four temporal sub-groups: Early Holocene (10,000–7,500 cal BP; $n = 297$), Middle Holocene (7,500–3,500 cal BP; $n = 556$), Late Holocene (3,500–130 cal BP; $n = 1409$), and modern (2014 monitoring data; $n = 395$). Since our data can be used to track changes in average mussel shell length by island, we conducted the Games-Howell statistical analyses for time period (Early, Middle, and Late Holocene and modern) for each island (San Miguel, Santa Rosa, and Santa Cruz). Additional tests included comparing the Late Holocene and modern period datasets for each island. No comparison was conducted for the Early Holocene because of the limited available data attained for this study.

A Brown-Forsythe and Welch test was conducted to assess the equality of the means; these tests are appropriate for use in statistical analyses when unequal sample sizes or unequal variance occurs (Tomarken and Serlin 1986). The Welch test result was preferred in all cases where Brown-Forsythe and Welch were disparate. We then applied the Games-Howell post hoc analysis to identify where statistically significant differences of means existed in our dataset. Significance level was consistent for all tests conducted ($p < 0.05$). All statistical analyses were conducted using SPSS software. Finally, these data were plotted against known periods of SST and marine productivity fluctuations, based on $\delta^{18}O$ analysis of *Globigerina bulloides* (surface-dwelling species of foraminifera) from varved sediments in the Santa Barbara Basin, to determine if variation in mean California mussel shell length could be attributed to natural climate variation (Kennett et al. 2007).

Results

Table 4.1 summarizes the results of the comparative analysis between the umbo-width method and the umbo-thickness method. Our results suggest that, although both the umbo-width regression formula and the umbo-length regression formula produced means that were statistically significant similar to the known mean for shell length, the umbo-width method was more similar to the known mean for length.

Table 4.2 summarizes data for the age, sample size, mean, minimum, maximum, and standard deviations of 2,262 California mussel shells from 16 prehistoric shell middens on Santa Cruz, Santa Rosa, and San Miguel islands. Table 4.3 summarizes data for the sample size, mean, minimum, maximum, and standard deviations of 395 California mussel shells from 9 of the 16 NPS monitoring locations. Of the 16 monitoring locations, 7 had fixed-plots devoid of California mussels, therefore, no mussel size data are available for these locations. The largest samples came from Late Holocene sites ($n = 1,409$), followed by Middle Holocene ($n = 556$), modern ($n = 395$), and a single Early Holocene site from San Miguel Island ($n = 297$). Our Santa Barbara Channel-wide sample of mussel shell measurements documents a long-term trend of variation

Table 4.1 Umbo-width and umbo-thickness method analysis

Shell length calculation method	Count (n)	Mean calculated shell length (mm)	St. dev (mm)	Max. length (mm)	Min. length (mm)
Known	50	34.65	10.35	76.37	20.45
Umbo-width	50	33.02	8.56	59.01	19.62
Umbo-thickness	50	38.12	9.58	62.55	20.44

Note: Millimeter (mm), standard (Std.), maximum (Max.) and minimum (Min.).

Table 4.2 Summary data for archaeological samples of California mussel

Site # (CA-)	Age (cal BP)	Time period*	Sample size	Mean calculated shell length (mm)	St. dev (mm)	Max. length (mm)	Min. length (mm)
SMI-232	1290	LH	409	37.76	14.69	91.55	10.95
SMI-396	4600	MH	89	53.17	15.74	89.69	18.03
SMI-575	6100	MH	108	42.84	17.98	122.89	12.31
SMI-657	6190	MH	34	46.49	17.11	114	21.72
SMI-608	9550	EH	297	45.96	20.49	106.45	12.97
SRI-87	>350	LH	200	36.8	9.86	100.96	20.82
SRI-2	1070	LH	259	46.55	13.49	114.44	17.32
SRI-77	1260	LH	49	37.14	8.62	66.92	22.57
SRI-163	1300	LH	121	50.31	16.69	103.88	24.37
SRI-62	2680	LH	88	54.61	14.12	101.78	29.62
SRI-667	4440	MH	200	40.22	10.74	100.49	18.17
SRI-109	5790	MH	100	54.77	13.75	89.2	27.85
SCRI-195	650	LH	98	50.51	15.19	112.63	22.7
SCRI-330	790	LH	100	50.58	14.04	87.86	20.27
SCRI-757	2860	LH	85	43.17	11.6	83.54	14.97
SCRI-770	5870	MH	26	42.49	11.31	77.8	29.98

Note: San Miguel Island (SMI), Santa Rosa Island (SRI), Santa Cruz Island (SCRI). *EH = Early Holocene; MH = Middle Holocene; LH = Late Holocene.

B. Campbell et al.

in shell size through the ancient record, followed by a rebound in shell size during the modern period for San Miguel and Santa Rosa islands. For Santa Cruz Island, mean mussel shell size has remained relatively constant through the Holocene. On San Miguel and Santa Rosa islands, there is a statistically significant difference in modern sizes compared to measurements from the Early, Middle, and Late Holocene (Table 4.4).

The San Miguel Island datasets expressed a statistically significant difference in mean shell length for all temporal periods with the exception of the Early and Middle Holocene where no difference was observed (Table 4.5). On Santa Rosa Island, statistically significant differences of means were observed for each time period. On Santa Cruz Island, our analysis produced a slight statistically significant difference in mean shell length from the Middle and Late Holocene assemblages and no significant difference in mean shell length when these periods were compared to the modern period.

The Welch test was statistically significant for all samples tested indicating that a post hoc test could be successfully used to identify statistically significant differences. A Games-Howell post hoc analysis was conducted using the Late Holocene data to identify statistically significant differences between the mean shell length for each of the three islands. The results indicate that mean shell length for each island during the Late Holocene was significantly different. Santa Cruz Island samples produced the largest mean shell length (48.3 mm), followed by Santa Rosa Island (44.8 mm) and San Miguel Island (37.8 mm). In contrast, the modern dataset revealed that San Miguel Island samples produced the largest mean shell length (67.5 mm), followed by Santa Rosa Island (65.0 mm) and Santa Cruz Island (46.2 mm). When considering only the

Table 4.3 Modern California mussel shell length data

Island	Age	Count (n)	Mean calculated shell length (mm)	St. dev (mm)	Max. length (mm)	Min. length (mm)
SMI	Modern	92	67.5	25.83	150	20
SRI	Modern	100	65	22.94	120	20
SCRI	Modern	208	46.21	27.57	110	10

Note: San Miguel Island (SMI), Santa Rosa Island (SRI), Santa Cruz Island (SCRI).

Table 4.4 Mean calculated shell length for California mussels

Island	Age	Count (n)	Mean calculated shell length (mm)	St. dev (mm)
SMI	EH	297	45.96	20.49
	MH	230	47.37	17.60
	LH	409	37.76	14.69
	M	92	67.50	25.83
SRI	MH	300	39.93	10.06
	LH	717	44.81	14.44
	M	100	65.00	22.94
SCRI	MH	26	42.49	11.31
	LH	283	48.33	14.15
	M	203	46.21	20.48

Note: San Miguel Island (SMI), Santa Rosa Island (SRI), Santa Cruz Island (SCRI), Early Holocene (EH), Middle Holocene (MH), Late Holocene (LH), Modern (M).

Trans-Holocene human impacts on mussels

Table 4.5 Games–Howell post hoc test results for archaeological and modern data of average California mussel size changes from San Miguel, Santa Rosa, and Santa Cruz Islands

(I) VAR00001		(J) VAR00001	Mean difference (I-J)	Std. error	Sig.	95% Confidence interval Lower bound	95% Confidence interval Upper bound
San Miguel Island	EH	MH	−1.41159	1.66164	0.831	−5.6942	2.8711
		LH	8.20075*	1.39354	0	4.6088	11.7927
		M	−21.53856*	2.94407	0	−29.2019	−13.8752
	MH	EH	1.41159	1.66164	0.831	−2.8711	5.6942
		LH	9.61234*	1.36915	0	6.0804	13.1443
		M	−20.12697*	2.93261	0	−27.7623	−12.4917
	LH	EH	−8.20075*	1.39354	0	−11.7927	−4.6088
		MH	−9.61234*	1.36915	0	−13.1443	−6.0804
		M	−29.73931*	2.78946	0	−37.0221	−22.4565
	M	EH	21.53856*	2.94407	0	13.8752	29.2019
		MH	20.12697*	2.93261	0	12.4917	27.7623
		LH	29.73931*	2.78946	0	22.4565	37.0221
Santa Rosa Island	MH	LH	−4.87901*	0.79253	0	−6.74	−3.018
		M	−25.06972*	2.36645	0	−30.6907	−19.4487
	LH	MH	4.87901*	0.79253	0	3.018	6.74
		M	−20.19071*	2.35654	0	−25.7894	−14.592
	M	MH	25.06972*	2.36645	0	19.4487	30.6907
		LH	20.19071*	2.35654	0	14.592	25.7894
Santa Cruz Island	MH	LH	−5.83632*	2.37275	0.049	−11.6616	−0.0111
		M	−3.71393	2.94414	0.421	−10.7589	3.3311
	LH	MH	5.83632*	2.37275	0.049	0.0111	11.6616
		M	2.12239	2.11011	0.574	−2.8497	7.0945
	M	MH	3.71393	2.94414	0.421	−3.3311	10.7589
		LH	−2.12239	2.11011	0.574	−7.0945	2.8497
Modern data	SMI	SRI	2.5	3.53779	0.76	−5.8597	10.8597
		SCRI	21.29310*	3.31642	0	13.4579	29.1283
	SRI	SMI	−2.5	3.53779	0.76	−10.8597	5.8597
		SCRI	18.79310*	3.00132	0	11.7135	25.8727
	SCRI	SMI	−21.29310*	3.31642	0	−29.1283	−13.4579
		SRI	−18.79310*	3.00132	0	−25.8727	−11.7135

Note: Early Holocene (EH), Middle Holocene (MH), Late Holocene (LH), Modern (M), San Miguel Island (SMI), Santa Rosa Island (SRI), Santa Cruz Island (SCRI).

*The mean difference is significant at the 0.05 level.

modern data, we used the Games–Howell post hoc analysis to determine if there was a statistically significant difference in average mussel shell length. The results suggest that a statistically-significant difference exists in the mean shell length of mussels measured at San Miguel and Santa Rosa islands compared to mussels from Santa Cruz Island (Table 4.5).

The mean shell length data for California mussels from each of the 16 sampled archaeological sites were compared to broad scale Holocene SST and marine productivity changes for the Santa Barbara Basin (Kennett et al. 2007). No correlations were observed between California mussel shell length and these cool and warm SST and high and low productivity trends (Figure 4.4).

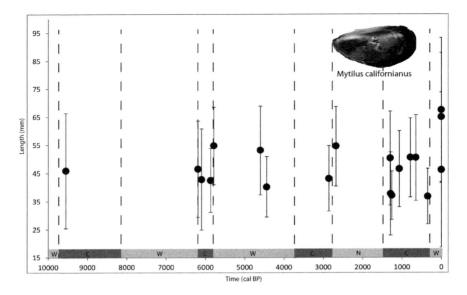

Figure 4.4 Trans-Holocene changes in mean California mussel shell length measurements for 16 Channel Island archaeological components compared to broad scale Holocene SST changes from the Santa Barbara Basin for the Early (10,000–7500 cal BP), Middle (7500–3500 cal BP), and Late Holocene (3500 cal BP–AD 1542). W = Warm, C = Cold, N = Neutral (Kennett et al. 2007).

Discussion and conclusions

Historical ecologists have argued for the critical importance of consulting archaeological and ethnographic records when building restoration and baseline targets for marine resource conservation (see Braje et al. 2005; Engelhard et al. 2015; Jackson et al. 2001; Kittinger et al. 2015; Lepofsky and Caldwell 2013; Mackenzie et al. 2011; McKechnie et al. 2014; Rick and Lockwood 2013; Thurstan et al. 2015). This is especially true in areas where human–environment interactions over the *longue durée* have led to widespread ecological changes. On the Channel Islands, thousands of years of settlement and subsistence activities including extensive fishing and shellfishing during the ancient and historical periods over millennia led to transformations of island seascapes. Studies from the Channel Islands have identified declines in the average shell size of several intertidal shellfish species over the last 10,000 years as the result of intense predation by humans (Braje et al. 2007, 2012a; Erlandson et al. 2008, 2011a, 2015a). For California mussels, Erlandson and colleagues (2008) demonstrated a reduction in mean shell length using archaeological samples from San Miguel Island. Using the umbo-width regression formula established by Campbell and Braje (2015), our study identified similar trends for California mussels from San Miguel Island with different patterns identified for Santa Rosa and Santa Cruz islands.

California mussel shell length on San Miguel Island decreases from the Middle to Late Holocene. This decline was followed by a rebound in modern mean shell length; modern mean mussel shell length on San Miguel Island is nearly twice that for the Late Holocene. Mean mussel size fluctuates on Santa Rosa Island during the Middle and Late Holocene, but the average prehistoric size of mussels were significantly smaller than modern mussels. On Santa Rosa Island, comparisons of the Late Holocene and modern data suggest a similar trend to San Miguel

Island; mean shell length increased approximately 21 mm when the Late Holocene sample was compared to the modern sample for the island. On Santa Cruz Island, despite thousands of years of intense human predation and subsequent release from both human and sea otter predation for the past 150 years, mean length of California mussels has remained relatively constant throughout the Late Holocene and modern period.

To determine if fluctuations in shellfish size correspond to SST or marine productivity trends, several researchers have investigated climatically driven causes for this reduction in mean shell length through time (Braje et al. 2011, 2012a; Erlandson et al. 2008, 2011a). These studies found no clear relationship between SST or marine productivity and the mean shell length of intertidal shellfish. Similarly, we were unable to identify a clear trend to suggest that SST was the driving force influencing changes in average California mussel shell length (see Figure 4.4). Rather, average size reductions of trans-Holocene mussel samples from San Miguel Island, especially during the Late Holocene, correlate with island population increases that occurred on the Northern Channel Islands during this time (Arnold 2001; Erlandson et al. 2001; Glassow 1999). The expansion of large Late Holocene coastal, residential villages would have placed tremendous predation pressure on local mussel beds, leaving little time for individuals to reach their maximum growth potential.

Trends in our modern dataset, on the other hand, suggest that environmental conditions such as localized marine upwelling and SST gradients likely exert strong influence over mussel growth and rebound rates following periods of intense predation or environmental pressure, possibly the result of anthropogenic climate change. Fenberg and colleagues (2015) suggest that the genus *Mytilus* is extremely sensitive to upwelling conditions, which can influence larval dispersal and food availability. The Santa Barbara Channel is a transitional zone where a confluence of circulation patterns, warm and cool water temperatures, and strong and weak upwelling occurs, especially in the waters off San Miguel Island (Wares et al. 2001). Our modern data shows a dramatic increase in mean shell length along an east-to-west Channel gradient suggesting that cooler SSTs and localized upwelling in the waters surrounding San Miguel and Santa Rosa islands may be heavily influencing the population structure and increase in mean shell length of California mussels in these areas, and the lack of increase at Santa Cruz Island (Blanchette et al. 2006; Figure 4.2).

Surprisingly, this east-to-west trend in mean shell length does not exist for our Middle or Late Holocene datasets. In fact, during the Late Holocene, there is a decrease in average mussel size from east to west along the Channel. It may be that the establishment of the intensive shell money bead trading network helped buffer the impacts of human predation on mussel beds on Santa Rosa and Santa Cruz islands. Since these islands acted as the prehistoric "mints" for bead production on the islands, trade for mainland foodstuffs may have helped buffer the heavy influence of human harvesting on these islands (see Arnold 1992, 2001; Kennett 2005). Although shell money beads were produced on San Miguel Island during the Late Holocene (see Braje 2010; Rick 2002, 2007), the island's considerable distance from the mainland and relatively fewer sandy beaches where purple olive snail shells (*Callianax biplicata*), the raw material essential for money bead production, are abundantly available may have made the island more peripheral to mainland trade networks.

Despite long-term predation pressure by the Chumash and their ancestors, California mussel populations remained an important protein source throughout the Holocene (Braje et al. 2012a). The fact that California mussels never disappear from the archaeological record suggests that this resource may have been actively managed by the Chumash, especially following the establishment of permanent villages and chiefdoms. After the establishment of large coastal villages during the Late Holocene and dramatic population increases, the Chumash demonstrated relatively little settlement mobility. This would have been the time when local intertidal systems came under the greatest human predation pressure. California mussels and other intertidal shellfish species remained a central component to the protein diet, with very little evidence of long-term impact, and islanders must have taken steps to manage the long-term viability of the resource. Chiefly ownership of resources within Chumash society has been documented ethnohistorically (see Arnold 2007 and Gamble 2008 for a discussion of *tomol* ownership). It is possible that as permanent settlements arose across the Northern Channel Islands, chiefs claimed ownership of marine resources located near or adjacent to their villages. Such ownership likely resulted in some form of management to ensure the stability of intertidal resources, including California mussel beds. Such a situation would not have been unique in prehistoric California, as ownership of local marine resources has been documented for other Native groups, including the Tolowa who claimed ownership over fishing places near Lake Earl and Lake Talawa (Gould 1975).

California mussels also may have remained relatively stable due to harvesting strategies. Plucking large or medium size mussels may have allowed a juvenile seed population that could rejuvenate mussel beds in a relatively short period of time. Human behavioral ecology studies suggest that plucking was an optimal strategy when compared to stripping an entire bed, leading some to believe it was likely the harvesting strategy used during prehistory (see Jones and Richman 1995). In much the same way, harder-to-access lower intertidal or upper subtidal California mussel populations may have remained relatively free from human predation pressure, maintaining a seed population to rejuvenate human harvested mussel beds.

For over 150 years, California mussels have been relatively free from human predation pressure on the Channel Islands. For nearly the same period of time, one of the primary non-human predators of the California mussel, the sea otter, has been absent since it was eradicated from the Northern Channel Islands during the historical fur trade. Only recently have otters been reintroduced to waters surrounding one of the nearby islands, San Nicolas Island. They have not been allowed, however, to re-establish populations along the Santa Barbara Channel over fears of their potential impacts to abalone recovery and commercial urchin fisheries, and they have been nearly absent around the Northern Channel Islands for over a century (Fanshawe et al. 2003).

Another key predator of California mussels, the ochre sea star, has historically undergone fluctuations in population density as a result of disease epidemics. The sea star recently suffered a massive die-off linked to Sea Star Wasting Disease (SSWD) and similar die-offs have been documented at various intervals over the past four decades (Hewson et al. 2014). First recognized in June 2013 in Washington state, this disease has caused significant damage to sea star populations along the Pacific Coast. As the main predator of California mussels today, sea stars control the habitat range of California mussels, particularly the lower boundaries of mussel beds—mussels tend to regress when sea stars are abundant and flourish when they are absent. Modern data for our study were collected prior to the most recent appearance of SSWD, however, and likely had little effect on our results. Continued study of modern California mussel populations in the coming years will be critical for assessing the ecological fallout due to SSWD.

Lobsters are also voracious predators of mussels, but their abundances decrease from east to west along the Santa Barbara Channel, so their predation effect would be minimal on San Miguel Island and, perhaps, the western end of Santa Rosa. It is possible that more intensive mussel predation by lobsters along Santa Cruz Island has resulted in smaller mean mussel sizes during the modern period and the apparent lack of a size rebound since the end of intensive Chumash harvesting.

Ultimately, the results of our historical ecological study suggest that California mussel populations on the Northern Channel Islands have rebounded when compared to the Early, Middle, and Late Holocene. This is especially true for Santa Rosa and San Miguel islands where there has been a tremendous recovery in the average size of mussels from the ancient to modern records. Mussel populations on Santa Cruz Island, however, have shown little sign of rebound during the modern period. This is despite the near lack of predation pressure by humans and sea otters, although a variety of organisms continue to predate on mussels. SST and marine productivity gradients, along with differences in modern predation pressure along east-to-west gradients, may play vital roles in both the micro- and macro-geographic differences in mean mussel size. It is important, however, to consider that although mussel populations on the Northern Channel Islands are doing favorably when compared to the Holocene, it is becoming increasingly apparent that over the past several decades other anthropogenic factors such as climate change and ocean acidification are contributing to a reduction in the health of mussel communities (Smith et al. 2008). Our study, then, represents the first step in investigating mussel size patterning through space and deep time. The decline in average mussel size on Santa Cruz from the Late Holocene to the modern period may be an important pattern for Channel Islands National Park biologists to carefully monitor in the coming years. Larger samples from archaeological sites adjacent to modern monitoring locations will be especially important for confirming or refuting this pattern.

As we rush towards an Anthropocene future, we must take care to consider that the state of our increasingly anthropogenic world is the result of millennia of human-environmental eco-dynamics. Even if geoscientists decide that the Anthropocene Epoch began in the last 50 years (which seems increasingly likely [Braje 2015, 2016]), it will be perspectives from deep history that can help us evaluate the modern world and better manage towards a more sustainable future. Historical ecological studies such as ours offer insights for evaluating the current state of marine and terrestrial ecosystems and making future projections about where we are headed, a task that remains impossible without understanding the history, magnitude, and drivers of past changes.

References

Alroy, J., 2001. A Multispecies Overkill Simulation of the End-Pleistocene Megafaunal Mass Extinction. *Science* 292, 1893–1896.

Arnold, J.E., 2007. Credit Where Credit Is Due: The History of the Chumash Oceangoing Plank Canoe. *American Antiquity* 72, 196–209.

Arnold, J.E., 2001. Social Evolution and the Political Economy in the Northern Channel Islands, in: Arnold, J.E. (Ed.), *The Origins of a Pacific Coast Chiefdom: The Chumash of the Channel Islands*. University of Utah Press, Salt Lake City, pp. 287–296.

Arnold, J.E., 1992. Complex Hunter-Gatherer-Fishers of Prehistoric California: Chiefs, Specialists, and Maritime Adaptations of the Channel Islands. *American Antiquity* 57, 60–84.

Bailey, G.N., Milner, N., 2008. Molluscan Archives from European Prehistory. In: Antczak, A., Cipriani, R. (Eds.), *Early Human Impact on Megamolluscs*. Archaeopress BAR International Series 1865, Oxford, pp. 111–134.

Bailey, G., 2004. World Prehistory from the Margins: The Role of Coastlines in Human Evolution. *Journal of Interdisciplinary Studies* 1(1), 39–50.

Bell, A.M., 2009. On the Validity of Archaeological Shellfish Metrics in Coastal California. Unpublished Master's Thesis, Department of Anthropology, California State University, Chico.

Blanchette, C.A., Broitman, B.R., Gaines, S.D., 2006. Intertidal Community Structure and Oceanographic Patterns around Santa Cruz Island, CA, USA. *Marine Biology* 149, 689–701.

Braje, T.J., 2016. Evaluating the Anthropocene: Is There Something Useful about a Geological Epoch of Humans? *Antiquity* 90, 504–18.

Braje, T.J., 2015. Earth Systems, Human Agency, and the Anthropocene: Planet Earth in the Human Age. *Journal of Archaeological Research* 23, 369–396.

Braje, T.J., 2010. *Modern Oceans, Ancient Sites: Archaeology and Marine Conservation on San Miguel Island, California*. University of Utah Press, Salt Lake City.

Braje, T.J., Erlandson, J.M., 2013. Looking Forward, Looking Back: Humans, Anthropogenic Change, and the Anthropocene. *Anthropocene* 4, 116–121.

Braje, T.J., Rick, T.C., Erlandson, J.M., Rogers-Bennett, L., Catton, C.A., 2015. Historical Ecology Can Inform Restoration Site Selection: The Case of Black Abalone (*Haliotis cracherodii*) along California's Channel Islands. *Aquatic Conservation: Marine and Freshwater Ecosystems*, doi: 10.1002/aqc.2561.

Braje, T.J., Rick, T.C., Erlandson, J.M., 2012a. A Trans-Holocene Historical Ecological Record of Shellfish Harvesting on California's Northern Channel Islands. *Quaternary International* 264, 109–120.

Braje, T.J., Rick, T.C., Erlandson, J.M., 2012b. Rockfish in the Longview: Applied Archaeology and Conservation of Pacific Red Snapper (Genus Sebastes) in Southern California, in: S. Wolverton, R. Lee Lyman (eds.), *Conservation Biology and Applied Zooarchaeology*. University of Arizona Press, Tucson, pp. 157–178.

Braje, T.J., Rick, T.C., 2011. *Human Impacts on Seals, Sea Lions, and Sea Otters: Integrating Archaeology and Ecology in the Northeast Pacific*. University of California Press, Berkeley.

Braje, T.J., Erlandson, J.M., Rick, T.C., Dayton, P.K., Hatch, B.A., 2009. Fishing from Past to Present: Continuity and Resilience of Red Abalone Fisheries on the Channel Islands, California. *Ecological Applications* 19, 906–919.

Braje, T.J., Kennett, D.J., Erlandson, J.M., Culleton, B.J., 2007. Human Impacts on Nearshore Shellfish Taxa: a 7,000 Year Record from Santa Rosa Island, California. *American Antiquity* 72, 735–756.

Braje, T.J., Erlandson, J.M., Kennett, D.J., Peterson, J.E., 2005. Deep History: Using Archaeology and Historical Ecology to Promote Marine Conservation. *Chemins Alternatifs* 21, 5–17.

Braun, D.R., Harris, J.W.K., Levin, N.E., McCoy, J.T., Herries, A.I.R., Bamford, M.K., Bishop, L.C., Richmond, B.G., Kibunjia, M., 2010. Early Hominin Diet Included Diverse Terrestrial and Aquatic Animals 1.95 Ma in East Turkana, Kenya. *Proceedings of the National Academy of Sciences* 107, 10002–10007.

Broughton, J.M., 2002. Pre-Columbian Human Impact on California Vertebrates: Evidence from Old Bones and Implications for Wilderness Policy, in: Kay, C.E., Simmons, R.T. (Eds.), *Wilderness and Political Ecology: Aboriginal Influences and the Original State of Nature*. University of Utah Press, Salt Lake City, pp. 44–71.

Broughton, J.M., 1999. *Resource Depression and Intensification during the Late Holocene, San Francisco Bay: Evidence from the Emeryville Shellmound Vertebrate Fauna*. University of California Press, Berkeley.

Broughton, J.M., 1997. Widening Diet Breadth, Declining Foraging Efficiency, and Prehistoric Harvest Pressure: Ichthyofauna Evidence from the Emeryville Shellmound, California. *Antiquity* 71, 845–862.

Broughton, J.M., 1994. Declines in Mammalian Foraging Efficiency during the Late Holocene, San Francisco Bay, California. *Journal of Anthropological Archaeology* 13, 371–401.

Campbell, B., Braje, T.J., 2015. Estimating California Mussel (*Mytilus californianus*) Size from Hinge Fragments: A Methodological Application in Historical Ecology. *Journal of Archaeological Science* 58, 167–174.

Claassen, C., 1998. *Shells*. Cambridge University Press, Cambridge.

Codding, B.F., Whitaker, A.R., Bird, D.W., 2014. Global Patterns in Exploitation of Shellfish. *Journal of Island and Coastal Archaeology* 2, 145–149.

Coe, W.R., Fox, D.L., 1942. Biology of the California Sea-Mussel (*Mytilus californianus*): Influence of Temperature, Food Supply, Sex and Age on the Rate of Growth. *Journal of Experimental Zoology* 90, 1–30.

Colonese, A.C., Collins, M., Lucquin, A., Eustace, M., Hancock, Y., de Almeida Rocha Ponzoni, R., 2014. Long-Term Resilience of Late Holocene Coastal Subsistence System in Southeastern South America. *PLoS ONE* 9(4), e93854. doi:10.1371/journal.pone.0093854.

Crumley, C.L. (Ed.), 1994. *Historical Ecology: Cultural Knowledge and Changing Landscapes*. School of American Research Press, Santa Fe, New Mexico.

Crutzen, P., 2002. Geology of Mankind. *Nature 415*, 23. http://dx.doi.org/10.1038/415023a.

Crutzen, P., and Steffen, E., 2003. How Long Have We Been in the Anthropocene Era? *Climatic Change* 61, 251–57. http://dx.doi.org/10.1023/B:CLIM. 0000004708.74871.62.

Engelhard, G.H., Thurstan, R.H., MacKenzie, B.R., Alleway, H.K., Bannister, R.C.A., Cardinale, M., Clarke, M.W., Currie, J.C., Fortibuoni, T., Holm, P., Holt, S.J., Mazzoldi, C., Pinnegar, J.K., Raicevich, S., Volckaert, F.A.M., Klein, E.S., and Lescrauwaet, A., 2015. ICES Meets Marine Historical Ecology: Placing the History of Fish and Fisheries in Current Policy Context. *ICES Journal of Marine Science*, 2–18.

Erlandson, J.M., 2001. The Archaeology of Aquatic Adaptations: Paradigms for a New Millennium. *Journal of Archaeological Research* 9, 287–350.

Erlandson, J.M., Ainis, A.F., Braje, T.J., Jew, N.P., McVey, M., Rick, T.C., Vellanoweth, R.L., and Watts, J., 2015a. 12,000 Years of Human Predation on Black Turban Snails (*Chlorostoma funebralis*) on Alta California's Northern Channel Islands. *California Archaeology* 7, 59–91.

Erlandson, J.M., Braje, T.J., Gill, K.M., and Graham, M.H., 2015b. Ecology of the Kelp Highway: Did Marine Resources Facilitate Human Dispersal From Northeast Asia to the Americas? *Journal of Island and Coastal Archaeology* 10, 392–411.

Erlandson, J.M., Braje, T.J., Rick, T.C., Jew, N.P., Kennett, D.J., Dwyer, N., Ainis, A.F., Vellanoweth, R.L., Watts, J., 2011a. 10,000 Years of Human Predation and Size Changes in the Owl Limpet (*Lottia gigantea*) on San Miguel Island, California. *Journal of Archaeological Science* 38, 1127–1134.

Erlandson, J.M., and Rick, T.C., Braje, T.B., Casperson, M., Culleton, B., Fulfrost, B., Garcia, T., Guthrie, D.A., Jew, N.P., Kennett, D.J., Moss, M.L., Reeder, L., Skinner, C., Watts, J., and Willis, L., 2011b. Paleo-Indian Seafaring, Maritime Technologies, and Coastal Foraging on California's Channel Islands. *Science* 331, 1181–1185.

Erlandson, J.M., and Rick, T.C., 2010. Archaeology Meets Marine Ecology: The Antiquity of Maritime Cultures and Human Impacts on Marine Fisheries and Ecosystems. *Annual Review of Marine Science* 2, 231–251.

Erlandson, J.M., Rick, T.C., Braje, T.J., Steinberg, A., and Vellanoweth, R.L., 2008. Human Impacts on Ancient Shellfish: A 10,000 Year Record from San Miguel Island, California. *Journal of Archaeological Science* 35, 2144–2152.

Erlandson, J.M., Graham, M.H., Bourque, B.J., Corbett, D., Estes, J.A., and Steneck, R.S., 2007. The Kelp Highway Hypothesis: Marine Ecology, the Coastal Migration Theory, and the Peopling of the Americas. *Journal of Island and Coastal Archaeology* 2, 161–174.

Erlandson, J.M., Rick, T.C., and Vellanoweth, R.L., 2004. Human Impacts on Ancient Environments: A Case Study from the Northern Channel Islands, in: Fitzpatrick, S.M. (Ed.), *Voyages of Discovery: The Archaeology of Islands*. Praeger, Westport, CT.

Erlandson, J.M., Rick, T.C., Kennett, D.J., and Walker, P.L., 2001. Dates, Demography, and Disease: Cultural Contacts and Possible Evidence for Old World Epidemics among the Island Chumash, Pacific Coast. *Archaeological Society Quarterly* 37, 11–26.

Erlandson, J.M., Rick, T.C., Vellanoweth, R.L., and Kennett, D.J., 1999. Marine Subsistence at a 9300 Year Old Shell Midden on Santa Rosa Island. *California Journal of Field Archaeology* 26, 255–265.

Fanshawe, S., Vanblaricom, G.R., Shelly, A.A., 2003. Restored Top Carnivores as Detriments to the Performance of Marine Protected Areas Intended for Fishery Sustainability: A Case Study with Red Abalones and Sea Otters. *Conservation Biology* 17, 273–283.

Faulkner, P., 2009. Focused, Intense and Long-Term: Evidence for Granular Ark (*Anadara granosa*) Exploitation from Late Holocene Shell Mounds of Blue Mud Bay, Northern Australia. *Journal of Archaeological Science* 36, 821–834.

Feder, H.M., 1970. Growth and Predation by the Ochre Sea Star, Pisaster ochraceus in Monterey Bay, California. *Ophelia* 8, 161–185.

Fenberg, P.B., Menge, B.A., Raimondi, P.T., and Rivadeneira, M.M., 2015. Biogeographic Structure of the Northeastern Pacific Rocky Intertidal: The Role of Upwelling and Dispersal to Drive Patterns. *Ecogeography* 38(1), 83–95.

Foley, S., Gronenborn, D., Andreae, M., Kadereit, J., Esper, J., Scholz, D., Poschl, U., Jacob, D., Schone, B., Schreg, B., Vott, A., Jordan, D., Lelieveld, J., Weller, C., Alt, K., S. Gaudzinski-Windheuser, S., Bruhn, K., Tost, H., Sirocko, F., and Crutzen, P., 2013. The Palaeoanthropocene: The Beginnings of Anthropogenic Environmental Change. *Anthropocene* 3, 83–88. http://dx.doi.org/10.1016/j.ancene.2013.11.002.

Gamble, L.H., 2008. *The Chumash World at European Contact: Power, Trade, and Feasting among Complex Hunter-Gatherers*. University of California Press, Berkeley.

Gill, K., and Erlandson, J.M., 2014. The Island Chumash and Exchange in the Santa Barbara Channel Region. *American Antiquity* 79, 570–572.

Glassow, M.A., 1999. Measurement of Population Growth and Decline during California Prehistory. *Journal of California and Great Basin Anthropology* 21, 45–66.

Glassow, M.A., 2016. Issues in the Identification of Umbones in California Mussel Shell Assemblages. *Quaternary International*. doi: 10.1016/j.quaint.2015.09.098.

Glassow, M.A., Sutton, E.A., Fernandez, C.F., and Thakar, H.B., 2016. Proxy Measurements of California Mussel Valve Length. *Advances in Archaeological Practice* 4(1), 31–40.

Gosling, E., 1992. Systematics and Geographic Distribution of Mytilus, in: Gosling, P. (Ed.), *The Mussel Mytilus: Ecology, Physiology, Genetics, and Culture*. Elsevier, Amsterdam, pp. 1–20.

Goudie, A., 2000. *The Human Impact on the Natural Environment*. The MIT Press, Cambridge, MA.

Gould, R.A., 1975. Ecology and Adaptive Response among the Tolowa Indians of Northwestern California. *Journal of California Anthropology* 2, 148–170.

Griffiths, C.L., and Branch, G.M., 1997. The Exploitation of Coastal Invertebrates and Seaweeds in South Africa: Historical Trends, Ecological Impacts and Implications for Management. *Transactions of the Royal Society of South Africa* 52(1), 121–148.

Hewson, I., Button, J.B., Gudenkauf, B.M., Miner, B., Newton, A.L., Gaydos, J.K., Wynne, J., Groves, C.L., Hendler, G., Murray, M., Fradkin, S., Breitbart, M., Fahsbender, E., Lafferty, K.D., Kilpatrick, A.M., Miner, C.M., Raimondi, P., Lahner, L., Friedman, C.S., Daniels, S., Haulena, M., Marliave, J., Burge, C.A., Eisenlord, M.E., and Harvell, C.D., 2014. Densovirus Associated with Sea-Star Wasting Disease and Mass Mortality. *Proceedings of the National Academy of Sciences* 111, 17278–17283.

Hudson, T., and Blackburn, T.C., 1985. The Material Culture of the Chumash Interaction Sphere, Vol. III: *Clothing, Ornamentation, and Grooming*. Ballena Press/Santa Barbara Museum of Natural History, Los Altos and Santa Barbara, CA.

Jackson, J.B.C., Kirby, M.X., Berger, W.H., Bjorndal, K.A., Botsford, L.W., Bourque, B.J., Bradbury, R.H., Cooke, R., Erlandson, J., Estes, J.A., Hughes, T.P., Kidwell, S., Lange, C.B., Lenihan, H.S., Pandolfi, J.M., Peterson, C.H., Steneck, R.S., Tegner, M.J., and Warner, R.R., 2001. Historical Overfishing and the Recent Collapse of Coastal Ecosystems. *Science* 293, 629–637.

Jazwa, C.S., Kennett, D.J., and Hanson, D., 2012. Late Holocene Subsistence Change and Marine Productivity on Western Santa Rosa Island, Alta California. *California Archaeology* 4, 69–98.

Jerardino, A., 1997. Changes in Shellfish Species Composition and Mean Shell Size from a Late-Holocene Record of the West Coast of South Africa. *Journal of Archaeological Science* 24, 1031–1044.

Johnson, J.R., Stafford, T.W., Ajie, H.O., and Morris, D.P., 2002. Arlington Springs Revisited, in: Browne, D.R., Mitchell, K.L., and Chaney, H.W. (Eds.), *Proceedings of the Fifth California Islands Symposium* (CD Publication), Santa Barbara Natural History Museum, Santa Barbara, CA.

Jones, T.L., and Richman, J.R., 1995. On Mussels: Mytilus Californianus as a Prehistoric Resource. *North American Archaeologist* 16, 33–58.

Kennett, D.J. 2005. *The Island Chumash: Behavioral Ecology of a Maritime Society*. University of California Press, Berkeley.

Kennett, D.J., Kennett, J.P., West, G.J., Erlandson, J.M., Johnson, J.R., Hendy, I.L., West, A., Culleton, B.J., Jones, T.L., and Stafford, T.W., 2008. Wildfire and Abrupt Ecosystem Disruption on California's Northern Channel Islands at the Allerød–Younger Dryas boundary (13.0–12.9 ka). *Quaternary Science Reviews* 27, 2530–2545.

Kennett, D.J., Kennett, J.P., Erlandson, J.M., and Cannariato, K.G., 2007., Human Responses to Middle Holocene Climate Change on California's Channel Islands. *Quaternary International* 26, 351–367.

King, C.D., 1990. *Evolution of Chumash Society*. Garland, New York, 20.

Kirch, P.V., 2005. Archaeology and Global Change: The Holocene Record. *Annual Review of Environment and Resources*. 30, 409–440.

Kirch, P.V., and Hunt, T.L., 1997. *Historical Ecology in the Pacific Islands: Prehistoric Environmental Landscape Change*. Yale University Press, New Haven, CT.

Kittinger, J.N., McClenachan, L., Gedan, K.B., and Blight, L.K. (Eds.) 2015. *Marine Historical Ecology in Conservation: Applying the Past to Manage for the Future*. University of California Press, Berkeley.

Lepofsky, D. and Caldwell, M., 2013. Indigenous Marine Resource Management on the Northwest Coast of North America. *Ecological Processes* 2(1), 1–12.

Love, M.S., 1996. *Probably More Than You Wanted to Know about the Fishes of the Pacific Coast*. Really Big Press, Santa Barbara, CA.

MacKenzie, B.R., Ojaveer, H., and Eero, M., 2011. Historical Ecology Provides New Insights for Ecosystem Management: Eastern Baltic Cod Case Study. *Marine Policy* 35(2), 266–270.

Marean, C.W., Bar-Matthews, M., Bernatchez, J., Fisher, E., Goldberg, P., Herries, A.I.R., Jacobs, Z., Jerardino, A., Karkanas, P., Minichillo, T., Nilssen, P.J., Thompson, E., Watts, I., and Williams, H.M., 2007. Early Use of Marine Resources and Pigment in South Africa during the Middle Pleistocene. *Nature* 449, 905–908.

Martin, P.S., 1973. The Discovery of America: The First Americans May Have Swept the Western Hemisphere and Decimated Its Fauna within 1000 Years. *Science* 179(4077), 969–974.

Martin, P.S., and Steadman, D.W., 1999. Prehistoric Extinctions on Islands and Continents. In: MacPhee R.D.E. (eds.), *Extinctions in Near Time: Advances in Vertebrate Paleobiology*, vol 2. Springer, Boston, MA.

McClenachan, L., Cooper, A.B., McKenzie, M.G., and Drew, J.A., 2015. The Importance of Surprising Results and Best Practices in Historical Ecology. *Bioscience* doi: 10.1093/biosci/biv100.

McKechnie, I., Singh, G.G., Braje, T.J., and Campbell, B., 2015. Measuring *Mytilus californianus*: An Addendum to Campbell and Braje (2015) and Singh and McKechnie (2015) including Commentary and an Integration of Data. *Journal of Archaeological Science* 30, 184–186.

McKechnie, I., Lepofsky, D., Moss, M.L., Butler, V.L., Orchard, T.J., Coupland, G., Foster, F., Caldwell, M., and Lertzman, K., 2014. Archaeological Data Provide Alternative Hypotheses on Pacific Herring (*Clupea pallasii*) Distribution, Abundance, and Variability. *Proceedings of the National Academy of Sciences* 111(9), 807–816.

Morrison, A.E., and Hunt, T.L., 2007. Human Impacts on the Nearshore Environment: an Archaeological Case Study from Kaua'i, Hawaiian Islands. *Pacific Science* 61, 325–345.

Myers, R.A., and Worm, B., 2003. Rapid Worldwide Depletion of Predatory Fish Communities. *Nature* 423, 280–283.

Pauly, D., 1995. Anecdotes and the Shifting Baseline Syndrome of Fisheries. *Trends in Ecology & Evolution* 10, 430.

Pauly, D., Christensen, V., Dalsgaard, J., Froese, R., and Torres, F., 1998. Fishing Down Marine Food Webs. *Science* 279, 860–863.

Pope, G.G., 1989. Bamboo and Human Evolution. *Natural History* October, 49–57.

Porcasi, P., Porcasi, J.F., and O'Neill, C., 1999. Early Holocene Coastlines of the California Bight: The Channel Islands as First Visited by Humans. *Pacific Coast Archaeological Society Quarterly* 35, 1–24.

Raab, L.M., 1992. An Optimal Foraging Analysis of Prehistoric Shellfish Collecting on San Clemente Island, California. *Journal of Ethnobiology* 12, 63–80.

Reddy, S.N., and Erlandson, J.M., 2012. Macrobotanical Food Remains from a Trans-Holocene Sequence at Daisy Cave (CA-SMI-261), San Miguel Island, California. *Journal of Archaeological Science* 39(1), 33–40.

Redman, C.L., 1999. *Human Impacts on Ancient Ecosystems*, University of Arizona Press, Tuscon.

Redman, C.L., James, S.R., Fish, P.R., and Rogers, J.D., 2004. *Archaeology of Global Change: The Impact of Humans on Their Environment*. Smithsonian Books, Washington, DC.

Reeder-Myers, L., Erlandson, J.M., Muhs, D.R., and Rick, T.C., 2015. Sea Level, Paleogeography, and Archeology on California's Northern Channel Islands. *Quaternary Research* 83, 263–272.

Rick, T.C., 2007. *The Archaeology and Historical Ecology of Late Holocene San Miguel Island*. Cotsen Institute of Archaeology, UCLA, Los Angeles.

Rick, T.C., 2002. Eolian Processes, Ground Cover, and the Archaeology of Coastal Dunes: A Taphonomic Case Study from San Miguel Island, California, California, U.S.A. *Geoarchaeology* 17(8), 811–833.

Rick, T.C., Ogburn, M., Kramer, M.A., and Hines, A.H., 2015. Archaeology, Taphonomy, and Historical Ecology of Chesapeake Bay Blue Crabs (*Callinectes sapidus*). *Journal of Archaeological Science*, doi: 10.1016/j.jas.2014.12.016.

Rick, T.C., and Lockwood, R., 2013. Integrating Paleobiology, Archaeology, and History to Inform Biological Conservation. *Conservation Biology* 27, 45–54.

Rick, T.C., and Erlandson, J.M. (Eds.), 2008. *Human Impacts in Ancient Marine Ecosystems: A Global Perspective*. University of California Press, Berkeley.

Rick, T.C., Erlandson, J.M., Vellanoweth, R.L., and Braje, T.J., 2005a. From Pleistocene Mariners to Complex Hunter-Gatherers: The Archaeology of the California Channel Islands. *Journal of World Prehistory* 19, 169–228.

Roy, K., Collins, A.G., Becker, B.J., Begovic, E., and Engle, J.M., 2003. Anthropogenic Impacts and Historical Decline in Body Size of Rocky Intertidal Gastropods in Southern California. *Ecology Letters* 6, 205–211.

Schoenherr, A., Feldmath, C.R., and Emerson, M., 1999. *Natural History of the Islands of California*. University of California Press, Berkeley.

Singh, G.G., and McKechnie, I., 2015. Making the Most of Fragments: A Method for Estimating Shell Length from Fragmentary Mussels (*Mytilus californianus* and *Mytilus trossulus*) on the Pacific Coast of North America. *Journal of Archaeological Science* 58, 175–183.

Smith, J.R., Fong, P., and Ambrose, R.F., 2008. The Impacts of Human Visitation on Mussel Bed Communities along the California Coast: Are Regulatory Marine Reserves Effective in Protecting These Communities? *Environmental Management* 41, 599–612.

Steadman, D.W., 2006. *Extinction and Biogeography of Tropical Pacific Birds*. University of Chicago Press, Chicago, IL.

Steele, T.E., and Álvarez-Fernández, E., 2011. Initial Investigations into the Exploitation of Coastal Resources in North Africa during the Late Pleistocene at Grotte Des Contrebandiers, Morocco, in: Bicho, N.F., Haws, J.A., and Davis, L.G. (Eds.), *Trekking the Shore*. Springer, New York, pp. 383–403.

Steffen, W., Grinevald, J., Crutzen, P., and McNeill, J., 2011. The Anthropocene: Conceptual and Historical Perspectives. *Philosophical Transactions of the Royal Society A* 369, 842–67. http://dx.doi.org/10.1098/rsta.2010.0327.

Stewart, K.M., 1994. Early Hominid Utilization of Fish Resources and Implications for Seasonality and Behavior. *Journal of Human Evolution* 27, 229–245.

Suchanek, T.H., 1985. Mussels and Their Role in Structuring Rocky Shore Communities, in: Moore, P.G., and Seed, R. (Eds.), *The Ecology of Rocky Coasts*. Hodder and Stoughton, London, pp. 70–96.

Suchanek, T.H., 1981. The Role of Disturbance in the Evolution of Life History Strategies in the Intertidal Mussels *Mytilus edulis and Mytilus californianus*. *Oecologia* 50, 143–152.

Suchanek, T.H., 1979. The Mytilus Californianus Community: Studies on the Composition, Structure, and Organization, and Dynamics of a Mussel Bed. PhD Dissertation, Department of Biology, University of Washington.

Thakar, H.B., Glassow, M.A., and Blanchette, C., 2015. Reconsidering Evidence of Human Impacts: Implications of Within-Site Variation of Growth Rates in Mytilus californianus along Tidal Gradients. *Quaternary International* 10(2), 184–206.

Thurstan, R.H., McClenachan, L., Crowder, L.B., Drew, J.A., Kittinger, J.N., Levin, P.S., Roberts, C.M. and Pandolfi, J.M., 2015. Filling Historical Data Gaps to Foster Solutions in Marine Conservation. *Ocean & Coastal Management* 115, 31–40.

Tomarken, A., and Serlin, R.C., 1986. Comparison of ANOVA Alternatives under Variance Heterogeneity and Specific Noncentrality Structures. *Psychological Bulletin* 99, 90–99.

U.S. Commission on Ocean Policy, 2004. An Ocean Blueprint for the 21st Century: Final Report.

Vitousek, P.M., Mooney, H.A., Lubchenco, J., and Melillo, J.M., 1997. Human Domination of Earth's Ecosystems. *Science* 277 (5325), 494–499.

Wares, J.P., Gaines, S., and Cunningham, C.W., 2001. A Comparative Study of Asymmetric Migration Events across a Marine Biogeographic Boundary. *Evolution* 55(2), 295–306.

White, G., 1989. A Report of Archaeological Investigations at Eleven Native American Coastal Sites, MacKerricher State Park, Mendocino County, California. Unpublished report on file with California State Parks.

Yamada, S.B., and Peters, E.E., 1988. Harvest Management and the Growth and Condition of Supermarket-Size Sea Mussels, *Mytilus Californianus*. *Aquaculture* 74, 293–299.

Zippay, M.L., and Helmuth, B., 2012. Effects of Temperature Change on Mussel, *Mytilus*. *Integrative Zoology* 7, 312–327.

5
DRIFT

Þóra Pétursdóttir

back to the edge of the sea, where the drama of life played its first scene on earth and perhaps even its prelude; where the forces of evolution are at work today, as they have been since the appearance of what we know as life; and where the spectacle of living creatures faced by the cosmic realities of their world is crystal clear
Carson 2015 [1955], 14

Prelude: Eidsbukta 70.96262°N 26.66342°Ø

This chapter gathers some thoughts and fragments from fieldwork conducted on a beach in Northern Norway. The fieldwork is part of a project reverberating around the phenomenon of the North Atlantic drift beach in past and present, its *nature*, its use and changing identity, and its implications for archaeological conduct and reasoning.

The beach, Eidsbukta, a small cove at the northern tip of Sværholt peninsula, is located at roughly 71° northern latitude, across the Porsanger fjord from North Cape, the northernmost point of Norway. Facing the open Barents Sea to the northwest, with the circulating surface waters of the North Atlantic current from the south and the Bear Island current from the northwest, Eidsbukta is ideally situated to capture large quantities of drift material from incoming tide and storm. Its effectiveness is bluntly recalled in the local name it was given by residents in the small, now long-abandoned, fishing hamlet on the east side of the barren Sværholt peninsula. 'We always called it the Driftwood beach [Rekvedfjæra]', Gunnlaug Sagen states, 'that is where we went for wood' (Sagen, pers. com.).

The aspirations of this chapter are to delineate, or hint at, some tensions, thoughts, and frictions provoked along this strip of land, in the tidal zone of Eidsbukta. Tensions that summon different species and kinds, other natures and ecologies and that may be of significance at the dawn of a new Anthropocene Era. Far removed from the hassle of civilization, the smog of urban centres, the spotlights of media and environmental discourse, and far removed from the comforts of modern lifestyles, Eidsbukta emits, in her own unkempt and unpretentious tongue, an argument both for and against an idea of this 'Age of Man'. With her indiscriminate collection of drift, resulting from a persistent collaboration with the forces of gravity, tide and storm, Eidsbukta both centres and decentres us humans. Through her worlding, her untiring gathering and making of her own environs, which also has sustained her valued legacy as a drift beach, she manifests the tensions between – and the strains within – notions of nature, culture, environment, pollution, resource, Anthropocene, archaeological record and time. And by so doing, by allowing things – species – of different kinds and origins to be 'thrown together' (Stewart 2008) she confronts, challenges and invites archaeological thinking.

Patina

Colours are not detached phenomena. Much like the taste, smell and texture of Proust's madeleine, colours may bring us beyond a moment, beyond what is seen. Colours recall, resonate, associate. And so it is that ecology, environment, eco, mostly resonates with various shades of green (Buell 2013). Green is the colour of life, of health and of a pristine inhuman nature. Green is the hope at the dawn of Anthropocene.

Grey, on the other hand, 'Grey is the fate of color at twilight' (Cohen 2013, 270). Grey's immediate association isn't hopeful and optimistic, but dull, lifeless, deprived. 'A grey ecology', as Cohen explains, 'might therefore seem a moribund realm, an expanse of slow loss, wanness, and withdrawal, a graveyard space of mourning' (ibid.). Grey is the shade of sickness. It may be the hue of Anthropocene, of anxiety, regret and bleakness. The lowering light preceding the apocalypse.

But grey is also a liminal shade, withdrawn in its prosaic patina it allows the elements to rest. It flattens the plane, soothes contrasts and brings differences closer. Grey brings us another landscape – not one that is colourless, dull and lifeless, but a landscape tinted by tranquillity, enabling the eye to glide unhindered between elements of different kind. Grey pacifies our preconceptions and tones down our definitions.

In reality, the colours of Eidsbukta are stark and faded, bright and bleached. Among its grey beach pebbles, whitewashed driftwood and kelp, is a dense decoration of foreign elements in fiery orange and yellow, bright green and blue. Radiating in stark contrast to what is considered the native patina of these northern latitudes these elements immediately stand out as foreign. As intruders. As contamination. As something opposing the environment.

But this is the *nature* of Eidsbukta. This is her worlding, her making of the environment, and her legacy as a drift beach. Her environment, her ecology has never discriminated between kinds or colours. Her ecology was always one of drift, gathering, and becoming. Hence, depicting Eidsbukta and her collection of drift in tones of grey is not a depriving of her nature, but an attempt to bring it closer – to actually see her.

Contours

The notion of Anthropocene brings forth a rhythmic tension, breechings in notions of time, frictions between what has been and what is becoming, between the abrupt and the gradual, the now and the distant. When is the dawn of the Anthropocene, and how deep lies its boundary?

Like contour lines on a map, or growth rings in wood, Eidsbukta's gathered topography delineates a geological, earthly biography. Repeating her contours like ripples in water, fossilized shorelines behold the faint and distinct silhouettes of her youth, her ageing, and infinity. Folding inland, like waves reaching shore they recall a telling of postglacial rebound, a rising of land, and the infinite return of the tide. The motion involved in her ever becoming – the rhythmic dance of pushing and pulling in the boundless affair of water and land.

Along the lowest of these fossilized ridges is the main wrack zone; a thick and coarse belt of debris, a tinted rosary stretching from one end of the cove to the other, draped in plastic, wood and shining colours, topographically reflecting the discrepancy and continuity between before and after, Holocene and Anthropocene.

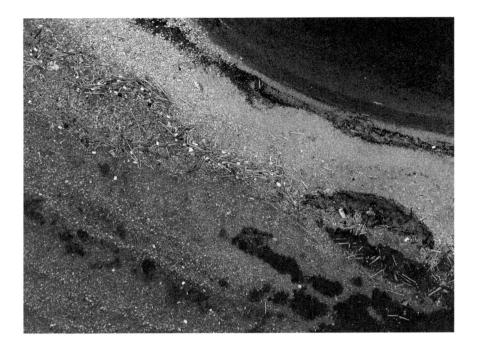

Walking this plane of temporal ridges folded against each other, rising and falling simultaneously, like waves in water, generates a different notion of time and event. Time becomes spatial and here becomes both distant and near, past and present, grounded and intangible, real and poetic – '*I dag er det prekambrium*' (Ulven 1981), today is Precambrian, and today is Anthropocene.

Tide

Time in Eidsbukta is tide, like *tid* in Norse is time. Time in Eidsbukta is neither linear nor cyclic, but rhythmic, spatial and enduring, folded through frequencies of currents and rapids, intensities and uproar, sometimes slow, sometimes fast, strong and vague, constructive and destructive.

The waves on the shore, like ripples in space-time, mount in a distance so infinite but break now and here. And then, to the roaring sound of rolling pebbles they pull back, to endure the becoming of new risings and breakings, again, and again. 'The very pulse of the sea, not only its perpetual motion,' Zerzan notes, 'has us imagining that it is drawing breath. Inspirations and exhalations of a living, if unimaginably vast animal' (Zerzan 2012, 2).

Time in Eidsbukta, tide in Eidsbukta, is tenacious and vast. It is now. Becoming rather than waning.

Its scale is not a lifetime, a generation, decades, centuries, millennia. Neither human, nor stretched, but magmatic, folded and pressed. Here.

Borderland

For many the coastline is home shore and the ocean an acquaintance that is respected and sometimes feared. The intensity of standing on the shore, breathing the overwhelming, 'absolute, (anti-)monumental There of it' (Zerzan 2012) makes you shrink and grow, bow and rise – as if

becoming one with the unceasing motions of this fluid infinity. The ocean is often spoken of as the last great wilderness, a 'last remaining lair of unparalleled wildness' (ibid.), to a human mind 'the best emblem of unwearied unconquerable power, the wild, various, fantastic, tameless unity of the sea' (Ruskin 1918, 35). The coastline, here, is a frontier and meeting place; an edge where imaginations are born and explorations launched.

It is almost too telling that along this imagined border, in the liminal zone between the known and unknown, the distant and proximate, we find things; accumulating in increasingly intimidating quantities – the unruly mongrel of *material culture*.

Acquainted with seaside landscapes you are familiar with the 'wrack zone'; the shelf mounting above the part of the shore that slopes down toward the water, where high tide and winter storms relentlessly deposit layer by layer of kelp, driftwood, things and debris. Childhood memories from days on the beach recall wondrous archaeological explorations in these exotic zones. Digging through salty, slimy and shrivelled piles to encounter strange things and creatures, washed ashore from faraway places: fishing nets, bottles and plastic containers, birds carcasses, glass balls, rubber boots and sandals, gutted fish, stranded seals, timber boards, and more.

Riches beyond compare.

Archaeological riches of unparalleled affluence. And yet, nostalgia set aside, these gathered deposits are unruly anomalies, contesting everything and all archaeology strives for. Thrown together in hybrid mixtures by forces beyond human control. Neither cultural nor natural, far removed from origin and function, in essence neither from here nor representing an anywhere.

Drift

Riches literally out of context.

The coastline, in Eidsbukta, is a frontier and meeting place. The intensity of standing on the shore, breathing the overwhelming, 'absolute, (anti-)monumental There of it' (Zerzan 2012) makes you wonder beyond cultural context, history and casualty, species and kinds, towards the potentials of a borderland archaeology.

Coincidence

Time – tide, in Eidsbukta is folded and pressed – here, gathered, thrown together and reordered. Exposed and inundated, brought in and acquired. 'Things arrive unannounced, then disappear again under the waves; buried history comes to the surface; traces of the past are exposed and erased' (Sprackland 2012, 236).

The riches of Eidsbukta fold space and time, distance and proximity, in a way archaeological chronology rarely tolerates. Things *don't just add up* (Stewart 2008), rationally, sequentially, stratigraphically. The assemblage remains infinitely unfinished, a gradual poesis of the before, the yet not, the possible, failed and lost. 'Something throws itself together and then floats past or *sticks*', as Stewart writes (ibid., 74). That is the coincidental challenge of Eidsbukta's collection.

It doesn't just add up. It doesn't *represent* anything evidently coherent, causal, meaningful – and is, above all, *presence*.

Therefore, attending to these riches, the rational of a borderland archaeology, is not one of suspicious scrutiny, aiming 'to get their representation "right"' (Stewart 2008, 73). Rather, it is to allow oneself to wonder what alternative ways of nearing and knowing may already radiate from this tumbled collective. A trust in sensation and presence beyond that of *re*presentation and reference. A sympathy for that which cannot be explained (Malpas 2012, 260).

Things are thrown together – they don't just add up. They drift. That is the condition of the real, our existential condition, and the condition of Anthropocene. 'Nothing is static. Nothing remains the same', Ryan states, which allows the spatial nature of the coastline to 'tangibly highlight the fluidity of the world – its ongoing and ever-emergent dynamic' (Ryan 2012, 9).

But fluid as it is, its ever-emergent potential and becoming is empowered through persistency. Not a static, inflexible persistency but a stubborn, boisterous volatility of matter – drifting, gathering, dispersing.

Drift

Until recently, drift matter was a natural resource and the drift beach valued and prized. In Old Norse mythology, drift was the matter of creation, and the drift beach the cradle of mankind. The first of men, Askur and Embla, were carved from driftwood found on the beach.

Approaching Icelandic shores towards the close of the ninth century, prospecting settlers, descendants of Askur and Embla, threw overboard their high-seat pillars, followed their drift and established their settlements where they washed ashore. Making their posts part of *drift matter* – the matter of creation – possibly rendered them rightful settlers, natives of the environment.

Drift matter is world making.

Think of dark matter, that utterly unseen and unknown density of everything that makes up the most. That unidentified, uncanny mass of dark energy that permeates space. Then think of drift matter. That unknown, drifting mass, that persists and worlds. Fluid as it is, its ever-emergent potential and becoming is empowered through its persistency. Not a static, inflexible persistency but a stubborn, boisterous volatility of matter – drifting, gathering, dispersing. A dark ecology (Morton 2016) – a dark energy, beyond human control, definition and knowledge.

The Anthropocene – the 'Age of Man' – is in essence an age of drift matter. Regardless of its anthropocentric labelling, the Anthropocene, above all, bears witness to the longevity and volatility of matter, things, big and small. A reminder not only of an exclusively human footprint, but also of an unruly heritage of material and more-than-human relations.

The problem is not that things become buried deep in strata but that they endure, outlive us, and come back at us with a force we didn't realize they had. A dark force of 'sleeping giants' (Harman 2016) that worlds in a way we did not and could not foresee.

Afterlife

We like to speak of the *after*life of things. How they carry on after we have produced them, used them, let them go, worn them out, disposed of them, lost them, forgotten them. We might see Eidsbukta as the terrain of such subsistence – meaningless, functionless, pointless.

But then, take a brief moment to think of all those places you have visited on your journeys. Some only briefly. Some only in passing, while rushing through an airport or gazing through the window of a running train. Then think of all the places you haven't visited. All those valleys, moors, islands and skerries that will never see your arrival.

Think of all those species you know, all those familiar and friendly, exotic and strange. Then think of all those creatures never seen, never known, because their being and scale doesn't comply with the complexity of your senses.

Think of gravitational waves washing past earth, incidentally detected in the blink of an eye, and through that minute collision forever changing our view upon the heavens. Then consider that they were formed through the merger of stellar ghosts, two gigantic black holes, 1.3 billion light years away.

We like to speak of the *after*life of things.

But take a brief moment to consider that speaking of the afterlife of things makes us central in their becoming and evolving. We become the authors, the axis of their lives. But the truth

often is that we only incidentally cross paths with them. We happen to them rather than the other way around.

Think of all those places you've only seen in passing.

Environment

Consider the *nature* of Eidsbukta, how she allows things, creatures of different kinds to gather on this verge of human realm. Imagine the journeys of these things, their stretched post-human lives. And picture the way they interact, how they drift and come together. You see that no

Drift

conventional archaeology or culture history is able to talk about these things? You see how our naming, definition, classification would be a violation of their being?

They do not belong to that context.

You see, that to talk about drift, which is an object agency, has nothing to do with intention? You see, that it has everything to do with potential, coincidence, contingency, sleeping giants and dark forces? You see the significance in acknowledging this agency?

This is the environment of Anthropocene – the climate of Anthropocene.

A paradox of this 'Age of Man', as argued by Liborion, is that it 'both centralizes and decentralizes humans' (Liborion 2016, 103). Not in the sense of questioning the gravity of the situation, or humans as actors, but by foregrounding how, in a world that is mixed and polluted, tropes of anthropocentric measures, human time and human pasts, are unable to fully articulate the intricacy of these relations.

Things don't just add up. Thrown together the *nature* of Eidsbukta may or may not involve human agency, but cannot be tackled without considering things' own endurance, their dark sides, and consequential affairs; affairs between plastic bags, sewages, fishing nets, currents, driftwood and drift ice, seagulls, temperatures, UV rays, winter storms, postglacial rebound and the moon's gravity.

Therefore, what a borderland archaeology – an environmental archaeology – calls the 'environment', must not be a web of harmonious, symmetrical relations between a multitude of species, between nature and culture, humanity and environ, but rather full of asymmetry, full of darkness, and full of regions devoid of human presence. Regions and affairs unmoved by our naming, knowledge and ignorance.

Acknowledgements

I would like to express my thanks to Bjørnar Olsen and Tim Flohr Sørensen for reading and discussing the passages of this chapter, to Ingar Figenschau for help with drone imagery, and to Stein Farstadvoll for his capturing of the whale carcass.

References

Buell, L. 2013. Foreword. *In*: J.J. Cohen, (eds.) *Prismatic Ecology: Ecotheory Beyond Green*, ix–xii. Minneapolis: University of Minnesota Press.

Carson, R. 2015. *The Edge of the Sea*. London: Unicorn Press Ltd.

Cohen, J.J. 2013. Grey. *In*: J.J. Cohen, (eds.) *Prismatic Ecology: Ecotheory Beyond Green*, 270–289. Minneapolis: University of Minnesota Press.

Harman, G. 2016. *Immaterialism*. Cambridge: Polity Press.

Liborion, M. 2016. Redefining pollution and action: The matter of plastics. *Journal of Material Culture*, 21(1), 87–110.

Malpas, J. 2012. *Heidegger and the Thinking of Place: Explorations in the Topology of Being*. Cambridge, MA: MIT Press.

Morton, T. 2016. *Dark Ecology: For a Logic of Future Coexistence*. New York: Columbia University Press.

Ruskin, J. 1918. *Selections and Essays*. Edited by F.W. Roe. New York: Charles Scribner's Sons.

Ryan, A. 2012. *Where Land Meets Sea: Coastal Explorations of Landscape, Representation and Spatial Experience*. Farnham: Ashgate.

Sprackland, J. 2012. *Strands: A Year of Discoveries on the Beach*. London: Vintage Books.

Stewart, K. 2008. Weak theory in an unfinished world. *Journal of Folklore Research*, 45(1), 71–82.

Ulven, T. 1981. *Forsvinningspunkt: Dikt*. Oslo: Gyldendal.

Zerzan, J. 2012. The Sea. *Anagnori* [online]. Available from: https://anagnori.wordpress.com/2012/09/08/featured-essay-the-sea-by-john-zerzan/ (accessed on 24 May 2014).

PART II

Multispecies ecology of the built environment

6
SYMBIOTIC ARCHITECTURES

Gavin Lucas

Introduction

It is hard to imagine an environment that humans inhabit that is not also host to other species. Of course, there is the contemporary discourse of hygiene in the home which is all about purification, a discourse which goes back to the nineteenth century (e.g. Shove 2003; Frykman & Löfgren 1987) and can no doubt be linked to the deep philosophical separation of nature and culture (Latour 1993). But even this discourse is somewhat riddled with arbitrary exceptions where some species (e.g. dogs, cats) are permitted into the enclave of culture or 'the human' while others (e.g. bacteria, mice) are not. But even more damaging to this imagined divide is the difference between public discourse and practice; I know (and have lived in!) many homes where people clearly put up with visible and co-habiting spiders, slugs, or other small fauna. Indeed, despite the practice of various hygiene regimes in the contemporary home, we all share an environment with a host of other species, albeit most of them invisible (Frantz 1988; Kembel et al. 2012).

Now this is saying nothing new. The problem emerges when the same discourse which drives us when cleaning our house to keep the human environment *human* (i.e. free of other species), also drives us to understand and explain human society and human history in the same way – in the absence of other species. This is not about ignoring their presence so much as their agency (Haraway 2003, 2007). It is difficult to imagine any study of human society which does not acknowledge the presence of cows, sheep, pigs, wheat, nuts, trees and so on. The danger rather lies in talking about them solely as either *resources* or *symbols*, as passive, inert objects subject to human exploitation or meaning. It is as if all human interaction with other species is solely explicable by recourse to human agency and intentionality, where *their* agency and being is suppressed. In one sense, the invocation of a multispecies archaeology is similar to the actor network theory perspective on actants. It is about giving other species agency in our stories.

I think this characterization is a useful one, but needs to be put in some perspective. When I was a student (in the early 1980s), environmental science was big in archaeology and one of the major issues was how to avoid environmental determinism. Thus explanations for the advent of farming or domestication might have used climate change as a prime agent of change. Humans were put in the role of being merely reactive or responsive. I do not think many archaeologists were very satisfied with that position, and you might even say the post-processual movement was partly about making humans more active in the face of environmental determinism, even to the extent in some cases of ignoring the agency of the environment altogether, assigning it a passive role. But some of the more processual-leaning archaeologists would not go that far; rather, they used the 'social' turn in archaeology to argue that human reaction to climate change also had its own agency; people can respond in different ways to climate change because of their 'culture' as well as adapting their culture to environmental change. This became the key way to combat charges of environmental determinism (e.g. Crumley 1994).

So what distinguishes the current approach to human-environmental relations, of which multispecies archaeology might be considered an aspect? Arguably, even when both human and natural agencies are acknowledged as in the above mentioned studies, there remains a sense in which they are also still separate; climate still changes – but on its own; humans still respond – but on their own. One of the key shifts, for example in the Anthropocene debate, is that this separation is no longer viable. Humans can *cause* climate change as much as be affected by it (Solli 2011; Edgeworth et al. 2014). The point is that agencies are always intertwined. The challenge is that whenever you invoke human agency you need to look a little closer and see what other non-human agents may be involved – and vice versa. For the rest of this chapter, I want to take a look at the archaeology of buildings in Iceland through the lens of a multispecies approach, that is, to explore the role of other non-human species as agents. To what extent can we unravel the talk about architecture as a purely human phenomenon and bring in the agency of other species? In sketching an answer, I will start with what I call a weak version of multispeciesism and then move on to a strong version.

Turf buildings and synanthropic species

Vernacular architecture in Iceland, even into the early twentieth century, was epitomized by the turf house (e.g. Ágústsson 2000; Mímisson 2016; Stefánsson 2013). The few stone houses that existed from the late eighteenth century were largely confined to the elite and the few timber houses tended to be built by foreign merchants – at least until the nineteenth century. Even in the capital city, Reykjavík, as late as 1910, over half the houses were still built from turf (Jónsson & Magnússon 1997, table 7.3). The turf house is basically characterized by turf (or stone and turf) walls with a turf roof, supported on a timber frame. Floors vary, even in the same house, but can be stone flags, wooden boards, or simply trampled ash and/or turf.

The turf, which constitutes a key part of the skin of the building, is alive. Grass grows on it, its roots taking nutrients from the soil which itself is aswarm with micro-organisms. Indeed, the organic content in turf has been shown to survive long after the building itself has been abandoned and even buried (Steinberg 2004). Moreover, turf houses are typically associated with a range of insects and fungi that are usually defined as synanthropes in the literature (see Forbes et al. 2014 for the most recent and detailed summary of the state of archaeoentomology in connection to turf architecture). Synanthropes are wild species that live in association with or in human-made habitats, and in fact there is even a specialized field which considers synanthropic habitats from an architectural perspective (e.g. Dodington 2013; also see http:// www.animalarchitecture.org). Beehives and birdhouses are classic examples of synanthropic architectures. Of course, even smaller organisms such as bacteria were present in turf houses, but archaeological research into the microbiome is only in its infancy (e.g. see Warinner et al. 2015). In short, turf buildings were host to a number of organisms, including people, insects, moulds and bacteria. They comprise an obvious example of multispecies habitat (as surely any house does), but also of course, a fairly unique one in terms of the particular composition of species.

Symbiotic architectures

Thus describing research on a contemporary turf farm now preserved as a museum, Dutch scholars found a number of species present:

> The inner walls are covered in a layer of fine brown dust, and show white traces caused by migration of salts leaching out of the turf. The high-salt contents influenced the flora and fauna indoors. However, the turf blocks contained nutrient media to allow for fungal growth. Edible mushrooms (genus *Armillaria*) were found on the turf walls during the building inspection. Dust samples from both walls, floors and furniture, contained few invertebrates. Parts of *Acaroidia, Laelaptidae* and *Araneae*, as well as four specimens of *Cryptostygmata*, were found in approximately 0.5 g of dust.
>
> *van Hoof & van Dijken 2008: 1028*

Archaeoentomological research on turf buildings in Iceland (and the North Atlantic) has been conducted for several decades now and has explored issues such as the impact of human colonization on habitats, both in terms of the introduction of new species (i.e. co-colonizers; see here the work of Crosby (1986) in general on ecological imperialism) and the effects on the biogeography of indigenous species (Forbes et al. 2014). Detailed research on the insect record from turf farms in Iceland has revealed a signature of typical insect species most commonly found co-habiting with people, including *Cryptophagus* spp., *Atomaria* spp., *Latridius minutus* (grp.), *Corticaria elongata* (Gyll.), and *Xylodromus concinnus* (ibid.: 9). Because a range of materials was also brought into houses as fuel, food, or bedding, a whole host of insect species can

Figure 6.1 Skálholt under excavation in 2004. Photograph: G. Lucas.

Gavin Lucas

also act as signatures of these materials – seaweed, eiderdown, cereals, etc., and their presence has even been used to infer specific activities and room functions (ibid.).

One of my projects in Iceland has involved the excavation of a large elite settlement in southwest Iceland, an episcopal seat dating from the eleventh century, although our excavations focused on the late seventeenth century and onwards (Figure 6.1). Analysis of the material and work towards a major publication is still in progress. Here, I want to focus on the microfauna from just one building – Building 1680 – at the settlement and will draw heavily on the primary research of the project archaeoentomologist, Hrönn Konráðsdóttir (2007). Analysis of insect remains from three samples taken from the floors of a storage/processing room (1680) and dating from the late seventeenth to late eighteenth century produced a large and diverse set of species (Table 6.1). About 20 to 30 per cent of these species are not typically synanthropic and appear to have come into the building mostly with peat blocks, cut and stacked to use as fuel. The building had three working ovens and, based on fuel residues, peat was the most common fuel used. These insect species generally favoured wet or damp environments and although some may have survived in the micro-habitats of peat stacks, many must have also died.

Table 6.1 List of insect species found in Building 1680 at Skálholt

Species name	Count
Acidota crenata (F.)	1
Agabus bipustulatus (L.)	1
Amara quenseli (Schön.)	6
Aphodius lapponum Gyll.	1
Aphodius sp.	1
Atheta (s.l.) spp.	10
Atomaria apicalis Er.	3
Atomaria sp.	5
Barynotus squamosus Germ.	2
Bembidion bipunctatum (L.)	1
Calathus melanocephalus (L.)	2
Catops fuliginosus Er.	5
Ceutorhynchus contractus (Marsham)	3
Colymbetes dolabratus (Payk.)	1
Corticaria elongata (Gyll.)	8
Cryptophagus sp.	9
Cytilus sericeus (Forst.)	1
Damalinia ovis (L.)	17
Epauloecus unicolor (Pill. & Mitt.)	10
Gabrius trossulus (Nord.)	1
Hydroporus sp.	1
Hypnoidus riparius (F.)	4
Latridius pseudominutus (Strand)	19
Latridius sp.	47
Melophagus ovinus (L.)	25
Melophagus ovinus (L.) puparia	28
Nebria rufescens (Ström.)	2
Notaris acridulus (L.)	1
Omalium excavatum Steph.	6
Omalium rivulare (Payk.)	3

Symbiotic architectures

Otiorhynchus arcticus (O. Fabricius)	3
Otiorhynchus nodosus (Müll.)	4
Otiorhynchus rugifrons (Gyll.)	1
Oxypoda sp.	16
Pediculus humanus L.	45
Philonthus sp.	4
Pterostichus nigrita (Payk.)	3
Pterostichus sp.	1
Quedius fulvicollis (Steph.)	5
Quedius mesomelinus (Marsham)	3
Quedius sp.	4
Rhinoncus pericarpius (L.)	1
Stenus carbonarius Gyll.	2
Stenus sp.	1
Tachinus corticinus Grav.	8
Tropiphorus obtusus (Bonsd.)	4
Typhaea stercorea (L.)	10
Xylodromus concinnus (Marsham)	21
Xylodromus sp.	1
Total count	361

Source: Hrönn Konráðsdóttir.

The remaining 70 to 80 per cent of the insect fauna were synanthropes and would have happily lived inside the building. Over a third of these were in fact ectoparasites, specifically lice – both human and two species of sheep lice. It is suggested their presence is indicative of the building being used for washing both clothing and wool/fleeces as part of wool processing, as the lice cannot live long without their host. Documentary sources consistently call the room a meat store for this period, although one mid-eighteenth-century map labels it as a tapestry store. The building probably was used for a variety of domestic processing and storage activities. Besides the lice, the other synanthropic species included flies, but also predominantly beetles associated with rotting vegetation and dung. The dung would probably have been fuel, but the rotting vegetation could be derived from wood, hay and food. One species in particular, the Icelandic *Epauloecus unicolor* (formerly known as *Tipnus unicolor*) (Figure 6.2), is associated with dry mouldy environments and fairly cool temperatures (17.5–20°C; Howe 1955; also see www.ni.is/poddur/hus/poddur/nr/13995). The adult insects feed on flour, bread, cereals, dead insects and dung from small rodents and humans (O'Farrell & Butler 1948, 361), while its larvae are often found in rodent excrement or in damp and decaying vegetation, including wood (Howe 1955; Larsson & Gígja 1959, 165–167).

The main point of such studies is largely to use microfauna such as insects as proxies or indicators for other things. The studies are usually quite explicit about this. Insects as evidence for the presence of grain, or the presence of human occupation. This is an important and useful approach, but it is also quite different from a multispecies angle. Although we can still use such studies to highlight the diverse organic composition of a building's inhabitants, to conduct a proper ecological or multispecies analysis of the building would require a shift in the way we look at these fauna. It also requires a lot *more* data – more samples on a high-resolution collection grid and information on other species, such as fungal spores or bacteria. A modern study, for example, has suggested that the bacterial composition of contemporary buildings is

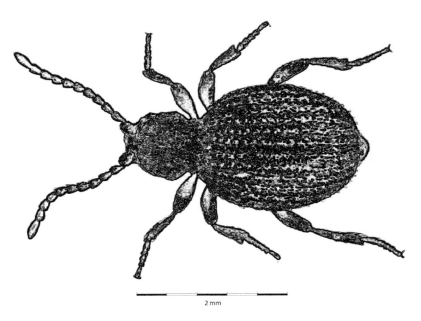

Figure 6.2   Epauloecus unicolor. Drawing: G. Lucas.

very dependent on the source of ventilation (Kembel et al. 2012). The goal would be to try to understand the specific building ecology of a turf house in terms of how other species can act as agents in understanding the way a building works. For Hrönn, who studied these insect remains, the *c.* 1:4 ratio of non-synanthropic to synanthropic species suggested that human presence in this room may have been much lower than in other rooms. For example, in an adjacent food store, the ratio was 1:5. What might this suggest about their different ecologies and their affect on the functioning of the buildings?

Turf building ecologies

Here I will take a very simple approach to the ecology of Building 1680 by considering the interconnection between different species. Looking at Figure 6.3, it is clear that humans operate as a keystone species. Keystone species are those that play a major role within an ecosystem, affecting species diversity and thus shaping the structure of the community (Paine 1995). Humans act either as direct carriers or conduits for other species such as human lice, or indirectly by introducing materials (such as wool or peat) that conduct other species such as sheep lice or *Agabus* sp. and *Hydroporus* sp. The exceptions are those synanthropic species like *Epauloecus unicolor* or fungi which could have equally entered the room carried by wind or flight, independent of human agency. The important question, though, is what do these different species *do* in terms of the building itself?

The non-synanthropes and ectoparasites – those which are largely dependent on human carriers, whether directly or indirectly – arguably do very little. Many of them no doubt perish rather quickly once they enter the room, especially once removed from their micro-habitat (e.g. peat, wool, hair). The important species are rather the more autonomous ones – humans

Symbiotic architectures

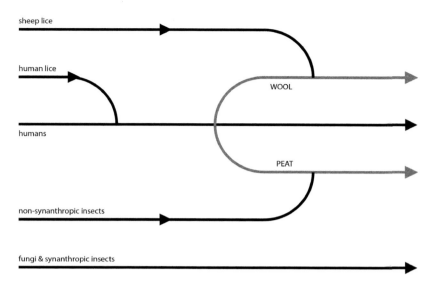

Figure 6.3 Species inter-relation diagram. Drawing: G. Lucas.

certainly, but also fungi and synanthropes like *Epauloecus unicolor*. To understand their agency, we need to effectively go beyond a multispecies approach and consider the building itself as an organism. To briefly explore this, I will summarize an argument I have put forward in another publication about architecture, one which draws on the concepts of metabolism and circulation (Lucas 2016; also see Lucas 2015). The basic idea is to view a building like an machine/organism, as a dynamic entity rather than an inert pile of turf, stone and wood. Its dynamism derives from the myriad processes occurring within and inside its body – organic, chemical, mechanical. Here, I want to think about the building in terms of two aspects: circulatory systems and organs. I will continue with my example of the storage/processing room from the settlement of Skálholt in Iceland to illustrate this approach.

Circulatory systems are about the regular movement of entities through a building; in the case of my example, I will look at six different things: water, air, insects, fungi, humans and peat. No doubt other organisms were present (e.g. mice), so this is merely a simplified example. There is a deliberate mix of the animate and inanimate here, but the animate is clearly multispecies in composition. In tracking the flow of these things, attention will also be directed to the architecture of the building and key elements that act as conduits and sometimes metabolic converters for these flows: the building's organs. These include a drain, three ovens, and openings (i.e. doors, chimney). I want to begin by summarizing separately the circulation of the seven things and their relation to the aforementioned organs, before overlaying them and considering their mutual entanglement.

- *Water*: the site has very clayey soils and ground water was clearly a major problem; it was when we were excavating, and it clearly was for its inhabitants in the past, as a complex network of sub-floor drains ran throughout most of the settlement. The drain in the building under consideration was rather short, ran just over half the length of the room and exited the western door out into the open and probably drained off downslope. Much of the ground water rising up would have been channelled through this drain. Some, however, would have been soaked up by the ash-rich floors; the use of ashes on floors was common practice historically in Iceland to absorb ground water or dampness, acting as a de-humidifier (Milek 2012). Finally, the heat generated by the ovens would have also helped dry any moisture derivative of ground water. Water circulation thus is directed by three different organs – the drain, the ovens and the floor.

- *Air*: the air circulating in the room was obviously flowing both in and out through openings, especially doors (it is unclear if the windows would have been openable) and was important not only as a carrier of organisms such as fungal spores and flying insects but also as an element of metabolism for many of the organisms (i.e. respiration). Moreover, the heat generated by the ovens would have also affected its convection as well as its humidity, the oven thus being a critical organ connecting the water and air systems.
- *Insects*: microfauna such as flies or beetles could have made their own way in (and out) of the building through openings, but a larger number were probably introduced via carriers such as people or peat. Once inside, a large proportion probably never left. However, they would have congregated in very specific locales – the ectoparasites and non-synanthropes probably confined to fleeces/wool, clothing, or peat stacks, while many of the synanthropes confined to wooden timbers or roofing material in the building, besides any foodstuff stored there.
- *Fungus/mould*: fungal spores, like insects, could have drifted in through openings on the wind, or come via carriers, including insects. Once settled on suitable plant matter – such as the timber posts or stored food – it could divide and grow into hyphae which fuse and then grow into moulds and mushrooms which decompose organic matter.
- *Humans*: people clearly used this building to do things, such as wash wool/clothing and prepare food; they may have spent many hours here but their ingress and egress would have been much more rapid and constant than most other organisms.
- *Peat*: peat came in via human carriers, but also acted as carriers of other organisms such as insects and fungi. Once inside, its main relation was with the ovens where it was ignited and combusted to create heat and smoke and, as a residue, ashes.

Just breaking down the inferred pathways of these six elements separately, one already discerns the connections between them. Let me now try and overlay them to build up a basic anatomical map of the building (Figure 6.4). In terms of day-to-day activities, two major systems are identifiable: the oven is the focal organ for human circulation while structural timbers (and stored food) are that for fungi and synanthropic insects. The floor is the common ground so to speak, insofar as it acts as the conduit for the metabolic output of both of these different activities while the doors into and out of the room facilitate circulation. However, it is important to recognize that these two systems (human-oven and insect/fungi-timber) are also entangled. The very structural integrity of the building is of course dependent on its posts, and the performance of these posts in turn is dependent on the temperature and especially humidity in the room which control the abundance of fungi and moulds and some insects which cause rot (e.g. Viitanen 1994; Viitanen & Burman 1995). The presence of three ovens in use at the same time would have made this room potentially much warmer and drier than any other in the settlement. Although direct analysis of moisture content and its impact on timbers is impossible in an archaeological context like this, evidence of a dry mould-loving insect like *Epauloecus unicolor* might well support this interpretation.

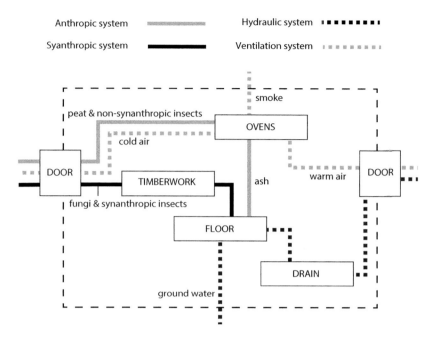

Figure 6.4 Room ecology/anatomy. Drawing: G. Lucas.

Although greatly simplified, both due to limited data and for ease of explanation, the outline sketched above reveals the complex ecology of Building 1680 and the importance of expanding a multispecies approach to consider the role of non-organic elements. In ending, let me take this one step further. Instead of seeing the building as a multispecies habitat or environment, what happens if we see the building as a multispecies organism itself – as a product of symbiosis?

Turf buildings and symbiosis: traversing the animate/inanimate border

Symbiosis is a concept from biology and refers to a variety of different ways that two species interact over long-term periods (Martin & Schwab 2013), which include both harmful, beneficial and neutral effects to one of the parties involved. Such relations can also be necessary to survival (obligate) or supplemental, and organisms can be physically attached or even inside another. More recently, the concept of the holobiont has been framed to capture the multispecies nature of many organisms (Ackerman 2012). The concept of holobiont was originally coined by Lynn Margulis and is useful in relation to time because she deployed it as a way to re-think evolution. Specifically, Margulis claimed that speciation largely occurs through symbiosis at the cellular level where genetic variation is produced not from random mutation but via bacteria and viruses (Margulis & Sagan 2003). Although Margulis's ideas on evolution are not widely shared (but see Shapiro 2011; also Clarke 2015), the idea of new entities emerging through symbiosis is a very provocative one, which I find useful in thinking about multispecies archaeology and architecture (also see Harman 2016). There are two aspects to consider if this notion is to be taken at all seriously. One concerns the idea of symbiosis as a type of assemblage – a fusion of previously separate objects; the other concerns the idea of life and the building as a *living* assemblage – an organism. Let me start with the first since it is perhaps the least contentious.

In what way do buildings constitute an assemblage? At a rather banal level, they of course are amalgamations of different materials. In the case of my building in Iceland, we have rocks, turf and timber as principal elements, alongside burnt wood, twigs and bark mashed together as floor. Each of these elements was once a separate entity: the rocks mostly collected from naturally weathered/fractured outcrops of solid geology, the turf cut from the ground into strips, the timber hewn mostly from driftwood. One could trace all these elements back even further if so desired, but the further back one goes, the less they look like the same object used in buildings. Indeed in the case of the turf and timber, they were largely modified or created from parent material in the process of building the room. Of course, none of these operations nor the assembling itself of a turf house would have been possible without people; people are certainly central agents in the process of assembling, but even here people did not act alone but in concert with other objects such as ropes, adzes, chisels, etc. But once the room was erected, the properties of the elements in the building itself acted to keep the room up and going: to counter any tensile and compressive forces, to retain warmth, keep out wind and rain, to channel movement, and so on. Once assembled, the room itself is auto-sustaining to a large degree.

The event I want to emphasize here then is not so much the process of assembling as the holding-together of the assemblage, once assembled. It is this holding-together or cohesion of elements which makes it possible to link the idea of an assemblage (which I have discussed in different ways in other texts; see Lucas 2012) to a multispecies archaeology and to symbiosis as a long-term relation. It is this cohesion which also makes it possible to talk about the building as a new entity; it is not merely a sum of its parts since most of these parts are simultaneously transformed once they enter into the specific relations with each other that constitute this building.

Turf, like skin, has been excised and grafted onto a new substrate; driftwood has been hewn and laid on end, its cellular structure combating new, compressive forces; rocks have been laid together, their irregular faces gripping those of adjacent rocks. It is not just the shape or form of these things that might have changed, but that some of their properties or affordances which previously lay dormant or unrealized, are now activated. Symbiosis makes old things act in new ways and in the process, sometimes engender a new entity. Particularly in the case of a multispecies approach, it is relevant to consider that the organic component of a building stays alive. The grass in the turf (especially on the roof) continues to grow, even if it needs periodically cutting or feeding. Its root structure helps to bind the turves together, to maintain its strength and coherence. Like some science fiction cyborg with human tissue grafted onto a metal skeleton, our turf building thus has a living skin grafted onto a skeleton of dead wood and stone. And it is not just the outside that is alive. Inside, in the gut of the building, live a variety of organisms from fungi to insects, as well as the occasional human of course – all of which establish an internal ecology, as we saw in the previous section. Like the bacteria in our stomach, is it not possible to see this as a type of endosymbiosis (where one organism lives inside another) than synanthropism? Where and why are we drawing the line?

To expand this idea, let me shift my focus from turf to concrete, fittingly so, given my study area of Iceland where concrete almost universally replaced turf as the main building material over the first half of the twentieth century. Experimental studies have recently explored the use of introducing calcite-precipitating bacteria (*Bacillus sphaericus*) in microcapsules in cement to create 'self-healing concrete'. When cracks or fissures appear in concrete, they expose the steel reinforcing to corrosion. These bacteria have the capacity to exude calcites when activated

Symbiotic architectures

and exposed to water, which then closes up the crack (Jonkers et al. 2010; van Tittelboom et al. 2010). In this example, the division between the organic and inorganic is blurred, as it is increasingly so in many instances in modern technology, such as with recent developments in bioprinting where scientists have recently successfully managed to manufacture a human vein using a 3D bio-printer (e.g. Jakab et al. 2010; Mironov et al. 2006, 2007).

Within biology, the idea of animacy – of life – has been extended to animal-built architectures such as termite nests, which have been dubbed part of the extended phenotype of the termite (Turner 2000, 2004). It is certainly no great leap to do the same for human-built architectures, a point in fact made by Marshal McLuhan some time ago in a different context (McLuhan 1964). The real question perhaps is not whether the building is alive or not, but whether it can be viewed as an organism in its own right – not just an extended organ of humans or an obligate symbiote. What this ultimately seems to come down to is auto-replicability. And buildings do not breed. If this is how we ultimately choose to define life, then clearly buildings are not alive; but it seems to me, this is a case of a general concept clouding a more particular one. The fact is, the building is a persistent entity which is self-sustaining in relation to its environment. It exists and persists through its relation with other entities, especially humans. In fact, biologists have no easy definition of life – unsurprisingly. It is often defined in terms of a number of physiological functions including metabolism, growth, adaptation, response and reproduction. Buildings can be said to include most of these functions except reproduction; on the other hand, other entities like viruses cannot metabolize even though they performs most of the other functions, and thus some prefer not to call them living things. What this ambiguity suggests, I would argue, is that life is not really a useful concept at all, since it divides reality into two blocks and while it seems to make sense to us at a very general level, once you look more closely, it is much more problematic.

In this chapter, I have been moving towards the idea that we see architecture as animate. Many contemporary scholars have embraced the idea of animacy in relation to things (e.g. Bennett 2010) and philosophers like Bergson have made it central to their ontology (Bergson 1911). At the same time, vitalism as an ontology is generally eschewed by scientists, even while they struggle with their own definitions of life. My purpose in adopting an approach which sees buildings as organisms is not to espouse vitalism but rather to challenge the distinction between living and non-living things, between the organic and inorganic. Simply put, there are too many affinities and similarities in terms of how we understand animate and inanimate complex systems, that the concept of life hinders more than it helps. Indeed, I wonder if the concept of life is rather a *political* concept first and foremost and derives from an opposition between animal life and social or political life – what the Greeks called *zoe* and *bios* respectively (Agamben 1998). We are back to that old dichotomy of nature and culture. It may seem as if the distinction between the organic and inorganic precedes that between biological life and social/political life, but the mediating concept here is really death, not life. What is capable of death? It is perhaps within necropolitics (rather than biopolitics) that the question of animacy or vitalism needs to be resolved (Mbembe 2003), not biology.

Acknowledgements

This chapter is deeply indebted to the primary research of Hrönn Konráðsdóttir on the insect assemblage from Building 1680; I would also like to thank her for sharing her data and commenting on a draft of this chapter, as well as the insightful comments of Chris Witmore and Suzie Pilaar Birch.

References

Ackerman, J. 2012. The Ultimate Social Network. *Scientific American* 306: 36–43.

Agamben, G. 1998. *Homo Sacer: Sovereign Power and Bare Life*. Stanford, CA: Stanford University Press.

Ágústsson, H. 2000. *Íslensk byggingararfleið I*. Reykjavík: Húsafriðunarnefnd ríkisins.

Bennett, J. 2010. *Vibrant Matter: A Political Ecology of Things*. Durham, NC: Duke University Press.

Bergson, H. 1911. *Creative Evolution*. London: MacMillan & Co.

Clarke, B. (ed.) 2015. *Earth, Life, and System: Evolution and Ecology on a Gaian Planet*. New York: Fordham University Press

Crosby, A.W. 1986. *Ecological Imperialism*. Cambridge: Cambridge University Press.

Crumley, C. (ed.) 1994. *Historical Ecology: Cultural Knowledge and Changing Landscapes*. Seattle: University of Washington Press.

Dodington, E.M. 2013. *How to Design with the Animal: Lessons in Cross-Species Architecture and Design*. Independent publisher: Houston, TX.

Edgeworth, M. et al. 2014. Archaeology of the Anthropocene. *Journal of Contemporary Archaeology* 1(1): 73–132.

Forbes, V., Dussault, F., & Bain, A. 2014. Archaeoentomological Research in the North Atlantic: Past, Present, and Future. *Journal of the North Atlantic* 26: 1–24.

Frantz, S.C. 1988. Architecture and Commensal Vertebrate Pest Management. In *Architectural Design and Indoor Microbial Pollution*, ed. R. Kundsin. Oxford: Oxford University Press, pp. 228–295.

Frykman, J. & Löfgren, O. 1987. *Culture Builders. A Historical Anthropology of Middle-Class Life*. New Brunswick, NJ and London: Rutgers University Press.

Haraway, D. 2003. *Companion Species Manifesto: Dogs, People and Significant Otherness*. Chicago, IL: Prickly Paradigm Press.

Haraway, D. 2007. *When Species Meet*. Minneapolis: University of Minnesota Press.

Harman, G. 2016: *Immaterialism: Objects and Social Theory*. Cambridge: Polity Press.

Howe, R.W. 1955. Studies on Beetles of the Family Ptinidae 12. The Biology of Tipnus Unicolor (Pill. & Mitt.). *Entomologist's Monthly Magazine* 91: 253–257.

Jakab, K., Norotte, C., Marga, F., Murphy, K., Vunjak-Novakovic, G., & Forgacs, G. 2010. Tissue Engineering by Self-Assembly and Bio-Printing of Living Cells. *Biofabrication* 2: 1–14

Jonkers, H.M., Thijssen, A., Muyzer, G., Copuroglu, O., & Schlangen, E. 2010. Application of Bacteria as Self-Healing Agent for the Development of Sustainable Concrete. *Ecological Engineering* 36: 230–235.

Jónsson, G., & Magnússon, M.S. (eds.) 1997. *Hagskinna. Sögulegar hagtölur um Ísland/Icelandic Historical Statistics*. Hagstofa Íslands, Reykjavík.

Kembel, S., Jones, E., Kline, J., Northcutt, D., Stenson, J., Womack, A., Bohannan, B., Brown, G., & J. Green. 2012. Architectural Design Influences the Diversity and Structure of the Built Environment Microbiome. *The ISME Journal* 6: 1469–1479.

Konráðsdóttir, H. 2007. An Archaeoentomological Contribution to the Skálholt Project, Iceland. Unpublished MSc dissertation, University of Edinburgh.

Larsson, S.G., & Gígja, G. 1959. Coleoptera 1. Synopsis. In Á. Friðriksson & S.L.Tuxen (eds), *The Zoology of Iceland*, pp. 1–218. Copenhagen: Ejnar Munksgaard.

Latour, B. 1993. *We Have Never Been Modern*. Cambridge, MA: Harvard University Press.

Lucas, G. 2012. *Understanding the Archaeological Record*. Cambridge: Cambridge University Press.

Lucas, G. 2015. Afterword: Archaeology and the Science of New Objects. In *Archaeology After Interpretation: Returning Materials to Archaeological Theory*, eds. B. Alberti, A. Jones, & J. Pollard. Left Coast Press: Walnut Creek, pp. 369–380.

Lucas, G. 2016. Building Lives. In *Elements of Architecture*, eds. B. Alberti, A. Jones, & J. Pollard. London: Routledge.

Margulis, L. & Sagan, D. 2003. *Acquiring Genomes: A Theory of the Origins of Species*. New York: Basic Books.

Martin, B.D. & Schwab, E. 2013. Current Usage of Symbiosis and Associated Terminology. *International Journal of Biology* 5(1): 32–45.

Mbembe, A. 2003. Necropolitics. *Public Culture* 15(1): 11–40.

McLuhan, M. 1964. *Understanding Media: The Extensions of Man*. London: Routledge.

Milek, K. 2012. Floor Formation Processes and the Interpretation of Site Activity Areas: An Ethnoarchaeological Study of Turf Buildings at Thverá, Northeast Iceland. *Journal of Anthropological Archaeology* 31: 119–137.

Symbiotic architectures

Mímisson, K. 2016. Building Identities: The Architecture of the Persona. *International Journal of Historical Archaeology* 20: 207–227

Mironov, V., Prestwich, G., & Forgacs, G. 2007. Bioprinting Living Structures. *Journal of Material Chemistry* 17: 2054–2060.

Mironov, V., Reis, N. & Derby, B. 2006. Review: Bioprinting: A Beginning. *Tissue Engineering* 12(4): 631–634.

O'Farrell, A.F., & Butler, P.M. (1948) Insects and Mites Associated with the Storage and Manufacture of Foodstuffs in Northern Ireland. *Economic Proceedings of the Royal Dublin Society* 3: 343–407.

Paine, R.T. (1995). A Conversation on Refining the Concept of Keystone Species. *Conservation Biology* 9(4): 962–964.

Shapiro, J.A. 2011. *Evolution: A View from the 21st Century*. Upper Saddle River, NJ: FT Press.

Shove, E. 2003. *Comfort, Cleanliness and Convenience: The Social Organization of Normality*. Oxford: Berg.

Solli, B. 2011. Some Reflections on Heritage and Archaeology in the Anthropocene. *Norwegian Archaeological Review* 44(1): 40–88.

Stefánsson, H. 2013. *Af Jörðu. Íslensk Torfhús*. Reykjavík: Crymogea.

Steinberg, J. 2004. Note on Organic Content of Turf Walls in Skagafjörður, Iceland. *Archaeologia Islandica* 3: 61–70.

Turner J. 2000. *The Extended Organism: The Physiology of Animal-Built Structures*. Cambridge, MA: Harvard University Press.

Turner J. 2004. Extended Phenotypes and Extended Organisms. *Biology and Philosophy* 19: 327–352.

van Hoof, J., & van Dijken, F. 2008. The Historical Turf Farms of Iceland: Architecture, Building Technology and the Indoor Environment. *Building and Environment* 4: 1023–1030.

van Titteleboom, K., De Belie, N., De Muynck, W., & Verstraete, W. 2010. Use of Bacteria to Repair Cracks in Concrete. *Cement and Concrete Research* 40: 157–166.

Viitanen, H. 1994. Factors Affecting the Development of Biodeterioration in Wooden Constructions. *Materials and Structures* 27: 483–493.

Viitanen H., & Bjurman, J. 1995. Mould Growth on Wood at Fluctuating Humidity Conditions. *Material und Organismen* 29(1): 27–46.

Warinner, C., Speller, C., Collins, M., & Lewis, C. 2015. Ancient Human Microbiomes. *Journal of Human Evolution* 79: 125–136.

7

THE ECO-ECUMENE AND MULTISPECIES HISTORY

The case of abandoned Protestant cemeteries in Poland

Ewa Domanska

Introduction

In the context of anthropocentric memory, socio-cultural history and identity politics, burial sites (cemeteries) and human remains are important to the formation of communities and nations, often contributing to the definition of their territorial limits. Thus the dead (their remains and graves), the earth and nationalism (necronationalism) are all closely related. Control over dead bodies is a litmus test for international politics. Dead bodies lay claim to soil. Exhumations, repatriations and reburials of remains resulting from archaeological investigation are akin to nationalistic appropriation of the soil. What is termed the politics of the dead body is fundamental to the formation of the ideology of a national community, while the relocation of remains and reburials (particularly of national heroes and enemies), as well as the construction of memorials or their destruction, remains closely associated with political transformations and the rewriting of history which follows (Verdery 1999; Ferrándiz and Robben 2015; Mihesuah 2000; Tarlow and Stutz 2013).

It is not the aim of this chapter, however, to consider the politics of the dead body or to write about how old non-Catholic cemeteries have become embodiments of the changing memory politics of the state and society. Instead, I propose exploring these cemeteries as particular ecosystems and/or as multispecies ecumenes. I suggest positioning discussion of this subject within the framework of the *longue durée* of ecological-necrological and multispecies relations, while also historicizing the idea of cemeteries as inviolable sites of eternal rest. I consider this issue strategic to the future of thought on the subject of the human condition and on relations between the human and non-human. I agree with New York lawyer Jason N. Summerfield, who recently stated that

> The systematic treatment of the dead – that is, how the state treats its deceased – is approaching an epoch of times, an age when the character of our treatment of the dead will have lasting consequences on humanity and mankind's memory of itself.
>
> *Summerfield 2014: 29*

I am thus interested in finding a way of thinking about human remains that would protect them from potential technological exploitation and/or recycling. Many individuals and communities in Europe, whether those that follow religious rules regulating approaches to the dead body and burial sites (Christian, Jewish and Muslim, for example) or those following cultural traditions, would consider such treatment a profanation of the remains and a violation of distinctly human customs and rites.

This chapter is based on case studies of disused former German Protestant cemeteries currently located in Poland but originally established in the nineteenth and early twentieth centuries in Pomerania, Silesia and Greater Poland, when the partitions of Poland (lasting from 1772 to 1918) resulted in these western and northern regions coming under Prussian and then German rule. Poles' particular attitude towards Protestant cemeteries after the Second World War followed the tendency of associating Protestants with Germans (Nazis). As such, they became particular sites of memory and sites in which memory politics played out. The policy of neglect and forgetting was thus part of a strategy of de-Germanizing (and consequently Catholicizing) territories associated with a traumatic past.[1]

By shifting the perspective on these old cemeteries away from the cultural-socio-political and towards a future-oriented ecological-necrological outlook instead (though I am not trying to claim that the two perspectives are mutually exclusive), we will uncover potential ways of dealing with these particular burial sites. The eco-necro perspective[2] encourages thinking about this phenomenon in its long-term contexts, which is something that I consider necessary in order to neutralize thinking (in the context addressed here) in frameworks defined by short-term interests and the memory politics, and/or historical politics, of dead bodies. The eco-necro approach will reveal that the neglected former German cemeteries in fact bear closer resemblance to the current spaces of natural or green cemeteries, which I believe will prove in the future to offer beneficial solution to dealing with human remains (in comparison, for example, to their chemical treatment in alkaline hydrolysis, a process also known more politely as bio-cremation [Olson 2014]), than to the now fading conception of cemeteries as romantic gardens or landscaped parks. Cemeteries were, as we know, an outcome of the growing denaturalization of burials, which was linked, for example, to the commercialization and industrial exploitation of the funeral industry. I am thus advocating the (re)naturalization of cemeteries and propose transforming the old cemeteries into contemporary eco-cemeteries, perhaps with the aim of cultivating them in this form and then (in future) again conducting burials in them.

I am not proposing here a kind of bio- or eco-centric approach to research on cemeteries. This is also not an attempt to re-establish an old binary between culture (seen as oppressive) and nature (perceived as healing scars inflicted by culture). My task here is to demonstrate the advantages of an ecological-necrological perspective that seeks to complement and supplement research conducted within the "soft sciences" (the humanities), which are usually preoccupied with problems of memory (*lieux de mémoire* and the politics of memory), representation, mourning, etc. Ecological perspectives inspire different research questions, different theoretical frameworks, while also helping to build a different metalanguage for researching this issue.

Multispecies history

While working on a book on the ontology of the human dead body, I came to realize at a certain point that the humanities and social sciences offer neither satisfactory answers nor relevant epistemological tools for engaging with these questions in a sufficient manner. This problem is also relevant to the issue of treating cemeteries as ecosystems and multispecies ecumenes, whether through a memory studies-based approach focused on the socio-cultural context, or through a framework that considers cemeteries as forgotten landscapes of (a culturally conceived) memory. If the question of these cemeteries is approached exclusively from the perspective of the humanities and social sciences, the understanding of what a cemetery essentially is, beyond its cultural significance, is consequently significantly limited. This creates barriers for considering their future. By focusing on what is above the ground, historians often forget that a body's existence does not end at the moment it is buried in a grave. Essentially, as American philosopher and literary scholar Robert P. Harrison writes, 'For all its grave stillness there is nothing more dynamic than a corpse. It is the event of passage taking place before our eyes. This phenomenon of passage . . . makes of the unalive body a relational "thing"' (2003: 93). While we often think of the cemetery space in binary terms of culture/nature and living/dead, the frameworks of the eco-necro and the eco-ecumene, meanwhile, encourage us to consider these spaces in terms of relations, commingling the constantly ongoing processes of life, for these spaces are brimming with a multispecies collective. It also allows us to reflect on death as a form of life.

Having observed this problem for years as a historian educated in the atmosphere of postmodern culturalism, I am now trying to unlearn socio-cultural determinism in creating knowledge about the past, while also trying to understand anew the role of the human being as part of the natural environment, as an element of the changes taking place in it and also as their agent. I am thus attempting to explore those research questions that enable (and indeed demand) a combination of reflections drawn from the humanities and the life and/or natural sciences. My research is thus intended as a contribution to the construction of a future-oriented knowledge of the past that is post-anthropocentric and post-secular.

I have coined the concept of 'multispecies history' as an analogy to the terms 'multispecies ethnography' and 'multispecies archaeology', which lends this volume its title (Domanska 2013; see also Onaga 2013; Hamilakis and Overton 2013; Kirksey and Helmrreich 2010). It undermines the traditional understanding of history as something that is focused on human beings and their history; instead, it is connected to contemporary research on animals, plants, fungi, microbes, as well as to ecological history, the ethnography and neurology of plants, and biology. In order to differentiate it from the way animals and plants have been explored in the past and also from environmental history, conducted within anthropocentric, Eurocentric and socio-cultural frameworks, I would like to reserve the concept of multispecies history for research that contests anthropocentrism and makes reference instead to posthumanism, as well as to other currently popular theories and approaches such as actor-network theory, theories of multispecies collectives, new materialism, new vitalism, object-oriented ontology, etc. (Bennett 2009; Braidotti 2013; Haraway 2003; Latour 2005; Wolfe 2010). This continues the critique of the humanist understanding of human beings that was evident in poststructuralist and deconstructionist thought (Jacques Derrida, Gilles Deleuze and Michel Foucault), which questioned humanism's faith in human exceptionalism that granted a central and dominant position to humans in the world, while also holding an essentialistic understanding of human nature. Historians have usually investigated the place of the human in culture, but now they are coming to speak of its place in nature, including co-evolution and relations to other species. Following in the footsteps of biologists (and sci-fi authors), posthumanists conceive of the human being as a particular ecosystem, a holobiont (Gilbert, Sapp and Tauber 2012: 327, 331, 334), that in effect forms a conglomerate (or assemblage) comprising the myriad of species that inhabit it while always remaining in a process of symbiosis with other forms of life, as well as with machines and things, too.

Multispecies history seeks 'innovative forms of agency' that go beyond human agency, finding them also in non-human factors – so, in animals, plants, objects, microorganisms (as well as in sound and light). From this perspective, multispecies history transcends anthropocentric visions (as they are understood in European culture), adopting instead a critical approach to the colonizing and instrumentalizing forms of the exploitation of nature, whose innate value is highlighted. It also takes a sceptical approach to the division of nature and culture by exploring questions that demonstrate the entanglement of human history with natural history (often to the extent that human history becomes natural history). Furthermore, this approach to history transcends the humanities and social sciences. Exploring, for example, the agency of microorganisms in shaping cultural heritage (and in particular its destruction) requires the application of findings from geomicrobiology and geomycology. Neglected cemeteries, I argue, are phenomena that embody and make observable both this transition and also the intersection of human and natural history. By taking an interest in anthropogenic environmental changes and the role of nature in shaping culture, multispecies history also generates a discourse that is critical in respect of human exceptionalism, mechanistic visions of the world and the instrumentalization of nature as a resource for satisfying human needs. In this way, multispecies history becomes part of the efforts to construct a post-anthropocentric knowledge of the past that seeks modes of conducting research and representing the past that would demonstrate ways of neutralizing human actions that lead to the devastation of the environment, the extinction of species and climate change. It thus inspires ways of thinking that are located not only in local and human categories, but also within the framework of the Anthropocene and the *longue durée* of big history (Smail 2008; Christian 2004; Spier 2011). Multispecies history thus invites a complementary approach to problems that incorporates both the humanities and the life sciences. Inscribing itself into the post-secular turn, meanwhile, multispecies history builds its theoretical framework with reference to fields including eco-theology and/or animal theology, animalism and totemism, as well as to concepts taken from discourses relating to various religions, faiths and beliefs (for example, gift, ecumene, human and non-human ancestry, hope, the persona, the ethics of reciprocity, etc.).[3]

The term 'ecumene' (Greek: οἰκουμένη/*oikoumene* – the inhabited world or territory) is used here with reference to anthropology, geography and theology.[4] I am exploiting the fact that both ecology and ecumene (and also economy) have the same root – *oikos*, or the house and the household. By using the concept eco-ecumene I combine the meaning of the word that relates to the natural environment with the one relating to terrain inhabited by humans, and so by conducting research on cemeteries I am expanding the concept of the ecumene to cover the cohabitation of post-human and non-human entities. I have also drawn on the theological meaning of ecumene, which refers to unity and reunification, as well as ecotheological ideas, including ecological ecumenism and deep ecumenism, which searches for a new paradigm for religion, one incorporating the partnership of various faiths in building new relations with the natural environment, while also exploring the role of religion in processes of adaptation (Stewart 1994; A. Kelly 2015; Hessel 1996; Moltmann 1993; Oelschlaeger 1994; Gottlieb 2006; Tucker, Jenkins and Grim 2016). In the framework proposed here, ecumene means a particular space (in this case, a cemetery) that provides not only the site for the decomposition of organic and non-organic remains, but also, and above all, a living habitat (and space for biosocial relations) that is absolutely essential to this process for animals, insects, plants and various microorganisms. The cemetery is thus a multispecies ecumene. What is important when defining it is the question of long-term belonging to this space and community, which, thanks to symbiotic co-mingling, enables the construction of particular relations of exchange, dependency, cooperation and reciprocity. In the same way that the Swedish anthropologist Ulf Hannerz has stated that the global ecumene will become the root metaphor for anthropology (Hannerz 1993: 56), it could be argued that the multispecies ecumene can become the root metaphor for multispecies history.

As I explore the phenomenon of cemeteries within the framework of multispecies history, I treat them as a form of ecosystem; as a habitat for a particular population of various life forms;

as a site that is typified both by the presence of decomposed human remains that have taken on the form of humus, as well as by the particular constellation of flora, insects and animals (Figure 7.1). In this context, soil might be perceived as a manufacturer – or perhaps better: producer of life and remains as effective 'dead agents' (which means that they cannot be treated as passive objects). From this perspective, historical research (humanities) cannot prosper without engaging complementary research drawn from the natural sciences, including the fields of ecology, etiology, botanical science (including dendrology) and taphonomy, which explores the posthumous fate of organic remains – including the influence of biological factors (the decomposition of bodies, bioerosion and bioturbation), physical factors (transport, mechanical erosion) and chemical factors (diagenesis) on the behaviour of remains and their fossilization, as well as on the formation of posthumous complexes known as necrocenoses. I locate my reflections in a long-term, non-human temporality, which if it has anything at all to do with memory then it is with the memory of microbes explored from the perspective of research on thanatomicrobiomes or grave microbiomes.[5] This would allow us to approach time in the context of the cemeteries and the burial sites not only in terms of short, chronological time, but also in the biological cycle of growth, blossom, reproduction, decline, death and decomposition, as well as in terms of very long (geological) time. Here, I am particularly interested in the status of non-humans, i.e. the condition of those forms of being that were once human but in the course of decomposition processes have become organic material forming part of the soil that is subject to further processes of mineralization and humification. As an element of the soil's carious substance, namely humus, remains form part of the natural environment, becoming a particular form of post-human multispecies 'collective subjectivity'. Essentially, then, we could argue – if we accept from the outset the idea that humans are a form of holobiont – that even after death humans retain this form of being, although they also undergo transhumanation (becoming humus), which means that their form also changes. Once human remains become commingled (an interesting term used in physical anthropology) with many other organic elements and create

Figure 7.1 Evangelical cemetery in Trzciel, Poland. Photo: Wojciech Olejniczak.

a biomass, they become non-human. Thus in the context of ecology, decomposition means dehumanization which – contrary to the world of culture – becomes a necessary condition of inclusion in the multispecies ecumene (existing below ground) (Domanska 2016). I am thus interested here in how these kinds of explorations can transform our thinking about the future of old cemeteries and the need to preserve and revitalize them.[6]

Humanitas *comes from the Latin* humando, *meaning 'burying'*

In his 1744 work *New Science*, Giambattista Vico wrote that there are three principle customs upon which human civilization is based – religion, marriage and the burial of the dead. He argued that maintaining these customs protected humanity from becoming animals. As Vico also claims, the word '*humanitas* in Latin comes first and properly from *humando*, "burying"' (Vico 1948: 8, 86).[7] These principles continue to apply in culture as particular forms of 'universals'. In a recent article by the French philosopher Françoise Dastur, I read that

> the most original manner of defining humans might be simply to say that they are strange animals who bury their dead, since that which characterizes humanity as such is the refusal to submit to the natural order, this cycle of life and death that rules over all living beings. This explains the importance in all cultures of the practice of funeral rites . . . Whereas most animals disregard the corpses of their congeners, humans have buried their dead since time immemorial. We could thus legitimately consider that the practice of funeral rites – more than the invention of language or the use of tools – is what characterizes the very advent of the human being.
>
> *Dastur 2015: 5–6*

I will not polemicize with Dastur here, since current research in ethology (the science of animal behaviour) argues that the notion that animals ignore the corpses of their relatives and do not conduct funerals for them is unsustainable (such behaviour has been noted not only in apes but also in elephants, dolphins and certain birds, for example, crows) (Anderson, Gillies and Lock 2010; Anderson 2016; King 2013).[8] I would, however, like to draw attention to Dastur's view that 'that which characterizes humanity as such is the refusal to submit to the natural order, this cycle of life and death that rules over all living beings.' Her unwillingness to think of the dead in terms of the food chain (or the trophic chain) is, as the Australian ecofeminist Val Plumwood notes, an expression of the anthropocentrism and species chauvinism that typifies Western culture. The very idea that the human body could constitute food for other lifeforms is considered repugnant. In Plumwood's view, European burial practices (inhumation, the use of coffins and sarcophagi, etc.) are designed to protect the body from becoming nourishment for other species for as long as possible (Plumwood 2012: 91–92). This is, though, not an entirely accurate view, at least not in light of current thought, since similar ideas are proclaimed, albeit for different reasons, by Christian theologians (in particular eco-theologians), including Richard Cartwright Austin and Matthew Fox. The latter, for example, writes that 'one of the laws of the Universe is that we all eat and get eaten. In fact, I call this the Eucharistic law of the Universe' (Linzey 2007: 53).

I cannot find a better way to illustrate the ideas outlined above than to cite the forensic scientists Franklin E. Damann and David O. Carter who write about 'decomposition ecology' and 'postmortem microbiology'. In a very telling way (at least for a humanist like me), they describe how the corpse becomes 'reincorporated within the landscape or it becomes sequestered within the biochemical footprint (e.g. fossilized remains)' (Damann and Carter 2014: 39):

Decomposition is the mobilization of nutrients bound to once-living organisms into the surrounding ecosystem *so that they may become recycled as living biomass* (Swift et al. 1979), be released into the atmosphere and soil, or become preserved as inorganic constituents of fossilization (Behrensmeyer 1984). Human decomposition is no exception to this process and lies at the centre of a complex web of cultural, physicochemical and biological reactions. The extent of preservation/destruction of a corpse is a function of the surrounding decomposer populations, the quality of the resource being decomposed, and the cultural and environmental modulators, all of which combine to form a unique and yet ephemeral *decompositional environment* (Carter et al. 2007) . . . [Carter et al.] explored the notion of a corpse as a rich source of nutrients and energy. In doing so, they reported on the contribution that carcass decomposition has on the terrestrial landscape by creating a heterogeneous hub of activity marked by an increase in carbon, nitrogen, and water (Carter et al. 2007). They suggested that this hub of activity is its own localized ecosystem that is bound in both time and space.

Damann and Carter 2014: 37–38; emphasis added

Reading this article I also learned of such terms as 'decomposer community' and biological agents (or biological consumers) that 'use a cadaver as a resource for acquiring essential nutrients and minerals' (bacteria and fungi, to mention only a few) (Damann and Carter 2014: 44). Other forensic science specialists present similar ideas, noting that 'soil systems process cadavers as "just" another form of organic matter; it is the human perspective that makes them a particularly special form of such material' (Barclay, Dawson et al. 2009: 507). Or that 'a cadaver is far from dead when viewed as an ecosystem for a suite of bacteria, insects, and fungi' (Hyde et al. 2013).

Cemeteries as an ecosystem and multispecies ecumene

The inspiring context of multispecies history encourages us to explore the particular phenomenon of cemeteries not only as an 'element of the cultural landscape' (Rydzewska 2008: 181) or of the ecological-cultural realm (which is often also known as the *deathscape*) (Maddrell and Sidaway 2010), but instead view it as a specific ecosystem (or rather a set of various diverse ecosystems) which forms an important store of biotic diversity (Barrett and Barrett 2001: 1820; Uslu, Barış and Erdoğan 2009). It is old, forgotten cemeteries that are no longer tended to that are of particularly great value to peacefully developing flora, as well as encouraging the presence of fauna.

On the other hand, climate change (in particular, rising temperatures) encourages us to think of cemeteries and the contents of graves, which exert a direct influence on the mineral content of soil, as 'an anthropogenic source of contamination' of the environment. There is a discipline known as necrogeography, which explores the morphology of cemeteries (Kniffen 1966) in a holistic manner, taking an interest not only in their architecture and aesthetic aspects, but also – and above all – in how they mould the terrain, their layout, trees and the other natural values of these sites. From the eco perspective, the deathscape becomes a space of dynamic life processes instead, thanks to the decomposition of organic remains, while also becoming a space that disrupts sustainable, balanced development. Simple observation of forgotten cemeteries allows us to state what happens to them on the surface: they are enveloped by the soil and subject to standard processes of both biodegradation (as is the case, for example, with wooden crosses), as well as to chemical and physical processes (the rusting of fences and metal elements on graves).

The eco-ecumene and multispecies history

Research on the influence of cemeteries on the environment and their polluting impact on groundwater and the air has been conducted around the world since the 1950s.[9] Such research has shown that the contaminating elements stem both from the decomposing bodies, as well as from the materials and objects used in burials. The most significant contaminants are coffins, owing to the materials that they are made from (hardwood or metal) and the chemical solutions that are used to preserve them, since these include heavy metals (iron, nickel and zinc, as well as chrome and copper). Another polluting factor is the clothes of the dead if they are made from synthetic materials (for example, nylon tights and the cushioning inside the coffins). Another solution that is especially environmentally harmful because it is particularly toxic and corrosive (even if it undergoes partial degradation) is formaldehyde, which is used for embalming bodies (with some nine litres used per corpse). Owing to the use of these materials and solutions, groundwater near cemeteries has been shown to contain above-average levels of phosphate, nitrogen, manganese, copper, potassium, calcium and lead ions (Żychowski 2011a; Żychowski 2011b).

Increasing ecological awareness is contributing to the growing popularity of environmentally friendly burials, which are often labelled as 'natural', 'green', or 'woodland' burials, or as 'low-impact' burials.[10] Such burials do not embalm the bodies, while non-biodegradable coffins and graves are avoided. The body is instead wrapped in a shroud made from natural materials (such as cotton, linen or silk) before being placed in a coffin made of softwood, wicker, or recycled cardboard (eco-coffins) that is then lowered into a fairly shallow grave in order to aid organic decomposition. Such graves are located in forests, parks and nature reserves and are placed close to trees, or directly beneath them – preferably close to trees with deep roots that do not create barriers to water flow or destroy bacteria but instead use the materials produced by decomposition to grow. Furthermore, such cemeteries avoid the use of artificial fertilizers and herbicides, while the grass is rarely mown (perhaps once or twice a year). It is a matter of ensuring that the burial has a minimal impact on the environment (in terms of potential contamination), while the grave itself becomes a way of preserving and/or conserving the (often rare) local flora growing in a particular place (Yarwood et al. 2015: 177).

There are no markers above the burial place. Graves are often left unmarked or a small plaque is attached to a nearby tree. Alternatively, a stone may be placed on the burial site. Plumwood has made an interesting observation on this point, noting:

> used to stress ecological continuity and traces, stone can be a comforting element in memorials, telling of continuity with a more enduring geological order. Stone can help mark and protect a wounded area in a way that is compatible with accepting the ecological body and the eventual dissolution of separate identity.
>
> *Plumwood 2007: 59*

Stone not only provides a link to the deep, geological past while also marking the site of active decomposition, but it also serves as a site of dynamic life processes, providing a microhabitat for various bacteria, algae and fungi that transform its surface (Gorbushina 2007). According to geomicrobiologists, stones are also inhabited by numerous lithobionts, including endoliths that live in the pores of stones (Sterflinger 2000; Sterflinger 2010; Scheerer, Ortega-Morales and Gaylarde 2009; Angel Rogerio-Candelera, Lazzari and Cano 2013).

By incorporating decomposing remains in the natural lifecycle, such burials, their supporters claim, offer eco-immortality. Humans' short lifecycle is thus transformed into the long cycle of a tree, lasting some 750 years, with the most significant portion of trees' existence coming after their death, as they take hundreds of years to fully decompose. When we think of the organic dead, then their lifecycle is extended significantly, since it also incorporates life in the form of organic existence, which is useful for the environment, and follows on from life in culture. The decision to opt for such burials is often determined by a dislike of large urban cemeteries, as well as the medicalization and commercialization of death and dying; other reasons stem rather from short-term perspectives (such graves require little attention), while those who opt for them tend not to fear that their grave will be reused. They also enable a degree of anonymity, a sense of closeness to nature and provide quiet, pleasant surroundings. Of course, a significant role is also played by the lower cost of natural burials compared to traditional funerals, and the low-maintenance graves.[11]

An environmentally conscious attitude has also penetrated the funeral industry, which is now full of competing offers for eco-burials, often making use of artistic projects. One such example comes from the Spanish artist and designer Gerard Moliné, who in 2006 designed a bio-urn made of coconut shells, peat and cellulose. It also includes the seed of a tree. After it is filled with the ashes of the dead, the bio-urn is placed in the ground and is to be treated as a sapling. The charred remains thus grow into a tree.[12]

A proposition for the future

So what can I offer in relation to dealing with the neglected, old Protestant cemeteries? In light of what I have written above, these cemeteries can be considered in their current form as kinds of proto-eco-cemeteries, similar to those that have been promoted since the 1990s and have proven particularly popular in the United Kingdom, Germany, the United States and Canada (where trees or stones often act as grave markers). Given growing ecological awareness, perhaps caring for such cemeteries will prove more appealing to people for ecological reasons (because old cemeteries form enclaves for unusual greenery and often endangered species), rather than for civilizational and cultural reasons (because of the burial of the dead and respect for the sanctity of cemeteries being an expression of humanity). It is worth remembering that because canonical law did not impose on Evangelicals the requirement to establish cemeteries only on sanctified ground they often chose attractive landscapes as settings for cemeteries, which now, even in their neglected state, as Agnieszka Rydzewska's research on Evangelical cemeteries in Greater Poland argues, 'constitute an element that diversifies their surroundings and they become ecological islands' (Rydzewska 2008a: 179; Rydzewska 2008b; Rydzewska 2013). Of course such cemeteries should be protected – but the real question is how? As Rydzewska's research conducted between 2002 and 2006 indicates, all of these cemeteries are neglected to some extent or even destroyed and overgrown with weeds. And it is not only the graves that are neglected, but also the plant cover. Rydzewska claims that in the north Greater Poland region alone there are thirty nine such cemeteries, with a total of almost three thousand trees growing in them, with some of these trees having reached the height of protected monumental trees. Furthermore, species typical of burial sites were noted on the territory of these old cemeteries, with particular 'permanent cemetery species' considered indicators of cemetery-type flora. These species include, for example, common ivy (*Hedera helix L.*), which is the Tertiary relict protected in Poland (Dębicz 2012: 151).

I must admit that I am more convinced by the solutions proposed by researchers investigating green spaces and the management of the cultural landscape, rather than those offered by historians (and politicians), whose perspective is limited to short-term political aims. What is important, I believe, is paying greater attention to environmental protection legislation and ensuring that these cemeteries acquire the legal status of 'protected natural landscape complexes'. I thus agree with what Agnieszka Konon, Michał Krzyżaniak and Piotr Urbański have argued in their

The eco-ecumene and multispecies history

2005 article, 'Stan cmentarzy poewangelickich na terenie Lednickiego Parku Krajobrazowego' [The state of former Evangelical cemeteries in the Lednicki Landscape Park]. They recommend ensuring as soon as possible that:

- visible information boards are installed;
- the cemeteries are cleared of litter and other waste;
- plants are tended to by eradicating weeds, forming hedges and removing dry branches;
- cemetery limits are marked out with plants or rocks;
- any remaining grave stones undergo conservation work;
- steps are taken to prevent the theft of timber from the cemeteries (Konon, Krzyżaniak and Urbański 2005: 50. See also Rydzewska 2008a: 181).

Since fragments of gravestones have survived in these cemeteries (particularly those from the nineteenth and early twentieth centuries), then those that can be rescued and subjected to conservation work could be transferred to specially constructed lapidaria (Rydzewska 2008a: 180), while others could be left to decay naturally (Figure 7.2).

Furthermore, it is important to note that the specialists in ecological matters (Konon, Krzyżaniak and Urbański), did not recommend the cleaning of old gravestones since they themselves constitute rich ecosystems and a natural habitat for various forms of lichens. Contrary to the view presented above and promoted by scholars working on landscape architecture, I am not convinced that cemeteries ought to be turned into parks (Rydzewska 2008a: 181): however, I do recognize that this might be an unavoidable outcome in urban areas.[13]

Of course, the question of documenting and creating inventories of cemeteries and individual graves is an important matter for heritage conservationists and historians. What is important, in my opinion, is the creation of mirror images of cemeteries in the form of virtual cemeteries, meaning that each site should have its own Internet portal containing the full archive of documents pertaining to a given cemetery, the people buried in it and the district to which it belonged.[14]

Figure 7.2 Evangelical cemetery in Trzciel, Poland. Photo: Wojciech Olejniczak.

Ewa Domanska

Conclusion

I would like to stress that what should be investigated by applying the *longue-durée* eco-necro and eco-ecumene perspective to the question of former Protestant cemeteries, is not just the entanglements with changing state policies but also, and perhaps above all, the changing attitudes of people towards death and burial customs, as well as also changing legal regulations. Eco-cemeteries are of course just one of many alternative ways of dealing with a dead body. Another important element is society's growing awareness of the fact that graves are temporary, i.e. they do not constitute a site of eternal rest.

In addition to the above-mentioned recommendations for dealing with former cemeteries, I would also suggest considering maintaining them in a state of controlled decay. This means that the sites should be cleared of litter, with information boards erected and their limits marked out (with stones, for example). In general, however, I would be in favour of the naturalization of these spaces. As I noted at the outset, my proposal is for old cemeteries to be transformed into contemporary eco-cemeteries, while perhaps also allowing new burials in future, without disturbing their natural state, by permitting green burials. I do of course recognize that this would be a difficult challenge, particularly because of legislation on cemeteries and burial of the dead. I should again stress, however, that this statement is directed towards the future, thus I ask you to treat it as a vision of a possible future, rather than as an immediate project for rescuing former cemeteries.

I would also like to stress my support for the principle of a dignified burial and care for burial sites that is an accepted part of many cultures, while also drawing attention not so much to this principle's cultural aspects (funeral rituals as rites of passage that enable the formation of new forms of relations with the dead) but rather to its natural aspects. My hypothesis is that including remains in the life cycle or in natural circulation might be a more effective guarantee of peace and protection from scientific and technological barbarianism than traditional burial with ornamented epitaphs. By protection against remains' profanation, I mean protection against their utilization and technological transformation, on the one hand, as well as against necro-aesthetics and necrophilia, on the other hand, while also offering protection against political instrumentalization in memory politics (for example, through exhumation). As a researcher and (bio/eco)humanist, I firmly believe that what has been put back in the earth ought to remain there.

Translated by Paul Vickers

Acknowledgements

This chapter is part of the book *Nekros. Wprowadzenie do ontologii martwego ciała* [Necros: An Introduction to the Ontology of Human Dead Body] (Warszawa: Wydawnictwo Naukowe PWN, 2017). The project is funded by the Polish National Science Centre (NCN: Narodowe Centrum Nauki), funding award number DEC-2013/11/B/HS3/02075.

Notes

1 For more information on abandoned protestant cemeteries in Poland, see: http://historia.luter2017. pl/k/cmentarze/; Lapidaria. For the forgotten cemeteries of Pomerania and the Kujawy region, see: https://www.facebook.com/lapidariakujpom/photos_stream?tab=photos_stream. See also Grzywa 2010; Kołacki and Skórzyńska 2017 eds.; Kłaczkow 2014.
2 I have borrowed this term from Sarah Bezan's article (Bezan 2015).
3 These are the ideals of 'new animism', which is not a belief in spirits inhabiting trees but rather a relational epistemology concerning relationships based on the ability to perceive non-humans as persons (Harvey 2006; Whiteley 2011).

4 I would agree with Michael Rectenwald and Rochelle Almeida who argue that 'the translation of religious language into a secular (or perhaps post-secular) discourse will be a vital component of secularisms in the future' (Rectenwald and Almeida 2015: 21).

5 In August 2014, the criminologist Gulnaz Javan of Alabama State University in Montgomery published together with his colleagues the very first study of thanatomicrobiomes. A more detailed description of the findings can be found in Finley, Benbow and Javan 2015.

6 For environmental historians like William J. Turkel, 'Every place is an archive that accumulates material traces of its past, and the continuity of that unwritten archive makes it possible to write very long-term histories of any place.' It is obvious that researchers specializing in geology, hydrology, dendrology, chemistry and physics present completely different information on the subject of place than do historians interested in politics, culture, or military history. With this chapter I am attempting to encourage historians to engage in complementary research on cemeteries which would combine the humanities with the natural sciences (Turkel 2006: 268).

7 Vico 1948: 8, 86. It is worth noting here that the Latin word *humanitas* comes in fact from *humanus* and *homo* – belonging to man, human, and not from *humando*. However, all these words are etymologically related to the world *humus* (Gr. χαμαί) – to cover with earth, to inter, bury. Vico was right in the sense that in the original usage of the term (anonymous *Rhetoric to Herennius* and Cicero's *For Publius Quinctius* and his *On Duties*), *humanitas* means belonging to the same species (*genus humanum*). Humanism as understood in opposition to the stage of animalism and barbarism, might be preserved by exercising human duties. For Vico, one of these duties (and a feature that make us human) is burying the dead.

8 Animals' responses to dead bodies of relatives and group members are deprived, however, of death-related symbols or rituals, which are important for human cultures (Anderson, Gillies and Lock 2010: 349).

9 Since 1996, Jan Lach has led a research team at the Geographical Institute of the Pedagogical University of Krakow which investigates the impact of cemeteries on burial sites and their environs (with a focus primarily on the arbitrary location of cemeteries and their polluting effect on groundwater).

10 The first cemetery of this kind was founded in the United Kingdom in 1993 in Carlisle, while the first equivalent in Germany was established in 2001. The Münchner Waldfriedhof near Munich is considered to be the first woodland cemetery. Opened in 1907, it was designed by Hans Grässel whose aim was to achieve a sense of closeness to nature without interfering significantly with the environment, which meant that the trees were allowed to grow over the graves. Another famous example is the network of woodland cemeteries in Germany known as FriedWald (www.friedwald.de), where ashes are placed in biodegradable urns among the roots of trees, which provide natural gravestones. The trees are marked only with small plaques engraved with information on the dead person. In Vienna, a woodland cemetery has been established alongside the Central Cemetery, where biodegradable urns are buried among the trees. Following a funeral the soil above the urn is evened out, thus no mound is left above the urns. The names of the dead are placed on a shared column in the shape of a tree (Harris 2007; S. Kelly 2015).

11 As research by Agnieszka Olechowska-Kotala has shown, the idea of creating eco-cemeteries is supported by 57 per cent of the young Poles that she surveyed. The planting of memorial trees rather than gravestones is supported by women to a greater degree than by men (Olechowska-Kotala 2011: 61–69).

12 The Bios Urn is made by a design studio from Barcelona directed by Gerard and Roger Moliné (https://urnabios.com/ – accessed 7 October 2017]. A similar urn, named Ovo, has been designed in Poland by Małgorzata and Marcin Dziembaj. It received a prize at the 2012 'Make me!' Łódź Design Festival (www.dizeno.pl/#!ovo/c24oe – accessed 7 October 2017).

13 Not a single Evangelical cemetery has survived within the city limits of Poznan, as they have been replaced by parks (Rydzewska, Krzyżaniak and Urbański 2011).

14 There are already attempts to establish such documentations – photographs, maps, historical documents (http://historia.luter2017.pl/cmentarz-staroluteranski-w-lesznie/ – accessed 7 October 2017).

References

Anderson, James R., 'Comparative Thanatology', *Current Biology*, vol. 26, no. 13, July 11, 2016: 543–576.

Anderson, James R., Gillies, Alasdair and Lock, Louise C., 'Pan Thanatology', *Current Biology*, vol. 20, no. 8, 2010: 349–351.

Angel, Miguel, Lazzari, Massimo and Cano, Emilio, eds. *Science and Technology for the Conservation of Cultural Heritage* (London: CRC Press, 2013).

Barclay, A. David, Dawson, Lorna A., et al., 'Soils in Forensic Science: Underground Meets Underworld', in: *Criminal and Environmental Soil Forensics*, edited by Karl Ritz, Lorna Dawson, David Miller (Dordrecht: Springer, 2009): 501–513.

Barrett, Gary W. and Barrett, Terry L., 'Cemeteries as Repositories of Natural and Cultural Diversity', *Conservation Biology*, vol. 15, no. 6, December 2001: 1820–1824.

Bennett, Jane, *Vibrant Matter: A Political Ecology of Things* (Durham, NC: Duke University Press, 2009).

Bezan, Sarah, 'Necro-Eco: The Ecology of Death in Jim Crace's *Being Dead*', *Mosaic: A Journal for the Interdisciplinary Study of Literature*, vol. 48, no. 3, September 2015: 191–207.

Braidotti, Rosi, *The Posthuman* (Cambridge: Polity Press, 2013).

Christian, David, *Maps of Time. An Introduction to Big History* (Berkeley and Los Angeles: University of California Press, 2004).

Damann, Franklin E. and Carter, David O., 'Human Decomposition Ecology and Postmortem Microbiology', in: *Manual of Forensic Taphonomy*, edited by James T. Pokines and Steve A. Symes (Boca Raton, FL: CRC Press, 2014): 37–49.

Dastur, Françoise, 'Mourning as the Origin of Humanity', *Mosaic: A Journal for the Interdisciplinary Study of Literature*, vol. 48, no. 3, September 2015: 1–13.

Dębicz, Regina, *Zieleń cmentarzy w krajobrazie wsi Dolnego Śląska* [Cemetery Greenery on the Landscape of Lower Silesian Villages] (Wrocław: Uniwersytet Przyrodniczy we Wrocławiu, 2012).

Domanska, Ewa, 'Dehumanisation through Decomposition and the Force of Law', trans. by Paul Vickers, in: *Mapping the 'Forensic Turn': The Engagements with Materialities of Mass Death in Holocaust Studies and Beyond*, edited by Zuzanna Dziuban (Vienna: New Academic Press, 2017): 89–104.

Domanska, Ewa, 'Wiedza o przeszłości – perspektywy na przyszłość' [Knowledge of the Past – Future Perspectives], *Kwartalnik Historyczny*, CXX (2), 2013: 221–274.

Ferrándiz, Francisco and Robben, Antonius C. G. M., eds. *Necropolitics: Mass Graves and Exhumations in the Age of Human Rights* (Philadelphia: University of Pennsylvania Press, 2015).

Finley, Sheree J., Benbow, M. Eric and Javan, Gulnaz, 'Microbial Communities Associated with Human Decomposition and Their Potential Use as Postmortem Clocks', *International Journal of Legal Medicine*, vol. 129, no. 3, May 2015: 623–632.

Gilbert, Scott F., Sapp, Jan and Tauber, Alfred I., 'A Symbiotic View of Life: We Have Never Been Individuals', *The Quarterly Review of Biology*, vol. 87, no. 4, December 2012: 325–341.

Gorbushina, Anna A., 'Life on the Rocks', *Environmental Microbiology*, vol. 9, no. 7, 2007: 1613–1631.

Gottlieb, Roger, *A Greener Faith: Religious Environmentalism and Our Planet's Future* (New York: Oxford University Press, 2006).

Grzywa, Jacek, 'Zapomniane "sacrum". Cmentarze ludności niemieckiej i żydowskiej jako problem społecznokulturowy współczesnego miasta' [The Forgotten "Sacrum": Cemeteries of German and Jewish populations as a Sociocultural Issue in Contemporary Towns], *Studia Etnologiczne i Antropologiczne*, no. 10, 2010: 386–404.

Hamilakis, Yannis and Overton, Nick J., 'A Multi-Species Archaeology', *Archaeological Dialogues*, vol. 20, no. 2, December 2013: 159–173.

Hannerz, Ulf, 'Mediations in the Global Ecumene', in: *Beyond Boundaries: Understanding, Translation and Anthropological Discourse*, edited by Gísli Pálsson (Oxford: Berg, 1993): 41–57.

Haraway, Donna, *The Companion Species Manifesto. Dogs, People and Significant Otherness* (Chicago, IL: Prickly Paradigm Press, 2003).

Harris, Mark, *Grave Matters: A Journey through the Modern Funeral Industry to a Natural Way of Burial* (New York: Scribner, 2007).

Harrison, Robert Pogue, *The Dominion of the Dead* (Chicago, IL and London: Chicago University Press), 2003.

Harvey, Graham, *Animism: Respecting the Living World* (New York: Columbia University Press, 2006).

Hessel, Dieter T., ed. *Theology for Earth Community: A Field Guide* (Maryknoll, NY: Orbis, 1996).

Hyde, Embriette R., Haarmann D.P., et al., 'The Living Dead: Bacterial Community Structure of a Cadaver at the Onset and End of the Bloat Stage of Decomposition', *PLoS ONE*, vol. 8, no. 10, October 2013 [e77733. doi:10.1371/journal.pone.0077733].

Kelly, Anthony J., 'The Ecumenism of Ecology', *Australian eJournal of Theology*, vol. 22, no. 3, December 2015: 193–205.

Kelly, Suzanne, *Greening Death: Reclaiming Burial Practices and Restoring Our Tie to the Earth* (Lanham, MD, Boulder, CO, New York and London: Rowman & Littlefied, 2015).

King, Barbara J., *How Animals Grieve* (Chicago, IL and London: University of Chicago Press, 2013).

Kirksey, S. Eben and Helmreich, Stefan, 'On the Emergence of Multispecies Ethnography', *Current Anthropology*, vol. 25, no. 4, November 2010: 545–576.

Kłaczkow, Jarosław, *The Evangelical Church of the Augsburg Confession in Poland in the Years 1945–1989* (Toruń: Marszałek, 2014).

Kniffen, Fred, 'Necrogeography in United States', *Geographical Review*, vol. 57, 1966: 426–427.

Kołacki, Jerzy and Skórzyńska, Izabela, eds. *"Ziemia skrywa kości". Zapomniane krajobrazy pamięci – cmentarze protestanckie w Wielkopolsce po 1945 roku* ["The earth contains many more bones". The forgotten landscapes of memory – Protestant Cemeteries in Greater Poland since 1945] (Poznan: Instytut Historii UAM, 2017).

Konon, Agnieszka, Krzyżaniak, Michał and Urbański, Piotr, 'Stan cmentarzy poewangelickich na terenie Lednickiego Parku Krajobrazowego' [The state of former Evangelical cemeteries in the Lednicki Landscape Park], *Roczniki Akademii Rolniczej w Poznaniu*, CCCLXX, 2005: 45–51.

Latour, Bruno, *Reassembling the Social. An Introduction to Actor-Network-Theory* (Oxford: Oxford University Press, 2005).

Linzey, Andrew, *Creatures of the Same God: Explorations in Animal Theology* (Winchester: Winchester University Press, 2007).

Maddrell, Avril and Sidaway, James D., eds *Deathscapes: Spaces for Death, Dying, Mourning and Remembrance* (Farnham: Ashgate, 2010).

Mihesuah, Devon A., ed. *Repatriation Reader: Who Owns American Indian Remains?* (Lincoln: University of Nebraska Press, 2000).

Moltmann, Jürgen, *God in Creation: A New Theology of Creation and the Spirit of God*, trans. by Margaret Kohl (Minneapolis, MN: Fortress Press, 1993).

Oelschlaeger, Max, *Caring for Creation: An Ecumenical Approach to the Environmental Crisis* (New Haven, CT and London: Yale University Press, 1994).

Olechowska-Kotala, Agnieszka, 'E-cmentarze, eko-cmentarze i spopielenie w diament – poglądy młodych Polaków' [E-cemeteries, eco-cemeteries and turning ashes into diamonds – the views of young Poles', in: *Problemy współczesnej tanatologii* [Issues in contemporary thanatology], vol. XV, edited by Jacek Kolbuszewski (Wrocław: Wrocławskie Towarzystwo Naukowe, 2011): 61–69.

Olson, Philip R., 'Flush and Bone: Funeralizing Alkaline Hydrolysis in the United States', *Science, Technology & Human Values*, vol. 39, no. 5, 2014: 666–693.

Onaga, Lisa A., 'Bombyx and Bugs in Meiji Japan: Toward a Multispecies History?', *The Scholar & Feminist Online*, no. 11, vol. 3, Summer 2013 [http://sfonline.barnard.edu/life-un-ltd-feminism-bioscience-race/bombyx-and-bugs-in-meiji-japan-toward-a-multispecies-history/ (accessed February 4, 2016)].

Plumwood, Val, 'Tasteless: Towards a Food-Based Approach to Death', in idem, *The Eye of the Crocodile*, edited by Lorraine Shannon (Canberra: Australian National University E Press, 2012): 91–99.

Plumwood, Val, 'The Cemetery Wars: Cemeteries, Biodiversity and the Sacred', *Local-Global: Identity, Security, Community*, vol. 3, 2007: 54–71.

Rectenwald, Michael and Almeida, Rochelle, 'Introduction: Global Secularisms in a Post-Secular Age', in: *Global Secularisms in a Post-Secular Age*, edited by Michael Rectenwald and Rochelle Almeida (New York and Berlin: Walter de Gruyter, 2015): 1–24.

Rydzewska, Agnieszka, 'Analiza dendroflory zabytkowych cmentarzy ewangelickich północnej części województwa Wielkopolskiego' [Analysis of the Dendroflora of Historical Evangelical Cemeteries of Northern Greater Poland], *Teka Komisji Architektury, Urbanistyki i Studiów Krajobrazowych – OL PAN*, 2008a: 172–182.

Rydzewska, Agnieszka, 'Cmentarze niekatolickie wielkopolski – Kłopotliwa spuścizna?' [Non-Catholic Cemeteries of Wielkopolska Region – Troublesome Heritage?], in: *Zarządzanie krajobrazem kulturowym* [Cultural Landscape Management], edited by Krystyna Pawłowska and Urszula Myga-Piątek, *Prace Komisji Krajobrazu Kulturowego PTG*, no. 10, Sosnowiec, 2008b: 241–247.

Rydzewska, Agnieszka, *Zabytkowe cmentarze ewangelickie północnej Wielkopolski* [The Historical Evangelical Cemeteries of Northern Greater Poland] (Poznań: Wydawnictwo Uniwersytetu Przyrodniczego w Poznaniu, 2013).

Rydzewska, Agnieszka; Krzyżaniak, Michał and Urbański, Piotr, 'Niegdyś *sacrum*, dziś *profanum* – dawne cmentarze ewangelickie Poznania i okolic' [Once Sacred, Now Profane – The Former Evangelical Cemeteries of the City of Poznan and the Surrounding Area], *Prace Komisji Krajobrazu Kulturowego*, no. 15, 2011: 64–72.

Scheerer, Stefanie, Ortega-Morales, Otto and Gaylarde, Christine, 'Microbial Deterioration of Stone Monuments: An Updated Overview', *Advances in Applied Microbiology*, vol. 66, 2009: 97–139.

Smail, Daniel Lord, *Deep History and the Brain* (Berkeley: University of California Press, 2008).

Spier, Fred, *Big History. History and the Future of Humanity* (Chichester: Wiley-Blackwell, 2011).

Sterflinger, Katja, 'Fungi as Geologic Agents', *Geomicrobiology Journal*, vol. 17, 2000: 97–124.

Sterflinger, Katja, 'Fungi: Their Role in Deterioration of Cultural Heritage', *Fungal Biology Reviews*, vol. 24, 2010: 47–55.

Stewart, James H., 'Deep Ecology and Deep Ecumenism: Religion and the New Paradigm. Reflections on the Theological Sources of our World-View', *Feminist Theology*, vol. 2, no. 6, May 1994: 103–117.

Summerfield, Jason N., 'Comments on the Potter's Field: The Future of Mass Graves', *Quinnipiac Probate Law Journal*, vol. 28, no. 1, 2014: 23–47.

Tarlow, Sarah and Stutz, Liv Nilsson, eds. *The Oxford Handbook of the Archaeology of Death and Burial* (Oxford: Oxford University Press, 2013).

Tucker, Mary E., Jenkins Willis and Grim, John, eds. *Routledge Handbook of Religion and Ecology* (London: Routledge, 2016).

Turkel, William J., 'Every Place Is an Archive: Environmental History and the Interpretation of Physical Evidence', *Rethinking History*, vol. 10, no. 2, 2006: 259–276.

Uslu, Aysel, Emin Bariş and Elmas Erdoğan, 'Ecological Concerns over Cemeteries', *African Journal of Agricultural Research*, vol. 4, no. 13, December 2009: 1505–1511.

Verdery, Katherine, *The Political Lives Of Dead Bodies: Reburial and Post-Socialist Change* (New York: Columbia University Press, 1999).

Vico, Giambattista, *The New Science of Giambattista Vico*, trans. by Thomas Goddard Bergin and Max Harold Fisch (Ithaca, NY: Cornell University Press, 1948).

Whiteley, Peter M., 'Epilogue: Prolegomenon for a New Totemism', in: *The Anthropology of Extinction: Essays on Culture and Species Death*, edited by Genese Marie Sodikoff (Bloomington, IN: Indiana University Press, 2011): 219–227.

Wolfe, Cary, *What Is Posthumanism?* (Minneapolis: University of Minnesota Press, 2010).

Yarwood, Richard, Sidaway, James D., Kelly, Claire and Stillwell, Susie, 'Sustainable Deathstyles? The Geography of Green Burials in Britain', *The Geographical Journal*, vol. 181, no. 2, June 2015: 172–184.

Żychowski, Józef, 'Geological Aspects of Decomposition of Corpses in Mass Graves from WW1 and 2, Located in SE Poland', *Environmental Earth Sciences*, vol. 64, no. 2, 2011a: 437–448.

Żychowski, Józef, 'The Impact of Cemeteries in Krakow on the Natural Environment: Selected Aspects', *Geographia Polonica*, no. 84, 2011b: 5–23.

8

ECOLOGIES OF ROCK AND ART IN NORTHERN NEW MEXICO

Benjamin Alberti and Severin Fowles

Introduction

Of the many branches of archaeological research, the study of rock art would seem to be particularly attentive to the lives of non-human species. Around the globe, most rock art traditions since the end of the Pleistocene have repeatedly returned to the theme of the animal, and this has led rock art researchers to repeatedly inquire into the nature of human-animal relations. Ancient representations of, say, a deer on the wall of a cave or on the side of a cliff prompt us to consider what it was about the relationship between deer and artist that led the latter to take up the former as the subject matter of his or her "art." Much rock art, indeed, seems to spring from indigenous meditations on interspecies relations and the hunter-prey relation in particular. Of course, it is also common to encounter iconography focused on human relationships with species that seem to have little to do with subsistence or the hunt. Exotic birds, horned serpents, dog-headed anthropomorphs, dragons—such creatures were presumably implicated in cultural discourses with deep symbolic resonances. But in each of these cases, a multispecies analysis of the *content* of rock art imagery can only take us so far.

Rather than examine multispecies rock art as a representational discourse, our goal in this chapter is to push toward an analysis of rock art as a multispecies *happening* in its own right, as a phenomenon that is forever caught up in creative and transformative relations with a great many other creatures and agencies. Put otherwise, the multispecies archaeology of rock art we are after is more akin to what Kathryn Miller refers to as "eco-art" (see Warshall 2000), insofar as it aims to destabilize the position of the artist from the start, re-imagining image production as an evolving ecological process that is always more-than-human.

This destabilizing move, we suggest, arises more easily in the study of rock art images than in the study of the canvas paintings and bronze sculptures of the modern museum. The latter reside in institutional spaces in which other-than-human processes are vigorously policed. Animals may be represented in museum artworks, but they are not permitted in the museum itself. Insects, fungi, and microbes of various sorts may have a better chance of penetrating the museum's security systems, but they are equally unwanted, and curators spend a great deal of effort attempting to minimize their visibility and effects. Rock art, in contrast, occurs "in the wild," in settings that are less governed by humans and more open to contributions of non-human species, as well as to ecological processes like mineralization and chemical weathering.

And one of our principal suggestions is that, for many non-modern rock artists, participation within these wider ecologies seems to have been what image production was all about (see also Yusoff 2015).

But there is a deeper argument we hope to advance as well, having to do with how a multi-species archaeology of rock art forces us to confront the ontological commitments that govern our analysis of images. In the modern West, it is not simply that image production tends to be regarded as an exclusively human affair; it is also typically assumed that the proper way to interpret an image is by placing it within its human context—which is to say, in its *historical* context. Western art is identified in books and on museum placards by its artist, title, and—crucially—by the year or time period of its creation. *When* the artwork was created matters a great deal, for this situates it within an unfolding sequence of human events. The artwork is made legible by its temporal position. Its spatial positionality, on the other hand, is almost never specified. Indeed, exactly *where* an artwork was created—in which kitchen or studio or meadow—is usually considered quite irrelevant to its interpretation. Often, one is not even sure on which continent a work of Western art was painted, let alone the specific ecologies that swirled around the image as it came into being. "Western" art need not be produced in Western Europe, and a "French" painting by Gauguin may well have been painted in Tahiti rather than France. Western art is regarded as fundamentally "of its time" in this sense; the date of a painting bestows upon it a historical identity rather than an ecological position. This is why universities have departments of Art *History* rather than Art Geography or Art Ecology.

The ontological priority placed on history and time—and by virtue of this, on the human—in the modern West makes it awkward to study rock art, much of which is notoriously difficult to situate chronologically. This is especially the case when subtractive technologies are employed (such as pecking, grinding, or incising) and when the glyphs remain exposed and unburied. Unable to determine the precise historical position of an image through chronometric dating, many archaeologists feel adrift and without a clear means of entering into interpretation. What rock art lacks in temporal precision, however, it more than makes up for in spatial precision, for in most cases we know the exact place where the image was made and where it was viewed. We know the image's relationship to rivers, to sunlight, to mountains, to trees, and to all the creatures that dwell therein. The interpretation of rock art begins to have robust possibilities, in other words, as soon as we shift the ontological weight from the *when* to the *where* of the image.

A multispecies approach helps us make this shift. But so too does a serious engagement with the knowledge and perspectives of indigenous traditions, particularly in the American Southwest where our research is situated. As we discuss below, a multispecies perspective already exists within much Native American philosophy as part of a broader theorization of place in which situated networks of ecological relations are considered ontologically constitutive. Before answering the question of what a multispecies archaeology of rock art might look like, then, we first explore what an *indigenous* archaeology of rock art might look like. As we will see, each looks a good deal like the other. And this, in the end, is our partial answer to both questions.

From history to place in the Rio Grande Gorge

Our research centers on the Rio Grande Gorge of north-central New Mexico, a visually dramatic rift valley that cuts through the sagebrush-covered plateau just west of the modern community of Taos (Figure 8.1). To the east of the gorge, the Sangre de Cristo mountain range rises to a height of over 13,000 feet. Blanketed with Ponderosa pine forests and aspen stands, the mountains are also home to Blue Lake, a key sacred node in the indigenous landscape, which in Taos Pueblo origin narratives is sometimes described as the place of emergence for

Ecologies of rock and art in New Mexico

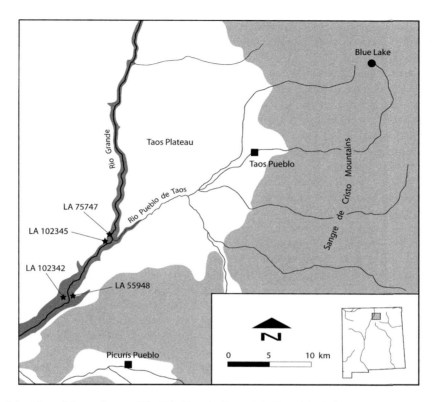

Figure 8.1 Map of the study area. The Rio Grande Gorge is indicated in dark gray.

the local community (see Bodine 1988). The waters of Blue Lake are also the point of origin for the Rio Pueblo de Taos, which flows west out of the mountain forests, straight through the heart of Taos Pueblo, and out onto the open sagebrush flats. Once there, the waters slowly descend, cutting away at the plateau until they eventually empty into the gorge where they join the Rio Grande.

The Rio Grande Gorge itself is a rugged landscape, filled with cliffs and talus ridges of basalt left behind by old volcanoes that can still be seen in the distance off to the northwest. Vegetation is sparse. Cottonwoods, willows, and dense grasses form a thin line along the Rio Grande; Ponderosa pines huddle in some of the side canyons; sagebrush, cactus, yucca, and scrubby juniper trees make footholds where they can throughout the rest of the landscape, creating sparse patches here and there in between great expanses of barren rock. Our surveys have demonstrated that humans rarely camped in the gorge for more than a night or two at a time; a few semi-sedentary pit houses were constructed in the southern portions of the region (see Fowles and Wilkinson forthcoming), but most of the gorge lacks evidence of long-term stays. No doubt the gorge was usually approached as an intimidating geological obstacle, complicating one's route to somewhere else. More often than not, that is our experience of the rift valley today. That said, some contemporary members of Taos Pueblo have emphasized that however much it serves as a barrier to movement, the gorge is also sacred as a place unto itself; they note in particular that the edge of the rim overlooking the rift valley has a shrine-like potency. Pueblo origin narratives typically include accounts of the emergence of the clans up through a hole in the ground, and one could speculate that a large part of the gorge's indigenous significance—past and present—has to do with the palpable sense of underworldliness when gazing down into its yawning depths.

Non-human animals spend much more time in the gorge. Mountain sheep, deer, prairie dogs, coyotes, foxes, rattlesnakes, lizards, and many others traverse its craggy interior; beavers groom themselves along the banks of the Rio Grande at sunset; trout, catfish, silvery minnows, otters, and various amphibians dwell within the river as well; turkey vultures and red-tailed hawks circle overhead (or 'underhead' if, as often as not, you are standing on the rim looking down); sparrows, piñon jays, and bushtits flit about the side canyons; ants can be seen crawling over most of the landscape when one zooms in for an intimate view. These are just a few of the permanent residents that make the gorge a lively place.

In 2013, the Rio Grande Gorge and its surrounding landscape were granted the status of a national monument by President Obama, primarily in recognition of its largely untrammeled beauty but also due to the many archaeological and historic sites within its boundaries. Foremost among the latter are tens of thousands of rock art panels produced by Native American visitors throughout the ages. Rock art occurs widely in the gorge, but it is particularly dense around heavily trafficked nodes in the landscape, resulting in what are commonly understood as historically charged places. Many would seem to be. At least, plenty of locations have been repeatedly visited and reworked over centuries and millennia. These are sites where images have accumulated on rock faces and where artifacts have propagated nearby beneath the sagebrush. In some cases, "history" seems to have pooled up around visually striking geological formations, which emerge as focal points within the broader landscape.

Consider one such place. On the west rim of the Rio Grande Gorge, a side-drainage has cut a sharp and widely visible notch that periodically transforms into a spectacular waterfall after a major spring snowmelt (Figure 8.2). Locals refer to this side-drainage as the "Kissing Fish" site (LA 102345), due to the presence of a rock art panel in which some see a scene of piscine amour (even as we see the characteristic goggle eyes of indigenous spirits known as *katsina*).[1] In fact, there are dozens of rock art panels at Kissing Fish. Archaic foragers, then Pueblo travelers, then Jicarilla and Comanche nomads on horseback, then Spanish and Anglo-American colonists, and finally tourists all visited the site, each leaving behind images on the rock walls of the small canyon where the drainage eventually cascades into the gorge.

We easily recognize this as a persistent place, marked by millennia of human action. But is it a "historically charged" place? This is a deceptively complicated question, for it invokes a notion of "history" that we commonly treat as universal but that, upon reflection, clearly is not. It should go without saying, we hope, that this little gully only has the potential to be experienced as a historically charged place for us, insofar as we possess a quite specific understanding of "history" as something that has the ability to "charge" places—a decidedly *human* history, that is, inscribed into and successively refiguring a more-than-human world. And here we arrive at the heart of the matter: if we are to move toward a multispecies perspective on rock art—or a multispecies archaeology more broadly—we must first overcome the Western understanding of history that emerged to overwrite ecologically specific places.

The history to which we refer is more precisely an Abrahamic or monotheistic ontology in which history rather than place is prioritized. It is this religiously derived "historical ontology" that has made possible the twinned missionary and colonial project that has amplified exponentially during the past half millennium (see Assman 2009). New Mexico has hardly escaped this struggle, which is plenty visible in the local rock art record when we turn to think about it ontologically rather than just stylistically. When Catholic settlers arrived in New Mexico at the close of the sixteenth century, for instance, they began pecking and scratching crosses on

Figure 8.2 A temporary waterfall erupts from the "Kissing Fish" site (LA 102345) as a warm day in early spring melts the remaining snow.

boulders up and down the Rio Grande, to the point that the cross is now the most common rock art icon in the region. Sites that have been repeatedly visited and marked by Catholics—as in the case of Figure 8.3—can certainly be referred to as historically charged places, and not simply because pecked images have accumulated in a single location over a period of time. Rather, such Catholic rock art sites are "historically charged" because the cross icon references an Abrahamic history that, despite its Near Eastern origins, was designed to be exported to every other landscape. For the faithful, Christ's passion was a transcendent event; He died for the sins of everyone

Figure 8.3 A boulder in the Rio Grande Gorge covered with pecked crosses.

everywhere, not just for those looking on in the Holy Land (Fowles 2013). This is why it made sense to the Spanish to peck a cross on a boulder halfway around the globe and to claim that this new and foreign land nevertheless had the same history as the Old World. They were reasserting a bedrock conviction that history—their history, the history of the Holy Land—travels and that local places have no real power of their own.

Most of us in the modern West (Christian or not) perpetuate this ontological priority of history over place. How else is one to explain the second most common form of rock art on the boulders in the gorge: rock art comprised simply of a name and a date (Figure 8.4). "Selsoe Martin, Nov. 4 1902. Jose D. Torres, Nov. 30, 1899"—could there be any stronger assertion of the vesting of identity in history than the bizarre compulsion to scratch a composite name/date over the indigenous imagery in a particular setting? These marks seem entirely disengaged with the Rio Grande Gorge and its indigenous ways of life. They seem instead to be the product of waves of individuals sweeping through and transforming—for a precisely defined chronological moment—this place into another place: their place. Sometimes the transformational effort goes a step further. A number of composite name/dates in the gorge are accompanied by place names, but these are exceptions that prove the rule insofar as the toponyms always refer to somewhere else. They overwrite the place onto which they have been inscribed. What something like "David Lambert. October 31, 1981. Texas" actually asserts is not just the priority of chronology or history but also the mutability or transferability of place. In the brief moment of graffiti production, "New Mexico" has been made into "Texas," just as this same landscape was once made into a "New" Mexico by the early Spanish colonists. Needless to say, even the local coyotes—the classic tricksters of so many Native American stories—wouldn't dream of attempting such a bizarre alchemy.

Figure 8.4   Names and dates in the Rio Grande Gorge at LA 102345.

Rock art begets rock art, however, due to the inescapable reality that it is, firstly, an emplaced phenomenon. As such, it begins to expose the cracks in ontological historicism itself. Consider the fact that Catholics and graffitists visiting the Rio Grande Gorge have often been prompted to make inscriptions on a specific rock face precisely because it had been previously inscribed. This simple fact unmasks the persistent sway of places even as the sovereignty of those places is being denied. In this way, the "modern Western" tradition seems to slide somewhat closer in line with an indigenous mode of image production. Catholics were drawn to and impacted by indigenous imagery, even as they attempted to remake those images into a chapter of Christian history. Likewise, Native American rock artists often imitated, transformed, or reinterpreted earlier rock art created by their predecessors.

There are many instances in which later indigenous artists selected lines or shapes from heavily repatinated imagery on a rock surface and repecked them, producing a fresh image of their own liking in the process. In Figure 8.5, for instance, we confront a case in which the iconographic elements of an "Archaic" (c. 5000 BCE–CE 900) panel were extracted and reinterpreted in a neighboring panel by a later Pueblo (c. CE 900–present) artist. Stacked wavy lines—a common Archaic motif in the region—became a serpent through the addition of a tail rattle, and the parallel lines just below were reorganized into a spider. Seemingly aniconic glyphs were thus construed as iconic. Figure 8.6 illustrates a quite similar set of Archaic wavy lines, although here they were transformed when a Pueblo rock artist added an anthropomorphic being to the same panel. The wavy lines now take on a wholly different interpretation, insofar as they seem to be shooting out of the hand of a human. Figure 8.7 presents yet another example of the indigenous remaking of ancient glyphs. Here, an eighteenth-century Comanche artist has modified a series of vertical wavy lines by scratching three parallel gun icons as an extension on the right side. The new image takes the form of a composite tally, the Archaic lines being repurposed to enumerate the booty acquired by a Comanche warrior during a successful battle or raid in the area.[2]

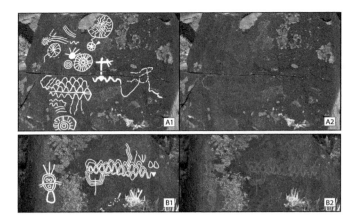

Figure 8.5 An Archaic panel (A) reinterpreted by a late pre-colonial artist on an adjacent Pueblo panel (B) at Site LA 75747.

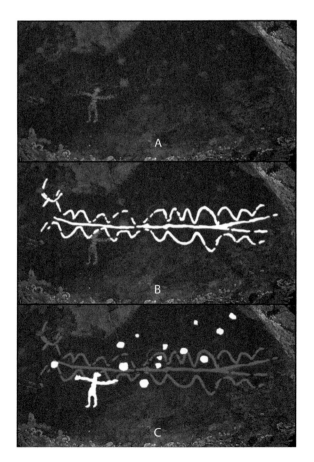

Figure 8.6 A boulder (A) hosting an Archaic panel (B) that was reinterpreted by a late pre-colonial Pueblo artist (C) at LA 102342.

Ecologies of rock and art in New Mexico

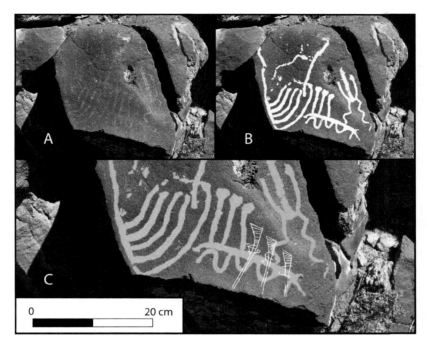

Figure 8.7 A boulder (A) hosting Archaic panel (B) reinterpreted by an eighteenth-century Comanche artist (C) at LA 102345.

We must resist the temptation to refer to Native American places such as these as "historically charged," for once again we risk smuggling in a specifically Abrahamic or Western ontology in which "history" is accepted as a transcendent force that travels and has the power to charge or remake places. As Vine Deloria Jr. (1994) so forcefully emphasized, most Native Americans consider this a very strange way of seeing things indeed. The alterity of Native American and Abrahamic ontologies vis-à-vis one another should not be underestimated, he cautioned:

> American Indians hold their lands—places—as having the highest possible meaning, and all their statements are made with this reference point in mind . . . [Christian European immigrants, on the other hand] review the movement of their ancestors across the continent as a steady progression of basically good events and experiences, thereby placing history—time—in the best possible light. When one group is concerned with the philosophical problem of space and the other with the philosophical problem of time, then the statements of either group do not make much sense when transferred from one context to the other.
>
> *Deloria 1994: 61–62*

The difference, to put it another way, has to do with the question of whether people (and their transcendent histories) remake places or whether places (and their immanent, more-than-human ecologies) remake people (Fowles 2013).

With respect to rock art, the ancestral Ute tradition provides an instructive example. Sally Cole (personal communication, 2013) has commented on the difficulty of recognizing a specifically Ute tradition of rock art in large part because Ute rock artists so often imitated the iconography already there. Ute rock art was chameleon-like; it responded to whatever local glyphs were encountered in a place rather than imposing foreign imagery that expressed a transcendent historical identity. The marks, then, emerged from what was already present. Little wonder, perhaps, that we have found it difficult to culturally affiliate rock art panels with the ancestral Ute in our own study area despite the fact that their presence is amply documented in early colonial records (but see Fowles et al. 2017; Montgomery 2017). The logic of Ute rock art production appears to have been highly situational. Even more so than in the Pueblo tradition, Ute iconographic practice seems designed to mimic—not efface—what was already there. The resulting rock art is radically of its place. In contrast, the endemic Catholic cross attempts to brand what is already there, hammering it into a local expression of a general history. Catholic rock art, in this sense, renounces the specificity of place.

But how are we to think about such dynamics when there was no earlier human tradition to interact with? How, in particular, did the earliest indigenous visitors to the Rio Grande Gorge iconographically engage with places when they were, as yet, unmarked by other humans? And what might such an inquiry tell us about the actors and processes we assume to be involved?

As discussed below, these questions reveal that what is at stake in the struggle against ontological historicism is the possibility of a multispecies archaeology itself. Ontological historicism emerged not just to make it possible for some humans (most notoriously, Europeans) to overwrite the sovereignty of other humans (those of the colonized world). It also emerged to make it possible for one species (humans) to overwrite the sovereignty of other species and the wider ecologies in which they participate. If anthropocentrism is the problem, then history, we propose, is its vehicle.

Natural signs

Clues to an alternative mode of conceptualizing history and place lie within the Archaic tradition, which left behind the earliest rock art identified in our study area.[3] Though highly mobile Paleoindian groups of the terminal Pleistocene were the first human occupants of northern New Mexico, rock art researchers in the region have not yet developed a means of distinguishing their rock art (if indeed they produced any) from that produced by Archaic hunter-gatherers during the Holocene. For our purposes, we follow the admittedly crude tradition of using "Archaic" to refer to all rock art originating prior to the tenth century CE when Pueblo agriculturalists finally entered the Taos region and transformed not just the local ecologies of humans, plants, and animals but the local iconographic traditions as well. In contrast to these later arrivals, most Archaic rock artists confronted canvases that lacked prior human traces. Theirs was a "bedrock" art, in this sense, pecked onto naked rock itself. If we regard images as necessarily human creations, then Early Archaic peoples would have regularly encountered "image-less" landscapes; similarly, if we regard *places* as necessarily human creations, then Early Archaic peoples regularly encountered "place-less" landscapes that had not yet been imbued with meaning. Would there have been nothing to imitate for these rock artists, then? Did Archaic image makers stand, almost by default, in the position that modern Western subjects have always sought to occupy: namely, in the position of the author confronting a blank slate upon which anything at all could be inscribed? In short, were the original inhabitants of our study area free agents who did not have to contend with local historical traditions (iconographic or otherwise) precisely because those traditions had yet to be constructed?

Surely not. From an ecological perspective, the history of a place is never a solely human history, and we suspect that Archaic inhabitants, in their own way, were especially attuned to this. Moreover, the meaningful traces that constitute a place-based history are never solely human products. This goes without saying, perhaps, for foragers who are constantly attending to what we, in the West, refer to as "natural signs": animal tracks, scat, evidence of ripening, and the like. The neuroscientist Stanislas Dehaene goes so far as to argue that a cognitive ability to "read" such ecological traces may have paved the way for—and, indeed, have been partly replaced by—an ability to read and interpret words. "It is possible," he proposes, "that reading of animal tracks is the cortical precursor for reading" in general:

> Years of experience with hunter-gatherers in the Amazon, New Guinea, or the African bush led anthropologists to marvel at the aborigines' ability to *read* the natural world. They decipher animal tracks with amazing ease. Meticulous inspection of broken branches or faint tracks in the dirt allows them to quickly figure out what animal has been around, its size, the direction in which it went, and a number of other details that will be invaluable for hunting. We are essentially "illiterate" about all these natural signs.
>
> *Dehaene 2009: 212*

The point, of course, is that for an ecologically literate community of Archaic hunter-gatherers, success in a new landscape probably depended upon an ability to join in a local history that was always already underway. The question then becomes how this "joining in" relates to the production of images.

Part of the answer to this question is clear enough: "natural signs" were regularly incorporated into Archaic image production. Indeed, the most common glyphic elements in Archaic rock art are the tracks of animals such as deer, elk, mountain sheep, and birds—as well as other humans, whose footprints are often presented right alongside those of other species with no obvious distinction (Figure 8.8). Insofar as dispersed and highly mobile hunter-gatherers spend a great deal of time tracking game, such rock art might seem to require little explanation. The Archaic rock artists, one might imagine, were simply projecting onto rocks the traces of animal (and human) movements they spent so much time studying underfoot.

Surely this is an inadequate explanation, however. Rock art is never a simple projection, particularly in the Rio Grande Gorge. Pecking even the simplest animal track glyph on the hard basalt boulders that serve as the rift valley's primary canvas involves first finding an expedient quartzite cobble, then knapping it into a pecking stone, and finally undertaking the muscular task of pecking itself. Many animal tracks in Archaic rock art panels are quite deeply pecked, in fact, suggesting that these exertions were undertaken with great purpose. Again we ask: why go to the work of crafting lithic imitations of the indexes of animal movements that had already been fashioned in the mud, dust, and snow of the surrounding landscape?

Here, it is useful to think about the mobile logics of the animals themselves, particularly the trail-blazing habits of species like mountain sheep and deer. The Rio Grande Gorge, as we have emphasized, is rugged and difficult to traverse even for those who have four legs rather than two. Birds may be able to travel "as the crow flies," but pedestrian creatures must constantly navigate the rift valley's many geographic obstacles. Thus when a route of potential movement up a cliff or around a craggy outcrop is seized upon it tends to be utilized repeatedly. Quadrupeds have been finding and marking such routes in the gorge for hundreds of thousands of years. Deer break branches and trample cacti as they pass. Mountain sheep, coyotes, and the occasional black bear add hoof and paw prints. And all of these species accentuate the path with their scat, left behind like breadcrumbs telling travelers how best to get from here to there.

Figure 8.8 Deer and human prints jumbled together on a water-worn boulder in the gorge.

The gorge is crisscrossed by well-marked animal trails of this sort, providing reliable least-cost routes across rough terrain.

One needn't spend more than a day on archaeological survey in the gorge to realize that human travelers would have always relied on these existing multispecies highways to assist in their own journeys. Lines of animal tracks leading up the side of a steep incline represent a kind of quadrupedal knowledge that has been embedded in the land and is now available to people on the move, whether or not they are actively pursuing game. Animal tracks mark trails and archive histories of movement, in other words, and it is reasonable to conclude that past rock artists, recognizing this, mimicked these same indexical signs on rock faces so as to participate

Ecologies of rock and art in New Mexico

in the construction of a knowledgeable landscape. It is surely significant, in this sense, that for thousands of years Archaic rock artists never actually depicted animal bodies themselves; they never sought to make a deer present in a place by pecking its bodily form on the side of a boulder (as was commonplace, for example, among later Pueblo rock artists). Rather, the goal seems to have been to lend greater permanence and visibility to the marks made by animals, shifting the medium from mud to stone. Such rock art did not impose itself on the local ecology so much as participate in an existing animal semiotics.

After animal tracks, the next most common elements in the Archaic rock art of the Rio Grande Gorge are "abstract" or "aniconic" glyphs: dots, squiggles, circles, meandering lines, and the like (Schaafsma 2003). Without many interpretive alternatives, most Southwestern rock art specialists have shrugged their shoulders and simply followed David Lewis-Williams's (2002) lead, treating any strange or inscrutable pattern as an effort to fix in stone the entoptic visions seen while in an altered state of consciousness. Some Archaic rock art panels may indeed have been implicated in what might be crudely referred to as "shamanic" practices. Certainly, the vision quest is a widespread component of hunter-gatherer traditions in the American West; it is frequently linked to image production (for example, the painting of visionary images on shields), and we can assume that such practices have a deep indigenous ancestry. Moreover, some of the Archaic rock art panels in the gorge with plausibly entoptic forms do occur in solitary shelters where one can easily imagine someone holing up in search of powerful visions.

But the "shamanic" interpretation falls apart when it leads us away from rather than toward a situated or place-based investigation of images. In the Rio Grande Gorge, for instance, we have had the opportunity to discuss certain panels with colleagues from local indigenous groups, and almost never does the topic of altered states arise. On one occasion, a friend from Taos Pueblo suggested that we would do well to think about the rows of dots—allegedly the most common entoptic images in the Southwest—on certain boulders as migration glyphs instead, each dot representing a different place the ancestors stopped en route to their present home in the Taos region (Bernardini and Fowles 2011). This is a decidedly Puebloan interpretation, however, linked to wider traditions of clan organization and semi-sedentary village life. The highly nomadic hunters and gatherers of the Archaic presumably would have had something quite different to say about the ancient dots pecked all over the region. Nevertheless, the point is that there are interpretive options to consider beyond altered states (see also McCall 2007).

Much of the seemingly aniconic imagery of the Archaic rock art tradition, in fact, may participate in the multispecies semiotics just noted. In Figure 8.9, what appears from a distance to be a progression of dots turns out to be a series of tiny hoof prints that circle around before being transformed into a pecked line. If the "dots" are tracks, then the line is perhaps a game trail and the entire human composition becomes a study of prior animal compositions in the landscape as both human and animal moved about in choreographic fashion. As if to comment upon this interpenetration of human and animal movements, the glyphic elements in this particular panel curve around to collectively define an oval form suggestive of a human foot or sandal print. Other Archaic rock art panels draw out these narrative possibilities of dots and lines more explicitly. In Figure 8.10, the upper face of the large boulder appears before us as a landscape that quadrupeds seem to have been frequenting. A long line of dots encircles the panel, following the rock's edges just as deer trails so often follow the tops of ridges. Entering into a slight recess in the rock art panel's center, the dots transform into legible hoof prints and seem to run about in chaotic directions.

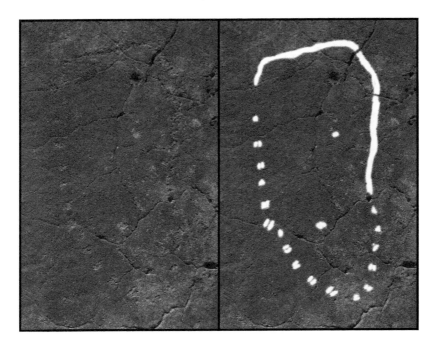

Figure 8.9 Small dot-like hoof prints emerge from a game trail, curving around to define the shape of a human foot or sandal.

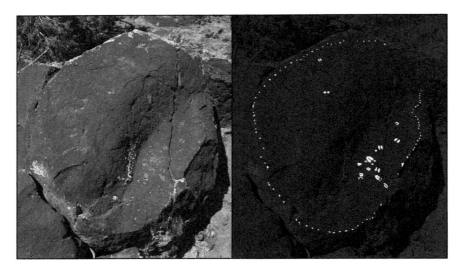

Figure 8.10 A hunt reenacted. Lines of dots follow a boulder's ridges before resolving into a chaos of deer tracks at LA 55948.

Our suggestion is that many of the enigmatic dots, lines, and shapes in Archaic rock art may have been less about altered states than about animals and their traces. In fact, the ever-present pecked dots may have participated in an even more mundane animal semiotics. Game trails, after all, are not only marked with hoof prints; they are also accentuated by scat. Some animals, like coyotes and bears, leave behind isolated fecal concentrations at infrequent intervals. But those species most commonly hunted by Archaic travelers defecate much more regularly. Small deer pellets, in particular, form seemingly endless dotted lines across the landscape, adding visibility and informational content to game trails. These are natural signs par excellence. Throughout the world, serious hunters always inspect animal feces intensely, rubbing it between the fingers, tasting it, and thereby discovering much about who passed through, when they did so, what they'd been eating, where they'd been, where they're going, and so on. Perhaps this, then, was the real source of all those dots in the Archaic rock art of the Rio Grande Gorge.

Be that as it may, much Archaic rock art clearly is about traces of movement in and through particular places.[4] Of course the mobile agencies involved are not just human and animal. In an arid world like northern New Mexico—where "Water is Life" is perhaps the most common expression—moisture has surely always been a target of desire, if not also of prayer. All species are drawn to rivers and drainages, and all species rejoice when the late summer rains finally arrive to awaken plant communities. Moreover, the movement of water—no less than that of humans and animals—leaves its indexical marks on places, carving out canyons, shaping rocks, and leaving behind mineral deposits that frequently take on imagistic qualities.

We find it significant, then, that Archaic rock art maps onto aquatic pathways throughout our study area, clustering around river confluences or along seasonal drainages. Such locations are where the densest communities of edible plants and game animals are also to be found so a superficial consideration of this correlation might regard it as mere coincidence. But the rock art itself often seems to engage with the traces of water in a more direct way. Along certain drainages, for instance, Archaic rock artists ground down rocks to create smooth "grinding slicks" that do not appear to have been used for processing foods (often they are at awkward angles and in awkward locations) and instead seem designed to mimic the rock surfaces in the drainages themselves, which have been worn smooth by the action of sediment-filled flash floods after a rain. So too might the many Archaic "cupules" in the region be linked to the motion of water. These small ground-out cavities bear a striking similarity to rock features all along the Rio Grande, where sand and pebbles have become caught in small eddies on a rock surface, eventually grinding out "natural cupules" that tell histories of early spring snowmelts, late summer monsoons, abundant flows of water, and the life that was afforded as a result (Figure 8.11).[5]

Needless to say, all places are filled with agencies that both precede and unfold alongside humans; ecology is simply another word for the situated histories those agents create, and the lives of all creatures are dependent to a great or lesser extent on their ability to read the eco-historical signs that were indigenous to the landscape around them. From an Abrahamic or Western perspective, in which histories are cut free from places and imposed hither and yon, this can be easy to forget. Our industrial ability to bulldoze over places—an ability that has come to characterize the modern world—has surely consummated the shift towards human illiteracy vis-à-vis natural signs, which, following Dehaene, seems to have been growing since the invention of textual signs. The *literacy* of Archaic hunters-and-gatherers, in contrast, was premised upon their repeated efforts to underline the natural signs around them, rather than to erase and write over these traces. In the process, human imagery contributed to the creation of a legible multispecies landscape that could be navigated both conceptually and physically.

Figure 8.11 Sculpted basalt boulder, the result of the action of water and humble pebbles.

Life on rocks

Rather than *creatio ex nihilo*, then, Archaic rock art reinterpreted, responded to, and took part in processes driven by a multitude of other-than-human agents. Paying close attention to the ecology of the rock surface reveals a host of other participants. Casting our eye—or hand—across the surface of the rock, we come into contact with the colors and textures of still other agencies. Microbial and fungal life worked on rock surfaces in different ways, producing either slow-moving patterns of various hues and textures, or extensive swathes of darkened or colored areas. Most apparent are the dry or slightly furry surfaces of crustose or foliose lichen—ancient, slow, co-inhabitants of the shady side of basalt boulders that line the gorge in great talus piles and ridges. Lichen alters rock surfaces, quickening the decay of rock rind or leaving stains and permanent discoloration (Chen et al. 2000). It may spread at as little as 0.1 mm annually. Conversely, rocks can re-patinate surprisingly quickly. A patina or desert varnish covers many of the rocky surfaces in the gorge with a shiny black or sometimes red veil, especially intense near water. Patination is a surface effect produced by the combined actions of microbes, airborne oxides, and clay, baked by the sun. Mixotroph microbes produce the patination, investing the surface with its black or red hue due to manganese or iron oxidization (Dorn and Oberlander 1981). Thus, layers of microbial communities have always been a constantly changing part of these sites, even though they unfold according to a much slower temporality than the lizard that quickly scampers overtop or the bird that perches, defecates, and—in a moment—leaves a white splotch of a scale it would take lichen decades to create.

Microbiota affect both rock and rock art, adding stable and durable organic pigments to the rock surface (Krumbein 2003: 39). The rock art itself would originally have been vibrant as quartzite hammerstones broke through the desert varnish. Archaic populations marked these rocks because of their extensive patinated surfaces. Not far from the gorge, on the sedimented plateau or among the rugged schists and granites of the Sangre de Cristo mountains, one does not find appropriate rocks and surfaces; hence, these areas attracted almost no rock art at all (Fowles 2004). The settings themselves, however, are not stable things and rock art relies—as images rely—upon changing surface conditions.

Focusing on these agencies and their relationship to the images suggests a way to think about the form and reproduction of the art. Rock art studies have been intimately connected to the existence of such life forms. Certain kinds of microbial life are recognized as the condition of possibility of the art itself. Yet other forms of life—the lichen in particular—are seen as pests that obscure the real art. Distinguishing image from lichen or pecking from lichen scars is some-times very difficult. Sweating in the heat reflected from a southward-facing boulder, one must concentrate intensely, feeling one's way to the image. The degree of repatination affects how the art is studied and understood. Tracing discrete images becomes challenging; the mystery and allure of the art seems to increase the more the contours and colors merge once again with the rock surface.

Microbes have recently become of great interest to ecological and multispecies thinking. A "microbial moment" (Paxson and Helmreich 2014: 166; Paxson 2014) has been pro-claimed; no longer the peril they once seemed to be, microbes are now being presented as models for truly relational living. Microbes seem to offer "not only model ecosystems, but also model *ecologies* – studies in how to frame the world" (Paxson and Helmreich 2014: 171, emphasis in the original). For example, through her ethnography of cheese and cheese-makers, Paxson (e.g., 2012, 2014) reveals the fear that microorganisms have engendered since Pasteur, as well as the contemporary recognition that there are beneficial microbes, cheese molds among them. It is a matter of distinguishing "friend" from "foe," statuses that turn out to be highly situational.

Rock art studies have much to gain from this new attention to microbial life. Descriptively, there are clear advantages; we could reframe rock art studies, moving away from the obser-vant gaze of the patient interpreter towards a model of the multispecies ethnographer (Kirksey and Helmreich 2010), exploring the inside of the ecologies in which the rock art participates. Microbes, in Latour's (1988: 37) language, "connect us through our intestinal flora, to the very things we eat." In our case, the connection is external. The algae and fungi that constitute lichen, the microbial action that produces and remakes black or red desert varnish, are all active players in the making of the rock art and the creation of these places. Such changes to rock surfaces cannot be distinguished on the basis of what causes them, whether tough, extremophile microbes that can survive in many inhospitable environments, or tough, extremophile hunter-gatherer bodies.

From a relational, ecological perspective, we could take seriously the similarity between art and life on the rocks as highly significant to the meaning of the rock art and as an extension of other natural signs. The patterning of lichen, and its slow growth, brings to mind the form and patterning of the rock art itself. Lichen leaves a shadow when it dies, over which even the most experienced student of rock art must pause. The net-like shapes and circles formed by lichen colonies are mirrored in Archaic geometric no less than the scatological trails of quadrupeds (e.g., Figure 8.12). The fact of that similarity, and the difficulty in distinguishing time-worn rock art from time-worn lichen, indicates that images that are similar in form to a putative natural original do more than point vaguely at an absent original. The question of what the art represents, or of what natural forms it is copying, thus becomes a question of what processes are being joined with or imitated (Ingold and Hallam 2014: 6).

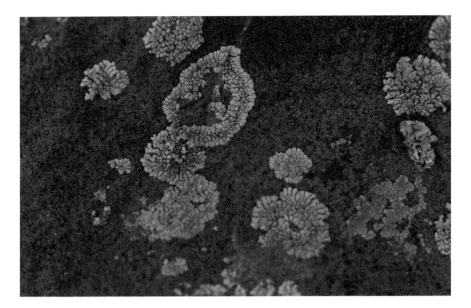

Figure 8.12   Rock plays host to vibrant lichen bodies.

The apogee of the conflation of rock art and life on rocks has been identified by rock art specialists working in the Kimberly region of western Australia (Pettigrew et al. 2010). Here, the surprisingly brilliant colors of the Bradshaw rock art tradition (also called *gwion gwion*), which is at least 46,000 years old, results not from durable pigment but from the existence of microbes and fungi that have entirely replaced the original paint. The conservative nature of the microorganisms involved means that exact outlines and details are largely maintained and stabilized. The color of the art will be a vivid "mulberry" or "cherry" depending on whether black fungi (probably belonging to the order Chaetothyriales) or a red organism (probably a species of Cynaobacteria) predominate on a given panel.

Even absent paint, such image colonization can be detected in the gorge rock art. Figure 8.13 includes one of the few explicitly anthropomorphic Archaic images (Fowles and Alberti 2017). The figure stands out clearly enough on its rock canvas; it has a distinct if wavy outline, large hand appendages with fingers spread apart, and a tapering torso and legs. Its most remarkable feature, however, is its face—or rather the brilliantly colored lichen that obscures its face. Here we encounter a multispecies graphical element: a lichen mask that has grown into the pecked space of the head. It was the human pecking that roughened the surface, of course, creating the slightly elevated moisture and shadow conditions that permitted the lichen colony to take hold. But it is both the human pecking and the lichen growth that together have resulted in the mysterious masked man that now confronts us. Hence, if we are to attribute a meaning to this "masked man"—and read it, for instance, as iconically related to the masked *katsina* spirits of the local Pueblo communities—then we have no choice but to conclude that this is a kind of hybrid art, an ecological happening (see Fowles and Alberti 2017).

The life that rocks host is not merely the condition for the possibility of art, though it is certainly that; it is also the natural history out of which rock art is born. Microbes are part of the surface ecologies that continually transform the rocky medium, which hosts both lichen

Ecologies of rock and art in New Mexico

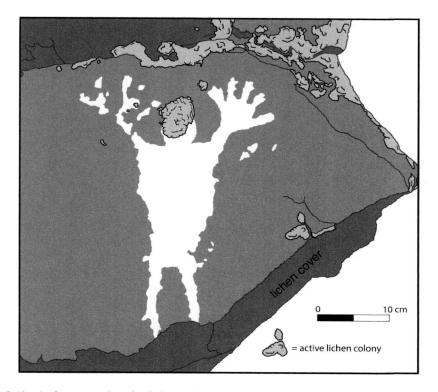

Figure 8.13 Anthropomorph with a lichen mask at LA 102345.

and image. Just as lichen is a composite of fungus and algae, the former playing host to the latter, lichen itself is a parasitic organism that transforms the rock that hosts it. Rock art plays the same role, adapting motile images set forth by the relationship between rock, lichen, artist, and surface. Perhaps, as Chapela (2015: 54) suggests, "inoculation" and "infection" capture this relationship better than the anthropocentric "incision." The anthropomorph with the lichen mask, then, is an index of the role of lichen and microbial life in the production of images.

Multispecies art

Rock art is as much ecology as it is art. We would do better to think of the Archaic geometrics and animal prints as ongoing engagements with the processes that engulfed the local itinerant population than as a rudimentary form of writing. The endless boulders in the gorge are dense with the marks of histories, the gestural traces of human and other agencies. Those who painted yesterday's graffiti, or scratched in last century's crosses, or pecked last millennia's hoof prints all partook in a rock art tradition that was already underway. They all annotated previous imagery, drawing it into their own surface work. As we have argued, it would have been no different when the very first rock artist entered the region and added her own marks to the deeply situated histories of the gorge's specific places.

It is a trick of hindsight to argue that a place is significant because it exhibits the traces of human agency. Distracted by the later images, it can be difficult to see the multiple other agencies at work. Perhaps a multispecies ethnography or a critical microbiology of rock art is what we need to gain new insight into the varied ecologies and the more-than-human semiotics of the petroglyph sites discussed above. On the other hand, perhaps all we need to do is pay more attention to the ontological understandings of the native communities whose ancestors produced so much of the imagery in question. "The structure of their religious traditions is taken directly from the world around them, from their relationships with other forms of life," wrote Vine Deloria Jr. (1994: 67) of the Native American relationship to place. "Context is therefore all-important for both practice and the understanding of reality . . . Hence revelation was seen as a continuous process of adjustment to the natural surroundings" (see Fowles 2013).

Thinking with mountain sheep and microbes about images, we see each site in the gorge as a place that has resulted from the subsuming of the human within a landscape that is already literate, filled with natural signs and unfolding according to a multispecies semiotics. We in the "modern West" may write our texts *as if* upon an empty world, and we may carry our histories about *as if* they are transcendent and sovereign, but like all others we inevitably get caught up in the interlinked ecologies that make places what they are: wind and water, algae and lichen, hoof prints and human pecks, and everything else that has come to clutter our surroundings. These larger ecologies are not just the backdrops for human dwelling and action; they are themselves art, history, and place—as well as a wellspring of revelation for those who have developed a means of attending to them.

Notes

1 On the *katsina* imagery of the Rio Grande Gorge, see Fowles 2013.
2 On the identification of Comanche rock art, see Fowles and Arterberry 2013; Fowles et al. 2017.
3 On the archaeology of the Archaic period in the vicinity of the Rio Grande Gorge, see Vierra and McBrinn 2016; McBrinn and Vierra 2017.
4 On the ontological significance of movement to local indigenous communities, see Fowles 2011.
5 On the cupules and grinding slicks of the Taos region, see Fowles 2009, 2013.

References

Assman, Jan. 2009. *The Price of Monotheism*. Stanford, CA: Stanford University Press.
Bernardini, W. and S. Fowles. 2011. Becoming Hopi, becoming Tiwa: Two Pueblo histories of movement. In *Movement, Connectivity, and Landscape Change in the Ancient Southwest*, edited by M. Nelson and C. Strawhacker, pp. 253–274. Boulder: University Press of Colorado.
Bodine, J.J. 1988. The Taos Blue Lake ceremony. *American Indian Quarterly* 12(2): 91–105.
Chapela, I. 2015. Symbiotic art and shared nostalgia. In *Allegory of the Cave Painting*, edited by M. Mircan and V.W.J. van Gerven Oei, pp. 49–66. Milan: Mousse Publishing.
Chen, J., H.-P. Blume, and L. Beyer. 2000. Weathering of rocks induced by lichen colonization: A review. *Catena* 39(2): 121–146.
Dehaene, S. 2009. *Reading in the Brain*. New York: Viking.
Deloria Jr., V. 1994. *God Is Red: A Native View of Religion*. Golden, CO: Fulcrum Publishing.
Dorn, R.I. and T.M. Oberlander 1981. Microbial origin of desert varnish. *Science* 213(4513): 1245–1247.
Fowles, S. 2013. *An Archaeology of Doings: Secularism and the Study of Pueblo Religion*. Santa Fe: School for Advanced Research Press.
Fowles, S. 2011. Movement and the unsettling of the Pueblos. In *Rethinking Anthropological Perspectives on Migration*, edited by G. Cabana and J. Clark, pp. 45–67. Gainesville: University of Florida Press.
Fowles, S. 2009. The enshrined Pueblo: Villagescape and cosmos in the northern Rio Grande. *American Antiquity* 74(3): 448–466.
Fowles, S. 2004. *The Making of Made People: The Prehistoric Evolution of Hierocracy among the Northern Tiwa*. Unpublished Ph.D. dissertation, University of Michigan.

Fowles, S. and B. Alberti. 2017. Surface revelations: Epistemologies and ecologies of rock art. In *Anthropology of the Arts: A Reader*, edited by Gretchen Bakke and Marina Peterson. London: Bloomsbury Academic.

Fowles, S. and J. Arterberry. 2013. Gesture and performance in Comanche rock art. *World Art* 3(1): 67–82.

Fowles, S., J. Arterberry, H. Atherton, and L. Montgomery. 2017. Comanche New Mexico: The eighteenth Century. In *New Mexico and the Pimería Alta: The Colonial Period in the American Southwest*, edited by J.G. Douglass and W.M. Graves, pp. 157–186. Boulder: University of Colorado Press.

Fowles, S. and D. Wilkinson. Forthcoming. Staging the Passion in a pagan land. In *Place and Performance: Theorizing Architectural Spaces in the Ancient World(s)*, edited by Ö. Harmanah and C. Becker. New York: Routledge.

Ingold, T. and E. Hallam. 2014. Making and growing: An introduction. In *Making and Growing: Anthropological studies of organisms and artefacts*, edited by E. Hallam and T. Ingold, pp. 1–24. London and New York: Routledge.

Kirksey, S.E. and S. Helmreich. 2010. The emergence of multispecies ethnography. *Cultural Anthropology* 25(4): 545–576.

Krumbein, W. 2003. Patina and cultural heritage: A geomicrobiologist's perspective. In R. Kozlowski (ed.) *Proceedings of the 5th European Commission Conference "Cultural Heritage Research: a Pan European Challenge."* Crakow: Polska Akademia, pp. 39–47

Latour, B. 1988. *The Pasteurization of France*, trans. Alan Sheridan and John Law. Cambridge, MA: Harvard University Press.

Lewis-Williams, D. 2002. *The Mind in the Cave: Consciousness and the Origins of Art*. London: Thames & Hudson.

McBrinn, M.E. and B.J. Vierra. 2017. The Southwest Archaic. In *Oxford Handbook of Southwest Archaeology*, edited by B. Mills and S. Fowles, pp. 231–246. New York: Oxford.

McCall, G.S. 2007. Add shamans and stir? A critical review of the shamanism model of forager rock art production. *Journal of Anthropological Archaeology* 26(2): 224–233.

Montgomery, L. 2017. When the Mountain People came to Taos: Ute archaeology in the northern Rio Grande. In *Spirit Lands of the Eagle and Bear: Numic Archaeology and Ethnohistory in the American West*, edited by R. Brunswig and D. Hill. Boulder: University of Colorado Press.

Paxson, H. 2012. *The Life of Cheese: Crafting Food and Value in America*. Berkeley: University of California Press.

Paxson, H. 2014. Microbiopolitics. In *The Multispecies Salon*, edited by S.E. Kirksey, pp. 115–121. Durham, NC: Duke University Press.

Paxson, H. and S. Helmreich. 2014. The perils and promises of microbial abundance: Novel natures and model ecosystems, from artisanal cheese to alien seas. *Social Studies of Science* 44(2): 165–193.

Pettigrew, J., C. Callistemon, A. Weiler, A. Gorbushina, W. Krumbein, and R. Weiler. 2010. Living pigments in Australian Bradshaw rock art. *Antiquity* 326, Project Gallery Article. http://antiquity.ac.uk/projgall/pettigrew326/ [accessed March 4, 2017].

Schaafsma, P. 2003. *Rock Art in New Mexico*. Santa Fe: Museum of New Mexico.

Vierra, B.J. and M.E. McBrinn. 2016. Resistant foragers: Foraging and maize cultivation in the Northern Rio Grande valley. In *Late Holocene Research on Foragers and Farmers in the Desert West*, edited by B.J. Roth and M.E. McBrinn, pp. 58–77. Salt Lake City: University of Utah Press.

Warshall, P. 2000. Eco-art. *Whole Earth*. Summer: 92–96.

Yusoff, K. 2015. Geologic subjects: Nonhuman origins, geomorphic aesthetics and the art of becoming inhuman. *Cultural Geographies* 22(3): 383–407.

9

OYSTERS AND MOUND-ISLANDS OF CRYSTAL RIVER ALONG THE CENTRAL GULF COAST OF FLORIDA

Victor D. Thompson and Thomas J. Pluckhahn

Introduction

We often think of the built environment as a phenomenon that people impose on the natural world. This perspective is rooted in the notion that there is a fundamental dichotomy between people and nature. As Ingold (2000) points out, this is usually not concordant with the ontology of the Native societies of the Americas. In contrast, such ontologies view humans and their actions as part of the world, rather than as distinct or separate. How do we understand the creation of the built environment in a manner that does not categorically rely upon viewing such features as separate from the "natural" world? We advocate an approach that considers a multiscalar consideration of both time and acts of creation (see Bailey 2007). In addition, we also suggest, following Ingold (2000, 2012), that such analyses situate these acts within the context of individuals dwelling in a broader landscape. Here, we define landscape as the various actions that are "collapsed into an array of features that must be understood as possessing different temporalities" that are "rooted in the movements of social life" (Ingold 1993: 162; Pluckhahn et al. 2015b: 20). By taking such a view, we rely on notions of structure, agency, and history (*sensu* Pauketat 2001a, 2001b) and a recursive view of the world, which includes anthropogenic constructions as a part of the world and not distinct from it (see Thompson 2014 for a discussion of these points).

We argue that the theoretical framework outlined above provides new avenues for questions and insight into the nature of the built environment generally and mound construction in the American Southeast specifically. In order to provide some context for these broader points, we apply this perspective to the Roberts Island Complex, an anthropogenic island with multiple mounds constructed out of shell located along Florida's central Gulf Coast (Figure 9.1). We consider the work, timing, and rhythms in the creations of not just the mounds, but also the entire landform itself. At the end of this chapter, we consider the relationships between the actions and traditions of mound building with that of the oyster—the primary constituent of both the mounds and the island. We suggest that to put this study in its proper context, we must consider the relationship of these actions to other species in the region. Of course, we cannot consider all of the species within the ecosystem in the span of one chapter; our consideration of oysters initiates a conversation regarding the relational aspects of traditions of mound building and island creation.

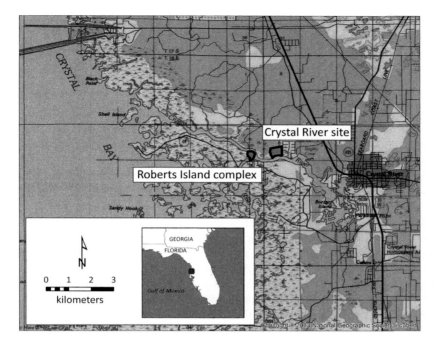

Figure 9.1 Location of Crystal River and Roberts Island in Florida, USA.

The building of land where there was no land before is perhaps one of the most dramatic acts of human constructions. Such processes would be highly symbolic and require a detailed knowledge of building materials and construction techniques (see Sherwood and Kidder 2011). Furthermore, the builders would also need to understand how such constructions work within specific geomorphological contexts (e.g., river floodplains, estuaries, freshwater wetlands). In the American Southeast, the most common expression of this is construction of earthen or shell mounds, a practice that dates back over 5,000 years (Saunders et al. 1997). In some areas of the central and southern Gulf Coast of Florida, Native Americans not only constructed mounds, but also the majority of the landform that supported them; we refer to such landscape features as "mound-islands" and define them as purposefully constructed landforms in wetland settings requiring the accumulation of human transported sediments (e.g., shell and earth) so as to create habitable dry lands. We note, however, that the creation of mound-islands need not have happened suddenly; these features can either develop gradually through the deposition of refuse or more quickly in association with larger-scale, planned construction episodes. Thus, some portions of the landforms were constructed with the intent of raising land above waters, whereas others occurred more by repeated deposition of shell refuse.

It is perhaps tempting to equate mound-islands as the ultimate imposition of human agency onto nature; however, we argue that such a perspective is actually counterproductive. Instead, we suggest that to understand the creations of mound-islands, we must view them as being part of what Ingold (2000, 2012) refers to as the builders' "lifeworld," which is always in the process of coming into being via the inhabitants' constant interaction and being in the world (see also Moore and Thompson 2012). From such a perspective, mound-islands are not anomalous, but rather come into being through actions and practices that are part of the lived world of the builders and their interactions with other species. Such a perspective forces us to consider the temporality of these features and not merely contemplate them as the product of an overarching grand design like some "prehistoric" skyscraper. To do this, we must also place such actions within the context of environmental changes on both small and large geographic and temporal scales.

Shell architecture in the American Southeast

In part, one of the reasons that we take the above approach to the Roberts Island Complex is that shell architecture and its use as a building material is a controversial subject in the American Southeast. Thompson and Worth (2011) summarize this debate, which centers on whether large deposits of shellfish remains represent monumental structures or if they are accumulations of refuse associated with everyday living. Arguments on this subject apply to sites of various periods and geographic areas of the region (e.g., Atlantic Coast), even extending to some interior shell sites along river valleys (see Moore and Thompson 2012). The extreme interpretations regarding this matter leave little room for debate. More recently, researchers engaged in these discussions realize that such sites exhibit considerable variation in form and layout, as well as scale (Thompson and Worth 2011: 68). Archaeologists use a number of different lines of evidence to argue either for or against the idea that shell deposits represent architecture, which include size and shape of the deposit, taphonomic processes, accumulation rates calculated via radiocarbon dating and stable isotope analysis, among others (see Thompson and Worth 2011 for a summary).

The issue with many of the debates surrounding the nature of shell architecture is that the extremes do not fully consider the complex actions by which individuals and groups created such deposits. Generally, when an archaeologist interprets a shell deposit to be formed via gradual accumulation of refuse, the interpretation stops there, and we learn little about the social and ritual lives of people. Conversely, if the shell deposits are interpreted as architecture, the archaeologist usually invokes one or more of a series of what are by now fairly stock explanations: competitive feasting, incipient hierarchies, and transegalitarian social relationships. The problem with this line of thinking is that the focus is on the final form of the deposit, an essentialist view which does not consider the rhythms of daily life, including all of the contestation, negotiation, and cooperation that happen in the course of dwelling in the landscape. In addition, while the function of such creations are important, there are other facets to the construction of such monuments, as well as simply dwelling within such landscapes, that archaeologists must consider in their broader analysis.

The perspective that we advocate requires careful consideration of the temporal scale of the deposition in order to better address how human actions and motives shape the landscape. We draw on our recent work regarding the timing of occupation and collection of mollusks to provide a more holistic temporal dimension to this discussion (Pluckhahn et al. 2015a, 2015b; Thompson et al. 2015). Traditionally, when archaeologists examine what they interpret to be monumental architecture, they often rely on notions of scale (Trigger 1990; see also Burger and Rosenwig 2012), and indeed this is a recurrent theme in the study of shell architecture in the Southeast (e.g., Marquardt 2010a, 2010b; Sassaman 2010). However, since we are concerned with an entire island, size alone and its connection to the timing of deposition are not the only factors we consider here. Elsewhere, we (Pluckhahn and Thompson 2013) use Smith's (2007) measures of greater planning and elaboration, axiality, orthogonality, and symmetry to examine the nearby Crystal River site. We employ these concepts again to examine elaboration and the way people moved through the island to get a sense of how the architecture and layout of the island came to be as part of the daily life and histories of the people who were part of their creation.

Crystal River and the Roberts Island Complex

By far the largest and most complex site in this area of the central Gulf Coast of Florida in terms of its architecture is the Crystal River site (Figure 9.2). This site encompasses seven hectares and has three flat topped mounds, two burial mounds (one a complex consisting of several parts), as well as other features (Pluckhahn et al. 2010). Crystal River is located along a river of the same name that flows a short distance downstream from the site into the Gulf of Mexico. Crystal River is perhaps one of Florida's most famous archaeological sites, due in part to its well-preserved architecture, elaborate, Hopewell-related, non-local burial artifacts, and three stone stelae at the site dating to the Middle and Late Woodland periods (Pluckhahn et al. 2010;

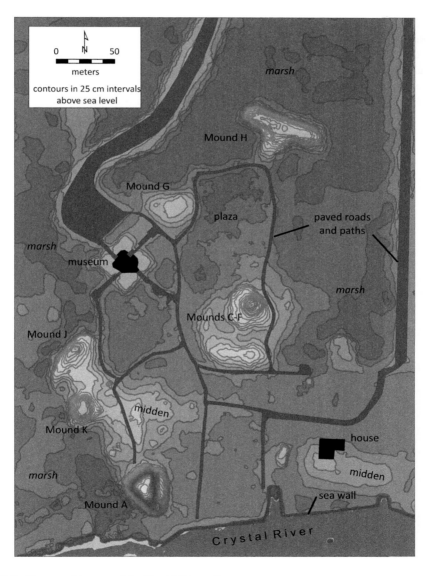

Figure 9.2 Topographic map of the Crystal River site.

Milanich 1999; Weisman 1995). However, numerous other impressive mound centers also dot the central Florida Gulf coastal landscape, particularly around the mouth of the Suwannee River (see Wallis et al. 2015).

Several other smaller mound centers are also in the immediate vicinity of Crystal River. One of these is the Roberts Island Shell Mound Complex, which incorporates five separately recorded sites (for simplicity we hereafter refer to the whole complex as Roberts Island) (Figure 9.3) (Weisman 1995). Located around one kilometer downstream from Crystal River, the complex encompasses approximately two hectares of anthropogenic deposits. It has three shell platform mounds and extensive midden deposits that form distinct features of the island that we refer to here as the platform mounds, mounded midden, linear ridge, and "water court". In some cases, where one of these features ends and another begins is not altogether clear, as we will discuss below.

Both Crystal River and Roberts Island date to the Woodland period (ca. 1000 BC to AD 1050). Our recent Bayesian analysis of radiocarbon dates from these two sites has refined our understanding of the chronology of their occupation, which we define as four phases of occupation and construction (Pluckhahn et al. 2015b). Of the two, Crystal River appears to have a much longer occupation with some of the initial earthworks at the site being constructed

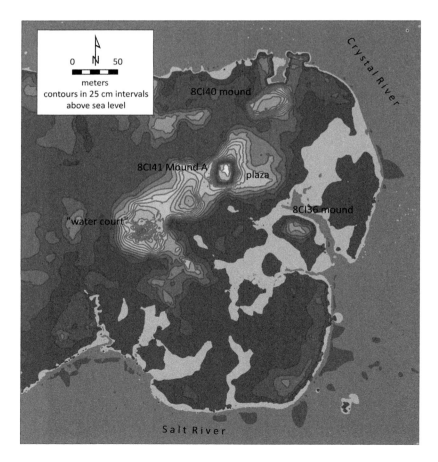

Figure. 9.3 Topographic map of Roberts Island.

around 800–420 cal. BC; however, this date on human bone is separated by 400 years from the next earliest radiocarbon assay (Pluckhahn et al. 2010: 173). It is during Phase 1[1] (start *cal. AD 65–224*; end *cal. AD 143–265*) that we see the earliest dated midden accumulation at Crystal River (Pluckhahn et al. 2015b: 31). During this time, it does not appear that groups occupied the site year-round and that the rapid midden accumulation appears to be related to mortuary feasts and possibly other rituals (Pluckhahn et al. 2015b; Thompson et al. 2015). During Phase 2 (start *cal. AD 221–321*; end *cal. AD 435–544*), it appears that occupation shifted to year-round habitation, and it was at this time that inhabitants constructed some of the first platform mounds (Pluckhahn et al. 2015; Thompson et al. 2015). During Phase 3 (start *cal. AD 479–634*; end *cal. AD 663–809*), Crystal River began its decline, and we see contraction of the middens (Pluckhahn et al. 2015; Thompson et al. 2015). It is also at this point that we see the beginning of occupation at Roberts Island. During Phase 4 (start *cal. AD 722–881*; end *cal. AD 890–1068*), we see the eventual abandonment of Crystal River and the elaboration of architecture at Roberts Island.

We examine these site histories, looking specifically at how the broader environmental context, movement, and changing landscape were intertwined with the spatial practices of the people who dwelled within the Crystal River landscape. In essence, the focus of our discussion is the nature of the decline of the Crystal River site and how a new center, Roberts Island, emerged quite literally from the waters.

Investigations at the Roberts Island Complex

Platform mounds

Perhaps the most intriguing features of Roberts Island are its three platform mounds. Earthen platform mounds are ubiquitous features of later time periods (ca. AD 1000–1500) in the American Southeast. Archaeologists, however, have found that these features were part of the Woodland period landscape as well (Pluckhahn 1996, 2003; Jefferies 1994; Wallis et al. 2015). Most of these Woodland platform mounds exhibit the classic truncated pyramidal form and were likely used as stages for display and ceremony (Knight 2001; Pluckhahn 2003). Several sites in Florida have such features, including Crystal River, McKeithen, and Fort Center, although the latter has circular flat top mounds (Pluckhahn and Thompson 2009, 2013; Milanich et al. 1997; Thompson and Pluckhahn 2012, 2014).

Mound A is the better preserved and larger of the three platform mounds at Roberts Island, possessing a 29 × 32 m base and a 14 × 21 summit (Pluckhahn et al. 2016) (Figure 9.4). The mound, standing over 3 m above the surrounding surface, is oriented with the cardinal directions with the long axis running N-S. The mound appears to have a ramp on its eastern side, similar to ones we have observed at Crystal River (Pluckhahn et al. 2016; Pluckhahn and Thompson 2009). Our 1 × 6 m trench excavated along the western side of this mound revealed that it is composed of whole, loosely consolidated shellfish, primarily oyster. While our excavations did not go deep into the mound (ca. 50 cm), ground penetrating radar (GPR) transects suggest that the rest of the structure exhibits a similar composition (i.e., dense shellfish deposits) as to what we observed in the trench.

Roberts Island Mound B is similar to Mound A in shape and size, although its sides are not as steep. The mound is oriented E-NE to W-SW and is 50 × 32 m at its base and 38 × 17 m at its summit. The summit of the mound is disturbed due to the construction of a modern house; however, its sides remain mostly intact. Unlike Mound A, it is not oriented along the cardinal directions, but offset to be 30 degrees north of east. Our 1 × 4 m trench down the side of the mound revealed that the mound is composed mostly of loosely consolidated, whole oyster shell

Figure 9.4 Photography of the excavation trench along the back of Mound A at Roberts Island.

at least up to the point of the maximum depth (ca. 40 cm) of our excavations. Again, while we could not excavate down to the base of the deposits, our GPR transect survey of the mound suggests that dense shell deposits are found throughout (Pluckhahn et al. 2016).

The construction material of these platform mounds and their age make them somewhat unusual for the region; the way in which Native Americans constructed them makes them unique in North America (Pluckhahn et al. 2016). Both Mounds A and B exhibit a stepped construction technique. Mound A has six observable risers and a possible seventh as indicated by the GPR transect survey at the bottom of the mound. Mound B has five risers as seen in our trench excavations (Pluckhahn et al. 2016).

It is likely that the builders constructed these platforms quite quickly, perhaps in a single building episode. Sampson (2015) found that oyster shells from the off-mound areas, in general, exhibit more variability in size than those found in the mounds. This suggests to her that relative to one another, the off-mound "midden" deposits suggest a slower period of accumulation than mound deposits (see also Thompson et al. 2015).

This construction technique thus elicits a form similar to some of the temple platform pyramids of Mesoamerica—though we would like to be clear that we posit no direct contact from such evidence. We do note that such constructions would have required different techniques and knowledge than other shell mounds in the region at the time. It is likely that the inhabitants of the region would have recognized such a striking difference between the Roberts' mounds and others in the region, considering such constructions symbolically distinct.

Mounded middens and plaza

While the larger platform mounds constitute much of the obvious architecture along the northeastern portion of the site, the surface upon which Mound A sits may have also been intentionally constructed architecture at some point in the history of the site. In this area, we did limited

Oysters and mound-islands in Florida

GPR survey transects as well as four shovel test units. Our GPR and shovel test results indicate large shell deposits in these areas. These deposits form a roughly rectangular area along the east side of Mound B, which is also the side that has the proposed ramp to its summit.

Recently, Kidder (2004) made the case for plazas as architecture for the Raffman site in the lower Mississippi River Valley. We believe that his points are relevant here. Mound A sits on shell-dense deposits that are roughly one meter deep. On both the western and eastern sides (the area of the possible plaza) of Mound A are two obviously discernible layers in the 50 × 50 cm test units, suggesting two occupations of dense oyster deposition (Gilleland 2013). The similarities between these two areas suggest, at least during the initial occupation, that Roberts Island consisted of a linear ridge of deposited shell. However, during the second discernible stage of dense shell deposition, the areas east and west of Mound B exhibit considerable differences in composition.

Gilleland (2013) note considerable differences in the number of oyster, marsh clam, and pottery from deposits east and west of the mound. In general, pottery in the test excavations west of the mound is present in moderate densities in some of the levels between the lower deposits and the surface. In addition, the diversity of shellfish taxa is greater in this area. It seems that the deposits to the west indicate creation through a series of multiple depositional episodes. In contrast, while oyster is the dominant species recovered in all the excavations, the units east of the mound exhibit the greater density. We recovered around 150,000 oyster shells, weighing over 2,700 kg, with units 3, 4, and 6 having a higher density than anywhere else (Gilleland 2013). All of this evidence in addition to the flat appearance of the area east of Mound A suggests a possible intentional construction of a plaza-like area for gatherings in "front" of the mound. In contrast, the area west of the mound appears to be mounded middens as the result of domestic occupation in this area.

The "water court" area

On the edge of the western side of Roberts Island are two other distinct features: the "water court" and a linear ridge extending into the marsh. Like other areas of the western side of the island, these two features appear to be mounded middens that either developed because of domestic occupation or were re-deposited midden making these specific forms. Regardless as to their formation processes, these two features are dramatically different from the rest of the island.

The water court is a roughly rectangular trough encircled by a wall of shell that is 18 × 9 m on a side. The court is 1 m deep, measured from the center of the depression to the highest point of the surrounding shell wall. Our resistance survey indicated that the trough of the water court contained more soil than shell, which we later confirmed through a small test excavation in the center of the court.

Although water courts are common in southwestern Florida, we know of no instances of these features appearing this far north along the Gulf Coast. Largely confined to the Ten Thousand Islands and Caloosahatchee regions, archaeologists are not clear on exactly how they functioned. The most recent and comprehensive work on these features is in Schwardron's (2010) dissertation on the Ten Thousand Islands region. She (2010: 58) summarizes both the past and most recent thinking on these features and most commonly interprets them as water impoundment facilities. However, what is unclear is exactly what kind of water and why. As Schwardron (2010: 58) notes, some suggest that these features held drinking water (Beriault et al. 2003; Moore 1900). Others note, however, that due to tidal inundation such features would be full of brackish water and likely functioned as fish traps (Beriault et al. 2003: 26–27; Cushing 2000; Dickel 1991: 144; Kolianos and Weisman 2005: 122–123). Yet another interpretation is that these served as short-term storage areas for surplus fish and shellfish (Schwadron 2010: 210).

For the Roberts Island water court, it is possible that this functioned as storage of live surpluses, although we readily admit this is a bit of speculation on our part, as we have not empirically tested this proposition. Another possibility is that the shape of the midden developed because there was some type of stilt house structure in the center, and shell midden developed around the platform. Again, this is speculation on our part; however, we do note that the excavation in the water court area contained some of the highest densities of pottery for the entire site, suggesting habitation of this area.

While we cannot point to a specific function for the water court area, there are a few ideas that we can rule out. First, there are no visible sluices into the court, which would allow fish access at high tide; thus, its possible function as a fish trap seems suspect. Second, at high tide, the soils are inundated with brackish water, and thus it is unlikely that the court functioned as a kind of cenote for holding fresh water. Furthermore, the Crystal River region is well known, indeed famous, for its freshwater springs throughout the landscape. In fact, Mound A at the Crystal River sits adjacent to one such spring (Pluckhahn and Thompson 2013). Therefore, we doubt that the inhabitants had a difficult time procuring fresh water. Finally, there is a linear ridge of shell which we hypothesize is a ramp from the marsh where resources might have been carried in from canoes, either to a domestic structure or storage area or both. Such shell pathways are not unknown in the region, as the Crystal River site also has one that leads from one of the platform mounds (Mound H) to one of the burial mounds (Mound G) (see Pluckhahn and Thompson 2009). Based on the ceramics from the excavations and dates from our excavations in the court, it appears the Roberts inhabitants constructed this feature around the same time as the mounds—around *cal. AD 774–897* (88.7%), *cal AD 926–943* (6.7%).

Dwelling in time and the watery landscapes of the Gulf Coast

Now that we have outlined the nature of the architecture at Roberts Island, we turn to consider the temporality of these activities on the landscape—particularly in the context of gathering mollusks for food, as well as construction materials. It is our intention here to explore how these structures are part of the life world (*sensu* Ingold 2012) of the inhabitants of the Crystal River landscape. To do this we must situate these structures within the long-term changes and short-term activities of the inhabitants of the region.

To begin to understand the long-term changes at this time, we must look to the available data on sea levels for the region. For Florida's low-laying Gulf Coast, any fluctuation in sea level can have dramatic effects. Although we do not understand in detail the large-scale processes affecting sea level and climate in the region, Walker (2013) has done an admirable job of synthesizing studies conducted in southeastern Florida and relevant studies from other regions that have potential teleconnections with the Florida Gulf Coast (e.g., Tanner 1991, 2000; Walker 1992, 2013). As noted above, we believe that the earliest occupation/creation of Roberts Island dates to around AD 500 and ends sometime after AD 1000. Interestingly, it appears that this period encompasses some rather dramatic changes in both sea level and climate.

Walker (2013: 40–41) notes that between AD 550 and 850, sometimes referred to as the "Vandal Minimum," there was generally a cooler climate and lower sea levels. However, shorter-term events may have punctuated this time. In contrast, the period between AD 850 and 1200, also referred to as the "Medieval Warm Period," included generally warmer and wetter periods and a sharp sea level rise similar to twentieth-century levels (Walker 2013: 42). While the exact pattern for the Florida Gulf Coast—and the central region specifically—is unknown, these broad patterns do appear to correspond roughly to the construction of Roberts Island.

Oysters and mound-islands in Florida

The creation of the lower portions of Roberts Island occurred during a time of lower sea levels, as water did not inundate these dense shell deposits. As we note above, there appears to be several occupational surfaces that the inhabitants of Roberts Island created through the piling of shells to create stable dry surfaces, for direct occupation, ceremonial gatherings, or both. Again, most of the upper levels of the island and the mounds seem to date to around or after AD 900, approximately matching the rising of sea levels during the Medieval Warm Period. Thus, while there are not direct measures of sea-level change and climate in the central Gulf Coast region, the archaeology of Roberts Island tends to follow patterns that archaeologists rely on elsewhere in Florida (see Marquardt and Walker 2012, 2013).

Although we note these general correlations in sea level and climate change, our intention is not to point out direct correlations between human action and environmental fluctuation. Indeed, finer resolution data may reveal even greater change than expected for the central Gulf Coast. Sea levels can change dramatically even on short-term decadal time scales (e.g., Colquhoun and Brooks 1986). Thus, our point here is to say the inhabitants of Roberts Island were keenly aware of their environment; indeed, they and their island were an intimate part of this world.

From the above discussion, it would seem that from a longer time perspective that Roberts Island emerged during a time of environmental fluctuation—of rising and falling sea levels. We argue that the lowering of sea levels may have contributed to the decline of Crystal River as a center for settlement and ceremony, and Roberts Island emerged to fill this gap (Pluckhahn et al. 2015). Recently, we conducted stable isotope analysis of oysters to examine both the timing of mound construction as well as the season of occupation of both the Crystal River site and Roberts Island (Thompson et al. 2015). Our results indicate collection of oysters occurred throughout the year for the midden areas of Roberts Island and the Crystal River site, during the later phases of occupation (Phase 3 and 4). The oysters that came from the mound contexts evidenced collection during the cooler months of the year, with the ones from Roberts Island either being collected during fall/winter or winter (Thompson et al. 2015: Figure 9). Such rapid feast events have been identified at other sites in the region as well (see Wallis and Blessing 2015).

While we did not sample deep into the core of the mound at Roberts Island, the radiocarbon dates and the stable isotope analysis of oysters all point towards rapid construction. In addition, the formality of these mounds with stepped pyramid appearance speaks to a planned architectural design. Given that the upper levels of Roberts Island emerged in a time of a fluctuation with rising sea level, we suggest that as the final abandonment of the Crystal River site was taking place, its inhabitants along with people from possibly other communities transposed the traditions established at the Crystal River site to Roberts Island in rapid fashion, thus re-creating and re-envisioning its landscape again. In the following section, we consider this the nature of the transposition of such traditions in more detail by examining the layout of both these sites to explore the historic connections between them.

Based on our above review of the data from Roberts Island, we consider it an anthropogenic landform, in other words, a mound-island—an island brought into being because of human action. It would be easy, of course, to discuss mound-islands simply in terms of the built environment. However, this would obscure what we think was an integral part of how such land forms in the first place. We view these features as not the imposition of some conceived plan on the landscape, or as a deterministic reaction to environmental change, but rather as a structured feature that people created as a result of dwelling in these places (*sensu* Heidegger 1971; Ingold 1993, 2000; Thomas 2001).

While we argue that mound-islands are a product of dwelling, we recognize that history and action structure the form that such islands take. Roberts Island as a whole represents flows of movement and creations at various time scales. Sometimes the actions that were at work to create the island operated over longer time scales, such as the accumulation of the midden-mounds. Others appear to be rapid events such as the construction of the stepped platform mounds during rituals and ceremonies in the winter months. These actions come together as part of a constructed landscape that incorporates both ceremonial events and daily life in one place.

As Ingold (2012: 160) notes, we can only understand the nature of things by focusing on the "history of relations that have brought it there." We argue the layout and form that Roberts Island eventually took represents such histories. We suggest that Roberts Island was part of a larger tradition among groups in the Crystal River area, which began with the founding of the Crystal River site itself. We concede that this proposition rests on the assumption that there were direct historical connections between the people of Roberts Island and Crystal River. However, the similarities in ceramics, close proximity of the sites, potential overlaps in occupation, and, as illustrated below, overall form make this a plausible scenario.

Traditions, as defined by Pauketat (2001a, 2001b) are actions brought from the past into the present. We suggest that paths of movement, particularly through places of dwelling, represent a type of tradition that archaeologists can infer through the analysis of site layout. In a recent paper, we (Pluckhahn and Thompson 2013) suggest that one of the distinguishing characteristics of the Crystal River site is the quality and form of its monuments, especially compared to other areas of the central Florida Gulf Coast (e.g., Cedar Key area). To illustrate this we draw on Smith's (2007) concepts of architectural planning and suggest that Crystal River exhibits a higher degree of axiality, orthogonality, symmetry, and use of plazas, formal entrances, and walls than other sites.

Similar to the Crystal River site, Roberts Island incorporates a degree of axiality, which we take as incorporating straight lines (Pluckhahn and Thompson 2013). Mound A, the larger midden-mound, and the water court form a central axis of the site, lending a certain degree of symmetry to the site as a whole. However, a few features are offset from this axis. In terms of orthogonality, this refers to the use of right angles; both the linear ridge and Mound B form perpendicular offsets to Roberts Island. At the level of individual architecture, Mound A exhibits a high degree of orthogonality and is paralleled only by other monuments at the Crystal River site, which itself is without peer in Florida (Pluckhahn and Thompson 2013). In addition, in terms of the vertical axis, mounds A and B incorporate orthogonality in their stepped construction. While these are not right angles, they are similar to angles represented in mound architecture at Crystal River.

We suggest several features that can be formal entrances and plazas at Roberts Island. First, Mound B fronts the waters of Crystal River, and all who entered from the river would have encountered this mound, moving over it to get to the rest of the island. We note that this would be an obvious marker for any traveler along the water. Once over the mound, visitors would encounter the plaza area, affronting Mound A, which also has a formal ramp on this side, as we note earlier. This parallels many of the formal ramps and areas at the Crystal River site (see Pluckhahn and Thompson 2013). Thus, anyone entering Roberts Island from the river on the western side of the island would encounter the stepped mounds and plaza. We doubt the symbolism of such encounters would be lost on visitors to the island. In contrast, the linear ridge of shell on the eastern side of the island allows direct access to the water court and the midden-mounds that make up the eastern portion of the island.

By no means are Roberts Island and the Crystal River site identical in their layouts. However, they do share more similarities with each other than any other site in the region thus far examined in terms of axiality, orthogonality, symmetry, and the use of plazas and formal entrances. We argue that such similarities were variations on historical traditions that were part of the lived experience of the inhabitants, in particular, how the arrangement of architecture at both places structured the way in which people moved through and within these landscapes. We argue that instead of replicating exactly the plan of Crystal River, the inhabitants of Roberts Island conformed to general themes of movement in both the architecture and middens they created through the work of daily life. The transposition of these traditions of movement and dwelling from the past (i.e., Crystal River) to the present (Roberts Island) represents a part of the history of relationships that brought Roberts Island into being. One of the key factors, as we will discuss, that played a large role in the transposition of these traditions from site to site is the importance of shellfishing—specifically oyster.

Traditions and shellfish

Rodning et al. (2016) recently invoked the creation myth of the Chitimacha to discuss the nature of mounds in wetlands for their work in Louisiana (see Charles et al. 2004 for an earlier reading of the earth diver creation myth to Hopewell mounds). In the myth, water covers the world, and there is no land for humans. The creator sends crawfish down to bring earth up and spread it around to create dry lands. Our point here is that like the crawfish, humans too create land. Again, not because of some master plan, but rather as a part of being in such environments. However, the Chitimacha myth, while instructive, is perhaps not relevant for this portion of the Gulf Coast. Therefore, we suggest to understand the relationships that people have with past monuments, we must not only look to the traditions that they carry over from their ancestors, but also their relationship with other species in the context of dwelling within their environments. For the present case, we suggest that one of the key things that we need to consider is the role of the oysters among the inhabitants of the Crystal River region.

It is perhaps tempting to view oysters as simply raw materials for the construction of land or mounds. In fact, one reviewer of another publication suggested that we had perhaps made too much of the relationship between the people and what they thought of oysters. After all, the reviewer noted, we build our houses out of wood, but I don't have a symbolic relationship with it. We feel that such a perspective fundamentally ignores the relational ontologies of Native societies and undertheorizes the role that species have in the shaping of traditions and cosmologies. In fact, there are several contextual reasons why shellfish, and oysters in particular, played a prominent role in Crystal River society.

One of the key indicators that oysters were symbolically important is their inclusion in burials in the region. Although there are no known burials at Roberts Island, numerous burials were excavated in the early 1900s and in the 1950s by archaeologists and antiquarians at the Crystal River site. In the burial mound complex (Mounds C–F), there were burials capped with oysters. Clearly their inclusion in some of the burials suggests some form of symbolic connections between the dead, the living, and these shellfish. It is tempting to speculate that because oysters spend part of their life underwater and another part exposed by the falling tide, the way in which they experience the world is much like that of humans. This cyclical ebb and flow of being among the living and then submerged in the underworld would not have been lost on the inhabitants of the region. Perhaps the inclusion and capping of burials with oysters was meant to reference this relationship.

In addition to burial traditions, we draw some parallels in the use of oysters to construct mound-islands and the way in which oysters grow along the Gulf Coast. The creation of mound-islands such as Roberts Island and mounds and middens of Crystal River involve the superpositioning of oyster deposits on top of other deposits. In some of these mounds, this involves the superpositioning of burials on top of older interments, in essence, placing the decedents over the ancestors. Again, the interesting parallel is that oyster bars also grow in this fashion; in fact, the health of a reef often depends upon a substrate made up of prior dead shells. Thus, in a way, oyster bars are a natural type of shell island. We admit this is a bit of speculation on our parts. Regardless of what oysters actually meant to the inhabitants of the region, it is clear that their inclusion in these traditions is to some degree intentional and meaningful. There are many ethnographic examples where decedents of particular groups view previous shell middens as the mounds of the ancestors, and part of the understanding of them as such involves referencing certain animals found in the middens. For example, Meehan (1982) notes older shell middens in parts of Australia were thought to be part of the dreamscape and created by the ancestors. McNiven (2013) also stresses the importance of middens' contents in the connection between food supply and the ancestors for the Torres Islanders. Thus, as McNiven and Wright state:

> Mounded midden features were constant visual reminders to the residents of Goemu that their everyday social activities, such as the use of cooking stones and the procurement and consumption of dugong, turtle, fish and shellfish, had historical continuities with the everyday social lives of their ancestors.
> *McNiven and Wright 2008: 145; McNiven 2013: 576*

In addition, the living oyster bars that gradually accrete with generations of new oysters could be viewed as an analog for the mound-islands as each new ritual feast and burial of the dead added to the histories of these places. Thus, both humans and oysters are history-dependent species.

Our final point regarding the importance of oysters in the Crystal River landscape is indicated by the shift and transposition of traditions from the Crystal River landscape to that of Roberts Island. As we point out above, during the sixth to ninth centuries AD we see the decline of Crystal River and the elaboration of architecture at Roberts Island. We link this shift to changes in sea levels and availability of oysters (see Thompson et al. 2015). We argue that as sea levels lowered, groups had to go farther towards the Gulf to gather oysters. However, Crystal River and Roberts Island are not that far apart, only around one kilometer. This does not seem to be such a significant distance. While there may be also other environmental factors that we cannot observe, the movement of the civic-ceremonial center might have been predicated, in part, for symbolical reasons, that is, to be closer to one of the most important entities in the landscape— the oyster beds. Again, whatever the case, the movement of the socio-political center closer to the beds out near the Gulf Coast indicates just how important oysters were to not only the maritime economy of the Crystal River region, but also the ritual and social aspects of these communities. In essence, this move could be interpreted as a statement of identity.

Conclusions

The nature of mound-island creation in the Crystal River area cannot be simply understood in economic and environmental terms. We suggest here that instead of viewing these places as static creations, they must be considered as part of a living landscape. In other words, we must understand these structures as being dynamically entangled with broader processes in the world of the inhabitants of the region. Such a perspective, as we point out, necessitates a reconceptualization of the built environment. This shift in thinking from western architectural terms to a more relational ontology allows us to explore the potential meanings of such structures and how the people who constructed them experienced such landscapes. As Hodder (2012: 10) notes, this line of thinking links us to the perspective that also considers such relationships from not only the viewpoint of people, but also of things, and in this case, the mounds and the species

Oysters and mound-islands in Florida

that comprise them. By taking this approach it also has forced us to consider the nature of the relationship that these people had with other species—the oyster in this case. We, of course, are not the first to consider this connection; however, our work in the Crystal River region indicates that there is more to the story than the oyster as being simply a lowly food or building material. This follows a worldwide pattern that traces a much more complex relationship with shellfish than earlier anthropological studies suggested.

Acknowledgments

This material is based upon work supported by the National Science Foundation under Grant No. 1026248. Additional support was provided by the Departments of Anthropology at the University of South Florida, the University of Georgia, the University of West Florida, and the Ohio State University. We thank the staff of the Crystal River Archaeological State Park, the Florida Department of Environmental Protection, the Florida Division of Historical Resources, and the Florida Public Archaeology Network for their support and enthusiasm. Finally, we appreciate the comments on our work by Suzie Pilaar Birch, Gavin Lucas, and Chris Witmore, which improved the overall quality of our chapter.

Note

1 All modeled start and end dates are reported at the 95% probability ranges. For details on the Bayesian modeling of these dates, see Pluckhahn et al. (2015).

References

Bailey, G. N. 2007. Time perspectives, palimpsests and the archaeology of time. *Journal of Anthropological Archaeology* 26, 198–223.

Beriault, J. G., R. S. Carr, M. Lance, and S. Bertone. 2003. A Phase I Archaeological Assessment of the Ten Thousand Islands Collier County, Florida (DHR Grant No. FO221). A.H.C. Technical Report No. 434. Archaeological and Historical Conservancy, Davie, Florida.

Burger, R. L., and R. M. Rosenswig (Eds.). 2012. *Early New World Monumentality*. University Press of Florida, Gainesville.

Charles, D. K., J. Van Nest, and J. E. Buikstra. 2004. From the earth: minerals and meaning in the Hopewellian world. In N. Boivin and M. A. Owoc (Eds.), *Soils, Stones, and Symbols: Cultural Perceptions of the Mineral World*. UCL Press, London, pp. 43–70.

Colquhoun, D. J. and M. J. Brooks. 1986. New evidence from the southeastern U.S. for eustatic components in the Late Holocene sea levels. *Geoarchaeology* 1, 275–291.

Cushing, F. H. 2000. *Exploration of Ancient Key-Dweller Remains on the Gulf Coast of Florida*. University Press of Florida, Gainesville.

Dickel, D. 1991. An Archaeological Survey of Collier County, Florida: Phase I. A.H.C. Technical Report #38. Archaeological and Historical Conservancy, Inc., Davie, Florida.

Gilleland, S. K. 2013. Finding the Floor: Construction History at Roberts Island. Unpublished honor's thesis, Department of Anthropology, University of South Florida, Tampa.

Heidegger, M. 1971. *Poetry, Language, Thought*, trans. A. Hofstadter. Harper and Row, New York.

Hodder, I. 2012. *Entangled: The Archaeology of the Relationships between Humans and Things*. Wiley-Blackwell, Oxford.

Ingold, T. 2012. *Being Alive: Essays on Movement, Knowledge, and Description*. Routledge, London.

Ingold, T. 2000. *The Perception of the Environment: Essays on Livelihood, Dwelling, and Skill*. Routledge, London.

Ingold, T. 1993. The temporality of the landscape. *World Archaeology* 25(2, Conceptions of Time and Ancient Society): 152–174.

Jefferies, R. W. 1994. The Swift Creek site and woodland platform mounds in the Southeastern United States. In *Ocmulgee Archaeology 1936–1986*, edited by D. J. Hally, pp. 71–83. University of Georgia Press, Athens.

Kidder, T. R. 2004. Plazas as architecture: an example from the Raffman site in northeast Louisiana. *American Antiquity* 69: 513–532.

Knight, V. J., Jr. 2001. Feasting and the emergence of platform mound ceremonialism in eastern North America. In *Feasts: Archaeological and Ethnographic Perspectives on Food, Politics, and Power*, edited by M. Dietler and B. Hayden, pp. 311–333. Smithsonian Institution Press, Washington, DC.

Kolianos, P. E., and B. R. Weisman. 2005. *The Lost Florida Manuscript of Frank Hamilton Cushing*. University Press of Florida, Gainesville.

Marquardt, W. H. 2010a. Shell mounds in the southeast: middens, monuments, temple mounds, rings, or works? *American Antiquity* 75: 551–570.

Marquardt, W. H. 2010b. Mounds, middens, and rapid climate change during the archaic–woodland transition in the southeastern United States. In *Trend, Tradition, and Turmoil: What Happened to the Southeastern Archaic?*, edited by D. H. Thomas and M. C. Sanger, vol. 93. Anthropological Papers of the American Museum of Natural History, New York, pp. 253–271.

Marquardt, W. H., and K. J. Walker. 2012. Southwest Florida during the Mississippian Period. In *Late Prehistoric Florida: Archaeology at the Edge of the Mississippian World*, edited by K. H. Ashley and N. M. White, pp. 29–61. University Press of Florida, Gainesville.

Marquardt, W. H., and K. J. Walker. 2013. The Pineland Site complex: An environmental and cultural history. In *The Archaeology of Pineland: A Coastal Southwest Florida Site Complex, A.D. 50-1710*, edited by W. H. Marquardt and K. J. Walker, pp. 793–920. Institute of Archaeology and Paleoenvironmental Studies, Monograph 4. University of Florida, Gainesville.

McNiven, I. J. 2013. Ritualized middening practices. *Journal of Archaeological Method and Theory*, 20(4): 552–587.

McNiven, I. J., and D. Wright. 2008. Ritualised marine midden formation in western Zenadh Kes (Torres Strait). In *Islands of inquiry: Colonisation, seafaring and the archaeology of maritime landscapes. Terra Australis 29*, edited by G. Clark, F. Leach, and S. O'Connor, pp. 133–147. Pandanus, Canberra.

Meehan, B. 1982. *Shell bed to shell midden* (No. 37). Australian Institute of Aboriginal Studies, Canberra.

Milanich, J. T. 1999. Introduction. In *Famous Florida Sites: Crystal River and Mount Royal*, edited by J.T. Milanich, pp. 1–28. University Press of Florida, Gainesville.

Milanich, J. T., A. S. Cordell, V. J. Knight, T. A. Kohler, and B. J. Sigler-Lavelle. 1997. *Archaeology of Northern Florida, AD 200–900: The McKeithen Weeden Island Culture*. University Press of Florida, Gainesville.

Moore, C. R., and V. D. Thompson. 2012. Animism and Green River persistent places: a dwelling perspective on the Shell Mound Archaic. *Journal of Social Archaeology* 12(2): 264–284.

Moore, C. B. 1900. Certain antiquities of the Florida West Coast. *Academy of Natural Sciences Journal* 11: 351–394.

Pauketat, T. R. 2001a. A new tradition in archaeology. In *The Archaeology of Traditions*, edited by T. R. Pauketat, pp. 1–16. University Press of Florida, Gainesville.

Pauketat, T. R. 2001b. Practice and history in archaeology: an emerging paradigm. *Anthropological Theory* 1(1): 73–98.

Pluckhahn, T. J. 2003. *Kolomoki: Settlement, Ceremony, and Status in the Deep South, AD 350 to 750*. University of Alabama Press, Tuscaloosa.

Pluckhahn, T. J. 1996. Joseph Caldwell's Summerour Mound (9FO16) and woodland platform mounds in the southeastern United States. *Southeastern Archaeology* 15(2), 191–211.

Pluckhahn T. J., V. D. Thompson, and W. J. Rink. 2016. Evidence for stepped pyramids of shell in the Woodland Period of eastern North America. *American Antiquity* 81(2): 345–363.

Pluckhahn, T. J., A. D. Hodson, W. J. Rink, V. D. Thompson, R. R. Hendricks, G. Doran, G. Farr, A. Cherkinsky, and S. P. Norman. 2015a. Radiocarbon and luminescence age determinations on mounds at Crystal River and Roberts Island, Florida, USA. *Geoarchaeology* 30: 238–260.

Pluckhahn, T. J., V. D. Thompson, and A. Cherkinsky. 2015b. The temporality of shell-bearing landscapes at Crystal River, Florida. *Journal of Anthropological Archaeology* 37: 19–36.

Pluckhahn, T. J., V. D. Thompson, and B. Weisman. 2010. Toward a new view of history and process at Crystal River (8CR1). *Southeastern Archaeology* 29(1): 164–181.

Pluckhahn, T. J., and V. D. Thompson. 2013. Constituting similarity and difference in the Deep South: the ritual and domestic landscapes of Kolomoki, Crystal River, and Fort Center. In *The Ritual and Domestic Landscapes of Early and Middle Woodland Peoples in the Southeast*, edited by Alice Wright and Edward Henry, pp. 181–195. University Press of Florida, Gainesville.

Pluckhahn, T. J., and V. D. Thompson. 2009. Mapping Crystal River: past, present, future. *The Florida Anthropologist* 62(1): 3–22.

Rodning, C. B., and J. M. Mehta. 2016. Resilience and persistent places in the Mississippi River Delta in Louisiana. In *Beyond Collapse: Archaeological Perspectives on Resilience, Revitalization, and Reorganization in Complex Societies*, edited by Ronald K. Faulseit. Southern Illinois University Press, Center for Archaeological Investigations Occasional Paper 42, Carbondale, IL.

Sampson, C. P. 2015. Oyster demographics and the creation of coastal monuments at Roberts Island Mound Complex, Florida. *Southeastern Archaeology* 34(1): 84–94.

Saunders, J. W., R. D. Mandel, R. T. Saucier, E. T. Allen, C. T. Hallmark, J. K. Johnson, . . . and R. Jones. 1997. A mound complex in Louisiana at 5400-5000 years before the present. *Science* 277(5333): 1796–1799.

Sassaman, K. 2010. *The Eastern Archaic, Historicized*. AltaMira, Lanham, MD.

Schwardron, M. 2010. Landscapes of Maritime Complexity: The Prehistoric Shell Works of the Ten Thousand Islands, Florida. Ph.D. Dissertation, Department of Archaeology and Ancient History, University of Leicester.

Sherwood, S. C., and T. R. Kidder. 2011. The DaVincis of dirt: geoarchaeological perspectives on Native American mound building in the Mississippi River basin. *Journal of Anthropological Archaeology* 30(1): 69–87.

Smith, M. E. 2007. Form and meaning in the earliest cities: a new approach to ancient urban planning. *Journal of Planning History* 6(1): 3–47.

Tanner, W. F. 1991. The "Gulf of Mexico" Late Holocene sea level curve and river delta history. *Gulf Coast Association of Geological Societies, Transactions* 41: 583–589.

Tanner, W. F. 2000. *Beach Ridge History, Sea Level Change, and the A. D. 536 Event. In The Years without Summer: Tracing the A.D. 536 Event and Its Aftermath*, edited by J. D. Gunn, pp. 89–97. BAR International Series 872. Archaeopress, Oxford.

Thomas, J. 2001. Archaeologies of place and landscape. In *Archaeological Theory Today*, edited by I. Hodder, pp. 165–186. Wiley-Blackwell, Oxford.

Thompson, V. D., T. J. Pluckhahn, O. Das, and C. F. T. Andrus. 2015. Assessing village life and monument construction *(cal. AD 65–1070)* along the Central Gulf Coast of Florida through stable isotope geochemistry. *Journal of Archaeological Science Reports* 4: 111–123.

Thompson, V. D. 2014. What I believe: reflections on historical and political ecology as research frameworks in Southeastern archaeology. *Southeastern Archaeology* 33: 246–254.

Thompson, V. D., and T. J. Pluckhahn. 2014. The modification and manipulation of landscape at Fort Center. In *Precolumbian Archaeology in Florida: New Approaches to the Appendicular Southeast*, edited by Neill Wallis and Asa Randall, pp. 163–182. University Press of Florida, Gainesville.

Thompson, V. D., and T. J. Pluckhahn. 2012. Monumentalization and ritual landscapes at Fort Center in the Lake Okeechobee Basin of South Florida. *Journal of Anthropological Archaeology* 31: 49–65.

Thompson, V. D., and J. Worth. 2011. Dwellers by the sea: Native American coastal adaptations along the southern coasts of eastern North America. *Journal of Archaeological Research* 19(1): 51–101.

Trigger, B. G. 1990. Monumental architecture: a thermodynamic explanation of symbolic behaviour. *World Archaeology* 22(2): 119–132.

Walker, K. J. 1992. The zooarchaeology of Charlotte Harbor's prehistoric maritime adaptation: spatial and temporal perspectives. In *Culture and environment in the Domain of the Calusa*, edited by W. H. Marquardt, pp. 265–366. Institute of Archaeology and Paleoenvironmental Studies, Monograph 1. University of Florida, Gainesville.

Walker, K. J. 2013. The Pineland Site Complex: environmental contexts. In *The Archaeology of Pineland: A Coastal Southwest Florida Site Complex, A.D. 50–1710*, edited by W. H. Marquardt and K. J. Walker, pp. 23–52. Institute of Archaeology and Paleoenvironmental Studies, Monograph 4. University of Florida, Gainesville.

Wallis, N. J., and M. E. Blessing. 2015. Big feasts and small scale foragers: Pit features as feast events in the American Southeast. *Journal of Anthropological Archaeology* 39: 1–18.

Wallis, N. J., P. S. McFadden, and H. M. Singleton. 2015. Radiocarbon dating the pace of monument construction and village aggregation at Garden Patch: a ceremonial center on the Florida Gulf Coast. *Journal of Archaeological Science: Reports*, 2: 507–516.

Weisman, B. R. 1995. The Roberts Island Shell Mound Complex and its archaeological significance. Manuscript 4365. Florida Mater Site File, Tallahassee.

10

MULTISPECIES DYNAMICS AND THE ECOLOGY OF URBAN SPACES IN ROMAN ANTIQUITY

Michael MacKinnon

Introduction

Urban environments host multiple organisms, which interact in myriad ways. Although this may seem obvious, dissecting the complexities surrounding this phenomenon proves challenging. Traditional accounts of the rise of urbanism typically focus upon the ancient Near East. Thereafter, various civilizations emerge in places such as Egypt, the Indus Valley, the Aegean and Mediterranean, China, Mesoamerica, and South America. It is beyond the scope of this chapter to detail developments across each setting; rather, attention here focuses upon urban contexts during Roman antiquity, broadly between c. 500 BC to c. 500 AD. This period certainly cultivates a range of urbanized places (here defined broadly as any nucleated settlement, from large cities, to smaller towns, and including military settlements; for brevity, 'city' is used loosely to collect all 'urbanized' spaces under one term) which variously may experience processes of evolution, development, transformation, disintegration, and decline. Within such settings, however, regardless of size or character, reside both humans and non-humans. But, who is influencing whom, and in what ways? How might incorporation of a multi- and inter-species perspective yield insight into the wider realm of ecological and cultural operations, attitudes, and behaviors among occupants—human and non-human? These questions shape the agenda, explored largely using zooarchaeological evidence from ancient urban sites (including Pompeii, Ostia, Athens, Carthage).

Animals, nature, numbers, and the ancient city

Roman cities variously characterized—physically and symbolically—the notion of civilization (Lomas 1997: 22). Still, as with many cultures, producer/consumer relationships interlinked town and country in antiquity. Defining the whereabouts of 'nature' in Roman antiquity is arguably complex, given 'nature' is a constructed concept (Sabloff 2001: 25), whose location, characteristics, and perception among individuals, let alone cultures, may vary. Is a city a place where 'nature is not?' (Sabloff 200: 12). At one level, urban environments can modify or disrupt natural environments; for example, turning grasslands into arable fields, clearing woodlands, adding pollutants into the biosphere, upsetting ecological niches among wild animals, and so forth. Alternatively, urban environments might create new kinds of 'nature,' such as parks,

Multispecies dynamics in Roman antiquity

gardens, yards, etc., with their own suite of species, introduced via human or other means. In some cases, this built environment may even be viewed as 'natural,' a concept that challenges notions of any bifurcation of nature. Animal 'inhabitants' in cities, thus, can arrive through various means, for various reasons. As pack animals, partners in labor, pets, or providers of consumable and/or non-consumable resources, animals may be considered perhaps more purposeful additions to a city. However, urban settings can also attract opportunistic and commensal species (some tolerated, other deemed as pests), which might be drawn to find food and shelter within the new environment, and for which competition may be reduced by the exclusion of less adaptable taxa. Overall, this diversity, in both scale and purpose, presupposes fairly commonplace incorporation of animals within Roman urban settings. Consequently, they do not seem 'out-of-place'; indeed, their relative omnipresence finds comment among some ancient sources (e.g., Ausonius, *Epistolarum liber* 18.6.25–26, remarks on urban traffic chaos caused by loose dogs, pigs, and ox-drawn carts).

How many animals might inhabit, or otherwise populate, a Roman city? Estimations are always problematic. Rough figures for consumable livestock to provision imperial Rome, annually, might range from a low of approximately 60,000 pigs, 2,000 sheep and goats, and 7,500 cattle, to a high of ten times these numbers (MacKinnon 2013: 122). Incorporate estimates for domestic fowl (100,000+ birds); horses, donkeys, mules and other traction animals (c. 5,000–10,000); pets (c. 5,000–10,000); exotics for shows and games (c. 1,000); sacrificial animals (c. 20,000–50,000), and the tally increases, augmenting more if one includes all types of birds, game animals and fish, stray cats and dogs, and rodents like mice and rats (MacKinnon 2013: 122). Rome, a unique 'mega-city,' tips towards figural extremes, but nonetheless highlights that the mix of animals transported to, and operating, or otherwise residing in, any ancient Roman urban setting clearly provides a rich foundation for exploration of inter- and multispecies dynamics. Focus here centers upon three domains: (i) commodity animals, (ii) pet animals, and (iii) commensal and scavenger animals.

Commodity animals in Roman urban environments

The notion of animals as representing or symbolizing concepts such as property, wealth, or commodity is not new (see Russell 2012 for greater discussion and further references; indeed, as regards Roman antiquity, the Latin terms for money/wealthy '*pecunia*' and livestock/flock '*pecus*' are interconnected). Furthermore, how such is codified or conceived may be multidimensional and complex (e.g., economic, social, spiritual, etc.). It is not my intent here to dissect this topic, but rather to illustrate how a multispecies initiative might frame newer perspectives for its investigation among Roman urban environments. The first example involves comparison of meat consumption between rural and urban sites for Roman Italy (MacKinnon 2004). Although not perfect, the ancient textual sources yield some indication of costs for various animals and their products (MacKinnon 2004: 204–11). Following those guidelines, available zooarchaeological evidence, in turn, indicates Roman cities in Italy imported relatively more animals and animal parts of greater wealth than their rural counterparts (MacKinnon 2004: 211–27). Rural sites, on average, contain a greater proportion of older livestock, implying relatively more younger-aged livestock could be marketed, for larger profit, in urban locales, where a wider concentration of elites resided. Urban sites further register, on average (and standardized for taphonomic biases), especially in the case for pigs and sheep/goats, a higher frequency of bones associated with 'primary cuts' of meat, arguably linked with better-quality, more succulent, fattier parts of the skeleton (e.g., ribs, upper limbs) (MacKinnon 2004: 192–204). The commoditization of animals with concomitant social-value or 'wealth' labeling attributed to age classes, resources, and body parts among these examples is not particularly restricted to Roman urban sites—rural sites might similarly desire and display these aspects—but available zooarchaeological evidence reinforces a central role of urban settings in catalyzing and concentrating such trends. Some manner of inter-species engagement may be postulated here with humans shaping livestock husbandry patterns (including manipulation of age and sex profiles), consequent with culturally defined systems of wealth and property.

This inter-species, co-shaping framework can be extended further if one considers that parts of animals, as well as whole animals, were variously marketed and consumed within Roman cities. Returning to the example of Roman Italy, the presence of faunal remains from all parts of cattle, sheep/goat, and pig skeletons within domestic assemblages from urban centers likely denotes that at least some of these animals were purchased whole. As such, some element of human choice in selection or manipulation of specific qualities these taxa exhibited may be at play (beyond age—as indicated above, assuming consumption of younger animals held social value more universally in Roman antiquity). A comparison of pig bone measurements for Roman Italy indicates a greater range in values among rural sites—a logical connection given this is where the bulk of breeding operations occurred (MacKinnon 2001: 661). Urban sites, by contrast, generally show more restricted size ranges, indicative perhaps of fairly regimented and organized systems, wherein only pigs of a certain weight or size were brought in and slaughtered (MacKinnon 2001: 657, 661). Correlative evidence for regularization as regards weights, quality, and condition of animals and meat cuts surfaces in ancient textual records for ancient Rome as well, most concretely within the Theodosian Code of AD 367. Overall, the notion of some degree of standardization of marketed/consumed livestock in urban settings provides an additional dimension to engage inter-species relationships. In part, standardization schemes may 'homogenize' choice among urbanites, perhaps leveling some measure of quality control or assurance to facilitate cultural cohesion. At the same time, however, such schemes can shape conditions among affected animals, for example, by breeding out diversity in livestock weights (among other traits), or by culling specific varieties/breeds of livestock that conform best to whatever culturally embedded value or choice is being subscribed.

Manipulation of traits highlights a much larger topic: creation of animal 'breeds' or 'varieties' (the latter, in the case of antiquity, perhaps a better term than 'breed' which connotes genetic understanding). Essentially, in 'breed' selection, potentially multidimensional aspects within the animal have been reduced to one or a few selected attributes deemed useful to human manipulation. Embedded within is not only agency in inter-species dynamics, but perhaps augmented perception of animals as artifacts—things to be created and developed by humans—than as uniquely sentient beings.

Investigating 'breed' development for Roman antiquity is complex (MacKinnon 2010b). Ancient textual and iconographic evidence provide some indication of different 'phenotypes' or 'varieties' within any single species of animal, but how these are described, classified, or represented can be vague, piecemeal, anecdotal, referential, or otherwise confusing. Zooarchaeological data can help to demarcate phenotypic ranges and clusters within species—economically, through assessment of morphometric patterns from recovered bones; in addition, through DNA analyses (where deeper genetic patterns can ultimately be isolated and explored). Human agency generally assumes an instrumental (if not sole) role in trait selection, but realities may be more multifaceted and interwoven, and greater appreciation should be given to contributions animals themselves may have in shaping trajectories (Sykes 2014). Additionally, deeper exploration of inter-species linkages might require a sub-branch examining sympatric relations between and among various 'breeds' within a species. To illustrate, available zooarchaeological metric data show patterns confirming the existence and cultural promotion of distinct 'varieties' of cattle across different regions of Roman Italy. New 'breeds' were created through selective manipulation of traits (e.g., taller, shorter, stronger, wider, heavier), choices of which largely catered to varying demands for aspects such as milk yield, meat, traction power, durability, and other characteristics, depending on temporal and regional circumstances. Multiple reasons might underlie such changes: military and demographic demands for foodstuffs; increasing implementation of ley farming; imports and generation of better-quality fodder, marketing regulations and decisions; competition among herders and farmers; import of new breeds, and cultural shifts in the care, value, or role of cattle (MacKinnon 2010b). No doubt numerous conditions might apply. Nevertheless, ultimately shaped in these landscapes are not simply new 'breeds' of animals, but new dynamics under which such 'breeds' now need to exist, co-exist, or even interact and interbreed, should the latter scenarios arise or be permitted.

Attention has focused thus far on domestic mammalian livestock (cattle, sheep/goat, pig) among Roman urban contexts. What role did other taxa play? Wild animals represent one important category, especially given such were generally luxury foods in Roman antiquity. Venison is specifically linked to wealthier diets, wild hare was an expensive delicacy, and wild boar is often mentioned alongside ostentatious feasting (MacKinnon 2004). Roman cities, thus, could capitalize on any socially constructed dietary demand for wild game; after all, they appear to be importing a larger frequency of more expensive types and cuts of meat from domestic livestock. Yet, curiously under-represented among such sites typically are remains of wild animals. Their NISP values among contexts for Pompeii, for example, remain relatively stable, under 1 percent, from the sixth century BC until the city's destruction in 79 AD (King 2002). Wild animals are equally insignificant at key urban sites including Ostia (MacKinnon 2014a), Rome (MacKinnon 2013) and Athens (MacKinnon 2014b). Whereas dietary requests for wild animals by the urban elite may potentially have been high, such might not have been met on a practical level, where neighboring lands were often utilized for other resources or simply not conducive to stocking wild animals. Competition by pigs, which could forage easily in forested regions and were in great demand as foodstuffs, may have further contributed to the reduction, possibly even extirpation, of wild game outside Roman cities.

A case study from Carthage, Tunisia adds further insight (MacKinnon 2010a). Similar to contexts in Italy, wild animals never constitute any significant portion of total NISP frequency values during occupation phases at ancient Carthage. Figures do rise over time, however, from 0.1 percent among Punic levels to 0.7 percent during Roman antiquity—a seven-fold increase, but still a minor contribution overall. Limited forested land existed around Carthage for game to inhabit naturally, and what was once there was probably destroyed very early on as agriculture expanded, especially during Roman times. Land or sea transport of wild animals from further abroad seems unlikely given associated complications and expenses. It seems Carthage satisfied urban demands for game by diversifying the stock consumed, through space-restricted aviaries, small game preserves, and most especially warrens for rabbits and hares. The latter constitutes the single most important wild animal taxon for Roman levels in Carthage, and could have been easily managed as a peripheral commodity alongside other crop and animal husbandry pursuits on suburban mixed farms. Also noteworthy is that Roman contexts see the broadest diversification of bird and fish species in the Carthaginian diet as well, compared to Punic levels. Clearly, the faunal data support an increased segment of elites at Roman Carthage, a social class cognizant of the importance of conspicuous consumption and gourmet foods, and with significant agency to shape animal husbandry operations in the city's hinterland.

As examples from Pompeii and Carthage indicate, large-sized wild mammals (e.g., deer, boar) were generally infrequent additions among urban assemblages. What about smaller-sized wild animals? Roman iconography provides numerous examples of landscape and garden scenes in which wild birds, including thrushes and other songbirds, factor (Toynbee 1973; Jashemski 1979; Sparkes 1997). Some specimens could derive from specialized aviaries set up in wealthier suburban or rural villas, smaller examples of which might also have existed in gardens, orchards, or vineyards of elite urban homes. Pigeons/doves were similarly maintained in aviaries, perhaps in cotes or pens on rooftops in urban areas remarked upon in several ancient sources (Juvenal 3.201–2; Plautus, *Miles Gloriosus* 162; Manilius, *Astronomica* 5.364–80). Dormice, another Roman culinary delicacy typically bred in suburban and rural locales, also need not be restricted solely to these places and could be raised within urban settings.

While urban sites provided potential (and culturally created) habitats for wild birds and consumed rodents, supportive archaeological evidence for such practices is more tenuous. Specialized jars (i.e., *gliraria, vivaria in doliis*) apparently used to fatten dormice were recovered among excavations at Pompeii, Rome, and other urban sites (Colonnelli et al. 2000). Various structures, including niches in walls, possible watering-troughs, garden fountains and makeshift shelters, all of which have been identified, especially among excavations in Pompeii, may provide some clues for birding (Johnson 1971: 78), but not without conjecture. Zooarchaeological evidence for production and consumption of smaller wild birds and dormice within Roman cities is equally problematic, due to biases associated with recovery, identification, and reporting of such taxa. Unusually high frequencies of dove bones from the sites of Dorchester and Caerwent in Roman Britain probably indicate some measure of husbandry for food and manure (O'Connor 2013: 54), but in most cases wild birds and dormice comprise only a tiny fraction of overall zooarchaeological counts. Nevertheless, despite concerns for drastic under-representation of smaller wild taxa, one still finds a remarkable array of them among Roman urban sites (Watson 2002; King 2002), many of which appear removed from their preferred ecological habitats, suggesting in turn some scheme of 'managing' these animals within an urban setting. Such efforts, inherently a display of control over nature, through, in some cases, inadvertent caging or mixing of taxa, certainly could act to enhance the cultural value of such animals, even if their overall caloric addition to the general diet was very minor.

Within the examples presented, humans obviously assume some agency in variously destroying, reshaping, creating, or otherwise modifying habitats for wild animals, but animals are not always passive in these processes. Different parameters may apply. At one level, inter-species competition, such as domestic pigs foraging in forested lands and upsetting ecological balances, yields a somewhat concrete application, fixed within Darwinian principles of competition and survival. At another level, animals may provide cultural incentives to initiate what might be considered 'unnatural,' 'artificial,' 'managed,' 'controlled' settings for their exploitation, in turn, prompting perhaps some reconsideration of the definition of 'wild animal' overall for taxa that might inhabit such spaces (be this on their own accord, or through human capture and placement). Additionally, by bringing 'nature' and its 'wild animals' into urban environments, calls to re-evaluate the wider concept of 'nature' might be warranted. Is 'managed' nature still nature or are there degrees to which this might be classified depending upon aspects such as location (rural/urban), scale, size, cultural philosophy, types of animals, etc.? Such questions are beyond the scope of this current overview, but nevertheless provide possible directions for future work. In this regard, the concepts developed by Latour (1991), who explores the dualistic divide modernity makes between nature and society, may prove fruitful in assessing patterns.

If Roman urban landscapes could be loci where wild taxa might be kept or otherwise 'managed,' might domestic food animals also be raised and 'managed' within cities? Clearly this occurred, but details are elusive. As regards types, domestic fowl and pigs factor among the better candidates as each might tolerate confined conditions or other restrictions or limitations

Multispecies dynamics in Roman antiquity

urban settings can present. Certainly this does not preclude sheep, goats, and cattle, but, notwithstanding traction or working cattle (and equids, not typically eaten), some of which were stabled specifically in cities for work within, these taxa typically associate with rural settings. Livestock numbers in and around Roman cities would obviously fluctuate on the basis of seasonal husbandry scheduling (e.g., transhumance), culling episodes, and festival events, among other cultural and ecological factors, but long-term, fixed urban residency for any significant number of livestock would likely be limited, excepting perhaps some domestic fowl and pigs.

Zooarchaeological investigation of domestic fowl among Pompeiian households indicates fairly consistent dietary contribution throughout antiquity. Values range from 3 percent at the House of Postumii to 9 percent at the House of the Gilded/Golden Cupids. To what degree recovery and taphonomic biases, cultural variables such as taste (i.e., dietary preference for fowl), economics (e.g., easier acquisition of chickens), or social constructs (i.e., birds as a dietary symbol of wealth), factor among results is difficult to prove; no doubt several reasons apply. Some urbanites may have raised poultry on their premises (e.g., garden, *atrium* and *peristyle* courtyards, or back rooms—with birds given free access, kept in smaller cages, or otherwise penned off); however, space was limited, and considerations for health, safety, escape of birds, and aesthetics of garden/*peristyle* settings would likely affect practices. Consequently, it seems reasonable to postulate that the bulk of domestic fowl consumed within Pompeii, and more broadly Roman cities in general, probably derived from birds imported from neighboring farms.

The sites of Ostia (MacKinnon 2014a) and Athens (MacKinnon 2014b) provide further texture to the issue. Although domestic fowl still comprise only a small percentage of NISP counts across Roman levels at these sites, their contribution increases slightly moving from Imperial times into late antiquity, and they are relatively more ubiquitous across contexts. Does this represent a greater incidence of intra-urban production of poultry birds? The presence now of juvenile domestic fowl adds further support for urban household production, given that typically such young birds would be relatively easily collected (alongside eggs) from birthing hens kept in a courtyard or household coop.

If some chickens were raised within urban settings in antiquity, what about other animals? Some of our best evidence for stalling or otherwise keeping animals within ancient cities comes from Pompeii. A number of excavated skeletons of equids and dogs, which perished in the AD 79 eruptions, are noted. Among these, five equid skeletons (four donkeys and one mule), all males, and aged between 4–9 years were recovered from a front room, bordering the street at the House of the Chaste Lovers (IX.12.6) (King 2002: 424). These were probably employed as pack animals to transport bakery goods at this household/shop. In another case, an articulated skeleton of a mule was found slumped over a wooden manger or trough against a back room in the House of Amarantus (I.9.12) (Fulford and Wallace-Hadrill 1998: 87). This individual was likely tethered to the wall, unable to escape. Pinned under its leg was a skeleton of a dog, itself showing no signs it was secured. Presumably this dog could have escaped, unless otherwise trapped or prevented. Regardless, this example illustrates that some animal stalls within the city were shared premises, in turn sparking curiosity of inter-species relationships. Did this mule and dog tolerate one another? What type of bond was created?

Excluding the cases above, no other skeletons of penned, chained, or otherwise trapped mammals (specifically cattle, pigs, sheep, and goats) have been recovered from Pompeiian houses. This does not imply none were kept or raised inside the city, just that such seems an uncommon event at domestic households *per se*. Nonetheless, some pigs likely rummaged the streets consuming urban waste, as is documented for medieval cities (Keene 1982), and inferred in several ancient sources (Plautus, *Captivi* 4.1.807–8; Horace, *Epist.* 2.2.72–5; Ausonius, *Epistolarum liber* 10.6.25–6). Zooarchaeological data indicate breeding of a larger, fat variety of pig in Roman antiquity that could best assume such a role (MacKinnon 2001: 665). Moreover, despite the noise they might make, the occasional stock was probably penned, even if temporarily in some houses. Back portions of houses adjacent to alleyway entrances provide possible spots, especially as suits larger animals like equids and cattle, while smaller stock could have been housed temporarily in back rooms, courtyards, or cellars, where present. Additionally, rooms damaged in the AD 62 earthquake at Pompeii could have been transformed into pens or holding yards fairly easily. In fact, opportune use of such damaged or neglected/abandoned spaces (themselves created through remodeling, decline, destruction, etc. of city settings) may have been rather commonplace among urban environments overall in antiquity. Recall above that the frequency of domestic fowl increases into late antiquity at both Ostia and Athens. While a number of factors might contribute to this pattern, both sites experienced periods of decline or flux at this time, in turn creating some disturbed/abandoned/neglected settings for opportunistic intra-urban poultry production.

Incorporation of food animals into urban networks certainly brings opportunities and challenges as regards their production, habitat, care and general livelihood. Humans assume active roles here, but animals are not passive in their otherwise economically based exploitation as 'wealth' or 'property.' Desired traits within animals act as enticers for humans to manipulate, creating 'breeds' of livestock. Such 'breeds,' in turn may assume larger roles in marking aspects such as territory, space, identity and power among humans: 'my prized, white Umbrian cow,' 'his strong, Campanian ox,' 'your snowy-white, soft-fleeced sheep,' 'her majestic, urban-stalled, horse.' Some reciprocal, behavioral, co-shaping is evident here. In another case, otherwise 'unnatural' urbanized settings may become new habitats for some animals (e.g., domestic fowl, selected livestock, 'managed' wild animals), with perhaps a greater degree of agency conferred upon these animals in shaping human behaviors, than vice-versa (e.g., 'I started it, and then it took a life of its own'). Even the fact that livestock engage in Roman urban life, overall—where they are not simply tolerated, but perhaps accepted and commonplace—helps shift understanding to reciprocal human/non-human interaction.

Pet animals in Roman urban environments

Perhaps no other topic carries as much potential for inter-species exploration than that of the pet. Abundant studies exist on pets, from surveys across the ages, including Roman antiquity (e.g., Toynbee 1973), to wider philosophical reflections about the role, meaning, place, and even definition of pet (MacKinnon 2014c). Undoubtedly, bonds are structured and experienced in particular ways, and often, at least in many modern contexts, modeled on relations between human beings (Sabloff 2001: 58). Pets can become 'kin,' which affords a whole set of metaphorical and symbolic associations to, and reactions from, humans.

Though this chapter does not offer an exhaustive review of pets among Roman sites, in large part, urban and rural sites show similarities as regards types and relative frequencies. Nonetheless, closer inspection for dogs reveals a pattern specific to urban sites. Although small lap- and toy-varieties of pet dogs register in fifth-century BC Aegean contexts, the Romans appear largely responsible for their subsequent breeding and spread (MacKinnon 2014c: 272). Such breeds, however, typically appear first in Roman cities, regardless of location, presumably reflecting principal trade networks, themselves fueled by augmented, or at least aggregate, demands from urban elite for novel products, including pet dogs. Here again, the metaphor of animal symbolizing wealth and prestige surfaces, but engrained within the concept of pet as opposed to product (although these can certainly be interwoven concepts). Urban centers appear to drive this phenomenon to a larger degree than other contexts in antiquity, with varieties of lap-dogs yielding particular influence (perhaps control) upon human behavior. The arthritic, and nearly toothless, Maltese-type, toy breed of dog recovered from a Roman cemetery at Carthage could not have survived into its old age with such advanced osteological ailments without human care and devotion (MacKinnon 2010c: 302–5). However, the burial of this animal among humans, in a separate grave, and with a special glass vessel (grave goods are scarce otherwise), elevates its status even more—probably to 'kin,' perhaps even 'master,' one might argue—considering the special and unique burial it received. Clearly, the inter-species dynamic between humans and pets can assume multiple levels of complexity, made even more tangible in urban settings where pressures for ostentation, competition, and status recognition may be quite strong.

Commensal and scavenger animals in Roman urban environments

While urban sites of antiquity incorporate their share of food, work, and pet animals, they also house varieties of commensal and scavenger animals. The numeric rise and spread of mice, rats, and other commensal animals, such as pigeons and sparrows, is often associated with urbanization. As urbanization advances, through colonization and expansion, so do commensals. Similarly, as urban centers expand, opportunities for scavenger animals can intensify. Through their rummaging, pigs and dogs can undertake such roles, but one must also factor in scavenging birds (e.g., raptors, vultures, among others) and rodents (including mice and rats) within this niche. Again, it is important in any study of commensal and scavenger animals in Roman cities to acknowledge fluidity in defining, and engaging with, concepts. For example, a pig may simultaneously assume duties as scavenger and commodity. Dogs may be pets, work animals, scavengers, and social symbols. Mice and birds can similarly blend or cross roles and responsibilities. Such multidimensionality underscores a hallmark of inter-species relations and affords great potential to examine subsequent effects upon ecological and cultural operations and patterns in ancient urban contexts.

With the exception of some wider studies about ravens and crows in Roman culture, little work exists on the role of scavenger and commensal birds within Roman urban contexts, especially in areas outside of Roman Britain (O'Connor 1993, 2013). Analyses of microfaunal remains (i.e., recovered faunal materials from smaller animal taxa, such as rodents, small birds, etc.) from Roman sites are more abundant, but not without concerns. Recovery biases largely restrict available samples, while reports for many sites tend to overview ecological data for various species represented, with less attention paid to how microfaunal and human communities might interact. The presence, within some Roman cities, of gardens, vineyards, and orchards must have allowed populations of various voles, shrews, moles, rats, and mice to become well established. The wide array of microfauna noted, for example, at Pompeii and Nicopolis, Bulgaria (two sites where enhanced recovery of faunal remains was conducted) attest to this (King 2002; Parfitt 2007). Voles, moles, and shrews are represented more often at Roman rural than urban sites (MacKinnon 2004: 60), perhaps, predictably, an indication of less amenable niches for them in cities overall, but data are insufficient to qualify and quantify patterns more completely.

Rats and mice often receive greater attention for their roles among urban contexts. Origins and dispersals (through human means) have been traced: the Phoenicians and Greeks apparently inadvertently brought the house mouse (*Mus musculus*) into the western Mediterranean during the last millennium BC, while the Romans appear responsible for importing and dispersing the black rat (*Rattus rattus*), among other pests, throughout their empire (Cucchi and Vigne 2006).

However, interaction of mice, rats and humans to broader urban ecologies is increasingly a topic addressed. For example, the black rat first appeared in assemblages soon after the site of Nicopolis was founded in c. AD 108 (Parfitt 2007: 210). Thereafter it registers in small numbers until late Roman times, when its frequency sharply increases, coincident with the peak phase of occupation at the site. Parallel patterns arise, triggering rats as potential proxies for intensity of human occupation and use of a site. By contrast, values for the house mouse at Nicopolis show no marked fluctuations, perhaps indicative of its less-dependant reliance upon human occupation for survival (Parfitt 2007: 221).

The dynamics among microfauna communities inhabiting Roman urban settings provide interesting avenues for exploring adaptation and competition among species. Sieved contexts from the site of Roman Winchester yielded only a few remains of house mice and no definite rats, while Roman York and London recorded much higher values of each taxon (O'Connor 2013: 53). That the latter sites were ports suggests their mice and rat populations were heavily linked to trade via ships and carts (O'Connor 2013: 54). Reduction in trade networks, coupled with decline in urban living into late antiquity in Britain produced two pressures for rats: one in the form of fewer introductions of ship rats to sites, the other a habitat change that favored reduced reliance on human refuse and shelter. Rat populations failed to cope under these circumstances, but the better-adapted house mice maintained at least some populations at this time (O'Connor 2013: 90).

Competition and adaptation among microfauna has been explored at Pompeii. Zooarchaeological data indicate that rats appear rarely among contexts at Pompeii, limited to different pockets of the city (King 2002). The rat's sedentary nature, and fear of crossing paved spaces (McCormick 2003: 10), may have restricted its foothold in Pompeii, in turn yielding a better environment for house mice. The more commensal house mouse gradually outcompeted and replaced the wood mouse (*Apodemus sylvaticus*) as the city developed (Holt and Palazzo 2013: 142). Clearly house mice were best adapted for the urban niche, but not so during all seasons. Periodic influxes of wood mice into the city during the summer months, when heat and drought can reduce resources in their natural wild environments, may inadvertently factor in disease ecology and human mortality. Wood mice can be very dangerous in transmitting disease, including tick-borne encephalitis and the Hantavirus. Their migration to Pompeii could have augmented contact with house mice and humans, and possibly factored among other disease agents (especially malaria) to account for higher mortality rates that register in the Roman Mediterranean context during early autumn (Holt and Palazzo 2013: 143–7).

The role of animals within disease ecologies begs larger questions about hygiene, health, safety, and waste management in Roman urban settings. How might adopting a multispecies perspective shed light on such operations? Both human and non-human inhabitants generate waste, with all manner of dung, filth, and carcasses potentially littering streets in ancient urban settings. A population of c. 1,000,000 in early imperial Rome, for example, might potentially generate over 50,000 kg of body wastes daily (Scobie 1986: 413). Factoring in animal dung and urine, butchery and food waste, dead carcasses and related garbage increases such amounts. While efforts were variously made by city inhabitants to remove waste, animals also helped in this regard by consuming organic refuse and even excrement.

Despite efforts at waste removal, no doubt ancient cities fostered numerous pathogens, which thrived in areas of poor sanitation. Animals exacerbated disease transmission under these conditions, not only through contamination of living conditions, foodstuffs, and water supplies, but also through more direct routes, such as vectors for rabies, plague, and malaria (if one considers mosquitoes and fleas), and transmitters of zoonotic diseases (i.e., those passed to humans from to animals), including bovine tuberculosis. Uncontrolled roaming of animals, such as dogs and pigs, coupled with close living conditions between humans and animals, would augment disease complications. No doubt ancient Roman cities saw their share of health problems, as testified in numerous complaints about diseases found in the ancient sources, as well as diagnoses and cures for many of these as outlined in medical (e.g., Celsus' *De medicina*; Galen's volumes) and veterinary (e.g., Vegetius' *Mulomedicina*) texts.

Although the negative effects, in terms of exacerbated disease incidence, contamination, and so forth, tend to be stressed when one links animals to environments of poor sanitation, it should also be appreciated that animals and humans share microbes that may be mutually beneficial in terms of strengthening immune systems or simply in the sharing of helpful microbiota. The constant exchange of both good and bad microbiota between humans and animals adds a deeper level of complexity to multispecies dynamics (see Weyrich, this volume for further discussion).

Whatever the interplay between animals, humans, and microbiota, tracking the incidence and prevalence of disease, within urban settings in antiquity, through zooarchaeology, is challenging. Evidence is drawn primarily from the field of animal paleopathology, which itself carries concerns linked to osteological representation of ailments, identification of conditions, diagnosis of etiologies, and lack of modern comparative material for assessment, not to mention complications associated with taphonomy, preservation, and reporting of affected faunal remains (Upex and Dobney 2012). Case studies of 'interesting/unusual' specimens currently dominate most paleopathological publications; more emphasis on larger syntheses of pathological conditions, which themselves incorporate broader questions about human-animal and animal-animal relationships in the past, is necessary to advance understanding.

Exploration of tuberculosis provides one means of understanding human-animal dynamics from the zooarchaeological record. Tuberculosis (TB) is an enzootic disease in mammals, commonly affecting cattle, pigs, and carnivores (Upex and Dobney 2012: 195). TB infection in cattle can spread to humans via respiratory pathways, as well as through consumption of infected milk products or tissues. Crowded urban settings certainly may exacerbate disease transmission, TB included. Isolated cases of tuberculosis have been noted in the zooarchaeological record (Mays 2005), but data are too piecemeal to infer any wider trends among site types in Roman antiquity. Proximity of cattle to humans in some urban settings can introduce this condition, but it seems unlikely this was a central means of transmission. Larger animals (i.e. equids, cattle) penned or stalled in Roman cities were probably done so with some degree of separation from humans. Ancient sources contrast this more 'civilized' practice to that of barbarians who pen horses, cattle, and humans (and the related infections such company contributes) together (Tacitus, *Annales* 4.49), or to the oddity of the Egyptians, who apparently keep their animals with them within their houses (Herodotus, *Histories* 1.2.36).

Detailed work in recording and interpreting joint arthropathies in cattle, as evidence for their use as traction beasts, provides another potentially fruitful direction to pursue as regards urban inter-species dynamics (Bartosiewicz et al. 1997). Although documented examples for this condition are minimal overall, a preliminary overview for Roman Italy shows no difference in its incidence between urban and rural contexts, suggesting perhaps some equivalence as regards potential traction stresses (MacKinnon, personal observation). Roman cities, thus, presented their fair share of laborious work duties for cattle.

Lastly, more nuanced investigations of general stress indicators, such as enamel hypoplasia, might be helpful in assessing health effects in urban settings, perhaps as a condition of overall scalar stress such environments may produce. Studies have linked the occurrence of enamel hypoplasia in pigs to effects of different feeding regimes and the related environmental conditions under which such operate (Vanpoucke et al. 2007). A general review among Roman contexts indicates some variation among site types, with urban centers displaying a smaller incidence of enamel hypoplasia among pigs than rural locations (MacKinnon, personal observation). Samples are insufficient to afford firm conclusions, but should this pattern prove real, it might suggest urban contexts imported healthier pigs, among further conditions for animals of a certain age, weight, or size, as indicated earlier.

Conclusions

Urban environments are both physical and cultural worlds that usher in a host of settings and circumstances for exploration of multispecies perspectives, wherein one might best view humans and animals interacting variously as both agents and participants. As regards physical alterations, investigation for urban settings in Roman antiquity shows that new niches can be created, or otherwise arise, for animals to inhabit. Some domestic livestock can be stabled within urban sites, essentially providing a structured habitat, but also a type of proximity, for better (e.g., convenience to exploit, control, monitor, care for the animal), or for worse (e.g., augmented potential for zoonotic disease transmission). Space restrictions for some domesticates in urban spaces might be loosened, for example, in the case of urban production of domestic fowl or pigs. The urban footprint of these taxa might in turn be linked to periods of decline within the city, as noted by the rise of domestic fowl during phases of late antiquity. Wild animals, such as wild birds and smaller game, might be 'managed' in Roman antiquity, through the use of aviaries, warrens, and other means of bringing 'nature' into the city. Scavenger and commensal taxa, domestic or wild, also inhabit Roman urban settings, themselves interwoven into communities that compete for space and resources, and whose numbers and interrelationships shift and fluctuate in response to the ebb and flow of urban physical surroundings.

Culturally, animals fulfill multiple roles within urban systems. Within such, the human-animal relationship itself is not, strictly speaking, metaphoric in any symmetric sense, but perhaps better considered in roles that are complementary rather than analogous. Among such roles commonly identified, animals might be classified as agent, artifact, commodity, status marker, companion, friend, helper, provider, scavenger, recycler, pest, annoyance, transmitter of disease, among other duties, roles themselves which can span multiple domains within human culture (e.g., ecological, psychological, economical, dietary, social, etc.). Such roles are not exclusive to urban settings in Roman antiquity, but denser populations and aggregate demands for animals and their products within Roman cities had significant impact on hinterlands to supply urban contexts, which in turn affected multispecies ecologies. Co-shaping of behaviors, animal and human, is exhibited. Humans variously acted as agents in selecting and breeding traits in animals that suited their interests, with urban sites perhaps intensifying this in narrowing the ranges among the types, weights, and parts of animals ultimately marketed and consumed within cities. The congregation of wealth in Roman cities, however, not only augmented dietary ostentation, but influenced demand for other status products, including pet animals. The higher relative incidence of small lap-dogs among Roman urban sites testifies to a specialized role of animal as kin, especially given the unique care and treatment some of these pets were afforded.

Overall urban environments—in their guise as both physical and cultural settings—impart a multitude of factors and conditions that subsequently affect multispecies dynamics. Cities in Roman antiquity were no different in this regard. Focus within this chapter has centered upon the assessment of three general categories of animals in ancient Roman urban settings: animals as (i) commodities, (ii) pets, and (iii) commensal species. Certainly, as argued above, urban

Multispecies dynamics in Roman antiquity

settings in antiquity variously modified, framed, and developed how animals factored within each of these categories, but perhaps more importantly discussion further highlights the dynamism sometimes inherent among these categories themselves. One need look no further than the multiple roles assumed, often simultaneously, among animals in antiquity to appreciate the multidimensional basis for their assessment in past cultures.

References

Bartosiewicz, L., W. Van Neer and A. Lentacker. 1997. *Draught Cattle: Their Osteological Identification and History.* Tervuren.

Colonnelli, G., M. Carpaneto and M. Cristaldi. 2000. Uso alimentare e allevamento del ghiro *Myoxus glis* presso gli antichi romani: materiale e documenti. In G. Malerba, C. Cilli and G. Giacobini (eds.), *Atti del 2° Convegno Nazionale di Archeozoologia.* Forli, 315–25.

Cucchi, T. and J. Vigne. 2006. Origins and diffusion of the house mouse in the Mediterranean. *Human Evolution* 21: 95–106.

Fulford, M. and A. Wallace-Hadrill. 1998. The House of Amarantus at Pompeii (I.9.11–12). An interim report on survey and excavations in 1995–96. *Rivista di studi pompeiani* 7: 77–113.

Holt, E. and S. Palazzo. 2013. The role of rodents in the disease ecology of the Roman city. *Archaeological Review from Cambridge* 28: 132–54.

Jashemski, W. F. 1979. *The Gardens of Pompeii.* New Rochelle, NY.

Johnson, L. R. 1971. Birds for pleasure and entertainment in ancient Rome. *The Maryland Historian* 2: 77–92.

Keene, D. J. 1982. Rubbish in medieval towns. In A. R. Hall and H. K. Kenward (eds.), *Environmental Archaeology in the Urban Context.* London, 26–30.

King, A. 2002. Mammals: evidence from wall paintings, sculpture, mosaics, skeletal remains, and ancient authors. In W. F. Jashemski and F. G. Meyer (eds.), *The Natural History of Pompeii.* Cambridge, 401–50.

Latour, B. 1991. *We Have Never Been Alone.* Cambridge, MA.

Lomas, K. 1997. The idea of a city: elite ideology and the evolution of urban form in Italy, 200 BC–AD 100. In H. M. Parkins (ed.), *Roman Urbanism: Beyond the Consumer City.* London, 21–41.

MacKinnon, M. 2001. High on the hog: linking zooarchaeological, literary, and artistic data for pig breeds in Roman Italy. *American Journal of Archaeology* 105: 649–73.

——. 2004. *Production and Consumption of Animals in Roman Italy: Integrating the Zooarchaeological and Textual Evidence.* Portsmouth, RI: *Journal of Roman Archaeology* Supplementary Series 54.

——. 2010a. 'Romanizing' ancient Carthage: evidence from zooarchaeological remains. In D. Campana, P. Crabtree, S. D. deFrance, L. Lev-Tov and A. Choyke (eds.), *Anthropological Approaches to Zooarchaeology: Complexity, Colonialism, and Animal Transformations.* Oxford, 168–77.

——. 2010b. Cattle 'breed' variation and improvements in Roman Italy: connecting the zooarchaeological and ancient textual evidence. *World Archaeology* 42: 55–73.

——. 2010c. 'Sick as a dog': zooarchaeological evidence for pet dog health and welfare in the Roman world. *World Archaeology* 42: 290–309.

——. 2013. Pack animals, pets, pests, and other non-human beings. In P. Erdkamp (ed.), *The Cambridge Companion to the City of Rome.* Cambridge, 110–28.

——. 2014a. Animals in the urban fabric of Ostia: initiating a comparative zooarchaeological synthesis. *Journal of Roman Archaeology* 27: 175–201.

——. 2014b. Animals, economics and culture in the Athenian Agora: comparative zooarchaeological investigations. *Hesperia* 83: 189–255.

——. 2014c. Pets. In G. Campbell (ed.), *The Oxford Handbook of Animals in Classical Thought and Life.* Oxford, 269–81.

Mays, S. A. 2005. Tuberculosis as a zoonotic disease in antiquity. In J. Davies et al. (eds.), *Diet and Health in Past Animal Populations.* Oxford, 269–81.

McCormick, M. 2003. Rats, communications, and plague: towards an ecological history. *Journal of Interdisciplinary History* 34: 1–25.

O'Connor, T. 1993. Birds and the scavenger niche. *Archaeofauna* 2: 155–62.

——. 2013. *Animals as Neighbors: The Past and Present of Commensal Animals.* East Lansing, MI.

Parfitt, S. A. 2007. The small mammals. In A. G. Poulter (ed.), *Nicopolis ad Istrum: A Late Roman and Early Byzantine City. The Finds and the Biological Remains.* Oxford, 199–223.

Russell. N. 2012. *Social Zooarchaeology: Humans and Animals in Prehistory*. Cambridge.

Sabloff, A. 2001. *Reordering the Natural World: Humans and Animals in the City*. Toronto.

Scobie, A. 1986. Slums, sanitation, and mortality in the Roman world. *Klio* 68: 399–433.

Sparkes, B. A. 1997. Painted birds at Pompeii. *International Journal of Osteoarchaeology* 7: 350–353.

Sykes, N. 2014. *Beastly Questions: Animal Answers to Archaeological Questions*. London.

Toynbee, J. M. C. 1973. *Animals in Roman Life and Art*. London.

Upex, B. and K. Dobney. 2012. More than just mad cows: exploring human-animal relationships through animal paleopathology. In A. L. Grauer (ed.), *A Companion to Paleopathology*. Oxford, 191–21.

Vanpoucke, S., F. Pigière, A. Defgnée and W. Van Neer. 2007. Pig husbandry and environmental conditions in north Gaul during Antiquity and the early Middle Ages: the contribution of hypoplasia analysis. *Archaeofauna* 16: 7–20.

Watson, G. E. 2002. Birds: evidence from wall paintings, mosaics, sculpture, skeletal remains, and ancient authors. In W. F. Jashemski and F. G. Meyer (eds.), *The Natural History of Pompeii*. Cambridge, 357–400.

11

MAMMALIAN COMMUNITY ASSEMBLY IN ANCIENT VILLAGES AND TOWNS IN THE JORDAN VALLEY OF ISRAEL

Nimrod Marom and Lior Weissbrod

Introduction

In this chapter, we apply indices of diversity from community ecology to long-term faunal data found within a confined geographical region – the northern Jordan Valley of Israel – in order to consider these data from a multispecies perspective. A substantial temporal gradient is seen here to represent the sequence through which sets of zooarchaeologically important species formed and were modified through time. Groups of taxa including wild game, domestic herd animals, and commensal animals coalesced into the communities of mammalian species of which humans were major players and that maintained a complex web of interactions among their members and with local ecologies.

By reassessing this substantial data set, we aim to highlight major developments in the formation of species communities and the way that this process interacted with human social organization within the Jordan Valley. Interpreting this faunal dataset benefits from the use of a long temporal frame, which considers a number of millennia (9th millennium BCE–1st millennium CE) both preceding and succeeding the development of urbanism, and of multiple assemblages from each of the major cultural periods in the local sequence, retrieved within our well-defined study region (Figure 11.1).

The trajectory through which mammalian species within increasingly anthropogenic environments were assembled into communities and recurring alterations in the composition of these communities should unravel an ecological history parallel and complementary to the one told from a purely anthropocentric perspective. Today urban centers and their adjacent agricultural hinterlands are viewed as human-dominated ecosystems, where social and economic decision-making dynamics exert an overriding pressure on ecological process and structure (Grimm et al. 2000; Marzluff et al. 2008; Zasada 2011). Contemporary urban landscapes are shaped from the ground up by humans to suit their needs, modifying in the process the fundamental nature of their geology, climate and ecology. In such settings, humans shape the complex web of ecological interactions which surrounds them, continually acting to improve its form and function for society's benefit while also adapting social and economic systems to special and temporal variation in ecological circumstances. By taking into account long-term faunal dynamics in the

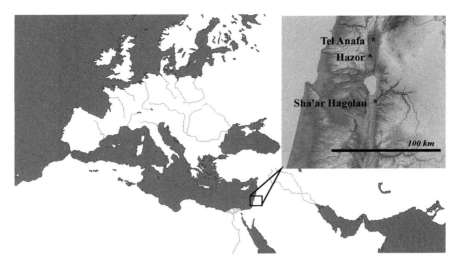

Figure 11.1 The study region with key sites.

archaeological record within a community framework, we can begin to assess to what extent the patterns and interactions of ecological communities are structured for human needs or made more complex by the interactions within communities.

The concept of the 'community', basic to ecological theory, is particularly useful as a lens through which to investigate the assembly process of animal species in human settlements, for two reasons. First, it encompasses by definition multispecies assemblages as well as the important requirement that all of the species within a given assemblage be engaged to a significant extent in a variety of types of direct and indirect interactions (Drake 1990). From this functional perspective, it is readily apparent that the ecological communities of ancient settlements and surrounding areas can be fairly easily conscribed because these island-like features of the landscape consisted of a relatively small area and possessed clear boundaries: the urban space and its economic hinterland (which could be spatially extensive and fragmented: Horden and Purcell 2000). It can be predicted that characteristics of the human-shaped environment, isolating it from its surroundings and influencing its ecological makeup, became especially pronounced with the rise of urbanism when settlements grew in size and, in many cases, walls were erected around them and the intensity of agro-pastoral activities at their peripheries increased.

Second, it is conceivable that the recruitment of different species into the communities of urban settlements and of interdependent satellite rural villages over time involved a limited set of processes, characterized ecologically as the interactions of domestication and commensalism. The former type implies some level of direct human control over animal reproductive processes, socially defined by ownership (Russell 2012), whereas in the latter type, animals benefit only indirectly from certain resources such as food and shelter, which are provided by humans unintentionally (Zeder 2012). An additional relevant interaction type involves game hunting, and although hunted animals did not coexist with humans inside settlements, they may be considered to have formed part of a wider web of ecological interactions among humans and other mammals within the study region by, for example, competition for limited grazing resource among wild and domestic herds.

The assembly of multispecies communities was a complicated process influenced by ecological, geographical, and socio-cultural factors. As such, reconstructing the dynamic of faunal association in an increasingly human-shaped environment can benefit from reference to the *particular* – a history, firmly grafted on a place-and-time grid. In this chapter, we will provide our view of the consolidation and development of human-animal associations in a particular region and a particular and long time-span: the northern Jordan Valley in Israel during the 9th millennium BCE–1st millennium CE.

The study region, comprising a narrow stretch of land ca. 5 km wide and 60 km long, extending between the Hula and Beit-She'an Valleys and encompassing the Sea of Galilee (Figure 11.1), has furnished evidence of human occupation going back at least to the Middle Pleistocene. The region lies at the edge of the Mediterranean climatic zone, with long, dry summers and wet winters. The levels of precipitation drop from approximately 600 mm to 400 mm annually along a north-south gradient. Perennial water sources are generally abundant, and comprised of rivers (the Jordan and its headwaters; Nahal Amud, Nahal Tsalmon and the Yarmuk, to name a few), standing freshwater lakes and wetlands (the Sea of Galilee, Lake Hula), and numerous springs. Present-day vegetation communities include the Mediterranean park forest with diverse herbaceous communities and Tabor oaks; widespread riparian elements; and also Irano-Turanian components from drier environments situated to the east and south.

Our study of trends in the dynamics of animal associations is based on 37 faunal assemblages from archaeological periods spanning early Holocene to Classical times (Table 11.1; Figure 11.1). Based on our experience in working on the zooarchaeology of the Jordan Valley, we are aware of potential pitfalls in interpretation of this record and take measures to sidestep them. Therefore, we do not treat the faunal data in published reports as directly reflecting the life assemblage from which it was drawn, and focus our attention on gross shifts in emphasis among ancient human societies of the region towards specialized utilization of broad taxonomic groups. This conservative approach allows us to avoid a number of potential biasing factors including different standards of bone recovery, inter-analyst variability in bone counting procedures, and differences between the contexts excavated at each site.

In order to reduce the risk of over-interpreting the available data, we conduct our study by first surveying the published zooarchaeological record using a very basic standardization to four taxonomic groups of large mammals: caprines, cattle, pigs, and wild game animals (fallow/ red deer and gazelle). By doing so, we sacrifice our capacity to interpret the occurrence of small-bodied taxa that occupy the end of the heavy-tailed taxonomic spectrum, which is particularly sensitive to sample size and recovery biases. Furthermore, the recovery of remains of mammals below the 'small' size category, including rodents (order Rodentia) and shrews (order Eulipotyphla), referred to as 'micro-mammals', has been highly uneven across sites, and unavoidably restrict our analysis to available data. This truncated dataset forms the grid through which we analyze large-scale changes in the structure of mammalian communities associated with ancient anthropogenic environments.

We further present case studies from specific sites and periods to help illustrate in detail the developmental stages along the continuum of evolving species associations. These case studies include faunal assemblages from the Neolithic (Sha'ar Hagolan), Bronze Age (Tel Hazor), Iron Age (Abel Beth-Maacha and Tel Hazor), and Hellenistic-Roman period (Tel Anafa). These are relatively large assemblages, retrieved from depositional contexts which are considered secure and well-defined, and, with the exception of Tel Anafa (Redding 1994), were analyzed by one of us (NM).

Table 11.1 Frequencies of large mammal taxonomic groups in the study region, in NISP

Period	Site	Sub-period	Reference	Caprine	Cattle	Pig	Deer/gazelle	Sheep:goat
Neolithic	Munhatta	Late Neolithic	Ducos (1968)	18	27	24	23	
Neolithic	Sha'ar Hagolan	PPNC	Marom and Bar-Oz (2013)	211	88	91	63	Goat
Neolithic	Sha'ar Hagolan	LNA	Marom and Bar-Oz (2013)	1011	246	329	237	Goat
Neolithic	Hagoshrim	PPNC	Haber (2001)	345	549	669	96	
Neolithic	Hagoshrim	LNA	Haber (2001)	1120	516	285	279	
Neolithic	Hagoshrim	LNB	Haber (2001)	1936	804	877	168	
Neolithic	Tel Te'o	LN	Horwitz (2001)	102	109	94	9	Goat
Chalcolithic	Tel Te'o	Chalcolithic	Horwitz (2001)	27	79	48	2	Goat
Chalcolithic	Tell Tsaf	Chalcolithic	Horwitz (2001)	53	40	20	4	
EBA	Tell Beth Yerakh	EB I	Cope (2006)	196	15	2	3	
EBA	Tell Beth Yerakh	EB IIA	Cope (2006)	85	85	27	14	
EBA	Yaqush	EB I	Hesse and Wapnish (2002)	343	100	22	35	Sheep
EBA	Yaqush	EB II	Hesse and Wapnish (2002)	292	91	4	4	Sheep
EBA	Yaqush	EB III	Hesse and Wapnish (2002)	215	113	4	7	Sheep
EBA	Tel Dan	EB II	Wapnish and Hesse (1991)	26	23			
EBA	Tel Dan	EB III	Wapnish and Hesse (1991)	15	20			
EBA	Tel Kinnrot	EB	Hellwing (1988)	188	89	26	1	
MBA	Qiryat Shmona	MBIIA-B	Raban-Gerstel and Bar-Oz (2012)	80	75	15	4	Sheep
MBA	Tel Dan	MBII	Wapnish et al. (1978)	53	9		3	Sheep
MBA	Hazor	MBII	Marom et al. (2014)	631	11	5	8	
LBA	Tel Kinrot	LB	Hellwing (1988)	280	133	8		
LBA	Tel Yenoam	LB	Lundelius (2003)	51	20	2		

LBA	Beth She'an	LB	Horwitz (2006)	95	39	18	5	Goat
IRA	Tel Dan	IR I	Wapnish and Hesse (1991)	33	14		3	Sheep
IRA	Abel Beth Maacha	IR I	Marom (unpublished data)	745	233		10	Sheep
IRA	Dan	IR II	Wapnish and Hesse (1991)	382	152		27	Goat
IRA	Hazor	IR II	Marom (2012)	41	48		32	sheep
IRA	Tel Kinnrot	IR II	Hellwing (1988)	1312	1506	66	487	Sheep
IRA	Tel Rehov	IR II	Tamar et al. (in press)	4348	1048		43	Sheep
Hellenistic	Beth Tsaida	Hellenistic	Fisher (2005)	610	484	34	113	Goat
Hellenistic	Tel Anafa	Hellenistic	Redding (1994)	203	172	57	28	Sheep
Hellenistic	Tel Beth Yerach	Hellenistic	Cope (2006)	56	10	11	2	
Hellenistic–Roman	Tel Dan Area T	Hellenistic	Wapnish et al. (1978)	1237	255		106	Sheep
Hellenistic	Beth Shean	Hellenistic	Wapnish et al. (1978)	27	25	2		
Roman	Tell Anafa	Roman	Redding (1994)	318	182	138	35	Sheep
Byzantine	Beth Shean	Byzantine	Horwitz (2006)	181	24	179	2	Goat
Early Islamic	Beth Shean	Early Islamic	Horwitz (2006)	68	4	53	1	Goat

The zooarchaeological record

The pre-urban background: 14th–5th millennia BCE

Sites dating to the terminal Pleistocene reveal the transformative process of transition of local hunter-gatherer societies from a mobile way of life to a more settled one. At the Epipaleolithic site of Ein-Gev (ca. 14,000 BCE), located on the eastern shore of the Sea of Galilee, some of the earliest known evidence of permanent stone construction was uncovered together with faunal remains representing 13 different species of large to small wild mammals (Davis 1972; Marom and Bar-Oz 2008). In addition, the remains of ten species of medium to small mammals were identified at the site of Ein-Mallaha, adjacent to Lake Hula and representing the final Epipaleolithic cultural unit before the onset of the Neolithic (ca. 13,000–9,500 BCE), and where evidence for permanent construction is considerably more abundant than in previous periods (Bouchud 1987; Bridault et al. 2008). In both of these sites, wild ungulates such as gazelle (*Gazella gazella*) and different species of deer (*Dama mesopotamica, Cervus elaphus*, and *Capreolus capreolus*) predominate. The site of Ein-Mallaha produced the earliest remains of a domesticated dog (*Canis lupus familiaris*) in Israel, found in association with a human burial (Davis and Valla 1978; Tchernov and Valla 1997). This site also yielded abundant remains of the common mouse believed to represent the earliest commensal house mouse (Tchernov 1984, 1991). Although domestication of the dog at an earlier period in Europe has been argued (Germonpré et al. 2012; Skoglund et al. 2015), in the Levant both the dog and house mouse are commonly thought to have initially developed commensal interactions with humans in the context of early semi-sedentary settlements, and in the case of the dog, this association quickly evolved entailed domestication evidenced by reduction in body size and co-burial (Tchernov 1984, 1991; Tchernov and Valla 1997).

From a faunal perspective, the earliest stages of the Near Eastern Neolithic 9,500–4,500 BCE, known as the Pre-Pottery and Pottery Neolithic periods, are not well-documented within our study region. During this time, intensified cultivation activities led to plant domestication and the emergence of sedentary agrarian economies in the Jordan Valley (Bar-Yosef and Belfer-Cohen 1989; Kislev and Bar-Yosef 1988; Kislev et al. 1986), and, correspondingly, the size and structural complexity of both human populations and their settlements continued to grow (Ben-Shlomo and Garfinkel 2009). In the early to mid-Neolithic, hunting persisted as a central component in the economy of incipient farmers, although a major and widespread shift in taxonomic emphasis is evidenced after ca. 6,500 BCE, by the Pre-Pottery Neolithic C phase. Intensified hunting focused on cattle or pigs rather than gazelle and deer – a pattern diametrically opposed to that of pre-Neolithic hunter-gatherers in the same region – suggests a growing conflict between sedentary farming communities occupying highly productive environments, such as riparian and alluvial areas, and the species of large to medium mammals common to those habitats (Marom and Bar-Oz 2009). Direct competition with wild cattle and boar over limited resources is conceivable in the context of sedentary crop farming, promoting the frequency of encounters and a more enhanced level of human-animal interaction within a wider community framework (Marom and Bar-Oz 2013). The wild gazelle and deer component of contemporary economies of the southern part of the study region, procured in grassland and woodland habitats, respectively, typically contracted to <20% of the recovered fauna.

Overview of trends from the 4th millennium BCE*–1st millennium* CE

Twenty-nine published assemblages dating from the 4th millennium BCE–1st millennium CE, each comprising at least 100 skeletal specimens identified to biological taxa were chosen from the study region in order to conduct an analysis of community diversity. First, we were interested in discerning changes in the abundance of four major taxonomic categories of livestock (caprines, cattle, and pig) and of game animals (deer, gazelle) to assess during which periods mammalian community structure was heavily dominated by particular taxa as opposed to having a more even distribution of taxonomic abundances. We interpret observed shifts in light of regional socio-political dynamics and the region's specific geographic position and structure.

The abundance of the four taxonomic groups within each assemblage was quantified using Shannon's Evenness index. This index was favored over the better-known Shannon diversity index because our restricted choice of taxonomic groups predetermined the richness component of the studied assemblages. In Figure 11.2, values of within-assemblage diversity (alpha diversity), shown along the horizontal axis of a scatterplot, are compared with values of between-assemblage diversity (beta diversity), expressed as means of Euclidean distance measures among all pairs of assemblages. The results of alpha diversity show overall significant variability with respect to

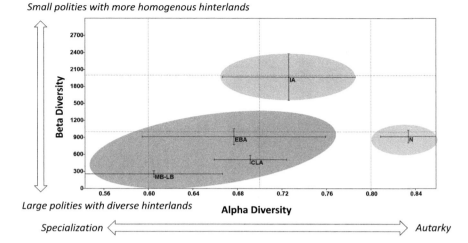

Figure 11.2 Alpha diversity (Shannon Evenness) and Beta diversity (Euclidean distance) of the different assemblages from the study region, with standard deviations. N = Neolithic cluster; EBA, MB-LB, and CLA = Bronze Age/Classical cluster; IA = Iron Age cluster.

period (Kruskal-Wallis H = 13.44, P = 0.02), with the difference between the Neolithic (high evenness) and later periods (low evenness) especially marked (based on Mann-Whitney's Pairwise Comparisons, P = 0.01 for Neolithic vs. Bronze Ages and P = 0.02 for Neolithic vs. post-Iron Age periods). The results show high intra- and inter-assemblage evenness in the Neolithic, particularly high homogeneity in the Bronze Ages and somewhat less even assemblages in the classical period, and a mosaic of particularly diverse faunal compositions in the Iron Age, wherein assemblages are not dominated to a great extent by any of the taxonomic groups but demonstrate considerable shifting in the internal structure from one assemblage to the next.

To better understand this result, the mean percentage values of the four taxonomic groups were plotted by period (Figure 11.3). Three diachronic trends of interest can be noted. First, the frequency of wild game species drops after the Neolithic, from about 9% of identified specimens on average to less than 3% in later periods. The increase in frequency of wild game during the Iron Age reflects a sampling bias: in one sample, from Tel Hazor (Marom 2012), much of the assemblage attributed to game animals was retrieved from a single pit at the site, and in all likelihood reflects a single hunting episode.

In a second trend, the frequency of caprines rises fairly abruptly with the transition from the Neolithic-Chalcolithic period (slightly less than 40% on average) to the Bronze Age (>60%), then reaches peak frequencies close to 70% during the Middle to Late Bronze Age and subsequently declines gradually in the Iron Age and Classical period. This shift appears to be associated with an increased emphasis on sheep rather than goat within the caprine component of livestock communities: assemblages from Neolithic and Chalcolithic periods for which there is published data regarding the sheep-to-goat ratio (N = 4) are all dominated by goats, whereas such Bronze Age assemblages (N = 7) are dominated by sheep, except for the Late Bronze Age site of Beth She'an. As the percentage of caprines decreases slightly from the Iron Age onwards, we start seeing a mixed pattern in which some assemblages are dominated by sheep (N = 8) and others by goats (N = 4).

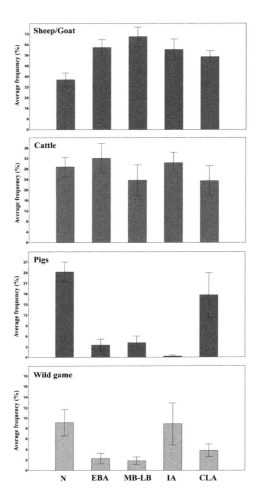

Figure 11.3 Relative frequencies of caprines, cattle, pigs and wild game in the study region through time.

In a third trend, pig frequencies are highest in the beginning of the sequence (Neolithic-Chalcolithic: ca. 24% on average), drop considerably for several thousands of years during the Bronze and Iron Ages (<5%), and finally rise substantially during the classical periods (ca. 18%). The strongly reduced role of pigs in these mammalian communities appears to be associated with the waxing interest in sheep in the Bronze Age beginning in the 3rd millennium BCE. The Hellenistic, Roman, and Byzantine assemblages of the classical period reflect a resurgence in the importance of pigs, lasting into the Early Islamic period, based on one assemblage from Beth She'an.

To summarize, three major temporal trends can be detected in the structure of mammalian communities along our sequence: (1) the pre-urban phase of the Neolithic-Chalcolithic is characterized by assemblages in which caprines (mostly goats), pigs, cattle, and large game animals are all well-represented in the economy, (2) in the Bronze Age, and especially its later part in the 2nd millennium BCE when full-blown urbanism emerges, assemblages are appreciably less diverse, dominated by caprines, mainly sheep during the Bronze Age, whereas pigs and game animals become negligible components; (3) this situation changes again after the Iron Age, when an emphasis on pigs re-emerges and the ubiquity of sheep-dominated assemblages declines.

Case studies

In this section we present assemblages which highlight details in the dynamic of long-term temporal changes described previously.

Neolithic Sha'ar Hagolan

The Neolithic village at Sha'ar Hagolan, occupied during the 5th–4th millennia BCE, may be seen as characteristic of an early phase in the assembly of human-animal communities in the Jordan Valley. Due to its location at the confluence of the rivers Jordan and Yarmuk, it was suggested (Marom and Bar-Oz 2009, 2013) that the settlement of early agriculturalists in this setting brought humans into direct competition with wild cattle and boar. This confrontation would have been the result of the limited extent of such alluvial habitats, preferred both by human cultivators and these fairly sedentary ungulates. The competition, proceeding through an initial phase of overhunting, transformed by the 5th millennium BCE to successful incorporation of cattle, pigs, and humans in a community where mutualism (+/+) rather than predation (+/-) is the dominant mode of association. Until that time, caprines constituted the sole member of Neolithic livestock communities, dogs would have become an established companion animal among early farming and hunting societies (Dayan 1994; Dayan and Galili 2000), and house mice seem to have constituted the main or sole member of the commensal community within human settlements as seen in Neolithic sites located in modern Syria and Turkey (Cucchi et al. 2012; Jenkins 2012).

Intensified pig exploitation at sites such as Sha'ar Hagolan and Munhatta marks an early start on a millennium-long path to domestication, which is evidenced later at the sites of Hagoshrim and Nahal Zehora (Haber and Dayan 2004; Davis 2012). The slow mosaic pattern by which pig husbandry was adopted suggests that multiple systemic changes in human ecological, economic, and social strategies had to have accrued over time to allow acceptance of the pig into the emergent Neolithic communities of humans and fauna. As both wild boar and cattle assumed the behavioral and morphological characteristics of the 'domestication syndrome', humans adapted to the new multispecies society by means of social plasticity: in the large Late Neolithic settlement of Sha'ar Hagolan in the early 6th millennium BCE, pig bones were significantly more common in one part of the settlement, whereas caprines were more common in another (Marom 2012). Provided that rates of animal consumption and discard in Neolithic settlements were related to patterns of animal ownership, this spatial organization may demonstrate the existence of a social division within the human community, maintaining near-settlement cattle and pig husbandry by one residential group and more mobile sheep/goat husbandry by another, likely through small-scale seasonal transhumance.

Sha'ar Hagolan can be viewed as a locality of interaction between humans and animals within a specific ecological context (Horden and Purcell 2000). In the fragmented landscape of the northern Jordan valley, where the distance between water-rich and semi-arid environments is very small, humans, cattle and pigs congregated in close proximity to water. The interaction with cattle, pigs and domestic caprines in this fragmented landscape provided motivation for diversification in the human social system and in turn influenced interactions with specific animals, with part of the group specializing in keeping cattle and pigs in proximity to the settlement, near water, while others specialized in keeping of caprines by utilizing more distal, drier habitats. The particular locality which we discuss, with its micro-ecological diversity comprising of areas of wetland and associated fauna, exerted its influence on the configuration of Neolithic human-animal multispecies society, and shaped the long-term legacy that such early associations possessed for economic and ecological processes within the region.

Middle Bronze Age Hazor

In the Middle Bronze Age, the city of Hazor was the greatest polity within the Jordan Valley, exerting its political and economic influence over extensive (if not well-defined) territories in and around the Hula Valley. A large assemblage of faunal remains from the acropolis of the mid-2nd-millennium BCE city has revealed a predominantly sheep-based economy (Marom et al. 2014). Because of the over-abundance of sheep (96%), it can be argued that Hazor's acropolis represents a setting of a particular mode of highly provisioned consumption, possibly associated with social elites. Contemporary faunal assemblages obtained from the lower city of Hazor (Marom and Zuckerman 2012) and from a small fort/village in nearby Qiryat Shmona (Raban-Gerstel and Bar-Oz 2012) show reduced sheep abundances and a more diverse taxonomic structure. These data combined suggest that the large assemblage from the acropolis of Hazor reflects provisioning from large flocks of sheep maintained by specialists, presumably situated in the polity's hinterland that would have abutted the ecological boundary with drylands of the Irano-Turanian zone in the Golan and Gilead regions. This ecotone has always provided rich grazing land. Further evidence from ancient documents in the royal archives of the Assyrian city of Mari supports the importance of particularly large-scale and region-wide sheep pastoralism within the Jordan Valley in the Middle Bronze Age (Malmat 1983).

An economy geared to wool production came at the expense of meat production based on pig husbandry. The movement from a autarkic village economy to a regional and even supra-regional economy of command orchestrated by a large polity controlling an ecologically varied geographic expanse may have branded pig husbandry less desirable (Zeder 1998); furthermore, it was less practical for local small-scale farmers once large settlements evolved in strategic locations away from convenient, water-rich micro-environments. The pull towards secondary production of wool would have encouraged specialized sheep pastoralism in marginal environments controlled by the Hazor polity. Furthermore, it is conceivable that wild game was no longer required as a dietary supplement in urban centers, and hunting could have become a prestigious pastime for the elites (Firmage 1992; Marom and Bar-Oz 2014).

The great city-state of Bronze Age Hazor was abandoned at the end of the 2nd millennium BCE (see also Lev-Tov and McGeough 2007) to re-emerge as a considerably smaller urban center affiliated with the Israelite kingdom of the early 1st millennium BCE. The faunal assemblage recovered from non-elite contexts of this Iron Age city is, on the whole, dominated by caprines, comprising a more even composition of both sheep and goats (Marom 2012). The reduced abundance of sheep between the Bronze and Iron Age assemblages of Hazor constitutes the main shift during this period, most likely instigated by a deep geopolitical change in the Jordan Valley and its economic consequences: wool production declined from its former standing as a major component of the region's economy. Even if demand for wool had persisted, the extensive pasture lands located to the east of Hazor were no longer directly available, as they became part of the ever-changing geographic collage of contending local polities (Panitz-Cohen et al. 2013).

Large-scale socio-political dynamics within the Upper Jordan Valley at the time of Hazor provided the necessary conditions for temporarily overriding long-established regularities in the structure of mammalian communities, extremely reducing taxonomic diversity. Geopolitical circumstances within the study region shifted again between the Late Bronze and Iron Ages, and a less centralized economy may have allowed the return of more diverse fauna, which expresses adaptations to local micro-ecological conditions. Data obtained from remains of small mammals found inside the houses of Hazor, including samples from both the Iron Age Acropolis and the Lower City of the Late Bronze Age, demonstrate ecological conditions similar to those observed in Neolithic villages: house mice dominate the assemblages, accounting for more than 80% of the small mammalian remains. They occur consistently with less abundant remains of insectivorous shrews (*Crocidura* sp.), together comprising the ecological communities of urban settlements across the Upper Jordan Valley and the broader region (Weissbrod et al. 2012, 2014). This apparent long-term consistency suggests that ecological conditions within urban settlements, including such aspects as settlement structure, size, and human residential density were fairly stable throughout especially long spans of time.

Hellenistic-Roman Tel Anafa

The site of Tel Anafa within the Hula Valley yielded a detailed faunal sequence spanning five separate phases of occupation in the Hellenistic-Roman periods, providing one of the most in-depth accounts of human-animal interactions after the Iron Age (Redding 1994). The faunal sequence reveals relatively high frequencies of cattle, and fluctuating frequencies of sheep, goats, and pigs through time. Redding (1994) concludes that sheep and cattle were imported into urban centers from specialist producers in rural areas and that demands exerted by urban-based and region-wide market systems were responsible for observed shifts in the abundance of different livestock species. He identifies a temporary breakdown of this economic network within the Hellenistic part of the sequence when a distinct pattern emerges of cattle herding combined with pig husbandry and deer hunting: again, demonstrating how configurations of multispecies societies more adapted to local ecological conditions can become reestablished once the influence of regional economic networks weakens.

Discussion

Our analysis of temporal changes in two components of diversity – within assemblages (alpha) and among them (beta) – produced three discreet patterns, which, we suggest, can be interpreted as the varying consequences of superimposing the effect of regional redistribution and exchange networks on an ecologically patchy landscape (Figure 11.2): the first includes the Neolithic sites; the second comprises the Bronze Age and Classical Period sites; while the third consists of the Iron Age faunas.

The Neolithic sample of assemblages is remarkable for its high alpha diversity. Because we used an evenness index as a measure of diversity, the high alpha indicates a highly balanced faunal composition of the Neolithic assemblages, characterized by nearly equal representation of the four taxonomic groups compared to other periods. Beta, between-assemblage diversity in the Neolithic is not remarkably high, which in combination with the pattern of an 'internally balanced' faunal composition indicated by alpha diversity, suggests local adaptations less affected by pressures to integrate into regional animal exchange networks. These emerging human-animal Neolithic communities employed rich alluvial environments available in local settings for the husbandry of livestock with high water requirements – cattle and pigs, combined with the herding of (mainly) goats, and for hunting. Absence of specialized production or a focus on any single group of livestock taxa reflects the fact that regional markets and resulting 'market pull' on local economies have not yet developed in this early period. The Neolithic period of the

Upper Jordan Valley was characterized by a patchy economic and political landscape, lacking the necessary integration of large-scale economic specialization.

The cluster of assemblages of the Bronze Ages and Classical period extends horizontally along the right-hand side of the graph in Figure 11.2, which is characterized by relatively low alpha diversity values. Especially low evenness coupled with an extreme dominance of sheep is particularly apparent at the Middle Bronze Age assemblage from the site of Hazor, which was retrieved from the acropolis of the ancient city – a context where provisioning of local urban consumers by distant rural producers is highly likely. Other assemblages belonging to this cluster are somewhat more internally diverse, although marked homogeneity in the basic pattern of sheep-dominated assemblages contributes to fairly low values of beta diversity. The observed patterns align with periods during which we can expect to see increasing vectors of unification of the political landscape, when economic considerations related to hierarchical interactions among settlements, their trade relations and local ecologies acquiesced to the pull of a broader regional market. Both political and economic hegemonies spread geographically across the Upper Jordan Valley to encompass peripheral areas where abundant grazing grounds for sheep encouraged pastoral specialization and wool production, which supplied the demands of a core polity. Temporary interruption in this system during a phase within the Hellenistic sequence at Tel Anafa resulted in reversion to a non-specialized, locally focused, independent and presumably more ecological pattern of livestock production and land use.

Faunal assemblages from the Iron Age show intermediate values of evenness lying between the more 'balanced' Neolithic pattern and the more specialized, sheep-dominated Bronze Age/ Classical period pattern. A particularly high beta diversity value for these assemblages indicates high variation in the internal structure among assemblages: some tend to an equitable composition of the taxonomic groups, similar to the Neolithic pattern, whereas others demonstrate dominance by a single taxon, as was seen to characterize on large scale assemblages of preceding and succeeding millennia. This period witnessed a shifting geopolitical scene marked by severe political perturbations, including frequent changes in the territorial boundaries between nation-state polities. Settlements in the Upper Jordan Valley frequently became cut off from expansive hinterlands in the Transjordan and the Golan Heights suitable for large-scale sheep pastoralism, and while centralized market forces continued to exert a certain pull towards production based on caprines for meat, milk and wool, and on cattle for draft animals in agriculture, this demand could be supplied only periodically and to a partial extent.

The urbanization of ancient landscapes was a millennia-long process involving the entanglement of larger sections of the landscape with the activity of social elites based in urban centers – locations that drew local communities of pastoralists, farmers and livestock into region-wide networks. Long-term data in the Upper Jordan Valley, when examined from the perspective of community diversity of mammalian assemblages, suggests a complex, non-linear and most likely cyclic relationship over time between two important factors illustrated in Figure 11.2: decreasing versus increasing patchiness in land use in relation to coalescence versus disintegration of regional exchange networks, respectively. This dynamic is seen by us to represent the hallmark of the evolution of an urban landscape and its correlate of increasing geopolitical complexity. Subject to regional processes of shifting political centralization and its effect on the extent of geographic expansion of urban-based hegemony, local economies fluctuated between a more open or closed state and could either function independent of, or were commandeered by, regional exchange hubs, responding by adjusting levels of specialization in livestock production. In this respect, the evolutionary trajectory revealed within the Upper Jordan Valley is of special interest because it clearly sets apart the Iron Age as a time of marked diversification in production systems and land use. This fundamental process underlined the resilience of

Mediterranean-type economies developed throughout history (Horden and Purcell 2000), and witnessed in a most pronounced manner with the transition to the Iron Age following the collapse of highly centralized economies and city-state polities based in palaces and temples of the 2nd millennium BCE (Broodbank 2013). We see that with the lapse of regionally interconnected economic exchange networks and large-scale political systems, patterns of community composition in the study region gravitate toward higher frequencies of pigs and cattle, highlighting the underlying significance of landscape structure and ecology in the Jordan Valley, including the relatively widespread distribution of wetland environments, in shaping local community assembly processes over time.

Within the framework of a multispecies zooarchaeology and a long-term perspective, our case study demonstrates the utility of working towards the bridging of persisting gaps among 'ecological' and 'social' approaches, and the synthesis of interrelated aspects of human history, political economy, and regional ecology, as advocated by the present volume.

References

Bar-Yosef, O. and Belfer-Cohen, A. (1989) The origins of sedentism and farming communities in the Levant. *Journal of World Prehistory* 3: 447–498.

Bar-Yosef, O. and Kislev, M. (1989) Early farming communities in the Jordan Valley. In D. Harris and G. Hillman (eds.) *Foraging and Farming: The Evolution of Plant Exploitation*, pp. 632–642. London, Unwin Hyman.

Ben-Shlomo, D. and Garfinkel, Y. (2009) Sha'ar HaGolan and new insights into Near Eastern protohistoric urban concepts. *Oxford Journal of Archaeology* 28: 189–209.

Bouchoud, J. (ed.) (1987) *La Faune du Gisement Natoufien de Mallaha (Eynan), Israel*. Paris, Association Paléorient.

Bridault, A., Rabinovich, R. and Simmons, T. (2008) Human activities, site location and taphonomic process: a relevant combination for understanding the fauna of Eynan (Ain Mallaha), level Ib (final Natufian, Israel). In E. Vila, L. Gourichon, A. M. Choyke and H. Buitenhuis (eds.) *Eighth International Symposium on the Archaeozoology of Southwestern Asia and Adjacent Areas, 2006, Lyon, France*, pp. 99–117. Lyon, Maison de l'Orient et de la Méditerranée.

Broodbank, C. (2013) *The Making of the Middle Sea: A History of the Mediterranean from the Beginning to the Emergence of the Classical World*. Oxford, Oxford University Press.

Cope, C. R. (2006) The fauna: preliminary results. In N. Getzov (ed.) *The Tel Bet Yerah Excavations, 1994–1995*, pp. 169–174. Jerusalem, Israel Antiquities Authority.

Cucchi, T., Auffray, J.-C. and Vigne, J.-D. (2012) Synanthropy and dispersal in the Near East and Europe: zooarchaeological review and perspectives. In M. Macholán, S. J. E. Baird, P. Munclinger and J. Piálek (eds.) *Evolution of the House Mouse*, pp. 65–93. Cambridge, Cambridge University Press.

Davis, S. J. M. (1972) Faunal Remains of Upper Paleolithic Sites at En-Gev. Unpublished thesis, Hebrew University.

Davis, S. J. M. (2012) Animal bones at the Nahal Zehora sites. In A. Gopher (ed.) *Village Communities of the Pottery Neolithic Period at the Menashe Hills, Israel: Archaeological Investigations at the Sites of Nahal Zehora*, pp. 1258–1320. Tel Aviv, Tel Aviv University.

Davis, S. J. M. and Valla, F. R. (1978) Evidence for domestication of the dog 12,000 years ago in the Natufian of Israel. *Nature* 276: 608–610.

Dayan, T. (1994) Early domesticated dogs of the Near East. *Journal of Archaeological Science* 21: 633–640.

Dayan, T. and Galili, E. (2000) A preliminary look at some new domesticated dogs from submerged Neolithic sites off the Carmel coast. In S. J. Crockford (ed.) *Dogs through Time: An Archaeological Perspective, Proceedings of the 1st ICAZ Symposium on the History of the Domestic Dog, Eight Congress of the International Council for Archaeozoology (ICAZ98), August 23-29, 1998, Victoria, B.C., Canada*, pp. 29–34. Oxford, BAR.

Drake, J. A. (1990) Communities as assembled structures: do rules govern pattern? *Trends in Ecology & Evolution* 5(5): 159–164.

Ducos, P. (1968) *L'origine des Animaux Domestiques en Palestine*. Bordeaux, Delmas.

Firmage, E. 1992. Zoology. In D. N. Freedman (ed.) *The Anchor Bible Dictionary*, pp. 1109–1167. New York, Doubleday.

Fisher, T. G. (2005) A Zooarchaeological Analysis of Change in Animal Utilization at Bethsaida from Iron Age II through the Early Roman Period. Unpublished thesis, University of Tennessee.

Germonpré, M., Lázničková-Galetová, M. and Sablin, M. V. (2012) Palaeolithic dog skulls at the Gravettian Předmostí site, the Czech Republic. *Journal of Archaeological Science* 39: 184–202.

Grimm, N. B., Grove, J. G., Pickett, S. T. and Redman, C. L. (2000) Integrated approaches to long-term studies of urban ecological systems: urban ecological systems present multiple challenges to ecologists—Pervasive human impact and extreme heterogeneity of cities, and the need to integrate social and ecological approaches, concepts, and theory. *Bioscience* 50(7): 571–584.

Haber, A. (2001) The Faunal Analysis of Hagoshrim: Biological and Economic Aspects of Prehistoric Agricultural Societies and the Process of Domestication. Unpublished thesis, Tel Aviv University.

Haber, A. and Dayan, T. (2004). Analyzing the process of domestication: Hagoshrim as a case study. *Journal of Archaeological Science* 31: 1587–1601.

Hellwing, S. (1988–1989). Faunal remains from the Early Bronze and Late Bronze Ages at Tel Kinrot. *Tel Aviv* 15–16: 212–220.

Horden, P. and Purcell, N. (2000) *The Corrupting Sea: A Study of Mediterranean History*. Oxford, Blackwell.

Horwitz, L. K. (2001) The mammalian fauna of Tel Teo. In E. Eisenberg, A. Gopher and R. Greenberg (eds.) *Tel Teo: A Neolithic, Chalcolithic and Early Bronze Age Site in the Hula Valley*. Jerusalem, Israeli Antiquities Authority.

Horwitz, L. K. (2006) Mammalian remains from Areas H, L, P and Q. In A. Mazar (ed.) *Excavations at Tel Beth-Shean 1989–1996, Volume I: From the Late Bronze Age IIB to the Medieval Period*, pp. 689–717. Jerusalem, Israel Exploration Society and the Institute of Archaeology of the Hebrew University.

Jenkins, E. (2012) Mice, scats and burials: unusual concentrations of microfauna found in human burials at the Neolithic site of Çatalhöyük, Central Anatolia. *Journal of Social Archaeology* 12(3): 380–403.

Kislev, M. and Bar-Yosef, O. (1988). The legumes: the earliest domesticated plants in the Near East? *Current Anthropology* 29(1): 175–179.

Kislev, M., Bar-Yosef, O.and Gopher, A. (1986) Early Neolithic domesticated and wild barley from the Netiv Hagdud region in the Jordan Valley. *Israel Journal of Botany* 35: 197–201.

Lev-Tov, J., and McGeough, K. (2007) Examining feasting in Late Bronze Age Syro-Palestine through ancient texts and bones. In K. C. Twiss (ed.) *The Archaeology of Food and Identity*, pp. 85–111. Southern Illinois University, Center for Archaeological Investigations.

Lundelius, E. L. (2003) Non-human bone material. In H. A. Liebowitz (ed.) *Tel Yin'am I: The Late Bronze Age*, pp. 255–263. Austin, Texas.

Malamat, A. (1983). Silver, gold, and precious stones from Hazor in a New Mari document. *The Biblical Archaeologist* 46(3). The American Schools of Oriental Research: 169–74. http://www.jstor.org/stable/3209828.

Marom, N. (2012) Archaeozoological analysis of animal bones from selected Iron Age contexts. In A. Ben-Tor (ed.) *Hazor IV*, pp. 604–623. Jerusalem, Israel Exploration Society.

Marom, N. and Bar-Oz, G. (2008) 'Measure for measure': a taphonomic reconsideration of the Kebaran site of Ein Gev I, Israel. *Journal of Archaeological Science* 35: 214–227.

Marom, N. and Bar-Oz, G. (2009) 'Man-made oases': Neolithic patterns of wild ungulate exploitation and their consequences for the domestication of pigs and cattle. *Before Farming* 2009(1): article 1.

Marom, N. and Bar-Oz, G. (2013) The prey pathway: a regional history of cattle (*Bos taurus*) and pig (*Sus scrofa*) domestication in the northern Jordan Valley, Israel. *PloS One* 8: e55958.

Marom, N. and Bar-Oz, G. (2014) Zooarchaeology and social identity in Bronze and Iron Ages Israel: a research framework. In B. De Cupere, V. Linseele and S. Hamilton-Dyer (eds.) *Archaeozoology of the Near East X*, pp. 227–241. Leuven, Peters.

Marom, N. and Zuckerman, S. (2012) The zooarchaeology of exclusion and expropriation: looking up from the lower city in Late Bronze Age Hazor. *Journal of Anthropological Archaeology* 31: 573–585.

Marom N., Yasur-Landau A., Zuckerman S., Cline E., Ben-Tor A. and Bar-Oz G. (2014) Shepherd kings? A zooarchaeological investigation of elite precincts in Middle Bronze Age Tel Hazor and Tel Kabri. *Bulletin of the American Schools of Oriental Research* 371: 59–82.

Marzluff, J., Shulenberger, E., Endlicher, W., Alberti, M., Bradley, G., Ryan, C., ZumBrunnen, C. and Simon, U. (eds.) (2008) *Urban Ecology: An International Perspective on the Interaction between Humans and Nature*. New York, SpringerVerlag.

Panitz-Cohen, N., Mullins, R. and Bonfil, R. (2013) Northern exposure: launching excavations at Tell Abil el-Qame (Abel Beth Maacah). *Strata* 31: 27–42.

Raban-Gerstel, N. and Bar-Oz, G. (2012) Zooarchaeological analysis of the faunal remains. In Y. Gadot and A. Yasur-Landau (eds.) *Qiryat Shemona (S): Fort and Village in the Hula Valley*, pp. 139–159. Tel-Aviv, Tel-Aviv University.

Redding, R. W. (1994) The vertebrate fauna. In S. Herbert (ed.) *Tel Anafa I: Final Report on Ten Years of Excavation at a Hellenistic and Roman Settlement in Northern Israel*, pp. 279–322. Ann Arbor, MI, Kesley Museum.

Russell, N. (2012) *Social Zooarchaeology: Humans and Animals in Prehistory*. New York, Cambridge University Press.

Skoglund, P., Ersmark, E., Palkopoulou, E., and Dalén, L. (2015) Ancient wolf genome reveals an early divergence of domestic dog ancestors and admixture into high-latitude breeds. *Current Biology* 25(11): 1515–1519.

Tamar, K. and Marom, N. (in press) The faunal remains from Tel Rehov, 2003–2005 seasons. In A. Mazar (ed.) *Tel Rehov 1*. Jerusalem, Israel Exploration Society.

Tchernov, E. (1984) Commensal animals and human sedentism in the Middle East. In J. Clutton-Brock and C. Grigson (eds.) *Animals and Archaeology 3: Early Herders and their Flocks*, pp. 91–115. Oxford, BAR.

Tchernov, E. (1991) Biological evidence for human sedentism in south-west Asia during the Natufian. In O. Bar-Yosef and F. R. Valla (eds.) *The Natufian Culture in the Levant*, pp. 315–340. Ann Arbor, MI, International Monographs in Prehistory.

Tchernov, E. and Valla, F. F. (1997) Two new dogs and other Natufian dogs from the southern Levant. *Journal of Archaeological Science* 24: 65–95.

Weissbrod, L., Bar-Oz, G., Cucchi, T. and Finkelstein, I. (2013) The urban ecology of Iron Age Tel Megiddo: using microvertebrate remains as ancient bio-indicators. *Journal of Archaeological Science* 40(1): 257–267.

Weissbrod, L., Malkinson, D., Cucchi, T., Gadot, Y., Finkelstein, I. and Bar-Oz, G. (2014) Ancient urban ecology reconstructed from archaeozoological remains of small mammals in the Near East. *PloS One* 9(3): e91795.

Zasada, I. (2011) Multifunctional peri-urban agriculture: a review of societal demands and the provision of goods and services by farming. *Land Use Policy* 28(4): 639–648.

Zeder, M. A. (1998) Pigs and emergent complexity in the ancient Near East. In S. M. Nelson (ed.) *Ancestors for the Pigs: Pigs in Prehistory*, pp. 109–122. Pennsylvania, MASCA Research Papers in Science and Archaeology.

Zeder, M. (2012) Pathways to animal domestication. In P. Gepts, T. R. Famula and R. L. Bettinger (eds.) *Biodiversity in Agriculture: Domestication, Evolution and Sustainability*, pp. 227–259. Cambridge, Cambridge University Press.

PART III

Agrarian commitments
Towards an archaeology of symbiosis

12

ANIMALS AND THE NEOLITHIC
Cui bono?

Terry O'Connor

Gordon Childe's concept of a Neolithic Revolution did archaeology both a favour and a disservice (Harris 1994). On the positive side, it was a bold attempt to view a cultural phenomenon that is clearly seen in the Eurasian archaeological record in an integrated way that considered all of the socioeconomic implications of settling down to farm. If the concept looks rather quaint and misguided now, it is because archaeology has moved on, in particular beyond Eurasia, and we now have a far greater and more complex data set to work with than was available to Childe. On the downside, by presenting the advent of agriculture as a Revolution, Childe encouraged a generation or more of prehistorians to think of the Neolithic in terms of old lifeways being overthrown and completely replaced. Childe's Marxist view of the world perhaps inclined him to think in terms of revolutionary rather than gradual change (Greene 1999; Thomas 1982). Whatever the underlying philosophy, the concept of a Neolithic Revolution gained appreciable traction (e.g. Simmons 2011). Even some more recent discussions of the subject that give due weight to pre-Neolithic developments towards cultural complexity nonetheless refer to the 'Neolithic Revolution' (e.g. Renfrew 2006).

The aim of this chapter is to examine the role of animals in the transition to the Neolithic, and to understand the emergence of what we call 'domesticated' animals. This is a subject that has already attracted a great deal of discussion and research (Zeuner 1963; Clutton-Brock 1981; Bökönyi 1989; O'Connor 1997; Russell 2002; Zeder et al. 2006; Vigne 2011; Vigne et al. 2011; Larson and Fuller 2014; McClure 2015; Zeder 2015), and a critical overview of the pertinent literature and its historiography would be a major research investigation in itself. Suffice to say that an initial research emphasis on domesticated caprines in southwest Asia (e.g. Hole 1996; Zeuner 1955) broadened to encompass other taxa and other regions of the world (e.g. MacDonald 1992; Grigson 1991). The broader context challenged any one-size-fits-all model of domestication, which would need to deliver a satisfactory explanation for the domestication of caprines, dogs, cats, reindeer and chickens, not to mention the working elephants of southern Asia (O'Connor 1997). Latterly, rapid developments in ancient and modern DNA analysis have taken the debate in new directions, tracking and dating the ancient genomic traces of domestication (e.g. Zeder et al. 2006; Gifford-Gonzales and Hanotte 2011; Flink et al. 2014), and reading the echoes of that process in modern genomes (e.g. Magee et al. 2014). Combined with increasingly sophisticated analysis of phenotypic traits, for example through Geometric Morphometrics (Evin et al. 2015), aDNA is contributing to a more informed modern synthesis regarding the emergence of domestic livestock.

That said, two particular criticisms can be levelled at current research in this field. The first is that the overwhelming majority of recent papers concern the what, when, and where of early domestication, with few tackling the questions of why and how. This may to some extent be because the main source of evidence has changed from bone morphometrics to aDNA, and hence from the agenda of zooarchaeology to that of archaeogenetics, leading to some renewed uncertainty as to the criteria for recognising 'domestication'. Those criteria and their practical application to the zooarchaeological record have been the subject of another fleet of papers over the last several decades (Larson and Burger 2013; Larson et al. 2014), with only sparse and optimistic reports that a consensus has been sighted on the horizon. Before we can address the question of why and how domestication came about, we would need to agree what it is we are looking for in the contextual, the morphometric and the genomic data. Few studies have attained that degree of integration at the time of writing, though Ottoni et al.'s (2012) study of pig domestication in western Europe is a notable exception. In contrast, Zhang et al. (2013) report aDNA from a bovine from northeast China in terms that carefully avoid stating whether it was a wild or a domestic animal. Unless otherwise stated, the remainder of this chapter uses terms such as 'domestication', and 'domesticated' in their general, vernacular sense, thereby ducking the issue for reasons that will become apparent.

The other criticism that can be made of many zooarchaeological studies of domestication is their anthropocentricity. To some extent this is inevitable. Whether we define archaeology as the study of the human past through surviving material evidence or as an engagement with 'old things' (Witmore 2013), then people are bound to be at the heart of any such research. However, the zooarchaeological record is the product of interactions between past humans and other sentient organisms. Domestication, however we define and understand it, was or is a renegotiation of the relationships that generated the zooarchaeological record, a renegotiation that was unlikely to have been one-sided. I have previously pointed out that a one-sided domestication process entirely of benefit to the human partners was unlikely to be an Evolutionarily Stable Strategy (ESS) (O'Connor 1997). The way that domestication and livestock husbandry have swept the world, with no successful replacement of animal domestication by another strategy, indicates that domestication is an ESS and therefore that a less anthropocentric explanation must be sought. Can we, therefore, develop a model for animal domestication in the Neolithic that understands domestication as an emergent property of a multispecies community, focusing neither on people nor goats, but on the faunal community of which both were a part? Such a model might usefully be based around two linked concepts that have proved their worth in behavioural ecology: niche construction theory (NCT) and gene-culture co-evolution (GCC).

NCT stems from the understanding that the niche of an organism is an integration of the needs and capacities of the organism and the opportunities and constraints of the environment in which it lives (Laland et al. 2000; Odling-Smee et al. 1996, 2003). Organisms, individually and collectively as populations, construct their niche as their circumstances require and allow. As they do so, a population of one species may act as an opportunity or a constraint acting on the population of another species. Some of that niche construction will be fundamental to the organisms' anatomy and physiology: lions are unlikely to adopt a niche as foliage browsers, whatever their circumstances. Some, on the other hand, will be locally contingent behavioural adaptations: a group of lions may develop a distinctive hunting strategy attuned to local prey and vegetation cover, a strategy that their young learn by experience and emulation. In this way, NCT requires due consideration to be given to the evolution of behavioural repertoire both by genetic inheritance and by the transmission of knowledge within a group – i.e. learning. GCC acknowledges this interdependence of genetic inheritance and learning, hence its alternative title Dual Inheritance Theory. In combining genetic and socially acquired inheritance and giving primacy to neither, GCC offers a potentially productive paradigm for considering the renegotiation of human-animal engagements in the Neolithic. To date, GCC has been applied in archaeology in a few quite specific cases, proving itself to be a valuable approach at a time when technical advances allow us to 'read' the genetic inheritance in such detail (Gerbault et al. 2013; Smith 2015).

NCT has been applied to studies of early plant and animal domestication with some success, though with varying degrees of acceptance. Bruce Smith, in particular, has been an effective advocate of this approach, demonstrating its advantages over, for example, arguments based on diet-breadth and other optimal-foraging models (Smith 2012, 2015; Zeder 2012). More nuanced arguments have been made, especially by Gremillion et al. (2014), who warn against what they see as a retreat from theory into empirically driven particularism, though their advocacy of "the use of theoretical frameworks that serve to link testable hypotheses to ultimate explanations for human behaviour" (ibid., 6176) would seem to necessitate empirical evidence particular to each specific hypothesis. Others have argued for endogenous social developments as a driver for early farming, such as Bowles and Choi (2013), and Collard et al. (2011) have applied NCT to analyses of artefact assemblages across the onset of the Neolithic. This present chapter is more aligned with Smith's approach than with the critique of Gremillion et al.. or Bowles and Choi's emphasis on social developments. Specifically, it will be argued that the primacy of inter-population engagements in evolutionary processes is unduly neglected by those who seek species-level generalisations, and should not be misunderstood as particularism. Furthermore, any detailed understanding of the origins of animal domestication has to incorporate the behaviour and culture of the animal populations concerned just as much as those of the human populations. Animal behaviour studies are showing just how varied that behaviour may be and the adaptive value of behavioural flexibility within species (e.g. Searle et al. 2010).

An NCT-GCC perspective has one particular advantage: it requires us to allow the possibility that behavioural attributes are disseminated other than by genetic inheritance within populations of species other than our own. Although the term 'culture' is as loaded and evasive as 'domestication', such transmission of ideas and behaviours, particular to a population and not species-wide, constitutes 'culture' of a sort (Whitehead and Lusseau 2012; Laland and Brown 2011). It is this perspective that focuses our discussion on populations, not on generalisations regarding species. That population focus is more consistent with the zooarchaeological record. Each sample of bones represents a given population of this or that species, not the totality of that species, world-wide. What we are seeking, then, when we seek the origins of animal domestication, is evidence of human niche-construction that shifts our species' role from that of a predator, whether highly specialised or broad-spectrum (Grayson and Delpech 1998, 2002), to an interventive manager of other species, with a more vested interest in maintaining living 'prey' and a behavioural repertoire that includes constraining and closely engaging with selected single-species populations. Populations of other species, meanwhile, have accommodated humans as their 'preferred predator', modified their flight reactions, and often adapted to residence for much of the year in an environment different to that typical of the species in the absence of people. When considering the origins of animal domestication, it is unhelpful to think in terms of a species having a 'natural environment', out of which it is taken by the domestication process. All species reduce and skew the fundamental niche that they are physiologically and behaviourally capable of occupying in response to factors such as competition and predation to achieve a realised niche that is defined in part by those constraining factors. Domestication moved animals from one set of constraints to another: which was the more 'natural' is a matter of semantics.

To set the broad environmental context, the early Holocene can most usefully be regarded as a sequence of profound environmental changes. Global temperatures oscillated widely at the end of the Pleistocene, then warmed rapidly but by no means evenly into the Holocene (Bos et al. 2007; Hou et al. 2012; Törnqvist and Hijma 2012). The palaeorecord shows that some of those climate changes were fast enough to have been evident within a human generation, and shows that their impact varied appreciably in different parts of the planet, much as we are seeing today (e.g. Magny et al. 2007). A form of particularism is necessary here, too, to understand climate change in terms of location-specific and population-specific impacts. The local consequences in terms of vegetation change would have been complex and contingent on more factors than global warming; factors such as soil formation and maturation and the history, and thus ecological inheritance (O'Connor and Evans 2005, 66), of the vegetation communities concerned. Rising sea levels affected all coastlines (Lambeck et al. 2014), especially in areas such as Southeast Asia, where huge areas of land were rapidly inundated (Hanebuth et al. 2000). Sea-level changes will in turn have affected the circulation of surface waters and hence the exchange of energy between hydrosphere and atmosphere. Sea-level movements and temperature rise will have required altitudinal adjustments of vegetation communities. At a smaller scale, generally higher temperatures will have had a marked effect on soil humus formation, and hence on fungal and invertebrate communities, not to mention changes in the timing and volume of snow-melt and thus local hydrologies (e.g. Snowball et al. 1999).

That summary barely scratches the surface. The point is that the Terminal Pleistocene and Early Holocene was a period of ecological perturbation at all scales, from global weather systems to the few square metres of a gravel point-bar. For larger-bodied animals, with lifespans measured in years rather than weeks, that rolling perturbation must have been especially challenging. A brown bear cub born in Britain at the end of the Younger Dryas may have encountered winter temperatures inimical to hibernation by the end of its adult life. The accumulated wisdom of human grandparents, based on the world as it had been 40–50 years previously, would have been useless at best, dangerous at worst. The realised niche occupied by a species at any time and place would have been relatively temporary, subject to adaptations as constraints and opportunities changed. Genetic adaptations and learned behaviour were constantly challenged, in an environment of climate change, ecological perturbation and disequilibrium biotas.

Faced with this challenge, human populations in different parts of the world adapted in different ways. In much of temperate Europe, the earliest post-glacial archaeology superficially resembles that of the Upper Palaeolithic. Some sophisticated hunter-gatherer groups targeted a particular prey ungulate, red deer and elk having replaced reindeer and horses (Leduc 2014), and the broad-spectrum foraging identified by some in the Upper Palaeolithic has its parallel in the coastal foragers of the Mesolithic (Zeder 2012; Price 2014). In a broad swathe of Eurasia, from the eastern Mediterranean to Balochistan, people adapted to the disturbances of the period by creating and maintaining patches of stability, stands of plants and animals that were predictable at a time of unpredictability. In this region, hunter-gatherers of the Magdalenian and Late Palaeolithic adapted to the climate swings of the Late Pleistocene by shifting prey and settlement locations (e.g. Jochim 2012). Human niche construction in the face of the challenges of the Early Holocene involved greatly increased ecosystem engineering, actively amending the composition and content of the human operational environment to generate patches of modified environment that had not previously existed. The *niche* construction element here is the process, not the outcome. The modified environment patches that emerged probably differed appreciably from place to place as different human populations acted on local biotas and abiotic resources to achieve an acceptable degree of predictable stability through ecosystem engineering. Those diverse and novel stable patches became potentially available to other species' populations, which will have responded in locally contingent ways according to other environmental constraints and, probably, to specific population histories.

In order to utilise the stable patches effectively, many people adopted a more sedentary life-way, and thus had a more focused and locally intensive impact on their immediate environment. The tendency to sedentism is seen in the Pre-Pottery Neolithic A (Finlayson et al. 2011) and in Terminal Pleistocene Natufian phases (Yeshurun et al. 2014). Comparing early (15–13ky BP) and late (13–11.7ky BP) Natufian, Yeshurun et al. argue that dense occupation and seden-tism are evidenced in the early Natufian, developing in complexity through into the PPNA. That in turn created new opportunities for species that could utilise semi-permanent dwellings and seasonal accumulations of food resources, such as pests of stored grain and their predators (Tchernov 1984; O'Connor 2013, 46–7). Maher et al. (2012) similarly make a strong case for the trend towards sedentism and cultural complexity having begun in the Epipalaeolithic. The 'Revolution' had very deep roots indeed.

One widespread feature of human niche construction in the Early Holocene was close man-agement of caprines. This could be seen as a means of attaining stability, by ensuring that a herd or flock of a prey species was immediately accessible. However, although wild caprines feature in some Terminal Pleistocene assemblages from the wider Middle East (e.g. Matthews et al. 2010; Arbuckle 2014; Stiner et al. 2014), one of the striking features of the PPNA is the switch from hunting gazelles *Gazella subgutterosa* to husbanding caprines (Makarewicz 2009; Sapir-Hen et al. 2009). This switch has preoccupied zooarchaeology since Garrard's thoughtful attempt to explain why early farmers would have preferred caprines to gazelles as domesticates (Garrard 1984). The migratory behaviour and territoriality of gazelles could have been problematic, though less so if suppressed or adapted in some populations as part of the gazelles' local culture. Perhaps, too, there was simply more to gain on the part of caprine populations than for gazelles? In the highland regions of the Zagros, in particular, topographic complexity must have ensured that habitat patches were fragmented across the wider landscape, and the species such as caprines that depended on a particular habitat were dispersed in small sub-populations – a metapopula-tion. Metapopulation dynamics are too distinctive and complex to be given full treatment here; papers in Gilpin (2012) give a useful introduction. One of the conclusions of recent metapopu-lation research has been that the consequences of increased extinction risk depend upon the age cohort that is particularly vulnerable to that risk, with elevated juvenile risk having more impact than elevated adult risk (Sutherland et al. 2014). Early farmers, who had a vested interest in maintaining goat numbers and therefore in optimising the recruitment of kids into the adult cohort, would thus have presented less of an extinction risk than would other predators. Not that a PPNA goat population would have known that, of course, but those demes within the metapopulation that adapted to people as a 'preferred predator' may have significantly reduced their extinction risk in the face of Early Holocene environmental changes.

The transition from predation to husbandry has been discussed by a number of authors as a route into domestication, most recently by Larson and Fuller (2014). In the case of gazelles, this transition clearly did not happen, for reasons that may have as much to do with the gazelles as with people. In the case of aurochs and pigs, Marom and Bar-Oz (2009) have argued that an increased intensity of hunting of both species in Southwest Asia in the Terminal Pleistocene led to an increased frequency of encounters. That increased frequency set the necessary preconditions for behavioural adaptation by aurochs and pigs, and for increased management of those two species by people. A transition from hunted prey to husbanded live-stock is perhaps most clearly seen in the zooarchaeological record of the llama *Llama llama* (e.g. López and Restifo 2012), and has been linked by Yacobaccio (2004) with social complexity within Andean hunter-gatherer groups. Llama populations that associated with people were able to extend into regions that might otherwise not have been ecologically available to them, for example moving to lower altitudes (Szpak et al. 2015). As caprine domestication emerged in some areas in which caprine predation was not a major aspect of earlier economies, something other than hunting encounters must have increased the frequency of contact between caprines and people, such as caprines actively seeking out the human modified environment as a relatively stable habitat patch.

Caprine populations that opportunistically utilised the human modified environment would have been subject to unusual pressures on their social structures, in particular reduction of intraspecies antagonism related to mating and to the consequences of increased population density. Bro-Jørgensen (2011) demonstrates that simple explanations based predominantly on male competitive strategies are inadequate for ungulates, and that behavioural interactions that may be specific to a population can drive phenotypic selection, becoming a GCC system. Close association with people is likely also to have favoured a reduction in flight distance. Modern data on flight distance in Eurasian wild sheep and goat species is sparse and unhelpful. Most of what we have derives from North American studies of bighorn sheep *Ovis canadensis* in reserves (e.g. Pelletier 2006) or from studies of guanaco *Llama guanocoe* (e.g. Malo et al. 2011). Although not directly relevant, these studies do at least show that wild ungulate populations can adapt if habituated to a regular and predictable form of disturbance that does not trigger a predator-recognition response. Thus bighorn sheep become fairly tolerant of tourist traffic, but react immediately to the presence of dogs. In a similar study of the behaviour of ungulates in African game parks, Kiffner et al. (2014) showed that zebras and most bovids became habituated to human disturbance and reduced their flight distance, but that gazelles did not. The capacity to become habituated to the close presence of people may have been what allowed caprines to enter into a domesticatory relationship, giving them the advantage of access to human-made patches of stability, possibly with exclusion of other predators and exclusion of competitive grazers by their lack of adaptation. It is not difficult to see this as the context for rapid natural selection favouring tolerance of people in such habituated populations. That brings us back to the question of individual population histories. Presumably some wild caprine populations had more frequent and intensive interaction with human populations than others. Different populations will have adapted behaviourally depending on the nature of that past interaction, developing a local 'culture' with regard to people. That may have been a factor in enabling or inhibiting the emergence of the specialised close affiliation that we call 'domestication', and may underlie the diversity of early husbandry strategies noted by Arbuckle and Atici (2013).

If animal domestication has its origins in mutual niche construction, it could in theory have occurred at any time or place in which conditions were suitable, not necessarily in the Early Holocene period conventionally associated with the origins of agriculture. Could animal domestication have occurred without the Neolithic context in which it took place? The point is often made that dogs were probably the first domesticated animals and the zooarchaeological and genetic records lend some support to this assertion (Larson et al. 2012; Frantz et al. 2016). As with all 'wild/domestic' differentiation, there are considerable difficulties inherent in trying to distinguish the bones of a free-living individual, or a small sample of such a population, from those of contemporaneous and possibly spatially co-existing individuals that had adapted to a close affiliation with people. In the case of dogs, this is complicated by the variation between modern populations of the presumed wild ancestor, the grey wolf *Canis lupus*, and thus the difficulty of defining a 'wild' prehistoric morphology (Dimitrijević and Vuković 2012). Some of the arguments for early records of dogs are therefore made on contextual rather than morphological grounds. The 'puppy' included in a Natufian burial at Ain Mallaha is a celebrated example (Davis and Valla 1978). Genomic studies have confirmed grey wolf as the ancestral species of dogs, *contra* Koler-Matznick (2002), and indicate multiple 'domestication' events from different wolf populations, usefully summarised by Honeycutt (2010) and clarified by Frantz et al. (2016).

Animals and the Neolithic

Some European canid specimens dated to as much as 30,000 BP have been argued to represent an early move towards domestication, a change of relationship that was temporary, perhaps local, and with no ancestral relationship to modern domestic dogs (Germonpré et al. 2009; Ovodov et al. 2011; Shipman 2012; Druzhkova et al. 2013). Taken at face value, a NCT-GCC model would predict exactly such localized and perhaps only temporary mutual accommodation by human and other animal populations that were in frequent contact. However, and somewhat regrettably, subsequent investigation has cast doubt on the domestic status of these specimens and the general consensus for now is that domestication of dogs from grey wolf arose at various places in Eurasia in the last few millennia of the Pleistocene (Boudadi-Maligne and Escarguel 2014; Freedman et al. 2014; Morey 2014). This is intriguing, as it places the change of relationship in the context of human hunter-gatherer populations, not incipient agriculturalists. The domesticatory relationship itself is exceptional, too, being between competing predators (wolves and people) rather than between herbivores and their potential predator (goats, sheep, cattle, llama, etc. and people). The Upper Palaeolithic of Eurasia records human populations increasing in number and in their capacity to construct a successful niche in diverse environments, most notably in the Gravettian (Brugère 2014; Simon et al. 2014). Increasing frequency and intensity of encounter with wolf populations presumably occurred, prompting a range of responses. Mutual avoidance may have been a successful strategy in some places: regrettably, a strategy that is unlikely to have left a zooarchaeological record. Deliberate extirpation of wolves by people is another: there is persuasive evidence that bears were deliberately sought out and killed in Upper Palaeolithic Europe (Wojtal et al. 2014). However, killing solitary bears during their hibernation is one thing, and killing a non-hibernating pack animal is quite another. The third possibility is that some wolf and human populations found a *modus vivendi* that avoided the worst effects of direct competition. Some evidence to this effect comes from Terminal Pleistocene deposits in northern England (Lord and O'Connor 2013). Bones from caves in karstic landscapes in this region frequently derive from wolf dens, with ample evidence of tooth-pits and other indications of wolf 'processing' of carcasses (O'Connor and Jacobi 2015). In a few instances, the tooth-marks can be shown to overlie, and thus to post-date, lithic cut-marks on the same specimen, indicating that wolves scavenged carcasses that had already been at least partly butchered by people (Lord et al. 2007). Significantly, those specimens are the largest-bodied ungulates in the local fauna: horses *Equus caballus* and aurochs *Bos primigenius*. It is possible that wolf populations in this region gained some trophic benefit by scavenging human kills to gain access to animals that would otherwise have been too large to be successfully hunted by the wolves alone. Such facilitation is recognised as an important factor in ecosystem function (Bruno et al. 2003). A similar form of facilitation has been observed in modern North America where wolves, not humans, act as the facilitating predator (Wilmers et al. 2003). In the presence of wolves, carrion availability changes in quantity and seasonal abundance, allowing scavengers such as coyote *Canis latrans* to adapt their niche. In the case of Upper Palaeolithic Europe, I suggest that the presence of human hunting bands allowed some wolf populations to similarly adapt their niche to take greater advantage of the scavenging opportunities. Might that have had other 'cultural' effects within the wolf population? At this point, the argument becomes informed speculation, as the evidence runs thin. However, it is at least plausible that smaller and therefore lower-ranking individuals within the wolf pack would have gained most advantage by closer association with people, enabling them to act outside the wolf pack hierarchy and providing a simple self-selection mechanism by which to account for the apparent size reduction and other morphological changes from grey wolves to early domestic dogs (Dayan 1994; Schmitt and Wallace 2014). In this model, wolf populations constructed a niche that accommodated predatory humans, leading to socio-cultural changes within wolf packs that allowed low-ranking individuals to benefit from closer association with people, and hence some genetic changes as smaller individuals thereby enhanced their breeding success. Niche construction by wolves and people led to a gene-culture co-evolution within the wolf populations, with smaller, more highly affiliative 'dogs' as an outcome.

This admittedly speculative model supposes the emergence of a form of commensalism on the part of some wolves. Commensalism has been proposed as one possible route to domestication by Larson and Fuller (2014) and is argued to have a greater time-depth than animal domestication (O'Connor 2013). Crucially, the zooarchaeological record shows the local emergence of commensal relationships between human and animal populations that did not develop into full domestication, underlining the importance of time- and location-specific factors. For example, Stewart (2004) draws attention to the high frequency of occurrence of foxes *Vulpes* spp. on Upper Palaeolithic sites. Stewart's data are taken further (O'Connor 2013, 42–4) to argue that the larger Upper Palaeolithic sites of Continental Europe allowed the development of a commensal scavenger niche amongst foxes *Vulpes* and birds of the crow family Corvidae. The same niche is utilised by some, but not all, populations of both taxa today, though neither has become a 'domesticate'. There is no inevitability about animal domestication. Some populations of some species have found, and continue to find, a niche that results in close affiliation with people, an ESS that does not develop into full domestication. In some cases, the adoption of a commensal 'culture' in non-domestic species can be shown to have led to genomic evolution, as seen in comparisons of wild and commensal populations of spiny mouse *Acomys cahirinus* (Nováková et al. 2008). Where such a GCC process has occurred, reversion of behaviour may be maladaptive in the population concerned.

The importance of examining the examples of canids and corvids is that mutual adaptation of populations did not necessarily lead to what we recognise as domestication. That end-point seems to have been more likely to occur in the context that we would recognise as 'Neolithic', i.e. with sedentary occupation, ceramics and plant cultivation. Something about that combination of attributes made a close affiliation advantageous both to some human populations and to some populations of some animal species. Given that, it is perhaps more helpful to see domestication arising as a property of certain multispecies communities, driven by mutual adaptation and niche-construction, and leading to varying degrees of gene-culture co-evolution as the domesticated ecomorphs diverged behaviourally and morphologically from non-domesticated demes of the same species. Something similar could be seen as having happened in human populations, too. The consequences of farming for human health have been chronicled at length (Armelagos and Cohen 1984; Larsen 2006), and Leach (2003) is one of several authors who have postulated a domestication process in our own species. Animal domestication and the emergence of livestock husbandry was very much a two-way street, and far more complex and locally contingent than discussion in the zooarchaeology literature has sometimes allowed. With the new insights provided by DNA analysis, this is the time to re-think our models for the origins of domestic animals, but to do so from a multispecies perspective that no longer treats animals as passive objects.

References

Arbuckle, B. S. (2014). Pace and process in the emergence of animal husbandry in Neolithic Southwest Asia. *Bioarchaeology of the Near East, 8*, 53–81.

Arbuckle, B. S., and Atici, L. (2013). Initial diversity in sheep and goat management in Neolithic southwestern Asia. *Levant, 45*(2), 219–35.

Armelagos, G. J., and Cohen, M. N. (Eds.). (1984). *Paleopathology at the Origins of Agriculture*. Academic Press, New York.

Bökönyi, S. (1989). Definitions of animal domestication. In J. Clutton-Brock (ed.), *The Walking Larder. Patterns of domestication, pastoralism, and predation.* Unwin Hyman, London, pp. 24–7.

Bos, J. A., van Geel, B., van der Plicht, J., and Bohncke, S. J. (2007). Preboreal climate oscillations in Europe: wiggle-match dating and synthesis of Dutch high-resolution multi-proxy records. *Quaternary Science Reviews, 26*(15), 1927–50.

Boudadi-Maligne, M., and Escarguel, G. (2014). A biometric re-evaluation of recent claims for Early Upper Palaeolithic wolf domestication in Eurasia. *Journal of Archaeological Science, 45,* 80–9.

Bowles, S., and Choi, J. K. (2013). Coevolution of farming and private property during the early Holocene. *Proceedings of the National Academy of Sciences, 110*(22), 8830–35.

Bro-Jørgensen, J. (2011). Intra-and intersexual conflicts and cooperation in the evolution of mating strategies: lessons learnt from ungulates. *Evolutionary Biology, 38*(1), 28–41.

Brugère, A. (2014). Not one but two mammoth hunting strategies in the Gravettian of the Pavlov Hills area (southern Moravia). *Quaternary International, 337,* 80–9.

Bruno, J. F., Stachowicz, J. J., and Bertness, M. D. (2003). Inclusion of facilitation into ecological theory. *Trends in Ecology & Evolution, 18*(3), 119–25.

Clutton-Brock, J. (1981). *Domesticated Animals from Early Times.* Heinemann, London.

Collard, M., Buchanan, B., Ruttle, A., and O'Brien, M. J. (2011). Niche construction and the toolkits of hunter-gatherers and food producers. *Biological Theory, 6*(3), 251–59.

Davis, S. J., and Valla, F. R. (1978). Evidence for domestication of the dog 12,000 years ago in the Natufian of Israel. *Nature 276,* 608–10 (December 7, 1978); doi:10.1038/276608a0.

Dayan, T. (1994). Early domesticated dogs of the Near East. *Journal of Archaeological Science, 21*(5), 633–640.

Dimitrijević, V., and Vuković, S. (2012). Was the dog locally domesticated in the Danube Gorges? Morphometric study of dog cranial remains from four Mesolithic–Early Neolithic archaeological sites by comparison with contemporary wolves. *International Journal of Osteoarchaeology, 25*(1), 1–30.

Druzhkova, A. S., Thalmann, O., Trifonov, V. A., Leonard, J. A., Vorobieva, N. V., Ovodov, N. D., Graphodatsky, A. S. and Wayne, R. K. (2013). Ancient DNA analysis affirms the canid from Altai as a primitive dog. *PloS One, 8*(3), e57754.

Evin, A., Flink, L. G., Bălăşescu, A., Popovici, D., Andreescu, R., Bailey, D., and Dobney, K. (2015). Unravelling the complexity of domestication: a case study using morphometrics and ancient DNA analyses of archaeological pigs from Romania. *Philosophical Transactions of the Royal Society B: Biological Sciences, 370*(1660); doi: 10.1098/rstb.2013.0616.

Finlayson, B., Mithen, S. J., Najjar, M., Smith, S., Maričević, D., Pankhurst, N., and Yeomans, L. (2011). Architecture, sedentism, and social complexity at Pre-Pottery Neolithic A WF16, southern Jordan. *Proceedings of the National Academy of Sciences, 108*(20), 8183–88.

Flink, L. G., Allen, R., Barnett, R., Malmström, H., Peters, J., Eriksson, J., Andersson, L., and Larson, G. (2014). Establishing the validity of domestication genes using DNA from ancient chickens. *Proceedings of the National Academy of Sciences, 111*(17), 6184–89.

Frantz, L. A. F., Mullin, V. E., Pionnier-Capitan, M., Lebrasseur, O., Ollivier, M., Perri, A., Linderholm, A., Mattiangeli, V., Teasdale, M. D., Dimopoulos, E. A., Tresset, A., Duffraisse, M., McCormick, F., Bartosiewicz, L., Gál, E., Nyerges, E., Sablin, M. V., Bréhard, S., Mashkour, M., Bălăşescu, A., Gillet, B., Hughes, S., Chassaing, O., Hitte, C., Vigne, J.-D., Dobney, K., Hänni, C., Bradley, D. G., and Larson, G. (2016). Genomic and archaeological evidence suggest a dual origin of domestic dogs. *Science 350*(6290), 1228–31.

Freedman, A. H., Gronau, I., Schweizer, R. M., Ortega-Del Vecchyo, D., Han, E., Silva, P. M., Galaverni, M., Fan, Z., Marx, P., Lorente-Galdos, B., Beale, H., Ramirez, O., Hormozdiari, F., Alkan, C., Vilà, C., Squire, K., Geffen, E., Kusak, J., Boyko, A. R., Parker, H., Lee, C., Tadigotla, V., Siepel, A., Bustamante, C. D., Harkins, T. T., Nelson, S. F., Ostrander, E. A., Marques-Bonet, T., Wayne, R. K., and Novembre, J. (2014). Genome sequencing highlights the dynamic early history of dogs. *PLoS genetics, 10*(1), e1004016.

Garrard, A. N. (1984). The selection of South-West Asian animal domesticates. In: Clutton-Brock, J. and Grigson, C., (eds.) *Animals and Archaeology. 3. Early Herders and their flocks.* BAR: Oxford; pp. 117–32.

Gerbault, P., Bollongino, R., Burger, J. Thomas, M. G. (2013). Inferring processes of Neolithic gene-culture co-evolution using genetic and archaeological data: the case of lactase persistence and dairying. In: Colledge, S., Connolly, J., Dobney, K., Manning, K., and Sheenan, S. (Eds.) *The Origins and Spread of Domestic Animals in Southwest Asia and Europe.* Left Coast Press, Walnut Creek, California, pp. 37–48.

Germonpré, M., Sablin, M. V., Stevens, R. E., Hedges, R. E., Hofreiter, M., Stiller, M., and Després, V. R. (2009). Fossil dogs and wolves from Palaeolithic sites in Belgium, the Ukraine and Russia: osteometry, ancient DNA and stable isotopes. *Journal of Archaeological Science*, *36*(2), 473–90.

Gifford-Gonzalez, D., and Hanotte, O. (2011). Domesticating animals in Africa: implications of genetic and archaeological findings. *Journal of World Prehistory*, *24*(1), 1–23.

Gilpin, M. (Ed.). (2012). *Metapopulation dynamics: empirical and theoretical investigations*. Academic Press, London.

Grayson, D. K., and Delpech, F. (1998). Changing diet breadth in the early Upper Palaeolithic of southwestern France. *Journal of Archaeological Science*, *25*(11), 1119–29.

Grayson, D. K., and Delpech, F. (2002). Specialized early Upper Palaeolithic hunters in southwestern France? *Journal of Archaeological Science*, *29*(12), 1439–49.

Greene, K. (1999). V. Gordon Childe and the vocabulary of revolutionary change. *Antiquity*, *73*(279), 97–109.

Gremillion, K., Barton, L., and Piperno, D. R. (2014). Particularism and the retreat from theory in the archaeology of animal origins. *Proceedings of the National Academy of Sciences 111*(17), 6171–77.

Grigson, C. (1991). An African origin for African cattle?—some archaeological evidence. *African Archaeological Review*, *9*(1), 119–44.

Hanebuth, T., Stattegger, K., and Grootes, P. M. (2000). Rapid flooding of the Sunda Shelf: a late-glacial sea-level record. *Science*, *288*(5468), 1033–35.

Harris, D. R. (1994). *The Archaeology of V. Gordon Childe: contemporary perspectives*. D. R. Harris (Ed.). University of Chicago Press, Chicago.

Hole, F. (1996). The context of caprine domestication in the Zagros region. *The Origins and Spread of Agriculture and Pastoralism in Eurasia*. Smithsonian Institution Press, Washington, DC, pp. 263–81.

Honeycutt, R. L. (2010). Unravelling the mysteries of dog evolution. *BMC Biology*, *8*(20), http://www.biomedcentral.com/1741-7007/8/20.

Hou, J., Huang, Y., Shuman, B. N., Oswald, W. W., and Foster, D. R. (2012). Abrupt cooling repeatedly punctuated early-Holocene climate in eastern North America. *The Holocene*, *22*(5), 525–29.

Jochim, M. (2012). Coping with the Younger Dryas in the Heart of Europe. In Meren, E. I. (ed.) *Hunter-Gatherer Behavior: Human Responses during the Younger Dryas*. West Coast Press, Walnut Creek, CA, pp. 165–178.

Kiffner, C., Kioko, J., Kissui, B., Painter, C., Serota, M., White, C., and Yager, P. (2014). Interspecific variation in large mammal responses to human observers along a conservation gradient with variable hunting pressure. *Animal Conservation*, *17*(6), 603–12.

Koler-Matznick, J. (2002). The origins of the dog revisited. *Anthrozoös 15*(2), 98–118.

Laland, K. N., and Brown, G. (2011). *Sense and Nonsense: Evolutionary perspectives on human behaviour*. Oxford University Press, Oxford.

Laland, K. N., Odling-Smee, J., and Feldman, M. W. (2000). Niche construction earns its keep. *Behavioral and brain sciences*, *23*(1), 164–72.

Lambeck, K., Rouby, H., Purcell, A., Sun, Y., and Sambridge, M. (2014). Sea level and global ice volumes from the Last Glacial Maximum to the Holocene. *Proceedings of the National Academy of Sciences*, *111*(43), 15296–303.

Larsen, C. S. (2006). The agricultural revolution as environmental catastrophe: implications for health and lifestyle in the Holocene. *Quaternary International*, *150*(1), 12–20.

Larson, G., and Burger, J. (2013). A population genetics view of animal domestication. *Trends in Genetics*, *29*(4), 197–205.

Larson, G., and Fuller, D. Q. (2014). The evolution of animal domestication. *Annual Review of Ecology, Evolution and Systemics 66*, 115–36.

Larson, G., Karlsson, E. K., Perri, A., Webster, M. T., Ho, S. Y., Peters, J., Stahl, P. W., Piper, P. J., Lingaas, F., Fredholm, M., Comstock, K. E., Modiano, J. F., Schelling, C., Agoulnik, A. I., Leegwater, P. A., Dobney, K., Vigne, J. D., Vilà, C., Andersson, L, and Lindblad-Toh, K. (2012). Rethinking dog domestication by integrating genetics, archeology, and biogeography. *Proceedings of the National Academy of Sciences*, *109*(23), 8878–83.

Larson, G., Piperno, D. R., Allaby, R. G., Purugganan, M. D., Andersson, L., Arroyo-Kalin, M., Barton, L., Climer Vigueira, C., Denham, T., Dobney, K., Doust, A. N., Gepts, P., Gilbert, T., Gremillion, K., Lucas, L., Lukens, L., Marshall, F. B., Olsen, K. M., Pires, C., Richerson, P. J., Rubio de Casas, R., Sanjur, O. I., Thomas, M. G., and Fuller, D. Q. (2014). Current perspectives and the future of domestication studies. *Proceedings of the National Academy of Sciences*, *111*(17), 6139–46.

Leach, H. (2003). Human domestication reconsidered. *Current Anthropology*, *44*(3), 349–68.

Leduc, C. (2014). A specialized Early Maglemosian site at Lundby Mose (Zealand, Denmark): a contribution to the understanding of Maglemosian patterns of animal resource exploitation. *Journal of Archaeological Science*, *41*, 199–213.

López, G. E., and Restifo, F. (2012). Middle Holocene intensification and domestication of camelids in north Argentina, as tracked by zooarchaeology and lithics. *Antiquity*, *86*(334), 1041–54.

Lord, T. C., O'Connor, T. P., Siebrandt, D. C., and Jacobi, R. M. (2007). People and large carnivores as biostratinomic agents in Late Glacial cave assemblages. *Journal of Quaternary Science*, *22*(7), 681–94.

Lord, T. C., and O'Connor, T. P. (2013). Cave palaeontology. In: T. Waltham and D. Lowe (eds.) *Caves and Karst of the Yorkshire Dales*. British Cave Research Association, Buxton, pp. 225–38.

MacDonald, K. C. (1992). The domestic chicken (*Gallus gallus*) in sub-Saharan Africa: a background to its introduction and its osteological differentiation from indigenous fowls (Numidinae and *Francolinus* sp.). *Journal of Archaeological Science*, *19*(3), 303–18.

Magee, D. A., MacHugh, D. E., and Edwards, C. J. (2014). Interrogation of modern and ancient genomes reveals the complex domestic history of cattle. *Animal Frontiers*, *4*(3), 7–22.

Magny, M., Vannière, B., De Beaulieu, J. L., Bégeot, C., Heiri, O., Millet, L., Peyron, O., and Walter-Simonnet, A.-V. (2007). Early-Holocene climatic oscillations recorded by lake-level fluctuations in west-central Europe and in central Italy. *Quaternary Science Reviews*, *26*(15–16), 1951–64.

Maher, L. A., Richter, T., and Stock, J. T. (2012). The Pre-Natufian Epipaleolithic: long-term behavioral trends in the Levant. *Evolutionary Anthropology: Issues, News, and Reviews*, *21*(2), 69–81.

Makarewicz, C. A. (2009). Complex caprine harvesting practices and diversified hunting strategies: integrated animal exploitation systems at Late Pre-Pottery Neolithic B'Ain Jamman. *Anthropozoologica*, *44*(1), 79–101.

Malo, J. E., Acebes, P., and Traba, J. (2011). Measuring ungulate tolerance to human with flight distance: a reliable visitor management tool? *Biodiversity and Conservation*, *20*(14), 3477–88.

Marom, N., and Bar-Oz, G. (2009). Man made oases. *Before Farming*, *2009*(1), 1–12.

Matthews, R., Mohammadifar, Y., Matthews, W., and Motarjem, A. (2010). Investigating the Early Neolithic of western Iran: the Central Zagros Archaeological Project (CZAP). *Antiquity*, *84*(323), http://www.antiquity.ac.uk/projgall/matthews323/.

McClure, S. B. (2015). The pastoral effect: niche construction, domestic animals, and the spread of farming in Europe. *Current Anthropology* *56*(6), 901–10.

Morey, D. F. (2014). In search of Paleolithic dogs: a quest with mixed results. *Journal of Archaeological Science*, *52*, 300–7.

Nováková, M., Palme, R., Kutalová, H., Janský, L., and Frynta, D. (2008). The effects of sex, age and commensal way of life on levels of fecal glucocorticoid metabolites in spiny mice (*Acomys cahirinus*). *Physiology & Behavior*, *95*(1), 187–93.

O'Connor, T. P. (1997). Working at relationships: another look at animal domestication. *Antiquity*, *71*(271), 149–56.

O'Connor, T. P. (2013). *Animals as Neighbors: The past and present of commensal animals*. MSU Press, East Lansing.

O'Connor, T. P., and Evans, J. G. (2005) *Environmental Archaeology: principles and methods*. Sutton Publishing, Stroud.

O'Connor, T. P. and Jacobi, R. (2015). Ossom's Cave, Staffordshire: an Upper Palaeolithic site reconsidered. In: Ashton, N. and Harris, C. (eds) *No Stone Unturned: Papers in honour of Roger Jacobi*. Lithic Studies Society, London, pp. 127–34.

Odling-Smee, F. J., Laland, K. N., and Feldman, M. W. (1996). Niche construction. *American Naturalist*, 641–48.

Odling-Smee, F. J., Laland, K. N., and Feldman, M. W. (2003). *Niche Construction: The neglected process in evolution* (No. 37). Princeton University Press, Princeton.

Ottoni, C., Flink, L. G., Evin, A., Geörg, C., De Cupere, B., Van Neer, W., Bartosiewicz, L., Linderholm, A., Barnett, R., Peters, J., Decorte, R., Waelkens, M., Vanderheyden, N., Ricaut, F.-X., Çakirlar, C., Çevik, O., Hoelzel, R., Mashkour, M., Mohaseb Karimlu, A. F., Seno, S. S., Daujat, J., Brock, F., Pinhasi, R., Hongo, H., Perez-Enciso, M., Rasmussen, M., Frantz, L., Megens, H.-J., Crooijmans, R., Groenen, M., Arbuckle, B., Benecke, N., Strand Vidarsdottir, U., Burger, J., Cucchi, T., Dobney, K. and Larson, G. (2012). Pig domestication and human-mediated dispersal in western Eurasia revealed through ancient DNA and geometric morphometrics. *Molecular Biology and Evolution*, doi: 10.1093/molbev/mss261.

Ovodov, N. D., Crockford, S. J., Kuzmin, Y. V., Higham, T. F., Hodgins, G. W., and van der Plicht, J. (2011). A 33,000-year-old incipient dog from the Altai Mountains of Siberia: evidence of the earliest domestication disrupted by the Last Glacial Maximum. *PLoS One*, *6*(7), e22821.

Pelletier, F. (2006). Effects of tourist activities on ungulate behaviour in a mountain protected area. *Journal of Mountain Ecology*, *8*, 15–19

Price, T. D. (2014). Affluent foragers of the Mesolithic. In: T. D. Price and J. A. Brown (eds.) *Prehistoric Hunter-Gatherers: The Emergence of Cultural Complexity*. Academic Press, New York, pp. 341–63.

Renfrew, C. (2006). Inception of agriculture and rearing in the Middle East. *Comptes Rendus Palevol*, *5*(1–2), 395–404.

Russell, N. (2002). The wild side of animal domestication. *Society & Animals*, *10*(3), 285–302.

Sapir-Hen, L., Bar-Oz, G., Khalaily, H., and Dayan, T. (2009). Gazelle exploitation in the early Neolithic site of Motza, Israel: the last of the gazelle hunters in the southern Levant. *Journal of Archaeological Science*, *36*(7), 1538–46.

Schmitt, E., and Wallace, S. (2014). Shape change and variation in the cranial morphology of wild canids (*Canis lupus, Canis latrans, Canis rufus*) compared to domestic dogs (*Canis familiaris*) using geometric morphometrics. *International Journal of Osteoarchaeology*, *24*(1), 42–50.

Searle, K. R., Hunt, L. P., and Gordon, I. J. (2010). individualistic herds: individual variation in herbivore foraging behavior and application to rangeland management. *Applied Animal Behaviour Science*, *122*(1), 1–12.

Shipman, P. (2012). Do the eyes have it? Dog domestication may have helped humans thrive while Neandertals declined. *American Scientist*, *100*(3), 198.

Simmons, A. H. (2011). *The Neolithic Revolution in the Near East: transforming the human landscape*. University of Arizona Press, Arizona.

Simon, U., Händel, M., Einwögerer, T., and Neugebauer-Maresch, C. (2014). The archaeological record of the Gravettian open air site Krems-Wachtberg. *Quaternary International*, *351*, 5–13.

Smith, B. D. (2012). A cultural niche construction theory of initial domestication. *Biological Theory*, *6*(3), 260–71.

Smith, B. D. (2015). A comparison of niche construction theory and diet breadth models as explanatory frameworks for the initial domestication of plants and animals. *Journal of Archaeological Research*, 1–48.

Snowball, I., Sandgren, P., and Petterson, G. (1999). The mineral magnetic properties of an annually laminated Holocene lake-sediment sequence in northern Sweden. *The Holocene*, *9*(3), 353–62.

Stewart, J. R. (2004). Neanderthal–modern human competition? A comparison between the mammals associated with Middle and Upper Palaeolithic industries in Europe during OIS 3. *International Journal of Osteoarchaeology*, *14*(3–4), 178–89.

Stiner, M. C., Buitenhuis, H., Duru, G., Kuhn, S. L., Mentzer, S. M., Munro, N. D., Pöllath, N., Quade, J., Tsartsidou, G. and Özbaşaran, M. (2014). A forager-herder trade-off, from broad-spectrum hunting to sheep management at Aşıklı Höyük, Turkey. *Proceedings of the National Academy of Sciences*, *111*(23), 8404–9.

Sutherland, C. S., Elston, D. A., and Lambin, X. (2014). A demographic, spatially explicit patch occupancy model of metapopulation dynamics and persistence. *Ecology*, *95*(11), 3149–60.

Szpak, P., Chicoine, D., Millaire, J. F., White, C. D., Parry, R., and Longstaffe, F. J. (2015). Early Horizon camelid management practices in the Nepeña Valley, north-central coast of Peru. *Environmental Archaeology*, doi: 10.1179/1749631415Y.0000000002.

Tchernov, E. (1984). Commensal animals and human sedentism in the Middle East. *Animals and Archaeology*, *3*, 91–115.

Thomas, N. (1982). Childe, Marxism, and archaeology. *Dialectical Anthropology*, *6*(3), 245–52.

Törnqvist, T. E., and Hijma, M. P. (2012). Links between early Holocene ice-sheet decay, sea-level rise and abrupt climate change. *Nature Geoscience*, *5*(9), 601–6.

Vigne, J. D. (2011). The origins of animal domestication and husbandry: a major change in the history of humanity and the biosphere. *Comptes rendus biologies*, *334*(3), 171–81.

Vigne, J. D., Carrere, I., Briois, F., and Guilaine, J. (2011). The early process of mammal domestication in the Near East. *Current Anthropology*, *52*(S4), S255–S271.

Whitehead, H., and Lusseau, D. (2012). Animal social networks as substrate for cultural behavioural diversity. *Journal of Theoretical Biology*, *294*, 19–28.

Wilmers, C. C., Crabtree, R. L., Smith, D. W., Murphy, K. M., and Getz, W. M. (2003). Trophic facilitation by introduced top predators: grey wolf subsidies to scavengers in Yellowstone National Park. *Journal of Animal Ecology*, *72*(6), 909–16.

Witmore, C. (2013). Which archaeology? A question of chronopolitics. In A. González-Ruibal (ed.) *Reclaiming Archaeology: Beyond the tropes of modernity*, Routledge, London and New York, pp. 130–44.

Wojtal, P., Wilczyński, J., Nadachowski, A., and Münzel, S. C. (2014). Gravettian hunting and exploitation of bears in Central Europe. *Quaternary International, 359/360*, 58–71.

Yacobaccio, H. D. (2004). Social dimensions of camelid domestication in the southern Andes. *Anthropozoologica, 39*(1), 237–47.

Yeshurun, R., Bar-Oz, G., and Weinstein-Evron, M. (2014). Intensification and sedentism in the terminal Pleistocene Natufian sequence of el-Wad Terrace (Israel). *Journal of Human Evolution, 70*, 16–35.

Zeder, M., Emshwiller, E., Smith, B. and Bradley, D. (2006). Documenting domestication: the intersection of genetics and archaeology. *Trends in Genetics 22*(3), 139–55.

Zeder, M. A. (2012). The broad spectrum revolution at 40: resource diversity, intensification, and an alternative to optimal foraging explanations. *Journal of Anthropological Archaeology, 31*(3), 241–64.

Zeder, M. A. (2015). Core questions in domestication research. *Proceedings of the National Academy of Sciences, 112*(11), 3191–98.

Zeuner, F. E. (1955). The goats of early Jericho. *Palestine Exploration Quarterly, 87*(1), 70–86.

Zeuner, F. E. (1963). *A History of Domesticated Animals*. Hutchinson, London.

Zhang, H., Paijmans, J. L., Chang, F., Wu, X., Chen, G., Lei, C., O'Connor, T. P., and Hofreiter, M. (2013). Morphological and genetic evidence for early Holocene cattle management in northeastern China. *Nature Communications, 4*(2755), doi:10.1038/ncomms3755.

13

MAKING SPACE FROM THE POSITION OF DUTY OF CARE

Early Bronze Age human-sheep entanglements in Norway

Kristin Armstrong Oma

Introduction

The Anthropocene is a term that is rapidly gaining momentum. It presupposes that humans stepped up and took a leading role in driving processes of change in a hereto-unprecedented scale. Domestication, of plants, animals and environments, is vital to this development. Domestication is, from this perspective, a process that presupposes mastery in the form of modification and manipulation of the behavioural dispositions, morphology and life world of other beings.

Archaeology has played a role in trying to explain these processes by way of environmental archaeology. This has epistemologically been informed by a fundamentally Cartesian, i.e. humanist/enlightenment paradigm, that presupposes that humans have conquered animals, plants and landscapes and subjected these to the human will, as though these are passive, even inanimate, matter (Johannsen 2012; van der Veen 2014). In this chapter, I question this approach and consider the domestication process and early agrarian commitments as steps of ever-changing human-animal engagements that created historically unique interspecies relationships. The agency of plants (e.g. Morehart and Morell-Hart 2013; van der Veen 2014) and animals (e.g. Brittain and Overton 2013) has only recently come under scrutiny, and I draw upon these ideas.

A number of questions are important when trying to grasp early agrarian commitments. In the first part of this chapter, I address relevant theoretical themes targeted to respond to questions like: what kinds of human-animal relationships existed in early stages of the domestication process? What were their natures? How were they carried out? What were their outcomes? In the second part, I explore how interspecies relationships – intangible bonds and sometimes surely fleeting moments – can be extricated from the archaeological record by considering the domestic life of Norwegian longhouses in the early Bronze Age (in Scandinavian archaeology, the early Bronze Age is dated to 1800–1100 BCE).

Interspecies relationships: the complexity

I understand interspecies relationships as commitments that are performed (Birke and Parisi 1999; Birke et al. 2004), and the performance can manifest in many ways. Thus, there are various scenarios in early husbandry practices regarding which species became entangled with humans, how material culture and practices became embodied, and how spatial set-ups were created to frame the engagements. These range from various species, geographical locations and different practices. One example is the cultural control over Barbary sheep during the early Holocene in the Sahara, where sheep were penned in caves by hunter-gatherer groups that clearly interacted with the sheep in other activities than hunting – possibly for ceremonies, considering nearby rock art (di Lernia 1998; Smith 2005: 84). Another famous example is the domestication of cattle and the cattle cult at the Neolithic Anatolian tell-site of Çatalhüyük, where cattle crania are integrated in the architecture, sometimes embedded in walls and benches, and deposited in burials (e.g. Russell et al. 2005; Twiss and Russell 2009). Further, the Natufian engagements with body parts of humans, gazelles and other animals is another interesting example (Boyd 2006). Common to these are that they involve two parts: the humans and the animals (domesticated, or in the process of becoming so). These brief examples demonstrate that there are many types of set-ups. What emerges from these can be described as different economic strategies or different forms of deeply entangled, and mutually constituted, becomings. I see no essential dissonance between these – they simply describe the same thing from different perspectives.

It is reminiscent of the famous Indian parable of the people who are blindfolded and are asked to identify an elephant, those that touch the trunk will give a very different description of it compared to those that touch the tusks. The inherent danger with perspectives is, however, when one dominates and there is an academic discourse in which the trunk is the only defining trait of the elephant. I have previously argued that environmental archaeology and zooarchaeology are often mainly focused on human-domestic animal relationships as expressive of economic strategies, and have thus tumbled down this rabbit-hole (Armstrong Oma 2007; Armstrong Oma and Birke 2013). This has potentially also had detrimental effects upon the ontological status and welfare of farm animals since the 1950s (Armstrong Oma 2013). I am not making a case for dismissing a line of inquiry into economic strategies, but merely stating that focusing on this as the only perspective gives a skewed impression of the complexity of human-domestic animal relationships.

Although many zooarchaeologists now also consider social aspects in relation to the animals they study (see Russell 2012 with references), they seem to not be interested in the animals *as themselves* – but rather the animals as props in a social play between humans. Rather, similar to the question asked by Mariejke van der Veen (2014) regarding plants – what do plants want? – I ask: what do animals want? And what do they need to do, to get what they want?

I do not, however, see this conundrum as a choice between 'hard-nosed' economic thinking, the use of animals in social practices, and sentimentalism – rather, these perspectives are, on their own, incomplete. I have previously argued that there is a space in between them that is left out – that of the deep-seated practice of, and construction of meeting points between, real-life people and real-life animals (Armstrong Oma 2012). The space of practice makes place (Parker Pearson and Richards 1994) and incorporates the relationship: what springs forth, what emerges, what is forever mutually becoming between the participating agents.

In this chapter, I discuss forms of relationships ranging from symbiosis to social contracts, and further the importance of recognising animal agency and introduce *duty of care* as fundamental to agrarian commitments. I have previously argued that humans and animals tacitly performed their dance of domestication within the framework of a social contract (Armstrong Oma 2007, 2010, 2013a, 2013b). In this contribution, I endeavour to extend this argument and discuss it within the domestication discourse.

Finally, in order to discuss the nature of such relationships and how they can be understood, I will draw upon a Scandinavian early Bronze Age case study to put forward a case for the importance of socialisation and development of trust between humans and animals as a basic building block for commitments fundamental to husbandry practices. This case study is but one link in the chain of development of the human-domestic animal engagement, and denotes a change that led to new ways of living for humans and sheep – and also physically altered their life-world.

Symbiosis and social contracts

Human-animal relationships are often described as a form of symbiosis, which denotes ways of living together in which two dissimilar organisms live in close physical proximity where each benefits the other. Their mutual advantage defines a relationship as symbiotic. This symbiotic perspective has sometimes been used to discuss human–farm animal relations (Zeuner 1963; Rindos 1984; Jarman et al. 1982; Bökönyi 1989; Budiansky 1992, 1994; Lund et al. 2004b). In anthropology, the human-animal relationship has been thought of as symbiotic growth between the family and the herd (Spencer 1998: 4, 11, 24–26; see also Budiansky 1992).

The term holds validity when describing agrarian commitments, but considering its strict definition, symbiosis upholds a one-sided focus on biological advantages, and leaves social and cultural factors out of the equation. This does not mean that a symbiotic relationship precludes social engagement, but a study of symbiosis does not consider social aspects of a relationship. Nor does it study individuals; rather, those individuals are regarded as representatives for behaviour rather than as subjects and agents. Although relationships are always somewhat symbiotic (the individuals that choose to enter it will wish to gain something from it), they are also something more: they are historically and contextually specific, and go into realms beyond the 'mere' mutual advantage to form truly unique relationships (Armstrong Oma 2007: 68–69).

The idea of symbiotic human-animal relationality is in some ways reminiscent of Donna Haraway's (2008) concept of companion species, which she uses to talk about myriad species, messmates, being at table with all kinds of beings, such as bacteria etc. While I do contend that animals and humans are companion species to each other as we dwell in the world in mutual co-habitation, my main focus lies in the kinds of becomings that emerge from specific and historically situated happenings that are physical meetings between beings that recognise each other's presence. Thus, it is my belief that to identify steps in the process of domestication, we must consider social and cultural factors as historically specific (e.g. Prescott 2012). Each group of beings that have entered a setting of domestication has brought its own requirements into the bargain, and subtly negotiated their own terms. Previously, I have referred to this as a social contract between humans and animals (Armstrong Oma 2007, 2010).

A social contract: socio-cultural ramifications

The idea of a human-animal contract differs fundamentally from a human-animal symbiosis because whereas a human-animal relationship as a symbiotic entity is essentially unspecific as its core drive is mutual biological benefits, the idea of a human-animal contract has socio-cultural ramifications for how the relationship is articulated. The notions of trust and reciprocity are at the core of the social contract. Animal agency is sometimes recognised by the way animals *act back*, buck, refuse (e.g. Warkentin 2009) – but in this respect, I suggest that the agency of animals is one of tacit agreement and cooperation, similar to how Gala Argent presents a compelling case for the horses' choice of cooperating and co-creating action by walking in step to human handlers (Argent 2012).

The idea of a social contract, a 'pact between man and beast, sought by each for their mutual aid' (Larrère and Larrère 2000: 55) goes back to antiquity and has been present through the ages (Larrère and Larrère 2000; Lund et al. 2004b: 37). It is identified in biology (Morris 1986: 3). It defines the terms of engagement and the duties, responsibilities and rights of the parts involved (Lund et al. 2004b: 35).

The ethical 'eco-contract' between humans and animals in organic farming (see Lund et al. 2004b: 38–43 for an outline of the content of this contract, and further: Larrère and Larrère 2000; Lund 2002; Lund et al. 2004b; Lund 2005) presupposes that humans and animals are partners in the agroecosystem, and is meant to regulate human-animal relations (Lund et al. 2004b: 35). It gives significance to animals *as themselves* and considers their particular needs in order to thrive (Alrøe et al. 2001; Lund and Röcklinsberg 2001: 409; Lund et al. 2004a; Lund 2005). Implicitly, the 'eco-contract' acknowledges animals as participants in contractual relations in which both humans and animals have rights and obligations towards each other. However, this does not imply that they are equal partners (Larrère and Larrère 2000: 55).[1] It is precisely because they are perceived as unequal in modern society that such a contract is meant to assure a fair and ethically sound treatment of animals. Today's organic 'eco-contract' does not correspond with contracts that existed in the past. But there is some common ground, such as a presupposition that there can be communication between humans and animals in a way that is meaningful to both – an exchange of affect, of emotion, and information interpretable by both (Larrère and Larrère 2000: 56).

Mary Midgley (1983: 83–87) suggests that the Hobbesian idea of a social contract between the sovereign and the people can be understood in two ways: as an existing body of law and custom, or as a deeper and more notional idea of unspoken trust and agreement, based upon tacit reciprocity and duties. It is the latter understanding of contract that I follow. Those who enter such a contract are bound solely by their trust in the other part and it creates a bond between unequal partners to secure the rights and duties of both and may also involve animals (cf. Rowlands 2006). Midgley (1983: 84) suggests that the contract should stand for an ideal area of unspoken trust and agreement. It therefore goes some way towards encouraging people towards encountering animals on their own terms, rather than on human terms.

The notion of contract has wider implications for considering human-animal relationships in prehistory, since it is negotiable and can take many forms. In the past, the same animals – within the locus of their present time – could simultaneously be symbols, companions and subsistence: meat, skin and bones and heavenly creatures. Allowing for human-animal relationships as social contracts opens up for an integration of factors that normally are not discussed together in the archaeological discourse. Economic strategies, cosmological institutions and performing relationships are incorporated within the same framework in the social contract. As participants in it, animals are given multiple roles and can simultaneously participate in different arenas. How does this perspective of human-animal relationality compare with traditional and recent understandings of the domestication process and its premises?

Domestication discourses

Domestication is normally understood as a series of events that led to changed lifeways for humans and animals, both as biological and morphological changes in domestic animals and humans, such as size, life expectancy and pathological changes. Domestication therefore goes beyond the taming of animals. We cannot pinpoint the exact causes that led to the sparks of domestication. Still, I hold that this process of change must have been rooted in embodied practice[2] and real-life experiences. The outcome is, however, known: over time, human understanding of animals changed, as did their way of being with animals.

I will not give a comprehensive overview here of the different explanations given for domestication (see Russell 2012: 207–220 for an in-depth analysis), but briefly paraphrase main lines of argument. The traditional discourse is one I term the *domination discourse*. Here, domestic animals are regarded as beings controlled by humans, for human consumption and other needs. This was succinctly expressed by Tim Ingold in his article 'From Trust to Domination' in which he described the transition from hunting to husbandry as one which involved a shift in the engagement with animals from reciprocal to domination, in which animals were kept as slaves (Ingold 2000; for critique, see Armstrong Oma 2007, 2010; Knight 2005). His maxim was, by many archaeologists, felt to voice their tacit understanding of the shift in perception of animals that domestication caused, and was widely quoted as an explanation of the nature of the relationship between humans and domestic animals as one of domination (for example, Wengrow 2006: 81; Denham and White 2007: 9–11).

Thus, the domination discourse runs deeper and goes beyond Ingold. It has its roots in the traditional way archaeologists have configured the concept of domestication from a biological and economic perspective, going at least as far back as Vere Gordon Childe's concept of the Neolithic revolution (Childe 1936). One salient example is Juliet Clutton-Brock's definition from her edited volume *The Walking Larder* (Clutton-Brock 1989: 7) where she puts it thus: 'a cultural and biological process . . . that can only take place when tamed animals are incorporated into the social structure of the human group and become objects of ownership'. And she goes on to say that domestic animals are 'bred in captivity for purposes of economic profit to a human community that maintains complete mastery over its breeding organization of territory and food supply'. More recently, Russell (2012: 214–215) similarly states that her stance is that 'the transformation of animals from shared resources to property is a critical transition.' Ingold's influential narrative has been instrumental in cementing this view. This discourse is bound up with a progressive view of human history as unidirectional, in which both the environment and animals were perceived to enter increasingly exploitative relations with humans (see also Cassidy 2007: 5–6).

Could there be alternative explanations? Several archaeologists claim greater complexity in the process (see Dransart 2002: 7; Jones and Richards 2003: 50; Whittle 2003: 80). One of the most notable voices is that of Steven Budiansky, who has swung the pendulum and credits animals and plants with the domestication of humans (Budiansky 1992, 1994). Others have chosen a middle ground, and emphasise mutuality, fallibility and chance in the development of humans and their environment (overview in Cassidy 2007; for example Zeuner 1963; Rindos 1984; O'Connor 1997). Terry O'Connor (1997) suggests an alternative model that gives greater agency to animals, and accentuates human and animal co-evolution as a process that is beneficial to both, thus sliding towards an explanation influenced by symbiotic thinking.

Natasha Fijn points out that domestication of animals in terms of 'making the animals into a being of human design, is likely to be a Western concept' (Fijn 2011: 18). In her work with Mongolian herders, she has come to a different conceptualisation of human-animal relations, and refers to this relationship as 'co-domestic', defined thus: 'the social adaptation of animals in association with human beings by means of mutual cross-species interaction and social engagement' (Fijn 2011: 19).

Domestication as an ethics of care

I argue that this led to a specific ethics of care in which humans responded to the needs of animals and instead of taking/using animals by killing them, there was a sense of, and possibly a need to, give back to the animals. Giving back could initially manifest in practices such as clearing areas for grazing and guarding water supplies, so that the animals were protected. And later, in more complex and entangled relationships, in building shelters, aiding during giving birth, providing food by collecting grass, leaves and bark, and ultimately more complex strategies that involved storage, such as haymaking. From the animals' perspective, what better servants could they have than these humans who clear and guard pastures, build shelters, bring water and food, and so on?

I understand such practices under the umbrella term *ethics of care*. This term is associated with *duty of care* and is normally used in social sciences and particularly in medicine and nursing, to denote the duty and practices of protecting, nurturing and caring for those who are weak, sick, injured, or disabled. But it is also a much wider term, and in UK legislation, duty of care is implemented in the Animal Welfare Act.[3] In a broader sense, it denotes the duty of behaving in such a way to others as to not do them harm, but to protect them – and it is in this sense that I extend this notion to animals in the past.

Introducing an ethics of care into the domestication discourse discloses an attitude in which the relationship between humans and domestic animals is seen as asymmetrical. However, this does not necessarily imply that animals are mindless creatures, Cartesian automata, or slaves devoid of agency that were completely dominated by humans. I acknowledge that animals have the capacity for agency, in line with the growing interdisciplinary recognition that many animals possess characteristics such as intelligence, emotion and awareness that vary from humans by degree rather than kind (Shapiro and DeMello 2010; DeMello 2012).

As in the humanities at large, human agency has been granted supremacy in archaeology. Ontologically, the nature of being is the nature of human being; the nature of action is of human action (Johannsen 2012: 305). However, the field of symmetrical archaeology has gone some way towards correcting this (see, for example Olsen et al. 2012). But animals are more than cultural abstractions: what is lacking is considerations of the animals *as themselves*. Animals are alive, active participants in their worlds, and the spaces where those worlds intersect and enmesh with humans are often messy and difficult to divide into clean compartments. In addition to how humans 'use' them, animals often take part in subjectified relationships with humans that impact both species at various levels of scale. For example, Birke, Bryld and Lykke (2004: 172–173) describe how rats in labs defy their definition as 'data' for animal experiments by requiring that humans facilitate their biological and social needs and perform accordingly.

Recognising animals as active co-creators of the world (Haraway 2003, 2008) has a particular relevance for farming societies. By way of their sentience, animals possess agency by their ability to purposefully act upon the world, unless severely physically restrained. On the farm, space is created, shared and mutually constituted by humans and domestic animals. Meanings arise and practices are constituted as joint actions unfold; whilst herding, milking, plucking wool, walking together, resting together, and creating spaces, thresholds (Armstrong Oma 2007). The consideration and care in which individuals are allowed to carve out their personal place is created everywhere on the farm.

I will briefly illustrate the implications of this by paraphrasing John Law and Annemarie Mol's (2010: 58) exploration of the agency of a Cumbrian sheep situated in time-space (2001 in England in the middle of the foot-and-mouth epidemic). Starting from material semiotics, they claim that entities give each other being, that they enact each other. Agency is thus 'ubiquitous, endlessly extended through webs of materialised relations'. This means that an actor does not act alone. It acts in relation to other actors, linked up with them. This means that it is also always being acted upon. To act is not to master, for the results of what is being done are often unexpected.

Law and Mol 2010: 57

This perspective slips away from the distinction between mastery and being-mastered (ibid.). This example connects the work of Science Studies, as advocated by Actor-Network Theory, with Human-Animal Studies. Similarly, I suggest that on farms, past and present, relations are managed by both farmers and animals, with their specific requirements to thrive and form a healthy flock, and by the animals' ability, by their agency, to choose whether to cooperate or resist.

Successful farming, then, depends upon acknowledging that animals' needs must be met in order for the animals to thrive. Further, I suggest that farmers, by way of duty of care, hold a self-imposed social obligation to the animals.

Identifying needs becomes an important aspect of this line of conjecture. In order to successfully carry out a duty of care, the need for care, and its specific ramifications, must be known. These needs are another aspect of animal agency; that they require specific set-ups in order to thrive. Examples are access to suitable feeds, the scope for movement, opportunity for shelter, and as a flock, they need the opportunity to reproduce. These needs are what the domestic animals bring into the social contract. Humans must cater to these needs in order to live in a successful agrarian commitment. Thus, in order to achieve a functioning household economy based upon husbandry, the needs of the animals are the main priority. The animals respond to the duty of care that humans bring to the table, as well as bringing their own. Consequently, by way of their needs, animals co-shape not only the social contract but also the spatial arrangements, daily and yearly cycles, engagement with the wider environment and so on, that shape the lives of all stakeholders in agrarian commitments. By this engagement, the process of mutual becoming unfolds.

A chain of domestications: changes in terms of engagement

Understanding the processes of domestication of animals goes beyond simply taming and ensuing genetic changes in animals, but addresses new ways of living, inter-species, both politically and socially (Armstrong Oma and Birke 2013: 113; see also Mlekuž 2013). I present an Early Bronze Age case study that renders a change in the terms of becoming between humans and domestic animals. In examining this case study, I draw upon Human-Animal Studies (Shapiro and DeMello 2010) as a way of investigating issues such as reciprocity, commitment, duty of care, socialisation and co-authored life-ways. Ultimately, new husbandry strategies that are evident in the archaeological record are all steps in the process of domestication, and in this case study I demonstrate how it brought humans and one other species – sheep – into greater proximity than before.

In northern Europe, the Neolithic two-aisled longhouse was replaced by the three-aisled longhouse in the early Bronze Age. This change is believed to coincide with the indoor stalling of domestic animals in one part of the house (Tesch 1992: 290; Rasmussen and Adamsen 1993: 138; Lagerås and Regnell 1999; Rasmussen 1999: 281; Årlin 1999; Armstrong Oma 2007, 2010, 2013a, 2013b). Together with the change in architecture, changes in ways of living occurred too, although it cannot be inferred that these came about because the Bronze Age farmers wanted to change their way of living. The reasons underlying this change are unknown.

Economic and functional reasons, such as the animals heating the house, are frequently given, but have been disproved by Zimmerman (1999). Both Årlin (1999) and Rasmussen (1999) suggest the cause to be an intensification of social relationships between humans and animals (tacitly assumed to be cattle). The new living arrangement certainly resulted in such deepening of relations, but I will venture forth with a more explicit explanation.

Trust, socialisation and habituation embedded in the architecture

I have studied early Bronze Age three-aisled longhouses in the region of Rogaland in South-western Norway. In this region, I argue that there is evidence for a strong presence of sheep and that they come to co-habit longhouses together with humans – and sheepdogs (Armstrong Oma 2016). This is based upon the majority of sheep/goat in faunal remains from the period (although assemblages are small due to the acidity of the soil; for reports, see Hufthammer 2002, 2004). For example, from the prehistoric village of Forsandmoen in Rogaland, a small number of bones were recovered from the whole life-span of the village, from the Early Bronze Age (c. 1500 BC) until the Migration period (c. 500 AD). The small size of the assemblage cannot be used to draw firm conclusions, but it is indicative of the species present at sites. The faunal remains were dominated by sheep/goat, with over half the assemblage identified to sheep/goat or sheep/goat size. Some of the bones were probably from pigs. Smaller numbers of wild animals, birds and fish were also present. Remarkably, no bones were identified to cattle, or large-size domesticates, and according to preservation bias, their bones should have been recovered if they had been there – after all, bird and fish bones have a much lower rate of recovery (for report, see Hufthammer 2004). At another Early Bronze Age site nearby, that of Kvåle in Rogaland, bone preservation was equally poor, but the few identified bones are all from sheep/goat (Hufthammer 2002; Soltvedt et al 2007: 56).

Another kind of animal materiality is the presence of sheep coprolites, which place sheep firmly within the house. Coprolites identified to be from sheep was found within a replaced roof-bearing posthole in an Early Bronze Age longhouse from Austbø, see Figure 13.1, whereas several more were found in the wall posts. The roof-bearing post had been replaced whilst the house was standing (Hemdorff 1989: 8), so the sheep dropping, found in the very bottom of the posthole (Hemdorff 1989: 11), must have fallen into the hole as the post was replaced, i.e. not during the initial construction of the house, but sometime during the lifespan of the standing house. This means that sheep were inside the house, and some quantity of dung must have been present for it to end up at the bottom of a posthole. I believe this demonstrates that sheep were indeed living inside the house. Sheep droppings are a by-product of living animals. I argue that this means that sheep were inside the house. The house seems to be separated into two parts by two closely set posts across in the middle of the house, these are supposedly doorposts for an opening between the two parts. There are two entrances, set asymmetrically at each long side. The postholes contained much charred material, notably in some cases copious amounts of charred grains, which led the excavator to believe that the house must have burnt at least once (Hemdorff 1989: 8). Based on this evidence, I conclude that humans had their main living space in the north-eastern part of the house, whereas sheep lived in the south-western part.

A factor that has frequently been overlooked when considering activities inside longhouses are smaller postholes located 'randomly' inside the house and are not part of the construction of the house. Such posts could represent tethering of animals or temporary, makeshift pens. The presence of smaller postholes near the posthole with the sheep dropping in Austbø House 1 could, further, indicate makeshift pens, consistent with lambing. Sheep

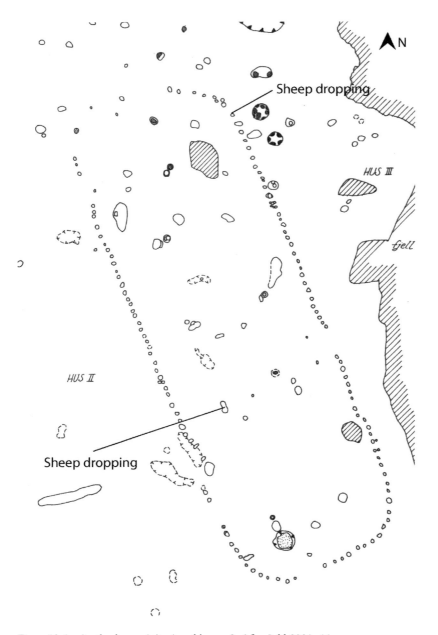

Figure 13.1 Austbø house 1 (top) and house 2. After Juhl 2001: 46.

are normally kept free-range inside the byre and at special times such as in the lambing season live in make-shift pens that are easily moved around to make space for ewes and newborn lambs. In a practical sense, a three-aisled construction is an obvious advantage in a sheep pen, and well suited to accommodate sheep, since the distribution of posts makes it easier to set up makeshift pens.

The dominance of sheep could well be connected to a new-fangled importance of textiles; this would require a development in the domestication process in this area that required large flocks of sheep, which were producers of fleece. In the Early Bronze Age, wool textiles start appearing in graves in Scandinavia. Famous examples are the Danish oak coffin graves, where women and men have been interred clad in wool costumes. In Rogaland, preservation is not so good, but there are wool textile fragments in graves from this period.

Obtaining wool requires manageability and sheep fleece was plucked rather than shorn at this stage. This practice necessitates an intense and close relationship that is highly dependent upon the development of trust between humans and sheep. This new practice needed a novel spatial framework, and I argue that the shift in building tradition, from two-aisled to three-aisled longhouses, was associated with a shift in the socio-economic household practice. This shift consists of an intensification of the human-sheep relationship, where sheep were drawn closer to the household and eventually taken into the house. But sheep were hardy and self-sufficient in the Bronze Age, so why would such a shift happen? I propose that keeping animals indoors, at least for part of their lives, have implications for how inter-species relationships are allowed to unfold. There are some clear advantages by keeping animals inside the house. One is that the animals become habituated with people, and I suggest that this allows for the development of mutual trust between human and animal on an individual as well as intimate level that would not happen with flocks kept outside (see below). This kind of relationship effectively makes the practice of obtaining wool possible. Such relationships can only be formed within the animal's biological 'window of opportunity'.

The power of early socialisation

Dogs must be socialised and habituated with humans early in life; this is crucial to develop positive feelings towards, and the ability to trust in, humans (also see O'Connor, this volume). A British study demonstrated that 68% of dogs that frequently showed behaviour dominated by fear-aggression had been reared outdoors in a stable, a kennel, or a shed, and not inside houses together with humans (Appleby et al. 2002; Solbakken 2010). This early socialisation, from birth until 16 weeks, is key to develop the kind of healthy social security that is so vital to create a strong working partnership (e.g. Price 2011).

Research on early socialisation in different animal species has shown that there is a window of opportunity in which the young will accept secondary caregivers, and its time-length varies from species to species. Scott (1962: 16) suggests that lambs 'form social attachments to their caretakers and associates' within the first ten days of life, whereas Markowitz et al. (1998) finds that in lambs, such attachments can be formed possibly only in the first three days. Despite artificial selection for tameness (Price 1984), a tendency to maintain some flight-distance and physiological stress responses to humans persist even today in domestic animals (Grandin 1987). For example, routine handling procedures of sheep, such as shearing and herding, leads to elevated stress levels (Markowitz et al. 1998: 573). Hutson (1985) has demonstrated that in sheep, stress can be alleviated by gentle handling and food rewards. Although tameness is to a certain degree heritable, environmental influences are important in animals' responses to humans, and one way of obtaining greater tameness is through increased contact and socialisation with humans in early life (Kilgour 1987).

This demonstrates that indoor stalling of animals, especially of the young, has a profound impact upon the animals' ability to develop positive feelings and trust towards humans, thus making the animals easier to handle later in life. Good stockmanship demands the development of a positive relationship between the caregiver and the animals in one's charge. This makes sense both regarding animal welfare (Dawkins 1980) and giving higher production yields (e.g. Seabrook 1972, 2001).

Studies have been conducted to assess whether early human handling of lambs leads to increased affinity for humans in lambs. Markowitz, Dally, Gursky and Price (1998: 580–581) found that 'handling and feeding of lambs, especially in the first 3 days of life, can strongly influence their responses to people as they mature.' Their study also shows that lambs can, in this early period, form a primary attachment to their mother, and a secondary social attachment to human handlers. The secondary attachment does not interfere with the primary attachment (ibid.: 584). In relation to the domestication process, Michael Ryder writes, in his magnum opus on sheep through the ages, that 'the key biological process appears to have been the "imprinting" on a young animal of a human being in place of its mother' (Ryder 1983: 3). However, I would argue that imprinting was not advantageous for the farmers in the Early Bronze Age. Imprinting would lead to a 'blended flock', in which species specificities would be lost. In a blended flock, the natural behaviour of the animals would be lost, due to lambs being imprinted by humans from birth. For example, this would cause problems with the fertility of the animals, as animals imprinted by humans want to mate with humans rather than their own species when they reach adulthood (Denenberg 1962: 112).

A different way of relating to sheep must have taken place, and rather than imprinting the lambs, humans and lambs must have been co-socialised, which would create a shared flock. Humans and sheep shared the house, but each had their own part. In a shared flock, the two kinds would be socialised with each other, and at the same time retain their species specificities that made them both thrive. I suggest that one of the reasons underlying the change to three-aisled longhouses was to create a setting in which co-socialisation, and inherently trust, could be nurtured. The way I see this tangibly happening is that at first, ewes about to give birth were taken into the house and the ewe, in a social setting where humans were present, reared their lambs. In this way, being around humans would be as natural to the lambs as breathing. This would be advantageous for both humans and sheep, as the sheep could be assisted in cases of difficult births and their lambs more sheltered and protected than they would have been outside. For the humans, this had the obvious advantage that the sheep became much more manageable and it would be much easier to pluck off the valuable fleece.

Bronze Age farmers both identified, and catered for the needs of sheep when they brought the pregnant ewes into the longhouse and let them give birth inside, so that the newborn lambs became socialised with humans from birth. In order to thrive and give up their wool, the sheep brought this need into the social contract. But also for the humans, this contact with the lambs must have led to a sense of wanting to care for them and to protect them – a duty of care. After all, mammals are biologically geared towards wanting to care for babies, across the species boundary (Bekoff 2012).

In Bronze Age Rogaland, Fijn's concept of 'co-domestic' is meaningful. The lack of fencing and divisions of the landscape point towards an untrammelled herding environment, reminiscent of Fijn's findings in Mongolia, that she describes thus: 'herders and herd animals live with each other in a shared landscape, inhabiting a co-domestic, ecosocial sphere' (2011: 19).

Conclusion: who's who in the Anthropocene

The secondary products revolution raises an important question: what implications would the use – following the procurement of – secondary products have for specific practices of a joint human-animal world? Clearly, a greater involvement, greater proximity and physical intimacy resulted. These factors would necessarily lead to an intimate knowledge of the animals in joint households. In this way, implications of economically based choices would lead to specific social entanglements. To answer the question posed at the outset – what kinds of human-animal relationships existed in early stages of the domestication process? – in Bronze Age Rogaland, entanglements between sheep and humans led to shared flocks in which all kinds of flock members lived under the same roof. The nature of this relationship could be understood as a social contract that created physical room for human-sheep socialisation, that in its turn led to an outcome in which the architecture facilitated a relationship based upon interspecies trust.

Returning to the beginning – what does this understanding of domestication and its processes bring to the discussion of the Anthropocene? In August 2016, *The Guardian* reported that scientists have now declared that we live in the dawn of a geological era called the Anthropocene.[4] The lead-in to the article states: 'Experts say human impact on Earth so profound that Holocene must give way to epoch defined by nuclear tests, plastic pollution and domesticated chicken.' Explicitly and implicitly, the Anthropocene is perceived as a human-only creation – even the domestic chicken is, according to this definition, a human construction. The Anthropocene is often associated with nuclear testing, plastic, concrete, air-borne pollution, and is thus dated to have started around 1950. In which case, the domestic chicken is a strange creature to throw into the mix. But processes leading up to the supposed start of this era from the 1950s onwards cannot be fully separated from the Anthropocene, such as the Industrial Revolution in the 1700s, and going further back in time, domestication of animals and even the use of fire by humans. Considering this time-depth, I argue that an understanding of the Anthropocene must be rooted in an acknowledgement that it is not a purely human enterprise (see also Armstrong Oma and Tønnessen 2016). The case study presented here shows that processes of making living arrangements were not shaped by humans alone, but also by animals and what their agency brought into the equation. I follow Anna Tsing (2012) in her description of traditional science as human exceptionalism, and this idea is a normative fantasy in our culture. She claims that

> science has inherited stories about human mastery from the great monotheistic religions. These stories fuel assumptions about human autonomy, and they direct questions to the human control of nature, on the one hand, or human impact on nature, on the other, rather than to species interdependence.
>
> *Tsing 2012: 144*

But, she posits, 'What if we imagined a human nature that shifted historically together with varied webs of interspecies dependence?' What, indeed? If so, I suggest that we understand this age we live in as having been co-authored by humans and animals, and it is the deep interspecies entanglements that are a defining trait rather than a speciesist understanding of humans as the sole doers and agents. Thus, there is no Anthropocene causing changes in the ecosphere without, or outside of, the dialectics of care between humans and their partners in domestication. In such a scenario, the exceptionalism of humans resides in their willingness to make space for other beings to flourish on their own terms.

Acknowledgements

I am indebted to Niall Armstrong for his close reading of this text, his invaluable comments and for countless discussions on the nature of human-animal relationships. Further, my deep gratitude goes to Savino di Lernia and Maryanne Tafuri for the Caldecote sessions in which the seeds to these ideas were sown. I am also grateful to my colleague Siv Kristoffersen for reading and commenting on an early draft of this text. I am also indebted to the editor for her very useful suggestions, and two anonymous reviewers for insightful comments. Any mistakes are my own. This research was funded by the Norwegian Research Council and the Norway Financial Mechanism 2009–2014 under project contract no EMP151.

Notes

1 Lund *et al.* (2004a: 36) point out that 'although the relation is essentially one between unequal contributors, both humans and farm animals are equal in the sense that they are members of the agroecological community, and their interdependence will at a closer look turn out to be greater than commonly assumed.'
2 Following feminist theory, experience is rooted in the body.
3 https://www.gov.uk/government/publications/animal-welfare-act-2006-it-s-your-duty-to-care.
4 https://www.theguardian.com/environment/2016/aug/29/declare-anthropocene-epoch-experts-urge-geological-congress-human-impact-earth accessed 18.09.2016.

References

Alrøe, H. F., et al. (2001). Does organic farming face distinctive livestock issues? A conceptual analysis. *Journal of Agricultural and Environmental Ethics* 14(3): 275–299.

Appleby, D., et al. (2002). Relationship between aggression and avoidance behaviour by dogs and their experience in their first six months of life. *The Veterinary Record* 150(14): 434–438.

Argent, G. (2012). Toward a privileging of the nonverbal: communication, corporeal synchrony and transcendence in humans and horses. *Experiencing animals: encounters between animal and human minds.* J. A. Smith and R. W. Mitchell. Animal Studies Series. New York, Columbia University Press: 111–128.

Årlin, C. (1999). Under samma tak – om "husstallets" uppkomst och betydelse under bronsåldern ur ett sydskandinaviskt perspektiv. *Spiralens öga. Tjugo artiklar kring aktuell bronsåldersforskning.* M. Olausson, Riksantikvarieämbetet. 25: 291–307.

Armstrong Oma, K. (2007). *Human-animal relationships: mutual becomings in the household of Scandinavia and Sicily* 900–500 BC. Oslo, Unipub.

Armstrong Oma, K. (2010). Between trust and domination: social contracts between humans and animals. *World Archaeology* 42(2): 175–187.

Armstrong Oma, K. (2012). Large-scale 'grand narratives' and small-scale local studies in the Bronze Age discourse: the animal perspective. *Local societies in Bronze Age Northern Europe.* N. Anfinset and M. Wrigglesworth. Sheffield, Equinox: 71–88.

Armstrong Oma, K. (2013a). Human-animal meeting points: use of space in the household arena in past societies. *Society & Animals* 21(2): 162–177.

Armstrong Oma, K. (2013b). Past and present farming: changes in terms of engagement. *Humans and the environment: new archaeological perspectives for the 21st century.* M. I. Davies and F. Nkirote. Oxford, Oxford University Press: 181–192.

Armstrong Oma, K. (2016). Sheep, dog and man: multi-species becomings leading to new ways of living in Early Bronze Age longhouses on Jæren, Norway. *The farm as a social arena.* Dommasnes, L. H., A. T. Hommedal and D. Gutschmidl-Schümann. Münster and New York, Waxmann Verlag: 25–58.

Armstrong Oma, K. and L. Birke (2013). Archaeology and Human-Animal Studies. *Society & Animals* 21(2): 113–119.

Armstrong Oma, K. and M. Tønnessen (2016). Once upon a time in the anthropocene. *Thinking about animals in the age of the anthropocene.* Tønnessen, M., K. Armstrong Oma and S. Rattasepp. London, Lexington Books: vii–xix.

Bekoff, M. (2012). Odd couples: compassion doesn't know species lines. *Psychology Today, Animal Emotions.* Blog post 28 October 2012 https://www.psychologytoday.com/blog/animal-emotions/201210/odd-couples-compassion-doesnt-know-species-lines.

Birke, L. and L. Parisi (1999). Animals, becoming. *Animal others: on ethics, ontology, and animal life.* H. P. Steeves. Albany, State University of New York Press: 55–73.

Birke, L., et al. (2004). Animal performances: an exploration of intersections between feminist science studies and studies of human/animal relationship. *Feminist Theory* 5(2): 167–183.

Bökönyi, S. (1989). Definitions of animal domestication. *The walking larder, patterns of domestication, pastoralism and predation.* J. Clutton-Brock. London and Boston, Unwin Hyman: 22–27.

Boyd, B. (2006). On 'sedentism' in the Later Epipalaeolithic (Natufian) Levant. *World Archaeology* 38(2): 164–178.

Brittain, M. and N. Overton (2013). The significance of others: a prehistory of rhythm and interspecies participation. *Society & Animals* 21(2): 134–149.

Budiansky, S. (1992). *The covenant of the wild: why animals chose domestication.* New York, William Morrow.

Budiansky, S. (1994). A special relationship: the coevolution of human beings and domesticated animals. *JAVMA* 204(3): 365–368.

Cassidy, R. (2007). Introduction: domestication reconsidered. *Where the wild things are now: domestication reconsidered.* R. Cassidy and M. H. Mullin. Oxford and New York, Berg: 1–25.

Childe, V. G. (1936) *Man makes himself.* London, Penguin.

Clutton-Brock, J., Ed. (1989). *The walking larder: patterns of domestication, pastoralism, and predation.* London, One World Archaeology.

Dawkins, M. S. (1980). *Animal suffering: the science of animal welfare.* London, Chapman & Hall.

DeMello, M. (2012). *Animals and society: an introduction to Human-Animal Studies.* New York and Chichester, West Sussex, Columbia University Press.

Denenberg, V. H. (1962). The effects of early experience. *The behaviour of domestic animals.* E. S. E. Hafez. London, Baillière, Tindall & Cox: 109–138.

Denham, T. and P. White (2007). *The emergence of agriculture: a global view.* London and New York, Routledge.

di Lernia, S. (1998). Cultural control over wild animals during the early Holocene: the case of Barbary sheep in central Sahara. *Before food production in North Africa.* S. di Lernia and G. Manzi. Forli, Italy, A.B.A.C.O.: 113–126.

Dransart, P. Z. (2002). *Earth, water, fleece, and fabric: an ethnography and archaeology of Andean camelid herding.* New York, Routledge.

Fijn, N. (2011). *Living with herds: human-animal coexistence in Mongolia.* Cambridge, Cambridge University Press.

Grandin, T. (1987). Animal handling. *Farm animal behaviour.* E. O. Price. Philadelphia, PA, Saunders: 323–338.

Haraway, D. (2003). *The companion species manifesto: dogs, people, and significant otherness.* Chicago, IL, Prickly Paradigm Press.

Haraway, D. (2008). *When species meet.* Minneapolis and London, University of Minnesota Press.

Hemdorff, O. (1989). *Innberetning til topografisk arkiv. Innberetning om arkeologisk undersøkelse af lokalitet 20 på Austbø gnr. 7, bnr. 7, Hundvåg, Stavanger kommune.* Stavanger, Arkeologisk museum i Stavanger.

Hufthammer, A. K. (2002). *Analyse av beinmaterialet fra Kvåle, Time kommune, Rogaland.* Rapport fra Zoologisk museum, Universitetet i Bergen, i Topografisk arkiv, Arkeologisk museum i Stavanger.

Hufthammer, A. K. (2004). *JS081 Rapport Forsandmoen, Forsand K., Rogaland,* Arkeologisk Museum i Stavanger.

Hutson, G. D. (1985). The influence of barley food rewards on sheep movement through a handling system. *Applied Animal Behaviour Science* 14(3): 263–284.

Ingold, Tim. 2000 From trust to domination: an alternative history of human-animal relations. In *The perception of the environment: essays in livelihood, dwelling and skill.* London and New York, Routledge: 61–76.

Jarman, M. R., et al. (1982). *Early European agriculture.* Cambridge, Cambridge University Press.

Johannsen, N. (2012). Archaeology and the Inanimate Agency Proposition: a critique and a suggestion. In *Excavating the mind: cross-sections through culture, cognition and materiality.* N. Johannsen, M. Jessen and H. Juel Jensen. Aarhus, Aarhus University Press: 305–347.

Jones, A. and C. Richards (2003). Animals into ancestors: domestication, food and identity in Late Neolithic Orkney. *Food, culture and identity in the Neolithic and Early Bronze Age.* M. Parker Pearson. Oxford, Archaeopress. 1117: 45–52.

Juhl, K. (2001). *Austbø på Hundvåg gennem 10 000 år. Arkeologiske undersøgelser i Stavanger kommune 1987–1990 Rogaland, Syd-Vest Norge.* Stavanger, AmS-Varia.

Kilgour, R. (1987). Learning and the training of farm animals. *Farm animal behaviour.* E. O. Price. Philadelphia, PA, Saunders: 269–284.

Knight, J. (2005). Introduction. *Animals in person: cultural perspectives on human-animal intimacy.* J. Knight. Oxford and New York, Berg: 1–13.

Lagerås, P. and M. Regnell (1999). Agrar förändring under sydsvensk bronsålder. *Spiralens öga. Tjugo artiklar kring aktuell bronsåldersforskning.* M. Olausson, Riksantikvarieämbetet. 25: 263–276.

Larrère, C. and R. Larrère (2000). Animal rearing as a contract? *Journal of Agricultural and Environmental Ethics* 12(1): 51–58.

Law, J. and A. Mol (2010). The actor-enacted: Cumbrian sheep in 2001. *Material agency: towards a non-anthropocentric approach.* C. Knappett and L. Malafouris. New York, Springer: 57–76.

Lund, V. (2002). Ethics and animal welfare in organic animal husbandry: an interdisciplinary approach. *Department of Animal Environment and Health.* Skara, Swedish University of Agricultural Sciences. Doctoral thesis.

Lund, V. (2005). The human-animal relationship in organic farming. *The human-animal relationship: forever and a day*. F. de Jonge and R. van den Bos. Assen, Royal van Gorcum: 231–246.

Lund, V., et al. (2004a). The ethical contract as a tool in organic animal husbandry. *Journal of Agricultural and Environmental Ethics* 17(1): 23–49.

Lund, V. and H. Röcklinsberg (2001). Outlining a concept of animal welfare for organic farming systems. *Journal of Agricultural and Environmental Ethics* 14(4): 391–424.

Lund, V., et al. (2004b). Natural behaviour, animal rights, or making money: a study of Swedish organic farmers' view of animal issues. *Journal of Agricultural and Environmental Ethics* 17(2): 157–179.

Markowitz, T. M., et al. (1998). Early handling increases lamb affinity for humans. *Animal Behaviour* 55(3): 573–587.

Midgley, M. (1983). *Animals and why they matter: a journey around the species barrier*. Harmondsworth, Penguin.

Mlekuž, D. (2013). The birth of the herd. *Society & Animals* 21(2): 150–161.

Morehart, C. T. and S. Morell-Hart (2013). Beyond the ecofact: toward a social paleoethnobotany in Mesoamerica. *Journal of Archaeological Method and Theory* published online: DOI 10.1007/s10816-013-9183-6.

Morris, D. (1986). *Catwatching: the essential guide to cat behaviour*. London, Jonathan Cape.

O'Connor, T. P. (1997). Working at relationships: another look at animal domestication. *Antiquity* 71: 149–156.

Olsen, B., M. Shanks, C. Webmoor and C. Whitmore (2012). *Archaeology: the discipline of things*. Berkeley, California University Press.

Parker Pearson, M. and C. Richards, Eds. (1994). *Architecture and order: approaches to social space. Material cultures*. London and New York, Routledge.

Prescott, C. (2012). The origin of a Bronze Age in Norway: structure, regional process and localized history. *Local societies in Bronze Age Northern Europe*. N. Anfinset and M. Wrigglesworth. Sheffield, Equinox Publishing: 215–231.

Price, C. (2011). Social security. *Your dog magazine*: 12–15.

Price, E. O. (1984). Behavioural aspects of animal domestication. *Quarterly Review of Biology* 59(1): 1–32.

Rasmussen, M. (1999). Livestock without bones: the long house as contributor to the interpretation of livestock management in the Southern Scandinavian Early Bronze Age. *Settlement and landscape*. C. Fabeck and J. Ringtved. Århus, Jutland Archaeological Society: 281–290.

Rasmussen, M. and C. Adamsen (1993). [The Bronze Age] Settlement. *Digging into the past: 25 years of archaeology in Denmark*. S. B. S. Hvass. Aarhus, Royal Society of Northern Antiquaries/Jutland Archaeological Society: 136–141.

Rindos, D. (1984). *The origins of agriculture: an evolutionary perspective*. New York, Academic Press.

Rindos, D., H. Aschmann, P. Bellwood, L. Ceci, M. N. Cohen, J. Hutchinson, R. S. Santley, J. G. Shaffer and T. Shaw (1980). Symbiosis, instability, and the origins and spread of agriculture: a new model. *Current Anthropology* 21(6): 751–772.

Rowlands, M. (2006). Out of contract. *Times Literary Supplement*: 26.

Russell, N. (2012). *Social zooarchaeology: humans and animals in prehistory*. Cambridge, Cambridge University Press.

Russell, N., et al. (2005). Cattle domestication at Çatalhüyük revisited. *Current Anthropology* 46, Supplement: 101–108.

Ryder, M. L. (1983). *Sheep and man*. London, Duckworth.

Scott, J. P. (1962). Introduction to animal behaviour. *The behaviour of domestic animals*. E. S. E. Hafez. London, Ballière, Tindall & Cox: 3–20.

Seabrook, M. F. (1972). A study to determine the influence of a herdsman's personality on milk yield. *Journal of Agricultural Labour Science* 1: 44–59.

Seabrook, M. F. (2001). *The effect of the operational environment and operating protocols on the attitudes of and behaviour of employed stockpersons. Human-animal relationship: stockmanship and housing in organic livestock systems*. Proceedings of the third NAHWOA workshop, Clermont Ferrand, 21–24 October 2000, Clermont Ferrand, University of Reading.

Shapiro, K. J. and M. DeMello (2010). The state of Human-Animal Studies. *Society & Animals* 18(3): 307–318.

Smith, Andrew B. (2005). *African herders: emergence of pastoral traditions*. Walnut Creek, CA, Altamira Press.

Solbakken, A. C. (2010). Atferdskonsultasjoner over en tiårsperiode. *Hundesport. Tidsskrift for norsk kennelklubb* 111(9–10): 50–51.

Soltvedt, E.-C., T. Løken, L. Prøsch-Danielsen, R.L. Børsheim and K. Oma (2007) *Bøndene på Kvålehodlene. Boplass-, jordbruks-, og landskapsutvikling gjennom 6000 år på Jæren, SV Norge.* AmS-Varia 47, Stavanger: Arkeologisk Museum i Stavanger.

Spencer, P. (1998). *The pastoral continuum: the marginalization of tradition in East Africa.* Oxford, Clarendon Press.

Tesch, S. (1992). House, farm and village in the Köpinge area from Early Neolithic to the Early Middle Ages. *The archaeology of the cultural landscape: field work and research in a South Swedish rural region.* L. Larson, J. Callmer and B. Stjärnquist. Stockholm, Almqvist & Wiksell. 4: 283–344.

Tsing, A. (2012) Unruly edges: mushrooms as companion species. For Donna Haraway. *Environment and Society* 1: 141–154.

Twiss, K. C. and N. Russell (2009). Taking the bull by the horns: ideology, masculinity, and cattle horns at Çatalhüyük (Turkey). *Paléorient* 35(2): 19–32.

Van der Veen, M. (2014). The materiality of plants: plant–people entanglements. *World Archaeology* 46(5): 799–812.

Wengrow, D. (2006). *The archaeology of Early Egypt: social transformations in North East Africa, 10,000 to 2650 BC.* Cambridge, Cambridge University Press.

Whittle, A. (2003). *The archaeology of people: dimensions of Neolithic life.* London and New York, Routledge.

Zeuner, F. E. (1963). *A history of domesticated animals.* London, Hutchinson.

Zimmermann, W. H. (1999). Why was cattle-stalling introduced in prehistory? The significance of byre and stable and of outwintering. *Landscape and settlement.* C. Fabeck and J. Ringtved. Århus, Jutland Archaeological Society: 301–318.

14

THE HISTORY OF THE HUMAN MICROBIOME

Insights from archaeology and ancient DNA

Laura S. Weyrich

The use of microbiology to examine multispecies archaeology

The primary focus of archaeology has historically centered around humans, and their actions and impacts on this earth. However, the focus of this book has revolved around understanding the multispecies interactions that have occurred throughout time. Intriguingly, many of the impacts and alterations from human life and adaptation have gone unseen, and remains largely unexamined to this day. Microorganisms coat every surface of the earth – the ground we walk on, the air we breathe, the bodies we live in, the water we drink, and the animals and artifacts we interact with on a daily basis. Every decision, movement, and interaction that humans have with the earth impacts these microorganisms. Therefore, it has become critical to examine these diverse microbial communities in the world, and examine how human activity altered and impacted these inter-species relationships. While a unique form of multispecies interaction, the relationship humans have with the microorganisms that live within the body – the microbiota – is a critical one for understanding the ramifications of human activity in the past.

The human microbiome

Microbial species coat nearly every surface of the human body, and outnumber human cells two to one! Although these 100 trillion microbiological cells in the human body only make up about three pounds of body mass, the roles they play in human health are absolutely critical (Cho and Blaser 2012). Over 1,800 species live in your gut, on your skin, in your mouth and lungs, and in your sexual organs, and provide more than 100 times the genetic information of the human genome (Gill et al. 2006), lending the human body extensive information to conduct and perform daily bodily functions. For example, bacteria in the gut help digest complex carbohydrates, produce essential vitamins (B and K), assist in developing and regulating the immune system, and compete with disease-causing microorganisms to limit infection (Conly and Stein 1992). Within three years of age, the microbiota acquired at birth, either from the vaginal flora of the mother or the environment and doctors performing the Caesarean surgery for birth (Dominguez-Bello et al. 2010), have nearly fully developed into the communities that will reside on and in the body for most of its adult human life. However, the community composition can also change throughout life, as it adapts to changes in the lifestyle and environment of the host. Microbial diversity in the human body can be altered through the introduction of new microbial species, changes in diet, exposure to different environments, co-habitation with animals, and disease (David et al. 2014; Fierer et al. 2008; Song et al. 2013; Chaban et al. 2013).

Recently, high-throughput DNA sequencing has allowed researchers to examine these diverse communities in greater detail, revealing a new approach to understanding disease on a holistic scale, rather than examining one single bacterial species at a time (Caporaso et al. 2011). Using this approach, these diverse microbial communities in the modern human body have now been linked to numerous ailments in the Western world. Alterations to the microbiota have been shown to include overall compositional shifts in the community or the loss and gain of single 'keystone' species. In the gut, microbiota alterations have been associated with several diseases, including obesity, necrotizing enterocolitis, inflammatory bowel disease, and susceptibility to infections, such as *Clostridium difficile* (Ley et al. 2005; Normann et al. 2013; Tlaskalova-Hogenova et al. 2011; Ray 2015). These gut microorganisms can also signal to the immune system to influence systemic inflammation or influence neurological diseases through the Gut-Brain axis (Flight 2014). Through these secondary mechanisms, heart disease, arthritis, cancer, depression, anxiety, and schizophrenia have now all been linked to alterations in the human microbiome (Dash et al. 2015; Spahr 2006; Scher and Abramson 2011; Schwabe and Jobin 2013; Jhamnani et al. 2013), and this list of diseases grows daily. Similarly, many of these diseases now associated with the human microbiota have increased in prevalence over the last several centuries. Furthermore, many of these diseases, such as obesity and heart disease, are largely absent in isolated Indigenous groups around the word, leading researchers to speculate about links between alterations in the human microbiota and disease prevalence in industrialized Western countries.

Several studies have investigated the mechanisms to explain how the modern microbiota becomes altered. A recent Harvard study demonstrated that changing the diet could alter microbial composition in as little as one week, resulting in both overall community shifts from nutrient differences and the introduction of new species (i.e. specialized bacteria found in fermented meats) (David et al. 2014). An entire bacterial species also may not survive in its new environment, but the gene content of the human microbiota can also be altered through diet. For example, carbohydrate-metabolizing genes were introduced from deep-sea microorganisms into the Japanese human gut through the consumption of sushi, providing the ability to breakdown complex carbohydrate structures within seaweed (Hehemann et al. 2010). In addition to diet, the environment also plays a large role in introducing new species. Within thirty minutes of entering a hotel room, the microbes on your body and the hotel room have mixed and intermingled (Lax et al. 2014). The same microbe swapping also occurs between you and your pet and the outside environment which your pet enjoys (Song et al. 2013). Finally, infectious diseases, such as the flu (influenza virus), food poisoning (*Salmonella* species), or even whooping cough (*Bordetella* species) can alter the microbiota via complex interactions with the immune system and direct interspecies competition (Chaban et al. 2013; Stecher et al. 2007; Weyrich et al. 2013). Even though mechanisms associated with diet, environment, or disease have been revealed, there are countless other imaginable scenarios, or mixtures of scenarios, that might also change the bacterial composition in the body. Critically, many are yet to be discovered.

While events and human influence can impact these microbial communities in the body, we must also ask how these changes in bacterial communities influenced us and how humans evolve. Because bacteria influence our susceptibility to disease, did microbiota impact our ability to survive during large epidemics in prehistory and history? Did our ability to digest food and obtain nutrients from the metabolism by microorganisms impact our health and how well we, as humans, survived harsh winters or droughts over tens of thousands of years? Did microorganisms impact our mental health, and were we more anxious to hunt wild game because of our microbiota? Interestingly, we are just beginning to investigate how bacteria influenced humans and their evolutionary history, and as a corollary, how human actions and large cultural events impacted our microbiota. This chapter will focus on how archaeological research and ancient DNA sequencing have been used to understand these interactions and influences, and identify the events in human history that may have altered these multispecies interactions in the past by changing bacterial communities within the body. We will discuss how researchers identified three large cultural transitions that impacted the bacteria in the body, and discuss the mechanisms behind these changes and how these changes ultimately altered human history. Through the intertwined applications of molecular biology, anthropology, history, and archaeology, we are now beginning to understand how the history of our microbiota impacted us, as well as what this history means for us today.

The evolutionary history of the human microbiome

While the microbiota and the human genome are tightly linked, the two can have very different evolutionary trajectories. The rate of mutation over long time periods is thought to be drastically different, simply due to reproduction times. For example, the human genome only mutates during reproduction, i.e. an average of every twenty years when humans reproduce. However, bacteria living within the human body can reproduce as quickly as twenty minutes (*Escherichia coli*) – that is over 400,000 bacterial reproduction events during a single human one! Due to this difference, bacteria have more opportunities to accumulate further mutations, and ultimately acquire more mutations over time. However, recent studies have shown that this may not be true, as strict environmental selection for bacteria in niches can limit the mutation rate by limiting the number of mutants that survive (such as in the gut, which is an acidic, anoxic environment) (Bart et al. 2014). The verdict is still out. However, bacteria have additional mechanisms that influence their evolutionary rate. Bacteria have secondary mechanisms of adding or removing genetic material from their genomes. These mechanisms allow microorganisms to swap DNA between related species or obtain environmental DNA that may provide them benefit (horizontal or lateral gene transfer) (Overballe-Petersen and Willerslev 2014). Due to this process, bacteria can adapt quickly to significant changes in the environment – changes that might cause the death of a higher-order organism, like a human, without help from the microorganisms in the body.

We must also remember that bacteria are rarely evolving alone, as most live in diverse communities that contain hundreds of interdependent species. Numerous ecological principles apply to these species on a micro-scale, and as one species changes, the others must adapt. For example, bacteria living together often feed from the other's waste products, and bacteria that utilize the same food source often have anti-microbial compounds to release on their competitors. Therefore, when an entire microbial community shifts, the microorganisms present must evolve ways of adapting on several levels. Further, most bacterial species are dependent upon the host, as the host is dependent upon microbes – a symbiotic relationship. The host and its microbes must work together during this evolutionary process, and disruptions for one likely lead to impacts on the other. Understanding the evolutionary links between the two, and how the microbiota have evolved in relationship to human genome, is critical for understanding modern human health and how it will change in the past. To investigate how these two entities have evolved through time, two very different strategies have been employed.

Examining alterations in the human microbiota through the use of out-groups

The first strategy for examining how microbiota and humans co-evolve is to study the microorganisms present in closely related host species, such as chimpanzees, bonobos, or gorillas. By comparing human microbiota to that in other apes and primates, researchers can estimate the differences that have occurred since the divergence or speciation of those species, i.e. the past five million years when comparing humans and chimpanzees (Soares et al. 2009). The first studies to examine the gut microbiota in wild, non-human primates detected significant differences in microbiota associated with specific host species. For example, microbiota from several Old World monkey species (the mantled colobus (*Colobus guereza*), red colobus (*Piliocolobus tephrosceles*), and red-tailed guenon (*Cercopithecus*)) were all distinct and indicated that each species had its own microbiota (Yildirim et al. 2010). Despite this, links and similarities to human microbiota were not evaluated. In a similar study, comparisons between chimpanzees and humans living in the same location were analyzed, and revealed both distinct differences and remarkable similarities. In this study, gut microbiomes from 32 chimpanzees (*Pan troglodytes)* in the Gombe Stream National Park, Tanzania (Moeller et al. 2012) were compared to humans working in the park. Chimp gut microbiota were structurally similar to humans, as both were dominated by various levels of three distinct bacterial taxa: *Bacteriodetes, Prevotella,* and *Ruminococcus* (Arumugam et al. 2011). This allowed researchers to categorize these communities in the same way, regardless of whether the sample was from a chimpanzee or a human, and group samples based on the overlap in the bacterial species present. The similar microbial community structures within these two closely related hominids highly suggested that many of the microbiota within the human body have been conserved over evolutionary time. Researchers were also able to identify some bacterial taxa unique to each host species, although at the time, these differences were largely dismissed. The chimpanzees and humans examined in this study were also followed over six months, and gut microbiota from both host species was able to change structurally over time, adapting to diet and other unidentifiable factors. These results demonstrate that microbiota in hominid species are distinct, and that additional factors, such as diet, can significantly alter the microbial species present in hominids.

Because of these factors, we must consider the environmental pressures that influence diversity of the human microbiota. First, there are internal, location-specific drivers that may select for specific bacteria; for example, the gut is a harsh, acidic, anaerobic environment that would strongly select for microorganisms that could thrive under those specific conditions. These internal drivers are likely significant for the similarities in bacterial community structure observed between chimpanzees and modern humans, despite the fact that physiological differences between hominid species may also contribute. Second, there are a myriad of outside, environmental factors that also must be considered, which include diet, location, exposure, or disease, that can drive variation and alterations in hominid microbiota (Yong 2012). It is likely these outside, environmental factors influence the variation we seen in hominid microbiota over time, and are responsible for the introduction and support of unique or distinct microbial species within the human body.

To examine how these secondary, environmental factors may contribute, chimpanzee, bonobo (*Pan paniscus*), gorilla (*Gorilla gorilla*), and human microbiota from the same (sympatric) and different (allopatric) geographical locations were examined (Moeller et al. 2013). When the microbiota from each host species were compared, each hominid could still be distinguished by their microbiota alone, identifying a level of host-specific selection on microbial species. However, gorillas and chimpanzees living in the same location (sympatry) shared more bacterial taxa than the same species that were living separately. This suggests that these secondary environmental exposures can significantly contribute to new species introductions and microbial success in hominids. This was subsequently confirmed to be true in the oral microbiota as well, as humans and chimpanzees and bonobos could still be distinguished, but sympatric hominids (same location) had more similar microbiota than their allopatric (different location) counterparts (Li et al. 2013). Even studies examining the impacts of captivity on animals species other than hominids identified significant contributions to the composition of gut bacterial communities that were attributed to diet alone, e.g. grass-eating animals had microbiota distinct from carnivores (Muegge et al. 2011). Together, these studies demonstrate that secondary environmental factors can contribute to alterations in hominid microbiota, even if humans and chimpanzees once shared a similar hominid microbiota. Therefore, we must investigate how these secondary factors contributed to alterations in the human microbiota over time, knowing that even slight changes in the composition of these microorganisms can have large impacts for human health and behavior.

Traditional lifestyles provide comparisons to identify alterations in human microbiota

After it was established that the human microbiome could be significantly influenced by environmental factors, researchers realized that differences in human lifestyles could have a major impact on the diversity in the human microbiota. In a landmark study, researchers compared microbiota from Amerindians in the Amazon basin, a rural culture in Malawi, and metropolitan children and adults from the United States (Yatsunenko et al. 2012). Marked differences could be seen between the three cultures, in both the species that were present (microbiota) and the functions that each bacterial community performed (microbiome). Similar findings were presented by researchers examining differences associated with diet in microbiota from European and Burkina Faso children in West Africa (Filippo et al. 2010). Entire species present in West African children were absent in comparison to samples collected from children in industrialized nations in Europe (*Prevotella* and *Xylandibacter*), suggesting that some microbiota are now absent or even extinct in some Westernized countries (Blaser and Falkow 2009). While these differences were all observed in the human gut, differences also exist in other body sites such as the mouth (Contreras et al. 2010). Further, these observations become even more complex when examining individuals within hunter-gatherer communities. For example, women in the Hadza hunter-gatherer community have different microbial species (*Treponema*) in the gut than their male counterparts, which is likely linked to the carbohydrates introduced from tubers that they consume raw during preparation (Schnorr et al. 2014). Although this second approach to examine how the bacteria in the human body has been very informative, it still does not disentangle the different evolutionary histories of different microbiota, identify which cultural or environmental shifts altered our microbiota, or explain how the microorganisms observed today were initially obtained. In order to do that, researchers would need a time machine to monitor bacterial communities that existed in the past. Today, researchers can now use ancient DNA analysis techniques to explore ancient bacterial communities.

Ancient DNA analysis

When trying to reconstruct the past history of health and disease, the next best thing to a time machine is sequencing ancient DNA to understand how these bacterial communities have changed through time. Ancient DNA is highly fragmented, damaged DNA that existed from a past time, preserved in fossils and biological materials. These preserved DNA fragments allow

The history of the human microbiome

molecular biologists and archaeologists to travel back into time, and explore the biological speciation events, investigate interbreeding and admixture, estimate demography, and identify evolutionary mechanisms and pressures that were present in the past. Despite this extraordinary value, working with ancient DNA has limitations (DNA sufficient for analysis only theoretically survives for about one million years – so sequencing any dinosaur DNA is *not* theoretically possible! (Allentoft et al. 2012)), and challenges, as fragmented and damaged DNA is lower in quantity, flooded with environmental DNA contamination, and difficult to accurately identify due to mutations introduced during DNA breakdown and oxidation (Shapiro and Hofreiter 2012; Hofreiter et al. 2001; Paabo 1989). To ensure the accuracy of ancient DNA studies, several guideline publications have been written (Cooper and Poinar 2000; Poinar 2003; Paabo et al. 2004). Inaccuracies in ancient DNA analysis can be avoided by following these steps:

1 Working in a clean environment, ideally a facility that is dedicated to ancient DNA analysis and is devoid of any modern DNA molecular or biochemical analysis, and collecting archaeological samples using sterile techniques when possible.
2 Monitoring background and environmental contaminants that are present in the facility, by examining DNA in the environment and including negative control samples in your analysis.
3 Replicating or duplicating your samples, to ensure you get the same answer more than once, or even in more than one laboratory.
4 Supporting your findings with logical statistical or analytical analysis, i.e. if you think your sample is a dinosaur, it should not be identified as a human (yes, this actually happened, and was published (Allard, Young, and Huyen 1995)).

By following these precautions, researchers can help ensure that ancient DNA analysis has been done as accurately as possible.

The analysis of ancient bacterial species is wrought with even further complications, and takes additional precautions and considerations to ensure the correct analysis of only ancient specimens. Microorganisms live on nearly every surface of the earth, from volcanic deep-sea vents to your lungs (Sogin et al. 2006; Beck, Young, and Huffnagle 2012). Therefore, researchers who examine ancient microbiota are at a higher risk of contaminating their samples, as nearly every utensil, reagent, laboratory technician, and dust particle can serve as a source of contamination. Furthermore, many ancient specimens have been buried underground and handled by countless museum curators, blurring the line between endogenous or 'real' DNA and bacterial DNA introduced from the ground or from the museum environment (exogenous). Even further precautions should be taken, such as sequencing extraction blank control samples and the laboratory environments to more closely monitor contamination during processing (Salter et al. 2014). Microbial species present in related soil or grave goods can also be analyzed to understand how much bacterial diversity observed is from environmental contamination (Warinner et al. 2014). Ancient specimens should be decontaminated in an attempt to remove any contaminant bacterial DNA on the outside of the samples, as a way of minimizing diversity contributed through exogenous sources (Weyrich, Dobney, and Cooper 2015). Lastly, ancient endogenous DNA can be identified based on the damage patterns and separated from bacterial DNA without DNA damage signatures (Ginolhac et al. 2011). Overall, microbial analysis of ancient specimens is arguably the most difficult field in ancient DNA research.

While decades of ancient DNA research were conducted utilizing simple DNA amplification by polymerase chain reaction, Next Generation Sequencing (NGS) technologies have now allowed researchers to obtain millions of sequences from a single sample. Two general NGS sequencing strategies have been developed to analyze bacterial DNA from ancient specimens: amplicon and shotgun DNA sequencing. Amplicon sequencing is an inexpensive and rapid approach to examining microbial community structure. One 'barcoding' gene conserved across all species of interest is sequenced, and differences within this single gene are utilized to estimate species diversity (Logares et al. 2013). For example, the 16S ribosomal RNA encoding genes is targeted to analyzed bacteria, while 18S ribosomal RNA or ITS (internal transcribed spacer) encoding regions can be sequenced from ancient samples to identify fungi, eukaryotes, or dietary components. However, this method requires some expectations from the sample type about the taxa of interest, and specific species cannot be identified using this method, due to the lack of resolution present from the analysis of only a single gene (Poretsky et al. 2014). The second method involves sequencing a random subset of DNA present in the sample, and then, like a puzzle, trying to reconstruct the fragments of genomes that have been obtained to identify taxa present (shotgun sequencing). This approach can be utilized to identify specific pathogens, investigate unknown species present in the sample, and explore the functions or genetic content available, but this method is much more expensive than amplicon sequencing due to the sheer number of DNA sequences needed to reassemble the genetic puzzle pieces (Sharpton 2014). Shotgun sequencing can also be utilized to simultaneously identify dietary and environmental components also locked in the bacterial matrix, providing an effective means of examining the cultural content in ancient samples (Warinner et al. 2014; Blatt et al. 2011).

Analysis of ancient microbiomes from preserved feces and dental plaque

To analyze ancient microbiota, there are two ancient sample types that have been examined: coprolites (preserved feces) or dental calculus (calcified dental plaque). Each sample has its disadvantages and benefits. Coprolites provide one of the only sources of evidence of intestinal microbiota present from ancient specimens, as modern feces have been shown to represent the bacteria in the intestinal track (Consortium 2012). However, coprolites can also contain large amount of environmental contamination, because the sample was likely directly exposed to the environment when it was deposited. For example, Tito and colleagues analyzed coprolites from two different cave locations in North and Central America, and while one of the caves was indicative of human intestinal microbiota, samples from another cave were more similar to cave soil microorganisms, unlike the human gut (Tito et al. 2012). Further, the organic content in the coprolites after deposition can provide an excellent living environment for microorganisms to grow outside of the host, altering bacterial community composition in the coprolites. Coprolites still preserved inside mummies in La Cueva de los Chiquitos Muertos in Mexico contained microbial communities similar to those from compost piles (Tito et al. 2012) rather than species found in the human gut. These impacts from taphonomy, or the degradation and alteration of a sample after the death of the organism occurred, can result in large experimental biases. Taphonomic processes can also occur much more rapidly in exposed coprolites than in bones or teeth (Allentoft et al. 2012), highlighting the significant technical issues that researchers must face when analyzing coprolites. Despite this, several groups have been able to analyze some microbiological information from ancient coprolites, and have even successfully obtained ancient human mitochondrial genomes from this material (Tito et al. 2008; Gilbert et al. 2008).

The second sample available for researchers to analyze ancient microbiota is dental calculus. Dental calculus is a calcified bacterial biofilm locked in place by calcification in the mouth, preserving up to 200 different bacterial species living together on the surface of teeth (Ennever, Vogel, and Benson 1973). This biofilm is the sticky layer that forms on the tooth surface after consuming sugary drinks, or not brushing the teeth for extend periods of time

(Arensburg 1996), and eventually becomes hardened if not removed/cleaned, encasing the bacteria within a solid matrix. Pieces of food debris and environmental material can also become enclosed in this bacterial matrix, allowing researchers to analyze diet, disease, and culture from one ancient calculus specimen (Weyrich, Dobney, and Cooper 2015). In modern populations, dental calculus is removed in regular dental cleanings, but in ancient populations, calculus builds up over the life of the individual, often resulting in large structures on the tooth surface. Therefore, the oral microorganisms present in a person throughout their life can be assessed in one sample. Because the calcified microorganisms are locked in place, and they are exquisitely preserved (the shapes of rods and cocci are in ancient calculus are still visible under a microscope (Dobney and Brothwell 1988)), providing one of the only reliable sources of ancient human microbiota.

In 2011, the first evidence that bacterial DNA was preserved in dental calculus was published and quickly followed by the first DNA sequencing analysis of the material (De La Fuente, Flores, and Moraga 2013; Preus et al. 2011). De la Fuente et al. were able to use polymerase chain reactions to identify four different oral species from ancient calculus samples (*Streptococcus*, *Porphyromonas*, *Actinomyces*, and *Fusobacterium* species), opening the door for further studies of oral microbiota. In 2013, Adler et al. were the first group to use NGS sequencing technologies to analyze whole bacterial communities preserved in calculus (Adler et al. 2013). Amplicon sequencing from ancient calculus specimens revealed oral microbial communities that are consistent with modern oral microbiomes, but also identified significant changes in microbial communities over the past 8,000 years in Europe, namely when agriculture was adopted (Neolithic Revolution) and when the invention of the machine markedly impacted human lives (Industrial Revolution). In 2013, Warinner et al. applied shotgun sequencing to medieval dental calculus, and were able to identify specific oral pathogens associated with disease, identify dietary components within calculus, and provide the first ancient protein sequences preserved within this matrix (Warinner et al. 2014). Analysis of ancient dental calculus is now a rapidly expanding field of bioarchaeology, as it promises to provide previously unavailable information about the diet and health of past cultures. The ancient DNA analysis of ancient dental calculus has truly revolutionized our ability to analyze ancient microbial communities and learn more about past cultures and health. In the next section, we will explore the mechanisms behind these changes, and why such significant alterations in the human microbiota were observed during two of the biggest human revolutions in history.

The 'Neolithic Revolution' and its impacts on human microbiome

Ancient DNA analysis of dental calculus has revealed marked changes in the oral microbiota associated with specific human cultural revolutions. The adoption of agriculture is one of the largest known cultural alterations in human existence, altering diet, lifestyle, environment, and species interactions. Hunting and gathering populations adopted agricultural practices, or were physically replaced when farming cultures moved into the same geographic location (Scarre 2013), as this lifestyle spread around the globe. However, this process was a very dynamic one, and occurred at different times in different locations around the globe. While agriculture is believed to have begun in the Fertile Crescent more than 10,000 years ago, it did not spread into central Europe until ~7,500 years ago, when the Linear Pottery Culture (LBK) migrated into the area (Brandt et al. 2013). In the Americas, maize domestication only occurred about 3,000 years ago, and in Africa, some evidence for domestication exists around 3,000 years ago, although many African cultures never adapted many aspects of the revolution (Scarre 2013). Despite these differences, the advent of agriculture supported large population booms, significantly altered the nutritional value of the human diet, resulted in new disease introductions and greater exposure to human waste, and over time, altered daily cultural practices and individual lifestyle habits.

The root of these changes stems from the alterations in diet. Hunter-gatherers consume large amounts of meat, as isotope data indicates that some hunting-gathering Neandertals were as carnivorous as polar bears (Richards et al. 2000). Hunter-gatherer diets, including Neandertals, in the Paleolithic also consisted of local fruits, tubers, insects, and other plants that were collected on opportunity-based circumstances, which is starkly different than the modern so-called 'paleo diet'. Across Europe, the Neolithic period resulted in the ability to grow wheat and barley, which increased in the levels of carbohydrates in the diet. In the human microbiota, carbohydrates can select for specific microbial species. For example, the microorganism that causes caries in the oral cavity, *Streptococcus mutans*, utilizes carbohydrates as a major food source. The metabolism of carbohydrates results in lactic acid production, which disintegrates enamel and results in oral decay (Ajdić et al. 2002). This scenario is true for other bacterial species, as carbohydrates are a rapid food source for many bacteria. This effective utilization of carbohydrates also likely explains many of the large shifts that we observed in the oral microbiota as individuals adopted farming (Adler et al. 2013), and likely had a significant impact on the types of species that were successful in the human body. For example, the presence of *S. mutans* increased through time (Adler et al. 2013), and was only observed in the human mouth after the introduction of carbohydrates during farming. Similarly, this alteration in diet also resulted in a reduction of iron, as the consumption of meat drastically decreased (Haviland et al. 2010), as evidence of anemia can be seen in the skeletal material in numerous Neolithic cultures across Europe. Iron is also a process-limiting mineral for microorganisms, and in environmental communities, can result in significant community alterations (Flint et al. 2007). The microorganisms in the body are subject to the same nutrients as humans, so these large dietary changes can ultimately impact the species that successfully thrive in the body.

Changes in diet occurred not only through the domestication and production of plant species, but also the domestication of several livestock species, to serve as a more reliable source of protein and meat and to pull plows and sow seeds (Scarre 2013). Cattle, swine, chickens, and goats were all likely domesticated during the early expansion of agriculture across the globe (Larson et al. 2007). These domestication events not only supported the growth of plants and provided direct protein dietary sources, but also provided a means for microorganisms to be shared between humans and animals, as many domesticated 'farm' animals lived in the same house or structure as early farmers (Scarre 2013). Several infectious diseases were likely introduced via this route from domesticated animals (zoonosis), and include diphtheria, influenza A, measles, mumps, pertussis, rotavirus, and smallpox (Wolfe, Dunavan, and Diamond 2007). It was once hypothesized that tuberculosis was also introduced during the Neolithic Revolution, but this has since been disproven. *Mycobacterium tuberculosis*, the microorganism that causes tuberculosis in humans, is closely related to the *Mycobacterium bovis*, which causes a very similar respiratory disease in bovids (Behr 2013), suggesting that the two diseases were once linked. However, when the full genomes of these closely related organisms were sequenced, it revealed that convergent evolution (evolving similar traits separately due to similar selection pressures) had resulted in two similar pathogens, without a recent shared history (Comas et al. 2013). This indicates that both cattle and humans likely already had tuberculosis before the onset of agriculture. A later study examining *M. tuberculosis* strains in the New World identified the source of this disease from wild sea lions, suggesting an introduction into humans in very ancient times from wild animals (Bos et al. 2014). In contrast, other diseases, like influenza, are still transferred between humans and domesticated animals, and without domestication, these diseases would have fewer routes of infection (Ferguson, Galvani, and Bush 2003). Nevertheless, the full list of microorganisms that were swapped and shared between humans and animals is still growing and being altered as more ancient DNA research is performed.

The domestication of mammals, such as cattle, horses, sheep, and goats, also provided easy access to the milk produced by them, which also likely had significant, yet different, impacts on the human microbiota. Until the Neolithic Revolution, many cultures did not have the ability to digest lactose and therefore could not drink raw milk from animals. Early farming cultures had to process and ferment the milk into cheese and yogurts to allow for longer storage, but also to break down the lactose (Curry 2013). Without the lactase genes to digest lactose, milk can serve as something analogous to a toxin, initiating diarrhea and vomiting in humans. Ancient DNA analysis of human genomic data determined that the ability to digest lactose arose during the later stages of the Neolithic Revolution, and spread in populations in Northern Europe and the Fertile Crescent that had increased access to cattle (Burger et al. 2007). The ability to drink raw milk from other species would have provided a great benefit to health in Neolithic populations, but could have also drastically impacted on the microbiota present in the human body. Milk from cattle and donkeys has been shown to alter gut microbiota (Trinchese et al. 2015), and milk has endogenous microorganisms that can be easily introduced into the body when it is consumed raw (Quigley et al. 2013). Further, select species within the human microbiota can utilize lactose as an efficient energy source, such as *Lactobacillus* species, providing a selective advantage over other species and resulting in alterations to the microbiota. *Lactobacillus* species are now commonplace in several locations in the body, and provide a very essential anti-inflammatory signal to the human immune system (Lorea Baroja et al. 2007). Together, this research suggests that the interactions between the human body, milk, and our microbes were likely established during these later parts of the Neolithic Revolution and played a key role in establishing some components of the modern human microbiota.

All of these alterations in diet and an increased availability to food provided a significant advantage for human health, which resulted in large population booms. With larger populations, the ability for infectious diseases to spread rapidly also grew, as more susceptible individuals provided more hosts for pathogens. In addition to the pathogens introduced through animal domestication, additional disease-associated microorganisms came through the lack of sanitation (exposure to human waste, introduction of pest animals, or contaminated food/water) and increases in population density. For example, *Yersinia pestis* (Black Death or Black Plague) was only introduced into human groups from rats, when populations became more sedentary and had greater waste exposure due to their immobile lifestyle. In medieval populations, the Black Death destroyed several large European cities during the Medieval Period (1,200–500 BP), killing up to 70% of London's population during the 1356 epidemic (Bos et al. 2011). While tuberculosis may have been present within humans before the Neolithic Revolution, it is also likely that this disease increased and spread with larger population numbers, and became a common infectious disease only after farming was introduced (Comas et al. 2013). Additional diseases now common in the modern world, such as whooping cough (*Bordetella pertussis*), also likely became mainstream only when population numbers grew large enough to sustain the pathogen (Diavatopoulos et al. 2005). The introduction of these pathogens into the microbiota and the inflammatory process associated with disease can also alter the microbiota, as pathogens can manipulate the immune system to deplete commensal microbiota (Weyrich et al. 2013; Stecher et al. 2007). Through these means, the introduction of new pathogens can have lasting impacts on the human microbiota.

The Neolithic Revolution was truly a mixture of several revolutionary events that irreversibly impacted human history, but also impacted the multispecies interactions between humans and their microorganisms. The diet was altered substantially, as carbohydrates and milk-based products became the staple food source of farming populations and supported novel microorganisms in comparison to hunter-gatherer populations. The domestication of animals, decreased sanitation from sedentary lifestyles, and population booms resulted in the introductions of disease-causing microorganisms each of which had distinct implications for the development of the human microbiota throughout this period. Through this diverse set of processes, the Neolithic Revolution remains one of the largest alterations to date in human microbiota, irreversibly altering the co-evolution that humans and their microorganisms had had for millions of years. Further studies will examine how specific events, i.e. epidemics or the admixture of different farming populations, influenced the microbiome that was later passed down into the modern period.

The Industrial Revolution impacts on the human microbiome

The second largest change identified in the human oral microbiota through time occurred after the Industrial Revolution, which is marked by the invention of machine tools and their implementation in mechanical manufacturing (Berg and Hudson 1992). This simple invention had irreversible consequences for human populations around the globe, and was the beginning of a great distinction between industrialized societies, Western cultures, and individuals living in other parts of the world practicing traditional lifestyles. The Industrial Revolution led to the widespread use of locomotion, textile and chemical manufacturing, iron production, and a laundry list of others (Berg and Hudson 1992), and permanently altered people's lifestyles in many countries, such as those in Europe and North America. These mechanical advancements led to some changes that were similar to those identified during the Neolithic Revolution (population growth, alterations to hygiene, and alteration to daily behaviors), but other changes were new, including large-scale pollution, alterations to food production, and globalization (Hermanussen 2006; Berg and Hudson 1992). This era marked the first time that coal (i.e. a fossil fuel) was burned for energy, and food was produced and processed on a scale that was truly never seen before. While all of these changes seem rather large scale, they all have radical implications for the bacteria that live on today in the human body.

In order to build, fuel, and power this new machinery, sources of energy were needed. Steam locomotion and the burning of coal provided the major sources of energy, but coal is a portable source of energy for urban societies and could burn at high temperatures, which is required for iron production. Coal also burns without the production of sulfur and ash, unlike wood-based furnaces – this was also required to produce pure iron free of impurities. In fact, so much coal was burned during the Industrial Revolution that several cities in Britain came to be described as the 'Black Country' for the outstanding black coal smoke and pollution in the air (Jones 2009). As a consequence of coal burning, heavy metals were also released into the atmosphere during this period, as the burning of coal releases lead, mercury, and nickel. These heavy metals were then incorporated into the human body, as well as the food and water sources available to people in these locations. In environmental microbiomes outside of the human body, heavy metal contamination can severely impact the composition of microbial communities, as heavy metals can be as toxic to microorganisms as they are to humans (Breton et al. 2013). Some bacterial species have unique biochemical pathways that allow them to export and/or deal with heavy metal contamination, but these genes must be shared and obtained by other microorganisms in the community to avoid significant community impacts (Hu et al. 2005). During the Industrial Revolution, microbial species with these unique pathways would have had a significant advantage over species that did not, and likely represent a mechanism for significant change in human microbiota.

The history of the human microbiome

Once mechanical processing was implemented on a widespread scale, food production and processing was also significantly altered. With machines, it was now possible to sterilize and preserve food in cans for later use (Graham 1981) and then transport it over long distances, increasing accessibility and availability of food to the general population. Before the Industrial Revolution, nutritional deficiencies linked to childhood deaths were common, and the lack of food resulted in regular famines, including the infamous potato famine in Ireland in the mid-nineteenth century (Donnelly 2008). After the invention of the machine, the nutritional quality, diversification, and distribution of food increased substantially. For example, the percentage of children in London who died before the age of five decreased by 40% during the Industrial Revolution (Berg and Hudson 1992). Alterations in nutritional content in the human diet can substantially alter the microbial communities present in the body, largely by regulating the immune system (Kau et al. 2011). Bacteria are susceptible to the same nutrients and therefore immune pressure applied by the health of the host, so altering the nutrient availability in the human diet would have significant implications for the bacteria living symbiotically with humans. These advances in nutrition and food availability also supported large population growths across industrialized nations, which would have also resulted in impacts similar to those discussed above regarding the Neolithic Revolution.

While increased nutrition would have been a positive effect on human lives, the sterilization of food may have had both positive and negative impacts. During the canning process, any microorganisms that can cause food spoilage must first be removed. This is commonly done by boiling or cooking the food under substantial pressure to destroy the microorganisms associated with the food. While canning fruits and vegetables can destroy the native microbiota, other processes like pasteurization of milk simply alter the microbial communities to those which support less fermentation and degradation of the food source (Quigley et al. 2013). The native microbial communities on the outside of fruits and vegetables are specific to farming method (organic vs. traditional) and host species (tomato vs. potato) (Leff and Fierer 2013), and, prior to the preservation of food through canning, they would have been introduced into the human body on a regular basis. Canning interrupts this natural process, which can often be good for the human body. For example, the introduction of a common soil microorganism, *Mycobacterium vaccae*, into the human body can support healthy mental activity (Lowry et al. 2007), and by removing these microorganisms during the canning process, vital microorganisms may not be introduced into human microbiota. In contrast, this canning process also introduced some new microorganisms into the human microbiota and exposed humans to novel diseases. For example, *Clostridium botulinum* is a common soil microorganism that is difficult to kill through traditional canning methods. If this microorganism is not killed during the canning process, it can grow in canned food items and acidic environments, and contains a lethal neurotoxin that can block muscle movement and cause death if ingested (the Botox beauty product developed to relax muscles and remove wrinkles from the face is indeed a purified form of this toxin!) (Sobel 2005). Ingesting pathogens or even less toxic microorganisms from processed foods became a normal part of daily life following the Industrial Revolution, and may even have impacted some commensal species that live in the human body.

In addition to impacts on individual daily lives, larger-scale changes also occurred as a result of the invention of the machine. Several European countries, including Britain, Spain, Portugal, France, and Holland, had successfully occupied foreign lands, and new improvements to locomotion, such as steam-powered ships and trains, provided easier access between Europe and elsewhere. This allowed access to foreign food sources and the introduction of modern food staples, such as sugar, in industrialized countries during this time period (Davis 1962). Sugar cane and sugar beets could now be produced in foreign lands and then processed and refined.

241

For example, sugar cane was cultivated nearly 10,000 years ago in New Guinea, but only became a European food staple when shipping and trade from the Pacific increased in the 1800s (Deer 1949). Steam engines were then used to process and refine the sugar back in Europe, producing larger quantities of purified sugar to meet the increasing demands. Sugar is a more accessible carbohydrate for many bacterial species, such as the pathogen responsible for caries in the mouth, *S. mutans*, which uses sugar to erode enamel and cause tooth decay (Ajdić et al. 2002). This large increase in refined sugar would have provided a significant advantage for species such as *S. mutans*, and therefore had irreversible impacts on the human microbiota, as sugar ingestion remains high in the modern human diet. This influx of sugar during the Industrial Revolution is likely to contribute to the drastic increase in oral decay observed in human populations over time (Aufderheide and Conrado 1998; Sajantila 2013). Large increases in sugar to the human diet have also impacted gut communities (Payne, Chassard, and Lacroix 2012), and is now tightly linked to several metabolic diseases in modern populations. The globalization of food certainly altered the human diet, and has secondary impacts on the bacteria living in the human body.

Increased transportation to foreign lands also provided a route for the introduction and mixture of microorganisms from different cultures. As discussed earlier, different cultural communities, each with their own daily rituals, diets, and environments, have their own distinct microbiota (Schnorr et al. 2014; Costello et al. 2009). Globalization meant the relocation and admixture of these cultures, as well as the introduction of old cultures to new environments. Because microbiomes can be shared between members of the same domain or family (Lax et al. 2014), the mixtures of cultures would have also meant the blending of microbiomes, swapping species and introducing new ones across cultural lines. While the impacts and mechanisms underlying the admixture of human microbiota are still being explored, this likely had downstream impacts on the microbiota present in individual cultures. For example, it is likely that European immigrants brought a new set of microorganisms to the New World and introduced these to indigenous peoples. While it is clearly known that pathogens, such as smallpox, were introduced to these populations (Campbell 2002), commensal microorganisms were also likely introduced at the same time. With the later introduction of European-based food sources and alterations in indigenous diets, it is then easy to imagine how new microorganisms may have been further supported in these new hosts.

The Industrial Revolution was a period of great change for human microbiota, as large-scale changes in food production, dietary nutrition, and availability and accessibility of food sources was altered substantially. These alterations, combined with the introduction of pollution and the intertwining of different microbiota from different cultures, irreversibly influenced the bacteria that we find in the body today. Despite these findings, there are still many other influences that remain uncharacterized. Researchers are still exploring how new food introductions, such as coffee or chocolate, influenced bacteria in the body, and how some novel medical practices during this time could have influenced human health, and ultimately human microbiota. Future research will identify further events and factors that impacted our microbiota during this period, and investigate how these changes contributed to the microbiota we find in the body today. Did this altered microbiota help protect us against disease, or are many of the diseases now associated with human microbiota a result of these most recent alterations?

Further alterations to human microbiota in the past century

While the Neolithic and Industrial Revolutions largely impacted the microbiota present in the human body, modern microbiomes are typically less diverse and drastically different than those identified from 100 years ago. In the past century, the alterations to human lifestyles have been boundless. Large-scale events, including the implementation of modern medicine, the invention of antibiotics in the 1950s, the 'Green Revolution' of the 1960s, and the introduction of food chemicals and preservatives are all factors that have likely had marked impacts on the human microbiota. While none of these processes have been examined to date, it is only a matter of time before the mechanisms and overall impacts of each of these events has been explored in great detail.

The introduction of modern medical practices likely left distinguished marks on the human microbiota. Vaccines were invented and introduced during the 1800s, and antibiotics were developed in the early 1900s. The first vaccine was against smallpox, and was developed against a closely related pox infection in cattle. Modern research has shown that specific microbes present in the microbiota are required for effective vaccine response (Oh et al. 2014, 5), but vaccinations have also been shown to alter both murine and primate microbiota (Seekatz et al. 2013; Eloe-Fadrosh et al. 2013). While vaccines are absolutely effective against curbing infectious disease, further research must investigate the interactions between vaccines and microbiota, and how the two are linked in modern humans. Second, the development of antibiotics also had irreversible effects on human microbiota. Sulfur drugs were developed in the early 1900s by Paul Ehrlich, and the now most widely used antibiotic, penicillin, was developed in 1929 by Alexander Fleming (Aminov 2010). As antibiotics are designed to limit bacterial growth, it should come as no surprise that their use drastically impacts human microbiota. However, recent evidence suggests that antibiotic use early in human life can cause irreversible effects on the development of human microbiota, and can select for species that support weight gain and obesity (Ley et al. 2005; Cho et al. 2012). While not initially obvious, this finding was verified by years of livestock research, as cattle and poultry producers across the United States added antibiotics to livestock feed as a means of increasing weight gain (Blaser 2014; also see Witmore, this volume).

As populations continue to grow and require animals for food consumption, the use of tools such as antibiotics, are necessary to support agrarian lifestyles in the modern era. However, this raises interesting questions about the human consumption of meat products that contain antibiotics, hormones, and other factors, which can have downstream impacts on the multitude of species that live within the human body. In addition to large-scale changes in the bacterial communities, these treatments, such as antibiotics, are also responsible for removing specific species from the human microbiota. For example, the presence of the stomach commensal bacteria, *Helicobacter pylori*, has been linked to a decreased prevalence with asthma, and removing this microorganism through the repeated use of antibiotics is likely one of the largest mechanisms feeding rising incidence rates of asthma in Western populations (Blaser 2014). Many other modern medicines have also been shown to markedly alter the human microbiota (Maurice, Haiser, and Turnbaugh 2013), but the effects of many more pharmaceuticals remain unexplored. In general, the use of antibiotics causes effects that are rather contrary to the alterations discussed before, as bacteria are being removed from the microbiota rather than introduced.

In addition to the modernization of medicine, similar alterations have also occurred in food production in the past century. The Green Revolution in the 1960s was the beginning of sweeping changes to global food production, as larger population sizes initially supported by the Industrial Revolution continued to grow and required increases in sustainable food production. This has transitioned into the implementation of genetically modified organisms (GMOs), which are now common in countries such as the United States. In addition, the requirements for food preservation and sustainability after processing have also increased. Each of these implementations and alterations has not been without impacts on our microbiota. For example, glyphosate, a common addition in GMO food crops to provide herbicide resistance, has been shown to block interactions between certain species in the human microbiota (Krüger et al. 2013). Further, the addition of food chemicals, such as emulsifiers, impacts the species diversity in the modern human gut (Chassaing et al. 2015), and the use of artificial sugars, such as fructose, can alter microbial communities and subsequently alter the ability of the body to metabolize sugars effectively (Payne, Chassard, and Lacroix 2012). Future research will examine whether or not other microbiota in the mouth or skin are equally affected, and whether or not these changes are detrimental or beneficial for human health. Nevertheless, these seemingly simple alterations to food production in the modern era have resulted in impacts similar to those observed during the Industrial Revolution.

As modern research continues to examine the effects of chemicals and modern lifestyle practices on the human microbiota, researchers will undoubtedly find more additives and compounds that can impact the species in the human body. New inventions and further alterations in food production and modern medicine will also likely come with their own set of impacts on the human microbiota. Further research will be required to determine the ultimate effects of these alterations, and whether or not these changes are linked to disease. It is likely that some changes may be good for our immune responsiveness or even our nutrient acquisition, while others could support systemic diseases, as has been shown with obesity, Type II diabetes, arthritis, and many others (Cho and Blaser 2012). The field of microbiome research is in its infancy. Only time will tell how all of these factors and alterations work together in a modern world.

Conclusion

Humans and their microorganisms have been evolving together for millions of years. Since the separation from our most recent common ancestor with chimpanzees nearly five million years ago, the extended human family tree developed and nurtured their own set of microbes, both beneficial and not. These microorganisms are essential for daily life, yet can be associated with disease when altered. The events and alterations to human lifestyles in the past have significantly and irreversibly impacted the bacteria that modern humans now carry with them. This story, one with outside influences and internal struggle, ends with the hundreds of species that each human carries and relies on every day. Using ancient DNA analysis, researchers are beginning to understand the events and factors that resulted in the modern human microbiota. The Neolithic and Industrial Revolutions occurred thousands of years apart, yet had similar and substantial influences on the microorganisms inside the human body. Today, researchers can ideally use these findings to predict how the microbiota will change in the future, and how these small changes in human lifestyle can be implemented in modern medicine to aid in microbiota health. By studying these past microbial communities, we may someday be able to reconstruct the microbial identity of each of the species in the human body, aiding in human health and preventing disease.

References

Adler, Christina J., Keith Dobney, Laura S. Weyrich, John Kaidonis, Alan W. Walker, Wolfgang Haak, Corey J. A. Bradshaw, et al. 2013. "Sequencing Ancient Calcified Dental Plaque Shows Changes in Oral Microbiota with Dietary Shifts of the Neolithic and Industrial Revolutions." *Nature Genetics* 45 (4): 450–55. doi:10.1038/ng.2536.

Ajdić, Dragana, William M. McShan, Robert E. McLaughlin, Gorana Savić, Jin Chang, Matthew B. Carson, Charles Primeaux, et al. 2002. "Genome Sequence of Streptococcus Mutans UA159, a Cariogenic Dental Pathogen," Proceedings of the National Academy of Sciences (PNAS), October, 14434–39.

Allard, M. W., D. Young, and Y. Huyen. 1995. "Detecting Dinosaur DNA." *Science* 268 (5214): 1192.

Allentoft, Morten E., Matthew Collins, David Harker, James Haile, Charlotte L. Oskam, Marie L. Hale, Paula F. Campos, et al. 2012. "The Half-Life of DNA in Bone: Measuring Decay Kinetics in 158 Dated Fossils." *Proceedings of the Royal Society B: Biological Sciences*, October, rspb20121745. doi:10.1098/rspb.2012.1745.

Aminov, Rustam I. 2010. "A Brief History of the Antibiotic Era: Lessons Learned and Challenges for the Future." *Frontiers in Microbiology* 1 (December). doi:10.3389/fmicb.2010.00134.

Arensburg, B. 1996. "Ancient Dental Calculus and Diet." *Human Evolution* 11 (2): 139–45. doi:10.1007/BF02437397.

Arumugam, Manimozhiyan, Jeroen Raes, Eric Pelletier, Denis Le Paslier, Takuji Yamada, Daniel R. Mende, Gabriel R. Fernandes, et al. 2011. "Enterotypes of the Human Gut Microbiome." *Nature* 473 (7346): 174–80. doi:10.1038/nature09944.

Aufderheide, Arthur C., and Rodreguez-Martin Conrado. 1998. *The Cambridge Encyclopedia of Human Paleopathology*. Cambridge: Cambridge University Press.

Bart, Marieke J., Simon R. Harris, Abdolreza Advani, Yoshichika Arakawa, Daniela Bottero, Valérie Bouchez, Pamela K. Cassiday, et al. 2014. "Global Population Structure and Evolution of Bordetella Pertussis and Their Relationship with Vaccination." *mBio* 5 (2): e01074-14. doi:10.1128/mBio.01074-14.

Beck, James M., Vincent B. Young, and Gary B. Huffnagle. 2012. "The Microbiome of the Lung." *Translational Research* 160 (4): 258–66. doi:10.1016/j.trsl.2012.02.005.

Behr, Marcel A. 2013. "Evolution of Mycobacterium Tuberculosis." *Advances in Experimental Medicine and Biology* 783: 81–91. doi:10.1007/978-1-4614-6111-1_4.

Berg, Maxine, and Pat Hudson. 1992. "Rehabilitating the Industrial Revolution." *The Economic History Review* 45 (1): 24. doi:10.2307/2598327.

Blaser, Martin J. 2014. *Missing Microbes: How the Overuse of Antibiotics Is Fueling Our Modern Plagues*. 1st edition. New York: Henry Holt and Co.

Blaser, Martin J., and Stanley Falkow. 2009. "What Are the Consequences of the Disappearing Human Microbiota?" *Nat Rev Micro* 7 (12): 887–94. doi:10.1038/nrmicro2245.

Blatt, S. H., B. G. Redmond, V. Cassman, and P. W. Sciulli. 2011. "Dirty Teeth and Ancient Trade: Evidence of Cotton Fibres in Human Dental Calculus from Late Woodland, Ohio." *International Journal of Osteoarchaeology* 21 (6): 669–78. doi:10.1002/oa.1173.

Bos, Kirsten I., Kelly M. Harkins, Alexander Herbig, Mireia Coscolla, Nico Weber, Iñaki Comas, Stephen A. Forrest, et al. 2014. "Pre-Columbian Mycobacterial Genomes Reveal Seals as a Source of New World Human Tuberculosis." *Nature* advance online publication (August). doi:10.1038/nature13591.

Bos, Kirsten I., Verena J. Schuenemann, G. Brian Golding, Hernán A. Burbano, Nicholas Waglechner, Brian K. Coombes, Joseph B. McPhee, et al. 2011. "A Draft Genome of Yersinia Pestis from Victims of the Black Death," October, 506–10.

Brandt, Guido, Wolfgang Haak, Christina J. Adler, Christina Roth, Anna Szécsényi-Nagy, Sarah Karimnia, Sabine Möller-Rieker, et al. 2013. "Ancient DNA Reveals Key Stages in the Formation of Central European Mitochondrial Genetic Diversity." *Science* 342 (6155): 257–61. doi:10.1126/science.1241844.

Breton, Jérôme, Sébastien Massart, Peter Vandamme, Evie De Brandt, Bruno Pot, and Benoît Foligné. 2013. "Ecotoxicology inside the Gut: Impact of Heavy Metals on the Mouse Microbiome." *BMC Pharmacology and Toxicology* 14 (1): 62. doi:10.1186/2050-6511-14-62.

Burger, J., M. Kirchner, B. Bramanti, W. Haak, and M. G. Thomas. 2007. "Absence of the Lactase-Persistence-Associated Allele in Early Neolithic Europeans." *Proceedings of the National Academy of Sciences of the United States of America* 104 (10): 3736–41.

Campbell, J. 2002. *Invisible Invaders: Smallpox and Other Diseases in Aboriginal Australia, 1780–1880*. Carlton South, Vic: Melbourne University Press.

Caporaso, J. Gregory, Christian L. Lauber, William A. Walters, Donna Berg-Lyons, Catherine A. Lozupone, Peter J. Turnbaugh, Noah Fierer, and Rob Knight. 2011. "Global Patterns of 16S rRNA Diversity at a Depth of Millions of Sequences per Sample." *Proceedings of the National Academy of Sciences of the United States of America* 108 Suppl. 1 (March): 4516–22. doi:10.1073/pnas.1000080107.

Chaban, Bonnie, Arianne Albert, Matthew G Links, Jennifer Gardy, Patrick Tang, and Janet E Hill. 2013. "Characterization of the Upper Respiratory Tract Microbiomes of Patients with Pandemic H1N1 Influenza." *PloS ONE* 8 (7): e69559. doi:10.1371/journal.pone.0069559.

Chassaing, Benoit, Omry Koren, Julia K. Goodrich, Angela C. Poole, Shanthi Srinivasan, Ruth E. Ley, and Andrew T. Gewirtz. 2015. "Dietary Emulsifiers Impact the Mouse Gut Microbiota Promoting Colitis and Metabolic Syndrome." *Nature* 519 (7541): 92–96. doi:10.1038/nature14232.

Cho, Ilseung, and Martin J. Blaser. 2012. "The Human Microbiome: At the Interface of Health and Disease." *Nature Reviews. Genetics* 13 (4): 260–70. doi:10.1038/nrg3182.

Cho, Ilseung, Shingo Yamanishi, Laura Cox, Barbara A Methé, Jiri Zavadil, Kelvin Li, Zhan Gao, et al. 2012. "Antibiotics in Early Life Alter the Murine Colonic Microbiome and Adiposity." *Nature* 488 (7413): 621–26. doi:10.1038/nature11400.

Comas, Iñaki, Mireia Coscolla, Tao Luo, Sonia Borrell, Kathryn E. Holt, Midori Kato-Maeda, Julian Parkhill, et al. 2013. "Out-of-Africa Migration and Neolithic Coexpansion of Mycobacterium Tuberculosis with Modern Humans." *Nature Genetics* 45 (10): 1176–82. doi:10.1038/ng.2744.

Conly, J. M., and K. Stein. 1992. "The Production of Menaquinones (Vitamin K2) by Intestinal Bacteria and Their Role in Maintaining Coagulation Homeostasis." *Progress in Food & Nutrition Science* 16 (4): 307–43.

Consortium, The Human Microbiome Project. 2012. "Structure, Function and Diversity of the Healthy Human Microbiome." *Nature* 486 (7402): 207–14. doi:10.1038/nature11234.

Contreras, Monica, Elizabeth K. Costello, Glida Hidalgo, Magda Magris, Rob Knight, and Maria G. Dominguez-Bello. 2010. "The Bacterial Microbiota in the Oral Mucosa of Rural Amerindians." *Microbiology (Reading, England)* 156 (Pt 11): 3282–87. doi:10.1099/mic.0.043174-0.

Cooper, Alan, and Hendrik N. Poinar. 2000. "Ancient DNA: Do It Right or Not at All." *Science* 289 (5482): 1139. doi:10.1126/science.289.5482.1139b.

Costello, Elizabeth K., Christian L. Lauber, Micah Hamady, Noah Fierer, Jeffrey I. Gordon, and Rob Knight. 2009. "Bacterial Community Variation in Human Body Habitats across Space and Time." *Science* 326 (5960): 1694–97. doi:10.1126/science.1177486.

Curry, Andrew. 2013. "Archaeology: The Milk Revolution." *Nature* 500 (7460): 20–2. doi:10.1038/500020a.

Dash, Sarah, Gerard Clarke, Michael Berk, and Felice N. Jacka. 2015. "The Gut Microbiome and Diet in Psychiatry: Focus on Depression." *Current Opinion in Psychiatry* 28 (1): 1–6. doi:10.1097/YCO.0000000000000117.

David, Lawrence A., Corinne F. Maurice, Rachel N. Carmody, David B. Gootenberg, Julie E. Button, Benjamin E. Wolfe, Alisha V. Ling, et al. 2014. "Diet Rapidly and Reproducibly Alters the Human Gut Microbiome." *Nature* 505 (January): 559–63. doi:10.1038/nature12820.

Davis, Ralph. 1962. "English Foreign Trade, 1700–1741." *The Economic History Review* 15 (2): 285–303. doi:10.1111/j.1468-0289.1962.tb02239.x.

De La Fuente, C., S. Flores, and M. Moraga. 2013. "DNA from Human Ancient Bacteria: A Novel Source of Genetic Evidence from Archaeological Dental Calculus." *Archaeometry* 55 (4): 767–78. doi:10.1111/j.1475-4754.2012.00707.x.

Deer, Noël. 1949. *The History of Sugar. Vol. 1.* London: Chapman and Hall Ltd.

Diavatopoulos, D. A., C. A. Cummings, L. M. Schouls, M. M. Brinig, D. A. Relman, and F. R. Mooi. 2005. "Bordetella Pertussis, the Causative Agent of Whooping Cough, Evolved from a Distinct, Human-Associated Lineage of B. Bronchiseptica." *PLoS Pathog* 1 (4): e45.

Dobney, Keith, and Don Brothwell. 1988. "A Scanning Electron Microscope Study of Archaeological Dental Calculus," in Olsen, S. L. (ed.) *Scanning Electron Microscopy in Archaeology. British Archaeological Reports International Series* 452. Oxford: BAR: 372–85.

Dominguez-Bello, Maria G., Elizabeth K. Costello, Monica Contreras, Magda Magris, Glida Hidalgo, Noah Fierer, and Rob Knight. 2010. "Delivery Mode Shapes the Acquisition and Structure of the Initial Microbiota across Multiple Body Habitats in Newborns." *Proceedings of the National Academy of Sciences*, June, 201002601. doi:10.1073/pnas.1002601107.

Donnelly Jr., James S.. 2008. *The Great Irish Potato Famine.* Thrupp, Stroud, Gloucestershire: The History Press.

Eloe-Fadrosh, Emiley A., Monica A. McArthur, Anna M. Seekatz, Elliott F. Drabek, David A. Rasko, Marcelo B. Sztein, and Claire M. Fraser. 2013. "Impact of Oral Typhoid Vaccination on the Human Gut Microbiota and Correlations with S. Typhi-Specific Immunological Responses." *PLoS ONE* 8 (4). doi:10.1371/journal.pone.0062026.

Ennever, J., J. J. Vogel, and L. A. Benson. 1973. "Lipid and Calculus Matrix Calcification In Vitro." *Dent Res* 52 (September): 1056–59.

Ferguson, N. M., A. P. Galvani, and R. M. Bush. 2003. "Ecological and Immunological Determinants of Influenza Evolution." *Nature* 422 (6930): 428–33. doi:10.1038/nature01509 nature01509 [pii].

Fierer, Noah, Micah Hamady, Christian L. Lauber, and Rob Knight. 2008. "The Influence of Sex, Handedness, and Washing on the Diversity of Hand Surface Bacteria." *Proceedings of the National Academy of Sciences* 105 (46): 17994–99. doi: 10.1073/pnas.0807920105.

Filippo, Carlotta De, Duccio Cavalieri, Monica Di Paola, Matteo Ramazzotti, Jean Baptiste Poullet, Sebastien Massart, Silvia Collini, Giuseppe Pieraccini, and Paolo Lionetti. 2010. "Impact of Diet in Shaping Gut Microbiota Revealed by a Comparative Study in Children from Europe and Rural Africa." *Proceedings of the National Academy of Sciences* 107 (33): 14691–96. doi:10.1073/pnas.1005963107.

Flight, Monica Hoyos. 2014. "Neurodevelopmental Disorders: The Gut-Microbiome-Brain Connection." *Nature Reviews Neuroscience* 15 (2): 104. doi:10.1038/nrn3669.

Flint, Harry J., Sylvia H. Duncan, Karen P. Scott, and Petra Louis. 2007. "Interactions and Competition within the Microbial Community of the Human Colon: Links between Diet and Health." *Environmental Microbiology* 9 (5): 1101–11. doi:10.1111/j.1462-2920.2007.01281.x.

Gilbert, M. T., D. L. Jenkins, A. Gotherstrom, N. Naveran, J. J. Sanchez, M. Hofreiter, P. F. Thomsen, et al. 2008. "DNA from Pre-Clovis Human Coprolites in Oregon, North America." *Science* 320 (5877): 786–89. doi:10.1126/science.1154116.

Gill, Steven R., Mihai Pop, Robert T. DeBoy, Paul B. Eckburg, Peter J. Turnbaugh, Buck S. Samuel, Jeffrey I. Gordon, David A. Relman, Claire M. Fraser-Liggett, and Karen E. Nelson. 2006. "Metagenomic Analysis of the Human Distal Gut Microbiome." *Science* 312 (5778): 1355–59. doi:10.1126/science.1124234.

Ginolhac, A., M. Rasmussen, M. T. Gilbert, E. Willerslev, and L. Orlando. 2011. "mapDamage: Testing for Damage Patterns in Ancient DNA Sequences." *Bioinformatics* 27 (15): 2153–55. doi:10.1093/bioinformatics/btr347.

Graham, J. C. 1981. "The French Connection in the Early History of Canning." *Journal of the Royal Society of Medicine* 74 (5): 374–81. doi:10.1177/014107688107400511.

Haviland, William, Dana Walrath, Harald Prins, and Bunny McBride. 2010. *Evolution and Prehistory: The Human Challenge*. Boston: Cengage Learning.

Hehemann, Jan-Hendrik, Gaëlle Correc, Tristan Barbeyron, William Helbert, Mirjam Czjzek, and Gurvan Michel. 2010. "Transfer of Carbohydrate-Active Enzymes from Marine Bacteria to Japanese Gut Microbiota." *Nature* 464 (7290): 908–12. doi:10.1038/nature08937.

Hermanussen, M. 2006. "Review of 'The Escape from Hunger and Premature Death, 1700–2100. Europe, America, and the Third World. By Robert William Fogel'." *Journal of Biosocial Science* 38 (4): 571–72.

Hofreiter, M., D. Serre, H. N. Poinar, M. Kuch, and S. Paabo. 2001. "Ancient DNA." *Nature Reviews Genetics* 2 (5): 353–59.

Hu, Ping, Eoin L. Brodie, Yohey Suzuki, Harley H. McAdams, and Gary L. Andersen. 2005. "Whole-Genome Transcriptional Analysis of Heavy Metal Stresses in Caulobacter Crescentus." *Journal of Bacteriology* 187 (24): 8437–49. doi:10.1128/JB.187.24.8437-8449.2005.

Jhamnani, Kapil, Venkataram Shivakumar, Sunil Kalmady, Naren P. Rao, and Ganesan Venkatasubramanian. 2013. "Successful Use of Add-on Minocycline for Treatment of Persistent Negative Symptoms in Schizophrenia." *Journal of Neuropsychiatry and Clinical Neurosciences* 25 (1): E06–7. doi:10.1176/appi.neuropsych.11120376.

Jones, Peter M. 2009. *Industrial Enlightenment: Science, Technology and Culture in Birmingham and the West Midlands, 1760-1820*. Manchester and New York: Manchester University Press.

Kau, Andrew L., Philip P. Ahern, Nicholas W. Griffin, Andrew L. Goodman, and Jeffrey I. Gordon. 2011. "Human Nutrition, the Gut Microbiome, and Immune System: Envisioning the Future." *Nature* 474 (7351): 327–36. doi:10.1038/nature10213.

Krüger, Monika, Awad Ali Shehata, Wieland Schrödl, and Arne Rodloff. 2013. "Glyphosate Suppresses the Antagonistic Effect of Enterococcus Spp. on Clostridium Botulinum." *Anaerobe* 20 (April): 74–8. doi:10.1016/j.anaerobe.2013.01.005.

Larson, G., U. Albarella, K. Dobney, P. Rowley-Conwy, J. Schibler, A. Tresset, J. D. Vigne, et al. 2007. "Ancient DNA, Pig Domestication, and the Spread of the Neolithic into Europe." *Proceedings of the National Academy of Sciences of the United States of America* 104 (39): 15276–81.

Lax, Simon, Daniel P. Smith, Jarrad Hampton-Marcell, Sarah M. Owens, Kim M. Handley, Nicole M. Scott, Sean M. Gibbons, et al. 2014. "Longitudinal Analysis of Microbial Interaction between Humans and the Indoor Environment." *Science* 345 (6200): 1048–52. doi:10.1126/science.1254529.

Leff, Jonathan W., and Noah Fierer. 2013. "Bacterial Communities Associated with the Surfaces of Fresh Fruits and Vegetables." *PLoS ONE* 8 (3): e59310. doi:10.1371/journal.pone.0059310.

Ley, Ruth E., Fredrik Bäckhed, Peter Turnbaugh, Catherine A. Lozupone, Robin D. Knight, and Jeffrey I. Gordon. 2005. "Obesity Alters Gut Microbial Ecology." *Proceedings of the National Academy of Sciences of the United States of America* 102 (31): 11070–75. doi:10.1073/pnas.0504978102.

Li, Jing, Ivan Nasidze, Dominique Quinque, Mingkun Li, Hans-Peter Horz, Claudine André, Rosa M. Garriga, Michel Halbwax, Anne Fischer, and Mark Stoneking. 2013. "The Saliva Microbiome of Pan and Homo." *BMC Microbiology* 13 (1): 204. doi:10.1186/1471-2180-13-204.

Logares, Ramiro, Shinichi Sunagawa, Guillem Salazar, Francisco M. Cornejo-Castillo, Isabel Ferrera, Hugo Sarmento, Pascal Hingamp, et al. 2013. "Metagenomic 16S rDNA Illumina Tags Are a Powerful Alternative to Amplicon Sequencing to Explore Diversity and Structure of Microbial Communities." *Environmental Microbiology*, October, n/a-n/a. doi:10.1111/1462-2920.12250.

Lorea Baroja, M., P. V. Kirjavainen, S. Hekmat, and G. Reid. 2007. "Anti-inflammatory Effects of Probiotic Yogurt in Inflammatory Bowel Disease Patients." *Clinical & Experimental Immunology* 149 (3): 470–79. doi:10.1111/j.1365-2249.2007.03434.x.

Lowry, C. A., J. H. Hollis, A. de Vries, B. Pan, L. R. Brunet, J. R. F. Hunt, J. F. R. Paton, et al. 2007. "Identification of an Immune-Responsive Mesolimbocortical Serotonergic System: Potential Role in Regulation of Emotional Behavior." *Neuroscience* 146 (2–5): 756–72. doi:10.1016/j.neuroscience.2007.01.067.

Maurice, Corinne Ferrier, Henry Joseph Haiser, and Peter James Turnbaugh. 2013. "Xenobiotics Shape the Physiology and Gene Expression of the Active Human Gut Microbiome." *Cell* 152 (1–2): 39–50. doi:10.1016/j.cell.2012.10.052.

Moeller, Andrew H., Patrick H. Degnan, Anne E. Pusey, Michael L. Wilson, Beatrice H. Hahn, and Howard Ochman. 2012. "Chimpanzees and Humans Harbour Compositionally Similar Gut Enterotypes." *Nat Commun* 3 (November): 1179. doi:10.1038/ncomms2159.

Moeller, Andrew H., Martine Peeters, Jean-Basco Ndjango, Yingying Li, Beatrice H. Hahn, and Howard Ochman. 2013. "Sympatric Chimpanzees and Gorillas Harbor Convergent Gut Microbial Communities." *Genome Research* 23 (10): 1715–20. doi:10.1101/gr.154773.113.

Muegge, Brian D., Justin Kuczynski, Dan Knights, Jose C. Clemente, Antonio González, Luigi Fontana, Bernard Henrissat, Rob Knight, and Jeffrey I. Gordon. 2011. "Diet Drives Convergence in Gut Microbiome Functions across Mammalian Phylogeny and within Humans." *Science* 332 (6032): 970–74. doi:10.1126/science.1198719.

Normann, Erik, Annika Fahlén, Lars Engstrand, and Helene Engstrand Lilja. 2013. "Intestinal Microbial Profiles in Extremely Preterm Infants with and without Necrotizing Enterocolitis." *Acta Paediatrica (Oslo, Norway: 1992)* 102 (2): 129–36. doi:10.1111/apa.12059.

Oh, Jason Z., Rajesh Ravindran, Benoit Chassaing, Frederic A. Carvalho, Mohan S. Maddur, Maureen Bower, Paul Hakimpour, et al. 2014. "TLR5-Mediated Sensing of Gut Microbiota Is Necessary for Antibody Responses to Seasonal Influenza Vaccination." *Immunity* 41 (3): 478–92. doi:10.1016/j.immuni.2014.08.009.

Overballe-Petersen, Søren, and Eske Willerslev. 2014. "Horizontal Transfer of Short and Degraded DNA Has Evolutionary Implications for Microbes and Eukaryotic Sexual Reproduction." *BioEssays* 36 (10): 1005–10. doi:10.1002/bies.201400035.

Paabo, S. 1989. "Ancient DNA: Extraction, Characterization, Molecular Cloning, and Enzymatic Amplification." *Proceedings of the National Academy of Sciences of the United States of America* 86 (6): 1939–43.

Paabo, S., H. Poinar, D. Serre, V. Jaenicke-Despres, J. Hebler, N. Rohland, M. Kuch, J. Krause, L. Vigilant, and M. Hofreiter. 2004. "Genetic Analyses from Ancient DNA." *Annual Review of Genetics* 38: 645–79. doi:10.1146/annurev.genet.37.110801.143214.

Payne, A. N., C. Chassard, and C. Lacroix. 2012. "Gut Microbial Adaptation to Dietary Consumption of Fructose, Artificial Sweeteners and Sugar Alcohols: Implications for Host–Microbe Interactions Contributing to Obesity." *Obesity Reviews* 13 (9): 799–809. doi:10.1111/j.1467-789X.2012.01009.x.

Poinar, H. N. 2003. "The Top 10 List: Criteria of Authenticity for DNA from Ancient and Forensic Samples." *International Congress Series* 1239: 575–79.

Poretsky, Rachel, Luis M. Rodriguez-R, Chengwei Luo, Despina Tsementzi, and Konstantinos T. Konstantinidis. 2014. "Strengths and Limitations of 16S rRNA Gene Amplicon Sequencing in Revealing Temporal Microbial Community Dynamics." *PLoS ONE* 9 (4): e93827. doi:10.1371/journal.pone.0093827.

Preus, Hans R., Ole J. Marvik, Knut A. Selvig, and Pia Bennike. 2011. "Ancient Bacterial DNA (aDNA) in Dental Calculus from Archaeological Human Remains." *Journal of Archaeological Science* 38 (8): 1827–31. doi:10.1016/j.jas.2011.03.020.

Quigley, Lisa, Robert McCarthy, Orla O'Sullivan, Tom P. Beresford, Gerald F. Fitzgerald, R. Paul Ross, Catherine Stanton, and Paul D. Cotter. 2013. "The Microbial Content of Raw and Pasteurized Cow

Milk as Determined by Molecular Approaches." *Journal of Dairy Science* 96 (8): 4928–37. doi:10.3168/jds.2013-6688.

Ray, Katrina. 2015. "Infection: Microbiota Reconstitution for Resistance to Clostridium Difficile Infection: Fight Fire with Fire?" *Nature Reviews: Gastroenterology & Hepatology* 12 (1): 4. doi:10.1038/nrgastro.2014.194.

Richards, Michael P., Paul B. Pettitt, Erik Trinkaus, Fred H. Smith, Maja Paunović, and Ivor Karavanić. 2000. "Neanderthal Diet at Vindija and Neanderthal Predation: The Evidence from Stable Isotopes." *Proceedings of the National Academy of Sciences* 97 (13): 7663–66. doi:10.1073/pnas.120178997.

Sajantila, Antti. 2013. "Major Historical Dietary Changes Are Reflected in the Dental Microbiome of Ancient Skeletons." *Investigative Genetics* 4 (1): 10. doi:10.1186/2041-2223-4-10.

Salter, Susannah J., Michael J. Cox, Elena M. Turek, Szymon T. Calus, William O. Cookson, Miriam F. Moffatt, Paul Turner, Julian Parkhill, Nicholas J. Loman, and Alan W. Walker. 2014. "Reagent and Laboratory Contamination Can Critically Impact Sequence-Based Microbiome Analyses." *BMC Biology* 12 (1). doi:10.1186/s12915-014-0087-z.

Scarre, Chris. 2013. *The Human Past: World Prehistory and the Development of Human Societies*. 3rd edition. New York: Thames & Hudson.

Scher, Jose U., and Steven B. Abramson. 2011. "The Microbiome and Rheumatoid Arthritis." *Nature Reviews: Rheumatology* 7 (10): 569–78. doi:10.1038/nrrheum.2011.121.

Schnorr, Stephanie L., Marco Candela, Simone Rampelli, Manuela Centanni, Clarissa Consolandi, Giulia Basaglia, Silvia Turroni, et al. 2014. "Gut Microbiome of the Hadza Hunter-Gatherers." *Nature Communications* 5 (April). doi:10.1038/ncomms4654.

Schwabe, Robert F., and Christian Jobin. 2013. "The Microbiome and Cancer." *Nature Reviews: Cancer* 13 (11): 800–12. doi:10.1038/nrc3610.

Seekatz, Anna M., Aruna Panda, David A. Rasko, Franklin R. Toapanta, Emiley A. Eloe-Fadrosh, Abdul Q. Khan, Zhenqiu Liu, et al. 2013. "Differential Response of the Cynomolgus Macaque Gut Microbiota to Shigella Infection." *PLoS ONE* 8 (6): e64212. doi:10.1371/journal.pone.0064212.

Shapiro, Beth, and Michael Hofreiter, eds. 2012. *Ancient DNA: Methods and Protocols*. 1st edition. New York: Humana Press.

Sharpton, Thomas J. 2014. "An Introduction to the Analysis of Shotgun Metagenomic Data." *Frontiers in Plant Science* 5 (June). doi:10.3389/fpls.2014.00209.

Soares, P., L. Ermini, N. Thomson, M. Mormina, T. Rito, A. Rã Hl, A. Salas, S. Oppenheimer, V. Macaulay, and M. Richards. 2009. "Correcting for Purifying Selection: An Improved Human Mitochondrial Molecular Clock." *American Journal of Human Genetics* 84 (6): 740–59. doi:10.1016/j.ajhg.2009.05.001.

Sobel, Jeremy. 2005. "Botulism." *Clinical Infectious Diseases* 41 (8): 1167–73. doi:10.1086/444507.

Sogin, Mitchell L., Hilary G. Morrison, Julie A. Huber, David Mark Welch, Susan M. Huse, Phillip R. Neal, Jesus M. Arrieta, and Gerhard J. Herndl. 2006. "Microbial Diversity in the Deep Sea and the Underexplored 'Rare Biosphere.'" *Proceedings of the National Academy of Sciences* 103 (32): 12115–20. doi:10.1073/pnas.0605127103.

Song, Se Jin, Christian Lauber, Elizabeth K. Costello, Catherine A. Lozupone, Gregory Humphrey, Donna Berg-Lyons, J. Gregory Caporaso, et al. 2013. "Cohabiting Family Members Share Microbiota with One Another and with Their Dogs." *eLife* 2 (April): e00458. doi:10.7554/eLife.00458.

Spahr, A., and E. Klein. 2006. "Periodontal Infections and Coronary Heart Disease: Role of Periodontal Bacteria and Importance of Total Pathogen Burden in the Coronary Event and Periodontal Disease (Corodont) Study." *Archives of Internal Medicine* 166 (5): 554–59. doi:10.1001/archinte.166.5.554.

Stecher, Bärbel, Riccardo Robbiani, Alan W. Walker, Astrid M. Westendorf, Manja Barthel, Marcus Kremer, Samuel Chaffron, et al. 2007. "Salmonella Enterica Serovar Typhimurium Exploits Inflammation to Compete with the Intestinal Microbiota." *PLoS Biol* 5 (10): e244. doi:10.1371/journal.pbio.0050244.

Tito, R. Y., D. Knights, J. Metcalf, A. J. Obregon-Tito, L. Cleeland, F. Najar, B. Roe. 2012. "Insights from Characterizing Extinct Human Gut Microbiomes." *PLoS ONE* 7 (12): e51146. doi:10.1371/journal.pone.0051146.

Tito, Raúl Y., Simone Macmil, Graham Wiley, Fares Najar, Lauren Cleeland, Chunmei Qu, Ping Wang, et al. 2008. "Phylotyping and Functional Analysis of Two Ancient Human Microbiomes." *PLoS ONE* 3 (11): e3703. doi:10.1371/journal.pone.0003703.

Tlaskalova-Hogenova, Helena, Renata Stepankova, Hana Kozakova, Tomas Hudcovic, Luca Vannucci, Ludmila Tuckova, Pavel Rossmann, et al. 2011. "The Role of Gut Microbiota (Commensal Bacteria) and the Mucosal Barrier in the Pathogenesis of Inflammatory and Autoimmune Diseases and Cancer: Contribution of Germ-Free and Gnotobiotic Animal Models of Human Diseases." *Cell Mol Immunol* 8 (2): 110–20.

Trinchese, Giovanna, Gina Cavaliere, Roberto Berni Canani, Sebastien Matamoros, Paolo Bergamo, Chiara De Filippo, Serena Aceto, et al. 2015. "Human, Donkey and Cow Milk Differently Affects Energy Efficiency and Inflammatory State by Modulating Mitochondrial Function and Gut Microbiota." *Journal of Nutritional Biochemistry*. Accessed September 21. doi:10.1016/j.jnutbio.2015.05.003.

Warinner, Christina, Joao F. Matias Rodrigues, Rounak Vyas, Christian Trachsel, Natallia Shved, Jonas Grossmann, Anita Radini, et al. 2014. "Pathogens and Host Immunity in the Ancient Human Oral Cavity." *Nat Genet* 46 (4): 336–44.

Weyrich, Laura S., Keith Dobney, and Alan Cooper. 2015. "Ancient DNA Analysis of Dental Calculus." *Journal of Human Evolution*, January. doi:10.1016/j.jhevol.2014.06.018.

Weyrich, Laura S., Heather A. Feaga, Jihye Park, Sarah J. Muse, Chetan Y. Safi, Olivier Y. Rolin, Sarah E. Young, and Eric T. Harvill. 2013. "Resident Microbiota Affect Bordetella Pertussis Infectious Dose and Host Specificity." *Journal of Infectious Diseases*, November, jit597. doi:10.1093/infdis/jit597.

Wolfe, Nathan D., Claire Panosian Dunavan, and Jared Diamond. 2007. "Origins of Major Human Infectious Diseases." *Nature* 447 (7142): 279–83. doi:10.1038/nature05775.

Yatsunenko, Tanya, Federico E. Rey, Mark J. Manary, Indi Trehan, Maria Gloria Dominguez-Bello, Monica Contreras, Magda Magris, et al. 2012. "Human Gut Microbiome Viewed across Age and Geography." *Nature* 486 (7402): 222–27. doi:10.1038/nature11053.

Yildirim, Suleyman, Carl J. Yeoman, Maksim Sipos, Manolito Torralba, Brenda A. Wilson, Tony L. Goldberg, Rebecca M. Stumpf, Steven R. Leigh, Bryan A. White, and Karen E. Nelson. 2010. "Characterization of the Fecal Microbiome from Non-Human Wild Primates Reveals Species Specific Microbial Communities." *PLoS ONE* 5 (11): e13963. doi:10.1371/journal.pone.0013963.

Yong, Ed. 2012. "Gut Microbial 'Enterotypes' Become Less Clear-Cut." *Nature*, March. doi:10.1038/nature.2012.10276.

15

AN ARCHAEOLOGICAL TELLING OF MULTISPECIES CO-INHABITATION

Comments on the origins of agriculture and domestication narrative in Southwest Asia

Brian Boyd

Introduction

Archaeology has not, thus far, featured very much in multispecies anthropology, and is entirely absent from most of its prominent contemporary writings (e.g. Haraway 2016; Kirksey 2014, 2015; Tsing 2015; Van Dooren et al. 2016). Given that the object of archaeological inquiry is the study of evidence for practices involving humans, animals, plants and materials, from the beginnings of humanity to the present day, and on a global scale, this oversight is notable. Archaeologists routinely carry out collaborative interdisciplinary research on multiple lines of human and nonhuman evidence, studying how communities of people, animals, plants, and materials came together in different (pre)historical contexts, and encountered each other in different networks and ecologies. But, despite recent acknowledgment that "organisms are situated within deep, entangled histories", and have "a shared heritage" (van Dooren et al. 2016: 2), there is relatively little historical depth to multispecies studies as currently formulated. "Deep history" is not and should not be confined to the study of the past few centuries of colonialism and capitalism; though this timespan may constitute deep history for sociocultural anthropology and human-animal studies as currently formulated, this timescale is not sufficient for long-term analysis of human-nonhuman relations. Archaeology is the discipline par excellence of the deep historical perspective, dealing with the contemporary, the pre-modern, and prehistoric worlds, including humanity's multi-millennia hunter-gatherer past. This endeavor involves study of the relationships between modern humans, other human species, nonhuman species, and material things, across tens of thousands of years and across vast geographical areas: "No other discipline can claim to work so great a canvas" (Barrett 1995: 3).

This is not to claim that archaeologists occupy some kind of privileged vantage point, or custodial role, from which to stake academic authority with regards to knowledge about the ancient/deep past and its materials (González-Ruibal 2013; Fowles in Alberti et al. 2011). But when a self-proclaimed "new approach to writing culture" emerges, seemingly unaware of the archaeological project's globally significant contribution to the anthropological purview of humanity's history of relationships with other species, and vice versa, then its claims of "paying attention to others" (van Dooren et al. 2016: 1) must be open to question. What kind of approach to writing culture "turns a blind eye to the wealth of studies, by anthropologists and archaeologists, of the manifold ways in which people in different parts of the world, and in different periods of history, have shared their lives with diverse animals and plants" (Ingold 2013: 16)?

That said, most archaeological studies of human–nonhuman relations and interactions are not explicitly articulated as "multispecies" in the ontological sense meant by advocates of the new approach. The stories archaeologists tell about such relationships may still tend to be dominated by systems (cultural, economic, and/or symbolic) and evolutionary thinking, but the study of multispecies interactions underpins a great deal of the work done by archaeologists in one way or another. A multispecies approach has much in common with perspectives developed in archaeology since the mid-twentieth century. For instance, Andre Leroi-Gourhan's influential concept of the technological *chaine operatoire* (e.g. Leroi-Gourhan 1964), while initially concerned with the reconstruction of networks of artifact production from raw material acquisition through production and use to discard, developed in more recent years into consideration of the social networks of relationships between humans and raw material sources in the landscape – e.g. lithic outcrops, animals, plants, and so on. The influence of this approach can be followed through to anthropological archaeology's adoption of Kopytoff's (1986) notion of object biographies (e.g. Gosden and Marshall 1999), which focuses on how the biographies of things, people, and nonhuman species are intimately entwined. But perhaps the closest theoretical similarities with a multispecies perspective lie in Ian Hodder's recent work on "entanglement" (e.g. Hodder 2012), in which long-term changes in the human condition are explained in terms of material (and non-material) mutualism: within which "human–thing relations . . . involve asymmetrical tensions and a mutual co-dependency" (2016: 2). But although Hodder takes the position that "entanglement sets out to turn our typically anthropocentric view of the world on its head" (2016: 129), his primary interpretive focus is on the human–thing relationship, with nonhuman species entanglements set apart (although still related) as "biological beings . . . entangled in ecological relations" (Hodder 2016: 3). In this respect, entanglement theory (and much of the "new materialisms") and a multispecies approach differ in their view of what constitutes anthropocentrism. A truly non-anthropocentric view of the nonhuman – even if this desired position is at all possible (Boyd 2017a) – requires acknowledgment that semiosis is not only a human cultural phenomenon but also a biological one (Crossland and Bauer 2017; Kohn 2013; Marom et al. 2016). As Bennett observes, "humans are always in composition with nonhumanity, never outside of a sticky web of connections or an ecology" (2004: 365).

So, the position taken here is that archaeology is, and has always been, a site of multispecies encounters; it can only be a multispecies investigation that brings together cognate interdisciplinary researchers (Boyd 2017a). The interpretive challenge is to decenter the human in such a way that places the historical complexities of the "sticky web" of human–nonhuman species relationships as the primary subject of archaeological inquiry. The following discussion addresses this challenge with specific reference to one of the dominant archaeological narratives about the relationships between humans and other species: the origins of agriculture and domestication in Southwest Asia (the "Fertile Crescent").

Neolithic origins narratives

Much of a history of archaeology could be written around the quest for origins, with plant and animal domestication and its consequences for the contemporary world being a major theme (e.g. for recent perspectives see *Current Anthropology* special issues 2009, 2011). In most parts of the world where a Neolithic phase is discernible, archaeologists have spent considerable efforts in identifying the preceding economic and cultural processes that ultimately led to the establishment of settled farming societies with a food resource primarily based on certain domesticated plant and animal species. Nowadays it is rare to read an academic or popular media article on aspects of the pre-Neolithic "transition" periods (the Epipalaeolithic, particularly the Natufian, and the Pre-Pottery Neolithic, PPN) of Southwest Asia that does not emphasize as its primary focus the "origins of agriculture", and the consequences and implications for the subsequent development of humanity. It seems that each and every element of pre-Neolithic archaeological sites – material culture, architectural features, evidence for diverse human activities and practices, and relationships with other species – must be deployed in the Neolithic transition narrative (e.g. Bar-Yosef and Belfer-Cohen 1999; Bar-Yosef Mayer and Porat 2008; Grosman et al. 2008; Nadel et al. 1994; Snir et al. 2015). Archaeologists' focus on this change from one way of eating to another has tended to overshadow other concomitant social changes that took place within hunter-gatherer communities in the millennia prior to those material signatures categorized as "the Neolithic". Further, the pre-Neolithic transition periods are invariably regarded through the retrospective lens of the Neolithic itself rather than in their own terms and with their own internal characteristics and historical trajectories independent of their perceived inevitable Neolithic destination. But the human communities of the pre-Neolithic inhabited a world where there was no prior knowledge of plant and animal domestication, sedentism, agriculture, and so on, developments that took place hundreds or thousands of years into their future. Their world was one of *being hunter-gatherer* (or however that mode of being we in the present call "hunter-gatherer" may have been apprehended by people in their own particular social and historical contexts) rather than one inevitably *becoming Neolithic*. Developing non–retrospective ways to view such contexts presents a considerable interpretive challenge for archaeologists. How can we think about pre-Neolithic ontologies and alterities that we in the present do not share and that differ so dramatically from our contemporary sociopolitical categories relating to sedentism, nomadism, population movement, and the control of plant and animal species that characterize the modern industrialized world?

Domestication and modernity

The concept of domestication looms large in archaeological Neolithic origins narratives, in which locating an initial temporal point of departure for direct human involvement in the reproductive cycles of plant and animal species is regarded essential to "understanding the roots of complex societies" (Larsen et al. 2014: 6139). In the biological sense, domestication is broadly conceptualized as management of the nonhuman by the human. It is regarded as something people did to make their world more secure and easier to manage; to make living in it better. Marom and Bar-Oz emphasize domestication as a process of *evolution*, rather than an event, which we need to detail archaeologically to understand "the role of humans as constant modifiers of their ecological niches" (2014: 1). Changes in the human–nonhuman relationship are signaled primarily by "demographic, biogeographic and morphological changes that occurred in the transformation of a wild species to a domesticated one" (2014: 1). This process seems to have begun around 11–12,000 years ago in different parts of the world, and according to Larsen et al. "encompassed a wide range or relationships, from commensalism/mutualism to low-level management, and direct control over reproduction" (2014: 6140). The traditional scenario (until the turn of the twenty-first century) placed the origins of crop domestication in the southern Levant around 11,400 cal BP, during the PPNA, with the domestication of goat and sheep around 10,000 cal BP (middle PPNB), and cattle and pig following slightly later. It has now become clear, in the light of recent archaeobiological and genetic analyses, that the earliest domestication of the "founder crops" of einkorn and emmer, and pulses, along with the initial domestication of sheep, pigs, and cattle (and possibly goats) took place much further north – in the Upper Tigris and Euphrates valleys of modern-day Syria and Turkey around 11 500 cal BP or perhaps slightly earlier (Zeder 2011). We need to bear in mind that these points of origin are in fact the "end point", the result, of the domestication processes. It is now apparent that in Southwest Asia these processes lasted many thousands of years (Maher et al. 2012), and so such gradual long-term changes may have gone largely unnoticed by people in their daily lives and interactions with plants and animals. It is only through our retrospective lens that we see the Neolithic point of arrival. In this sense, the established archaeological narrative or concept of plant and animal domestication as a key component in human social evolution is part of the origins "trope of modernity" (González-Ruibal 2013). The human–nonhuman species relationship represented within this trope is still one of human mastery over nature. In discussing this relationship as one of "our existing great divides" (in Alberti et al. 2011: 906), Severin Fowles has argued that archaeologists'

> major contribution [to the modernist project] has been the evolutionary ontostory of how the modern liberal humanist subject has come to be and of how the world of nonhumans has been drawn increasingly into his (the gendering is necessary) sphere of control.
>
> *Alberti et al. 2011: 899*

Of course, it is widely acknowledged amongst scholars that domestication is not simply a case of human mastery over, or ownership of, nonhuman species (e.g. Cassidy 2007; Ingold 1994; Marder 2013). Rather, it involves types of mutualism and symbiosis, changing relationships, an engagement between different forms of life. But archaeologists still tend to express these changing relationships in terms of human control or management and species instrumentalism. Helen Leach argues that "most definitions of domestication still portray it as a process that was driven by humans to satisfy human needs, often stating or implying in their choice of terms that humans 'created' their domesticates through conscious intervention" (Leach 2007: 71). Ultimately, as Hartigan points out, "the core certainty and conceit behind a long tradition of narrating the history of domestication is that, simply, it's something we did to them" (Hartigan 2015: 72). Those histories tend to revolve primarily around the consequences for humans: the archaeological narrative of the road from domestication to civilization is well-worn, but the mutualism of the human–plant–animal relationship, while acknowledged, remains subsumed in the overarching evolutionary trope of the shift from wild to domestic, from nature to culture. These histories reveal little about the historically specific nature of the human–nonhuman relations that constitute what we construct with hindsight as one of the most significant transformations in human history.

Despite extensive anthropological critique (e.g. MacCormack and Strathern 1980; Descola 2013), claims to the contrary (e.g. Fitzgerald 2013), and an apparent widespread desire to acknowledge non-anthropocentric ways of thinking about human–nonhuman relations, the nature/culture concept has proven tenacious in archaeological/anthropological approaches to plant and animal domestication, especially in those narratives relating to the Neolithic transition. F.R. Valla has argued that "the Natufian saw domestication as an appealing way in which to introduce the animal into society. They thereby opened the way to the unlimited expansion of the 'humanized' world at the expense of nature" (1995: 187). Similarly, Belfer-Cohen and Goring-Morris observe:

> This was the time when humans took upon themselves not only the domestication
> of plants and animals, but also the domestication of the landscape – nothing remained
> "natural" or immutable anymore. While places within the landscape were most prob-
> ably also previously imbued with symbolic significance, there were now conscious
> efforts to tame and/or influence localities within the landscape that were not necessar-
> ily beneficial in terms of the purely functional mechanisms of optimal foraging.
>
> *Belfer-Cohen and Goring-Morris 2002: 144*

Discussing early Neolithic Gobekli Tepe in southeast Anatolia/Turkey, Hodder and Meskell (2011) have argued that the animal imagery depicted on the monumental carved stone pillars at the site were an expression of a desired domination by male humans over dangerous male wild animals: masculine human control of wild nature. They suggest that

> The ability to kill a dangerous wild animal or a large wild bull, to use and overcome its
> masculinity, and to control the distribution of its meat and mementoes was as impor-
> tant to creating the agricultural revolution as domesticating plants and animals.
>
> *Hodder and Meskell 2011: 251*

This reiteration of the term "wild", referring to a world where animals were only wild (in our terms, not theirs), draws a distinction between wild animal nature and human culture, placing the animal ontologically in a place where they are always constitutively outside the human.

Similarly, Lewis-Williams (2004) has argued for the figure of the "shaman" as an authorita-tive mediator between people and the nonhuman world at Neolithic Çatalhöyük in Turkey. This role was linked directly to the control of wild animals. Initially, it is argued, shamans gained their status and supernatural – super *nature* – power partly from their control of, and domination over, wild sheep, goats, and pigs. As these animals gradually became "ordinary" (domesticated), the shamans turned their attentions to the control of wild cattle, aurochs, which over time also became domesticated, thus signaling the end of the dominant social role of the shaman in both human and animal communities. So, the human-animal relationship here is of interest only insofar as it underwrites a changing resource base, whether economic or symbolic. This tells us nothing about the agency or role of animals apart from being "wild" or "domesticated", categories that are inescapably embedded in western notions of nature and culture.

The Neolithic world archaeologists reach for and attempt to categorize and apprehend is, presently, largely articulated through these concepts, but the people who inhabited that world did not share "our" conception of "their" world. Western concepts do not travel that well even in the modern world, so why should they be appropriate with which to explain modes of human-nonhuman relations in the deep past? Further, the concept of domestication works as a metaphor as well as a tracing of material transformations. But we need to cast the human and the nonhuman together in more than a metaphorical sense in our histories of species relations. One possible approach is to take seriously the evidence for human-nonhuman mutualism and write histories of *co-domestication* rather than of human mastery over nature/the nonhuman. This may not sidestep the dominant evolutionary domestication narrative entirely, but such a perspective begins to move the human from the eco/geo-historical center towards a condition of shared, mutual, (e)co-existence with nonhuman species, acknowledging that "the hybrid community sharing meaning, interests and affects is more often the norm than the exception" (Lestel 2006: 150).

Troubling the Neolithic narrative

Rethinking the overarching concept of plant and animal domestication with a "multispecies attitude" necessarily involves a reformulation of existing fields of archaeological inquiry into the changing conditions in human and nonhuman ecologies during the millennia from ca. 23,000 to 10,200 cal BP, the perceived "Neolithic transition" periods. And, yes, we can be certain that changes in those conditions – material and non-material – happened during this long timespan. We know unequivocally that some human communities became sedentary for periods of time, investing in certain places in the landscape, and that some people became intimately involved in the lives of certain plants and animals to the extent that the behavioral and reproductive lives of such species were irreversibly altered. We now call the overall combination of these changes "the Neolithic", but an archaeological "multispecies attitude" offers other ways to think through those changes in human-nonhuman relationships. What forms of life were made possible by, and emerged from, the changing conditions of species co-habitation within those past ecologies? This is not simply a question of geographically and temporally charting human modification or instrumentalization of certain plant and animal species. Nor is it adequate in relational terms to frame certain animal species merely as non-agentive "indicators" of human modes of landscape/place inhabitation (e.g. Boyd 2006). Rather it is an investigation into the material contexts where human and nonhuman species met, encountered each other, and created new forms of relationships. In archaeological terms, these were the specific material contexts where certain people, plants, animals, and objects were brought together through particular interactions and practices and, ultimately, deposited. A number of Epipalaeolithic objects and mortuary contexts provide interesting sites of multispecies encounters, and regularly confront us with evidence that does not sit easily with the existing Neolithic transition or domestication narratives, thus opening the way for consideration of different ontologies whereby some human and nonhuman species may have been regarded or categorized through their participation, inclusion or incorporation in certain representational and depositional practices, rather than through our own retrospective "Neolithic lens".

When (some) species meet – object(s) 1: carved animal bones

Interestingly, for a "culture on the threshold" of animal domestication, there is very little in the way of figurative representation of animals from the late Epipalaeolithic Natufian. There are similarly few human representations, and no depictions of plants or plant use, trees, and so on. There are, however, a few instances where the human, the animal, and the plant are drawn together in different ways.

A series of excavation projects from the 1940s to the early 1970s at Nahal Oren (Wadi Fellah) cave and terrace, Mount Carmel, revealed a Late Natufian settlement with circular stone structures and around 50 human burials (Stekelis 1942; Stekelis and Yizraeli 1963; Noy et al. 1973).

From the 1950s excavations (exact provenance unpublished), an animal long bone with a human head carved on one end and an animal head on the other is the only object from the Epipalaeolithic explicitly displaying some form of human-animal association (Noy 1991: Figure 5). Beyond the representational, there is no visible evidence of other obvious uses of the object, although there are traces of polish and burning/heat treatment on much of the bone surface. Given the occurrence of the objects from other nearby Mount Carmel sites described below, it is possible that the Nahal Oren piece is an unfinished bone haft.

Multispecies co-inhabitation in Southwest Asia

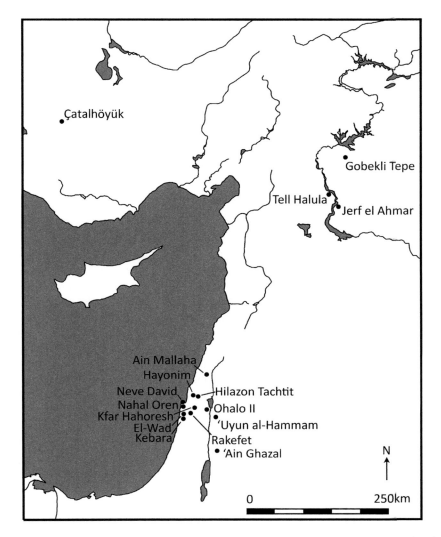

Figure 15.1 Map of Epipalaeolithic and Pre-Pottery Neolithic sites in Southwest Asia mentioned in the text.

Predating the Nahal Oren excavations, the European archaeologists Dorothy Garrod, Rene Neuville, and Francis Turville-Petre had each directed projects that had established the seemingly pivotal position of the Natufian in the Southwest Asian prehistoric cultural sequence:

> In 1928 the cliffs of the Wady el-Mughara were threatened by quarrying operations for the construction of the new harbour at Haifa . . . Mr. Charles Lambert . . . of the Department of Antiquities . . . dug three trenches at the Mugharet el-Wad . . . His most notable find was the carving in bone of Natufian date, which was the first example of Stone Age art to be discovered in the Near East.
>
> *Garrod and Bate 1937: 3–4*

Lambert's find – a carved long bone depicting the head of an animal on one end, is directly comparable to a similar object from Turville-Petre's excavations at nearby Kebara Cave, also on Mount Carmel: "Probably the most important object found [at Kebara] was a grooved bone sickle-blade haft" (Turville-Petre 1932: 272). This well-known artifact from Kebara measures 38 cm in length, and has an animal head carved on one end and a semicircular projection on the opposite edge of the blade-edge near the tip, possibly representing the animal's sexual organs.

Garrod described these bone objects from el-Wad and Kebara in technological/functional terms as "sickle hafts", although Turville-Petre and Neuville suggested that they were also "possibly ritual objects" (Turville-Petre 1932: 72; Neuville 1934). Of all the archaeological objects from the first excavations of Natufian sites in 1920s and 1930s Palestine, the sickle hafts, sometimes found in association with flint blades (some with silica gloss on their cutting edges), have been afforded special attention due to their perceived central role in the emergent "Neolithic narrative": "the Lower [Early] Natufian people were probably the first agriculturalists" (Garrod, 1957: 216).

For this reason, Natufian "sickles" continue to contribute to the Neolithic narrative (e.g. Astruc et al. 2012; Hodder 2017; Maeda et al. 2016), but these composite tools have other stories to tell, not just one overarching explanation about the "origins of agriculture". And it is here that we can begin to flesh out the network of connections, the multispecies ecologies, within which such objects were embedded/entangled. What can be said about possible interspecies relationships embodied in an animal bone object, carved on both ends to depict a human and a nonhuman animal? We could begin with the observation that during the Early (pre-Younger Dryas) Natufian at least, the human communities that lived between the Mediterranean coast and the Jordan Valley were primarily *forest-dwellers*. Forest communities of oak species, terebrith, hawthorn, pistachio, pine, wild cereal grasses (e.g. wheat, barley) and so on, would have constituted places of species co-inhabitation – the social ecologies of human and other animal species (e.g. gazelle, red, fallow and roe deer, wild boar, tortoise, fox, and other large and small "game"). The complexity of human-forest relationships beyond simple subsistence scenarios have been clearly demonstrated by recent posthumanist ethnographic studies and new ecological thinking about human-plant co-dependence (e.g. Kohn 2013; Marder 2013; Mortimer-Sandilands and Erickson 2010). These multi-disciplinary approaches to plant-life can be characterized as having a concern with vegetal modes of being, that is: paying attention to plants in much the same way as non-anthropocentric perspectives have begun to enrich research in human-animal studies. As an alternative to the "Neolithic transition" narrative, we can draw upon these perspectives to help make connections and associations between, for example, human technologies (knowledge and skills), animal bone objects, plants, and so on. For example, in Epipalaeolithic and early Neolithic contexts, hafted implements – made partly from the bones of dead animals – were used to acquire not only wild cereals and other plant foods, but probably also reeds, rushes, and grasses required for clothing and shelter, and for the craft practices of weaving and basketry. It has also become clear through recent phytolith studies that some plant species gathered with animal bone (and flint) tools were used to produce technologies of body containment – baskets and cloth wrappings/bindings – for use in mortuary practices (e.g. Wendrich and Ryan 2013; Power et al. 2014; Ryan 2011). It appears that baskets and textiles were intimately involved in a number of related practices, carrying objects, materials, and human and animal bodies, to and from specific locations across Epipalaeolithic/PPN landscapes (Boyd 2017a), locations with long histories of multispecies relationships between the living and the dead, human and nonhuman.

When (and where) species meet 2: mortuary/burial contexts

Firmly rooted in the "Neolithic transition" narrative, Belfer-Cohen and Goring-Morris have written that the adoption of sedentism amongst some human communities during the Epipaleolithic/Early Neolithic resulted in "tensions" which had to be resolved by "mechanisms" of some kind: "There is a wide-ranging consensus that the search for these mechanisms should be focused in particular on the ritual and symbolic aspects of the archaeological record" (Belfer-Cohen and Goring-Morris 2002: 144). This perceived consensus has come about through necessity rather than choice. Until relatively recently, "ritual" and "symbolism" were not *en vogue* in archaeological discussions of the circumstances surrounding the origins of the Neolithic in Southwest Asia. Over the last twenty years, however, excavations at a number of archaeological sites from across the region have yielded overwhelming evidence of complex and elaborate "ritual and symbolic aspects" of pre-(full) Neolithic social life. We can cite examples from PPNB Kfar HaHoresh in Lower Galilee, Israel (Goring-Morris 2005; Simmons et al. 2007), with its extraordinary range of human and animal mortuary deposits, or PPNA Jerf el Ahmar's (Syria) remarkable large-scale "kiva-like" stone architecture (Stordeur 2000). Then there are the unique anthropomorphic lime plaster statues from PPNB 'Ain Ghazal, Jordan (Rollefson 2000), and, most dramatically, the monumental stone circles of PPNA Gobekli Tepe (southeast Anatolia/ Turkey) with carved pillars depicting (for the most part) a diversity of nonhuman creatures (Schmidt 2004, 2012). All these defy the traditional environment/economy-driven "Neolithic narrative". There are also hundreds of recently discovered human burials from the sites of Körtik Tepe (PPNA) in southeastern Anatolia (Erdal 2015) and Tell Halula (PPNB) in the Euphrates Valley, Syria (Molist et al. 2009), testifying to the scale and diversity of mortuary practices in the centuries before the "fully settled" Neolithic.

This plethora of "symbolic" evidence raises important questions that complicate traditional social/cultural evolutionary perspectives on the nature of pre-Neolithic human communities and their relationships with nonhuman species. We are now witnessing a troubling of the Neolithic transition narrative by the archaeological mainstream, even if it is not couched in such terms. But perhaps we should be cautious about creating a Neolithic that is primarily the product of an archaeology of ritual practices and symbolic associations. Undoubtedly such a narrative is just as biased as a Neolithic based on environmental and economy-driven scenarios. This is a topic for further discussion elsewhere, so let us turn to some specific mortuary sites of multispecies encounter.

Animals

Human-animal associations can be seen throughout the long sequence of Epipalaeolithic Natufian inhabitation at 'Ain Mallaha (Eynan) in the Upper Jordan Valley. A lakeside settlement initially founded on the presence of the dead – 'Ain Mallaha was repeatedly visited and architecturally embellished for many centuries in the same secluded location, a place of long-term inhabitation carved out of the forest. Around 120 human burials have been excavated since the site's initial discovery in the mid-1950s (Bocquentin 2007; Perrot et al. 1988). In terms of animal associations, gazelle horn cores were included in the grave pit of the collective burial H (Homo)1, H25, H26, H27, H31, and in the pit of H70. This latter example lay on top of a ground stone mortar. Animal bones were also associated with burial H52, and the grave fill of H72 contained a deer antler. Elsewhere, grave 10 at Hayonim Cave, western Galilee, yielded a wild boar tusk, and gazelle remains were recovered from graves H2 and, possibly H3 at late

Natufian Hayonim Terrace (Valla 2013, and see below). Animal bones were found in all the graves in late Natufian Raqefet Cave, Mount Carmel (Power et al. 2014).

There are, however, a number of Natufian human–nonhuman animal associations that seem to suggest a more explicit relationship between species. The Early Natufian "Cemetery B" at 'Ain Mallaha contained around twelve primary individual human burials underlying at least three superimposed circular stone "houses" (Perrot et al. 1988; Valla 2008). Several of the human bodies (adult females, adult males and one child) wore various decorations made from *Dentalium* shell – a species from the Mediterranean or Red Seas and an ubiquitous element of bodily adornment throughout the Natufian across the region. Most archaeological attention, however, has been afforded to burial H104, in which an adult woman was interred with a 4–6-month-old canid, in all probability a domesticated dog (Tchernov and Valla 1997). At the time of excavation (mid-1970s) until quite recently, this was generally accepted as the earliest known morphologically domesticated canid (Davis and Valla 1978). The human–dog association is also seen at Late Natufian Hayonim Terrace. Excavated in the late 1980s, a collective human-animal interment (Burial H.7-8-10) contained the skeletons of three people, their bodies in direct contact with those of two domesticated dogs, gazelle horn cores, and the remains of two tortoise carapaces (*Testudo graeca*). The hind paw of one of the fully articulated dogs lay on one of the human skulls. It has been suggested that "the humans were probably buried with clothes" (Tchernov and Valla 1997: 71; Valla 2013). This is supported by archaeothanatological analysis which also suggests that the corpses were clothed or wrapped in shrouds (Bocquentin 2003: 228), comprising a humans-animals-plant fiber wrappings/clothes assemblage. In addition, two of the humans and both dogs appear to have been "pinned down", or at least accompanied by, unmodified stones, thus including another nonhuman material element in the grave.

The 'Ain Mallaha example, often referred as "the puppy burial", especially in the popular media, is regularly cited as evidence for the earliest known "pet". The headlines often refer to "man's best friend", despite the accompanying human being a woman. Descriptions of this burial are often empathetic – the woman's hand rested on the body of the curled-up puppy. The overall picture is one of the dog being brought into the human world through domestication/taming. The two 'Ain Mallaha and Hayonim Terrace burials are the only examples of complete animals (mammals) deposited/buried with humans. Gazelles are represented only by disarticulated bones. Valla has written that this differential treatment of gazelle and dog

> confirms the new closeness of humans and dogs . . . It reveals that the Natufian saw domestication as an appealing way in which to introduce the animal into society. They thereby opened the way to the unlimited expansion of the "humanized" world at the expense of nature.
>
> *Valla 1995: 187*

But beyond this dichotomous anthropocentric nature/culture perspective, the Hayonim Terrace human-dog-gazelle-tortoise association raises the issue of the relationship between these different creatures. Valla suggests that dogs "acquired a different status to that of other mammals . . . The Natufians would have understood that the connection which they maintained with the animal world was already in the process of changing" (Valla 1999: 232). Presumably peoples' awareness of such changes would have depended on how rapidly they occurred or became visible. Unlike gazelles, dogs probably would have been present in everyday living spaces, within settlements, feeding on human food remains (and on other commensal species such as rats). Their assimilation into the human community could have happened relatively quickly but this does not in itself explain why dogs occasionally ended up in graves with humans and parts of gazelle and tortoise bodies. This anthropocentric concern that gives primacy to the human and instrumentalized domesticate highlights the shortcomings of the Neolithic narrative approach. A multispecies perspective, on the other hand, interrogates equally the human, the dog, the tortoise, and the gazelle, and even the stones. These creatures and things are part of the same mortuary practice that led to their incorporation in the grave assemblage.

In studies of the Natufian, the mountain gazelle (*Gazella gazella*) has long held a special place. The gazelle is by far the most common animal species represented in Natufian (and other Epipalaeolithic) contexts. It has an archaeological history as an environmental indicator (Bate 1937; Hartman et al. 2017; Henton et al. 2017), as evidence that the Natufians were specialized gazelle hunters (Campana and Crabtree 1990; Legge and Rowley-Conwy 1987), and as part of the domestication debate (Bar-Oz et al. 2004; Cope 1991; Legge 1972; Simmons and Ilany 1975). Of course, the gazelle was not, and never has been, domesticated, but they were clearly drawn into relationships with humans and other animals at certain times and places. Bar-Oz et al. have argued recently that "cultural factors seem to account for the increased emphasis on gazelle hunting in the Natufian. We suggest looking at both economic and social patterns in the Natufian to further elucidate these cultural factors" (2013: 692). It is unclear what these cultural and social factors may have been, but we can recall the decorated "sickle hafts", the multispecies objects, discussed earlier. As we have seen, these objects made from gazelle bones, occasionally decorated with possible gazelle representations, were used in an array of activities from food gathering to architectural construction, gendered craft activities and mortuary practices.

In the pre-Natufian Epipalaeolithic context, and moving beyond traditional subsistence and mobility scenarios, Maher et al. (2012) and Henton et al. (2017) have eschewed abstract and uniform models of mobility (which is of course a complex mode of relationship between people, animals, plants, and materials in the landscape), and instead place analytical emphasis on the human–gazelle relationship within an agentful inhabited landscape where people and gazelles aggregated and dispersed together at certain times throughout the year. This insightful perspective invokes different ways of mutual multispecies "living with" in the seasonal life of relatively mobile communities.

Also in the pre-Natufian Epipalaeolithic (traditionally labeled "Geometric Kebaran"), another animal species has been recognized as a participant in mortuary practices: the fox. Dating to ca. 15,000–14,200 cal BP, one of the earliest known "cemeteries" in the region, the site of 'Uyun al-Hammam in Wadi Ziqlab, northern Jordan, displays a remarkable series of primary and secondary burials, many with accompanying worked bone and stone objects, and nonhuman animal remains – fox, deer, gazelle, tortoise, aurochs, and other species (Maher et al. 2011). Fox remains (mainly teeth) are known from some Natufian graves (e.g. Hayonim Cave), but 'Uyun al-Hammam is the only example of the placement of fox bodies in graves alongside humans (and other animals and animal body parts). Grave I included a fox skull and humerus, lying underneath the articulated ribs of a human. Large pieces of red ochre adhered to the human ribs and further ochre fragments were found adhering to the fox skull. A fox skeleton, missing the skull and right humerus, was discovered in Grave VIII, which also included a worked animal bone object, a red deer antler, flint blades and flakes, and a number of flat, unworked stone cobbles. The excavators suggest that the fox skull and the postcranial bones are from the same animal (Maher et al. 2011: 6).

Before the discovery of the 'Uyun al-Hammam burial, and the occasional fox teeth and isolated mandibles in Natufian contexts notwithstanding, foxes were discussed by zooarchaeologists as part of the wider Epipalaeolithic animal "subsistence economy", probably hunted, butchered and eaten (Yeshurun et al. 2013). It is now clear that their relationships with humans and other nonhuman animals went beyond the quotidian. It may be also worth reflecting on the fox's relationship to the dog. Although foxes and dogs do not appear together in mortuary assemblages, perhaps the inclusion of the dog in later "human burials" such as those of 'Ain Mallaha and Hayonim Terrace, although temporally separated by hundreds if not a couple of thousand of years, relates to some kind of ancestral memory or tradition involving the fox-human relationship in death. The obvious difference is that the dogs we encounter in the Natufian graves are "domesticated", the pre-Natufian fox of 'Uyun al-Hammam is "wild". But perhaps it does not really matter if an animal was wild or domestic; these are our categories, they were not understood or categorized as such by the people who entered into relations with them.

But what of the tortoise? Again, as with the gazelle and the fox, this creature has long been recognized as a (relatively small) component of the Epipalaeolithic animal economy. An intriguing possible multispecies interrelationship between humans, birds and tortoises exists in a scenario where tortoise carcasses may have acted as lures to capture raptors such as buzzards and eagles at Wadi Jilat 22, eastern Jordan (Martin et al. 2013). The birds' feathers were possibly worn by people as bodily adornment. Yet even its participation in the mortuary ritual, as in the Hayonim Terrace burial discussed above, has not been sufficient to warrant the tortoise's inclusion in recent considerations of postulated Natufian symbolic schemes. In formulating a "coherent thought?" for the Natufian, centered on the Hayonim Terrace grave assemblage, Valla discusses how "the Natufians, consciously or not, established association/opposition relationships between the diverse elements employed in this tomb" (Valla 1999: 232). He goes on to lay out the perceived relationships worthy of investigation:

1   humans and unmodified stones
2   dogs and unmodified stones
3   humans and dogs
4   humans and gazelle horn-cores
5   dogs and gazelle horn-cores.

As mentioned earlier, Valla sees humans and dogs as receiving equal treatment, their complete bodies deposited, then covered or pinned down by stones. Gazelles, however, are represented only by horn-cores. No place is reserved in this scheme for the tortoises, which appear in the same number (two) as the dogs. The relationship between the human, the dog, the gazelle, and the tortoise is thus unclear. We have to turn to the nearby and broadly contemporaneous site of Hilazon Tachtit, a small cave used primarily as a burial location in the Late Natufian phase, ca. 12,000 cal BP (Grosman and Munro 2016; Grosman et al. 2008). Among the 28 human burials, one grave, probably the earliest placed in the cave, is remarkable for its diverse range of human-animal associations and depositions in its various phases of construction. In this grave, an elderly (ca. 45 years old) woman was buried with the horn-core and frontal bone of a gazelle, marine cockle shells (some fashioned into pendants), a wild boar radius and ulna, half of a stone marten skull, an auroch's tail, the wing tip of a golden eagle, a leopard pelvis, a worked animal bone point, the remains of at least 86 tortoises, and an articulated human foot. These human and nonhuman animal remains were accompanied by a worked limestone pebble, a fragment of a basalt bowl, and a limestone scraper. Numerous other animal remains, including those of young gazelles, formed part of the grave fill (Grosman and Munro 2016).

The Hilazon Tachtit grave assemblage and fill contents have been interpreted as the combination of the remains of a funeral feast (particularly the gazelle and tortoise remains), and collected items brought to the grave by people attending the funeral, or perhaps belonging to the dead woman herself (Munro and Grosman 2010). This much is uncontentious. Given the detailed contextual information and the remarkable species diversity of the grave assemblage, the opportunity exists for a rich multispecies interpretation of the human-nonhuman-object relationships represented in this high, secluded place overlooking the east Mediterranean landscape of western Galilee. Disappointingly, however, we are presented with yet another typically anthropocentric Neolithic transition narrative that serves to instrumentalize the nonhuman animal and privilege the human presence. Specifically, the diversity of animal species (and other materials) deposited in the grave are used not to elucidate the vibrant range of human-animal relations clearly evident in the complexity of the archaeological remains, but to confer social status and identity upon the human. Plucking a social persona from the ethnographic rack, the authors make a speculative leap and claim that "the interment rituals and the method used to construct and seal the grave suggest that this was the burial of a shaman, one of the earliest known from the archaeological record" (Grosman and Munro 2016: 312). From this distinctly anthropocentric perspective, the grave's nonhuman animals are instrumentalized with the sole purpose of investing identity upon, and emphasizing, the singularity of "the human"; and yet, each of these animals would have held a different place or significance – socially, culturally, and historically – in the ecologies in which the burial cave was situated.

By de-centering the speculated persona of the human, we could instead narrate stories about how the range of animals were brought together in this particular mortuary locale. By this, I do not mean an estimate of the individual or collective effort/labor involved in acquiring the tortoises and gazelles for the "funerary" feast (Grosman and Munro 2016). If the animal body parts – leopard, aurochs, boar, marten, eagle, and so on – were brought by people from neighboring communities, by visitors, what was significant about those particular animals and the nature of their relationships with the people carrying them, and with the woman who accompanied them in the grave? Were these specially selected animals, or their culturally selected parts, "totemic", perhaps distributing (in the sense of Gell) aspects of local or more distant communities and persons? This entangled network of human-nonhuman animal relationships goes far beyond any one person, whether a "shaman", a "witch", a "sorcerer", or some other arbitrary ethnographic epithet. Even if the Hilazon Tachtit woman was a "shaman", close reading of the relevant ethnographic sources – rather than deploying an archaic form of ethnographic comparison – would demonstrate that shamanic ritual practices themselves are *interspecies relationships*. In such relationships, shamans live with and through other species, and vice versa. A non-anthropocentric interpretation would consider how, for example, people may have been chosen by animals to act as cross-species mediators, rather than animals being harnessed by humans for human purposes.

By definition, a multispecies approach to the Hilazon Tachtit human-nonhuman assemblage would critically consider a range of possible social permutations but, like "the puppy burial" of 'Ain Mallaha, the multispecies mortuary assemblage of human (the woman plus the disarticulated single foot) and other animals' bodies has been reduced to serve the traditional narrative of a "revolutionary cultural entity [the Natufian]" on the "eve of the Neolithic transformation" (Grosman et al. 2008: 17668).

One crucial point to highlight regarding both the 'Ain Mallaha and Hilazon Tachtit humans – and always bearing in mind the temporal distance of at least several centuries separating them – both individuals are women of around 45 years old. With so much concentrated archaeological focus on the domesticated dog at Mallaha, the social persona of the Hilazon Tachtit individual, and the general concern with how these factors relate to the origins of the Neolithic, some rather obvious gender and age-related issues have been overlooked (see Boyd 2002, 2017b for discussion of gender-focused human-animal Natufian/PPN contexts). Further discussion on this aspect of the human-nonhuman animal relationship is clearly required.

Plants and related things

Turning to plants and plant-related objects, direct evidence for the former in pre-Natufian contexts is limited, with only Ohalo II on the southwestern shore of the Sea of Galilee yielding well-preserved *in situ* botanical remains (e.g. Weiss et al. 2004). This Early Epipalaeolithic site provides evidence for wild plant gathering by a hunter-gatherer-fisher community as far back as ca. 23,000 cal BP. Ohalo II consists of the remains of six brush huts, possibly evidence for a settlement occupied year-round, according to the results of the faunal and botanical analyses. The exceptional preservation conditions at the lakeshore site, created by charring/burning during or after occupation, and regular postdepositional silting in anaerobic conditions, have allowed for a rare glimpse into the range of plant and other organic resources available to the human community (or communities) who lived at this location – wild cereals, fruits, nuts, grasses, and so on. No other Early Epipalaeolithic site in the "Fertile Crescent" has such a wealth of well-preserved organic deposits, and so inevitably the Ohalo II material has been harnessed into the Neolithic origins narrative, as exemplified by a recent article, "The Origin of Cultivation and Proto-Weeds, Long before Neolithic Farming" (Snir et al. 2015) – 10,000 years before, to be precise.

There are as yet no comparable macrobotanical remains from other Epipalaeolithic contexts, but at late Natufian Raqefet Cave, Mount Carmel, the quotidian use of wild grass species is well attested by the presence of microbotanical remains (Power et al. 2014). Phytolith analysis of the Raqefet sediments also demonstrates that reeds (Phragmites) and flowering plants (seen as impressions in sediment) were used in mortuary contexts to line several graves (Power et al. 2014: 59). There are also numerous ground stone associations at Raqefet, a feature of Natufian (and earlier) mortuary practices that now seems fairly widespread.

Kaufman (1986, 1989), was amongst the first scholars to suggest that ground stone objects such as pestles and mortars, traditionally associated with plant-processing activities, were entwined with non-quotidian practices prior to the Natufian. At the Middle Epipalaeolithic/ Geometric Kebaran site of Neve David, Mount Carmel, the burial of an adult male was accompanied by a ground stone mortar fragment that lay directly over his skull. Behind the head and shoulder stood a basalt bowl, and between the legs lay a piece of a basalt milling stone (Kaufman 1989). These associations suggest "continuity in ritual behaviour between the Geometric Kebaran and the Natufian" (Kaufman 1986: 122), based upon evidence from Natufian levels at Jericho in the lower Jordan Valley, and the late Natufian cemetery at Nahal Oren on Mount Carmel. The Nahal Oren excavations uncovered several graves that appear to have been "marked" by limestone mortars (Noy 1989: 56), around 70 cm in height, pierced through the base, and inserted into the grave in such a way as to protrude above the ground surface to a height of around 20 cm. Drawing upon ethnographic accounts, the original excavators of the site initially speculated that these mortars may have served as tombstones and/ or as a means by which the soul of the dead could leave the body (Stekelis and Yizraeli 1963: 5–6). Kaufman has argued that the association of "food processing" artifacts with the dead indicates that "these implements took on a special significance beyond their economic importance" (Kaufman 1986: 122), suggesting that the tradition of associating non-functional "dead" mortars with human burials began during the Geometric Kebaran, becoming more ritualized and standardized in the Natufian. However, until recently, it seemed that most ground stone objects or fragments from Natufian mortuary deposits come from grave fills rather than, as at Neve David, in direct association with the body itself.

At Mallaha/Eynan, a number of burials from the occupation levels have been tentatively associated with mortars or mortar fragments (burials H59, H70, H89), and a basalt pestle (H19) (Perrot et al. 1988). There are further examples recovered from graves. From el-Wad, Mount

Carmel, Dorothy Garrod described mortar (H. Group 57, in which four of the skeletons lay in a semicircle around a broken limestone, and H60) and pestle (H5) grave associations (Garrod and Bate 1937). She also noted the proximity of burials to an enclosed stone platform into which was cut a V-shaped basin or mortar. Three similar, but smaller, bedrock mortars were situated outside the platform area. The interior surfaces of these mortars displayed no signs of use-wear, prompting Garrod to suggest that the entire construction may have been "connected with a cult of the dead" (ibid.: 102). The excavations at Hayonim Cave have produced numerous basalt mortar fragments, some conjoinable, from the fills of, and structures associated with, Graves 6, 7, and 8, as well as several ochre-stained basalt pestles (or fragments of) in Graves 3, 4, 6, and 7. The pestle from Grave 7, similar to an example from el-Wad, had been worked to form the shape of an animal hoof (Belfer-Cohen 1988, 1991), an animal-mineral artifact association.

The association of processing artifacts with graves or grave fills (perhaps placed by participants during the burial event) could be taken to suggest that people placed significance on notions of transformation (Boyd 1992): for example, the transformation of plants into food, of the person from life to death, the physical transformation of the body post mortem, and so on. I developed this interpretation further some years ago (Boyd 2005), and it is now further supported by the evidence from Raqefet, and 'Uyun al-Hammam, Jordan (Maher 2007; Maher et al. 2011, 2012; Rosenburg and Nadel 2014). It now seems incontrovertible that ground stone objects were a primary component of the mortuary practice at many burial locales during the Epipalaeolithic and, along with the presence of animal remains and body decoration in the form of marine and freshwater shells, it seems clear that a multispecies mortuary assemblage – a drawing together of human and nonhuman animal bodies and parts, feasting remains, food-related objects, bodily adornment, and so on – was a relatively regular (perhaps "seasonal") feature at some sites (Boyd 2002, 2005, 2006; Nadel et al. 2012, 2013; Yeshurun et al. 2013). And yet, the Neolithic narrative continues to dominate and suppress such ways of thinking about human-animal-object relationships: "Directly preceding the transition to agriculture, Raqefet Cave contains evidence for elaborate mortuary behavior and probably testifies to increasingly numerous and complex Natufian populations" (Yeshurun et al. 2013: 524).

Emphasis on the social role of plants within a multispecies ecology does not necessarily entail the abandonment of important questions of pre-Neolithic plant collecting and gathering, Rather, those quotidian/economic practices can be situated within broader ecologies that recognize the ways that associations between domains that we might view as separate were intimately connected with other life forms. A focus on "human-animal-plant-object" brings different kinds of relations into view, entwining tools and the animals that provided them, plant worlds, people, and their activities.

Endwords

Archaeologists' longing to create seemingly overarching explanations that stifle often small-scale, local, intimate histories of past social lives, human and nonhuman, need to be critically evaluated. It is essential to critically and carefully think through the material evidence for the moments and places where human and nonhuman species came together, and through different practices (technological, mortuary, craft, quotidian, and so on), enabled different forms of sociality. Sometimes, those practices were routine, familiar, and habitual; at other times, they may have involved encounters with strangers, unfamiliar people, animals, and things relating to wider social and cultural currents. Some of those encounters may have involved consideration of people, animals, objects, and events in the past, spoken about or remembered. It seems highly unlikely, however, that such encounters, familiar or otherwise, can be related to events and processes thousands of years in a future they would never experience or even envisage. Only archaeologists construct such retrospective narratives about past humanity. A multispecies – or interspecies – approach to human-nonhuman relations in the deep past is part of a larger political archaeology project that seeks to undermine such disciplinary convention and conservatism. Interpretations of past multispecies encounters will not necessarily pertain to the Neolithic narrative because there were/are always other stories to tell, particularly stories that do not favor human exceptionalism.

Acknowledgments

I would like to thank Suzanne Pilaar Birch, Gavin Lucas and Chris Whitmore for their kind invitation to contribute to this timely volume. Particular thanks to Suzanne for her optimism and sorely tested patience in awaiting the final draft. I am grateful to Zoe Crossland for her unfailingly incisive thoughts and comments on the numerous drafts of the chapter.

References

Alberti, B., Fowles, S., Holbraad, M., Marshall, Y., and Witmore, C. (2011) "'Worlds otherwise': archaeology, anthropology, and ontological difference", *Current Anthropology*, 52(6): 896–912.

Astruc, L., Ben Tkaya, M., and Torchy, L. (2012) "De l'efficacite des faucilles neolithiques au Proche-Orient: approche experimentale", *Bulletin de la Societe prehistorique francaise*, 109(4): 671–87.

Bar-Oz, G., Yeshurun, R., and Weinstein-Evron, M. (2013) "Specializing hunting of gazelle in the Natufian: cultural cause of climatic effect?", in O. Bar-Yosef and F.R. Valla (eds.), *Natufian Foragers in the Levant: terminal Pleistocene social changes in Western Asia*, Ann Arbor, MI: International Monographs in Prehistory, pp. 685–98.

Bar-Oz, G., Dayan, T., Kaufman, D., and Weinstein-Evron, M. (2004) "The Natufian economy of el-Wad Terrace with special reference to gazelle exploitation patterns", *Journal of Archaeological Science*, 31: 217–31.

Barrett, J.C. (1995) *Some Contemporary Challenges in Archaeology*, Oxford: Oxbow.

Bar-Yosef, O. and Belfer-Cohen, A. (1999) "Encoding information: unique Natufian objects from Hayonim Cave, Western Galilee, Israel", *Antiquity*, 73: 402–10.

Bar-Yosef Mayer, D.E. and Porat, N. (2008) "Green stone beads at the dawn of agriculture", *Proceedings of the National Academy of Sciences*, 105(25): 8548–51.

Bate, D.M.A. (1937) "Paleontology: the fossil fauna of the Wadi el-Mughara caves", in D.A.E. Garrod and D.M.A. Bate (eds.), *The Stone Age of Mount Carmel*, Oxford: Clarendon Press, pp. 137–240.

Belfer-Cohen, A. and Goring-Morris, N. (2002) "Recent developments in Near Eastern Neolithic research", *Paléorient*, 28(2): 143–48.

Bennett, J. (2004) "The force of things: steps towards an ecology of matter", *Political Theory*, 32(3): 347–72.

Bocquentin, F. (2003) *Pratiques funéraires, paramètres biologiques et identités culturelles au Natoufien: une analyse archéo-anthropologique.* Ph.D. thesis. Université Bordeaux 1.

Bocquentin, F. (2007) "A final Natufian population: health and burial status at Eynan-Mallaha", in M. Faerman, L.K. Horwitz, T. Kahana and U. Zilberman (eds.), *Faces from the Past: diachronic patterns in the biology of human populations from the Eastern Mediterranean*. Papers in Honour of Patricia Smith, Oxford: British Archaeological Reports, International Series 1603, pp. 66–81.

Boyd, B. (1992) "The transformation of knowledge: Natufian mortuary practices at Hayonim, western Galilee", *Archaeological Review for Cambridge*, 11(1): 19–38.

Boyd, B. (2002) "Ways of eating/ways of being in the Later Epipalaeolithic (Natufian) Levant", in Y. Hamilakis, M. Pluciennik, and S. Tarlow (eds.), *Thinking through the Body: archaeologies of corporeality*. New York: Kluwer/Plenum, pp. 137–52.

Boyd, B. (2005) "Transforming food practices in the Epipalaeolithic and Pre-Pottery Neolithic Levant", in J. Clarke (ed.), *Archaeological Perspectives on the Transmission and Transformation of Culture in the Eastern Mediterranean*, Oxford: Oxbow, pp. 106–12.

Boyd, B. (2006) "On sedentism in the Later Epipalaeolthic (Natufian) Levant", *World Archaeology*, 38(2): 164–78.

Boyd, B. (2017a) "Ecologies of fiber-work: animal technologies and invisible craft practices in prehistoric Southwest Asia", *Quaternary International*, https://doi.org/10.1016/j.quaint.2017.06.050.

Boyd, B. (2017b) "Archaeology and human-animal relations: thinking through anthropocentrism", *Annual Review of Anthropology*, 46: 299–316.

Campana, D.V. and Crabtree, P.J. (1990) "Communal hunting in the Natufian of the southern Levant: the social and economic implications", *Journal of Mediterranean Archaeology*, 3(2): 223–43.

Cassidy, R. (2007) "Introduction: domestication reconsidered", in R. Cassidy and M. Mullin (eds.), *Where the Wild Things Are Now: domestication reconsidered*, Oxford and New York: Berg, pp. 1–25.

Cope, C. (1991) "Gazelle hunting strategies in the southern Levant", in O. Bar-Yosef and F.R. Valla (eds.), *The Natufian Culture in the Levant*, Ann Arbor: International Monographs in Prehistory, pp. 341–58.

Crossland, Z. and Bauer, A. (2017) Im/materialities: things and signs, *Semiotic Review*. 4: January 2017. https://www.semioticreview.com/ojs/index.php/sr/article/view/9.

Current Anthropology (2009) "Rethinking the origins of agriculture", 50(5).

Current Anthropology (2011) "The origins of agriculture: new data, ideas", 52(S4).

Davis, S.J.M. and Valla, F.R. (1978) "Evidence for the domestication of the dog in the Natufian of Israel 12 000 years ago", *Nature*, 276(5688): 608–10.

Descola, P. (2013) *Beyond Nature and Culture*, Chicago, IL: University of Chicago Press.

Erdal, Y.S. (2015) "Bone or flesh: defleshing and post-depositional treatments at Körtik Tepe (Southeastern Anatolia, PPNA period)", *European Journal of Archaeology*, 18: 4–32.

Fitzgerald, D. (2013) "Philippe Descola's *Beyond Nature and Culture*", *Somatosphere*, http://somatosphere.net/2013/10/philippe-descolas-beyond-nature-and-culture.html.

Garrod, D.A.E. (1957) "The Natufian culture: the life and economy of a Mesolithic people in the Near East", *Proceedings of the British Academy*, 43: 211–27.

Garrod, D.A.E. and Bate, D.M.A. (1937) *The Stone Age of Mount Carmel*, Oxford: Clarendon Press.

González-Ruibal, A. (2013) "Reclaiming archaeology", in A. González-Ruibal (ed.), *Reclaiming Archaeology: beyond the tropes of modernity*, New York: Routledge, pp. 1–29.

Goring-Morris, N. (2005) "Life, death and the emergence of differential status in the Near Eastern Neolithic: evidence from Kfar HaHoresh, Lower Galilee, Israel", in J. Clarke (ed.), *Archaeological Perspectives on the Transmission and Transformation of Culture in the Eastern Mediterranean*, Oxford: Oxbow, pp. 89–105.

Gosden, C. and Marshall, Y. (1999) The cultural biography of objects, *World Archaeology*, 31(2): 169–78.

Grosman, L. and Munro, N.D. (2016) "A Natufian ritual event", *Current Anthropology* (Online-Only Material Supplement A), 57(3): doi:10.1086/686563.

Grosman, L., Munro, N., and Belfer-Cohen, A. (2008) "A 12,000-year-old shaman burial from the southern Levant (Israel)", *Proceedings of the National Academy of Sciences*, 105(46): 17665–9.

Haraway, D.J. (2016) *Staying with the Trouble: making kin in the Chthulucene*, Durham, NC and London: Duke University Press.

Hartigan Jnr., J. (2015) *Aesop's Anthropology: a multispecies approach*, Minneapolis: University of Minnesota Press.

Hartman, G., Bar-Yosef, O., Brittingham, A., Grosman, L. and Munro, N.D. (2017) "Hunted gazelles evidence cooling, but not drying, during the Younger Dryas in the southern Levant", *Proceedings of the National Academy of Science*, 113(15): 3997–4002.

Henton, E., Martin, L., Garrard, A., Jourdan, A.-L., Thirwell, M., and Boles, O. (2017) "Gazelle seasonal mobility in the Jordanian steppe: the use of dental isotopes and microwear as environmental markers, applied to Kharaneh IV", *Journal of Archaeological Science: Reports*, 11: 147–58.

Hodder, I. (2012) *Entangled: an archaeology of the relationships between humans and things*, Oxford: Blackwell.

Hodder, I. (2016) *Studies in Human-Thing Entanglement*, Creative Commons.

Hodder, I. and Meskell, L. (2011) "A 'curious and sometimes a trifle macabre artistry': some aspects of symbolism in Neolithic Turkey", *Current Anthropology*, 52(2): 235–63.

Ingold, T. (1994) "From trust to domination: an alternative history of human-animal relations", in A. Manning and J. Serpell (eds.), *Animals and Human Society: changing perspectives*, London: Routledge, pp. 1–22.

Ingold, T. (2013) "Anthropology beyond humanity", *Suomen Antropologi: Journal of the Finnish Anthropological Society*, 38(3): 5–23.

Kaufman, D. (1986) "A reconsideration of adaptive change in the Levantine Epipalaeolithic", in L.G. Straus (ed.), *The End of the Palaeolithic in the Old World*, Oxford: BAR I.S. 284, pp. 117–28.

Kaufman, D. (1989) "Observations on the Geometric Kebaran: a view from Neve David", in O. Bar-Yosef and B. Vandermeersch (eds.), *Investigations in South Levantine Prehistory*, Oxford: British Archaeological Reports I.S. 497, pp. 275–85.

Kirksey, E. (2015) *Emergent Ecologies*, Durham, NC and London: Duke University Press.

Kirksey, E.S. and Helmreich, S. (2010) "The emergence of multi-species ethnography", *Cultural Anthropology*, 25(4): 545–76.

Kohn, E. (2013) *How Forests Think: toward an anthropology beyond the human*, Berkeley: University of California Press.

Kopytoff, I. (1986) "The cultural biography of things: commoditization as a process", in A. Appadurai (ed.), *The Social Life of Things: commodities in cultural perspective*, Cambridge: Cambridge University Press, pp. 64–91.

Larsen, G. (2014) "Current perspectives and the future of domestication studies", *Proceedings of the National Academy of Sciences*, 111(17): 6139–46.

Leach, H.M. (2007) "Selection and the unforeseen consequences of domestication", in R. Cassidy and M. Mullin (eds.), *Where the Wild Things Are Now: domestication reconsidered*, Oxford and New York: Berg, pp. 71–99.

Legge, A.J. (1972) "Prehistoric exploitation of the gazelle in Palestine", in E.S. Higgs (ed.), *Economic Prehistory*, Cambridge: Cambridge University Press, pp. 170–77.

Legge, A.J. and Rowley-Conwy, P.A. (1987) "Gazelle killing in Stone Age Syria", *Scientific American*, 257(2): 76–83.

Leroi-Gourhan, A. (1964) *Le geste et la parole I: technique et langage*, Michel: Paris.

Lestel, D. (2006) "Ethology and ethnology: the coming synthesis. A general introduction", *Social Science Information*, 45(2): 147–53.

Lewis-Williams D. (2004) "Constructing a cosmos: architecture, power and domestication at Çatalhöyük", *Journal of Social Archaeology*, 4(1): 28–59.

MacCormack, C. P. and Strathern, M. (eds.) (1980) *Nature, Culture and Gender*, Cambridge: Cambridge University Press.

Maeda, O., Lucas, L., Silva, F., Tanno, K. I., and Fuller, D. Q. (2016) "Narrowing the harvest: increasing sickle investment and the rise of domesticated cereal agriculture in the Fertile Crescent", *Quaternary Science Reviews*, 145: 226–37.

Maher, L.A. (2007) "2005 excavations at the Geometric Kebaran site of" Uyun al-Hammam, al-Koura District, northern Jordan", *Annual of the Department of Antiquities of Jordan*, 51: 263–72.

Maher, L.A., Richter, T., and Stock, J. (2012) "The pre-Natufian Epipalaeolithic: long-term behavioral trends in the Levant", *Evolutionary Anthropology*, 21: 69–81.

Maher, L.A., Stock, J.T., Finney, S., Heywood, J.J.N., Miracle, P.T., and Banning, E.B. (2011) "A unique human-fox burial from a pre-Natufian cemetery in the Levant (Jordan)", *PLoS One*, 6 (1): doi:10.1371/journal.pone.0015815.

Marder, M. (2013) *Plant-Thinking: a philosophy of vegetal life*, New York: Columbia University Press.

Marom, N. and Bar-Oz, G. (2014) "The prey pathway: a regional history of cattle (*Bos taurus*) and pig (*Sus scrofa*) domestication in the northern Jordan Valley", *PLoS One*, 8(2): doi:10.1371/journal.pone.0055958.

Marom, N., Yeshrun, R., Weissbrod, L. and Bar-Oz, G. (eds.) (2016) *Bones and Identity: zooarchaeological approaches to reconstructing social and cultural landscapes in southwest Asia*, Oxford and Philadelphia, PA: Oxbow Books.

Martin, L., Edwards, L., and Garrard, A. (2013) "Broad spectrum or specialized activity? Birds and tortoises at the Epipalaeolithic site of Wadi Jilat 22 in the eastern Jordan steppe", *Antiquity*, 87: 649–65.

Molist, M., Montero-Ruiz, I., Clop, X., Rovira, S., Guerrero, E., and Anfruns, J. (2009) "New metallurgic findings from the Pre-Pottery Neolithic: Tell Halula (Euphrates Valley, Syria)", *Paléorient*, 35(2): 33–48.

Mortimer-Sandilands, C. and Erickson, B. (eds.) (2010) *Queer Ecologies: sex, nature, politics, desire*, Bloomington and Indianapolis: Indiana University Press.

Munro, N.D. and Grosman, L. (2010) "Early evidence (ca. 12,000 BP) for feasting at a burial cave in Israel", *Proceedings of the National Academy of Sciences*, 107(35): 15362–6.

Nadel, D., Danin, A., Werker, E., Schick, T., Kislev, M.E., and Stewart, K. (1994) "19,000-year old twisted fibers from Ohalo II", *Current Anthropology*, 35(4): 451–8.

Nadel, D., Lambert, A., Bosset, G., Bocquentin, F., Rosenberg, D., Yeshurun, R., Weissbrod, L., Tsatskin, A., Bachrach, N., Bar-Matthews, M., Ayalon, A., Zaidner, Y., Beeri, R., and Grinberg,

H. (2012) "The 2010 and 2011 seasons of excavation at Raqefet Cave", *Journal of the Israel Prehistoric Society*, 42: 35–73.

Nadel, D., Danin, A., Power, R.C., Rosen, A.M., Bocquentin, F., Tsatskin, A., Rosenberg, D., Yeshruven, R., Weissbrod, L., Rebollo, N.R., Barzilai, O., and Boaretto, E. (2013) "Earliest floral grave lining from 13,700-11,700-y-old Natufian burials at Raqefet Cave, Mt. Carmel, Israel", *Proceedings of the National Academy of Sciences*, 110(29): 1174–8.

Neuville, R. (1934) "Les débuts de l'agriculture et la faucille préhistorique en Palestine", *Extrait du Receuil de la Société Hebraïque d'Exploration et d'Archéologie Palestiniennes*. Jerusalem.

Neuville, R. (1951) *Le Paleolithique et Mesolithique du Deseret de Judee*, Masson: Paris.

Noy, T. (1989) Some aspects of Natufian mortuary behavior at Nahal Oren, in I. Hershkovitz (ed.) *People and Culture in Change*, Oxford: BAR I.S. 508, pp. 53–7.

Noy, T. (1991) "Art and decoration of the Natufian at Nahal Oren", in O. Bar-Yosef and F.R. Valla (eds.), *The Natufian Culture in the Levant*, Ann Arbor: International Monographs in Prehistory, pp. 557–68.

Noy, T., Legge, A.J., and Higgs, E.S. (1973) Recent excavations at Nahal Oren, Israel, *Proceedings of the Prehistoric Society*, 39: 75–99.

Perrot, J., Ladiray, D., and Solivères-Massei, O. (1988) *Les Hommes de Mallaha (Eynan), Israel*, Paris: Association Paléorient.

Power, R.C., Rosen, A.M., and Nadel, D. (2014) "The economic and ritual utilization of plants at the Raqefet Cave Natufian site: the evidence from phytoliths", *Journal of Anthropological Archaeology*, 33: 49–65.

Rollefson, G.O. (2000) "Ritual and social structure at Neolithic 'Ain Ghazal", in I. Kuift (ed.), *Life in Neolithic Farming Communities: social organization, identity, and difference*, New York: Kluwer/Plenum, pp. 165–90.

Rosenberg, D. and D. Nadel (2014) "The sounds of pounding: boulder mortars and their significance to Natufian burial customs", *Current Anthropology*, 55(6): 784–812.

Ryan, P. (2011) "Plants as material culture in the Near Eastern Neolithic: perspectives from the silica skeleton artifactual remains at Çatalhöyük", *Journal of Anthropological Archaeology*, 30(3): 292–305.

Schmidt, K. (2004) "Frühneolithische zeichen vom Göbekli Tepe", *Tuba-AR*, 7: 93–106.

Schmidt, K. (2012) *Göbekli Tepe: a Stone Age sanctuary in South-Eastern Anatolia*, Berlin: ex oriente.

Simmons, A.H. and Ilany, G. (1975) "What mean these bones? Behavioral implications of gazelles' remains from archaeological sites", *Paléorient*, 3: 269–74.

Simmons, T., Goring-Morris, N., and Horwitz, L.K.,(2007) "'What ceremony else?' Taphonomy and the ritual treatment of the dead in the Pre-Pottery Neolithic B mortuary complex at Kfar HaHoresh, Israel", in M. Faerman, L.K. Horwitz, T. Kahana, and U. Zilberman (eds.), *Faces from the Past: diachronic patterns in the biology of human populations from the Eastern Mediterranean. Papers in Honour of Patricia Smith*, Oxford: British Archaeological Reports, International Series 1603, pp. 1–27.

Snir, A., Nadel, D., Groman-Yaroslavski, I., Melamed, Y., Sternberg, M., Bar-Yosef, O., and Weiss, E. (2015) "The origin of cultivation and proto-weeds, long before Neolithic farming", *PLoS One*, 10(7): doi:10.1371/journal.pone.0131422.

Stekelis, M. (1942) "Preliminary report on soundings in prehistoric caves in Palestine", *Bulletin of the American School of Oriental Research*, 867: 2–10.

Stekelis, M. and Yizraeli, T. (1963) "Excavations at Nahal Oren: preliminary report", *Israel Exploration Journal*, 13(1): 1–12.

Stordeur, D. (2000) "New discoveries in architecture and symbolism at Jerf el Ahmar (Syria), 1997–1999", *Neo-Lithics*, 1(00): 1–4.

Tchernov, E. and Valla, F.R. (1997) "Two new dogs, and other Natufian dogs, from the Southern Levant", *Journal of Archaeological Science*, 24: 65–95.

Tsing, A. (2015) *The Mushroom at the End of the World: on the possibility of life in capitalist ruins*, Princeton, NJ: Princeton University Press.

Turville-Petre, F. (1932) "Excavations at the Mugharet el-Kebarah", *Journal of the Royal Anthropological Institute*, 62: 271–6.

Valla, F.R. (1999) "The Natufian: a coherent thought?", in W. Davies and R. Charles (eds.), *Dorothy Garrod and the Progress of the Palaeolithic: studies in the prehistoric archaeology of the Near East and Europe*, Oxford: Oxbow, pp. 224–41.

Valla, F.R. (1995) "The first settled societies: Natufian (12,500–10,200 BP)", in T. Levy (ed.), *The Archaeology of Society in the Holy Land*, London: Leicester University Press, pp. 169–87.

Valla, F.R. (2008) *L'homme et l'habitat: l'invention de la maison durant la prehistoire*, Paris: CNRS editions.

Valla, F.R. (dir.) (2013) *Les Fouilles de la Terrasse d'Hayonim (Israel)*, Paris: De Boccard.

Van Dooreen, T., Kirksey, E., and Munster, U. (2016) "Multispecies studies: cultivating arts of attentiveness", *Environmental Humanities*, 8(1): 1–23.

Weiss, E., Wetterstrom, W., Nadel, D., and Bar-Yosef, O. (2004) "The broad spectrum revisited: evidence from plant remains", *Proceedings of the National Academy of Sciences*, 101/26: 9551–5.

Wendrich, W. and Ryan, P. (2013) "Phytoliths and basketry materials at Çatalhöyük (Turkey): timelines of growth, harvest and objects' life histories", *Paléorient*, 38(1): 57–65.

Yeshurun, R., Bar-Oz, G. and Nadel, D. (2013) "The social role of food in the Natufian cemetery of Raqefet Cave, Mount Carmel, Israel", *Journal of Anthropological Archaeology*, 32(4): 511–26.

Zeder, M.A. (2011) "The origins of agriculture in the Near East", *Current Anthropology*, 52(4): S221–35.

PART IV

The ecology of movement

16

LEGS, FEET *AND* HOOVES

The seasonal roundup in Iceland

Oscar Aldred

Just as humans have a history of their relations with animals, so also animals have a history of their relations with humans. Only humans, however, construct narratives of this history.

Ingold 2000: 61

Introduction

Archaeology, like many disciplines, has a preoccupation in studying just one species of interest: in our case humans. In this respect even the recovery of skeletal remains of animals from excavations are usually studied in terms of *human* consumption and use. This is as one might expect, given humans' place at the helm of the Anthropocene (Ruddiman 2013; Edgeworth et al. 2014; Edgeworth et al. 2015). After all, humans have a central role in the life cycles of nurture and slaughter of many animals. Those that take a more balanced view, who have explored the interrelationships between humans and animals, tend to place humans as carers, or put animals as victims, or as both as adaptors to external behaviours, or each as the subjects in violence (Hodder 2012; Tinbergen 1963; Netz 2004). These responses try to address the centuries of imbalance in thinking and writing that has emphasised the vertical hegemony of humans over other animals. In this chapter, I want to turn the tables slightly, and ask what if we were to re-position the status of animals not below us or above, but alongside us; less as subjects for care, but as companions? Arguably, such a perspective allows for greater symmetry between species (e.g. Haraway 2003; Witmore 2015).

To do this, what I suggest is that to really get to know an animal, or human for that matter, one needs to walk *with*, not ahead or behind, and what this demands are two things. First, realigning the relationship by turning the ontological table from a vertical to horizontal position, and second, viewing this relationship through the filtered lens of movement (Aldred 2014; Edgeworth 2014). In doing so, animals become one of the constitutional parts of a mobile, extended community – a multispecies assemblage – of human and nonhuman entities. Thus, by conjoining movement with an extended community, a multispecies archaeology is brought to the foreground.

To make this happen, in this chapter I describe and reflect on the movements associated with the seasonal roundup of sheep in the district of Skútustaðahreppur, northeast Iceland. The roundup is an annual event, and although medieval in origins, it still continues today in a reduced form. As a part of a medieval system of transhumance, sheep were driven and left to graze in the summer pasture areas – upland heath areas – before being rounded up at the end of the summer by an assemblage of farmers on horses, dogs, and helpers on foot. Once the sheep were rounded up, they were driven back to the settlement area, and then allocated to their respective farms on the basis of defined markings at the sorting fold (Aldred 2006).

Becoming *with* is becoming worldly: landscape inhabitation

A multispecies archaeology of the roundup is underpinned by two theoretical positions. First, I am concerned with the way archaeology separates an activity such as the roundup into discrete analytical units, usually defined by natural or cultural forms and processes. A most telling example is the way that sheep are considered passive in the roundup process, alongside other nonhuman entities such as the landscape. While there are advantages in creating an analytical distance through this form of partitioning, because a greater understanding of totalities, say, that constitute an ecosystem consisting of humans, animals and plants, is gained, it also brings disadvantages. The partitioning creates a synthetic division that binds what are mutually *inter-dependent* entities into an abstract system of cultural:natural. The former part is active while the latter is passive. Furthermore, after such detailed examination, the reassembling of the forms and processes under scrutiny never quite produce the original experienced arrangement; in a redacted partitioning, gaps will always remain. As Ingold (1974, 1980, 1986, 2000), Latour (1993, 1999, 2004), Descola and Pálsson (1996) and others, remind us, such a partitioning divorces the actual experience of carrying out practical tasks when compared to how an activity such as the seasonal roundup appears when it is perceived through a 'scientific' gaze – for example, the system of taxonomy that has been used to divide animals and plants since the eighteenth century (Linnaeus 1735; Ingold 1994). Re-working this partitioning may lead not only to a multispecies perspective, but a unified-species one (Ingold 2000: 61–76; Skúlason 2005: 21–3). However, in order for this to work successfully, what is needed is a second way to keep the analysis of the parts, say of the practical experiences of living and working with animals, or more directly the roundup, and the landscape, enchained.

A second theoretical position used in this chapter argues for a wider view of the human-animal relationship, and specifically that between sheep and farmers, as a distributed system of an extended ecology (Bennett 2010). An extended ecology has a character that is assemblage-like (Lucas 2012), a form of community (Harris 2012, 2014), and a type of 'bundle' (Zedeño 2008: 364). Delanda's assemblage theory of society is explicitly an expanded concept like the extended ecology, not just because it is a good fit with the politics inherent in this chapter, but rather because it takes heed of the implications of what an expanded view of the assemblage does: linking micro- to macro- scales of practices as entities 'drift' into forming new assemblages (DeLanda 2006; Deleuze and Guatarri 1983, 2004). The currency of this second position for a multispecies archaeology permits the drifting and reconfiguration of new assemblages with the same entities involved, which is what happens during the roundup, as I will explain. Furthermore, assemblage-thinking addresses the challenge of overcoming territorialisations; many of these lie at the heart of archaeology.

This Deleuzian concept of territory is a reaction against the categorisation and forming of boundaries and fixing of things into solids (Edgeworth 2011: 87–8). Examples of territorialised

The seasonal roundup in Iceland

archaeologies are approaches that rely on structures in material patterning that use archaeology's common tools such as stratigraphy, seriation, ordering, and taxonomies, to pre-determine the capacities of things that may have been quite fluid in character, where boundaries between fixed typologies may have been much more diffuse than they appear to have been. At macro-landscape-scales, such solid structures are defined by the strictly defined boundaries or territories in which sheep graze; yet where sheep graze is fluid, but inter-dependent on nonhuman topographies, vegetation cover, climate and weather systems. Studies that have brought an inter-dependent, assemblage-like, fluid and more entangled perspective on the connections between animals and humans have *deterritorialised* the fixed set of relations in at least two ways. Examples such as Haraway's emotional entanglements with animals have a political mode of thinking (Haraway 1991, 2004, 2008), and another study is Ingold's re-stating of the ecology and productive practices of Circum-Arctic reindeers and Saami herders (Ingold 1974, 1976, 1980). While the former has a moral foundation, and the latter a neo-Marxist economic perspective, in this chapter I straddle these two poles.

These two theoretical positions, *inter-dependent* and *deterritorialising*, create the possibility for a deeper examination of the inter-connected and ecological relational networks that occur between farmers and sheep during seasonal roundups. Arguably, it gets underneath the often superficial responses to questions on how humans and animals become entwined together, and pull apart while still remaining entangled. A key factor is attached to the movements that occur at different stages in their entanglement. Utilising archaeology, ethnography and historical sources, the investigation of the human-animal relation uses movement to keep the activities and the constitutive parts of the moving assemblage linked *together* from several perspectives by examining: (1) the different flows that converge during the roundup; (2) human movements alongside co-constitutive companion species such as dogs, horses and sheep; (3) the locales where species congregate and meet, and what properties become swapped. These perspectives are the basis for a lively and relational ontology that breaks down the subsets and dichotomies of 'humans in nature' or 'culture versus nature', that tend to hold people and other animals apart. The ontological flow that I use for the roundup is flat, in which differences between sheep and farmers emerge through the relations that exist between them at various stages during the roundup, in which properties become assigned and power is acted out (agency) through their entanglement with each other, and other allies (Latour 1999, 2005; Harman 2007: 43, 2009; Morton 2013: 14).

To explore the roundup from a multispecies perspective, three irreducible practical stages are examined: the organisation of the roundup, the roundup itself, and the sheep-sorting into farms.[1] While these stages are the gears within the black-box of human-animal relations, in this chapter, these are distributed and examined amongst three networks: spatial and temporal networks, and the network of social practices.

Spatial networks

The spatial network is the scene and action of the roundup, where the organisation of the activity focuses its attention, where paths are laid out into the grazing areas, and where flows of humans and animals tangle and converge.

The district of Skútustaðahreppur is a dynamic system, characterised by the shallow eutrophic Lake Mývatn that sits in the centre of the area and around which the majority of the farms that support the seasonal roundup are located (McGovern et al. 2007). The lake is 37 km^2 and about 50 km from the coast, and is surrounded by dry lava fields on one side and extensive

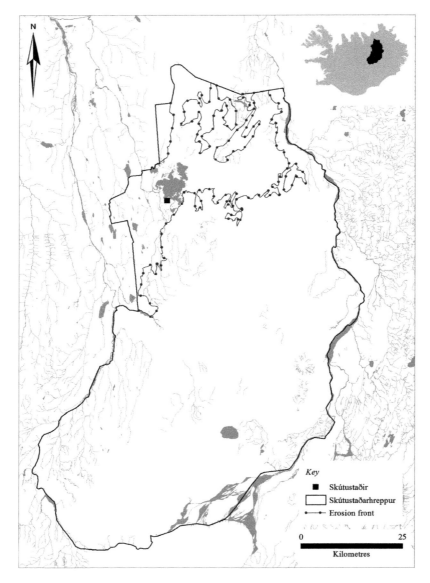

Figure 16.1 Study area, showing main erosion front (the area in which Skútustaðir is placed in is the area with most vegetation; the other area is greatly denuded). The two grazing areas are located in the north and east of Lake Mývatn (central grey shaded area), and south of Skútustaðir.

wetlands fed by the river Kráká, that winds its way from south to north, on the other. However, Skútustaðahreppur is a highly sensitive environment. At 400 m above sea level, fluctuations in one part of the ecosystem have a significant impact on many of the other inter-connected features – none the more so than for Skútustaðahreppur's two grazing areas. The first grazing area is called *Austurafrétt* – 'eastern common land'; and the second is called *Suðurafrétt* – 'southern common land' (Figure 16.1).

The seasonal roundup in Iceland

Table 16.1 Grazing areas within Skútustaðahreppur, collective grazing area, and historical connections

Grazing area	Grazing zone	Historical rights	Area (km²)
Austurafrétt	Gæsafjallastykki	Reykjahlið & Grimstaðir	168
	Norðufjall	Reykjahlið	348
	Neðri Miðfjall	Reykjahlið	88
	Austari Miðfjall	Reykjahlið	133
	Veggjastykki	Reykjahlið	272
	Grafarlandstykki	Reykjahlið	1521
	Miklimó	Skútustaðir & Grænavatn	894
Suðurafrétt	Austurdalur and Grafarlönd	Skútustaðir	526
	Framdalur	Einarstaðir & Reykjahlið	965

The two grazing areas, called Austurafrétt and Suðurafrétt, lie to the north and east of Lake Mývatn, and to the south, respectively. They are subdivided into several smaller zones, defined by lava, rivers and mountains; Austurafrétt has six zones, whilst Suðurafrétt has three (Table 16.1). Knowing about these grazing areas was important for organising the roundup because they helped to predict where the paths would be, and where the likely areas were where sheep would graze; this allowed the calculations about how many people and other animals such as dogs and horses, would take part in the roundup. But as we will see, these territories were, and are, not fixed, bounded states, but blend and flow into one another.

While the tradition of grazing sheep in the upland summer pastures is at least as old as the twelfth century in some parts of Iceland (Dennis, Foote and Perkins 2000), the first known documentary reference to the activity in Skútustaðahreppur is in the eighteenth century. Earlier activity is indicated by archaeology, however. It is probable that a transhumance practice – seasonal movement of animals to summer grazing lands and back again – similar to the one practised today, was developed after an eleventh-century extensive system of earth and turf-built boundaries in the region fell out of use, probably in the fourteenth century. The boundaries system comprised enclosures for land management that was probably connected with controlling the movement of sheep in and out of grazing areas (Einarsson et al. 2002; Einarsson and Aldred 2011; Aldred et al. 2007). In its place, a 'new' system was developed in the fourteenth century, as a more community-orientated system, but continuing the control of sheep movement, and by extension human movement, in and out of the grazing areas.

A key feature of this control was not physically constructed boundaries, but the earmark (*fjámörk*), which was used to identify the sheep as belonging to a particular farm. While today the marking is identified by serial numbers and coloured tags pierced into the ear, in medieval times and up until later, a specific cut was made into the ear. A standardised set of symbols was used that denoted ownership. The practice is at least as old as the thirteenth century (Dennis, Foote and Perkins 2000: 346–8 Nos. 405, 409, 414, 415i, ii, 416; for other places cf. Ryder 1983: 242, 537–8, 543, 668–70; Svabo 1782; Aðalsteinsson 1981: 79; Gosset 1911; Fenton 1978; Sanderson 1971; Cabanel-Leduc 1975; Barth 1961). A similar practice occurred with the Saami: when different family members inherited reindeer, each one would add new ear marks to the animals that they inherited, to distinguish theirs from the other heirs' reindeer (Ingold 1976: 50–3; 1980: 115–16 (Figure 17), 195; 2007: 45–6 (Figure 2.3)). The form of earmarking is likely to have become more complex through time as the system developed and with an

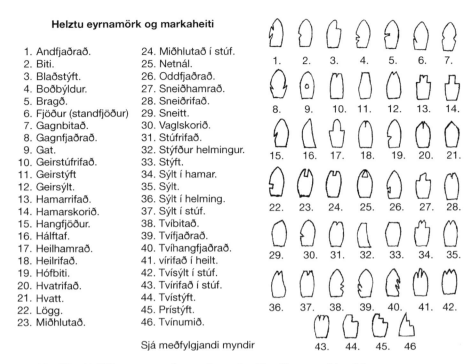

Figure 16.2 The 46 different types of earmarks used to identify ownership of sheep.

increase in sheep numbers. They became combinations of markings usually involving three or more elements in either or both ears from 46 different marks (Figure 16.2). The sheep's earmark was both a liberating feature of their identity – that allowed them to move unhindered during the summer – but was also one that incarcerated them on their return to their respective farms at the end of the summer.

The entanglement of farmers and sheep, of landscape, earmarks, grazing patterns, vegetation growth, and other fauna – cultural and natural forces – illustrates the various spatial extensions and multiple movement flows amongst the different entities involved in the roundup. There are processes of dispersal, gathering and collecting, as well as semi-autonomous flows of herding animals, as well as other animals, as well as the sorting of both in the farms, as well as passage along pre-determined flows with pre-scribed stages. These multiple, emergent, semi-autonomous and highly choreographed movements are indicative of a multispecies archaeology. They require examination of the contractive and expansive spatial flows of *inter-dependent* entities along enchained networks. As such, assessing what effect the network has in shaping practices and material outcomes, and considering what happens when a model of flow is devised, can be applied to an archaeology that has up to now really only been understood largely in terms of solid, fixed materials (Edgeworth 2011: 88, 137). A multispecies account of the roundup is a re-articulation of an activity that has been considered spatially linear: from farm to grazing area, and back to the farm. As we will see, the spatial dimensions of the roundup are more characteristically thought of as non-linear, and this is partly to do with their inherent temporal complexities.

Temporal networks

The roundup is made up of several different temporal scales, but for this chapter two are important: the year-on-year operation; and the minutiae set within a roundup in a particular year. Where the sheep grazed was based in part on a pre-eighteenth-century system, that had developed over many years, and therefore was a tried and tested practice that had a particular knowledge derived from a path dependency with a much longer history. For example, a small group of medieval farms (Einarsstaðir, Reykjahlíð, Skútustaðir, Arnavatn, Þverá, Grænavatn and Grimsstaðir (Vésteinsson 2004: 8)) had individual rights to the grazing areas that were used by the community of Skútustaðahreppur. Furthermore, these farms were the old, established power base in the region. In addition, sheep from neighbouring communities also had long-term rights to graze in Skútustaðahreppur: sheep from Helgastaðahreppur, Kelduhverfi and Ljósavatnshreppur in Bárðadalur. And some farms in Skútustaðahreppur also had the right to graze in other communities' grazing areas, such as Helgastaðahreppur. In 1882, Skútustaðahreppur had 723 sheep, and contributed 23 gatherers to the roundup (Sigurjónsson 1987: 108). The mixture of rights along with sheep from Skútustaðahreppur produced a complex system. One of the effects was fluctuating sheep numbers year on year, though the general trend shows a consistent increase in numbers from the eighteenth century until the middle of the twentieth century (Table 16.2).

An additional feature was needed for the human organisation of the roundup, more than just earmarks. It needed more human control, or a formal organisation. Skútustaðahreppur's roundup committee, *Skútustaðahreppsnefnd*, assessed sheep numbers at the start of the summer, decided on the numbers of people needed for the roundup, and discussed, amongst other matters, the observations made by the gatherers in the grazing areas during the roundup and the requirements for the maintenance of the sorting folds.

The organisation of the roundup was an important function for the community, as it was the primary means by which to ensure successful grazing and gathering of sheep each year; a vital component for the local economy, for sustenance and commerce activities, such as those involving wool production (Robertsdóttir 2008). But control was not so much in the hands of

Table 16.2 Sheep numbers derived from documentary sources: 1703 and 1712, and the rest from the *fjallskílabók*, the committee's book, for Skútustaðahreppur

Year	Skút total	Other total	Total
1703	1662	/	1662★
1712	2122	/	2122
1868	3212	/	3212
1869	3401	/	3401
1902	5200	1575	6775
1906	5590	1412	7002
1907	5750	1080	6830
1908	5890	975	6865
1909	6495	953	7448
1910	7485	908	8393

Note: ★ without lamb numbers

the farming community; for the roundup was directed by the sheep, altering and re-shaping the human system of gathering through their numbers. Furthermore, sheep were central for reproducing the social ties year on year, that brought community-wide co-ordination by establishing what was, and still is, a major social event in the calendar for the community – the equivalent of the harvest festival (Björnsson 1995: 56–8; Hastrup 1998: 154–6).

The close relationship between sheep and farmers also manifested itself through one of the committee's major challenges: reducing the stress on vegetation from overgrazing. Empirical evidence derived from fieldwork and subsequent soil models suggest that while sustainable practices in managing vegetation stress were already occurring locally on farms in the community in the eighteenth century (Simpson et al. 2004), they may not have been as successful in the grazing areas. In a meeting that took place on 13 March 1878 about Suðurafrétt's decimation by erosion, it was stated that some parts were no longer suitable for grazing because of a loss of two to three metres of soil (Sigurjónsson 1987: 31–2). As a result, it was decided that there was a need to manage the grazing areas, rotating their use rather like a field rotation system that operated in British medieval arable farming to ensure the continued fertility of the land (Astill and Grant 1992: 62–85).

Once the numbers of sheep and people needed for the roundup were calculated, and decisions made on where sheep were likely to be grazing, it was time to map out pre-scribed paths into the grazing areas. Skútustaðahreppur had at least five paths (Table 16.3), though contemporary accounts suggest seven paths were used (Sigurjónsson 1950: 129). The different number of paths probably reflect seasonal changes in the paths and possibly changes in practice between historical accounts and Sigurjónsson's contemporary one. The five gathering paths were also further divided into the distinct grazing areas within Austurafrétt and Suðurafrétt.

The ethnographic accounts suggest that the roundup was a 'going around the mountain' (*kring í fjall*), a kind of pre-visualised arrangement of the roundup along these paths, when the movements were to be undertaken, as it were, and the co-ordination of timings and other movements with respect to the wider farming community. These brought together both a fixed and inflexible form of movement, yet required some negotiation in its application. Here was a series of flows that were highly orchestrated, in which people and animals were spatially and temporally choreographed, but in which elements of improvisation occurred. An important calculation was the expected end time of the gathering, so that the rest of the farming community arrived *en masse* at the sorting fold to divide the sheep. Traditionally the gathering started on the

Table 16.3 Gathering paths taken by Skútustaðahreppur with other communities which are listed

Path no.	Sorting fold	Other communities	Gatherers	Days
1 Framdalaleit	Réttartorfa &Viðiker	Bárðadalur	22	3
2 Hafursstaðaheiði	Grænavatnsrétt or Garðsmýrarrétt	Bárðadalur	23	3
3 Gæsafjallstykki	Gæsadal & Hraunsrétt	Helgastaðahreppur	23	2
4 Norðurfjöll	Réttargrund & Svinadalur	Kelduhverfi	47	2
5 Grafarlandagöngur	Dalsrétt or Hlíðarétt		22	4

Note: Gatherer estimates are derived from Skútustaðahreppur's sheep numbers in 1902 using the gatherer-to-sheep ratio from Helgastaðahreppur 1882. And number of days derived from an article in one of Iceland's national newspapers, *Morgunblaðið*, 5 September 1989. Note that Baldursheimarétt was not constructed in 1902

The seasonal roundup in Iceland

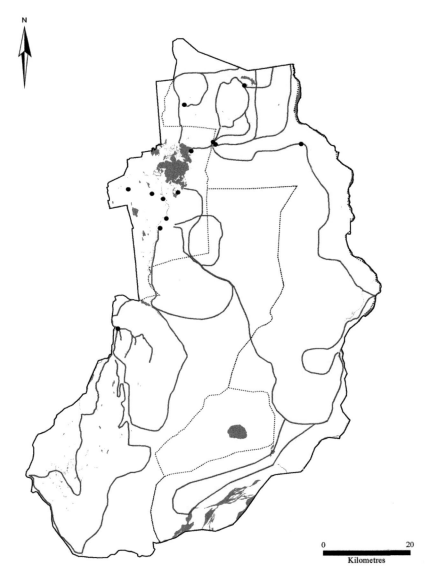

Figure 16.3 Hypothetical gathering paths reconstructed from Sigurjónsson (1950) and several ethnographic accounts.

twenty-first week of summer, approximately 5–11 September, although it was later assigned a specific day, first 11 September and then 14 September (Sigurjónsson 1950). However, this was not only a co-ordination point for one farming community but several. Skútustaðahreppur's grazing areas were also used by several of its neighbouring communities, which meant that the co-ordination was always a process that took into account multiple demands; a negotiation that took place *before* movement. Thus, the community's committee were attuned to the decisions, timings and movements happening not only in their own community and the others around them. In many ways, a single community's roundup was always linked to a much broader network, operating across the whole of Iceland where successive neighbouring communities would know the date and timing of the neighbouring roundup. Thus, each seasonal roundup was a part of a much larger enchained hyper-network.

There were 137 gatherers who were involved in the movements for Skútustaðahreppur's five gathering paths, and in Helgastaðahreppur there were 23 from Skútustaðahreppur. Although it is uncertain how many people took part from Kelduhverfi in Skútustaðahreppur's gathering, it may have been that while the gatherers from Kelduhverfi gathered the sheep to the north and those from Skútustaðahreppur gathered the sheep around Gæsadal and Hágöng, the two communities met at a sorting or holding fold in the grazing area, such as Svinadalur, for example. This was a sorting made on-the-move, so to speak, with the herd in tow, rather than a specific allocation of gatherers to Skútustaðahreppur or Kelduhverfi.

As I have already suggested, the timing of movements during the gathering operation was a complicated process that was highly orchestrated, and so in addition to the external consideration of other community practices, and the destination date for the wider community at the sorting fold, the gathering paths also needed different start times so that their convergence in the grazing areas were aligned and they arrived at the sorting fold more or less at the same time. And because the duration of each path differed, how the movements were organised was a kind of temporal rather than spatial choreography that required local knowledge of distances travelled, the amount of time this would take with the number of sheep being herded, and the accommodation of contingency in unforeseen events. The number of gatherers and the timing of these movements mattered. Thus, the gathering process can be thought of as a set of inter-connected events that gradually brought sheep and farmers back together again. Furthermore, the gathering process was repeated several times during a single season, perhaps three or more times according to the landscape conditions (Sigurjónsson 1950: 130).

With a large multispecies assemblage comprising farmers, sheep and an assortment of other animals, it became hard to control the competing flows of movement. There was a particular kind of agency in sheep movements, imbued by the wider landscape, that required the moving assemblage to be reactive to the conditions occurring in any one particular moment. These flows extended across the entirety of the roundup process. Furthermore, the assemblage was prone to fragmentation and divergence, with a number of smaller groups taking different landscapes to check for sheep – an example of assemblage drift. Thus, the movement assemblage was characterised both by its dispersal along multiple paths, and the forming of different assemblages and their drift, as it was about convergence along pre-scribed paths with a number of staging posts and shelters where the assemblage would rest over the duration of the gathering.

From another perspective, the roundup is a kind of species itself: an inter-dependent organism, comprising multiple moving legs, understood through the inter-relationships between its parts, year on year, and at the micro-scale movements, occurring at each stage in a particular gathering. The roundup is therefore a highly temporal entity, not necessary defined by just a linear practice, from one stage to the next, but a non-linear entity, not so much pre-determined but a long-term temporal project that has the potential to take many paths. The moving multispecies assemblage was constantly being defined and re-defined *before*, *after* and *during* the actual roundup practice occurred. Arguably this was made possible because the roundup was an annual event, repeated and based on a tried and tested practice, in which the certain types of conditions could be predicted, while others happened spontaneously. The combination of a particular structure and improvisation was shaped by and produced social relations between farmers and sheep. Thus, other kinds of operations besides spatial and temporal networks were set in motion.

Networks of social practice

As I have suggested, there were several emergent forms resulting from the entanglement between sheep and farmers, for example, the amount of labour that each farm contributed to the roundup, where they went, when it was to start, and what day the sorting was to take place (see Figure 16.3). So as to ensure the transfer of knowledge between its participants, a document listing the numbers of gatherers that each farm should provide and along which paths they were to gather sheep, was circulated. The gathering was not radically different from year to year. It would have used some of the same riders, horses and dogs, that moved along similar paths though each was negotiated each time in different ways. Physical changes might occur in the two grazing areas, which were often subject to physical change; new lava flows or the moving soil erosion front around Sandættur (literally translated as 'sand-eater') in the Miklimór zone in Suðursafrétt, could disrupt the roundup traditions. While landscape knowledge was used to ensure the stability of the roundup, the sheep themselves demanded a degree of flexibility. In this respect, there were social forces on two fronts. First, the way in which every year the list that was circulated between farms at the start of the roundup formalised the social bonds between farmers by its communal effects, demanded co-operation. And second, the sheep – as well as other nonhuman entities – were a disruptive force in the relationship, but nevertheless formed specific kinds of social ties with the farmers.

What we know about the relationship between animals and humans since the colonisation of Iceland in the ninth century AD comes mainly from the archaeological record. What this tells us is that the relationship between animals and humans was one of mutual inter-dependence. However, while a common narrative considers the important role that animals have had for humans, this has largely been concerned with examining subsistence strategies, and the economics and power dynamics amongst the early settlers through to the later medieval periods. The same can be said about more recent periods from the histories of the organisation of the seasonal roundup. Indeed, from the late nineteenth century to today, our knowledge of the seasonal roundup comes from oral and written histories, and from ethnographic accounts of the current practices (cf. Sigurjónsson 1950, 1987), rather than archaeology. But the examination of the roundup through an archaeological lens suggests a multi-layered practice. For example, the roundup consisted of multiple flows, the remnants of which are evident in the committee's

Table 16.4 Proportions of farms, herds, sheep and gatherers for Skútustaðahreppur's gathering in 1902

Community	Farms	Herd groups	Sheep	Gatherers
Skútustaðahreppur (A)	8	9	1580	36
Helgastaðarhreppur (A)	6	7	515	17
Skútustaðahreppur (S)	19	33	3181	85
Barðadalur (S)	8	8	1575	22

Note: A is Austurafrétt, S is Suðurafrétt

book, in the names given to parts of the landscape and the monuments that are left along the edges and inside the two grazing areas. These flows are of several different scales: from the birth to death of the sheep, and the entanglement of the farmer with them; to the repetitive movements that occurred season after season – the dispersion of sheep in the grazing areas in the spring, which were then gathered in the late summer, and divided into farms at the sorting fold. While many parts of the roundup remained stable in its outward appearance, each time it was performed subtle differences crept in, eroding earlier traditions and forming new ones. Old and new hands were involved in gathering the sheep; the gathering was a kind of rite of passage, and the status of the community was enhanced (Hastrup 1998: 154). Within this group were an assortment of different animals such as dogs and horses, and all operating under subtly different landscape and weather conditions. Most profound was the different configuration of the sheep herd – consisting of several winter wethers, young sheep, and sheep from multiple farms, both within and outside of the community.

The calculation of how many gatherers for the roundup was made on the basis of the sheep numbers for each farmer that were logged in the spring before sheep were moved to the grazing areas and represented a social contract of sorts; there was approximately a ratio of forty sheep to one gatherer. There seem to be at least two different results of the calculation: a sheep number range and a tax value assigned to each sheep, as in Skútustaðahreppur's 1902 roundup (Table 16.4).

The roundup was a process that would have shaped the people involved, along with the animals. Moving through the landscape transformed the farmers' social structure, for instance through the transfer of knowledge between young and old hands. Furthermore, the moving also transformed the social ties between sheep and farmers. Here was a process that turned free roaming sheep into herded animals. In addition, the roundup's importance in enhancing, as well as maintaining, the social bonds between people within the community gradually turned from one where there was an investment in maintaining lost ties with the landscape, to vested interests for a successful gathering, to one in which the emphasis was placed on sheep as commodities – viewing them as a product rather than as beings. The prevailing arrangement, perhaps up until the eighteenth century, was one in which sheep provided for a community's dietary needs, as well as reinvigorating the social bonds between people. After the eighteenth century, emphasis was placed on secondary product requirements which were linked with the growing industrialisation of sheep production for wool and meat exports.

What is interesting here for a multispecies archaeology is that the system of taxing farmers for the number of sheep they owned was probably a response to the demand for sheep, as a result of the commoditising forces associated with Iceland's industrial development. The previous system of managing the stock of sheep, vegetation stress, and the personnel used to gather sheep in the grazing areas during the roundup was circumvented by a more inter-connected system, of which a sheep tax was the effect. Here was a system of extra control – beyond boundaries and earmarks – but one applied to humans, which was nonetheless derived from sheep. Furthermore, this introduced a new kind of mobility – itinerant gatherers were hired where individual farms did not have enough people who could contribute to the roundup. Alternatively, the sheep tax may have been used to accommodate others who perhaps preferred to hire hands for gathering instead of trekking themselves; an example of 'impersonal' transhumance (Fox 2012: 46ff.). Furthermore, while taxing farmers was a commercial incentive, or disincentive depending on your point of view, it also changed the social dynamic of the gathering from one where all concerned had a personal investment to one where it became a more impersonal commercial venture. The effect of removing the personal and invested relationship from the roundup meant that the community's focus shifted away from the grazing areas to the sorting fold, where sheep were divided up to be sent to their respective farms. Thus, the roundup in the late nineteenth and early twentieth century was transformed not only by the institutional politics of communities, but also by what the sheep had come to represent in human eyes, but not in themselves. Thus, the roundup was related to several inter-related forces that emerged through a dynamic inter-play within the extended community.

There were a number of different forces that acted on and within the community during the roundup. For instance, there was a *social force* that shaped and organised the roundup, regulating the grazing areas and the impact of sheep on vegetation quality. There was a *relational force* constituted by an increased sheep presence and the numbers of gatherers that influenced the group dynamic during the roundup, for example how the movement assemblage moved along the paths into the grazing areas. And there was an *environmental force*, an imperative that determined the quality of the vegetation in the grazing over the short and longer term. These combined forces produced particular types of social responses, and as a result, varying communities. These different communities – communities within a community – also established new kinds of social relations between their members, that had a range of mobile requirements: farmers depended on where their sheep were grazing; where sheep were grazing depended on the predicted season-on-season vegetation growth; the success or otherwise of a farmer depended on sheep and the environments in which they grazed. Any changes in the configuration of the entities involved in the roundup – human or nonhuman – also affected all others. For instance, an increase in sheep numbers and their increasingly commoditisation affected the vegetation growth, but it also altered the social structure of the farming community. The way in which a whole series of movements were altered because of sheep also influenced the location of the sorting fold. And it is the sorting fold that the chapter turns to next – a place where the social, temporal and spatial networks converged.

Sorting fold and earmarks: convergences and transformations

Within the three networks discussed above, focus has been on two of the three stages of roundup: the organisation of the roundup, and the gathering itself. The last stage is located at

Table 16.5 Sorting and holding folds related to Skútustaðahreppur; distance from closest farm

Fold	Type	Nearest farm	Distance (km)	Location
Réttartorfa	Sorting	Svartakót	22.6	Grazing area
Réttargrund	Sorting	Reykjahlíð	18.9	Grazing area
Rétt í Gæsadal	Holding	Reykjahlíð	10.5	Grazing area
Péturskirkja	Holding	Reykjahlíð	25.2	Grazing area
Strengjarétt	Sorting	Baldursheimar	3.1	Border
Dalsrétt	Sorting	Reykjahlíð	5.2	Border
Sellandarétt	Sorting	Baldursheimar	5.5	Border
Gautlandarétt	Sorting	Gautlönd	0.9	Farm zone
Hlíðarétt	Sorting	Reykjahlíð	1.1	Farm zone
Réttartangi	?Sorting	Þuríðarnes	0.4	Farm zone
Baldurheimsrétt	Sorting	Litlaströnd	0.8	Farm zone

the sorting fold, where the different paths and activities connected with the roundup converge, and at the same time have the greatest transforming potential for all of the participants involved. As Matt Edgeworth reflects, animal enclosures are good sites to examine social practices and organisation and the entanglement of humans, animals and environments amongst the flows of human and animals (Edgeworth 2011: 119–20). In Skútustaðahreppur, there are approximately 77 archaeological sites interpreted as folds, which can be divided into three main groups: local folds (which are lesser types associated with single farms, where everyday activities take place), holding folds (whereby sheep are gathered and held overnight before being moved on during the roundup), and sorting folds (where sheep and farmers become fully entangled after several months of grazing and perhaps a few weeks of gathering) (Table 16.5). While there are many local folds, in theory there should be just two sorting folds – one for each grazing area, i.e. Austurafrétt and Suðurafrétt. However, in Skútustaðahreppur, nine have been identified, suggesting temporal-depth, perhaps as early as 1300. Furthermore, what I am concerned with in this section is how a multispecies archaeology lends itself to understanding the spatial location and design of the fold.

The sorting fold operated at several nested scales and movements. This included movements at the scale of the landscape, and at the scale of flesh of the gatherers and the sheep (Merleau-Ponty 1968). The movements of the multispecies assemblage also influenced the location of the sorting fold several times. Over a 300-year period, the fold location shifted from within the grazing area (earlier) to the margins of the settlement zone (later). The reason for the shift depends on the point of view offered, but using a conventional narrative, writ small, it can be suggested that the increase in sheep numbers depleted the vegetation more rapidly due to the environment's fragile conditions, which further acerbated soil erosion, resulting in a greater regulation of the grazing practices and a need to relocate the sorting fold. But it may be that the relocation was also as a result of changes in the organisational structure of the roundup, especially a response from outside of the community such as commercial forces.

Besides controlling where sheep were dispersed in the spring for grazing, another form of controlling regulation involved moving the sorting fold out of the grazing areas and into the farming zone. This was done to suit the requirements of grazing practices for the long-term sustainability of the community's grazing practices, as the closer the fold was to the settlement zone the easier it was to divide the flock to disperse to their respective farms. Furthermore, a new construction accommodated increases in flock sizes. And while this would mean that the distances over which sheep had to travel at any one time may have been a factor in relocating the sorting fold: closer to farms meant that movements were more node-like, perhaps stopping with the gathered flock at strategic places such as holding folds, on the way to the main sorting fold.

Several stopping places were required as the distance from the northern tip of the grazing area of Austurafrétt to the south of Suðurafrétt is c. 120 km, and between the eastern and western edges defined by the glacial rivers Skjálfandafljót and Jökulsá á Fjöllum, the distance is c. 60 km. Therefore, it may have been simply easier and more productive to move sheep from the grazing area along multiple gathering paths, at which points there was a convergence forming a mass at strategic places within the grazing areas, and then sorting them near or in the settlement zone. An affect of the change in location also influenced the community-level event of sorting the sheep that was a part of the seasonal re-affirming and creation of social ties between its members (cf. Aldred 2006). By creating an iterative seasonal, structured roundup, practice became habitual, a *habitus* developed, and certain kinds of social orders within the community were further instilled.

The seasonal roundup in Iceland

As I have suggested, the whole roundup was a transformative experience not only for farmers, or the landscape, but also for sheep. The spring dispersal of the sheep into the grazing areas separated the dependence of the sheep on the farmer. And during the roundup, the sheep were further transformed by moving from the grazing areas into the domestic space of the settlement zone. At the fold, sheep were moved through the sorting enclosures and individually separated from the larger herd into their respective farms. This was achieved through an incarceration, and harm in the form of an earmark. The sorting fold and earmark were intimately related, and as two central features of the roundup, they were mechanisms for the transformation of the relations between sheep and farmers.

However, at the sorting fold in particular, sheep and farmers were transformed in multiple ways. As sheep passed through the various holding areas of the sorting fold from their collective state as a flock and separated off individually by the human community into their respective farms, the bonds that tied them to their owners were reaffirmed. Therefore, the sorting fold embodied the transformative process in quite a direct way through its control of movement and the spaces involved, regulating animal bodies; movements and space different from the more fluid and improvised state in the grazing area, became a more fixed, solid and structured existence at the fold and thereafter (see Figure 16.4).

The design of the sorting fold is also a representation of the relationship that sheep and farmers had to one another. The sorting fold is a device that reunited sheep and farmer, acting as a kind of filtering system. The sheep flowed through the sorting fold but was caught up in movements that were controlled by the farmers through a space designed and structured to

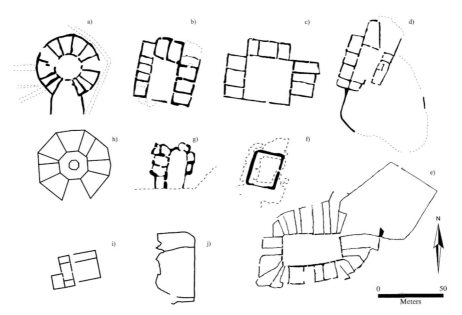

Figure 16.4 All sorting folds in the study area that have been surveyed (except rétt í Gæsdalur – see Figure 16.6). Key: (a) Gautlandaréttir; (b) Sellandarétt; (c) Strengjarétt; (d) Dalsrétt; (e) Hliðarétt; (f) Réttartorf; (g) Réttargrund; (h) Baldursheimarétt; (i) Stöng; (j) Péturskirkja.

maximise this behaviour. The fold is made up of several partitions – a central area and a number of smaller compartments offset from the central area. The sorting process was itself a kind of holding area, but one in which sheep passed through, and in which the ties between sheep and farmers became increasingly closer. However, the sorting fold was also a place at which farmers became tied to their sheep again, after several months of attending to other activities on the farm. Flows are a built-in feature of the design, enabling a funnel movement to take place that also constrained other mobilities, whether for transformation or the passage of sheep through the sorting fold. Thus, there was a close relation and agency from the movements of sheep to the design and requirements of farmers.

Even though it was the sheep that were rounded up, divided and returned to their respective farms, the farmer was also processed because of the way in which they moved from scene to scene: from the organised preparation, along the gathering path, to the collection of sheep in the central holding area and literally the dragging of individual sheep to the individual farm compartments in the fold, and then back to the farm again, reforging old ties with the sheep. In this sense, sheep and farmers were transformed *together* along similar trajectories: from taking part in movements together towards the grazing areas, and then separated at the level of the flesh, both permitted freer movements when apart, as it were, and then the bonds of association were re-forged during the roundup, though on opposite sides of this relationship. During the gathering and its culmination at the sorting fold, these two trajectories in movement rejoined where the symmetry between them came about through movement. In many ways, these movements were like a squeeze-box: a spatial expansion and contraction series that was directly related to the type of relationality between sheep and farmers. The sorting fold acted as a lynch-pin in the gathering operation, directing a series of gravitational movements, but it was also a hub for a series of transformative movements that altered the relations between the sheep and farmers. This effect was also mirrored in the wider community. The event was an important seasonal happening, bonds were not only retied but could also be remade with other members of the community through small trade, social transactions and stimuli for the winter ahead. So at one level, there was a circulation of movements through the sorting fold, but also around it.

After the reforging of their ties to farmers, there were two possible journeys for sheep. The first was a repetition of the cycle again the following summer, and the second, slaughter. Before the eighteenth century, several considerations were taken into account when deciding which sheep were to repeat the cycle and which were to be slaughtered. A main concern was to maintain a sustainable sheep number balance with respect to the available winter fodder as well as the expected quality of the winter grazing. In the early twentieth century, it has been suggested that to sustain the flock, sixteen lambs per one hundred sheep would need to be kept. This suggests that sheep were usually six to seven years old when they were slaughtered. Older ewes needed little maintenance alongside wethers (Aðalsteinsson 1991: 286). Thus, the sheep that were slaughtered may have been a mixture of lambs, young ewes and older sheep, which is broadly consistent with detailed archaeological research on sheep population (e.g. McGovern 2009: 197–215). At least it is suggested that the farming strategy in the medieval period was flexible to several different scenarios, whether for milking, wool production or meat.

A species that incarcerates another forges its own chains

The three networks and their convergence illustrate the spatial, temporal and social character and form of entanglements that took place between sheep and farmers (Figure 16.5). These

The seasonal roundup in Iceland

1. landscape ⟶ grazing areas ⟶ grazing zones ⟶ gathering paths ⟶ sorting fold ⟶ farm ⟶ earmark

2. [April] cuckoo-month (*gaukmánuður*) ⟶ egg-time (*eggtíð*) ⟶ sowing (*sáðtíð*) ⟶ lambing (*stekktíð*) ⟶ sun-month (*sólmanauður*) ⟶ sheiling or upland grazing (*sélmánuður*) ⟶ hay-time (*beyannir*) ⟶ corn-cutting (*kornskurðarmánuður*) ⟶ harvest (*hbaustmánuður*) ⟶ slaughtering (*gormánuður*) [October]

3. land-use and ownership ⟶ designation of grazing areas ⟶ monitoring by committee ⟶ gatherers & organisation (committee & 'king of mountain') ⟶ social gathering by community at the sorting fold

Figure 16.5 Three networks (1) Spatial, (2) Temporal, (3) Social.

Violence	Freedom	Eating	Imprisoned	Separated	Killed
1. Marking ⟶	2. Releasing ⟶	3. Grazing ⟶	4. Gathering ⟶	5. Sorting ⟶	6. Slaughtering
Property	Freedom	Tasks	Collected	Reforged	Subsistence

Figure 16.6 Operational chain of Icelandic sheep farming practice (specific to the discussion in this chapter) with reference to the experiential difference between sheep (above) and farmers (below).

indicate at least three features. First, the spatial network operated from the macro level of the landscape, to the micro scale of the earmark. The movements attached to each part of the operational flow or chain (Leroi-Gourhan 1993) are related to these spatial arenas and defined by the circulation around them. In other words, a series of nested mobilities connected each spatial node. Second, the temporal network is related to a sequence of events reflecting a time-line that follows a particular internal logic along prescribed paths, but which could be disrupted, revealing other sets of strategic operations. The relations associated with these operations are characterised by the movements inherent in events that are directly tied to the rhythmic, seasonal cycle of spatial expansion (summer) and contraction (winter). Furthermore, the flows in this network structured the marking of time by the associated naming of the months reflecting the type of task happening during the yearly cycle. This is reminiscent of Bourdieu's structured practices that were reciprocated through the social meanings given to a society that are represented by *habitus*: the abstract calendar, the farming cycle and the mythical year (Bourdieu 1977: 99 (Figure 2), 134 (Figure 3)). Third, a network of social practices is produced through the mobilities that bonded the different parts of the extended community together, from the organisation of the roundup, through to the gathering operation and then the bringing of the wider community to the sorting fold. This was to some extent based on a degree of anticipation of an already established series of traditional seasonal movements, and in their application during the gathering and sorting.

Different types of movements were then associated with each point along these three networks: (1) the social landscape and its histories which established the traditions behind the practice and its mechanism that acted as a kind of genealogy; (2) the designation of grazing areas after monitoring which determined where movements were taking place; (3) the monitoring by a committee which led to the level of grazing and thus the gathering movements; (4) the definition of the number of gatherers and the appointment of a locally situated 'king of the mountain', and (5) the community gathering at the sorting fold to separate sheep into their respective farms based on a system of earmarking. A kind of 'taskscape' coalesces around the three networks, forming a single, mutual system, held between sheep and farmers, on either side of which is placed a kind of experiential difference and repetition for sheep and farmers (Figure 16.6).

While the releasing of sheep made possible other movements, this was predicated on the violence and harm done by the earmark. On the one hand, the earmark conferred the status of property and ownership on the sheep as a *living* commodity, and on the other, bound a sheep to its owner in a self-sustaining relationship. What I mean by this is that the relations between farmers and sheep were entirely reciprocal, bringing to mind Netz's quote: 'a species that incarcerates another forges its own chains' (Netz 2004: 230). Freedom was gained because now both the sheep and the farmer could become independent of one another, but in some ways they were constantly enchained which resulted in a loss on both sides of the relationship. The relationship between the sheep and the farmer were made whole again through a reunion during the gathering and then again at the sorting fold. The relationship between the farmer and sheep is like a pendulum, with all the reciprocal ties that this entailed, and where the earmark was a concrete reality which helped to shape the terms of the relation between farmers and sheep. While the sorting fold marked the transition back to the incorporated relationality between sheep and farmers after the gathering that defined that relation in terms of its pendulum nature, the earmark was a permanent feature of this relation. The earmark was immutable and marked the deeper division between the virtual or potential relation (during the summer grazing period) and the actualised relation (after the fall, during the winter and spring period). In a real sense, the sorting fold and the earmark were both transitional 'sites' that can only be really understood together, as their different mobilities converged and intertwined together.

Each irreducible part of the roundup gives 'body' to the relationship between sheep and farmers (see Figure 16.6). Thus the discussion about the roundup can take place on an equal hooving/footing where there is no straightforward power relation or hegemony, such as humans dominating animals. Instead, power is distributed and emerges through the materialising actions and the sets of relations, beyond the more usual narratives of subjugation; humans are as dependent on animals, as animals are on humans. The virtual path that connects sheep and farmers was also one predicated on two opposing mobile directionalities: separation and coming together. By casting a wider net, other types of relations and mobilities are revealed where the conspicuous and hidden entanglements between humans and animals involved the exchange and swapping of properties (Latour 1996). For example, the sheep defined the work that farmers do during the grazing period, and the push and pull of relations at different stages during the roundup. In other words, while sheep and farmers were and will always be two distinctively defined bodies – as different species – they each articulated the other, forming a single, coherent body where they combined and acted as one; pendulum-like, swinging one way with the relation (in constituting *a* single body) and then the other way without one another but still defined by the other (not visible, or expressed as two separate but entangled bodies). Consequently, the movement of sheep and farmers and their release from one another is a material dimension of a process of socialisation. Seen in this way, it is not the separate flows of different bodies that constituted the roundup, but the way that the flows were entangled, dispersed and converged through multiple mobilities that shaped and defined the nature of the bound/unbound set of relations between farmer and sheep.

The intimate ties between sheep and farmers were most visible at the sorting fold. The sorting fold was also the culmination of a much longer process of relationality characterised by the roundup's operational chain, from the earmarking to the slaughtering. But the circulating reference, to coin a Latourian phrase (Latour 1999: 24ff.), was also most evident during the sorting process, which was where the earmarking came into its own as a tangible indicator of the relationship between sheep and farmers; in a sense, the earmark was a latent feature which was forgotten when the sheep were released into the grazing areas, but came into being *at* the sorting fold. So while the sorting fold was a site for the separation and division of sheep, it was also a site that reaffirmed older set of relations between farmers and sheep, reconfirming their mutual relationship to one another. Many sheep of course would have passed several times through the gates of the sorting fold, and were named accordingly after the number of winters that they had lived (one, two, three winters – Björnsson 1995: 6). Yet, in one way or another, the sorting fold was also a closing of particular lifecycles or paths, if not in death, then a loss in mobility, a *re-incarceration*, as it were.

Conclusions

Giving greater account of the relations between farmers and sheep in this chapter has been based on considering the roundup from a multispecies perspective, with a central feature in the chapter associated with an assemblage of materials and moving bodies, or people, animals and landscape that comprised an unity, an *extended community*. As such, the chapter has revealed the constitutional role of movement and the constitutive parts of the roundup as an inter-dependent ecology of practices (Stengers 2010). An ecology in the sense that was responsive to and reacted with any changes occurring within and outside of the inter-connected system of the roundup. The concept of an extended community addresses a mutual concern for animals and humans, as well as other nonhuman things, such as landscape, rather than presenting as a series of discrete independent entities. The constitutional parts of this community although inter-dependent, are, also, not neutral. Each part has an active role in shaping the workings of the community. This is partly because in this multispecies approach – that is, 'archaeological' in both the literal and metaphorical sense of 'excavating' the surface of the practice – I have put movement at centre stage. That is to say, sheep and farmers at different times in the roundup have different roles, acting as differential agents with the power to influence the other. But it is through movement, in particular, that much of this power emerges, linking the constitutional parts of the community that are usually placed into 'the obscure background of social activity' (cf. de Certeau 1984: xi). What has been revealed are the actions of the community without deference to *a priori* construction of what constitutes animal or human, allowing traditional vertical social schemes that define human-animal relations in a vertical ontology. Instead, I have examined the spatial, temporal, social and mobile bonds between humans and animals through a series of horizontal relations. What this has done is to keep the social grounded in an ontology that is on a par with the materiality of the evidence. Arguably, a real, concrete shape to an emergent social that demonstrates the inter-connectedness and reciprocation of multiple species through a single practice has been offered, and upon this ground the paths for further archaeological work in the future have been created.

Note

1 Much has been left out from the description of the seasonal roundup and its historical context. A more detailed description may be found in several papers (Aðalsteinsson 1991; Aldred 2006, 2012, 2013).

References

Aðalsteinsson, S. 1981. Origin and conservation of farm animal populations in Iceland. *Zeitschrift für Tierzüchtung und Züchtungsbiologie* 98, 258–64.

Aðalsteinsson, S. 1991. Importance of sheep in early Icelandic agriculture. *Acta Archaeologica* 61, 285–91.

Aldred, O., Einarsson, Á., Hreiðarsdóttir, E. Ó. and Lárusdóttir, B. 2007. *Forn garÐlög í SuÐur-Þingeyjarsýslu. A System of Earthworks in North-east Iceland*. Reykjavík: Fornleifastofnun Íslands.

Aldred, O. 2006. Réttir in the landscape: a study on the context of focal points, in Arneborg, J. and Gronnow, B. (eds) *Dynamics of Northern Societies: Proceedings of the SILA/NABO Conference on Arctic and North Atlantic Archaeology*. Copenhagen, Denmark: Aarhus Universitetsforlag. Pp. 353–63.

Aldred, O. 2012. Mobile communities: the gathering and sorting of sheep in Skútustaðarhreppur, North-east Iceland. *International Journal of Historical Archaeology* 16.3, 488–508.

Aldred, O. 2013. Farmers, sorting folds, earmarks and sheep in Iceland, in Beaudry, M. C. and Parno, T. G. (eds) *Archaeologies of Mobility and Movement*. London: Springer. Pp. 47–63.

Aldred, O. 2014. Past movements, tomorrow's anchors: on the relational entanglements between archaeological mobilities, in Leary, J. (ed.) *Past Mobilities: Archaeological approaches to movement and mobility*. London: Ashgate. Pp. 21–47.

Astill, G. G. and Grant, A. (eds) 1992. *The Countryside of Medieval England*. Oxford: Blackwell.

Barth, F. 1961. *The Nomads of South Persia*. Oslo: University of Oslo Press.

Bennett, J. 2010. *Vibrant Matter: A political ecology of things*. Durham, NC: Duke University Press.

Björnsson, Á. 1995. *High Days and Holidays in Iceland*. Reykjavík: Mál og menning.

Bourdieu, P. 1977. *Outline of a Theory of Practice*. Cambridge: Cambridge University Press.

Cabanel-Leduc, R. 1975. L'Elevage et la marquage du mouton en l'île d'Ousessant (Finistére), in Pujol, R. and Laurans, R. (eds) *L'Homme et l'animal*. Paris: Inst. Int. d'Ethnosciences. Pp. 543–59.

de Certeau, M. 1984. *The Practice of Everyday Life*. Berkeley: University of California.

DeLanda, M. 2006. *A New Philosophy of Society: Assemblage theory and social complexity*. London: Continuum.

Deleuze, G. and Guattari, F. 1983. *On the Line*. Cambridge, MA: MIT Press.

Deleuze, G. and Guattari, F. 2004. *A Thousand Plateaus*. London: Continuum.

Dennis, A., Foote, P. and Perkins, R. 2000. *The Laws of Early Iceland: Gragas*. Translated by Dennis, A., Foote, P. and Perkins, R. (eds.). Winnipeg: University of Manitoba Press.

Descola, P. and Pálsson, G. (eds) 1996. *Nature and Society: Anthropological perspectives*. London: Routledge.

Edgeworth, M. 2011. *Fluid Pasts: Archaeology of flow*. London, Bloomsbury Academic.

Edgeworth, M. 2014. Enmeshments of shifting landscapes and embodied movements of people and animals, in Leary, J. (ed.) *Past Mobilities: Archaeological approaches to movement and mobility*. London: Ashgate. Pp. 49–61.

Edgeworth, M., Benjamin, J., Clarke, B., Crossland, Z., Domanska, E., Gorman, A., Graves-Brown, P., Harris, E., Hudson, M., Kelly, J., Paz, V., Salerno, M., Witmore, C., and Zarankin, A. 2014. Forum on 'Archaeology of the Anthropocene'. *Journal of Contemporary Archaeology* 1.1, 73–132.

Edgeworth, M., Richter, D., Waters, C., Haff, P., Neal, C., and Price, S. 2015. Diachronous beginnings of the Anthropocene: the lower bounding surface of anthropogenic deposits. *Anthropocene Review* 2, 33–58.

Einarsson Á. and Aldred O. 2011. The archaeological landscape of Northeast Iceland: a ghost of a Viking Age society, in Cowley, D. (ed.) *Remote Sensing for Archaeological Heritage Management in the 21st Century*. Brussels: Archaeolingua. Pp. 243–58.

Einarsson, Á., Hansson, O., and Vesteinsson, O. 2002. An extensive system of medieval earthworks in northeast Iceland. *Archaeologia Islandica* 2, 61–73.

Fenton, A. 1978. *The Island Blackhouse*. Edinburgh: HMSO.

Fox, H. 2012. *Dartmoor's Alluring Upland: Transhumance and pastoral management in the Middle Ages*. Exeter: University of Exeter Press.

Gosset, A. 1911. *Shepherds of Britain: Scenes from shepherd life past and present, from the best authorities*. London: Constable and Company.

Haraway, D. J. 1991. *Simians, Cyborgs and Women: The reinvention of nature*. London: Free Association.

Haraway, D. J. 2003. *The Companion Species Manifesto: Dogs, people, and significant otherness*. Chicago, IL: Prickly Paradigm Press.

Haraway, D. J. 2008. *When Species Meet*. Minneapolis: University of Minnesota Press.

Harman, G. 2007. The importance of Bruno Latour for philosophy. *Cultural Studies Review* 11.1, 31–49.

Harman, G. 2009. *Prince of Networks: Bruno Latour and metaphysics*. Prahran: re.press.

Harris, O. 2012. Relational communities in Prehistoric Britain, in Watts C. (ed.) *Relational Archaeologies*. London: Routledge. Pp. 173–89.

Harris, O. 2014. (Re)assembling communities. *Journal of Archaeological Method and Theory* 21, 76–97.

Hastrup, K. 1998. *A Place Apart: An anthropological study of the Icelandic world*. Oxford: Clarendon Press.

Hodder, I. 2012. *Entangled*. London: Wiley-Blackwell.

Ingold, T. 1974. On reindeer and men. *Man (N.S.)* 9, 523–38.

Ingold, T. 1976. *The Skolt Lapps Today*. Cambridge: Cambridge University Press.

Ingold, T. 1980. *Hunters, Pastoralists and Ranchers: Reindeer economies and their transformation*. Cambridge: Cambridge University Press.

Ingold, T. 1986. *Evolution and Social Life*. Cambridge: Cambridge University Press.

Ingold, T. 1994. From trust to domination: an alternative history of human-animal relations, in Manning, A. (ed.) *Animals and Human Society: Changing perspectives*. London: Routledge. Pp. 1–22.

Ingold, T. 2000. *The Perception of the Environment: Essays in livelihood, dwelling and skill*. London: Routledge.

Ingold, T. 2007. *Lines: A brief history*. London: Routledge.

Latour, B. 1993. *We Have Never Been Modern*. Cambridge, MA: Harvard University Press.

Latour, B. 1996. Pragmatogonies. A mythical account of how humans and nonhumans swap properties. *American Behavioural Scientist* 37.6, 791–808.

Latour, B. 1999. *Pandora's Hope: Essays on the reality of science studies*. Cambridge, MA: Harvard University Press.

Latour, B. 2004. *Politics of Nature: How to bring the sciences into democracy*. Cambridge, MA: Harvard University Press.

Latour, B. 2005. *Reassembling the Social: An introduction to Actor-Network-Theory*. Oxford: Oxford University Press.

Leroi-Gourhan, A. 1993. *Gesture and Speech*. Translated by A. B. Berger. Cambridge, MA: MIT Press.

Linnaeus, C. 1735. *Systema naturae, sive Regna tria naturae. Systematice proposita per Classes, Ordines, Genera, & Species*. Leiden: Lugduni Batavorum, Apud Theodorum Haak.

Lucas, G. 2012. *Understanding the Archaeological Record*. Cambridge: Cambridge University Press.

McGovern, T. 2009. The archaeofauna, in Lucas, G. (ed.) *Hofstaðir. Excavations of a Viking Age Feasting Hall in North-Eastern Iceland*. Reykjavík: Institute of Archaeology. Monograph No. 1. Pp. 168–252.

McGovern, T. H., Vésteinsson, O., Friðriksson, A., Church, M. J., Lawson, I. T., Simpson, I. Á., Einarsson, A., Dugmore, A. J., Cook, G. T., Perdikaris, S., Edwards, K. J., Thomson, A. M., Adderley, W. P., Newton, A. J., Lucas, G., Edvardsson, R., Aldred, O., and Dunbar, E. 2007. Landscapes of settlement in northern Iceland: historical ecology of human impact and climate fluctuation on the millennial scale. *American Anthropologist* 109, 27–51.

Merleau-Ponty, M. 1962. *Phenomenology of Perception*. London: Routledge.

Morton, T. 2013. *Hyperobjects: Philosophy and ecology after the end of the world*. Minneapolis: University of Minnesota Press.

Netz, R. 2004. *Barbed Wire: An ecology of modernity*. Middleton, CT: Wesleyan University Press.

Róbertsdóttir, H. 2008. *Wool and Society: Manufacturing policy, economic thoughts and local production in 18th-century Iceland*. (Centrum för Danmarksstudier 21), Göteborg: Makadam.

Ruddiman, W. 2013. The Anthropocene. *Annual Review of Earth and Planetary Science* 41, 45–68.

Ryder, M. L. 1983. *Sheep and Man*. London: Duckworth.

Sanderson, S. 1971. Sheep marks in Lakeland. *Folk Life* 9: 135–9.

Sigurjónsson, B. 1987. *Göngur og réttir*. Reykjavík: Skjaldborg Akureyri.

Sigurjónsson, B. 1950. *Göngur og réttir. Þingeyjar- og Múlaþing III*. Akureyri: Bókaútgáfan Norðri.

Simpson, I., Guðmundsson, G., Thomson, A. M., and Cluett, J. 2004. Assessing the role of winter grazing in historic land degradation, Mývatnssveit, Northeast Iceland. *Geoarchaeology* 19.5, 471–502.

Skúlason, P. 2005. *Meditations at the Edge of Askja*. Reykjavík: University of Iceland Press.

Stengers, I. 2010. *Cosmopolitics I*. Minneapolis: University of Minnesota Press.

Svabo, J 1782 [1959]. *Indberetninger fra en Reise i Færøe 1781 og 1782*. Copenhagen: Kildeskrifter og studier.

Tinbergen, N. 1963. On aims and methods of ethology. *Zeitschrift fur Tierpsychologie* 20.4, 410–33.

Vésteinsson, O. 2004. *Krókdalur fornleifaskráning*. Reykjavík: Fornleifastofnun Íslands FS258-04191.

Witmore, C. 2015. Bovine urbanism: the ecological corpulence of *Bos urbanus*, in Clarke, B. (ed.) *Earth, Life, and System. Evolution and ecology on a Gaian planet*. New York: Fordham University Press. Pp. 225–49.

Zedeño, M. N. 2008. Bundled worlds: the roles and interactions of complex objects from the North American plains. *Journal of Archaeological Method and Theory* 15, 362–78.

17

THE RHYTHM OF LIFE

Exploring the role of daily and seasonal rhythms in the development of human-nonhuman relationships in the British Early Mesolithic

Nick J. Overton

Introduction

The removal of the traditional Cartesian divisions between humans and animals, which served to characterise animals as homogenous, static, non-sentient autonoma, opposed to a unique and separate humanity, has opened up the space for new explorations of human-nonhuman relationships (e.g. Cartmill 2008: 837; Wolfe 2003: xv; Agamben 2004; Calarco 2008). No longer inhabiting separate human and animal realms, relationships can instead be explored as emerging through daily interactions and engagements; humans and nonhumans are both just 'ordinary knotted beings' who are all mundanely here on earth, engaging in a 'shaping dance of encounters' (Haraway 2008: 3–5). Archaeology has engaged within this 'animal turn', with numerous studies focusing on tracing the engagements and relationships between humans and nonhumans in the past (e.g. Argent 2010, 2013; Armstrong Oma 2010, 2013; Jones 2009; Overton and Hamilakis 2013; Brittain and Overton 2013). By acknowledging the significance of nonhuman actions in relationship-forming human-nonhuman engagements, it is necessary to progress beyond a monolithic 'human-animal' relationship, to explore the vast array of potential relationships between specific nonhumans and humans. The question now presented is how might archaeology explore specific encounters, in a way that may elucidate how living relationships in daily life are manifest within archaeologically recovered materials? This chapter presents the concept of rhythm as a tool that can, in conjunction with faunal materials, be used to explore such engagements and relationships.

Human and nonhuman rhythms

Living within a world consisting of many other living beings in mutually constituting relationships, exploring humans' relationship with nonhumans requires the consideration of a shared past, in which humans and nonhumans interacted with one another in diverse and seemingly contradictory ways (Jones 2009: 75). In such accounts, where human-nonhuman relationships emerge through encounter and engagement within this shared past, the temporal rhythm of these meetings is key in forming particular relationships and understandings. Considering rhythm as a common ground through which species cohabit, the dynamic push and pull of individuals' particular rhythms are significant in regulating and structuring intra-active engagements, through which different species emerge and live together in the shared world (Brittain and Overton 2013: 138). In order to progress beyond abstract 'human-animal' accounts and focus instead on specific human-nonhuman relationships, it is imperative to start with the actual, physical encounters and understand the particular rhythms, those repeated movements and actions that crafted relationships between living humans and nonhumans (Armstrong Oma 2013: 164; cf. Brittain and Overton 2013; Overton and Hamilakis 2013; also see Aldred, this volume). Considering human-nonhuman relationships in Bronze Age Scandinavia, Armstrong Oma has considered how, through processes including milking, herding and shearing, humans were required to develop particular daily, task-specific, and seasonal rhythms. In turn, by tracing these rhythmic entanglements in detail, nonhumans are revealed as an embedded and structuring principle within the space of co-habitation (2010: 186; also see Armstrong Oma, this volume). In the Iron Age burials of the Pazyryk culture in the Altai Mountains, the tattoos of horses on a number of human bodies are interpreted by Argent as representations of actual, biographical horses, a horse of that person's lifetime (Argent 2013: 189). The inscription of these horses onto the flesh is a physical manifestation of the significant relationships between specific humans and horses, borne out of, at least in part, the synchrony between horse and human through riding, the anticipation and prediction of the other's actions and the sharing of rhythms (ibid.: 180). In the Late Bronze Age of Britain, red deer antler cheekpieces, which held the organic mouthpiece or bit, have also been considered as material traces of the synchronisation of rhythms in the participative encounter between humans and horses (Brittain and Overton 2013: 139). Within the Early Aceramic Neolithic of Cyprus, the shared rhythms of humans and caprids, developed and performed through their continual mutual engagement as herd and herder, were reflected in the collective deposition of caprid and human remains: at Mylouthkia, the deposition of 23 whole, unbutchered caprids and the remains of a minimum of five humans in Well 133 has been interpreted by Jones (2009) as a material acknowledgement of human and caprid inseparable 'everydayness'; no doubt connected and intertwined in living worlds, they were equally entangled in death (85, 93).

Such studies have notably focused on the pastoral relationships; however, exploration of rhythm in human-nonhuman relationships is not restricted to post-domestication periods. Hunting requires humans to attune and engage with the specific and different rhythms of the species they track and hunt (Hamilakis 2003: 240). This can be thought of not as a simple shift from one abstract rhythm to another, but instead as a synchronisation of distinct human and nonhuman rhythms (Brittain and Overton 2013: 143). At the Late Mesolithic site of Aggersund in Denmark, the hunting of whooper swans required humans to engage in their daily and seasonal temporal habits; this bound a suite of places, tasks and material together, tied to the distinctive rhythm of the swans. This, in turn, may have developed human understanding of these swans as sentient and intentional, capable of undertaking their own movements in patterns and at times particular to themselves (Brittain and Overton 2013: 144; Overton and Hamilakis 2013: 124). However, not all human-nonhuman interactions can be considered in terms of the synchronisation of rhythms; engagements in which humans experience discord between their own rhythms and those of nonhumans are equally important. At the site of Shillourokambos, also dating to the Early Aceramic Neolithic of Cyprus, the individual burial of cats, in stark contrast to the commingled deposition of caprids and humans at Mylouthkia, is suggested to signify their distinctiveness in daily engagements. As a nocturnal species, it is extremely unlikely that human and cat rhythms were synchronised. Instead, they were likely to encounter each other sporadically, at liminal moments, as the cat ventured out to hunt and the human came in from a day of work. Such encounters would lead to an understanding that each were bound into their own distinct temporal rhythms, developing a recognition of the 'otherness' of cats, which was materially acknowledged in the individual burial of cats (and humans) at the site (Jones 2009: 90).

'Otherness' in this context should not be understood as highlighting an essential difference, as an exclusive 'other-to-humans'; instead, it cites an intrinsic similarity, as an inclusive 'an-other'. Therefore, an 'Other' is not a category opposed to humans, it includes humans; in this sense, any human or nonhuman that is understood as a capable and intentional agent is an 'Other', akin to Haraway's 'significant other' (2008). However, 'otherness' is not a homogenising category; whilst individuals share a commonality as agents, their character as specific 'others' is a product of the particular ways they behave in encounters. Therefore, many different species and individuals may be understood as 'Others', but this does not remove the potential for humans to understand differences between them. It is the development of specific understandings of particular nonhumans through the intersection of distinct rhythms in the human-nonhuman encounter that this chapter seeks to explore further, specifically considering meetings in the Early Mesolithic of Southern Britain.

Tracing Mesolithic rhythms

Archaeology holds the extremely lucrative position of recovering, analysing and interpreting the material remains of the very nonhuman individuals humans engaged with in the past, which offer the unparalleled opportunity to trace emerging relationships. Recently, the development of Social Zooarchaeology has offered the opportunity to examine human-animal relationships through the analysis of animal remains in more depth, with the clear aim to move away from considering animals and their remains exclusively as food (e.g. Marciniak 1999; deFrance 2009; Russell 2012). Instead, studies have explored how animals and their remains were wrapped up in systems of wealth, status, power, ritual and belief systems, and lifeways of humans in the past (e.g. deFrance 2009; Russell 2012), including new analytical methods to elucidate such social patterns from zooarchaeological data (e.g. Orton 2012). However, whilst these 'social zooarchaeologies' sidestep the anthropocentrism of economic reductionism, they do not fully acknowledge the agentic potential of nonhumans; too often animals remain static resources, as symbols, units of wealth, or measures of status. In this 'Social Zooarchaeology', the 'social' refers to human-human social relations; animal remains are considered as the materials through which human relationships are negotiated (cf. Overton and Hamilakis 2013; Overton 2014b). More recently, the acknowledgement of the significance of nonhuman actions in the formation of relationships has led Social Zooarchaeology to establish frameworks that explore how nonhuman actions affected human interactions with them, and understandings of them, shifting the 'social' lens to consider human-nonhuman, as opposed to human-human, relations (cf. Overton and Hamilakis 2013). These frameworks use species, age, sex and seasonal data generated through established zooarchaeological analyses and combine it with ethological studies to elucidate how these species and individuals behaved. In using ethological studies, multiple studies of geographically separate populations is necessary, where possible, to avoid the inherent problems of imposing modern parallels onto past populations, akin to direct ethnographic parallels in archaeological interpretations. By characterising the habits, actions and movements of nonhumans, it is possible to explore the intersection of humans and nonhuman rhythms, and consider how different engagements and experiences led to humans developing specific or different understandings of particular species.

As hunter-fisher-gatherers, the lives of humans in Mesolithic Britain would include regular and frequent encounters and engagements with a number of nonhuman species living within their shared environment. In order to explore the nature of the specific human-nonhuman interactions, the faunal material from two sites in Southern Britain will be presented here. In turn, the characterisation of specific human-nonhuman interactions will be used to explore the development of subsequent relationships and human understandings.

Site background and assemblage data

The sites of Thatcham and Faraday Road are located in the Kennet Valley in Southern Britain (see Figure 17.1). The faunal material from Thatcham, divided into five 'sites' relating to the five excavated areas, indicate intensive and repeated occupation along a gravel bluff on the edge of the floodplain, returning dates[1] ranging from 9650–8790 cal BC to 8630–8260 cal BC (Wymer 1962; Overton 2014a; Gowlett et al. 1987; Roberts et al. 1998; cf. Chisham 2004). This discussion will focus on the assemblages from sites I–III, as sites IV and V returned very low frequencies of osseous remains. The Faraday Road assemblage evidenced material from multiple, temporally discrete hunting events, collated and deposited in a natural hollow, returning a date of 9120–8500 cal BC (Overton 2014a; Ellis et al. 2003). At both sites, the faunal data (Table 17.1) indicates human interaction and encounter with a wide range of different species. This discussion will focus on tracing the engagements between humans and three different species: wild boar, beaver and wildcat.

Figure 17.1 Map of Great Britain and Ireland, showing the location of the sites of Thatcham and Faraday Road in the Lower Kennet Valley.

Table 17.1 Relative frequency of species at Thatcham sites I–III and Faraday Road, presented as number of identified specimens (NISP) and the minimum number of individuals (MNI)

	Thatcham Site I		Thatcham Site II		Thatcham Site III		Faraday Road	
	NISP	MNI	NISP	MNI	NISP	MNI	NISP	MNI
Aurochs	3	1	2	1	7	2	16	1
Elk	–	–	1	1	2	1	–	–
Red Deer	58	7	51	4	86	3	56	1
Roe Deer	9	2	6	1	38	6	25	2
Wild Boar	6	1	50	3	109	6	637	12
Beaver	–	–	12	2	65	4	36	3
Wildcat	–	–	–	–	1	1	3	1
Fox	2	1	–	–	3	1	–	–
Pine Marten	3	1	–	–	–	–	–	–
Badger	–	–	1	1	7	2	–	–
Wolf	–	–	–	–	3	1	–	–
Total	81	13	123	13	321	27	774	20

Daily rhythms

In daily life, humans came into contact with nonhumans in the local environment; however, it is unlikely humans only met nonhumans when they chose to, in a series of humanly dictated and pre-planned hunting events. In reality, the timing and location of encounters would be largely dependent on each species' daily actions, their habitat selections, activity cycles and movements – in short, their individual rhythms. After all, humans would not be able to meet species if they were not there to meet. Therefore, it is necessary to outline the daily rhythms and activities of wild boar, beaver and wildcat, to characterise how, where and when humans may have encountered and interacted with individuals of these species.

Of the Mesolithic fauna, wild boar were potentially the most conspicuous ungulate; females, young and sub-adults live together in large matrilineal groups, with only older males being truly solitary (Truve and Lemel 2003: 52). Furthermore, with the highest reproduction rates for ungulates, local populations can double within a year (Massei and Genov 2004: 135). Although now primarily nocturnal in areas of Europe, this has been attributed to modern intensive hunting pressure (Lemel et al. 2003: 34); communities not under heavy hunting pressures engage in diurnal rhythms (Keuling et al. 2008: 729). Showing no clear shifts in activity through the day, wild boar regularly seek cover, utilising marsh and wetland environs if available (Dardaillon 1986: 251–2); however, they also forage in deciduous/mixed woodlands (Massei and Genov 2004: 138). In contrast to wild boar, beavers are largely nocturnal (Coles 2006: 11). Although in areas where they are not intensively hunted they may emerge during the day, feeding activity intensifies throughout the night, reaching a peak around midnight (Kitchener 2001: 63, 71). Furthermore, the beaver is predominantly aquatic, remaining in lodges and ponds during the day, moving to local terrestrial feeding grounds at dusk (Coles 2006: 6; Mills 1913: 106). European wildcat are extremely cryptic and elusive, present in low densities and are highly mobile within their home ranges (Monterroso et al. 2009: 27; Klar et al. 2008: 310). They are closely bound to forest habitats offering extremely sheltered diurnal resting sites, either on the ground or in arboreal cavities (Jerosch et al. 2010: 51; Sarmento et al. 2006: 86), only moving to forest-edge conditions in darkness to hunt rodents (Monterroso et al. 2009: 33).

Human encounters with these species in the Kennet Valley would therefore occur at specific and different times of the day, as a result of the animals' particular rhythms. At Thatcham and Faraday Road, human encounters with wild boar would be potentially regular and cyclical during the day, as they both engaged in predominantly diurnal rhythms. The sharing of similar diurnal rhythms may have led humans to understand themselves as temporally bound together with these species. However, such meetings were not isolated events, and it is unlikely wild boar did not change their behaviour to avoid future encounters. In ungulate species, disturbances stimulate an adjustment of habitat selection to minimise mortality risk and the effects of stress (Jayakody et al. 2008: 82); even in the absence of physical attacks, the presence of predators will scare ungulate species and elicit both spatial and temporal shifts in order to spend more time in the lower-risk areas of what is termed the 'landscape of fear' (Hernandez and Laundre 2005: 218; Laundre et al. 2001: 1409). Therefore, whilst the diurnal rhythms of this species may have highlighted inherent similarities between humans and wild boar, encounters over longer periods of time would also evoke a sense of intentionality on the part of the wild boar, as they altered their own daily rhythms and places as a reaction to human actions.

In contrast to the diurnal wild boar, encounters with beavers would be at dusk, as they emerged from their lodges, feeding into the night, offering a clear distinction to the rhythms of the local ungulates, and potentially humans too. Similarly, encounters with wildcat would only occur during the hours of darkness, as these shy and sparse species emerged from their shelters within dense vegetation, stealthily entering forest-edge and open conditions, which would continue to provide cover for these small species. Encounters would be dark, snatched, fleeting and potentially rare. Like the cats at Shillourokambos (Jones 2009), the distinctive nature of beaver and wildcat rhythms may have elicited an understanding of the 'otherness' of individuals of these species, beings undertaking their own activities, distinct from humans.

The particular timings of human encounters with nonhumans would reveal species wrapped up in their own daily lives, some temporally bound together with humans, others engaged in distinctively different rhythms. However, this is not to suggest that human understandings were the result of simply 'seeing' nonhumans' distinctive rhythms; this gives the impression of humans abstractly observing nonhumans as they run parallel alongside each other. Instead, it is the intersection of these rhythms, the entanglement of humans and nonhumans, and the subsequent human experiences, that are key. As previously discussed, in hunting species, humans have to engage in, or synchronise with, the specific and different rhythms of their prey (Hamilakis 2003: 240; Brittain and Overton 2013). The faunal material from Thatcham and Faraday Road contain multiple individuals of both wild boar and beaver (see Table 17.1), indicating these species were intentionally hunted. Therefore, to hunt these species, humans would necessarily become wrapped up in alternative, nonhuman rhythms: the hunting of wild boar may have been undertaken during the day, reinforcing similarities between humans and wild boar rhythms. However, to hunt nocturnal beaver a more significant alteration would be required, leaving diurnal activities to become active during hours of darkness. To move through the environment at these different times would elicit different experiences. Whilst moving in daylight to hunt wild boar may feel familiar, moving in the dark may present distinctly different experiences, where the lack of light can render the familiar unfamiliar (Davies et al. 2005: 283). In engaging in alternative rhythms as part of hunting specific species, the nature of the experience is intimately bound to the species they hunt; by moving at times particular to each species, unusual or distinct experiences would lead humans to recognise the 'otherness' of these species, agentic beings living at times specific to themselves. In contrast to wild boar and beaver, the remains of wildcat in the Thatcham and Faraday Road faunal assemblages indicate single individuals, represented by very few specimens, and present only at some sites. This scarcity, and the solitary and shy nature of the species suggests wildcat was not regularly hunted at these sites in the Kennet Valley. Instead, humans and wildcat may have met through chance encounters, which, being unpredictable in their nature, would not include the synchronisation of human rhythms with those of the wildcat. Such encounters may still have allowed humans to develop understanding of the 'otherness' of wildcats; however, this would develop from the discord between their rhythms. Not furnished with experiences facilitated by ongoing synchronisation with nonhuman rhythms, the 'otherness' of wildcats may have been distinctly different to wild boar or beaver, characterised more by the unknown than the known.

Inter-personal meetings

Through processes of encounter and hunting, the synchronisation of human rhythms with particular nonhumans, or indeed the discord between human and nonhuman rhythms, led to the formation of specific human understanding of different species. However, these processes did not just offer temporal or environmentally orientated experiences: by hunting and killing nonhumans, humans would be afforded intimate and close sensorial bodily encounters. Whilst 'traditional' narratives of hunting present a utilitarian view of killing nonhumans, to the point that the moment of dispatch is rarely discussed, others have suggested this to be an extremely significant moment. For example, Hamilakis has argued that the close proximity and constant contact of humans and nonhumans in Bronze Age Greece would make the killing of domestic species a highly charged and emotional event (2008: 7–8). Although human–nonhuman relationships in the Mesolithic were not born out of the same co-habitation that is afforded by the pastoral herder-herd relationship, by considering humans developing understanding of nonhumans as intentional 'others' through their interactions, the moment of killing can still be considered as a significant event (cf. Overton and Hamilakis 2013: 128).

Crucially, many of the hunting methods used by Mesolithic groups, such as spears, nets, snares, pitfalls, traps, or poison (Magnell 2006b: 64; Noe-Nygaard 1974: 218) required close proximity for final dispatch. The particular abundance of archaeological evidence for the use of flint-tipped projectiles (e.g. Noe-Nygaard 1975; Leduc 2012) has led to the suggestion that the bow and arrow existed as a surgical shock weapon (Churchill 1993: 18), both in ambush hunting, and more protracted processes of tracking and pursuit. However, the bow and arrow is also likely to require close-range encounter; particularly when hunting larger ungulates, a high level of accuracy and power is required to penetrate major organs whilst avoiding parts of the skeleton that would otherwise deflect the projectile, potentially suggesting an effective range of 5–15 metres (Churchill 1993: 18; Friis-Hansen 1990: 494; Triplett 2004: 62).

The close-proximity nature of hunting events would not only afford intimate and close sensorial bodily encounters, they would also be greatly shaped by the specific behaviours of the nonhuman species involved. As a gregarious species living in large multi-family groups (Truve and Lemel 2003: 52), wild boar were potentially encountered and hunted in groups, a suggestion supported by the frequency of individuals in the Kennet Valley assemblages, particularly Faraday Road and Thatcham III (see Table 17.1). Furthermore, in close-quarters hunting, wild boar are a dangerous prospect; when cornered, or hit with non-fatal shots, individuals will round on pursuers and attack, making these hunting episodes the ultimate test of skill and nerve for hunters (Triplett 2004: 7, 30). Maxwell described the wild pig of the Iraq marshes as huge and evil-tempered, in a moment becoming a 'raging tornado of slashing tusks that rip flesh like knives, leaving white bone open to the sky' (1957: 72). With the ability to take great damage and still turn to fight pursuers, modern sport hunters disturbing a large boar or a sow with young would rather shimmy up a tree than face them when attacking (Triplett 2004: 1). It is of particular interest to note that a number of wild boar skulls from the Danish Mesolithic sites of Aldersro, Hastrup Mose, Søborg Mose and Fuglekjæ Mose, exhibit lesions or wounds on the cranium, which, based on their size and elongated morphology, seem to represent axe impacts, or other blunt force trauma (Noe-Nygaard 1974: 229–237). These attest not only to the close-quarter nature of hunting events, but may also suggest blows that are less of an intended kill shot, but instead a moment of self-defence by the hunter (Noe-Nygaard 1974: 238), giving wild boar hunting a distinctly melee-like flavour. Therefore, at Faraday Road, and Thatcham II and III, we may imagine hunters embroiled in a dangerous and frantic melee, some killing young, screaming and thrashing in distress and pain, desperately trying to seek safety with their mothers, whilst others attempted to dispatch violent and explosive adults turning with retaliatory intent. This rich, emotive and dangerous encounter would reinforce humans' understanding of wild boar as intentional beings, very much actors within genuinely mutual encounters, who had the ability to act and react as 'others' within their shared environment.

Whilst characterisations of beaver as nocturnal rodents may appear to present a great contrast to the potentially volatile and dangerous wild boar, they should not be thought of as easy to kill; they can be as pugnacious as they are industrious. When cornered or pursued, beaver can turn on their assailant, brandishing their large razor-sharp incisors with such ferocity and skill that any predator is glad to retreat. On occasions, beaver have been known to confront and kill large predators such as bobcat (Mills 1913: 35), and human fatalities have been recorded in modern times: confronting and killing a beaver may have been a task that required as much wariness and care as any other nonhuman. As an alternative to direct hunting, trapping may have been used to catch beaver, however, they are renowned for avoiding paths where an individual has previously been trapped (Nelson 1973: 252), making it difficult to trap this species in any great number. The frequencies of individuals at Faraday Road and Thatcham (see Table 17.1) may, therefore, suggest direct hunting over trapping. However, in both cases, the killing would be a close range encounter, more so if the individuals were killed partly for the pelts, which would encourage the use of a blunt trauma weapon over a projectile to avoid puncturing the skin. Accounts of killing beaver in this way suggest this would be a highly affective event. 'A thousand trappers unite' to tell the same story; when confronted by a human with a weapon to dispatch the individual, the beaver raises up on hind legs, with hands up-raised to desperately ward off the death blow, dying while vainly trying to shield their head with both hands (Mills 1913: 14). The potentially dangerous nature of confronting a beaver at close quarters, and the emotive nature of the moment of dispatch, including a suite of movements and actions the hunter may have understood as inherently similar to their own, would not only have made this a distinctive event, but also emphasised their intentionality and 'otherness'.

In contrast, inter-personal hunting encounters with wildcats may have been notably different; for such small, shy, sparse and nocturnal species, different strategies, such as trapping, may have been used (Leduc 2012: 12; Charles 1997: 259; Holliday 1998: 711). Ethnographic surveys of contemporary indigenous societies suggest all groups within the Northern Boreal Forests engage widely in trapping, and high frequencies of smaller carnivore species such as wildcat, pine marten and fox at Danish Mesolithic sites have been used to suggest widespread trapping in the past (Holliday 1998; Richter 2005). The trapping process would have led to encounters that were somewhat different to the hunting encounters of wild boar or beaver; instead of the direct and immediate interactions and experiences of hunts, in which humans and nonhumans are entangled together in specific moments, trapping, in which a trap is set, left, then returned to after a period of time, presents a more dislocated process. In trapping, an empty trap is left and an ensnared nonhuman is returned to, the moment of capture occurring at an unknown, and un-experienced moment. This distinction would be particularly apparent if the trapped individual was dead on inspection. This dislocated nature of trapping may have reinforced humans' understandings of wildcats as different, previously developed through their experience of them engaged in distinct nocturnal rhythms. Furthermore, in lacking the immediacy of direct hunting, trapping would not afford the same experiences of individuals acting, reacting, panicking, or retaliating, echoing the lack of experience of wildcats in daily life. This is not to say trapping would be devoid of experience: captured individuals may still be alive when the traps are checked, presenting an injured, distressed and desperate individual, terrified, weak and bleeding, requiring a final blow from the hunter to dispatch them. This too would be a potentially emotive situation, eliciting an understanding that these species also experienced a range of emotions, conferring a sense of sentience and intentionality. However, it would also be distinctly different to direct hunting encounters, a contrast that was ultimately born out of wildcats' distinctive daily rhythms and behaviours, which would further reinforce the 'otherness' of this species.

Environmental rhythms

Hunting not only required humans to alter the times that they moved through the environment; they also had to travel to particular places. As outlined above, each species used different habitats, at different times of the day. To hunt wild boar, humans had to move into marsh and sedge conditions, or mixed woodland during the day, all places which may change during the course of a day, or over longer periods as the wild boar adapted and changed their movements. However, to hunt beaver, humans would have to move to the River Kennet's water's edge, or small groves of trees on the riverbank at night. In hunting, humans would be taken to places specific to each species, some known, but some potentially unknown, or rarely visited. Some of the habitats may have been less understood, or less easy to move through and within; the aquatic habitat of the beaver may have offered particular distinction to the terrestrial habitat of humans. Beavers' physiological adaptations to water are still noted as distinctive and unusual (Coles 2006: 3); their ability to swim up to 800 m underwater undetected (Kitchener 2001: 83) must have made some beavers seem to simply vanish, in a habitat not necessarily favoured by humans. Furthermore, discussions of Mesolithic people 'at one' with their environment has led to an assumption that 'wilderness', land outside one's immediate knowledge, did not exist, and all space was available to move in. However, we may instead consider an environment that contained malevolent forces, places and agents, in which areas may not have been regularly entered, where fear was a primary motivator for action (Davies et al. 2005: 283). Whilst wildcat may not have been intentionally or intensively hunted at Thatcham or Faraday Road, it is interesting to consider that the environmental settings for chance encounters, the impenetrable and dense woodland understory habitats favoured by wildcats, may have been unknown, avoided, or potentially malevolent places. As such, the snatched, fleeting and shadowy encounters of wildcat emerging from these areas may have developed an understanding of these species as malevolent, or at the least different 'others' (Overton 2016).

Although some of the places humans experienced whilst engaging with nonhumans may have been unfamiliar, many others would have been known and regularly visited, such as particular openings, specific stands of trees or riverbanks. Humans and nonhumans would have also shared edible materials; autumnal fruits and nuts are targeted by wild boar and beaver (Massei and Genov 2004: 138; Coles 2006: 4), a plentiful resource that must have also been used by humans. In particular, wild boar are known to target high-energy acorns and hazelnuts (Massei and Genov 2004: 138), both of which have been cited as potential key Mesolithic foodstuffs (e.g. Mason 2000) and of which the latter have been found as burnt food waste at both Faraday Road and Thatcham III (Ellis et al. 2003; Wymer 1962). However, although humans and non-humans shared a number of places and tasks in the landscape, they may have also used them in different ways: both beaver and humans may have used beaver ponds, but in ways specific to themselves. Therefore, whilst humans and nonhumans existed together in a single, shared environment, humans experienced nonhumans engaged in their own lives, in ways, at times and in places specific to them; this specificity of different species persistently developed humans' understating of intentional nonhumans within the environment.

In the Kennet Valley, humans' understandings emerged through processes of hunting, where different nonhuman species were experienced as engaging in their own rhythms, undertaking their own tasks and using a range of places. However, preceding hunting events at Thatcham and Faraday Road, humans prepared: they knapped flints, hafted tools and gathered necessary materials and items. These preparations may have been temporally specific to their quarry: were they early, prior to hunting wild boar, or later in the day, to hunt beaver at night? Once ready, hunters would move to certain places in the landscape, which their prey frequented at that time. These tasks, objects and movements are material and performative acknowledgements of the intentionality of the 'other'. In the Danish Later Mesolithic, it has been argued that seasonal movement of humans to hunt migratory species is predicated on understanding that nonhumans possessed the agency to determine their own movements to the sites (Overton and Hamilakis 2013). In the same way, preparations for hunting events are carried out in the knowledge that species are engaged in their own practices, making agentic decisions to move at certain times, to specific places. If not, intentional hunts would be a futile practice, hoping on a chance encounter with a rhythm-less quarry that exhibits completely random and unpredictable movements.

Through the synchronising of rhythms, humans in the Kennet Valley experienced non-humans engaged in their own daily rhythms, bound into particular activities and networks of specific places and materials. On one level, this would offer a parallel with human action: many species, including humans, were intrinsically similar in that they engaged in daily rhythms and actions within landscape. However, nonhumans did not represent a mirror of human action. Different species engaged in their own temporalities, visited their own places and spaces, and undertook their own tasks. Repeated encounters with wild boar that engaged in regular daily rhythms between dawn and dusk, moving through woodlands and openings also used by humans, may have elicited strong similarities to humans' own daily activities, drawing parallels between these species and humans. Encounters with crepuscular and nocturnal beaver may have been more regular, as they swam in the pools and fed in riverside groves surrounding Faraday Road and Thatcham. However, whilst not necessarily rare, humans would experience beaver engaging in rhythms and habitats that sharply contrasted their own, marking them as distinctive. Through encounter and synchronisation with these species, humans were taken to places known and unknown, at times familiar and unfamiliar, searching for material used and unused. They would come to be understood as simultaneously intrinsically similar to, but specifically different from humans – as 'Others'. Preparations for hunting were material acknowledgements of this 'otherness'; an understanding of nonhumans as intentional agents, which was learnt through daily engagement, interactions and experiences. In contrast, encounters with wildcats would be sporadic and unpredictable meetings at night with small, stealthy and shy species inhabiting dense and potentially avoided places. The lack of human synchrony with wildcat rhythms in such meetings may have presented a clear discord, enforcing their distinctive 'otherness', but one that contrasts the 'otherness' of wild boar or beaver, borne out of more detailed and entangled engagements.

It is interesting here to note that in contemporary hunter-gatherer groups that understand humans and nonhumans as sharing a common, unifying essence, not all species are considered as 'persons' (Hill 2011: 407; Willerslev 2004: 633; Viveiros de Castro 1998: 471; Pedersen 2001: 414); instead, a species must show a capacity and responsibility in order to be considered as such (Bird-David 2006: 43). Whilst human experiences in the Kennet might have led to recognising the 'otherness' of all species, the difference in experiences and engagements provided contrasts that developed specific understandings of nonhumans. Perhaps only some species, such as wild boar or beaver that presented parallels to human behaviour, or those that were encountered and engaged with frequently, were understood as 'persons'. This is not to deny the agentic potential of wildcat; however, the infrequent, fleeting and liminal nature of encounter may have led to humans understanding them in distinctively different ways (cf. Overton: 2016).

Seasonal rhythms

Daily engagements between humans and nonhumans played a central role in emerging relationships and understandings, but human understanding of nonhumans also developed over larger temporal scales; in the Kennet Valley, nonhumans were engaged in seasonal, as well as daily rhythms. The beaver presents one of the clearest example of seasonal activity: in the autumn, groups will gather green wood, dragging it across land and floating it along channels from up to a mile away, storing it in their pond as a winter food source (Mills 1913: 12). This forms a guaranteed food source in areas where heavy winter freezing makes access in and out of the lake impossible; however, beavers continue to collect and store food even in mild climates (Coles 2006: 47). Wild boar also exhibit seasonal activities, preferentially visiting different environments through the year; for example, they show marked peaks in rooting activity in dryer areas during winter (Welander 2000: 269) and focus on nuts and seeds in autumn (Massei and Genov 2004: 138). They are also wrapped up in social and reproductive seasonal activities. Wild boar males, which are primarily solitary for much of the year, move to join social groups in order to mate in November and December (Groot Bruinderink and Hazebroek 1994: 634). These seasonal movements and aggregations would also be characterised by conspicuous social interactions between individuals; vocalisation, displaying and fighting of males would make these distinctive events. The potential year-round occupation at Faraday Road (see Table 17.2) would result in humans experiencing wild boar seasonally changing: feeding widely in wetlands and woodlands during the summer as groups or solitary males, as the days became shorter, they would move to focus on fruits and nuts in the woodlands. Males arrived to join groups, where they fought and mated, before dispersing again, as the groups spread more widely in the landscape as the cold of winter receded. No direct seasonal data was available based on the beaver remains present; however, indicators from other species at Faraday Road and Thatcham III (see Table 17.2) suggest humans would have been present whilst beavers engaged in their annual harvest, travelling across the local area to gather branches and logs and store them in their ponds.

The experience of beaver and wild boar engaging in seasonal behaviours must have elicited general parallels with humans' own movement around the landscape throughout the year, building on human understandings of specific species as agents. Certainly the flux of autumnal activity, with beavers harvesting and wild boar focusing on the nuts, seeds and fruit that were presumably also a key resource for humans, offers a picture of very similar human and nonhuman practices. Therefore wild boar did not just offer similarities to humans in their daily activities; they also shared wider practices of seasonal movement, adding to the perception of these as agentic individuals. However, whilst humans and wild boar were similarly bound into seasonal practices, they were unique to each species; the places, timings and actions undertaken were

Table 17.2 Seasonal indicators in the faunal assemblages from Thatcham sites I–III and Faraday Road

	J	F	M	A	M	J	J	A	S	O	N	D
Faraday Road												
–Wild Boar (tw)												
Thatcham I												
–Red Deer (tw)												
–Roe Deer (tw)												
–Roe Deer (ua)												
Thatcham II												
–Red Deer (ua)												
–Wild Boar (tw)												
Thatcham III												
–Red Deer (tw)												
–Red Deer (ua)												
–Roe Deer (ua)												
–Wild Boar (tw)												

Note: (tw) denotes season indicated by individuals aged by toothwear, (ua) denotes season indicated by unshed antler

manifestations of their 'otherness'. Although the daily rhythms of the beaver starkly contrast those of humans, their autumnal gathering offers one of the tightest parallels, showing individual and intentional 'thought for the morrow' (Mills 1913: 30), clearly illustrating their ability as sentient agents, again reinforcing their 'otherness'. In contrast, wildcat do not exhibit clear seasonal changes; indeed, encounters may have been so infrequent, fleeting and dark that there was little chance to develop any detailed understanding of them, on both a daily and seasonal scale. This would further build on the perception of these species as distinctly different.

Conclusions

Mesolithic hunter–gatherers in the Kennet Valley came to understand nonhumans through their daily interactions and engagements. Furthermore, the specific rhythms of nonhumans played a key structuring role in these meetings, experience and engagements, which subsequently led to the formation of specific human understanding of, and relationships with nonhuman species and individuals. By using faunal remains within a multispecies framework, archaeology can consider how human and nonhuman rhythms intersected in the past, and explore the emergence of a multitude of different human–nonhuman relationships. Wild boar, regularly encountered, may have elicited numerous parallels between their rhythms, tasks and actions and those of humans, developing an acknowledgement that they were bound into similar lifeways and practices as humans, and therefore were intentional and sentient beings. Beavers offered a contrasting experience, inhabiting distinctly different rhythms and habitats, yet engaging in many tasks also undertaken by humans, although in ways specific to themselves. By synchronising with these alternative rhythms, entering different areas and habitats, humans would experience the 'otherness' of beaver, as intentional beings wrapped up in their own, distinctive lives. The distinctive rhythms of wildcats may also have elicited an understanding of their 'otherness', however, developed through fleeting, shadowy and infrequent encounters, they may have been understood as distinctly different from more regularly encountered species.

Beyond producing narratives of living human-nonhuman interactions and engagements, what is at stake in such studies? In essence, the emergence of these relationships is the first step in a string of actions and interactions that have significant material consequences; human understanding of nonhumans is crucial in guiding and shaping the treatment of nonhumans, both as living individuals and as material remains. For example, contemporary hunter-gatherer groups' treatment of nonhuman remains, in practices of butchery, consumption, distribution and deposition, are guided by the understandings of these individuals developed through living encounters. The remains of those individuals and species that come to be understood as 'persons' are treated in specific and respectful ways, in order to maintain ongoing human-nonhuman social relationships (cf. Hill 2011; Nadasdy 2007: 27; Jordan 2008: 240–41). Therefore, human understandings of nonhumans in the past, stemming from the intersection of rhythms, have the potential to greatly structure the patterns in material remains that archaeological analyses strive to interpret.

Acknowledgements

This research originated as part of my doctoral research, which would not have been possible without funding from the Arts and Humanities Research Council. I also wish to thank Marcus Brittain, with whom I began to start thinking about rhythm in human-nonhuman relationships; the discussions we shared remain at the heart of how I think about these ideas and themes.

Note

1 All dates presented at 95.4% probability, calibrated with Oxcal v4.2.4 (Bronk-Ramsey 2009) with the IntCal13 atmospheric curve (Reimer et al. 2013).

References

Agamben, G. 2004. *The Open: Man and Animal*. Stanford, CA, Stanford University Press.

Argent, G. 2010. Do the Clothes Make the Horse? Relationality, Roles and Statuses in Iron Age Inner Asia. *World Archaeology* 42 (2); 157–174.

Argent, G. 2013. Inked: Human-Horse Apprenticeship, Tattoos, and Time in the Pazyryk World. *Society & Animals* 21; 178–193.

Armstrong Oma, K. 2010. Between Trust and Domination: Social Contracts between Humans and Animals. *World Archaeology* 42 (2); 175–187.

Armstrong Oma, K. 2013. Human-Animal Meeting Points: Use of Space in the Household Arena in Past Societies. *Society & Animals* 21; 162–177.

Bird-David, N. 2006. Animistic Epistemology: Why Do Some Hunter-Gatherers not Depict Animals? *Ethnos* 71 (1); 33–50.

Brittain, M. and Overton, N. 2013. The Significance of Others: A Prehistory of Rhythm and Interspecies Participation. *Society & Animals* 21; 135–150.

Bronk Ramsey, C. (2009). Bayesian Analysis of Radiocarbon Dates. *Radiocarbon* 51 (1); 337–360.

Calarco, M. 2008. *Zoographies: The Question of the Animal from Heidegger to Derrida*. New York, Columbia University Press.

Cartmill, M. 2008. Animal Consciousness: Some Philosophical, Methodological and Evolutionary Problems. *American Zoologist* 40 (6); 835–846.

Charles, R. 1997. The Exploitation of Carnivores and Other Fur-Bearing Mammals during the North-Western European Late and Upper Palaeolithic and Mesolithic. *Oxford Journal of Archaeology* 16 (3); 253–277.

Chisham, C. 2004. *Early Mesolithic Human Activity and Environmental Change: A Case Study of the Kennet Valley*. Unpublished PhD Thesis, University of Reading.

Churchill, S.E. 1993. Weapon Technology, Prey Size Selection, and Hunting Methods in Modern Hunter-Gatherers: Implications for Hunting in the Palaeolithic and Mesolithic. *Archeological Papers of the American Anthropological Association* 4 (1); 11–24.

Coles, B. 2006. *Beavers in Britain's Past*. Oxford, Oxbow books.

Dardaillon, M. 1986. Seasonal Variations in Habitat Selection and Spatial Distribution of Wild Boar (*Sus scrofa*) in the Camargue, Southern France. *Behavioural Processes* 13; 251–268.

Davies, P., Robb, J.G. and Ladbrook, D. 2005. Woodland Clearance in the Mesolithic: The Social Aspects. *Antiquity* 79 (304); 280–288.

deFrance, D.S. 2009. Zooarchaeology in Complex Societies: Political Economy, Status and Ideology. *Journal of Archaeological Research* 17; 105–168.

Ellis, C.J., Allen, M.J., Gardiner, J., Harding, P., Ingrem, C., Powell, A. and Scaife, R.G. 2003. An Early Mesolithic Seasonal Hunting Site in the Kennet Valley, Southern England. *Proceedings of the Prehistoric Society* 69; 107–135.

Friis-Hansen, J. 1990. Mesolithic Cutting Arrows: Functional Analysis of Arrows Used in the Hunting of Large Game. *Antiquity* 64; 494–504.

Gowlett, J.A.J., Hedges, R.E.M., Law, I.A. and Perry, C. 1987. Radiocarbon Dates from the Oxford AMS System: Archaeometry Datelist 5 (Thatcham). *Archaeometry* 29 (1); 127.

Groot Bruinderink, G.W.T.A. and Hazebroek, E. 1994. Diet and Conditions of Wild Boar, *Sus scrofa scrofa*, Without Supplementary Feeding. *Journal of Zoology London* 233; 631–648.

Hamilakis, Y. 2003. The Sacred Geography of Hunting: Wild Animals, Social Power and Gender in Early Farming Societies. In Kotjabpoulouy, E., Hamilakis, Y., Halstead, E., Gamble, P. and Elefanti, V. (eds). *Zooarchaeology in Greece: Recent Advances*. London, British School at Athens.

Hamilakis, Y. 2008. Time, Performance and the Production of a Mnemonic Record: From Feasting to an Archaeology of Eating and Drinking. In Hitchcock, L., Laffineur, R. and Crowley, J. (eds). *DAIS: The Aegean Feast*, 3-17. Liege and Austin, University of Liege and University of Texas at Austin.

Haraway, D. 2008. *When Species Meet*. Minneapolis, University of Minnesota Press.

Hernandez, L. and Laundre, J.W. 2005. Foraging in the 'Landscape of Fear' and its Implications for Habitat Use and Diet Quality of Elk *Cervus elaphus* and Bison *Bison bison*. *Wildlife Biology* 11 (3); 215–220.

Hill, E. 2011. Animals as Agents: Hunting Ritual and Relational Ontologies in Prehistoric Alaska and Chukotta. *Cambridge Archaeological Journal* 21 (3); 467–426.

Holliday, T.W. 1998. The Ecological Context of Trapping among Recent Hunter-Gatherers: Implications for Subsistence in Terminal Pleistocene Europe. *Current Anthropology* 39 (5); 711–719.

Jayakody, S., Sibbald, A.M., Gordon, I.J. and Lambin, X. 2008. Red Deer *Cervus elaphus* Vigilance Behaviour Differs With Habitat and Type of Human Disturbance. *Wildlife Biology* 14; 81–91.

Jerosch, S., Gotz, M., Klar, N. and Roth, M. 2010. Characteristics of Diurnal Resting Sites of the Endangered European Wildcat (*Felis silvestris silvestris*): Implications for its Conservation. *Journal for Nature Conservation* 18; 45–54.

Jones, P. 2009. Considering Living-Beings in the Aceramic Neolithic of Cyprus. *Journal of Mediterranean Archaeology* 22 (1); 75–99.

Jordan, P. 2008. Northern Landscapes, Northern Minds: On the Trail of an 'Archaeology of Hunter-Gatherer Belief'. In Hays-Gilpin, K. and Whitley, D. S. (eds). *Belief in the Past: Theoretical Approaches to the Archaeology of Religion*, 227–246. Walnut Creek, CA, Left Coast Press.

Keuling, O., Stier, N. and Roth, M. 2008. How Does Hunting Influence Activity and Spatial Usage in Wild Boar *Sus scrofa* L.? *European Journal of Wildlife Research* 54; 729–737.

Kitchner, A. 2001. *Beavers*. Stowmarket, Whittet Books.

Klar, N., Fernandez, N., Kramer-Schadt, S., Herrmann, M., Trinzer, M., Buttner, I. and Niemitz, C. 2008. Habitat Selection Models for European Wildcat Conservation. *Biological Conservation* 141; 308–319.

Laundre, J.W., Hernandez, L. and Altendorf, K.B. 2001. Wolves, Elk and Bison: Reestablishing the 'Landscape of Fear' in Yellowstone National Park, U.S.A. *Canadian Journal of Zoology* 79; 1401–1409.

Leduc, C. 2012. New Mesolithic Hunting Evidence from Bone Injuries at Danish Maglemosian Sites: Lundby Mose and Mullerup (Sjælland). *International Journal of Osteoarchaeology* Early View Online Version: doi:10.1002/oa.2234.

Lemel, J., Truve, J. and Soderberg, B. 2003. Variation in Ranging and Activity Behaviour of European Wild Boar *Sus scrofa* in Sweden. *Wildlife Biology* 9; 29–36.

Magnell, O. 2006. *Tracking Wild Boar and Hunters: Osteology of Wild Boar in Mesolithic Scandinavia*. Lund, Wallin & Dalholm.

Marciniak, A. 1999. Faunal Materials and Interpretive Archaeology: Epistemology Reconsidered. *Journal of Archaeological Method and Theory* 6 (4); 293–320.

Mason, S.L.R. 2000. Fire and Mesolithic Subsistence-Managing Oaks for Acorns in Northwest Europe? *Palaeogeography, Palaeoclimatology, Palaeoecology* 164; 139–150.

Massei, G. and Genov, P.V. 2004. The Environmental Impact of Wild Boar. *Galemys* 16; 135–145.

Maxwell, G. 1957. *A Reed Shaken by the Wind*. London, Longman, Green and Co.

Mills, E.A. 1913. *In Beaver World*. Boston, MA and New York, The Riverside Press Cambridge.

Monterroso, P., Brito, J.C., Ferreras, P. and Alves, P.C. 2009. Spatial Ecology of the European Wildcat in a Mediterranean Ecosystem: Dealing with Small Radio-Tracking Datasets in Species Conservation. *Journal of Zoology* 279; 27–35.

Nadasdy, P. 2007. The Gift of the Animal: The Ontology of Hunting and Human-Animal Sociality. *American Ethnologist* 34 (1); 25–43.

Nelson, R.K. 1973. *Hunters of the Northern Forest: Designs for Survival Among the Alaskan Kutchin*. Chicago, IL, University of Chicago Press.

Noe-Nygaard, N. 1974. Mesolithic Hunting in Denmark Illustrated by Bone Injuries Caused by Human Weapons. *Journal of Archaeological Science* 1; 217–248.

Noe-Nygaard, N. 1975. Two Shoulder Blades with Healed Lesions from Star Carr. *Proceedings of the Prehistoric Society* 41; 10–17.

Orton, D.C. 2012. Taphonomy and Interpretation: An Analytical Framework for Social Zooarchaeology. *International Journal of Osteoarchaeology* 22; 320–337.

Overton, N.J. 2014a. Memorable Meetings in the Mesolithic: Tracing the Biography of Human-Nonhuman Relationships in the Kennet and Colne Valleys with Social Zooarchaeology. Unpublished PhD Thesis, University of Manchester.

Overton, N. 2014b. Review of Russell, N. Social Zooarchaeology: Humans and Animals in Prehistory. *Journal of Field Archaeology* 39 (1); 108–109.

Overton, N.J. 2016. More than Skin Deep: Reconsidering Isolated Remains of 'Fur Bearing Species' in the British and European Mesolithic. *Cambridge Archaeology Journal* 26(4); 561–578.

Overton, N.J. and Hamilakis, Y. 2013. A Manifesto for a Social Zooarchaeology: Swans and Other Beings in the Mesolithic. *Archaeological Dialogues* 20 (2); 111–136.

Pedersen, M.A. 2001. Totemism, Animism and North Asian Indigenous Ontologies. *Journal of the Royal Anthropological Institute* 7 (3); 411–427.

Reimer, P. J., Bard, E., Bayliss, A., Beck, J. W., Blackwell, P. G., Bronk Ramsey, C., Grootes, P. M., Guilderson, T. P., Haflidason, H., Hajdas, I., Hatt, C., Heaton, T. J., Hoffmann, D. L., Hogg, A. G., Hughen, K. A., Kaiser, K. F., Kromer, B., Manning, S. W., Niu, M., Reimer, R. W., Richards, D. A., Scott, E. M., Southon, J. R., Staff, R. A., Turney, C. S. M., and van der Plicht, J. 2013. IntCal13 and Marine13 Radiocarbon Age Calibration Curves 0–50,000 Years cal BP. *Radiocarbon*, 55 (4); 1869–1887.

Richter, J. 2005. Selective Hunting of Pine Marten, *Martes martes*, in Late Mesolithic Denmark. *Journal of Archaeological Science* 32; 1223–1231.

Roberts, A.J., Barton, R.N.E. and Evans, J.G. 1998. The Early Mesolithic Mastic Radiocarbon Dating and Analysis of Organic Residues from Thatcham III, Star Carr and Lackford Heath. In Ashton, N. M., Healy, F. and Pettie, P. B. (eds). *Stone Age Archaeology: Essays in Honour of John Wymer. Lithics Studies Occasional Paper 6, Oxbow Monograph 102*, 185–192. Oxford, Oxbow Books.

Russell, N. 2012. *Social Zooarchaeology: Humans and Animals in Prehistory*. Cambridge, Cambridge University Press.

Sarmento, P., Cruz, J., Tarroso, P. and Fonseca, C. 2006. Space and Habitat Selection by Female European Wild Cats (*Felis silvestris silvestris*). *Wildlife Biology in Practice* 2 (2); 79–89.

Triplett, T. 2004. *The Complete Book of Wild Boar Hunting*. Guilford, CT, The Lyons Press.

Truve, J. and Lemel, J. 2003. Timing and Distance of Natal Dispersal for Wild Boar *Sus scrofa* in Sweden. *Wildlife Biology* 9; 51–57.

Viveiros de Castro, V. 1998. Cosmological Dexis and Amerindian Perspectivism. *The Journal of the Royal Anthropological Institute* 4 (3); 469–488.

Welander, J. 2000. Spatial and Temporal Dynamics of Wild Boar (*Sus scrofa*) Rooting in a Mosaic Landscape. *The Zoology Society of London* 252; 263–271.

Willerslev, R. 2004. Not Animal, Not Not Animal: Hunting, Imitation and Empathetic Knowledge among the Siberian Yukaghirs. *Journal of the Royal Anthropological Institute* 10 (3); 629–652.

Wolfe, C. 2003. Introduction. In Wolfe, C. (ed.). *Zoontologies: The Question of the Animal*, ix–xxiii. Minneapolis and London, University of Minnesota Press.

Wymer, J.J. 1962. Excavations at the Maglemosian Sites at Thatcham, Berkshire, England. *Proceedings of the Prehistoric Society* 28; 329–361.

18

SEASONAL MOBILITY AND MULTISPECIES INTERACTIONS IN THE MESOLITHIC NORTHEASTERN ADRIATIC

Suzanne E. Pilaar Birch

Introduction

The traditional archaeological narrative surrounding the early Holocene in the Balkans tends to focus on changes in human cultural material, technology, and subsistence from the Mesolithic into the Neolithic. Demographic continuity—or lack thereof—has been a central debate, but recent models in the eastern Adriatic have increasingly recognized the spatially and temporally nuanced nature of this shift (e.g., Bass 2008; Forenbaher et al. 2013; Forenbaher & Miracle 2005; Orton et al. 2016; Robb & Miracle 2007; Pilaar Birch & Vander Linden 2017). Human lifeways were embedded in local ecologies, which in turn were structured not least by the climatic and environmental conditions that governed the presence and seasonal abundance of myriad plant and animal species. Local environments were affected by changes in seasonal temperature ranges, vegetation, and freshwater availability during this time. In the Adriatic, the sea level increased rapidly following the end of the last ice age, with a short hiatus at the very end of the Pleistocene corresponding with the Younger Dryas (12,900–11,700 BP) (Lambeck et al. 2002, 2004; Surić et al. 2005). It then steadily increased from the initial Holocene until current sea levels were reached between 8,000 and 6,000 years ago, causing the formation of the northern third of the Adriatic Sea and the inundation of the Great Adriatic Plain (Lambeck et al. 2004; Surić 2005; Colantoni et al. 1979). In response to these dramatic transformations at the Pleistocene-Holocene transition, the seasonal mobility and subsistence strategies of red and roe deer, chamois, ibex, wild boar, and humans would have had to adapt in both the short and long term.

In this chapter, I will consider the role of multispecies interactions in determining landscape and resource use, especially on a seasonal basis, in response to large-scale climate change and sea-level rise that altered the regional landscape and local environment during the early Holocene, using zooarchaeological evidence from three cave sites located in the Istrian Peninsula and on the island of Lošinj, Croatia (Nugljanska, Pupićina, & Vela Špilja; Figure 18.1). Decisions about mobility and subsistence for both humans and animals were intimately linked and shaped by seasonal resource availability.

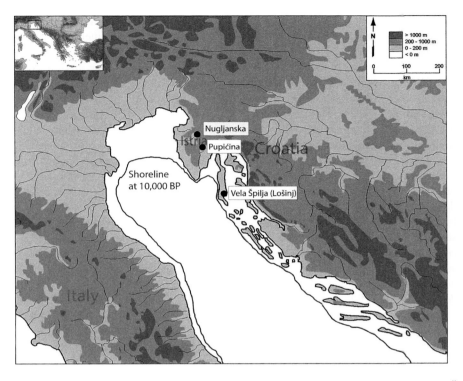

Figure 18.1 Map showing the locations of the three case study sites, Nugljanska, Pupićina, and Vela Špilja on the island of Lošinj.

Environmental context and seasonality

The early Holocene was a time of warming and increased precipitation, and mixed deciduous woodland expanded throughout the region (Balbo et al. 2006; Willis 1994; Andrić et al. 2008; Favaretto et al. 2008). This period was punctuated by very short cool oscillations, the most notable of these the 8.2kya event, when winters became colder and summers drier, and forested areas in higher elevations became dominated by less palatable drought- and cold-resistant plant species. Palynological records place the formation of the present-day vegetation in the Istrian mountains at approximately 8,000 BP, while the later expansion of Mediterranean climate-adapted species reflects the introduction of domestic plants and forest clearing by around 6,000 BP (Schmidt et al. 2000). By the end of this period, the climate approached modern conditions as winters became significantly cooler and summers warmer (Huntley & Prentice 1993).

Caves have a long history of use as habitation sites, temporary shelters, seasonal camps, and sacred places. Location, the physical environment surrounding the cave, its proximity to local resources, and amount of protection from the elements all influence site selection and the activities taking place there, such as hunting, butchery, and tool-making by humans, but also denning, sheltering, and birthing by animals. Seasonal availability of these local resources would determine when to use which site within the wider regional settlement system.

The term "seasonality" is often used for a number of different concepts in prehistory and archaeology. This includes intra-annual climatic variation (increased differences or extremes in seasonal weather patterns); the seasonal nature of site use (is it used in many seasons, or just one?); and the season of site use (spring, summer, autumn, winter). We use this term when discussing the nature of residential mobility and the duration of site use—do people move nightly, weekly, or on a monthly basis? How many times per year do groups relocate, and does this coincide with seasonal fluctuations, or something else? To some extent a discussion of seasonally mediated residential mobility depends on characterizing the first definition: what is the degree of environmental seasonality? This is an important consideration, but is not the central question explored here, where a broadly temperate climate regime persisted throughout the early Holocene. Instead, the objectives are to consider the seasonal nature of site use, and season of site use, within a multispecies perspective that takes into account prey species mobility, seasonal availability and harvest, and the role of novel marine ecologies.

In order to give full consideration to the interconnectedness of landscape, environment, and those inhabiting it, it is crucial to have an understanding of the behavioral ecology of those species found in archaeological sites—where human remains are often conspicuously lacking—including red deer (*Cervus elaphus*), roe deer (*Capreolus capreolus*), ibex (*Capra ibex*), chamois (*Rupicapra rupicapra*), and boar (*Sus scrofa*), as well as smaller animals like hare (*Lepus europaeus*), fox (*Vulpes vulpes*), birds, fish, and insects. Even factors such as parasites, which are difficult to quantify in the archaeological record, influence herbivore behavior (e.g., Clutton-Brock et al. 1982). Likewise, the seasonal appeal of coastal environments plays a role in mobility, the life cycles of sessile molluscs influencing harvest and selection. In addition, underlying geology may affect animal distribution patterns based on the vegetation types they support (Sturdy et al. 1997) and the forage preferences of different ungulate species (cf. Hofmann 1984, 1985). For example, in Paleolithic northwestern Greece, bedrocks such as limestone and alluvial gravel fans were argued to be supportive of open vegetation such as steppe and grasses, with medium grazing capabilities, whereas limestone and flysch may have offered a vegetation ideal for a number of grazers, and harsh, bare scree a habitat for chamois and ibex (Sturdy et al. 1997). The study region of the Istrian Peninsula and island of Lošinj possess complex geologies, with mixed flysch and limestone bedrocks supportive of a mixed vegetative community attractive to many herbivore species.

Multispecies paleoecology

Mammals

Inferring the seasonal ecology and ethology of species in the past, even when those species persist into the present day, is problematic in the best of circumstances. For example, the season of birth estimates used in this chapter are based on the modern birth periods for each taxon discussed below. Yet, studies have shown that increases in the length of the growing season could cause some species to shift births earlier in the season (e.g. Ozgul et al. 2010). Since we have little in-depth knowledge of the length and duration of the growing seasons during the early Holocene, it is not possible to resolve the issue of the accuracy of birth season based on modern animals, yet they remain our best estimates.

Red deer (Cervus elaphus)

This species today has wide distribution across Europe, where they thrive in open woodland and woodland-edge habitats (Geist 1998). Their feeding ecology is particularly important to consider, as it has broad implications for movement and migration within regional landscapes, and subsequently deer availability and use by human populations. In general, red deer can be considered opportunistic feeders with a wide dietary range (Sturdy et al. 1997). Mating occurs during the annual rut, from mid-September to mid-November (Clutton-Brock et al. 1982; Fletcher 1974). Calving occurs approximately eight months later, in late May and early June, with one calf per hind. In non-migratory populations, individuals can use seasonal home ranges as small as 5–6 hectares (Yanushko 1957) and up to 200 ha (Clutton-Brock et al. 1982). In contrast, migratory populations can move between summer and winter ranges more than 5,000 hectares (50 km) apart (e.g. Knight 1970). Because there can be substantial variability in both the occurrence and distance of herd migration, hunter-gatherers whose specialized subsistence economy relied on this species would have had to take this factor into account.

Roe deer (Capreolus capreolus)

Roe deer can efficiently exploit a range of habitats and their edges. They are found throughout Europe at elevations ranging from sea level to 2,400 m. They can be found in deciduous, mixed, and coniferous woodland, as well as open moors and arable land, but prefer mosaic landscapes (Geist 1998). They are more selective in choosing their forage than red deer and are more often associated with wooded environments (Sturdy et al. 1997). The rut occurs in the summer, between late July and early August. Fawns are born in May or June. Roe deer can have mixed and variable migration strategies. In cold latitudes, this can be influenced by the amount of snowfall each year, and variability in climate may be responsible for variable spatial strategies within a population (Ramanzin et al. 2007). In densely populated areas, non-overlapping summer and winter ranges have been measured to be as little as 4 km (Wahlström & Liberg 1995); in a low-density area migration distances were approximately 12 km (Mysterud 1999). This included both a seasonal altitudinal shift as well as lateral change in home range size.

Caprids (chamois, Rupicapra rupicapra *and ibex,* Capra ibex*)*

Both chamois and ibex are native to mountainous regions in continental Europe that have been extensively modified by human use, so their modern behavioral ecology and habitat choice is not necessarily reflective of the past; in fact, many modern populations exist as the result of repopulation efforts in the early twentieth century (Phoca-Cosmetatou 2002). Modern chamois are known to occur in the Alps at altitudes ranging from 500 to 3,100 m above sea level and have home ranges up to 74 hectares in size. A subspecies, *balcanica*, is found in Croatia today (Shackleton 1997). In contrast, at the Late Pleistocene archaeological site of Bandaj in Herzegovina, chamois have been recorded at only 100 m (Miracle & Sturdy 1991). Ibex have been also traditionally been regarded as a high-altitude species, living at or above the treeline from 1,600 to 3,200 m above sea level in the Alps (Phoca-Cosmetatou 2002 and references therein). However, this is more likely due to the present-day distribution of steep, craggy rock faces at high altitudes rather than the altitudinal preference itself (Choisy 1994) and this is supported by archaeological evidence from the Italian Upper Palaeolithic as well as modern-day examples of populations of Spanish and Walia ibex occupying lower altitudes with suitable craggy habitat (Phoca-Cosmetatou 2002). Females and males usually gather together in October for the autumn rut. Kids are born at the end of May and early June. Chamois and ibex do not migrate laterally across large distances, but they are known to move through altitudes during the year (Shank 1985). One to two weeks following the birth of young in the late spring, mothers and kids move up to summer ranges that are slightly higher in altitude than winter and spring ranges to avoid heat and insects. In the autumn, groups return to lower elevations for the rut.

Boar (Sus scrofa)

Boar are remarkably adaptable omnivores, and so it is no surprise that they have a wide geographic distribution, from steppic environments in central Asia to broad-leafed forests in southern and central Europe (Grubb 2005). In Europe, they prefer forested areas and evergreen oak forests, though they will also inhabit more open shrubland habitats if they have nearby access to tree cover (Spitz & Janeau 1995). They inhabit elevations ranging from sea level up to 2,400 m and would likely have been available throughout the northeastern Adriatic region (Spitz & Janeau 1990). Populations of boar still inhabit Croatia today. There can be multiple birthing seasons depending on climate and resource availability. Although boar are known to move over considerable distances, they do not migrate per se. Estimates of home ranges have varied from 20 to 150 ha for a modern population in southern France to ranges of 500–1,000 ha for female groups and 1,000–2,000 ha for males (Oliver & Leus 2008 and references therein). These ranges may cover large distances but have not been documented as seasonal movements of populations.

Marine Molluscs

Shellfish have been shown to be an important dietary component in Mesolithic coastal environments throughout Europe (e.g., Milner et al. 2004, 2007). Deith (1983) asserts that in the Mesolithic, the time of collection and eating of shellfish are essentially synonymous and are therefore useful for reconstructing both paleodiet and season of site use. There is not much caloric yield per shell and they can in many cases be seen as supplemental. When shells occur in large middens and lensed concentrations, this may be indicative of a more integral role in the diet. Marine mollusc ecology is perhaps more "passive" than that of terrestrial mammals, and is considered here in the context of their desirability and availability for human collectors. It should be noted that most of these species reproduce by spawning in the late spring and early summer, and so are at their nutritional optimum during that time (Little & Kitching 1996). Below, I present a brief summary of the ecology of the taxa found at the case study sites discussed in this chapter.

Limpets (Patella spp.)

Limpets have a global distribution and are aquatic "grazers", eating microalgae and kelp (Little & Kitching 1996). Animals living on low-level bare rock generally have a lifespan of 4–5 years, whereas those living on high level, barnacle-covered rock have a life expectancy of up to 15 years or more and are thus larger and more desirable for human collectors. Their main predator defense is to clamp down. This means that when limpets are being gathered, they must be prised off quickly. The relative difficulty of collection in relation to other species might make them a second—or even third or fourth—option when food-getting, although their abundance during low tide may make them an easy target. Once the shell has been prised off the rock, they are easy to eat raw. They also detach from the shell easily within a few minutes of cooking.

Seasonal mobility and multispecies interactions

Mussels *(Mytilus spp.)*

Mussels are suspension feeders that dominate the low and mid-intertidal region, and are found worldwide. They form extensive beds, strips, and patches with other species. Individuals in the center of the bed grow at the slowest rates, but faster growing animals on the edge are subject to increased levels of predation (Little & Kitching 1996). These species have a large variety of predators, including dog whelks, crabs, starfish, birds, and humans. Mussels in sheltered waters tend to suffer greatest predation from crabs, whereas those on more exposed coasts are less preyed upon. This has implications for gathering, as one may need to forage in rougher areas to get the amount and size of mussels desired. Mussels are harvested regularly in the present day and are easier to collect than limpets, so could be considered a priority species for collecting when available.

Cockles *(Cerastoderma spp.)*

The common cockle also has wide geographic distribution and is found throughout the Atlantic Ocean and the Mediterranean, Adriatic, and Black Seas (Laurie 2008). They live in high densities in sheltered bays and estuaries, and colonies have the potential to migrate in response to climate change. They are burrowing filter feeders, but generally go no deeper than 5 cm in the intertidal zone. With some digging, they can be collected in large quantities soon after the tide has gone out. It is interesting to note that they occupy sandy or muddy beaches, whereas the other taxa found at the study sites are all rocky intertidal species.

Terrestrial molluscs

Edible land snail *(Helix spp.)*

Lubell (2004a, 2004b) provides in-depth overviews of land snail ecology as well as their archaeological significance throughout the circum-Mediterranean region in the late Pleistocene and early Holocene. The brief synopsis of their ecology provided here is based on his summaries in these publications. Land snails hibernate during cold periods and aestivate in hot and arid conditions. They lay large clutches of eggs in holes in the ground during periods of increased moisture and are most active in warm, moist conditions. In temperate regions, they generally hibernate in the late autumn and winter and are active during the spring and summer. Mesolithic human foragers would have required an understanding of seasonal availability of plants preferred by snails as well as their reproductive cycles. Abundances can be influenced by the number of daylight hours as well as temperature; the highest rates of reproduction occur in temperatures of 20–25°C. Modern ecological studies have also suggested that abundances are higher in ungrazed grassland and shrubland. Based on these characteristics, it is likely that snails were an abundant, easily collected resource during the spring and summer months in the early Holocene in the temperate conditions of the northeastern Adriatic.

Plants

A variety of plants and plant material would have made up some component of forager diet in the early Holocene. Grove (2009) asserts that the relocation of residential bases is primarily caused by the exhaustion of plants within a foraging radius based on multiple ethnographic examples (e.g., the Hadza, Vincent 1985). The lack of any plant remains at the case study sites despite careful recovery methods precludes their further discussion here. It is likely that fruits and berries, nuts and tubers could have been an important part of the diet, and were probably easily collected and transported.

Human foraging ecology

One of the most resilient aspects of human behavioral ecology models is the general assumption that hunter-gatherer behavior is closely related to the structure of food resources in a given environment. The use of optimal foraging theory (MacArthur & Pianka 1966; Smith & Winterhalder 1992; Winterhalder & Smith 1981) is prevalent as a framework for interpreting the prehistoric zooarchaeological record left by foragers, particularly the occurrence of broad-spectrum diets. However, in niche construction theory, organisms (including humans) shape their own environment through behavior that takes advantage of intergenerational knowledge to maximize towards a variety of goals (Zeder 2012). It allows for more complex relationships between humans, plants, animals, and their environments to be explored in the archaeological record and may be a more appropriate explanatory paradigm for a truly multispecies approach.

In the archaeological record, a "broad spectrum" diet is one in which a wide range of animal and plant species are consumed. The "broad spectrum revolution" (BSR) is archaeologically visible as both an increase in species diversity (Flannery 1969) as well as the exploitation of "low-ranked" prey (Stiner 2001). However, whether the occurrence of broad spectrum diets is environmentally mediated or caused by other factors such as demography is still a matter of some debate (Flannery 1969; Stiner 2001; Stutz et al. 2009). Flannery (1969) had originally argued (for Late Upper Paleolithic assemblages in the Near East) that it was caused by over-population and the movement of human groups into "marginal" environments, who were then forced to exploit an increasing range of small game. By his definition, ungulates could still dominate the food supply, but additional, predictable resources would supplement the diet. This was later exemplified at the cave of La Riera in the Cantabria region of Spain, where diversification of resources was attributed to population growth in the Late Pleistocene (Straus & Clark 1986). Flannery revisited the BSR in 1986 at the site of Guilá Naquitz as a strategy for dealing with the unpredictability of resources in the face of an unstable environment in the late Pleistocene when the ability to relocate was reduced, primarily due to social factors. Redding (1988) agreed with the notion of the BSR as linked to risk reduction and increasing resource predictability in an unpredictable environment, but still saw the driving force as disequilibrium between carrying capacity and population size.

The BSR is often cited as prime example of optimal foraging theory in application, particularly in explaining diet breadth models (e.g. Kennett 2005; Marin-Arroyo 2009) and most notably by Stiner (2001) and Stiner and Munro (2002), who emphasize the importance of handling costs in prey ranking. Stiner and colleagues offer Mesolithic Greece as an example for this application, citing population packing caused by sea-level rise as a factor in reduced mobility, driving the adoption of the use of less efficient resources at Franchthi and the other Peloponnesian site of Klissoura I (Starkovich 2009; Starkovich & Stiner 2010; Stiner & Munro 2011).

I argue that while broad spectrum adaptations visible in the archaeological record can be indicative of more intensive resource use in some cases, these additional resources are not necessarily less efficient if the mobility strategy has been modified to accommodate for exploiting resources at optimal seasons throughout the year, accompanied by other ways of mediating

Seasonal mobility and multispecies interactions

efficiency such as technology and gender or age-based roles. Essentially, a broad spectrum diet may suggest more efficient use of a landscape by humans at different parts of the year, which could be in response to shifts in resource predictability. In other words, efficiency can be mediated by adjustments in seasonal movements; coastal resources can be exploited when they are at a nutritional peak in early summer, potentially by children, and hare can be trapped by snares in large numbers during the winter, when their coats are thicker and can add to their net return. Thus, prey species ecology and predictability is an integral part of human decision-making regarding where to move and what to eat, and these mobility decisions may be considered a type of niche construction.

Human decisions about mobility depend on knowledge about resource accessibility and seasonal monitoring of those resources within a given site catchment area. Intertwined with decisions about mobility are decisions about foraging, which depend not only on energy and nutrition but also information; as Jochim (1998) defines it, as awareness of where, when, and how to obtain a given resource, which can be considered synonymous with the knowledge of the seasonal resource accessibility and importantly, predictability (*sensu* Kelly 1983, 1992). From this perspective, seasonal planning allows for increased foraging efficiency in the long term. On the other hand, foraging decisions made once a given mobility strategy is employed may still be optimized for efficiency, so that prey are still ranked within a subsistence economy. Decisions regarding mobility are then resource-predictability determined, and decisions about subsistence are resource-efficiency determined. For example, the exploitation of red deer is energetically expensive, but provides a good return. To some extent, if this species was moving on a seasonal basis, they were also predictably available in certain locations on a seasonal basis—a reliable resource that was abundant at certain times of the year. Thus we can assume that these animals would have been a likely prey choice for Late Pleistocene hunter-gatherers in the study region, and their behavior framed human mobility decisions and niche construction, not the other way around. With the loss of the Great Adriatic Plain and a change in the mosaic of local habitats in the early Holocene, the seasonal movements of herds may have become less reliable, necessitating adjustments in not only energy-motivated subsistence patterns, but also knowledge-determined patterns of mobility.

Following this logic, the mobility of certain prey species may have influenced or even dictated human mobility. We might expect that a specialized faunal assemblage targeting a migratory species suggests site use at a certain time of year to primarily hunt the animal in the season it is most abundant and accessible in that environment. This single-season site use is expected to occur in a predictable but not necessarily productive environment (i.e. the climate conditions of the terminal Pleistocene may not have been most productive, but the cessation of sea-level rise made for a stable landscape). A more diverse faunal assemblage, in contrast, may suggest multiple-season site use as groups return periodically or stay longer to exploit certain taxa at different times of year. Multi-season site use is expected to occur in a somewhat unpredictable but productive environment (i.e. the early Holocene may have offered amiable climate conditions punctuated by short-term cold oscillations, and sea-level rise caused rapid localized habitat change, reducing predictability). In addition, there would likely be an increase of marine fauna, particularly molluscs, at sites closer to the coastline in the Holocene assemblages; not due to the "resource stress" that would be inferred following optimal foraging theory, but instead reflecting the incursion of the Adriatic Sea and the availability of a new resource. These conjectures can be further substantiated in the archaeological record using evidence of the season of death for terrestrial species, and season of collection of marine molluscs.

Suzanne E. Pilaar Birch

Archaeological context

The archaeology of cave sites in the northeastern Adriatic has been well documented by long-term field projects beginning in the mid-1990s (Forenbaher & Miracle 2005; Miracle & Forenbaher 2000). The cave sites of Vela Špilja on the island of Lošinj and Nugljanska and Pupićina on the Istrian Peninsula in Croatia provide evidence for long sequences of use (Table 18.1), dating to the Late Upper Paleolithic, Mesolithic, Neolithic and extending into modern day (Komšo 2006, Miracle 2001).

Table 18.1 Radiocarbon dates for the case study sites

Cultural period	Climate period	Site	^{14}C BP	cal BP (1σ)	Sample number	Reference
Neolithic	Atlantic	VSL	6,175±37	6,955–7,170	OxA–26174	Pilaar Birch et al. 2016
Neolithic	Atlantic	VSL	7,134±37	7,930–8,020	OxA–18118	Forenbaher et al. 2013
Mesolithic	Atlantic	VSL	6,240±37	7,150–7,259	OxA–26173	Pilaar Birch et al. 2016
Mesolithic	Atlantic	VSL	6,224±36	7,155–7,235	OxA–32823	Pilaar Birch et al. 2016
Mesolithic	Boreal	VSL	9,494±39	10,650–10,830	OxA–26060	Forenbaher et al. 2013
Mesolithic	Preboreal	VSL	9,805±50	11,160–11,315	OxA–18041	Forenbaher et al. 2013
Mesolithic	Boreal	NUG	8,170±50	8,980–9,320	BETA–127704	Miracle & Forenbaher 2000
Mesolithic	Atlantic/Boreal	NUG	7,992±39	8,716–9,007	OxA–26347	Pilaar Birch & Miracle 2015
Mesolithic	Atlantic/Boreal	NUG	8,032±38	8,770–9,020	OxA–26060	Pilaar Birch & Miracle 2015
Mesolithic	Boreal	NUG	8,248±39	9,345–9,400	OxA–26059	Pilaar Birch & Miracle 2015
Paleolithic	Younger Dryas/ Bølling-Allerød	NUG	11,160±50	12,845–13225	OxA–X–2462–26	Pilaar Birch & Miracle 2015
Paleolithic	Bølling-Allerød	NUG	11,520±90	13,200–13,600	BETA–127705	Miracle & Forenbaher 2000
Mesolithic	Boreal	PUP	8,770±310	9,090–10,665	Z–2578	Miracle 2001
Mesolithic	Boreal	PUP	9,200±170	9,905–10,820	Z–2634	Miracle 2001
Mesolithic	Preboreal	PUP	10,000±170	11,100–12,155	Z–2635	Miracle 2001
Mesolithic	Preboreal	PUP	9,590±180	10,385–11,400	Z–2572	Miracle 2001
Mesolithic	Preboreal	PUP	9,840±60	11,150–11,400	BETA–129332	Miracle 2001
Mesolithic	Younger Dryas/ Preboreal	PUP	10,000±270	10,760–12,426	Z–2576	Miracle 2001
Paleolithic	Younger Dryas/ Preboreal	PUP	10,020±180	11,135–12,223	Z–2631	Miracle 2001
Paleolithic	Younger Dryas	PUP	10,150±60	11,600–12,050	BETA–131626	Miracle 2001
Paleolithic	Younger Dryas	PUP	10,610±200	11,953–12,960	Z–2574	Miracle 2001

Establishing the taxa present in the faunal assemblage and recording modification of specimens allows for a consideration of the role of different species in the human diet, as well as their broader ecology. It is an essential first step in considering the role of these species in shaping the seasonal round. Estimating ages at death using established protocols provides insight into seasonality of site use. The use of stable isotope analysis to investigate animal migration has become more commonplace in recent years (Balasse et al. 2002; Britton et al. 2009, 2011; Mashkour et al. 2005; Pilaar Birch et al. 2016; Pellegrini et al. 2008) and can be applied towards understanding the mobility patterns of prey species. Sampling marine shells to determine season of collection is also well established, and methods are increasingly becoming more sophisticated and of a higher resolution (e.g., Burchell et al. 2012a, 2012b; Deith 1983; Mannino et al. 2003, 2007; Milner 2002). These data must be considered within their environmental and archaeological contexts in order to interpret past animal and human behavior. Below, I add to the existing body of zooarchaeological data on these sites (Pilaar Birch & Miracle 2015; Pilaar Birch & Miracle 2017; Pilaar Birch 2017; Miracle 1997, 2001, 2002) by presenting season of death data from terrestrial fauna and summarizing season of collection data from marine molluscs.

Vela Špilja Lošinj

The island of Lošinj formed in the early Holocene. The cave of Vela Špilja (VSL) sits at 268 m on the peak of Televrin, an ideal outpost for surveying what was first surrounding grassland and later, estuary and then open water as the coast transformed in the early Holocene.

In the Late Pleistocene and Late Upper Paleolithic, over half (about 60%) of the assemblage was comprised of red deer, followed by chamois and ibex and few specimens of hare, wild boar, equids, and fox (Pilaar 2009; Pilaar Birch & Miracle 2017). In the early Holocene, during the Mesolithic, chamois and ibex, which would have been especially well adapted to the rocky terrain surrounding the cave, make up about a third of the assemblage. The remaining two-thirds is comprised, in order of abundance, by hare, red deer, wild boar, roe deer, fox, and a few specimens of hedgehog (Pilaar Birch & Miracle 2017). In stark contrast to the Mesolithic, over 90% of remains are of domestic sheep and goat throughout the Neolithic (Pilaar Birch 2017).

The Mesolithic composition of fauna reflects a "broad spectrum" diet. This is contrary to the biased pattern of specialization that might be expected based on the small overall sample size. The potential movement of red deer further inland as the sea level rose may have affected both prey availability and choice, as additional smaller resources were exploited. As the sea level rose and the site became isolated from the mainland, the island may have become less suitable for red deer, leading to an increase in human predation on chamois and ibex, accompanied by diversification that would have included small game as well as marine and terrestrial molluscs.

As might be expected through the lens of optimal foraging theory, there is an increase in species richness and the inclusion of "low-ranked" prey like hare in the Mesolithic diet; however, there is less support for intensification in terms of increased processing of carcasses (Pilaar Birch & Miracle 2017) that might suggest dietary stress (cf. Miracle 1995). Instead, it is argued that changes in annual and seasonal predictability of resource availability probably necessitated a change in dietary practices in tandem with adjustments in seasonal mobility patterns.

Marine molluscs appeared for the first time in the Mesolithic horizon and included limpets (*Patella* spp.), mussels (*Mytilus galloprovincialis*), and topshells (*Gibbula* and *Phorcus* spp.).

There were also isolated occurrences of *Murex*, *Columbella*, *Ostrea* and *Cerastoderma*. Edible land snails (*Helix*) are also found in great abundance in the Mesolithic. Relative proportions of bone (by weight) are lowest during the Mesolithic (21%) when land snails are most abundant (75%) and marine shells appear (4%). Marine shell follows a pattern of increasing density through time. When only molluscs are compared, terrestrial snails comprise the majority of the assemblage in the Mesolithic, while marine molluscs are dominant in the Neolithic.

What is most interesting in the Mesolithic at VSL is how the overall taxonomic composition from different types of resources (i.e. terrestrial mammals and land snails) shifts rather than there being only an increase in taxonomic richness of terrestrial mammals. When proportions of terrestrial mammal bone, land snail, and marine shell are considered by weight and horizon at VSL, land snail and marine shell are important contributors to the overall assemblage. The spike in land snail abundances in the Mesolithic in tandem with a rise in marine resources and small game suggests snails were a foodstuff rather than a natural denizen of the cave at this time. It is likely that increases in proportions of land snails are associated with increased dietary breadth during the Mesolithic, whereas the gradual increase in marine mollusc proportions are more likely associated with increased access to coastal resources through time, as they reach their maximum proportions in the Neolithic after Lošinj had become an island.

Nugljanska

Nugljanska sits at a higher elevation than VSL and Pupićina, about 550 m above sea level (Miracle & Forenbaher 2000). Its earliest archaeological contexts date to the late glacial, suggesting early re-occupation of the uplands at this time (Komšo & Pellegatti 2007). The archaeology of the cave suggests more opportunistic or occasional use during the late Pleistocene and an increase in intensity of use, perhaps even becoming a base camp, in the Mesolithic (Komšo 2006; Miracle 2007; Pilaar Birch & Miracle 2015). Like VSL, red deer are the most abundant in the Pleistocene/Late Upper Paleolithic, just over half of the entire assemblage (60%). Red deer decrease in abundance in the early Holocene, where they represent about a third of the remains and wild boar are instead the dominant taxon (Pilaar Birch & Miracle 2015). Small numbers of other prey species like roe deer, aurochs, chamois, and hare are also present in both the late Pleistocene and the early Holocene, along with individual specimens of carnivores like bear, lynx, fox, badgers, and martens. The site is not close to the coast, and marine shell is rare throughout the Holocene sequence. In the earliest Mesolithic, land snails are more abundant than marine molluscs, which include the gastropod *Columbella rustica* and bivalves *Cerastoderma edule* and *Mytilus galloprovincialis* (Pilaar Birch & Miracle 2017).

Pupićina

The archaeology of Pupićina Cave has been extensively published (Miracle 1997, 2001; Miracle & Forenbaher 2000, 2006). The cave is located in the canyon of Vela Draga at an elevation of 220 m, about 10 km from the coast (Miracle 1997). Diversification occurred throughout the Mesolithic and there is also evidence for episodic feasting (Miracle 2001). In contrast to the relatively higher proportions of red deer in the late Pleistocene/Late Upper Paleolithic at VSL and Nugljanska, boar and roe deer are just as numerous at Pupićina during this time. These taxa continue to occur in the early Holocene/Mesolithic, with an increase in relative abundances of roe deer and boar as compared to red deer. Small game such as hare

Seasonal mobility and multispecies interactions

and badger also increase, and are accompanied by marine and terrestrial molluscs (Miracle 2002). Miracle (1997) notes the importance of considering whether the appearance of a "broad spectrum" diet in the Mesolithic is due to the inclusion of additional food resources in the diet or whether small game may appear for other reasons. Miracle (1997) notes that cut marks have been observed on both hare and badger, suggesting their use by humans, whether for meat or fur or both.

The use of both terrestrial and marine molluscs increased throughout time at Pupićina. Miracle (2001) noted that frequencies of *Mytilus* remained relatively stable throughout the Mesolithic, with a surge in abundances towards the end of the sequence. As at VSL and Nugljanska, there are no large middens and remains are found scattered throughout the contexts. Terrestrial mammals were always the most important resources at Pupićina and the rarity of marine molluscs and the abundance of terrestrial snails suggest that marine food items were never a main resource in the diet during any period at the site. The addition of marine foods was more likely supplementary, but Miracle warns against their dismissal as a "famine food" (2001). Instead, they may represent "special foods" or a resource that was consumed soon after people made the trip from the coast to Pupićina and brought the molluscs with them. Based on butchery patterns and other contextual information, Miracle suggests that some of the Mesolithic food refuse at Pupićina is the result of periodic feasting, which supports its designation as a central place in the landscape at which people may have aggregated in more than one season.

Seasonality and terrestrial fauna

Determining the age at death of an animal is not always possible, but there are several ways of estimating it using known lengths of time of tooth eruption and wear, and long bone fusion (cf. Ruscillo 2006; Wilson et al. 1982; Klein et al. 1983; Davis 2000; Zeder 2006; Miracle & O'Brien 1998). This allows for season of death to be extrapolated if a birth season can be assumed. It is important to stress that these can only be estimates within a range of time, but these ranges can sometimes be determined at a useful resolution for investigating season of occupation.

Vela Špilja Lošinj

Overall sample sizes at VSL were small, so reconstructing seasonality was challenging. Only caprids and red deer were able to be aged, and age at death could not be determined within a useful scale of months for any specimen. However, it was possible to reconstruct age curves based on broad determinations of long bone fusion. As with all seasonality analyses, this cannot rule out seasons of occupation, but it can be useful for determining spring use (cf. Miracle & O'Brien 1998). In the late Pleistocene and Late Upper Paleolithic, there were 13 caprid specimens that could be assigned to an age class: one was identified as an infant, seven as juvenile, and five as adults. There were 19 cervids assigned to age class: one infant, twelve juveniles, and six adults. These patterns may have more to do with procurement strategies during this time, but may also suggest that the site was used to target young animals in the autumn. The rare occurrence of infant remains may indicate a spring visit but may just as well be incidental. Out of eight ageable remains identified to chamois or ibex in the early Holocene Mesolithic, three were identified

as "foetal" or "infant" based on the condition of the bone. Two elements were classified as "juvenile", and three recorded as "adult". The presence of very young animals
suggests potential spring use. Juveniles and adults can be obtained in any season, so their
relative abundances are less useful for seasonality determinations. Based on the archaeological evidence, it appears use of VSL was sporadic and ephemeral during all time periods. Nevertheless, we can draw some limited conclusions from the age representations of
the fauna. Juvenile animals of red deer as well as caprids could suggest a cull during the
autumn, when young animals from the previous birth season were abundant (cf. Pilaar Birch
& Miracle 2017). Killing off young animals just before the rut may have implications for the
mating behavior of females, who are more likely to reproduce without dependent offspring.
In contrast, the foetal and infant remains found in the Mesolithic horizon, along with adults,
may suggest the taking of young animals or pregnant females during the spring. Based on the
small sample size and broad age classes, this is highly speculative. Spring use is also inferred
during the Neolithic, when the cave was used for herding activities (Pilaar Birch 2017).

Nugljanska

The only terrestrial mammal remains suitable for estimating age at death within a useful time
resolution for estimating season of procurement at Nugljanska were from ageable dentitions
of red deer and wild boar. Age at death was estimated based primarily on tooth eruption for
red deer (Brown & Chapman 1991) and wear for wild boar (Grant 1982; see also Wright et
al. 2014). The birthing season for red deer lasts from late May into early June, so date of birth
was estimated to be 1 June for this taxon. One red deer hemi-mandible and a maxilla were
determined to originate from two different individuals in the early Mesolithic and were estimated to be 13–19 months old at death. This suggested a summer or autumn kill, since rates
of eruption for the upper jaw are assumed to be relatively synchronous with the lower jaw. In
addition, one maxilla from the late Mesolithic was also aged 13–19 months, indicating a summer–autumn death. Sample size was slightly larger for boar. The date of birth is estimated at 1
April based on Miracle's (1997) estimate for boar at Pupićina. However, this taxon may have
multiple birth seasons throughout the year. Age at death of four boar from the early Mesolithic
could be determined. Three of the specimens appeared to be yearlings (12–14 months) and also
suggest a spring death. One individual was aged to 21–33 months based on a recently erupted,
unworn third molar, so it is speculative to estimate a season of death for this individual. In the
late Mesolithic, one specimen of boar was estimated to have been 6–8 months old, indicating
an autumn death.

Based on the ageable tooth rows of red deer and boar, there is evidence for multiple seasons
of use at Nugljanska. In the earliest Holocene and early Mesolithic, specimens identified to boar
indicate spring use. These estimations are based on tooth rows determined to be from three
separate individuals. The two red deer samples fall from mid-summer to autumn, suggesting use
of these taxa in two different seasons or an extended period of availability over a few months.
In the late Mesolithic, one individual of each taxon overlaps in the autumn, although summer
use is possible. Based only on the limited remains of terrestrial fauna, we can deduce that the
site was potentially used in the spring, summer, and autumn during the Mesolithic. That there
are no remains which fall into winter is interesting, because the elevation of this site and slightly
exposed aspect (as compared to Pupićina, for example) may have made it an undesirable choice
for winter use despite its south-west orientation.

Seasonal mobility and multispecies interactions

Pupićina

The reconstruction of seasonal procurement at Pupićina using tooth eruption and wear to estimate age at death summarized below is derived exclusively from Miracle (1997). An autumn death was estimated for a single red deer mandible in the early Mesolithic horizons. Four roe deer mandibles also suggested procurement in the autumn during the Mesolithic. Assuming one birth season per year for boar, 25 out of 27 aged mandibles indicated late summer-early winter deaths. Twenty-two of these dated to the Mesolithic. Mesolithic finds are only attributed to the autumn based on tooth eruption, but this does not rule out use in other seasons.

Using data provided to me by P. Miracle (pers. comm.), I collated existing age at death determinations made for Pupićina based ojn long bone fusion of red and roe deer. Assuming a birth date for both taxa of 1 June, an interesting pattern of seasonal procurement emerges. Roe deer are killed in late autumn and winter ($n = 14$). Red deer overlap with this period, but also extend to include summer and early autumn use ($n = 19$). These estimations could be combined to provide a narrow period of use when most of the evidence overlaps, November–January, but also provide evidence for distinctly separate summer use in June–August and the potential availability of red deer in multiple seasons.

Miracle (1997) had concluded that Pupićina appeared to be used in the autumn during the Mesolithic and that people were targeting woodland and wood-edge habitats in the canyon below and plateau above the site. He then questioned the seasonal procurement of terrestrial and marine molluscs and reasoned that while they could also have been obtained in the same season as ungulates, land snails can only be collected when they are active, which requires warm and moist conditions. Lubell et al. (1976) had shown for species of *Helix* in the Mediterranean that this period of activity encompasses spring and autumn (see also Lubell 2004a, 2004b). Furthermore, Miracle (1997) asserted that marine molluscs are at their nutritional peak in the summer months. Taken together, these lines of data potentially suggest a long duration of use through the summer and autumn. Using age at death estimates based on long bone fusion, a similar pattern of use emerged for red and roe deer. Evidence for season of use falls primarily in the late autumn and winter, with as many as eight red deer specimens indicating early to mid-summer use. It is interesting to note that there is no evidence for spring use based on any of the available data. The springtime flooding of the canyon may have made Pupićina an unreliable place to stay during that time of the year, while its sheltered location and aspect may have been especially desirable during the autumn and winter.

Seasonality of marine mollusc collection

Marine molluscs occurred in small numbers at Nugljanska during the Mesolithic, increased in relative abundance during the Mesolithic at VSL, and were also found in Mesolithic horizons at Pupićina. Evidence for the mass consumption of marine molluscs in the form of shell middens is absent. Shellfish probably formed a supplementary part of the diet as they became increasingly accessible due to the encroaching shoreline, and their season of collection can be inferred from the isotopic sampling of shell edges. Because the timing of shell collection and consumption are likely to be synchronous, taking place within a few days of each other, it is possible to infer season of site use from this data if it is considered in context with other archaeological evidence.

Suzanne E. Pilaar Birch

Table 18.2 Season of collection of molluscs from the case study sites

Sample	Horizon/level	Taxon	Season of collection	Confidence	Alternate season of collection
NUGS 1	Level 3	*Cerastoderma*	Summer	High	
NUGS 2	Level 3	*Cerastoderma*	Summer	High	
NUGS 3	Level 3	*Cerastoderma*	Autumn	Medium	Winter
NUGS 4	Level 3	*Cerastoderma*	Summer	Medium	Autumn
VSL 12	Horizon 4 Level 60	*Mytilus*	Winter	Medium	Early Spring
VSL 13	Horizon 4 Level 60	*Mytilus*	Winter	Medium	Early Spring
VSL 14	Horizon 3 Level 50	*Patella*	Autumn	High	
VSL 15	Horizon 3 Level 50	*Patella*	Autumn	Medium	Winter
VSL 18	Horizon 3 Level 50	*Patella*	Autumn	Medium	
PUPS 4	Horizon M1	*Mytilus*	Summer	High	
PUPS 9	Horizon M1	*Mytilus*	Summer	High	
PUPS 10	Horizon M1	*Mytilus*	Winter	High	
PUPS 2	Horizon M2	*Mytilus*	Winter	High	
PUPS 6	Horizon M2	*Mytilus*	Summer	High	
PUPS 8	Horizon M2	*Mytilus*	Spring	High	

The seasonality determinations presented in Table 18.2 are derived from $\delta^{18}O$ and $\delta^{13}C$ stable isotope results from mussels, *Mytilus galloprovincialis*; limpets, *Patella rustica* L.; and cockles, *Cerastoderma edule* (Pilaar Birch 2012).

As an island site, VSL had the highest overall proportion of shell remains. The marine mollusc assemblage at VSL was dominated by limpets, *Patella* and mussels, *Mytilus*, so specimens from both of these taxa were selected for sampling. Individuals of the topsnails *Gibbula* and *Phorcus* were also found, but were not analyzed isotopically. Of the case study sites, Nugljanska is located furthest from the coast and its assemblage yielded the least marine mollusc remains. The cockle, *Cerastoderma edule* was most abundant and chosen for isotopic sampling. Upon further consideration of the inland location of the site, the intact condition of the shells, and their small number, it is not possible to confirm whether they were brought to the site for consumption or another purpose. However, the shells did not show any evidence of human modification. It is likely that if they were collected dead, for a purpose other than consumption, they may have exhibited some form of alteration, such as drilling for jewelry or edge-wear from use. Since cockles open upon cooking and the meat is easily extracted, it is plausible that the animals were consumed and the shells discarded without damage. As noted above, it is interesting to note the differential ecology of *Cerastoderma* found at Nugljanska from the *Mytilus* and *Patella* found at VSL and Pupićina. Cockles burrow in sandy beaches or mudflats and prefer estuarine conditions with low salinity. This is in contrast to the rocky intertidal habitat that makes up the majority of the Istrian coast today, which is preferred by *Mytilus* and *Patella*. There are some sand beaches on the western coast of Istria, but this coast would not have come into existence until the sea had reached near-present levels after 8,000 years ago. This suggests that people at Nugljanska had collected cockles on the western coast or that some sand beaches and similar habitats were present along the southern coast; alternatively, the empty shells could have been traded or brought from somewhere further south. Pupićina also had a variety of marine mollusc remains, but only *Mytilus* shells were suitably preserved for incremental isotopic sampling.

Seasonal mobility and multispecies interactions

Table 18.3 Combined estimations of season of procurement for terrestrial faunal remains and marine molluscs during the Mesolithic

Site	Marine molluscs	Terrestrial mammals
VSL	Winter–Spring($n = 2$)	Spring (caprids, $n = 3$)★
	Autumn only ($n = 2$)	Autumn (caprids, $n = 3$)★
	Autumn–Winter ($n = 1$)	
Nugljanska	Summer only ($n = 3$)	Summer–Autumn (red deer, $n = 3$)
	Summer–Autumn ($n = 1$)	
	Autumn–Winter ($n = 1$)	
Pupićina	Winter ($n = 2$)	Summer only (red deer, $n = 8$)
	Spring ($n = 1$)	Summer–Autumn (red deer, $n = 6$)
	Summer ($n = 3$)	Autumn–Winter (red and roe deer, $n = 15$)
		Winter only (roe deer, $n = 6$)

Note: Season of site use data from terrestrial mammal data is particularly speculative for VSL and estimates derived from age curves are starred (★).

Season of site use

Here, I combine data derived from terrestrial fauna with season of collection data from marine shells in order to present a unified discussion of season of site use based on multiple proxies (Table 18.3).

Vela Špilja Lošinj

Based on the combined terrestrial fauna and marine mollusc data for the Mesolithic, VSL has evidence for spring, autumn, and potentially winter use. It should be restated here that the sample size for terrestrial mammal remains is very limited. This could be due to the extent of excavation at this site, but could also reflect a real pattern of repeated, ephemeral visits in different seasons. Despite the small dataset, there is evidence for procurement in more than one season in the Mesolithic.

Nugljanska

During the Mesolithic, combined evidence from marine molluscs and terrestrial fauna at Nugljanska supports use in summer and autumn. This evidence derives primarily from both the early (Level 5) and later (Level 3) Mesolithic, and there is evidence for obtainment of different resources in more than one season within each level. In the later Mesolithic Level 3, there is evidence for both summer and autumn collection of cockles, perhaps brought along from the coast when groups arrived at the site, rather than representing the results of a logistical foray. There was a peak in the abundance of land snails, which are most likely to be collected during warm, moist conditions through the late spring and early autumn, in early Mesolithic Level 5. We can conclude that the site may have been used in multiple seasons during the Mesolithic, although it cannot be discounted that these episodes may have occurred far apart in time. Nevertheless, multiple seasons of procurement can be suggested based on the seasonality of marine and terrestrial molluscs and terrestrial mammal remains.

Suzanne E. Pilaar Birch

Pupićina

Based on marine molluscs, long bone fusion, and dental eruption, there is a sizeable amount of evidence for use in different seasons during the Mesolithic, and more importantly, evidence for use in multiple seasons within individual horizons from the same type of proxy. For example, long bone fusion data from Horizon M3 suggest late summer–early autumn procurement of red deer and late autumn–early winter procurement of roe deer, while Horizon M2 suggests summer, autumn, and winter collection of marine molluscs.

Discussion: the seasonal round

Vela Špilja Lošinj

There is a broad spectrum diet in the Mesolithic at VSL, but evidence for seasonal use from the long bone fusion data is limited. Land snails are found in abundance and would likely have been collected in spring or summer. There is evidence for autumn use based on marine molluscs. Taken together, there does appear to be some limited support for use in multiple seasons during the Mesolithic based on the diversity of the faunal assemblage and presence of non-migratory species, and some evidence for more than one season of procurement of resources. That being said, use in the Mesolithic was most likely sporadic, and though there are signs it occurred in different seasons, these may have been years apart.

Nugljanska

The area around Nugljanska may have become more forested in the early Holocene. This is supported by the increase in boar in the Mesolithic assemblage, which prefer woodland habitat; and by regional paleoenvironmental proxies. Boar, which are assumed to have large home ranges but do not migrate seasonally, became the main targeted species in the assemblage in the Holocene. Red deer were still important. A significant increase in the range of variation of $\delta^{18}O$ values in red deer teeth suggests they may have been moving within a more restricted zone as the Great Adriatic Plain became inundated (Pilaar Birch et al. 2016). This change in behavior may have led to decreased predictability of migratory routes. The diet also includes non-migratory terrestrial prey species such as roe deer. The data presented in this chapter and discussed above support multiple seasons of procurement. This suggests the site may have been used in different seasons to target different prey. Taken together, the diverse taxonomic composition of the faunal assemblage, targeting of non-migratory taxa, and multiple seasons of procurement of marine and terrestrial resources suggest site use in multiple seasons in the Mesolithic.

Pupićina

Pupićina provided the most archaeological evidence for multiple season use during the Mesolithic based on combined mollusc and faunal remains. This is amenable to the existing interpretation of Pupićina as a central place. It would have been returned to throughout the year, perhaps with longer stays. In general, the Mesolithic terrestrial mammal assemblage is diverse throughout, with relative proportions of small game and small carnivores such as fox increasing steadily through time, leading to a more species-rich assemblage. In addition, the use of land snails and small proportions of marine molluscs increase, so that diversification appears to be occurring throughout the Mesolithic period. While there may be subtle variations between faunal assemblage composition (including marine and terrestrial molluscs) and season of death proxies for seasonal site use between horizons, taken together there is strong evidence for all three parameters of multiple season site use in both the early and later Mesolithic.

Conclusion

Overall, there is evidence for multi-season site use at the case study sites during the Mesolithic. The extent to which this is a shift from the Late Upper Paleolithic is debatable, given the limited evidence for inferring seasonality at that time, but there does seem to be a change in season of use (based wholly on terrestrial mammal remains) from spring to summer, autumn, and winter at Pupićina; the addition of spring to autumn at VSL; and spring, summer, and autumn use at Nugljanska. The addition of seasonal data from marine molluscs adds depth to the understanding of the nature of seasonal site use in this region during the Mesolithic. This is supported by the faunal data from terrestrial mammals and the variable mobility of prey species such as red deer and chamois/ibex (cf. Pilaar Birch 2017; Pilaar Birch & Miracle 2015; Pilaar Birch & Miracle 2017; Pilaar Birch et al. 2016).

The Mesolithic is often characterized as a period where coastal elements are incorporated into a broad spectrum diet, based on both zooarchaeological and stable isotope evidence throughout Europe (e.g., Bailey & Spikins 2008; Richards & Hedges 1999). This does not necessarily appear to be the case in Istria and the eastern Adriatic more broadly (e.g., Lightfoot et al. 2011), and it may be that these resources were supplementary or exploited at now-inundated open air sites closer to the coasts in certain seasons. Radiocarbon dates suggest dietary diversification and multi-season site use occurred during climatically favorable and resource-rich, albeit potentially unpredictable, periods in the early Holocene, demonstrating that broad-spectrum changes in diet are not necessarily caused by "resource stress" but rather, that multiple season site use may have evolved to more effectively exploit game during seasons when they were abundant and accessible, as a form of multispecies niche construction.

References

Andrić, M., B. Kroflič, M.J. Toman, N. Ogrinc, T. Dolenec, M. Dobnikar & B. Čermelj. 2008. Late quaternary vegetation and hydrological change at Ljubljansko barje (Slovenia). *Palaeogeography, Palaeoclimatology, Palaeoecology* 270: 150–165.

Bailey, G. & P. Spikins (ed.). 2008. *Mesolithic Europe*. Cambridge: Cambridge University Press.

Balasse, M., S.H. Ambrose, A.B. Smith & T.D. Price. 2002. The seasonal mobility model for prehistoric herders in the south-western Cape of South Africa assessed by isotopic analysis of sheep tooth enamel. *Journal of Archaeological Science* 29: 917–932.

Balbo, A.L., M. Andrič, J. Rubinič, A. Moscariello & P.T. Miracle. 2006. Palaeo-environmental and archaeological implications of a sediment core from Polje Čepic, Istria, Croatia. *Geologia Croatica* 59: 107–122.

Bass, B. 2008. Early Neolithic communities in southern Dalmatia: farming seafarers or seafaring farmers? *European Journal of Archaeology* 11: 245–265. doi:10.1177/1461957109106376.

Britton, K., V. Grimes, J. Dau & M.P. Richards. 2009. Reconstructing faunal migrations using intra-tooth sampling and strontium and oxygen isotope analyses: a case study of modern caribou (*Rangifer tarandus granti*). *Journal of Archaeological Science* 36: 1163–1172.

Britton, K., V. Grimes, L. Niven, T.E. Steele, S. McPherron, M. Soressi, T.E. Kelly, J. Jaubert, J.-J. Hublin & M.P. Richards. 2011. Strontium isotope evidence for migration in late Pleistocene *Rangifer*.

implications for Neanderthal hunting strategies at the Middle Palaeolithic site of Jonzac, France. *Journal of Human Evolution* 61: 176–185.

Brown, W.A.B. & N. Chapman. 1991. Age assessment of red deer (*Cervus elaphus*): from a scoring scheme based on radiographs of developing permanent molariform teeth. *Journal of Zoology* 225: 85–97.

Burchell, M., A. Cannon, N. Hallmann, H.P. Schwarcz & B.R. Schöne. 2012a. Intersite variability in the season of shellfish collection on the central coast of British Columbia. *Journal of Archaeological Science.* doi:10.1016/j.jas.2012.07.002.

Burchell, M., A. Cannon, N. Hallmann, H.P. Schwarcz & B.R. Schöne. 2012b. Refining estimates for the season of shellfish collection on the Pacific Northwest Coast: applying high-resolution oxygen isotope analysis and sclerochronology. *Archaeometry.* doi:10.1111/j.1475-4754.2012.00684.

Choisy, J.P. 1994. Reintroduction de bouquetins—Capra sp.: condition de reussite, choix des massifs, enseignements: l'exemple du Vercors. *Ibex Journal of Mountain Ecology* Speciale Gruppo Stambecco Europa I: 15–33.

Clutton-Brock, T.H., F.E. Guinness & S.D. Albon. 1982. *Red deer: Behaviour and ecology of two sexes.* Chicago, IL: University of Chicago Press.

Colantoni, P., P. Gallignani & R. Lenax. 1979. Late Pleistocene and Holocene evolution of the North Adriatic continental shelf (Italy). *Marine Geology* 33: M41–M50.

Davis, S.J.M. 2000. The effect of castration and age on the development of the Shetland sheep skeleton and a metric comparison between bones of males, females and castrates. *Journal of Archaeological Science* 27: 373–390.

Deith, M.R. 1983. Molluscan calendars: the use of growth-line analysis to establish seasonality of shellfish collection at the Mesolithic site of Morton, Fife. *Journal of Archaeological Science* 10: 423–440.

Favaretto, S., A. Asioli, A. Miola & A. Piva. 2008. Preboreal climatic oscillations recorded by pollen and foraminifera in the southern Adriatic Sea. *Quaternary International* 190: 89–102.

Flannery, K. 1969. Origins and ecological effects of early domestication in Iran and the Near East, in P.J. Ucko & G.W. Dimbleby (eds.), *The domestication and exploitation of plants and animals.* Chicago, IL: Aldine, pp. 73–100.

Flannery, K. 1986. *Guila Naquitz: Archaic foraging and early agriculture in Oaxaca, Mexico.* New York: Academic Press.

Fletcher, T.J. 1974. The timing of reproduction in red deer (*Cervus elaphus*) in relation to latitude. *Journal of Zoology* 172: 363–367.

Forenbaher, S., T. Kaiser & P.T. Miracle. 2013. Dating the East Adriatic Neolithic. *European Journal of Archaeology* 16: 589–609. doi:10.1179/1461957113Y.0000000038.

Forenbaher, S. & P.T. Miracle. 2005. The spread of farming in the Eastern Adriatic. *Antiquity* 79: 514–528.

Geist, V. 1998. *Deer of the world: Their evolution, behaviour, and ecology.* Mechanicsburg, PA: Stackpole Books.

Grant, A. 1982. The use of tooth wear as a guide to the age of domestic ungulates, in B. Wilson, C. Grigson & S. Payne (eds.), *Ageing and sexing animal bones from archaeological sites* (British Archaeological Reports Series 102). Oxford: Archaeopress, pp. 91–108.

Grove, M. 2009. Hunter-gatherer movement patterns: causes and constraints. *Journal of Anthropological Archaeology* 28: 222–233.

Grubb, P. 2005. Order Artiodactyla, in D.E. Wilson & D.A.M. Reeder (eds.), *Mammal species of the world: A taxonomic and geographic reference.* Third edition. Baltimore, MD: Johns Hopkins University Press, pp. 637–722.

Hofmann, R.R. 1984. Feeding habits of mouflon (*Ovis ammon musimon*) and chamois (*Rupicapra rupicapra*) in relation to the morphophysiological adaptation of their digestive tract, in M. Hoefs (ed.), *Whitehorse Conference on Wild Sheep and Goats.* Whitehorse, Yukon, pp. 341–355.

Hofmann, R.R. 1985. Digestive physiology of the deer-their morphophysiological specialisation and adaptation, in P.F. Fennessy & K.R. Drew (eds.), *Biology of deer production* (Bulletin 22). Wellington: Royal Society of New Zealand, pp. 393–407.

Huntley, B. & I.C. Prentice. 1993. Holocene vegetation and climates of Europe, in H.E. Wright, J.E. Kutzbach, T. Webb, W.F. Ruddiman, F.A. Street-Perrott & P.J. Bartlein (eds.), *Global climates since the Last Glacial Maximum.* Minneapolis: University of Minnesota Press, pp. 136–168.

Jochim, M.A. 1998. *A hunter-gatherer landscape: Southwest Germany in the Late Paleolithic and Mesolithic.* New York: Plenum.

Kelly, R.L. 1983. Hunter-gatherer mobility strategies. *Journal of Anthropological Research* 39: 277–306.

Kelly, R.L. 1992. Mobility/sedentism: concepts, archaeological measures, and effects. *Annual Review of Anthropology* 21: 43–66.

Kennett, D.J. 2005. *The island Chumash: behavioural ecology of a maritime society*. Berkeley: University of California Press.

Klein, R.G., K. Allwarden & C. Wolf. 1983. The calculation and interpretation of ungulate age profiles from dental crown heights, in G. Bailey (ed.), *Hunter gatherer economy in prehistory: A European perspective*. Cambridge: Cambridge University Press, pp. 47–57.

Knight, R.R. 1970. The sun river elk herd. *Wildlife Monographs* 23: 1–66.

Komšo, D. 2006. The Mesolithic in Croatia. *Opuscula archaeologica* 30: 55–92.

Komšo, D. & P. Pellegatti. 2007. The Late Epigravettian in Istria: Late Paleolithic colonization and lithic technology in the northern Adriatic area, in R. Whallon (ed.), *Late Paleolithic environments and cultural relations around the Adriatic*, British Archaeological Reports, International Series 1716, pp. 27–39.

Lambeck, K., T.M. Esat & E.-K. Potter. 2002. Links between climate and sea levels for the past three million years. *Nature* 419: 199–206.

Lambeck, K., F. Antonioli, A. Purcell & S. Silenzi. 2004. Sea-level change along the Italian coast for the past 10,000 yr. *Quaternary Science Reviews* 23: 1567–1598.

Laurie, E.M. 2008. An investigation of the common cockle (*Cerastoderma edule L.*): collection practices at the kitchen midden sites of Norsminde and Krabbesholm, Denmark, British Archaeological Reports International Series 1834. Oxford: Archaeopress.

Lightfoot, E., B. Boneva, P.T. Miracle, M. Šlaus & T.C. O'Connell. 2011. Exploring the Mesolithic and Neolithic transition in Croatia through isotopic investigations. *Antiquity* 85: 73–86.

Little, C. & J.A. Kitching. 1996. *The biology of rocky shores*. Oxford: Oxford University Press.

Lubell, D. 2004a. Prehistoric edible land snails in the circum-Mediterranean: the archaeological evidence, in J. Brugal & J. Desse (eds.), *Petits Animaux et Societes Humaines. Du Complement Alimentaire Aux Resources Utilitaires. XXIVe rencontres internationales d'archéologie et d'histoire d'Antibes*. Antibe: Éditions APDCA , pp. 41–62.

Lubell, D. 2004b. Are land snails a signature for the Mesolithic-Neolithic transition? *Documenta Praehistorica* 31: 1–24.

Lubell, D., F.A. Hassan, A. Gautier & J.-L. Ballais. 1976. The Capsian escargotieres. *Science* 191: 910–920.

MacArthur, R.H. & E. Pianka. 1966. On optimal use of a patchy environment. *The American Naturalist* 100: 603–609.

Mannino, M.A., B.F. Spirob & K.D. Thomas. 2003. Sampling shells for seasonality: oxygen isotope analysis on shell carbonates of the inter-tidal gastropod *Monodonta lineata* (da Costa) from populations across its modern range and from a Mesolithic site in southern Britain. *Journal of Archaeological Science* 30: 667–679.

Mannino, M., K.D. Thomas, M.J. Leng, M. Piperno, S. Tusa & A. Tagliacozzo. 2007. Marine resources in the Mesolithic and Neolithic at the Grotta dell'Uzzo (Sicily): evidence from isotope analyses of marine shells. *Archaeometry* 49: 117–133.

Marin-Arroyo, A.B. 2009. Economic adaptations during the Late Glacial in northern Spain: a simulation approach. *Before Farming* 2: article 5.

Mashkour, M., H. Bocherens & I. Moussa. 2005. Long distance movement of sheep and goats of Bakhtiari nomads tracked with intra-tooth variations of stable isotopes (^{13}C and ^{18}O), in J. Davies, I. Mainland & M. Richards (eds.), *Diet and health in past animal populations: Current research and future directions. Proceedings of the 9th Conference of the International Council of Archaeozoology, Durham, August 2002*. Oxford: Oxbow, pp. 113–124.

Milner, N. 2002. *Incremental growth of the European oyster Ostrea edulis: Seasonality information from Danish kitchenmiddens*, British Archaeological Reports International Series 1057. Oxford: Archaeopress.

Milner, N., O.E. Craig, G.N. Bailey, K. Pedersen & S.H. Andersen. 2004. Something fishy in the Neolithic? A re-evaluation of stable isotope analysis of Mesolithic and Neolithic coastal populations. *Antiquity* 78: 9–22.

Milner, N., O.E. Craig & G.N. Bailey (eds.). 2007. *Shell middens in Atlantic Europe*. Oxford: Oxbow.

Miracle, P. 1995. Broad spectrum adaptations re-examined: hunter-gatherer responses to Late-Glacial environmental changes in the eastern Adriatic. Unpublished PhD dissertation, Department of Anthropology, University of Michigan.

Miracle, P.T. 1997. Early Holocene foragers in the karst of northern Istria. *Porocilo o raziskovanju paleolitika, neolitika in eneolitika v Sloveniji* 24: 43–61.

Miracle, P. 2001. Feast or famine? Epi-Paleolithic subsistence in the northern Adriatic basin. *Documenta Praehistorica* 26: 177-197.

Miracle, P.T. 2002. Mesolithic meals from Mesolithic middens, in P.T. Miracle & N. Milner (eds.), *Consuming passions and patterns of consumption*. Cambridge: McDonald Institute for Archaeological Research, pp. 65–88.

Miracle, P. 2007. The Late Glacial "Great Adriatic Plain": "Garden of Eden" or "No Man's Land"during the Epipaleolithic? A view from Istria (Croatia), in R. Whallon (ed.), *Late Paleolithic environments and cultural relations around the Adriatic*, British Archaeological Reports, International Series 1716, pp. 41–51.

Miracle, P. & D. Sturdy. 1991. Chamois and the karst of Herzegovina. *Journal of Archaeological Science* 18: 89–108.

Miracle, P. & C. O'Brien. 1998. Seasonality of resource use and site occupation at Badanj, Bosnia-Herzegovina: subsistence stress in an increasingly seasonal environment?, in T.R. Rocek & O. Bar-Yosef (eds.), *Seasonality and sedentism: Archaeological perspectives from Old and New World sites*. Cambridge, MA: Peabody Museum of Archaeology and Ethnology, pp. 41–74.

Miracle, P.T. & S. Forenbaher. 2000. Pupićina Cave Project: brief summary of the 1998 season. *Histria Archaeologica* 29: 27–48.

Miracle, P.T. & S. Forenbaher (eds.). 2006. Prehistoric herders of northern Istria. *The Archaeology of Pupićina Cave. Volume 1*. Pula: Arheološki Muzej Istre.

Mysterud, A. 1999. Seasonal migration pattern and home range of roe deer (Capreolus capreolus) in an altitudinal gradient in southern Norway. *Journal of Zoology* 247: 479–486.

Oliver, W. & K. Leus. 2008. Sus scrofa: IUCN Red list of threatened species. Version 2011.2. Available at: http://www.iucnredlist.org.

Orton, D., J. Gaastra & M.V. Linden. 2016. Between the Danube and the Deep Blue Sea: Zooarchaeological meta-analysis reveals variability in the spread and development of Neolithic farming across the Western Balkans. *Open Quaternary* 2. doi:10.5334/oq.28.

Ozgul, A., D.Z. Childs, M.K. Oli, K.B. Armitage, D.T. Blumstein, L.E. Olson, S. Tuljapurkar & T. Coulson. 2010. Coupled dynamics of body mass and population growth in response to environmental change. *Nature* 466: 482–485.

Pellegrini, M., R.E. Donahue, C. Chenery, J. Evans, J. Lee-Thorp, J. Montgomery & M. Mussi. 2008. Faunal migration in Late-Glacial central Italy: implications for human resource exploitation. *Rapid Communications in Mass Spectrometry* 22: 1714–1726.

Phoca-Cosmetatou, N. 2002. A zooarchaeological reassessment of the habitat and ecology of the ibex (*Capra ibex*), in R.C.G.M. Laurewerier & I. Plug (eds.), *The future from the past: Archaeozoology in conservation and heritage management*. Proceedings of the 9th Conference of the International Council of Archaeozoology, Durham, August 2002. Oxford: Oxbow, pp. 64-78.

Pilaar Birch, S.E. 2009. The fauna of Vela Špilja on the Island of Lošinj, Croatia: taphonomy, ecology, and subsistence. MPhil. University of Cambridge.

Pilaar Birch, S.E. 2012. Human adaptations to climate change and sea level rise at the Pleistocene-Holocene transition in the Northeastern Adriatic. PhD. University of Cambridge.

Pilaar Birch, S.E. 2017. Neolithic subsistence at Vela Špilja on the island of Lošinj, Croatia, in D. Serjeantson, P. Rowley-Conwy, & P. Halstead (eds.), *Bone Man: Essays in Memory of Tony Legge – Fisherman, Fowler, Hunter and Zooarchaeologist*. Oxford: Oxbow, pp. 263–268.

Pilaar Birch, S.E. & M. Vander Linden. 2017. A long hard road . . . Reviewing the evidence for environmental change and population history in the eastern Adriatic and western Balkans during the Late Pleistocene and Early Holocene. *Quaternary International*. doi: 0.1016/j.quaint.2016.12.035.

Pilaar Birch, S.E. & P.T. Miracle. 2015. Subsistence continuity, change, and environmental adaptation at the site of Nugljanska, Istria, Croatia. *Environmental Archaeology* 20(1): 30–40.

Pilaar Birch, S.E., P.T. Miracle, R.E. Stevens & T.C. O'Connell. 2016. Reconstructing late Pleistocene/early Holocene migratory behavior of ungulates using stable isotopes and its effects on forager mobility. *PloS ONE* 11(6): e0155714. doi:10.1371/journal.pone.0155714.

Pilaar Birch, S.E. & P.T. Miracle. 2017. Human response to climate change in the Northern Adriatic during the late Pleistocene and early Holocene, in G. Monks (ed.), *Climate change and past human responses: An archaeozoological perspective*. Vertebrate Paleobiology and Paleoanthropology Series. New York: Springer, pp. 87–100.

Seasonal mobility and multispecies interactions

Ramanzin, M., E. Sturaro & D. Zanon. 2007. Seasonal migration and home range of roe deer (*Capreolus capreolus*) in the Italian eastern Alps. *Canadian Journal of Zoology* 85: 280–289.

Redding, R. 1988. A general explanation of subsistence change: from hunting and gathering to food production. *Journal of Anthropological Archaeology* 7: 56–97.

Richards, M.P. & R.E.M. Hedges. 1999. A Neolithic revolution? New evidence of diet in the British Neolithic. *Antiquity* 73: 891–897.

Robb, J. and P.T. Miracle. 2007. Beyond "migration" versus "acculturation": new models for the spread of agriculture. *Proceedings of the British Academy* 144: 99–115.

Ruscillo, D. 2006. *Recent advances in ageing and sexing animal bones. Proceedings of the 9th Conference of the International Council of Archaeozoology, Durham, August 2002.* Oxford: Oxbow.

Schmidt, R., J. Müller, R. Drescher-Schneider, R. Krisai, K. Szeroczynska & A. Barić. 2000. Changes in lake level and trophy at Lake Vrana, a large karstic lake on the island of Cres (Croatia), with respect to palaeo-climate and anthropogenic impacts during the last approx. 16,000 years. *Journal of Limnology* 59: 113–130.

Shackleton, D.M. 1997. Conservation priorities and options, in D.M. Shackleton (ed.), *Wild sheep and goats and their relatives*. Cambridge: IUCN, pp. 318–330.

Shank, C.C. 1985. Inter-and intra-sexual segregation of chamois (*Rupicapra rupicapra*) by altitude and habitat during summer. *Z. Säugetierkunde* 50: 117–125.

Smith, E.A. & B. Winterhalder. 1992. *Evolutionary ecology and human behavior*. New York: Aldine.

Spitz, F. & G. Janeau. 1990. Spatial strategies: an attempt to classify daily movement of wild boar. *Acta Theriologica* 35: 129–149.

Spitz, F. & G. Janeau. 1995. Daily selection of habitat in wild boar. *Journal of Zoology* 237: 423–434.

Starkovich, B.M. 2009. Dietary changes during the Upper Palaeolithic at Klissoura Cave 1 (Prosymni), Peloponnese, Greece. *Before Farming* 3: article 4.

Starkovich, B.M. & M.C. Stiner. 2010. Upper Palaeolithic animal exploitation at Klissoura Cave 1 in southern Greece: dietary trends and mammal taphonomy. *Eurasian Prehistory* 7: 107–132.

Stiner, M.C. 2001. Thirty years on the "Broad Spectrum Revolution" and Paleolithic demography. *Proceedings of the National Academy of Sciences* 98: 6993–6996.

Stiner, M.C. & N.D. Munro. 2002. Approaches to prehistoric diet breadth, demography and prey ranking systems in time and space. *Journal of Archaeological Method and Theory* 9: 181–214.

Stiner, M.C. & N.D. Munro. 2011. On the evolution of diet and landscape during the Upper Palaeolithic through Mesolithic at Franchthi Cave (Peloponnese, Greece). *Journal of Human Evolution* 60: 618–636.

Straus, L.G. & G.A. Clark (eds.). 1986. *La Riera Cave: Stone Age hunter-gatherer adaptations in Northern Spain*. Tempe: Arizona State University Press.

Sturdy, D., D. Webley & G. Bailey. 1997. The Palaeolithic geography of Epirus, in G. Bailey (ed.), *Klithi: Palaeolithic settlement and Quaternary landscapes in Northwest Greece. Volume 2: Klithi in its local and regional setting*. Cambridge: McDonald Institute for Archaeological Research, pp. 587–614.

Stutz, A.J., N.D. Munro & G. Bar-Oz. 2009. Increasing the resolution of the Broad Spectrum Revolution in the southern Levantine Epipaleolithic (19–12 ka). *Journal of Human Evolution* 56: 294–306.

Surić, M., M. Juracic, N. Horvatincic & I. Krajcarbronic. 2005. Late Pleistocene–Holocene sea-level rise and the pattern of coastal karst inundation: records from submerged speleothems along the eastern Adriatic Coast (Croatia). *Marine Geology* 214: 163–175.

Vincent, A.S. 1985. Plant foods in savanna environments: a preliminary report of tubers eaten by the Hadza of Northern Tanzania. *World Archaeology* 17: 131–148.

Wahlström, L.K. & O. Liberg. 1995. Patterns of dispersal and seasonal migration in roe deer (*Capreolus capreolus*). *Journal of Zoology* 235: 455–467.

Willis, K.J. 1994. The vegetational history of the Balkans. *Quaternary Science Reviews* 13: 769–788.

Wilson, B., C. Grigson & S. Payne. 1982. *Ageing and sexing animal bones from archaeological sites* (British Archaeological Reports Series 102). Oxford: Archaeopress.

Winterhalder, B. & E.A. Smith (eds.). 1981. *Hunter-gatherer foraging strategies: Ethnographic and archaeological analyses*. Chicago, IL: University of Chicago Press.

Wright, E., S. Viner-Daniels, M. Parker-Pearson & U. Albarella. (2014). Age and season of pig slaughter at late Neolithic Durrington Walls (Wiltshire, UK) as detected through a new system for recording tooth wear. *Journal of Archaeological Science* 52: 497–514.

Yanushko, P.J. 1957. The way of life of Crimean deer and their influence on the natural cycle. *Transactions of the Moscow Society of Naturalists* 35: 39–52.

Zeder, M.A. 2006. Reconciling rates of long bone fusion and tooth eruption and wear in sheep (*Ovis*) and goat (*Capra*), in D. Ruscillo (ed.), *Recent advances in ageing and sexing animal bones. Proceedings of the 9th Conference of the International Council of Archaeozoology, Durham, August 2002*. Oxford: Oxbow, pp. 87–118.

Zeder, M.A. 2012. The Broad Spectrum Revolution at 40: resource diversity, intensification, and an alternative to optimal foraging expectations. *Journal of Anthropological Archaeology* 31: 241–264.

19

THE ROLE OF OSTRICH IN SHAPING THE LANDSCAPE USE PATTERNS OF HUMANS AND HYENAS ON THE SOUTHERN COAST OF SOUTH AFRICA DURING THE LATE PLEISTOCENE

Jamie Hodgkins, Petrus le Roux, Curtis W. Marean, Kirsty Penkman, Molly Crisp, Erich Fisher, and Julia Lee-Thorp

Introduction

How have prey species structured the way modern humans (*Homo sapiens*) and other social carnivores utilize the landscape? The availability, location, diversity, and abundance of food resources play a critical role in influencing hunter-gatherer and carnivore mobility (Kelly, 1983). Thus, the behavioral patterns of other living organisms are powerful forces in shaping human behavior. In this chapter, we will explore the role that ostrich play in shaping subsistence patterns in early modern humans and brown hyena (*Parahyaena brunnea*) 'at two sites located in the Pinnacle Point (PP) cave and rock shelter complex in South Africa: PP5-6 and PP30. This project tracking multispecies behavioral ties is aided by a bioavailable $^{87}Sr/^{86}Sr$ isoscape map created for the region surrounding Pinnacle Point. The map was generated by determining the $^{87}Sr/^{86}Sr$ values found in bedrock along the South African coast, coastal forelands, and into the inland mountain chains. Ostrich breed within defended territories, consuming plant food within those territories, and thus their tissues acquire $^{87}Sr/^{86}Sr$ values from a restricted area. The $^{87}Sr/^{86}Sr$ values obtained from ostrich eggshell fragments deposited at PP5-6 and PP30 should therefore provide information about where on the landscape human hunter–gatherers and social carnivores encountered and collected eggs.

There is no question that ostrich eggs are a desirable food (Romanoff and Romanoff, 1949; Cook and Briggs, 1977; Bertram, 1992; Cooper et al., 2009; Sebei et al., 2009). Each ostrich egg is a rich source of protein (12.2 g/100 g of liquid), calories (~2000 kcal/egg), fat (11.7 g/100 g liquid), minerals, vitamins, and amino acids, which make them sought after by both carnivores and humans (Romanoff and Romanoff, 1949; Cook and Briggs, 1977; Bertram, 1992; Sales et al., 1996). Archaeological ostrich eggshell (OES) fragments are commonly found along with refuse from other meals at occupation sites located across the Old World from China (Boaz and Ciochon, 2004) to the South African Coast (Robbins et al., 1996; Halkett et al., 2003; Texier et al., 2010, 2013; Vogelsang et al., 2010; Steele and Klein, 2013), with early evidence of ostrich egg exploitation dating back to 2.34 million years ago at sites associated with early *Homo* (Roche et al., 1999). Ostrich eggs are a predictable, seasonally available resource for an average of three months per year (Bertram, 1992; Sebei et al., 2009). Additionally, they are easy to carry (either in the mouth by large carnivores or by hand or bag), can be stored for a month, and when emptied by humans can be used as liquid storage containers (Bertram, 1992; Wadley, 1992; Hitchcock et al., 1996; Texier et al., 2010, 2013). OES was a highly valued raw material for the production of pendants and beads, the latter dating back to at least ~40 ka (e.g. Ambrose, 1998). OES beads were a key component of gifting exchange networks among recent southern African hunter-gatherers (Wiessner, 1986), and we expect a similar pattern of exchange in the past. It is clear from modern records and archaeological remains that ostrich eggs have been utilized for millennia, but to more clearly understand the relationship between ostrich, humans, and carnivores, it is important to understand ostrich ecology.

Ostrich ecology

Ostrich (*Struthio camelus*) have a geographically expansive range stretching throughout Africa and into the Middle East (Cooper et al., 2009). South Africa is home to the subspecies *S. c. australis*, which ranged across the country from the Atlantic to the Indian Ocean and as far north as the neighboring countries of Namibia, Botswana, and Zimbabwe (Cooper et al., 2009) for more than a million years based on OES fragments from Wonderwerk Cave (Ecker, 2016). Due to farming and human population pressures, the range of wild ostrich has contracted since the 1900s.

As evidenced by their large geographical range, ostrich populations can thrive in diverse habitats ranging from coastal environments (including the Greater Cape Floristic Kingdom of South Africa) to shrublands (e.g. the succulent Karoo of South Africa), to grasslands, and semiarid savannahs (Milton et al., 1994). Eggshells are semipermeable, as pores in the shell allow moisture and air to pass through the egg (Tullett and Board, 1977; Cooper et al., 2009). Thus, for ostriches to reproduce in each of these diverse habitats, the pore structure of ostrich eggs changes in terms of their size and distribution across the egg to suit each environment (Tullett and Board, 1977; Cooper et al., 2009).

Ostrich are omnivores that primarily eat a mix of fresh green C_3 and C_4 plants, and a small proportion of large seeds, shells, insects, small mammal bones, and antelope fecal pellets (Milton et al., 1994; Johnson et al., 1998). Ostrich can acquire most of their water from the plants they consume, but will drink at local ponds when water is available (Williams et al., 1993; Milton et al., 1994; Johnson et al., 1998). During the breeding season, ostrich acquire these food and water resources in more restricted areas. Males defend territories that range in size from 0.09 km² to 19 km², depending on space available (Sauer and Sauer, 1966; Bertram, 1992; Kimwele and Graves, 2003; Sebei et al., 2009). Female ostrich range between the territories of multiple males. Dominant females lay eggs within the protected territory of a dominant male; the couple then take turns incubating the eggs (Sauer and Sauer, 1966; Kimwele and Graves, 2003; Cooper et al., 2010). Non-dominant females lay eggs in the nests of dominant females, in the expectation that the eggs will be incubated (Sauer and Sauer, 1966; Kimwele and Graves, 2003; Cooper et al., 2010).

Predation of ostrich eggs occurs from the time the egg is laid until it hatches (Bertram, 1992). However, the easiest time for carnivores and humans to access eggs is shortly after

Late Pleistocene landscape use in South Africa

they are laid, during an 11–18 day window before the dominant female and male begin to incubate the eggs by sitting on top of them; this is also when the internal egg is mostly liquid, before substantial embryonic development begins (Bertram, 1992; Kimwele and Graves, 2003). During this time, the eggs are left in the nest and guarded from a distance, but the ostrich do not yet sit on top of the nest. The predation rate for nests is high; it has been reported that before incubation, eggs in the nest have a 24% survival rate, while after incubation, any remaining eggs have a 54% survival rate (Bertram, 1992). At the time of incubation, the dominant female pushes some eggs out of the nest, making those eggs more vulnerable to predation (Bertram, 1992).

Brown hyenas are known to raid ostrich nests. Hyenas have been observed transporting eggs over a distance of 6.8 km back to a den to provision their young (Mills, 1977), but they have also been observed consuming multiple eggs at the nest when they find them (Mills, 1977; Bertram, 1992; Kandel, 2004; Sebei et al., 2009). Hyenas also scatter eggs into the bush, some at a sizeable distance from the nest (up to 600 m), and will consume those eggs over time (Mills, 1977). Because ostrich eggs are a regular food item for hyenas, these social carnivores provide a useful comparison with humans when examining how ostrich egg exploitation may have influenced landscape use patterns.

Background

Sites

Pinnacle Point 5-6 is a slit-cut rock shelter preserved in the Pinnacle Point quarzitic cliffs off the Indian Ocean in Mossel Bay, South Africa (Karkanas et al., 2015). The Indian Ocean coastal inter-tidal zone is currently ~50 m from the main sediment stack. PP5-6 preserves a tall (15 m) vertically stacked stratigraphic sequence dating from ~90 ka at the bottom to ~50 ka at the top (Karkanas et al., 2015). Sediments at the site preserve a high-resolution archaeological record composed of stone tools, faunal remains, OES fragments, mollusks, hearth deposits, ochre, fire-modified rock, etc. (Brown et al., 2012). For this study, a total of 70 OES fragments were sampled from stratigraphic levels dated between 81 and 51 ka. These samples span the warmer interglacial cycle of marine oxygen isotope stage (MIS) 5 (N = 12 OES) to the colder glacial transition of MIS 4 (N = 52 OES), with a small sample (N = 6 OES) excavated from MIS 3. Thus, sampling OES across these MISs will allow us to determine if the location where OES were collected changed over time, and between global climate cycles.

PP30 is a paleontological cave site formed in calcrete above the Pinnacle Point cliffs—calcretes, dunes, and aeolianites are stratified above the quarzitic cliffs at Pinnacle Point (Copeland et al., 2016; Rector and Reed, 2010). PP30 is thought to have had a short occupation by hyenas (*Parahyaena brunnea*) at ~151 ka (Rector and Reed, 2010). Because brown hyenas also utilize ostrich eggs as a food source (Mills, 1977), this site was selected because it was hypothesized that the cave might provide a baseline for the Pleistocene hyena collection range, and that the OES samples would be less likely to have been affected by fire. At 151 ka, hyenas occupying PP30 could have had an extensive range on the South African coastal shelf, as the cave would have been approximately 89 km from the coast at that time (Fisher et al., 2010).

Pinnacle Point is centrally located on the south coast of South Africa and currently receives both summer and winter rain averaging about 450 mm per year. The current vegetation at Pinnacle Point includes several vegetation types of the Greater Cape Floristic Region, dominated by shrubby evergreen sclerophyllous plants. The slopes below the cliffs have pockets of thicket with trees and shrubs, and in some nearby areas there are substantial active dune-fields interspersed with thicket vegetation. During the occupation of the sites, conditions would have been substantially different (Marean et al., 2014). The continental shelf at this location slopes gradually and thus even small drops in sea level exposed significant landmass, so that during the times discussed here there was typically a coastal plain between 3 and 95 km wide (Fisher et al., 2010). Grass-eating species like the Cape hartebeest (*Alcelaphus buselaphus*) and black wildebeest (*Connochaetes gnou)* dominate the Pleistocene faunal assemblages (Rector and Reed, 2010), and many of the species were likely migratory—a faunal composition atypical of the region in the historic period. It has been hypothesized that these lowered sea levels were accompanied by changes in rainfall patterns and created a now extinct ecosystem called the Paleo-Agulhas Plain (Marean, 2010; Marean et al., 2014), with ungulates migrating to the east for the summer rains and west for the winter rains on a predominantly grassland plain. At the two sites and time periods sampled here, that Paleo-Agulhas Plain ecosystem would have been in place, though it likely varied in character over time. This grassy plain would have been a favored habitat for ostriches.

Strontium isotope distribution in the southern Cape zone

The geographically limited ranges traversed by ostrich during the breeding season (up to 19 km^2), which lasts on average three months, is useful for the interpretation of radiogenic strontium isotope analysis, as it could narrow the probable location of egg-laying. Radiogenic strontium isotope ratios ($^{87}Sr/^{86}Sr$) are used to track the movement of animals across the landscape (Hoppe et al., 1999; Blum et al., 2000; Copeland et al., 2008), because the bedrock of a particular geological region has a characteristic isotopic signature (Price et al., 2002; Koch, 2007). Older rocks (e.g. granites) tend to have higher values (~0.710–0.740), and younger rocks (e.g. sedimentary rocks such as limestone) tend to have lower values (~0.707–0.709) (Bentley, 2006). Values present in bedrock are eroded by water, carried into water systems and taken up by plants. This bioavailable strontium is then ingested by herbivores and preserved in their tissues (i.e. teeth, bones, eggs) (Hoppe et al., 1999; Blum et al., 2000; Copeland et al., 2008). Water from the ocean ($^{87}Sr/^{86}Sr$ = 0.7092) in the form of sea spray and ocean fog also contributes to the bioavailable strontium taken up by plants and animals. Sea spray has a strong effect in coastal areas (Chadwick et al., 2009; Evans et al., 2009; Whipkey et al., 2000). In ostrich, strontium is incorporated into the crystalline component of the eggshell as a substitute for calcium; consequently, the $^{87}Sr/^{86}Sr$ value in an ostrich egg is generally indicative of the location where female ostriches were foraging before and during egg production (Blum et al., 2000; Bentley, 2006).

Eggshell is fairly resistant to diagenetic changes (Brooks et al., 1990; Demarchi et al., 2016). The organic matrix is 3% of the mass of the shell and is predominantly made of proteins, while the inorganic crystalline component is calcite (Johnson et al., 1998; Koch, 2007; Stewart et al., 2013). Amino acid analysis can determine if OES has been diagenetically altered (Johnson et al., 1998; Crisp, 2013), and so this was undertaken on each sample to investigate the effect of heating on the $^{87}Sr/^{86}Sr$ values.

Methods

Strontium analysis

The $^{87}Sr/^{86}Sr$ isotope ratio compositions of the eggshell samples were determined following routine methods employed in the Multicollector-ICP-MS facility in the Department of Geological Sciences, University of Cape Town (e.g. Copeland et al., 2010; Copeland et al., 2016).

Below is a brief account of this method used for the $^{87}Sr/^{86}Sr$ isotope ratio measurements of the eggshell samples.

The eggshell samples were first ultrasonicated in ultra-clean MilliQ water to remove any material adhering to the surface. After drying in an oven at $\pm 60°C$, approximately 4–40 mg of eggshell, depending on available material, was weighed into a 7 ml Teflon beaker and 2 ml of two-bottled distilled, concentrated (65%) HNO_3 added. The beakers were closed and placed on a hotplate at 140°C for an hour to ensure dissolution, then opened and dried. The residue was re-dissolved in 1.5 ml of 2 M HNO_3, and the strontium fraction isolated using columns containing 0.2 ml of Triskem Sr.Spec resin, after the procedure originally developed by Pin et al. (1994). The resulting strontium fraction of each sample was dried down again, and re-dissolved in 2 ml of 0.2% HNO_3. These strontium-fractions of individual samples were diluted to yield final solutions of ± 200 ppb Sr appropriate for analysis by MC-ICP-MS.

The $^{87}Sr/^{86}Sr$ isotope ratio analyses of these solutions were performed on a Nu Instruments NuPlasma HR in the MC-ICP-MS facility. NIST SRM987 was used as the reference standard and analyzed after every 4–6 analyses of the unknowns. All resulting $^{87}Sr/^{86}Sr$ isotope data of the eggshell samples were normalized to a reference $^{87}Sr/^{86}Sr$ value of 0.710255 for the bracketing NIST SRM987 analyses. All $^{87}Sr/^{86}Sr$ isotope data produced in this facility are corrected for isobaric interference of ^{87}Rb on ^{87}Sr, using the measured signal for ^{85}Rb and a natural abundance $^{87}Rb/^{85}Rb$ ratio of 0.38506. Instrumental mass fractionation is corrected for during each analysis using the exponential law, the measured $^{86}Sr/^{88}Sr$ ratio, and a natural abundance $^{86}Sr/^{88}Sr$ isotope ratio value of 0.1194.

Amino acid analysis

OES samples were cleaned in ultra-pure H_2O, ground and bleached for 72 hr (NaOCl 12% wt/vol) in order to isolate the functionally intra-crystalline proteins, following the methods of Crisp et al. (2013). Sample preparation for chiral amino acid analyses (total hydrolysable and free amino acids fractions: THAA and FAA) was carried out following the method of Crisp et al. (2013). Separation of the chiral forms (D and L) of multiple amino acids was performed by RP-HPLC with fluorescence detection using a modified method of Kaufman and Manley (1998). The amino acids reported here are among those detected routinely with good chromatographic resolution in OES: Asx and Glx (Asp + Asn and Glu + Gln due to irreversible deamidation during sample preparation), alanine (Ala), valine (Val), and isoleucine (Ile). Serine (Ser) is not reported as its decomposition patterns are complicated by decomposition and a reversal in D/L values, therefore its utility decreases for older samples (Vallentyne, 1964).

Results

Alteration

The amino acid compositions showed that a high proportion (about 50%) of the PP5-6 samples had been heated to some degree (Crisp, 2013, Table 1), likely through human activity resulting in the OES samples being exposed to human-created fire. However, there was no correlation between heating and the $^{87}Sr/^{86}Sr$ value (Figure 19.1), indicating that these elevated temperatures had not compromised the integrity of the original isotopic signature. At PP30 only a couple samples were heated, which may be caused by natural fire (Table 19.2). It is also relevant to note the range of $^{87}Sr/^{86}Sr$ values of OES at PP5-6 and PP30 (0.7082–0.7124), are similar to the range of values obtained from faunal enamel samples at PP5-6 and PP13B

(0.7092–0.7112), a site located within the PP complex (Copeland et al., 2016). Dentin samples extracted from the teeth of 55 individuals belonging to twelve different herbivore taxa at PP5-6 and PP13B confirmed that the enamel samples were not significantly affected by diagenesis (Copeland et al., 2016).

Table 19.1 [87]Sr/[86]Sr results of ostrich egg shell fragments from PP5-6

AAR number	Sp. number	87/86Sr	±2s internal	Age est. (ka)	Dist. from coast (km)	Heating criteria[1]
4603	273468	0.709322	0.000015	51	20	0
4647	164179	0.709247	0.000011	64	30	3
4599	163872	0.709248	0.000011	64	30	3
4646	164005	0.709317	0.000009	64	30	3
4676	273532	0.709324	0.000012	64	30	3
4649	165702	0.709334	0.000015	64	30	0
4650	166717	0.709514	0.000011	64	30	3
4677	273544	0.709341	0.000014	69	0	1
4669	273464	0.709690	0.000012	69	0	0
4666	246164	0.709693	0.000012	69	0	1
4602	248682	0.709869	0.000013	69	0	3
4637	140936	0.709802	0.000017	72	15	0
4598	160369	0.709617	0.000016	72	15	0
4624	118977	0.709459	0.000014	72	15	3
4643	160487	0.709628	0.000010	72	15	0
4644	160672	0.709637	0.000014	72	15	3
4605	273489	0.709471	0.000016	73	15	3
4586	131618	0.709597	0.000017	73	15	0
4587	132475	0.709613	0.000012	73	15	3
4606	273492	0.709676	0.000013	73	15	0
4625	119321	0.709678	0.000013	73	15	3
4626	132531	0.709712	0.000015	73	15	—
4632	134423	0.709591	0.000013	73	15	0
4630	134343	0.709778	0.000014	73	15	3
4590	136905	0.709554	0.000012	73	15	3
4636	139618	0.710332	0.000016	73	15	0
4642	159001	0.709599	0.000012	74	1	3
4579	173917	0.709370	0.000017	74	1	3
4634	137831	0.709412	0.000014	74	1	1
4576	137314	0.709514	0.000014	74	1	0
4594	140814	0.709581	0.000012	74	1	0
4594	140814	0.709581	0.000012	74	1	0
4616	106511	0.709617	0.000012	74	1	1
4595	151055	0.709624	0.000016	74	1	0
4615	106510.5	0.709665	0.000013	74	1	0
4614	106505	0.709723	0.000016	74	1	0
4635	138416	0.709741	0.000012	74	1	0
4641	156147.1	0.709475	0.000010	74	1	0
4663	212920	0.709834	0.000011	74	1	3
4583	106625	0.709688	0.000012	74	1	0
4621	107248	0.709470	0.000013	74	1	3
4639	156114	0.709326	0.000013	74	1	0
4622	107317	0.709643	0.000016	74	1	3
4640	156147	0.709471	0.000015	74	1	0
4584	107236.1	0.709457	0.000016	74	1	3

4617	106638	0.709696	0.000011	74	1	0
4618	106777	0.709671	0.000015	74	1	0
4620	106975	0.709536	0.000013	74	1	2
4675	273514	0.709541	0.000010	74	1	0
4619	106965	0.709630	0.000012	74	1	0
4597	158651	0.709735	0.000014	74	1	0
4568	107246	0.709488	0.000012	74	1	3
4567	106779	0.709540	0.000013	74	1	0
4566	106760	0.709667	0.000016	74	1	0
4623	107390	0.709687	0.000011	74	1	0
4596	152029	0.709722	0.000014	74	1	0
4578	158651.1	0.709733	0.000012	74	1	0
4585	107448	0.709764	0.000012	74	1	3
4582	273548	0.709697	0.000014	76	1	0
4629	133721.1	0.709613	0.000013	77	5	0
4571	133643	0.709637	0.000012	77	5	1
4572	134114	0.709615	0.000012	78	5	0
4610	273616	0.709619	0.000013	78	5	2
4679	273632	0.712483	0.000011	78	5	—
4645	163432	0.710147	0.000013	80	5	0
4648	165476	0.710151	0.000011	80	5	0
4611	273665	0.709714	0.000011	80	5	1
4612	273667	0.709722	0.000012	80	5	0
4601	233435	0.709738	0.000013	80	5	0
4680	273675	0.709591	0.000014	81	5	1

Note: [1]Heating criteria = 0 (unburned) to 3 (severely burned).

Table 19.2 [87]Sr/[86]Sr results of ostrich egg shell fragments from PP-30

AAR number	Sp. number	87/86Sr	±2s internal	Age est. (ka)	Dist. from coast (km)	Heating criteria[1]
4604	67591	0.709390	0.000011	151	89	0
4687	66107	0.709584	0.000010	151	89	0
4700	66924	0.709561	0.000011	151	89	0
4703	67049	0.709512	0.000013	151	89	0
4711	67870	0.709310	0.000011	151	89	0
4699	67110	0.709084	0.000015	151	89	0
4702	67048	0.708623	0.000025	151	89	0
4712	67874	0.708297	0.000028	151	89	0
4713	67001	0.709467	0.000010	151	89	0
4715	66274	0.709303	0.000012	151	89	0
4684	65808	0.709378	0.000013	151	89	0
4685	65288	0.709441	0.000010	151	89	0
4686	65314	0.709426	0.000009	151	89	0
4692	65166	0.709395	0.000011	151	89	0
4694	65170	0.709367	0.000014	151	89	0
4696	Sieved	0.709304	0.000014	151	89	3
4697	Sieved	0.709398	0.000012	151	89	3
4705	67308	0.709352	0.000014	151	89	0
4706	67450	0.709498	0.000013	151	89	0
4716	66473	0.709314	0.000017	151	89	0

Note: [1]Heating criteria = 0 (unburned) to 3 (severely burned).

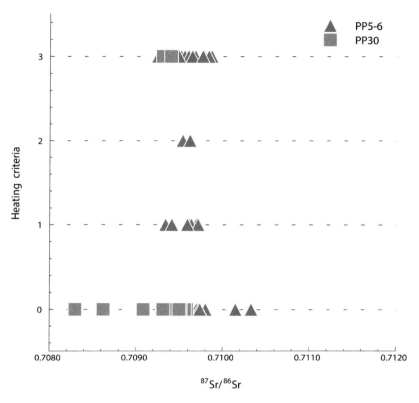

Figure 19.1 Graph indicating that elevated temperatures in PP5-6 samples did not affect their original isotopic signature.

OES results

This study benefits from existing interdisciplinary research efforts to reconstruct the location of the South African coastline over time, and to map the modern bioavailable strontium isotope values present around the sites of Pinnacle Point, creating an isoscape map (Fisher et al., 2010; Copeland et al., 2016). Specifically, Fisher et al. (2010) described and presented a detailed reconstruction of the transgression and regression of the Indian Ocean over the last 430,000 years, which shows that at 151 ka when brown hyena were occupying PP30, the coast was ~89 km from the site (Figure 19.2). OES from PP5-6 were sampled from time intervals in which the coast ranged from 0.5 to 30 km from the coast, and thus humans at PP5-6 had a narrower coastal shelf on which to forage. Data from the coastline model was also compared against an isoscape map of the area surrounding PP (Figure 19.3). This bioavailable $^{87}Sr/^{86}Sr$ map was created by sampling modern vegetation growing on all known geological units surrounding PP and analyzing the samples for $^{87}Sr/^{86}Sr$ (Copeland et al., 2016). Mapping the modern bioavailable strontium around the sites demonstrated that $^{87}Sr/^{86}Sr$ values increase inland from the coast (Figure 19.4): a pattern driven by the influence of rainfall and sea spray (Copeland et al., 2016).

When $^{87}Sr/^{86}Sr$ values from OES at PP30 and PP5-6 are plotted with modern vegetation samples collected around Pinnacle Point (Copeland et al., 2016), and with the reconstructed distance from the coast estimated by Fisher et al. (2010), it is clear that most of the eggs at both sites were laid on the Paleo-Agulhas Plain (Tables 19.1 and 19.2, Figure 19.4). This Paleo-Agulhas

Late Pleistocene landscape use in South Africa

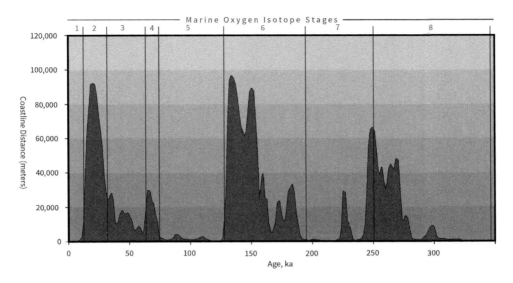

Figure 19.2 Graph showing isotope stages and the distance of Pinnacle Point site from the coast over the last 430,000 years.

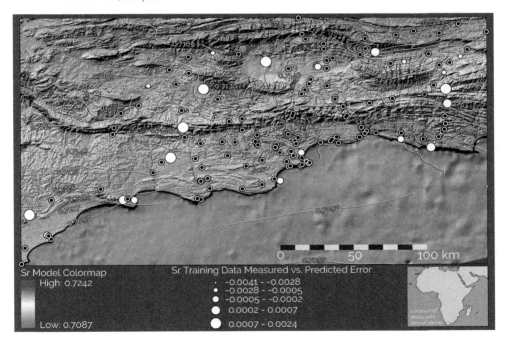

Figure 19.3 A ^{87}Sr/^{86}Sr isoscape map generated by sampling the ^{87}Sr/^{86}Sr values in modern vegetation growing on all known geological units surrounding PP (Copeland et al., 2016).

Plain would have provided a rich expansive grassland ecosystem perfect for ostrich and African mammals, and would have been an attractive target location for humans and carnivore to hunt and forage (Marean, 2016). At PP5-6, three OES samples (specimens 163432, 165476, and 139618) have values more than one standard deviation (0.0003) above the mean (0.7095).

Jamie Hodgkins et al.

In addition, one OES sample (Specimen 273632) has a value (0.7125) more than two standard deviations (±0.0078) higher than the mean (Table 19.1, Figure 19.5). These elevated ratios

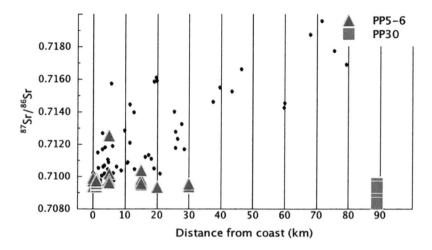

Figure 19.4 The y-axis represents [87]Sr/[86]Sr values for modern vegetation samples (black circles), OES samples from PP5-6 (gray Triangles), and OES samples from PP30 (gray squares). The x-axis represents the distance from the coast. For the modern vegetation samples, the distance is the modern distance from the coast, and for the fossil OES samples, the distance is the reconstructed distance from the coast (see Fisher et al., 2010; Copeland et al., 2016.

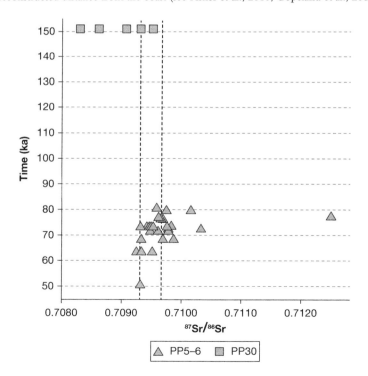

Figure 19.5 Graph showing instances of deviation in [87]Sr/[86]Sr values for eggs at PP5-6.

could suggest that (1) the eggs were laid on the Paleo-Agulhas Plain closer to the mountains; (2) they were laid on alluvial sediments from rivers washing sediment from the mountains toward the coast, and/or (3) these shells were gifted/traded from slightly different geological areas than other shells at the site. This third possibility will be explored with future analyses. In contrast, PP30 does not have any eggs with elevated values; rather, this site preserves two samples (specimens 67048 and 67874) with values more than two standard deviations (0.0006) lower than the mean (0.7093) (Table 19.2, Figure 19.5). However, since it is known that PP30 was positioned 89 km from the ocean at 151 ka, it is possible that these lower values come from sediments far out on the shelf, perhaps from Quaternary alluvium/cover sand/calcrete deposits. This is a hypothesis that could be tested on marine sediment cores in the future.

Discussion and conclusions

The results of our analysis show that ostrich breeding territories existed on the Paleo-Agulhas Plain, an environment similar to areas of Africa today characterized by grasslands cut by riverine environments. These locations provide key habitats for multiple species because they provide ample food and water. This ecosystem would have supported ostrich, whose eggs would have added to an already resource-rich environment attractive to multiple hunters including both modern humans at PP5-6 and brown hyena at PP30. While ostrich likely did have breeding territories inland from the Paleo-Agulhas Plain, neither the hyenas nor human foragers appear to have collected eggs from the Cape Folded Mountains and their foothills, although humans likely collected some eggs along the rivers that dissect the coastal plain or received them as part of an exchange network. It should be reemphasized that we sampled OES across the MIS5-MIS3 transitions at PP5-6. It is interesting that ostrich must have continued to breed on the Plain through these major MIS stages even as the ocean transgressed close to the mouth of the cave, and then regressed 30 km from the site. The data from PP30 suggest that hyenas were equally attracted to ostrich breeding sites on the Paleo-Agulhas Plain; however, ostrich may have taken advantage of the greater expanse of the plain in the period sampled at PP30, during which the exposed shelf stretched out 89 km to the south, allowing extended breeding territories causing hyenas to venture further in pursuit of eggs than the humans at PP5-6 were permitted.

The findings that the Paleo-Agulhas Plain provided an ecologically rich habitat populated by ostrich and other terrestrial fauna, establishing an irresistible locale for carnivores and human hunters, is consistent with results from a recent study by Copeland et al. (2016). In that study, the $^{87}Sr/^{86}Sr$ values of faunal enamel samples from PP30 and PP13B (a cave site within the Pinnacle Point complex) showed that butchered animal bones found at the sites came from fauna that had spent their early years living on the coastal plain. Again, no evidence was found among the faunal remains to suggest that humans were hunting animals away from the coast.

This study allows us to assess whether any OES fragments could be identified that deviated from the mean $^{87}Sr/^{86}Sr$ OES value at each site. As noted, several samples were found from each site that were one or two standard deviations from the mean. These findings will allow us to explore the possibility that some of the OES were collected during longer foraging rounds by humans and hyenas, or, in the case of human foragers from PP56, that the ostrich eggs were part of a gifting or trade network. Thus, we have now laid the groundwork to explore how ostrich were involved in exchange networks amongst modern humans as early as 80 ka ago. This study as a whole demonstrates that multispecies archaeology can provide a detailed reconstruction of past environments and human and animal behaviors.

Acknowledgements

We recognize the support of a grant from the National Science Foundation (BCS-1138073), Hyde Family Foundations, the Institute of Human Origins (IHO) at Arizona State University, and the John Templeton Foundation to the Institute of Human Origins at Arizona State University, and the NERC grant NE/G004625. The opinions expressed in this publication are those of the author(s) and do not necessarily reflect the views of any of these funding organizations.

References

Ambrose, S.H., 1998. Chronology of the Later Stone Age and food production in East Africa. *Journal of Archaeological Science*. 25, 377–392.

Bentley, R.A., 2006. Strontium isotopes from the earth to the archaeological skeleton: A review. *Journal of Archaeological Method and Theory*. 13, 135–187.

Bertram, B., 1992. *The ostrich communal nesting system*. Princeton University Press, Princeton, NJ.

Blum, J., Taliaferro, E., Weisse, M., Holmes, T., 2000. Changes in Sr/Ca, Ba/Ca and 87Sr/86Sr ratios between trophic levels in two forest ecosystems in the Northeastern U. S. A. *Biogeochemistry*. 49, 87–101.

Boaz, N., Ciochon, R., 2004. *Dragon Bone Hill: An Ice-Age saga of Homo erectus*. Oxford University Press, New York.

Brooks, A., Hare, P., Kokis, J., Miller, G., Ernst, R., Wendorf, F., 1990. Dating Pleistocene archeological sites by protein diagenesis in ostrich eggshell. *Science*. 248, 60–64.

Brown, K.S., Marean, C.W., Jacobs, Z., Schoville, B.J., Oestmo, S., Fisher, E.C., Bernatchez, J., Karkanas, P., Matthews, T., 2012. An early and enduring advanced technology originating 71,000 years ago in South Africa. *Nature*. 491, 590–593.

Chadwick, O.A., Derry, L.A., Bern, C.R., Vitousek, P.M., 2009. Changing sources of strontium to soils and ecosystems across the Hawaiian Islands. *Chemical Geology*. 267, 64–76.

Cook, F., Briggs, G., 1977. Nutritive value of eggs. In: Stadelman, W., Cotterill, O. (Eds.), *Egg science and technology*. AVI Publishing Company Inc., Westport, CT, pp. 92–108.

Cooper, R.G., Horbańczuk, J.O., Villegas-Vizcaíno, R., Sebei, S.K., Mohammed, A.E.F., Mahrose, K.M.A., 2010. Wild ostrich (*Struthio camelus*) ecology and physiology. *Tropical Animal Health and Production*. 42, 363–373.

Cooper, R.G., Mahrose, K.M.A., Horbańczuk, J.O., Villegas-Vizcaíno, R., Sebei, S.K., Mohammed, A.E.F., 2009. The wild ostrich (*Struthio camelus*): A review. *Tropical Animal Health and Production*. 41, 1669–1678.

Copeland, S.R., Cawthra, H.C., Fisher, E.C., Lee-Thorp, J.A., Cowling, R.M., le Roux, P.J., Hodgkins, J., Marean, C.W., 2016. Strontium isotope investigation of ungulate movement patterns on the Pleistocene Paleo-Agulhas Plain of the Greater Cape Floristic Region, South Africa. *Quaternary Science Reviews*. 141, 65–84.

Copeland, S.R., Sponheimer, M., Lee-Thorp, J.A., le Roux, P.J., de Ruiter, D.J., Richards, M.P., 2010. Strontium isotope ratios in fossil teeth from South Africa: assessing laser ablation MC ICP-MS analysis and the extent of diagenesis. *Journal of Archaeological Science*. 37, 1437–1446.

Copeland, S.R., Sponheimer, M., Roux, P.J., Grimes, V., Lee-Thorp, J.A., de Ruiter, D.J., Richards, M.P., 2008. Strontium isotope ratios (^{87}Sr / ^{86}Sr) of tooth enamel: a comparison of solution and laser ablation multicollector inductively coupled plasma mass spectrometry methods. *Rapid Communications in Mass Spectrometry*. 22, 3187–3194.

Crisp, M. 2013. Amino acid racemization dating: method development using African ostrich (*Struthio camelus*) eggshell. Unpublished PhD thesis, University of York.

Crisp, M., Demarchi, B., Collins, M.J., Morgan-Williams, M., Pilgrim, E., Penkman, K.E.H., 2013. Isolation of the intra-crystalline proteins and kinetic studies in *Struthio camelus* (ostrich) eggshell for amino acid geochronology. *Quaternary Geochronology*. 16, 110–128.

Demarchi, B., Hall, S., Roncal-Herrero, T., Freeman, C.L., Woolley, J., Crisp, M.K., Wilson, J., Fotakis, A., Fischer, R., Kessler, B.M., Rakownikow Jersie-Christensen, R., Olsen, J. V, Haile, J., Thomas, J., Marean, C.W., Parkington, J., Presslee, S., Lee-Thorp, J., Ditchfield, P., Hamilton, J.F., Ward, M.W.,

Wang, C.M., Shaw, M.D., Harrison, T., Domínguez-Rodrigo, M., MacPhee, R. DE, Kwekason, A., Ecker, M., Kolska Horwitz, L., Chazan, M., Kröger, R., Thomas-Oates, J., Harding, J.H., Cappellini, E., Penkman, K., Collins, M.J., 2016. Protein sequences bound to mineral surfaces persist into deep time. *eLife*. 5, 1–50.

Ecker, M. 2016. Two million years of environmental change: a case study from Wonderwerk Cave, Northern Cape, South Africa. PhD thesis, University of Oxford.

Evans, J.A., Montgomery, J., Wildman, G., 2009. Isotope domain mapping of ^{87}Sr/^{86}Sr biosphere variation on the Isle of Skye. *Scotland. J. Geol. Soc.* 166, 617–631.

Fisher, E.C., Bar-Matthews, M., Jerardino, A., Marean, C.W., 2010. Middle and Late Pleistocene paleoscape modeling along the southern coast of South Africa. *Quaternary Science Reviews.* 29, 1382–1398.

Halkett, D., Hart, T., Yates, R., Volman, T., Parkington, J., Orton, J., Klein, R., Cruz-Uribe, K., Avery, G., 2003. First excavation of intact Middle Stone Age layers at Ysterfontein, Western Cape Province, South Africa: implications for Middle Stone age ecology. *Journal of Archaeological Science.* 30, 955–971.

Hitchcock, R.K., Yellen, J., Gelburd, D., Osborn, A., Crowell, A., 1996. Subsistence hunting and resource management among the Ju/'Hoansi of Northwestern Botswana. *African Study Monographs.* 17, 153–220.

Hoppe, K.A., Koch, P.L., Carlson, R.W., Magnetism, T., 1999. Tracking mammoths and mastodons: reconstruction of migratory behavior using strontium isotope ratios. *Geology.* 27, 439–442.

Johnson, B.J., Fogel, M.L., Miller, G.H., 1998. Stable isotopes in modern ostrich eggshell: a calibration for paleoenvironmental applications in semi-arid regions of southern Africa. *Geochimica et Cosmochimica Acta.* 62, 2451–2461.

Kandel, A.W., 2004. Modification of ostrich eggs by carnivores and its bearing on the interpretation of archaeological and paleontological finds. *Journal of Archaeological Science.* 31, 377–391.

Karkanas, P., Brown, K., Fisher, E., Jacobs, Z., Marean, C.W., 2015. Interpreting human behavior from depositional rates and combustion features through the study of sedimentary microfacies at the site of Pinnacle Point 5-6 South Africa. *Journal of Human Evolution.* 85, 1–12.

Kaufman, D.S., Manley, W.F. 1998. A new procedure for determining DL amino acid ratios in fossils using reverse phase liquid chromatography. *Quaternary Science Reviews.* 17, 987–1000.

Kelly, R.L., 1983. Hunter-gatherer mobility strategies. *Journal of Anthropological Research.* 39, 277–306. www.jstor.org/stable/3629672.

Kimwele, C., Graves, J., 2003. A molecular genetic analysis of the communal nesting of the ostrich (*Struthio camelus*). *Molecular Ecology.* 12, 229–236.

Koch, P.L., 2007. Isotopic study of the biology of modern and fossil vertebrates. In: Michener, R., Lajtha, K. (Eds.), *Stable Isotopes in Ecology and Environmental Science*. Blackwell Publishing, Oxford, pp. 99–154.

Marean, C.W., 2010. Pinnacle Point Cave 13B (Western Cape Province, South Africa) in context: the Cape Floral kingdom, shellfish, and modern human origins. *Journal of Human Evolution.* 59, 425–443.

Marean, C.W., 2014. The origins and significance of coastal resource use in Africa and Western Eurasia. *Journal of Human Evolution.* 77, 17–40.

Marean, C.W., 2016. The transition to foraging for dense and predictable resources and its impact on the evolution of modern humans. *Philosophical Transactions of the Royal Society* B. 371, 1–12.

Marean, C.W., Cawthra, H.C., Cowling, R.M., Esler, K.J., Fisher, E., Milewski, A., Potts, A.J., Singels, E., De Vynck, J., 2014. Stone Age people in a changing South African Greater Cape Floristic Region. In Allsopp, N., Colville, J.F. Verboom, T. (Eds.), *Fynbos: Ecology, evolution, and conservation of a megadiverse region*. Oxford University Press, Oxford, pp. 164–199.

Mills, M., 1977. Diet and foraging behavior of the brown hyaena (*Hyaena brunnea Thunberg*, 1820) in the southern Kalahari. University of Pretoria.

Milton, S.J., Dean, W.R.J., Siegfried, W.R., 1994. Food selection by ostrich in Southern Africa. *Journal of Wildlife Management.* 58(2), 234–248.

Pin, C., Briot, D., Bassin, C., Poitrasson, F., 1994. Concomitant separation of strontium and samarium neodymium for isotopic analysis in silicate samples, based on specific extraction chromatography. *Analytica Chimica Acta.* 298, 209–217.

Price, T.D., Burton, J.H., Bentley, R.A., 2002. The characterization of the biologically available strontium isotope ratios for the study of prehistoric migration. *Archaeometry.* 1, 117–135.

Rector, A.L., Reed, K.E., 2010. Middle and late Pleistocene faunas of Pinnacle Point and their paleoecological implications. *J. Hum. Evol.* 59, 340–357. doi:10.1016/j.jhevol.2010.07.002.

Robbins, L., Murphy, M., Stevens, N., Brook, G., Ivester, A., Haberyan, K., Klein, R., Milo, R., Stewart, K., Matthiesen, D., Winkler, A., 1996. Paleoenvironment and archaeology of Drotsky's Cave: Western Kalahari Desert, Botswana. *Journal of Archaeological Science*. 23, 7–22.

Roche, H., Delagnes, A., Brugal, J.-P., Feibel, C., Kibunjia, M., Mourre, V., Texier, P.-J., 1999. Early hominid stone tool production and technical skill 2.34 Myr ago in West Turkana, Kenya. *Science*. 399, 57–60.

Romanoff, A., Romanoff, A., 1949. *The Avian Egg*. John Wiley & Sons Inc., New York.

Sales, J., Poggenpoel, D.G., Cilliers, S.C., 1996. Comparative physical and nutritive characteristics of ostrich eggs. *World's Poultry Science Journal*. 52, 45–52.

Sauer, E., Sauer, E., 1966. The behavior and ecology of the South African ostrich. *Living Bird*. 5, 45–75.

Sebei, S.K., Bergaoui, R., Hamouda, M. Ben, Cooper, R.G., 2009. Wild ostrich (*Struthio camelus australis*) reproduction in Orbata, a nature reserve in Tunisia. *Tropical Animal Health and Production*. 41, 1427–1438.

Steele, T.E., Klein, R.G., 2013. The Middle and Later Stone Age faunal remains from Diepkloof Rock Shelter, Western Cape, South Africa. *Journal of Archaeological Science*. 40, 3453–3462.

Stewart, J.R.M., Allen, R.B., Jones, A.K.G., Penkman, K.E.H., Collins, M.J., 2013. ZooMS: making eggshell visible in the archaeological record. *Journal of Archaeological Science*. 40, 1797–1804.

Texier, P.-J., Porraz, G., Parkington, J., Rigaud, J.-P., Poggenpoel, C., Miller, C., Tribolo, C., Cartwright, C., Coudenneau, A., Klein, R., Steele, T., Verna, C., 2010. From the cover: a Howiesons Poort tradition of engraving ostrich eggshell containers dated to 60,000 years ago at Diepkloof Rock Shelter, South Africa. *Proceedings of the National Academy of Sciences of the United States of America*. 107, 6180–5.

Texier, P.-J., Porraz, G., Parkington, J., Rigaud, J.P., Poggenpoel, C., Tribolo, C., 2013. The context, form and significance of the MSA engraved ostrich eggshell collection from Diepkloof Rock Shelter, Western Cape, South Africa. *Journal of Archaeological Science*. 40, 3412–3431.

Tullett, S.G., Board, G.R., 1977. Determinants of avian eggshell porosity. *Journal of Zoology* (London). 183, 203–211.

Vallentyne, J.R. 1964. Biogeochemistry of organic matter – II Thermal reaction kinetics and transformation products of amino compounds. *Geochimica et Cosmochimica Acta*. 28, 157–188.

Vogelsang, R., Richter, J., Jacobs, Z., Eichhorn, B., Linseele, V., Roberts, R.G., 2010. New excavations of Middle Stone Age deposits at Apollo 11 rockshelter, Namibia: stratigraphy, archaeology, chronology and past environments. *Journal of African Archaeology*. 8, 185–218.

Wadley, L., 1992. Reply to Barham: aggregation and dispersal phase sites in the Later Stone Age. *South African Archaeological Bulletin*. 47, 52–55.

Whipkey, C., Capo, R., Chadwick, O., Stewart, B., 2000. The importance of sea spray to the cation budget of a coastal Hawaiian soil: a strontium isotope approach. *Chemical Geology*. 168, 37–48.

Wiessner, P. 1986. !Kung San networks in a generational perspective. In Biesele, M., Gordon, R. and Leechman, D. (Eds.), *The Past and Future of !Kung San Ethnography*. Helmut Buske Verlag, Hamburg.

Williams, J. B., Siegfried, W. R., Milton, S. J., Adams, N. J., Dean, W. R. J., du Plessis, M. A., Jackson, S., Nagy, K. A., 1993. Field metabolism, water requirements, and foraging behavior of wild ostriches in the Namib. *Ecology*. 74, 390–404.

20

PREY SPECIES MOVEMENTS AND MIGRATIONS IN ECOCULTURAL LANDSCAPES

Reconstructing late Pleistocene herbivore seasonal spatial behaviours

Kate Britton

Introduction

Movements, defined as spatial changes in the location of an animal in time, are a core aspect of an animal's life and its interactions within the ecosystem. A wide variety of movement types have evolved in different species, and can be seen as a key aspect of an organism's adaptive capacity and evolutionary potential. Animal movements occur over a range of scales, from 'station-keeping'-type residency, to 'classic' long-distance migrations, with substantial variability in the scale, timing, duration and periodicity of movement modes (Dingle 1996). For ecologists and biologists today, the study of faunal movements – particularly migrations – is important for a variety of reasons: not only do ranging behaviours and migrations shape the distributions and actions of individuals or groups of organisms, but they also act to influence community and ecosystem structures and dynamics, evolutionary processes, and even global biodiversity (Nathan et al. 2008).

Understanding the behaviours of extinct and ancestral species has important implications in studies of palaeoecology and evolutionary biology. When considering palaeontological samples, an appreciation of the palaeoethology and behavioural palaeoecology of an animal could prove integral to palaeoenvironmental or palaeoclimatic studies, and also to understanding long-term biological processes such as evolutionary change, speciation and extinction (see discussion in Hoppe et al. 1999). An assessment of feeding and spatial behaviours through time and space allows insight into the stability/conservation of niche behaviours in specific taxa (Feranec et al. 2009). Where multiple species are studied, palaeoecological studies also have implications for our understanding of faunal community structures and dynamics within ecosystems (Feranec and MacFadden 2006; Feranec et al. 2007).

For archaeologists, understanding the temporal and spatial aspects of the seasonal biogeography of the animals should – like any other palaeoenvironmental or palaeoclimatic proxy – be viewed as an essential component in reconstructing the broader ecological and environmental suites in which humans lived. However, beyond providing the 'backdrop' for human activity, understanding the dietary ecology and movement behaviours of prey species at archaeological sites is also important in understanding the behaviours and subsistence choices of ancient human hunters. This is because, at archaeological sites, and unlike natural accumulations, animal remains normally derive from activities directly associated with human action. In this sense, the behaviours and life-histories of those animals can be seen as forming an essential part of the interpretative framework for the reconstruction and understanding of those human actions. Aspects of animal migratory or ranging habits could directly influence contemporary human movements and behaviours, both ecological and cultural, and therefore form a vital part of both the landscapes and the human lives we are endeavouring to understand. This is especially relevant to Palaeolithic archaeology in the late Pleistocene of Europe (~130,000–12,000 years BP), where presumed or elucidated animal behaviour have been used to explain relationships between sites, landscape use, seasonal human movements and ranging, hunting strategies and even worldviews in both the Middle (Gaudzinski 1996; Gaudzinski and Roebroeks 2000; Gaudzinski 2006) and Upper Palaeolithic (Bahn 1977; Gordon 1988; Bratlund 1996; Fuglestvedt 2014).

Focusing on herbivores and the species commonly exploited in the European Palaeolithic in particular, this chapter provides an introduction to ungulate movement behaviours and explores the influence these might have had for late Pleistocene European hunter-gatherer groups. A critique of the use of modern analogues to infer the behaviours of extinct and ancestral taxa is formed, drawing on modern examples that highlight the behavioural plasticity and variability observed within single species today, and the influence of local ecological, environmental and climatic context. The need for direct methods for reconstructing prey species' palaeomigratory behaviour, and the potential implications of such studies for archaeology and other fields is explored. The potential and current limitations of intra-tooth strontium isotope techniques is discussed using the case study of late Pleistocene reindeer movements in Europe. Finally, the prospect of spatial isotope palaeoethology or palaeoecology as a field is considered, and possible future directions are highlighted.

Spatial aspects of herbivore ethology and behavioural ecology

The spatial and temporal distribution of a species are an important component of its physical fitness and reproductive success (MacArthur 1984; Avgar et al. 2013). While genetic (and thus morphological) changes permit long-term adaptation to changing climatic and biotic conditions, changes in the distribution of a species are far more easily and immediately achievable. Physical movement allows the tracking of habitat, and adjustments to environmental variations, helping to avoid species extinction (Pease et al. 1989). Other demands, such as inbreeding avoidance, mate selection, and predation and parasitic avoidance, can also influence the biogeography of a species. Therefore, animal movements and migrations have evolved in response to a combination of ecological and selective pressures (Dobson 1982, 1985).

There are a variety of different movement behaviours that can be seen as contributing to the lifetime tracks of different organisms (Baker 1978), including plants, invertebrates and vertebrates (see Dingle 1996: 10, Table 1-1). Many animal species, including mammal taxa, spend their lifetimes in a limited (circumscribed) area or home range (Dingle 1996: 9). Other species undertake different types of movements outside the usual parameters of their home range boundaries. Animals may disperse permanently or periodically into new ranges; such dispersals are likely to be unpredictable in direction (Sinclair 1992) and are normally undertaken due to the selective pressures of inbreeding avoidance, mate competition, or resource availability, and also to reduce the immediate risks of predation and disease (Dobson 1982, 1985; Waser 1985). However, some animals move more deliberately (and even repeatedly) between different spatial units or ranges throughout life. Such movements are often described as migrations (Baker 1978), although the precise definition and core attributes of migration are variable and debated (Dingle 1996). Some movements, when irregular or only loosely defined, may be described with the epithet of nomadic (migration) or rather as 'seasonal ranging'. For example, many modern ungulates in mountainous regions often move seasonally, although this is rarely considered a 'true' migration. Such behaviour is commonly seen in some modern populations of bison (*Bison bison*) in western North America. This altitudinal seasonal ranging is often driven by snow cover, temperature changes and seasonal food abundances – with higher-altitude summer ranges and lower-altitude winter ranges (e.g. van Vuren 1983; van Vuren and Bray 1986).

Other species may move in a more defined way, the same pattern recurring year after year – these are seasonal migrations, and often considered 'true' migrations, featuring a specific to-and-fro aspect. Such movements normally occur between two or more different environments (at an ecological, if not physical, distance) and truly migratory species are those adapted to several distinct habitat types that fluctuate in suitability (Baker 1978). While these are often undertaken with annual or seasonal regularity, with a to-and-fro aspect, and over long distances (relative to station-keeping or ranging movements), it has been argued that these are not defining features of all migrations (Dingle 1996: 16–17). Furthermore, mixed movement modes have been observed, where populations of animals are composed of both resident and migratory individuals, known as partial migrations (Chapman et al. 2011). Although simplistic, the basic model of two habitats and two seasons, with repeated to-and-fro movements between the two habitats on a seasonal basis is consistent with many examples of herbivore migrations (Fryxell and Sinclair 1988; Fryxell and Holt 2013); for example, seasonal migrations of barren-ground caribou (*Rangifer tarandus groenlandicus*) between vast summer and winter ranges (Banfield 1954; Kelsall 1968), or the seasonal migratory behaviour of wildebeest (*Connochaetes taurinus*) in the Serengeti between wet and dry seasons (Wilmshurst et al. 1999; Holdo et al. 2009).

Faunal migrations can therefore be understood as a strategy used by a variety of species to cope with seasonally variable environments, with the costs and benefits (and therefore the temporal and spatial nature) of migrations highly dependent on local ecological conditions (MacArthur 1959). Migrations have evolved multiple times in multiple taxa (Dingle 1996; Cresswell et al. 2011), and the global occurrence of migratory behaviours in modern large herbivorous species suggests common underlying causes. Migratory behaviour is often selected for when resource distributions are seasonally restricted (Shaw and Couzin 2013), but is also influenced by spatial distribution of resources and resource density dependence (Fryxell and Holt 2013: 1277). These include the gaining of access to high-quality forage, the avoidance of predation, thermal stress, insect harassment, and contact with disease or parasitic vectors (Fryxell and Sinclair 1988; Coughenour 2008). The fact that many migrations occur during transitional seasons (for example, during spring and autumn at mid- and high latitudes) appears to confirm that movements may often be due to the changing availability of resources throughout the year. Furthermore, at latitudinal extremes, such movements can also be driven by immediate climatic pressures and such thermostress migrations usually involve movements along latitudinal or elevation gradients (which tend to be climatic gradients), e.g. the north–south migration of some modern barren-ground caribou herds (Banfield 1954).

Prey species' movements and migrations in human niche and cultural geographies

Faunal materials at archaeological sites are (usually) predominantly anthropogenically derived, and therefore are directly related to human site use. In this sense, their study – from species identification to chemical analysis – forms an essential component of reconstructing the broader ecological and environmental suites in which humans lived. However, zooarchaeological remains are also connected to past human activities and decisions, from late Pleistocene selective hunting and butchering practices, to Neolithic animal husbandry, to Medieval tanning. At hunter-gatherer sites in particular, the life-histories of prey species – such as their spatial ecology and migratory behaviour – form an essential part of the interpretative framework for the reconstruction and understanding of contemporaneous human actions. Rather than simply providing the 'backdrop' for human activity, the movements of migratory species, such as reindeer or caribou (Figure 20.1), can be useful in understanding the relationships between sites, human landscape use, seasonal human movements and ranging, and, through this, hunting behaviours (Britton 2010; Britton et al. 2011).

The relationship between human activities, such as landscape use and hunting, strategies, and prey species' mobility, could be described as 'niche geography' (Binford 1987). 'Niche geography' is a form of landscape use whereby human mobility is understood to be primarily derived from resource availability and is determined by the feeding niche of humans and therefore also by the geographical niche of the animal species exploited. Given that the movements of ungulates are rarely random and include specific ranging, and even seasonally repetitive movements, it is unlikely that the 'niche geography' of early humans would involve random or unplanned movements and actions. Human movements can also be understood in terms of 'cultural geography' (Binford 1987), a framework which has been favoured with regards to anatomically modern humans in late glacial and early Holocene groups in Europe. This term describes a form of landscape use based around socially and culturally constructed centres, rather than occupying the environment and undertaking any movements through the satisfying of immediate physical and subsistence needs. 'Cultural geography' implies the addition of wider social parameters and more complex spatial contexts to human subsistence, aided by technology and centred around hunting camps and home-bases (see discussions in Kolen 1999; Gaudzinski and Roebroeks 2000).

Figure 20.1 A pictorial representation of a caribou engraved onto caribou antler from the precontact Yup'ik site of Nunalleq, western Alaska. Animals such as caribou, seals and salmon remain at the heart of subsistence activities in the region today, and are central to traditional Yup'ik society, culture, and philosophy. Image: Rick Knecht.

Where 'niche geography' determines human group mobility, an understanding of the seasonal movements and foraging habits of herbivorous prey species is essential for understanding the behaviours of contemporary hominins. However, this is also true of instances of 'cultural geography'. Even where clear physical ordering of the landscape and more complex spatial and social organisation is apparent (i.e. 'cultural geographies'), resource availability often still provides the broader framework and is an ultimately restrictive influence, for example, with the technologically, socially and culturally complex landscape of south-west France during the late glacial period. Here, sites in the Périgord and the Pyrenees have been described as representing the different seasonal bases for the same groups of highly mobile Magdalenian 'reindeer followers' (Bahn 1977: 255). The theory of seasonally moving populations, dependent on the migrations of reindeer, draws relationships between archaeological sites and material culture – tying human movements to animal migrations, inextricably knotting the 'cultural' and 'niche' landscapes. Such theories have been developed further by some (e.g. Gordon 1988), but also contested by others (Burke and Pike-Tay 1997).

In this sense, the dichotomy of 'niche' and 'cultural' human geographies, or the notion that cultural geographies somehow exclude or supersede 'natural' ones is artificial. 'Ecological life' attitudes (Ingold 2000) and 'animic' (Fuglestvedt 2014: 42) approaches to the environment highlight that human cultures and worldviews can be shaped by the environment in the widest sense of the word and that animals as living co-inhabitants of the land are as much part of that environment as humans and the physical landscape. The dualism of animal-human relationships is fundamental to standard Western notions that humans are set apart from 'inert' nature. Non-Western perspectives, however, often emphasise fundamental similarity between humans, animals and nature (Scott 1989: 194–195). Indeed, the notion that, rather than set apart, humans are 'one species of person in networks of reciprocating persons' (Scott 1989: 195), including animals, who can choose whether or not to give humans what they need to live is widely reported among northern hunting peoples (Ingold 2000: 48). As Fuglestvedt (2014) argues, with reference to the late Upper Palaeolithic Ahrensburgian culture, high dependency on game hunting structures and reinforces such animic attitudes, particularly in pioneer contexts and in a world of physical and environmental flux (i.e. post-glacial northern Europe).

Amongst other late Pleistocene hunting societies, relationships to animals would be pivotal, and social and ecological relations may therefore be seen as inextricably tied. Whether purely being considered in practical and economic terms, or as part of the broader culturally mediated landscapes, a focus on other living inhabitants of the landscape, and their movements, should be viewed as an intrinsic part of understanding hunter-gatherer lifeways (and perhaps even lifeworlds) in the past. It is clear that throughout the Middle Palaeolithic, Upper Palaeolithic, and Mesolithic of Europe, understanding the seasonal availability and distribution of archaeologically important prey species could be pivotal to interpreting human landscape movements and subsistence choices – whether we are considering migratory interception/mass kill sites (such as the Middle Palaeolithic site of Salzgitter Lebenstedt, Germany, or the Late Glacial sites of Stellmoor, Germany, and Meiendorf, Germany), the total 'niche geography' of early hominin groups, or the 'cultural geography' of specialised techno-socio–cultural complexes (such as the Magdalenian or Ahrensbergian 'reindeer hunters').

The insufficient analogue

One of the most common ways in which faunal behaviour is alluded to in archaeological studies is, either explicitly or not, through the use of modern analogue. However, this is a problematic practice in archaeology and palaeoecology, particularly when applied to estimates of seasonal migrations or ranging habits of extinct and ancestral species. Perhaps the most immediate issue with this approach is that, for extinct species, there are no suitable modern analogues. This is especially relevant to Europe and North America in the Pleistocene, where cold-adapted proboscidians and other megafauna were common. These large mammals would not only have been game and raw material resources (meat, ivory, hide, etc.) but also their physical presence, dietary and range-size demands would have shaped the physical landscape and the early human world. This would include the creation of trails, thus allowing access to useful resources such as water sources, fruit patches, mineral licks and optimal feeding tracts for other species, including humans. The dietary and migratory movements of these animals would also serve to create grasslands, attracting non-migratory grazers and helping to maintain high biotic productivity through seed distribution (Guthrie 1990; Haynes 2002). An understanding of the ranging habits of such animals – as well as other, now extinct species, or ancestral extant herbivore species – is therefore essential for accurate reconstructions of the landscape ecology of the past and understanding how this may have influenced human populations. It must also be noted that a number of modern migratory animal species also have sedentary ecotypes. For example, both wildebeest (*Connochaetes* sp.) (Serneels and Lambin 2001) and reindeer/caribou (*Rangifer tarandus* ssp.) (Banfield 1961) have migratory and non-migratory populations. Furthermore, mixed strategies or partial migrants have been observed within the same populations of some animal (Chapman et al. 2011). There may, however, not be any significant morphological or genetic distinctions that can be made between the two forms in the archaeological or palaeontological record. Movement variability (from migration to nomadism) has been observed in other extant species of northern ungulate, such as moose (*Alces alces*), across their latitudinal range, largely in response to local environmental conditions (Singh et al. 2012).

The use of modern analogues is also limited by the range of modern environments available for comparison. Given this, even in cases where there is species continuity, faunal behavioural analogues cannot be drawn. For example, there is no suitable modern analogue for the mammoth steppe ecosystem of the European, Siberian and North American Palaeolithic. This is also true of the continental arctic tundra environments of Eurasia during recent cold phases. Unlike modern day barren-land or arctic tundra, these were ecotones combining glacial tundra with fertile loess soils. Furthermore, unlike today's northern plains, these ancient habitats were at low latitudes, were fully continental and fully terrestrial – favouring high bioproductivity (Guthrie 1990; Goebel 1999; Hoffecker 2002). Modern arctic environments are clearly not suitable analogues for the vast plains of Palaeolithic Central and Eastern Europe. Therefore, the migratory behaviour of the modern caribou in the extreme northwest of Alaska, for example, may not be analogous for the seasonal ranging habits of Palaeolithic reindeer in Europe.

In addition to the issue of a lack of similar environments, it is also important to note that many modern environments (from which analogies are drawn) are in some way directly or indirectly influenced by modern human actions. This includes the very direct influences of infrastructure, range restriction and land partitioning, and the shrinking of available resources and habitable areas through competition. Developments within migratory corridors, such as roads, fencing and energy development can present physical barriers to long-distance animal movement and impede migration (Seidler et al. 2015). This has been demonstrated in studies of the influence of roads, high-voltage power lines, pipelines and tourist resorts on the winter foraging habits of wild reindeer (*Rangifer tarandus tarandus*) in south central Norway (Dahle et al. 2008). Another such example is the relationship between the caribou winter territory and the incidence of anthropogenically controlled wildland burning. Such burning practices serve to

Prey species movements and migrations

increase vegetative diversity and productivity, but destroy the lichen mats that form the bulk of caribou winter forage. GPS radio-collar tracking of individuals from the Alaskan Nelchina caribou (*Rangifer tarandus granti*) herd demonstrate that caribou will avoid tracts of land for decades after burning (Joly et al. 2002). The impact of controlled vegetation fires on species substitution, extinction, distribution and migration has been observed in Canadian boreal forest ecosystems elsewhere (Weber and Flannigan 1997) and may even have been relevant in the past, where anthropogenically controlled forest/wildland burning may have occurred (Lewis and Ferguson 1988). Other direct human actions, such as supplementary feeding, can substantially alter ungulate migrations and these anthropogenic resource changes in one season can have unintended behavioural consequences in the next: for example, changes in the summer range in populations of elk in western Wyoming due to winter supplementary feeding regimes (Jones et al. 2014).

In addition to these obvious anthropogenic influences, there are other, global, human-induced changes which have the potential to alter mass herd behaviour. Examples include anthropogenically derived atmospheric and environmental pollutants, or the global rise in temperatures and increasingly erratic weather patterns (known to be the result of the combustion of fossil fuels) (IPCC 2013). There is growing evidence that recent global climate change has altered species' distribution patterns, extending growing seasons, and the phenology of animal breeding and migration (e.g. Pitelka et al. 1997; Cotton 2003; Jenni and Kery 2003; Travis 2003; Joly et al. 2007; Levinsky et al. 2007; Rivalan et al. 2007; Klein et al. 2008; Joly et al. 2011). Therefore, behaviours drawn from modern species, at a time when human behaviour has invariably altered their physical, biological and chemical environment, are not likely applicable to Palaeolithic species.

Another factor which must be taken into account when applying models of modern animal behaviour to the species of the past is that – even in relatively recent history – significant variations have been observed in the migratory behaviour of the same species. For example, pre-nineteenth-century documents and ethnographic accounts indicate that plains bison in North America undertook long-distance, seasonal migrations (e.g. Bamforth 1987; Hamilton et al. 2006). Today, many populations are sedentary or undertake seasonal altitudinal ranging (e.g. van Vuren 1983; van Vuren and Bray 1986). It is not known whether such changes result from natural distribution and behavioural fluctuations in these populations, or whether such differences are the product of the influence of modern humans (or indeed, climatic or environmental changes). Bison were hunted to almost total extinction in the wild in the nineteenth century and most modern herds are bred and managed within conservation areas. Therefore, perhaps in the case of bison, historical records can provide a better indication of the natural spatial ecology of this species. However, the use of historical plains bison as an analogue for the migratory behaviour of European Palaeolithic bison populations remains inappropriate for reasons previously discussed (i.e. the stark differences between the environment of the recent North American mid-west and Europe during the last glaciation).

Changes in the distribution and movement habits of other species have also been observed in recent centuries, even where there is no clear human-derived cause, for example, the regular demographic fluctuations (or cycles) that have been observed in populations of Greenland caribou. These herds have been shown to expand and contract enormously, with range expansion and long-distance migratory behaviour correlating with large populations. These 'boom-bust' cycles may be triggered by broad-scale climatic variations, forage availability and reproductive behaviours. These cycles have been documented over the last 250 years, using historical, ethnohistorical and game-statistics sources (Figure 20.2, based on Meldgaard 1986: 58, Figure 57), with cycles showing a complicated, but likely periodic, synchronicity (Meldgaard 1986).

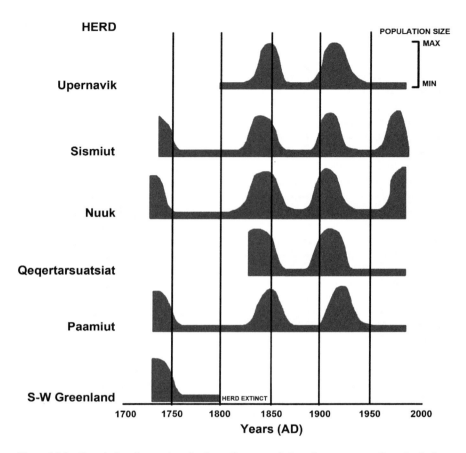

Figure 20.2 Population fluctuations in six caribou populations from western Greenland, from c. 1730 until 1985. Image adapted from Meldgaard 1986: 58, Figure 57.

As well as such cycles of behaviour, climatic variations also account for large variations in the geographical spread of species in relatively recent history. For example, changes in the distribution of populations of woodland caribou (*Rangifer tarandus caribou*) in eastern North America have been observed over the last few hundred years. In the early and mid-nineteenth century, woodland caribou resided in Maine, northern Vermont, New Hampshire, northern Minnesota, Wisconsin, Michigan, and throughout Atlantic Canada – the southern extent of the geographical distribution of the species being much further south than today (Banfield 1961; Bergerud and Mercer 1989). This pattern coincides with the later phase of the last global cooling period or 'Little Ice Age' (Mann 2007). This variation is therefore likely to have been climatically induced, with favoured climatic conditions extending northward during the following warming period, opening up the landscape for other competing species and pushing the caribou further north into their suitable biome. The relationship between decadal climatic shifts and range use/geographical distributions have also been noted more recently in Alaskan caribou herds (Joly et al. 2007; Joly et al. 2011). Such studies give us some indication of what to expect in the behaviour of ancient animal populations during periods of climatic change, but also reiterate that modern behavioural analogues may not be appropriate when applied to the past.

Prey species movements and migrations

Given the issues outlined above, it appears that the use of modern analogues is not an ideal solution to understanding the behaviours of ancient animals. In some cases, there are no available analogous species (e.g. woolly mammoths) and, even where the species is extant, the modern physical, environmental and climatic suites are unlikely to be comparable to those in the past. It must be noted that, even in relatively recent history, variations in the demography and distribution of populations can be observed: Whatever the causes of such shifts, these century-level changes are on significantly smaller timescales than those that may have occurred during the many millennia of the Middle and Upper Palaeolithic. Given the significant (and potentially unknown) local and global climatic and environmental fluctuations associated with such long periods of time, the migratory and seasonal feeding behaviours of past mammalian species (even those that are extant) cannot be sufficiently elucidated from present-day observations. Conversely, with appropriate analytical approaches in place to reconstruct faunal mobility habits directly from their physical remains, the archaeological record could be seen as a vital archive to investigate variability in faunal movement behaviours through time and in relation to climatic and environmental change.

Reconstructing animal life-histories, past and present

There are a number of methods available to study the extent and path of migratory movements in modern faunal populations. These including field methods, such as direct observations and counts, and trapping to sample animals for genetic and chemical markers of origin or life-history. Trapping may also include marking and releasing animals (e.g. ringing birds), and their subsequent recapture at different passage points to trace migratory pathways. Radio and satellite telemetry is also an important tool in tracking the behaviours of individuals and herds, along with radar observations of large groups (Dingle 1996: 64–84).

Beyond their presence (or absence) in the faunal records, there are few techniques that can provide insights into the biogeography or spatial palaeo-ethology/-ecology of different species commonly found at archaeological sites. Morphometric traits can – in a general sense – also be utilised to estimate the spatial ecology of a species, for example, the relationship between body size and that of the geographical range of a species (reviewed in Gaston and Blackburn 1996).

This relationship shows that larger-bodied taxa will have a larger range size due to the requirement for more food resources (due to their larger body and higher energy expenditure). Given this, populations with larger home ranges would also need to have larger total geographical ranges in order to maintain minimum viable population sizes (McNab 1963; Lindsted et al. 1986). Analysis of the body size, range size and biomic specialisation of African large mammals indicates a relationship between latitudinal extent and body size, which has also been observed in other species from other areas (e.g. Olifiers et al. 2004). Such models could therefore be applied to archaeological and palaeontological materials through morphometric analysis. However, it has also been suggested that much of the observed modern variation in the variables of specialisation and geographical range size in large mammals cannot always be attributed immediately to body size but is also the product of local biome-specific factors (Fernandez and Vrba 2005). Furthermore, although general information about the size of a species' range can be estimated from body size, and computational models can be used to elucidate the range sizes of archaeological animals from their physical remains, this approach cannot provide any information about the direction or phenology of ranging or migration habits.

Over the past twenty years, the frequency of the use of stable isotope analysis in animal ecology has grown significantly (Wolf et al. 2009), and these approaches have been used to investigate many aspects of ecosystem, physiology, population, nutritional and migratory ecology

(Hobson 1999; Hobson and Wassenaar 1999; Rubenstein and Hobson 2004; Hobson and Wassenaar 2008). This has been mirrored by the increasing use of these techniques in archaeology (Makarewicz and Sealy 2015; Britton in press), and in more recent years, zooarchaeology (Pilaar Birch 2013; Makarewicz 2016). In ecology, isotope methods are valuable as they can be applied across different taxa and the most commonly used analytes are found across different species (e.g. blood, fur, etc.). This can allow the analysis of multiple species within different ecosystems, allowing the assessment of behavioural and feeding ecology at many levels of the food chain. The standardisation of sampling and measurement procedures on similar analytes allows the comparison of multiple species and across multiple geographical areas (Hobson and Wassenaar 2008). Furthermore, stable isotope methods can permit a temporally integrated approach to the reconstructing of foraging behaviour and animal ecology. Compared to other methods, stable isotope approaches do not rely on the re-capture or re-sighting of previously sampled individuals (Rubenstein and Hobson 2004). When a large-enough survey is conducted, data is meaningful on a population level, with data archiving allowing the assessment of temporal trends. Although isotope analysis can offer lower resolution results than other methods of reconstructing foraging and ranging behaviour in modern animals (e.g. tagging, satellite collaring, etc.), the use of multiple isotopes in combination can increase this resolution (Hobson and Wassenaar 2008).

A large number of stable light isotope studies have been conducted on modern wild mammalian fauna to assess feeding habits, with some including archaeologically relevant analytes (i.e. tooth and bone). This includes the reconstruction of diet and grazing behaviours (Copeland et al. 2009), resource partitioning (Feranec 2007), trophic relationships (Sealy et al. 1987; Ambrose 1991), and seasonal foraging habits (Koch et al. 1995; Ben-David et al. 2001; Drucker et al. 2001; Kielland 2001; Cerling et al. 2004; Drucker et al. 2010). Such studies have led to the analysis of wild archaeological fauna, both as a means of establishing 'baselines' for human dietary interpretation, and for better understanding ancient foodwebs and investigating niche feeding behaviours (e.g. Bocherens 2003; Feranec et al. 2010; Britton et al. 2012). However, few studies – modern or archaeological – have focused on the use of isotopic techniques to document the ranging and movement habits of ungulates and other important archaeological prey species. Strontium isotope analysis (a method utilised by geologists to characterise rocks for over half a century, see Faure and Powell 1972) has great potential for the investigation of human and animal provenance (Beard and Johnson 2000; Bentley 2006). It has been applied to modern elephant ivory to demonstrate the origin, and thus illegal trade, of ivory (van der Merwe et al. 1990). Strontium isotope approaches are particularly powerful when combined with incremental sampling approaches, and limited modern experimental studies on wild caribou and bison from North America have demonstrated the potential of these techniques to document migratory habits and movement histories (Britton et al. 2009; Britton 2010). However, there are relatively few studies that incorporate strontium isotope analysis and intra-tooth sampling to address the issue of animal movement and ecology in modern samples, potentially due to the relatively high costs of traditional strontium isotope analysis compared to other methods (e.g. carbon/nitrogen isotope analysis of bone collagen and carbon/oxygen isotope analysis of tooth enamel). This could also be due to the more complex sampling techniques and preparation methods involved in strontium isotope analysis. These factors may also explain why very little modern observational experimental work incorporating strontium isotope analysis and archaeologically relevant analytes has been conducted. Therefore, as with other, more established areas of isotope archaeology, it is essential that more modern experimental work be undertaken using strontium isotope analysis and intra-tooth sampling.

Despite the lack of a large body of proof-of-concept work based on modern samples, strontium isotope approaches have been utilised to explore the ranging and movement habits of extinct and ancestral animal species. In one such study, bulk strontium isotope analysis of calcified tissues in 3,000-year-old mammals from Yellowstone National Park have been used to investigate their landscape use (Feranec et al. 2007). Feranec and colleagues determined that strontium isotope ratios in small and mid-sized mammals correlated with the values of local substrates. Large-body-sized individuals demonstrated $^{87}Sr/^{86}Sr$ ratios indicative of foraging behaviours that incorporated variable lithologies. When compared to modern mammals, the data suggests continuity in the behaviour and foraging radii of different animal species at Yellowstone and, therefore, that the niches of species can be conserved over considerable periods of time (Feranec et al. 2007). In a study by Hoppe et al. (1999) $^{87}Sr/^{86}Sr$ analysis of bulk enamel samples from mastodon (*Mammut americanum*) and mammoth (*Mammuthus* sp.) from late Pleistocene Florida were used to assess differences in their movement and (potentially) migratory behaviour. Analysis of the bulk samples revealed that $^{87}Sr/^{86}Sr$ values in mastodons were universally higher than mammoths, indicating that mastodons spent considerable periods of time in Georgia as well as Florida (Hoppe et al. 1999). Intra-tooth strontium data from a mastodon molar revealed a cyclical pattern, indicating this species made regular seasonal migrations between Florida and the Georgian foothills (Hoppe et al. 1999).

European reindeer in the late Pleistocene: a case study in isotope palaeoethology using intra-tooth strontium isotope analysis

In more recent years, strontium isotope approaches and intra-tooth sampling of prey species' dental enamel from archaeological sites has been used to explore faunal landscape use and, through this, elucidate human subsistence strategies. For example, strontium isotope analysis (combined with oxygen) evidenced different ranging behaviours in horse (*Equus hydruntinus*) and red deer (*Cervus elaphus*) in late Upper Palaeolithic central Italy, but also that data were consistent with a transhumance model that had been proposed for the region (Pellegrini et al. 2008). A study at the late Pleistocene site of Amvrosievka, eastern Ukraine, utilised similar approaches to argue that European steppe bison (*Bison priscus*) – a species often assumed to be migratory – were largely sedentary with limited evidence of inter-seasonal movement (Julien et al. 2012). The ready availability of steppe bison throughout the year may even explain its key role in Palaeolithic human subsistence (Julien et al. 2012: 117). Similar conclusions were drawn from a previous study of a single bison sample from an earlier Middle Palaeolithic site in south-west France (Britton et al. 2011).

The species that has received most attention in late Pleistocene isotope zooarchaeological studies of faunal movements is, perhaps unsurprisingly, reindeer (*Rangifer tarandus* spp.). European Palaeolithic reindeer are commonly considered to be a seasonally (bi-annually) migrating taxa (Bahn 1977), their behaviours likened to modern North American caribou herds. However, wild herds of extant caribou and reindeer include both sedentary and migratory ecotypes, with some herds occupying herd ranges of a few hundred square kilometres and others occupying enormous annual ranges and undertaking extensive seasonal movements over thousands of kilometres (Bergman et al. 2000). Some herds undertake the 'classic' long-distance thermostress migrations (north on a north-south trajectory), although the phenomena of migratory behaviour (its direction, distance, organisation, philopatry, route fidelity and persistence) is thought to be triggered by a range of factors including population size, forage abundance, predation avoidance and insect pestilence (Bergerud and Luttich 2003). There is a clear relationship between environment (i.e. forage availability), population size and the need for seasonal migration. Without regular, long-distance movements, it is unlikely that a single, local environment could support the vast numbers of animals seen in some modern migratory caribou herds.

Populations of modern sedentary (or short-distance-migratory) woodland and barren-ground caribou are normally smaller than their long-distance-migratory counterparts by several orders of magnitude. For example, the sedentary Red Wine Mountains caribou herd occupy a herd range of approximately 25,000 km² in central Labrador and had a population of ~150 animals in 1997 (Schaefer et al. 1999). By contrast, the migratory George River herd (Labrador and northern Québec) has a total herd range of around 700,000 km² and was estimated to have a population of between 600,000 and 800,000 in 1996 (Schaefer et al. 2000). Population densities are also unstable through time, and have been shown to fluctuate hugely due to relatively small climatic and environmental changes (see above, and Meldgaard 1986; Joly et al. 2007; Klein et al. 2008). These variations observed in modern and historical caribou biogeography indicate the need for direct methods for reconstructing the seasonal movements of Pleistocene reindeer.

Abundance of prime-aged reindeer accumulated over a short window of time at sites have been used to argue for a seasonally restricted, migratory resource, for example at the Middle Palaeolithic sites of Salzgitter-Lebenstedt (Gaudzinski and Roebroeks 2000), Jonzac (Niven et al. 2012) and Les Pradelles (Costamagno et al. 2006). Similar approaches have also been applied to 'reindeer specialization' (Mellars 2004) in the Upper Palaeolithic of south-west France and elsewhere (Bratlund 1996; Burke and Pike-Tay 1997; Enloe and David 1997; Thacker 1997). Osteometrics have been used to distinguish between different Palaeolithic reindeer populations, and these data have been used to rule out some proposed reconstructions of reindeer seasonal movements (Delpeche 1983; Weinstock 2000).

To date, a small number of studies have sought to directly assess reindeer migrations in Palaeolithic Europe using strontium isotope analysis of sequentially sampled dental enamel (see Figure 20.3), including studies from Middle Palaeolithic south-west France (Kelly 2007; Britton 2010; Britton et al. 2011) and in late Upper Palaeolithic northern France and Germany (Price et al. 2015; Waterman et al. 2015).

While intra-tooth strontium data from the published studies suggest to-and-fro movements between different lithological units (Britton et al. 2011; Price et al. 2015), and thus concluded behaviour was migratory, both studies found directionality and distance of movement difficult

Figure 20.3 Late Pleistocene reindeer lower third molar (M3) with broken roots, sequentially-sampled ahead of strontium isotope analysis. The selected surface was abraded prior to sampling in order to remove cementum and surficial contaminants, before enamel was removed as powdered samples. Measurements taken from the enamel-root junction (indicated with an arrow) allow the isotope data to be plotted as a time-series sequence. Image: Kate Britton.

to assess. On the basis of local bioavailability data in the two regions studied, reindeer movements do seem to have other commonalities – for example, the avoidance of upland areas. The limited body of work undertaken to date has also served to emphasise that co-analysis of oxygen isotopes in intra-tooth samples is an important component of interpreting seasonal ranging behaviours (Britton et al. 2009; Price et al. 2015); that birthing grounds may be straightforward to discern by analysis of the early forming parts of the second molar (Britton et al. 2009), and also that strontium isotope data have the potential to reveal changes in migratory behaviour in a species through time. At the Middle Palaeolithic Neanderthal butchery site of Jonzac, reindeer sampled from earlier (Quina Mousterian) levels demonstrated intra-tooth strontium isotope variability consistent with seasonal migratory behaviour (as they move between areas of different strontium isotope 'signatures'); a single reindeer tooth was also analysed from the more recent (Denticulate Mousterian) cultural phase and demonstrated lower (local) values and decreased intra-tooth variation (suggesting a lack of movement) (see Figure 20.4, and Britton 2010). These data from two different phases of the same site may provide the first tentative evidence for changes in reindeer migratory behaviour through time, and may indicate that this species was more 'local' and less vagile during this later, warmer period (Britton 2010).

Significantly, the data from the earlier, Quina Mousterian levels at Jonzac, when combined with season-of-death and seasonality data, help evidence the mode of Neanderthal hunting at the site. The isotope and zooarchaeological data suggest Neanderthals intensively exploited the reindeer as the herds passed through the area, with the rock shelter of Jonzac located near their migration routes (Britton et al. 2011). From Jonzac, and other sites (e.g. Salzgitter-Lebenstedt – Gaudzinski and Roebroeks 2000), we can deduce that targeted monospecific exploitation and

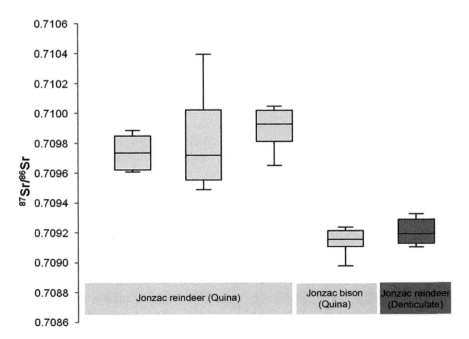

Figure 20.4 Sequential $^{87}Sr/^{86}Sr$ data from Rangifer and Bison/Bos enamel from Quina (Level 22) and Denticulate (Level 8) phases of Jonzac. Box plots display the first and third quartile, median, minimum and maximum values. Adapted from Britton 2010: 222.

interception hunting (a behaviour often attributed to later societies) were subsistence strategies practised by Neanderthals as well as by anatomically modern humans. This implies more complex subsistence strategies, landscape use, and animal–human relationships than are commonly ascribed to Middle Pleistocene hominins. While the elaborate social, cultural and symbolic significance of prey species are (literally) written on the walls of the Upper Palaeolithic, the lack of similar parietal art and material culture attributed to the Neanderthals is exemplary of the trap of negative evidence that is commonly used to reconstruct Neanderthal behaviours and to 'evaluate' them (Speth 2004). This highlights the prevalence of human exceptionalism in Middle Pleistocene archaeology and the study of extinct human 'Others', as well as in the study of animal species.

While the dataset is currently very limited, the potential change in reindeer migratory behaviour over time hinted at in the Jonzac study is also important. This highlights the dynamism and plasticity we must consider in multispecies archaeology, and also raises questions about the implications of continuity and change in prey species' behaviour for past human groups. Meat-eating is deeply rooted in the human story (McPherron et al. 2010), with profound ecological and evolutionary consequences for the genus *Homo*, ultimately enabling wider habitat tolerance and distribution of *H. ergaster/erectus* out of Africa and into Eurasia (Foley 2001). The entangled nature of this cross-species dependency for all hominins (as social primates) must be considered central to later Pleistocene archaeology too, and as 'more than just a question of calories' (Foley 2001: 325). For Neanderthal reindeer-hunters, Upper Palaeolithic 'Ice Age' *artistes*, or pioneer populations in post-glacial northern Europe, the implications of differences in prey species' behaviour and distribution occurring over short timespans, and especially in periods of rapid climatic change, could have been profound for the social, cultural and symbolic.

Concluding thoughts: towards a framework for prey species spatial palaeoethology and palaeoecology

The intra-tooth strontium isotope analysis of herbivore teeth from archaeological sites has, in recent years, highlighted the potential of this method for reconstructing the seasonal movements of important prey species in the past. Underpinned by modern experimental studies, these methods permit the investigation of wild animal spatial palaeoethology and palaeoecology, and through this, allow more detailed reconstruction of the ecological and cultural landscapes of the human past. Using these techniques, it is possible to identify to-and-fro migratory behaviour within a seasonal framework; to isotopically characterise calving grounds, and winter and summer ranges, and also to reveal relative changes in migratory behaviour through time. However, the identification of winter and summer ranges *geographically* and the identification and characterisation of migratory corridors are clearly more difficult to infer, and are currently a clear limitation on these approaches. Furthermore, as highlighted by modern work on a herd currently undergoing a population crash and migratory disturbance (the George River herd, Canada), inconsistent behaviours lead to equally inconsistent isotope data in terms of inter-individual variability (Britton 2010).

There are also limitations inherent to the archaeological record that limit the nature and scope of isotopic investigations at any particular site. For example, the identification of herd behaviours is only meaningful where either behaviour is very constant or where the deposition of a particular assemblage/component of a site is chronologically highly restricted (such as with a mass-kill site). Studies on sites that represent multiple 'events' may reveal a variability in behaviour that can be difficult to interpret without more restrained dating (Price et al. 2015). There are also issues with sample size and sample requirements. In the case of reindeer,

Prey species movements and migrations

as low-crowned herbivores, two teeth (normally, the second and third molar) are required to reconstruct a full annual cycle (Britton et al. 2009). Therefore, two teeth from the same animal are required from multiple animals to conduct the most basic assessment of intra-annual movements in a single assemblage/single phase. With partial or complete hemi-mandibles required from multiple individuals, the investigation of prey species' behaviour may not always be feasible. Underlying lithology can also be a restrictive consideration, especially in areas with very little (or conversely very great) lithological, and thus isotopic, variability. Furthermore, even where suitable materials are available, the costs of strontium isotope analysis and the availability of local strontium 'bioavailability' data can further limit data analysis and data interpretation. Although there are countries for which large baseline datasets have been published, from soils, plants, or fauna (e.g. in Britain, Evans et al. 2010; in France, Willmes et al. 2014), these are the exception and more studies are required.

In spite of these limitations, intra-tooth strontium isotope approaches do show great potential for the reconstruction of prey species' migratory behaviours in the past, for both archaeologists and ecologists wanting to exploit a deep time archive of biological materials which archaeology represents. One way for archaeological studies to go beyond what recent studies have achieved could be with the formulating of truly cross-disciplinary research projects, incorporating not only archaeologists and geochemists but also spatial ecologists. For example, in order to more fully utilise isotope data evidencing faunal mobility habits (and through this, human behaviours and experiences), new ways of contextualising isotope data are going to be required. GIS tools, or computational models, for example, are commonly used in spatial ecology, and could prove useful in plotting seasonal migrations and herd routes from intra-tooth strontium data. Working with spatial ecologists will allow the incorporation of discrimination factors, for example, the common topographical attributes seen in migratory corridors of modern caribou. Other archaeological datasets could also be useful in defining these and other parameters, such as palaeoenvironmental or palaeoclimatic proxy data. As with many other areas of isotope archaeology, development of these tools within a proof-of-concept experimental framework with modern materials using archaeologically relevant analytes will be key. However, for a co-created field of faunal spatial palaeoecology to emerge, cross-disciplinary methodologies and epistemologies will need to be reconciled. Challenges of study design and sample size are obvious sources of discrepancy in archaeological and ecological isotope data sets, along with methods of analysing, visualising and interacting with data, as well as the theoretical frameworks used to interpret data. In order to move forward, an understanding of the archaeological record, taphonomy and diagenesis will need to be coupled with theoretical and practical approaches to understanding spatial patterns and their relationships to ecological factors drawn from landscape (spatial) ecology (Britton 2017).

The establishing of frameworks for studying prey species spatial palaeoecology using archaeological materials will have a clear benefit for both archaeologists and palaeoecologists. This must begin with the rejection of the modern analogue (for animals, as for humans), the expectation of plasticity in faunal behaviours in deeper time, and the development of methodologies to reconstruct those behaviours. The results from the incremental strontium isotope analysis of modern, and archaeological, faunal enamel are very promising, and suggest this is a powerful tool for the reconstruction of animal seasonal palaeobiogeography. Further applications, particularly in areas with published strontium 'baseline' datasets, and the development of these techniques within a spatial ecology framework, will lead to better ways of understanding anthropologically accumulated faunal deposits, and the movements of archaeological prey species. Through this, the subsistence choices, hunting strategies, and 'seasonal rounds' of past human groups will be better accessed, permitting greater insights into eco- and socio-cultural connections across the living landscapes of the past.

Kate Britton

Acknowledgements

This chapter is based on research from the doctoral thesis of the author (Britton 2010), which was supported by the Max Planck Society (MPI-EVA), University of Durham, and the Natural Environment Research Council (ref: NER/S/A/2006/14004). Thanks to Mike Richards (SFU); Jean-Jacques Hublin and Shannon McPherron (MPI-EVA); Andrew Millard, Mark White and Peter Rowley-Conwy (Durham). Special thanks to Suzanne Pilaar Birch for inviting me to contribute to this volume, and to Suzanne and the series editors for comments on earlier versions of this manuscript. Thanks to Rick Knecht (Aberdeen) for permission to use Figure 20.1, and also to the University of Aberdeen, for professional and financial support during the preparation of this chapter.

References

Ambrose, S. H. 1991. Effects of diet, climate and physiology on nitrogen isotope abundances in terrestrial foodwebs. *Journal of Archaeological Science* 18:293–317.

Avgar, T., Street, G. and Fryxell, J. 2013. On the adaptive benefits of mammal migration. *Canadian Journal of Zoology* 92:481–490.

Bahn, P. 1977. Seasonal migration in South-west France during the late glacial period. *Journal of Archaeological Science* 4:245–257.

Baker, R. R. 1978. *The evolutionary ecology of animal migration*. London: Hodder and Stoughton.

Bamforth, D. B. 1987. Historical documents and bison ecology on the Great Plains. *Plains Anthropologist* 32:1–16.

Banfield, A. W. F. 1961. *A revision of the reindeer and caribou, genus Rangifer*. Ottawa: Department of Northern Affairs and National Resources.

—— 1954. *Preliminary investigation of the barren ground caribou*. Ottawa: National Parks Branch, Department of Northern Affairs and National Resources.

Beard, B. L. and Johnson, C. M. 2000. Strontium isotope composition of skeletal material can determine the birth place and geographic mobility of humans and animals. *Journal of Forensic Science* 45:1049–1061.

Ben-David, M., Shochat, E. and Adams, L. G. 2001. Utility of stable isotope analysis in studying foraging ecology of herbivores: examples from moose and caribou. *ALCES* 37:421–434.

Bentley, R. A. 2006. Strontium isotopes from the earth to the archaeological skeleton: a review. *Journal of Archaeological Method and Theory* 13:135–187.

Bergerud, A. T. and Mercer, W. E. 1989. Caribou introductions in eastern North America. *Wildlife Society Bulletin* 17:111–120.

Bergerud, A. T. and Luttich, S. N. 2003. Predation risk and optimal foraging trade-off in the demography and spacing of the George River Herd, 1958 to 1993. *Rangifer Special Issue* 14:169–191.

Bergman, C. M., Schaefer, J. A. and Luttich, S. N. 2000. Caribou movement as a correlated random walk. *Oecologia* 123:364–374.

Binford, L. R. 1987. Searching for camps and missing evidence? Another look at the Lower Palaeolithic. *In*: Soffer, O. (ed.) *The Pleistocene Old World: Regional perspectives*. New York: Plenum Press.

Bocherens, H. 2003. Isotopic biogeochemistry and the palaeoecology of the mammoth steppe fauna. *Deinsea Annual of the Natural History Museum Rotterdam* 9:57–76.

Bratlund, B. 1996. Hunting strategies in the Late Glacial of northern Europe: a survey of the faunal evidence. *Journal of World Prehistory* 10:1–48.

Britton, K. in press. 2017. A stable relationship: isotopes and bioarchaeology are in it for the long haul. *Antiquity* 91: 853–864.

Britton, K. 2010. *Multi-isotope analysis and the reconstruction of prey species palaeomigrations and palaeoecology*. Doctoral thesis, Durham University.

Britton, K., Grimes, V., Dau, J. and Richards, M. P. 2009. Reconstructing faunal migrations using intra-tooth sampling and strontium and oxygen isotope analyses: a case study of modern caribou (*Rangifer tarandus granti*). *Journal of Archaeological Science* 36:1163–1172.

Britton, K., Gaudzinski-Windheuser, S., Roebroeks, W., Kindler, L. and Richards, M. P. 2012. Stable isotope analysis of well-preserved 120,000-year-old herbivore bone collagen from the Middle Palaeolithic site of Neumark-Nord 2, Germany reveals niche separation between bovids and equids. *Palaeogeography, Palaeoclimatology, Palaeoecology* 333–334:168–177.

Prey species movements and migrations

Britton, K., Grimes, V., Niven, L., Steele, T., McPherron, S., Soressi, M., Kelly, T. E., Jaubert, J., Hublin, J.-J. and Richards, M. P. 2011. Strontium isotope evidence for migration in late Pleistocene Rangifer: Implications for Neanderthal hunting strategies at the Middle Palaeolithic site of Jonzac, France. *Journal of Human Evolution* 61:176–185.

Burke, A. and Pike-Tay, A. 1997. Reconstructing "L'Âge du Renne'". *In*: Jackson, L. T. and Thacker, P. T. (eds.) *Caribou and reindeer hunters of the Northern Hemisphere*. Aldershot: Avebury.

Cerling, T. E., Passey, B. H., Ayliffe, L. K., Cook, C. S., Ehleringer, J. R., Harris, J. M., Dhidha, M. B. and Kasiki, S. M. 2004. Orphans' tales: seasonal dietary changes in elephants from Tsavo National Park, Kenya. *Palaeogeography, Palaeoclimatology, Palaeoecology* 206:367–376.

Chapman, B. B., Brönmark, C., Nilsson, J. Å. and Hansson, L. A. 2011. The ecology and evolution of partial migration. *Oikos* 120:1764–1775.

Copeland, S. R., Sponheimer, M., Spinage, C. A., Lee-Thorp, J. A., Codron, D. M. and Reed, K. E. 2009. Stable isotope evidence for impala *Aepyceros melampus* diets at Akagera National Park, Rwanda. *African Journal of Ecology* 47:490–501.

Costamagno, S., Meignen, L., Beauval, C., Vandermeersch, B. and Maureille, B. 2006. Les Pradelles (Marillac-le-Franc, France): A mousterian reindeer hunting camp? *Journal of Anthropological Archaeology* 25:466–484.

Cotton, P. A. 2003. Avian migration phenology and global climate change. *Proceedings of the National Academy of Sciences of the United States of America* 100:12219–12222.

Coughenour, M. B. 2008. Causes and Consequences of Herbivore Movement in Landscape Ecosystems. *In*: Galvin, K. A., Reid, R. S., Behnke Jr, R. B. and Thompson Hobbs, N. (eds.) *Fragmentation in semi-arid and arid landscapes: Consequences for human and natural systems*. Amsterdam: Springer.

Cresswell, K. A., Satterthwaite, W. H. and Sword, G. A. 2011. Understanding the evolution of migration through empirical examples. *In*: Milner-Gulland, E. J., Fryxell, J. M. and Sinclair, A. R. E. (eds.) *Animal migration: A synthesis*. Oxford: Oxford University Press.

Dahle, B., Reimers, E. and Colman, J. E. 2008. Reindeer (*Rangifer tarandus*) avoidance of a highway as revealed by lichen measurements. *European Journal of Wildlife Research* 54:27–35.

Delpeche, F. 1983. *Les faunes du Paléolithique supérieur dans le sud-ouest de la France*. Paris: Éditions du C.N.R.S.

Dingle, H. 1996. *Migration: The biology of life on the move*. New York: Oxford University Press.

Dobson, F. S. 1985. Multiple causes of dispersal. *The American Naturalist* 126:855–858.

—— 1982. Competition for mates and predominant juvenile male dispersal in mammals. *Animal Behaviour* 30:1183–1192.

Drucker, D., Bocherens, H., Pike-Tay, A. and Mariotti, A. 2001. Isotopic tracking of seasonal dietary change in dentine collagen: preliminary data from modern caribou. *Earth and Planetary Sciences* 333:303–309.

Drucker, D. G., Hobson, K. A., Münzel, S. C. and Pike-Tay, A. 2010. Intra-individual variation in stable carbon ($\delta13C$) and nitrogen ($\delta15N$) isotopes in mandibles of modern caribou of Qamanirjuaq (*Rangifer tarandus groenlandicus*) and Banks Island (*Rangifer tarandus pearyi*): implications for tracing seasonal and temporal changes in diet. *International Journal of Osteoarchaeology* (doi: 10.1002/oa.1220).

Enloe, J. G. and David, F. 1997. *Rangifer* herd behaviour: seasonality of hunting in the Magdalenian of the Paris Basin. In: Jackson, L. T. and Thacker, P. T. (eds.) *Caribou and reindeer hunters of the Northern Hemisphere*. Aldershot: Avebury.

Evans, J. A., Montgomery, J., Wildman, G. and Boulton, N. 2010. Spatial variations in biosphere 87Sr/86Sr in Britain. *Journal of the Geological Society* 167:1–4.

Faure, G. and Powell, J.L. 1972. *Strontium Isotope Geology*. New York: Springer-Verlag.

Feranec, R., Garcia Garcia, N., Diez, J. C. and Arsuaga, J. L. 2010. Understanding the ecology of mammalian carnivorans and herbivores from Valdegoba cave (Burgos, northern Spain) through stable isotope analysis. *Palaeogeography Palaeoclimatology Palaeoecology* 297:263–272.

Feranec, R. S. 2007. Stable carbon isotope values reveal evidence of resource partitioning among ungulates from modern C-3-dominated ecosystems in North America. *Palaeogeography Palaeoclimatology Palaeoecology* 252:575–585.

Feranec, R. S. and MacFadden, B. J. 2006. Isotopic discrimination of resource partitioning among ungulates in C-3-dominated communities from the Miocene of Florida and California. *Paleobiology* 32:191–205.

Feranec, R. S., Hadly, E. A. and Paytan, A. 2009. Stable isotopes reveal seasonal competition for resources between late Pleistocene bison (*Bison*) and horse (*Equus*) from Rancho La Brea, southern California. *Palaeogeography Palaeoclimatology Palaeoecology* 271:153–160.

—— 2007. Determining landscape use of Holocene mammals using strontium isotopes. *Oecologia* 153:943–950.

Fernandez, M. H. and Vrba, E. S. 2005. Body size, biomic specialization and range size of African large mammals. *Journal of Biogeography* 32:1243–1256.

Foley, R. A. 2001. The evolutionary consequences of increased carnivory in hominids. *In*: Stanford, C. B. and Bunn, H. T. (eds.) *Meat-Eating and Human Evolution*. Oxford: Oxford University Press.

Fryxell, J. M. and Holt, R. D. 2013. Environmental change and the evolution of migration. *Ecology* 94:1274–1279.

Fryxell, J. M. and Sinclair, A. R. E. 1988. Causes and consequences of migration by large herbivores. *Trends in Ecology and Evolution* 3:237–241.

Fuglestvedt, I. 2014. Humans, material culture and landscape: outline to an understanding of developments in worldview on the Scandinavian Peninsula, ca. 10,000-4500 BP. *In*: Cannon, A. (ed.) *Structured Worlds: The archaeology of hunter-gatherer thought and action*. London and New York: Routledge.

Gaston, K. J. and Blackburn, T. M. 1996. Range size-body size relationships: evidence of scale dependence. *Oikos* 75:479–485.

Gaudzinski, S. 1996. On bovid assemblages and their consequences for the knowledge of subsistence patterns in the Middle Palaeolithic. *Proceedings of the Prehistoric Society* 62:19–39.

Gaudzinski, S. and Roebroeks, W. 2000. Adults only. Reindeer hunting at the Middle Palaeolithic site of Salzgitter-Lebenstedt, Northern Germany. *Journal of Human Evolution* 38:497–521.

Gaudzinski, S. 2006. Monospecific or species-dominated faunal assemblages during the Middle Paleolithic in Europe. *In*: Hovers, E. and Kuhn, S. L. (eds.) *Transitions before the transition: evolution and stability in the Middle Paleolithic and Middle Stone Age*. New York: Springer US.

Goebel, T. 1999. Pleistocene human colonization of Siberia and peopling of the Americas: an ecological approach. *Evolutionary Anthropology* 8:208–227.

Gordon, B. C. 1988. *Of Men and Reindeer Herds in French Magdalenian Prehistory*. Oxford: British Archaeological Reports (International Series 390).

Guthrie, R. D. 1990. *Frozen fauna of the Mammoth Steppe: The story of Blue Babe*. Chicago, IL and London: University of Chicago Press.

Hamilton, S., Wiseman, N. and Wiseman, D. 2006. Extrapolating to a more ancient past: ethnohistoric images of northeastern Plains vegetation and bison ecology. *Plains Anthropologist* 51:281–302.

Haynes, G. 2002. The catastrophic extinction of North American mammoths and mastodons. *World Archaeology* 33(3, Ancient Ecodisasters): 391–416.

Hobson, K. A. 1999. Tracing origins and migration of wildlife using stable isotopes: a review. *Oecologia* 120:314–326.

Hobson, K. A. and Wassenaar, L. I. 1999. Stable isotope ecology: an introduction. *Oecologia* 120:312–313.

Hobson, K. A. and Wassenaar, L. I. 2008. *Tracking animal migration with stable isotopes*. Amsterdam: Academic Press.

Hoffecker, J. F. 2002. *Desolate landscape: Ice-age settlement in Eastern Europe*. New Brunswick, NJ: Rutgers University Press.

Holdo, R. M., Holt, R. D. and Fryxell, J. M. 2009. Opposing rainfall and plant nutritional gradients best explain the wildebeest migration in the Serengeti. *The American Naturalist* 173:431–445.

Hoppe, K. A., Koch, P. L., Carlson, R. W. and Webb, D. S. 1999. Tracking mammoths and mastodons: reconstruction of migratory behaviour using strontium isotope ratios. *Geology* 27:439–442.

Ingold, T. 2000. *The Perception of the Environment: Essays on livelihood, dwelling and skill*. London: Psychology Press.

IPCC 2013. *Climate Change 2013: The Physical Science Basis. Contribution of Working Group I to the Fifth Assessment Report of the Intergovernmental Panel on Climate Change. In*: Stocker, T. F., Qin, D., Plattner, G.-K., Tignor, M., Allen, S. K., Boschung, J., Nauels, A., Xia, Y., Bex, V. and Midgley, P. M. (eds.). Cambridge, UK and New York: IPCC.

Jenni, L. and Kery, M. 2003. Timing of autumn bird migration under climate change: advances in long-distance migrants, delays in short-distance migrants. *Proceeding of the Royal Society of London Series B-Biology* 270:1467–1471.

Joly, K., Adams, L., Dale, B. and Collins, W. 2002. Evaluating the impacts of wildland fires on caribou in interior Alaska. *Arctic Research of the United States* 16:63–67.

Joly, K., Jandt, R. R., Meyers, C. R. and Cole, M. J. 2007. Changes in vegetative cover on Western Arctic Herd winter range from 1981 to 2005: potential effects of grazing and climate change. *Rangifer Special Issue* 17:199–207.

Joly, K., Klein, D. R., Verbyla, D. L., Rupp, S. and Chapin III, F. S. 2011. Linkages between large-scale climate patterns and the dynamics of Arctic caribou populations. *Ecography* 34:345–352.

Jones, J. D., Kauffman, M. J., Monteith, K. L., Scurlock, B. M., Albeke, S. E. and Cross, P. C. 2014. Supplemental feeding alters migration of a temperate ungulate. *Ecological Applications* 24:1769–1779.

Julien, M.-A., Bocherens, H., Burke, A., Drucker, D., Patou-Mathis, M., Krotova, O. and Péan, S. 2012. Were European steppe bison migratory? 18O, 13C and Sr intra-tooth isotopic variations applied to a palaeoethological reconstruction. *Quaternary International* 271:106–119.

Kelly, T. E. 2007. *Strontium isotope tracing in animal teeth at the Neanderthal site of Les Pradelles, Charente, France*. B.Sc. Thesis Master's Thesis, The Australian National University.

Kelsall, J. P. 1968. The migratory barren-ground caribou of Canada. *Canadian Wildlife Service Monograph* 3.

Kielland, K. 2001. Stable isotope signatures of moose in relationship in relation to seasonal forage composition: a hypothesis. *ALCES* 37:329–337.

Klein, D. R., Bruun, H. H., Lundgren, R. and Philipp, M. 2008. Climate change influences on species interrelationships and distributions in high-Arctic Greenland. *In*: Meltofte, H., Christensen, T. R., Elberling, B., Forchhammer, M. C. and Rausch, M. (eds.) *High-Arctic Ecosystem Dynamics in a Changing Climate*. San Diego, CA: Elsevier Academic Press Inc.

Koch, P. L., Heisinger, J., Moss, C., Carlson, R. W., Fogel, M. L. and Behrensmeyer, A. K. 1995. Isotopic tracking of change in diet and habitat use in African elephants. *Science* 267:1340–1343.

Kolen, J. 1999. Hominids without homes: on the nature of Middle Palaeolithic settlement in Europe. *In*: Roebroeks, W. and Gamble, C. (eds.) *The Middle Palaeolithic Occupation of Europe*. Leiden: Leiden University.

Levinsky, I., Skov, F., Svenning, J. C. and Rahbek, C. 2007. Potential impacts of climate change on the distributions and diversity patterns of European mammals. *Biodiversity and Conservation* 16:3803–3816.

Lewis, H. T. and Ferguson, T. A. 1988. Yards, corridors, and mosaics: how to burn a boreal forest. *Human Ecology* 16:57–77.

Lindsted, S. L., Miller, B. J. and Buskirk, S. W. 1986. Home range, time, and body size in mammals. *Ecology* 67:413–418.

MacArthur, R. H. 1959. On the breeding distribution pattern of North American migrant birds. *The Auk* 76:318–325.

MacArthur, R. H. 1984. *Geographical Ecology: Patterns in the distribution of species*. Princeton, NJ: Princeton University Press.

Makarewicz, C. A. and Sealy, J. 2015. Dietary reconstruction, mobility, and the analysis of ancient skeletal tissues: expanding the prospects of stable isotope research in archaeology. *Journal of Archaeological Science* 56:146–158.

Makarewicz, C. A. 2016. Toward an integrated isotope zooarchaeology. *In*: Grupe, G. and McGlynn, C. G. (eds.) *Isotopic Landscapes in Bioarchaeology*. Berlin and Heidelberg: Springer Berlin Heidelberg.

Mann, M. E. 2007. Climate over the past two millennia. *Annual Review of Earth and Planetary Sciences* 35:111–136.

McNab, B. K. 1963. Bioenergetics and the determination of home range size. *American Naturalist* 97:133–140.

McPherron, S. P., Alemseged, Z., Marean, C. W., Wynn, J. G., Reed, D., Geraads, D., Bobe, R. and Bearat, H. A. 2010. Evidence for stone-tool-assisted consumption of animal tissues before 3.39 million years ago at Dikika, Ethiopia. *Nature* 466:857–860.

Meldgaard, M. 1986. *The Greenland Caribou: Zoogeography, taxonomy, and population dynamics*. Copenhagen: Meddelelser om Grønland.

Mellars, P. A. 2004. Reindeer specialization in the early Upper Palaeolithic: the evidence from south west France. *Journal of Archaeological Science* 31:613–617.

Nathan, R., Getz, W. M., Revilla, E., Holyoak, M., Kadmon, R., Saltz, D. and Smouse, P. E. 2008. A movement ecology paradigm for unifying organismal movement research. *Proceedings of the National Academy of Sciences* 105:19052–19059.

Niven, L., Steele, T. E., Rendu, W., Mallye, J. B., McPherron, S. P., Soressi, M., Jaubert, J. and Hublin, J.-J. 2012. Neandertal mobility and large-game hunting: the exploitation of reindeer during the Quina Mousterian at Chez-Pinaud Jonzac (Charente-Maritime, France). *Journal Of Human Evolution* 63:624–635.

Olifiers, N., Vieira, M. V. and Grelle, C. E. V. 2004. Geographic range and body size in Neotropical marsupials. *Global Ecology and Biogeography* 13:439–444.

Pease, C. M., Lande, R. and Bull, J. J. 1989. A model of population growth, dispersal and evolution in a changing environment. *Ecology* 70:1657–1664.

Pellegrini, M., Donahue, R. E., Chenery, C., Evans, J., Lee-Thorp, J., Montgomery, J. and Mussi, M. 2008. Faunal migration in late-glacial central Italy: implications for human resource exploitation. *Rapid Communications in Mass Spectrometry* 22:1714–1726.

Pilaar Birch, S. E. 2013. Stable isotopes in zooarchaeology: an introduction. *Archaeological and Anthropological Sciences* 5:81–83.

Pitelka, L. F., Gardner, R. H., Ash, J., Berry, S., Gitay, H., Noble, I. R., Saunders, A., Bradshaw, R. H. W., Brubaker, L., Clark, J. S., Davis, M. B., Sugita, S., Dyer, J. M., Hengeveld, R., Hope, G., Huntley, B., King, G. A., Lavorel, S., Mack, R. N., Malanson, G. P., McGlone, M., Prentice, I. C. and Rejmanek, M. 1997. Plant migration and climate change. *American Scientist* 85:464–473.

Price, T. D., Meiggs, D., Weber, M.-J. and Pike-Tay, A. 2015. The migration of Late Pleistocene reindeer: isotopic evidence from northern Europe. *Archaeological and Anthropological Sciences* 9:1–24.

Rivalan, P., Frederiksen, M., Lois, G. and Julliard, R. 2007. Contrasting responses of migration strategies in two European thrushes to climate change. *Global Change Biology* 13:275–287.

Rubenstein, D. R. and Hobson, K. A. 2004. From birds to butterflies: animal movement patterns and stable isotopes. *TRENDS in Ecology and Evolution* 19:256–263.

Schaefer, J. A., Veitch, A. M., Harrington, F. H., Brown, W. K., Theberge, J. B. and Luttich, S. N. 1999. Demography of decline of the Red Wine Mountains caribou herd. *Journal of Wildlife Management* 63:580–587.

Schaefer, J. A. C., Bergman, C. M. and Luttich, S. N. 2000. Site fidelity of female caribou at multiple spatial scales. *Landscape Ecology* 15:731–739.

Scott, C. 1989. Knowledge construction among the Cree hunters: metaphors and literal understanding. *Journal de la Société des Américanistes* 75:193–208.

Sealy, J. C., van der Merwe, N. J., Lee-Thorp, J. A. and Lanham, J. L. 1987. Nitrogen isotopic ecology in southern Africa: implications for environmental and dietary tracing. *Geochimica et Cosmochimica Acta* 51:2707–2717.

Seidler, R. G., Long, R. A., Berger, J., Bergen, S. and Beckmann, J. P. 2015. Identifying impediments to long-distance mammal migrations. *Conservation Biology* 29:99–109.

Serneels, S. and Lambin, E. F. 2001. Impact of land-use changes on the wildebeest migration in the northern part of the Serengeti-Mara ecosystem. *Journal of Biogeography* 28:391–407.

Shaw, A. K. and Couzin, I. D. 2013. Migration or residency? The evolution of movement behavior and information usage in seasonal environments. *The American Naturalist* 181:114–124.

Sinclair, A. R. E. 1992. Do large mammals disperse like small mammals? *In*: Stenseth, N. C. and Lidicker Jr., W. Z. (eds.) *Animal Dispersal: Small mammals as a model*. London: Chapman and Hall.

Singh, N. J., Börger, L., Dettki, H., Bunnefeld, N. and Ericsson, G. 2012. From migration to nomadism: movement variability in a northern ungulate across its latitudinal range. *Ecological Applications* 22:2007–2020.

Speth, J. 2004. News flash: negative evidence convicts Neanderthals of gross mental incompetence. *World Archaeology* 36:519–526.

Thacker, P. T. 1997. The significance of *Rangifer* as a human prey species during the Central European Upper Palaeolithic. *In*: Jackson, L. T. and Thacker, P. T. (eds.) *Caribou and Reindeer Hunters of the Northern Hemisphere*. Aldershot: Avebury.

Travis, J. M. J. 2003. Climate change and habitat destruction: a deadly anthropogenic cocktail. *Proceedings of the Royal Society of London Series B-Biological Sciences* 270:467–473.

van der Merwe, N. J., Lee-Thorp, J. A., Thackeray, J. F., Hall-Martin, A., Kruger, F. J., Coetzee, H., Bell, R. H. V. and Lindeque, M. 1990. Source-area determination of elephant ivory by isotopic analysis. *Nature* 346:744–746.

van Vuren, D. 1983. Group-dynamics and summer home range of bison in Southern Utah. *Journal of Mammalogy* 64:329–332.

van Vuren, D. and Bray, M. P. 1986. Population-dynamics of bison in the Henry Mountains, Utah. *Journal of Mammalogy* 67:503–511.

Waser, P. M. 1985. Does competition drive dispersal? *Ecology* 66:1170–1175.

Waterman, A. J., Thomas, J. T., Enloe, J. G. and Peate, D. W. 2015. The influence of prey availability on ice age hunting strategies: tracing Magdalenian reindeer migratory patterns using strontium isotope (87Sr/86Sr) analysis of reindeer teeth from Verberie (Oise, France). *80th Annual Meeting of the Society for American Archaeology (15-19 April, 2015)*. San Francisco, CA.

Weber, M. G. and Flannigan, M. D. 1997. Canadian boreal forest ecosystem structure and function in a changing climate: impacts on fire regimes. *Environmental Reviews* 5:145–166.

Weinstock, J. 2000. *Late Pleistocene Reindeer Populations in Western and Central Europe: An osteometrical study of* Rangifer tarandus. Tübingen: Mo-Vince Verlag.

Willmes, M., McMorrow, L., Kinsley, L., Armstrong, R., Aubert, M., Eggins, S., Falguères, C., Maureille, B., Moffat, I. and Grün, R. 2014. The IRHUM (Isotopic Reconstruction of Human Migration) database – bioavailable strontium isotope ratios for geochemical fingerprinting in France. *Earth Syst. Sci. Data* 6:117–122.

Wilmshurst, J. F., Fryxell, J. M., Farm, B. P., Sinclair, A. and Henschel, C. P. 1999. Spatial distribution of Serengeti wildebeest in relation to resources. *Canadian Journal of Zoology* 77:1223–1232.

Wolf, N., Carleton, S. A. and Martínez de Rio, C. 2009. Ten years of experimental animal isotpe ecology. *Functional Ecology* 23:17–26.

INDEX

abandoned cemeteries 118–132
abstract imagery 145–147
aDNA 201–202, 234–237; *see also* "ancient DNA"
Adriatic Sea 310, 311, 318–327
afterlife of things 97–98
age at death, animals' 321–323
agency: animals 3, 14, 219–220, 225; human 105–106, 219; innovative forms of 105–106, 120–121; multiple agencies and rock art 151–152
agrarianism 5; animals and the Neolithic 201–213; Bronze Age Norway 214–229; end of the Neolithic 26–46; human microbiome 230–250; multispecies co-inhabitation in Southwest Asia 251–270
agriculture 5; decline of 27–28; impact of its advent on the human microbiome 237–240; organic 217; origins in Southwest Asia 251–270
'Ain Mallaha (Ein-Mallaha) 187–188, 206, 257, 259, 260, 263, 264
air 112, 113
alpha diversity 188–189, 193–194
amino acid analysis 336, 337
amplicon DNA sequencing 236, 237
Anacapa 67–68, 71
analogues, modern 351–355
Anavolos canal system 33
ancient DNA analysis (aDNA) 201–202, 234–237
aniconic imagery 145–147
animacy 115
animal agency 3, 14, 219–220, 225
animal bones: carved 256–258; stable isotope analysis of 356–357; worked 261–262
animal rights 14
animal tracks 143–145, 145–147
animic attitudes 351

Anthropocene 1, 4, 12, 41, 66, 214, 225; California mussels 65–84; drift 85–101; dynamics 57–59; emergence of 26–46; as present singular or past plural 47–49; Remote Oceania 47–64; as rupture 38–40
Anthropocene Working Group 12
anthropocentrism 11–25, 123, 252
anthropomorphic rock art 150, 151
antibiotics 36–37, 243
anti-predator adaptation 51
antiquarianism 12–15
Archaic rock art 142–151
architectural planning concepts 164–165
Argent, G. 217, 296
Argive Plain, Greece 29–34, 38–39, 40
Armstrong Oma, K. 296
art: rock art 133–153; multispecies 151–152; Western 134
artificial selection 49
Askur 96
assemblage drift 282
assemblages: extended ecology 274; mammalian communities in the Jordan Valley 153–197; turf buildings and symbiosis 113–115
Athens 175, 176
aurochs 205, 255
Austurafrétt 276–277
Australia 150
axiality 164

bacteria 109–110; calcite-precipitating 114–115; human microbiome 230–250
Bar-Oz, G. 253
basketry 258
Bate, D.M.A. 257
beach 85–101
bears 207

Index

beavers 299–301, 302, 303–305, 305–306
beef cattle industry 29, 34–38, 38–39
beetles 109, 110
Belfer-Cohen, A. 254–255, 259
beta diversity 188–189, 193–194
Big Bone Lick 13, 22
bighorn sheep 206
bio-urn 126
birds: commensal and scavenger 177; impact of
    Pacific Rat 53, 56–57; wild for consumption 174
bison 349, 353, 357
Black Death 239
blended flock 224
Blue Lake, New Mexico 134–135
boar *see* wild boar
bones *see* animal bones
bonobos 233–234
borderland archaeology 91–93, 98–100
borehole irrigation 31–33
Boulanger, N.-A. 18, 20–21
Bourdieu, P. 289
bows and arrows 301
Boyd, B. 265
Bradshaw rock art tradition 150
Braje, T.J. 67, 68, 72
breeds, animal 172–173, 176
British Early Mesolithic 295–309
broad spectrum diet 316–317, 319
Bronze Age: Jordan Valley 185, 186–187,
    189–190, 192–193, 194; Norway 220–225
brown hyenas 333, 335, 343
Buffon, Comte de 11–12, 13, 14, 15–24
built environment 4–5; abandoned cemeteries
    118–132; Jordan Valley 183–197; oyster
    mound-islands 154–169; rock art 133–153;
    Roman cities 170–182; turf buildings 105–117
burials 259–265; abandoned cemeteries 118–132;
    custom of burial of the dead 123; eco-burials
    119, 125–126, 128, 129; origins of the
    Neolithic in Southwest Asia 259–265; oysters
    and 165–6; with animals 259–263; with plants
    and other objects 264–265
burning of wildland 353–354

calcite-precipitating bacteria 114–115
California mussels (*Mytilus californianus*) 65–84;
    ecology 69–70; shell length measurements 60,
    70–77
Calydonian boar hunt myth 13
Campbell, B. 67, 71, 72
canning 241
caprines: community assembly in the Jordan Valley
    186–187, 188–193; husbanding in the Neolithic
    205–206
carbohydrate-metabolizing genes 231
carbohydrates 238
care: duty of 219, 224; ethics of 219–220, 224

caribou 350, 352–353, 353–354, 357–358
Carson, R. 85
Carter, D.O. 123–124
Cartesian paradigm 214
Carthage 173, 177
Çatalhöyük/Çatalhüyük 215, 255, 257
Catholic rock art 136–138, 139, 142
cats 296–297; wildcats 299–301, 302–303, 304,
    305, 306
cattle 215; Cattle City in Texas 29, 34–38, 38–39;
    community assembly in the Jordan Valley
    186–187, 188–193; Roman cities 171, 172,
    173, 179
cattle cult 215
cemeteries: abandoned 118–132; as an ecosystem
    124–126; green 119, 125–126, 128, 129;
    virtual 127
chamois (*Rupicapra rupicapra*) 313–314, 319–321,
    321–323
Childe, V.G. 1, 26, 27, 201
chimpanzees 233–234
Chitimacha creation myth 165
Chronika, Argive Plain 31–34
Chukchi people 20
Chumash people 66, 68, 77–78
circulatory systems 111–113
cities *see* urbanism
citrus crops 31–34, 38
civilization, human 123
Classical (Hellenistic-Roman) faunal assemblages
    185, 187, 189–190, 193, 194
climate change 59, 79, 105–106, 353–354;
    Paris Agreement 49
Clostridium botulinum 241
Clutton-Brock, J. 218
coal 240
cockles (*Cerastoderma* spp.) 315, 324
co-domestication 218, 224, 255
co-evolution 22; co-evolutionary trajectories
    in Neolithic packages 49–50; gene-culture
    co-evolution (GCC) 202–203, 206, 207–208
coffins 125
coincidence 94–96
co-inhabitation, multispecies 251–270
colonization, human 52, 58
colours 87
commensalism 184, 208; Roman cities 171,
    177–180
commodity animals 171–176
community assembly of mammalian species
    183–197
companion species 216
concentrated/confined animal feeding operations
    (CAFOs) 14–15, 34–38
concrete 114–115
Constantinople 27
contours 87–90

369

Index

controlled decay 128
coprolites: human microbiome analysis 236; and rock art 143, 147; sheep 221, 222
corvids 208
crop domestication 253–254
cross-disciplinary research 361
crosses 136–138, 142
Crossland, Z. 15
Crystal River 154–169
cultural geography 349–351
cupules 147, 148
customs 123
Cuvier, G. 13
Cyprus 296

daily rhythms 299–303, 304
dark matter 96
dates and names rock art 138, 139
dead, the: abandoned cemeteries in Poland 118–132; burials *see* burials; treatment of the dead 118–119
decomposition 122–123, 123–124
deconstructionism 120
deer 143, 144; community assembly in the Jordan Valley 186–187, 188, 188–191; red deer 312–313, 317, 319–321, 321–323, 326; roe deer 313, 319–321, 321–323
deforestation 54–55, 56, 57, 60
Dehaene, S. 143
dehumanization 122–123
DeLanda, M. 274
Deloria, V., Jr 141, 152
dental calculus 236–237
deterritorialization 274–275
diet 231; broad spectrum 316–317, 319; impact of Industrial Revolution 241–242; impact of Neolithic Revolution 238–239, 240
disease 178–179, 231; Neolithic Revolution and 238–239, 240; TB 179, 238, 239
DNA 4; ancient DNA analysis 201–202, 234–237; high-throughput DNA sequencing 231
dogs 13–14, 22, 188, 191; burials with humans in Southwest Asia 260–261, 262, 263; domestication 206–208; need for early socialization 223; pets in Roman cities 176–177, 180; Pompeii 13, 22, 23, 175
domestic fowl 174–175
domestication 21, 26, 49–50, 184; chain of domestications 220–221; discourses 217–218; as ethics of care 219–220; human-animal relationships in the early domestication process 214–229; and the human microbiome 238–239; and modernity 253–255; origins in Southwest Asia 251–270; socialization 221–224; transition to the Neolithic 201–213
domination 255; discourse 218
donkeys 175

dormice 174
dots 145–147
drift matter 96–97
dual inheritance theory 202–203
duty of care 219, 224

early socialization 223–224
earmarks 277–278, 285–288, 290, 291
East Turkana, Kenya 66
eco-cemeteries 119, 125–126, 128, 129
eco-contract 217
eco-ecumene 121
ecological insulation 50–52
ecological life attitudes 351
ecological novelty 1
eco-necro approach 119
ecosystem engineering 204
ecosystems, cemeteries as 124–126
ectoparasites 109, 110
ecumene 121; multispecies 124–126
Edgeworth, M. 286
Eidsbukta beach, Norway 85–101
Ein-Gev 187–188
Ein-Mallaha ('Ain Mallaha) 187–188, 206, 257, 259, 260, 263, 264
El-Wad 257–258, 264–265
'elephants' *see* mammoths
Embla 96
enamel hypoplasia 179–180
Enlightenment 14, 21
entanglements 215, 252; sheep-human 220–225
environment: borderland archaeology 98–100; contamination by cemeteries 124–125; impact of human activity on 352–354; modern analogues 352
environmental change 41
environmental determinism 105–106
environmental force 285
environmental rhythms 303–305
Epauloecus unicolor 109, 110
Erlandson, J.M. 76
ethics of care 219–220, 224
ethnography, multispecies 2, 6
Etna 23
Euclidean distance 188–189
evolution 113; evolutionary history of the human microbiome 232–234
Evolutionary Stable Strategy (ESS) 202
'Ewa plain, O'ahu 54, 55, 56
exchange networks 334, 343
experiential difference 289–290
extended community 291
extended ecology 274
extinction 22

Fabris, P. 14
Faraday Road site, Britain 298–306

370

Index

Feranec, R.S. 357
Fertile Crescent 237; origins of agriculture and domestication 251–270
Flannery, K. 316
flight distance 206
flood 18, 22
Flores, S. 237
Florida 154–169
food production 241–242, 243–244
food processing 241–242, 243–244; artifacts in graves 264–265
foraging: ecology 316–317; optimal foraging theory 3, 316; for ostrich eggs 333–346
forest 54–55, 56, 57, 60
forest-dwellers 258
formal entrances 164
formaldehyde 125
Forster, J.R. 11, 12, 19, 22, 23
fossil archive, species memory and 20–24
fossil fuels 33, 37, 240
fossil ivory 11, 15–17
Fowles, S. 254
fowls, domestic 174–175
foxes 208, 261–262
fragility 50–52
France 351, 358–361
fungi 4, 112, 113; rock art 148–151

game animals 184, 186–187, 188–191
Games-Howell post hoc analysis 72, 74–75
Garrod, D. 257–258, 265
gatherers for sheep roundup 282, 284
gathering paths 280, 281, 282
gazelles 205; burials with humans in Southwest Asia 259–260, 260–261, 262; community assembly in the Jordan Valley 186–187, 188, 188–191
gene-culture co-evolution (GCC) 202–203, 206, 207–208
gene flow, limited 51
generalism 50
genetically modified organisms (GMOs) 243–244
geological time scale 21–22
George River herd, Canada 358, 360
German Protestant cemeteries 118–132
gigantism 13; and human origins 18–20
Gilleland, S.K. 161
global warming 59
glyphosate 243–244
goats 58, 171, 172, 186–187, 188–193
Gobekli Tepe 255, 257
Goliath 19
gorillas 233–234
Goring-Morris, N. 254–255, 259
graves *see* burials, cemeteries
gravestones 127

gravitational waves 97
grazing areas 276–277; management of 280
Greece 38–39; Argive Plain 29–34, 38–39, 40; Neolithic 26
green cemeteries 119, 125–126, 128, 129
Green Revolution 243
greenhouse gases 37, 59
Greenland 353, 354
Gremillion, K. 203
grey colours 87
grey wolf (*Canis lupus*) 206–208
grinding slicks 147
groundwater pollution 124–125

habituation 221–223
Hadza hunter-gatherer community 234
Hamilakis, Y. 301
Haraway, D. 13–14, 216
Harrison, R.P. 27, 28, 39, 120
harvesting strategies for mussels 78
Hayonim 257; Cave 259, 265; Terrace 259–260
Hazor 184, 192–193
heating of ostrich eggs 337–340
heavy metals 240
Helicobacter pylori 243
Hellenistic-Roman (Classical) faunal assemblages 185, 187, 189–190, 193, 194
Helmreich, S. 2
herbivores 347–367
Herculaneum 13
high-throughput DNA sequencing 231
Hilazon Tachtit 257, 262–263
history: multispecies history 119–123; and place 134–142
Hodder, I. 252, 255
holding folds 285, 286
holobiont 113, 120, 122
Holocene, early 203–206
Hoppe, K.A. 357
horses 31, 34; tattoos of 296
house mice 178, 191, 193
human agency 105–106, 219
human colonization 52, 58
human exceptionalism 1, 120, 225
human genome 232
human microbiome 230–250
human origins, giant species and 18–20
'human revolution' 1
humanity, characterizing 123
Hunt Krater 13
hunter-gatherers 50, 234, 238, 253; Archaic rock art 142–151; contemporary groups 305, 307
hunting 296, 300, 303, 304; inter-personal encounters 301–303; preparations for 304
hydrological organization 57
hyenas 333, 335, 343
hygiene in the home discourse 105

Index

ibex (*Capra ibex*) 313–314, 319–321, 321–323
Iceland: seasonal roundup 273–294; symbiotic architecture 105–117
imprinting 224
indoor stalling of animals 220–224
Industrial Revolution 240–242
Ingold, T. 154, 155, 164, 218, 273
insects 107–109, 112, 113
insulated ecologies 50–52
interactions, multispecies 310–332
inter-dependence 274, 275, 283, 290–291
inter-personal hunting encounters 301–303
interspecies relationships 214–29, 263; complexity 215–216
intra-tooth strontium isotope analysis 356–361
iron 238
Iron Age faunal assemblages 185, 187, 189–190, 194–195
Island Chumash 66, 68, 77–78
islands: fragility in island ecosystems 50–52; Neolithization 47–64; oysters and mound-islands 154–169
isoscape map 340, 341
isotope analysis 163, 355–356; strontium isotope analysis *see* strontium isotope analysis
Israel 183–197
Istrian Peninsula 310, 311, 318–327
ivory, fossilized 11, 15–17

joint arthropathies 179
Jonzac, France 358, 359–361
Jordan Valley, Israel 183–197
Jubaea palm forest 54, 60

Kao Pah Nam Cave, Thailand 66
Kaufman, D. 264
Kebara Cave 257, 258
Kennet Valley sites, Britain 298–306
keystone species 110
Kidder, T.R. 161
Kimberly region, Australia 150
Kirch, P.V. 56
Kirksey, S. 2
'Kissing Fish' site, Rio Grande Gorge 136, 137
Konon, A. 126–127
Konráðsdóttir, H. 108–109
Kopytoff, I. 252
Krzyżaniak, M. 126–127

lactose 239
Lambert, C. 257–258
land snails 53–54, 315, 320, 321, 326
landscape inhabitation 274–275
landscape use patterns 333–346
lap-dogs 177, 180
Latour, B. 15
Law, J. 219–220

Lehmann, H. 29, 30, 31, 32–33
Lewis-Williams, D. 145, 255
lice 109
lichen 148, 149, 150–151
life 113–114, 115
limpets (*Patella* spp.) 314, 324
lines (in rock art) 139, 140, 141, 145–147
livestock: indoor stalling 220–224; Roman cities 171–173, 174–176, 180; seasonal roundup in Iceland 273–294; standardization schemes 172; urban herds 29, 34–38, 38–39; *see also* domestication, *and under individual animals*
lizards 54
llamas 205
lobsters 78
local folds 286
London 178
longhouses, Norwegian 220–224
Lošinj 310, 311, 318, 319–320, 321–322, 323–325, 327
Lubbock, J. 26

Malpas, J. 95
mammals: community assembly in the Jordan Valley 183–197; modern analogues 357; seasonal mobility and multispecies interactions 312–314, 319–323, 325–327; *see also under individual mammals*
mammoths 11, 13, 14, 15–17, 18, 22, 357
Manis Mastodon site, Washington 22
Margulis, L. 2, 113
marine molluscs *see* shellfish
marine productivity 67, 75, 76, 77, 79
marine upwelling 77
Markowitz, T.M. 223, 224
Marom, N. 253
marriage 123
mastodons 357
McCollum, A. 22, 23
McNiven, I.J. 166
meat consumption 171–172
mechanization 240–242
medicine 243
Meehan, B. 166
Meskell, L. 255
Mesolithic: rhythms 295–309; seasonality and multispecies interactions 310–332
metapopulation dynamics 205
methane 37, 59
mice 177–178, 188; dormice 174; house mice 178, 191, 193; wood mice 178
microorganisms 2, 4; bacteria *see* bacteria; human microbiome 230–250; rock art 148–151
middens, mounded 158, 160–161, 166
migration: of giant species 19; prey species movements and migrations 347–367
migration glyphs 145

milk 239
Miracle, P. 320, 321, 323
mixtures of cultures 242
modern analogues 351–355
modernity 253–255
Mol, A. 219–220
Moliné, G. 126
molluscs: marine *see* shellfish; terrestrial *see* snails
money bead trading 77
monkeys 233
Moraga, M. 237
morphometric analysis 355
mortars and pestles 264–265
mortuary deposits *see* burials
mound-islands 154–169
mounded middens 158, 160–161, 166
Mount Carmel 256–258
movement 5–6; landscape use patterns in South Africa 333–346; prey species 347–367; rhythms in the British Early Mesolithic 295–309; seasonal mobility in the Adriatic 310–332; seasonal roundup in Iceland 273–294; traces of and rock art 143–145, 145–147; traditions of and mound-islands 164–165
mules 175
multi-component generalism 50
multispecies art 151–152
multispecies co-inhabitation 251–270
multispecies ecumene 124–126
multispecies ethnography 2, 6
multispecies history 119–123
multispecies interactions 310–332
museums 133
mussels (*Mytilus* spp.) 315, 324; California mussels 65–84
mutation 232
Mycobacterium vaccae 241
Mylouthkia 296

Nahal Oren 256, 257, 264
names and dates rock art 138, 139
Native Americans 152; microbial impact of European immigrants 242; rock art 136, 139–142, 150–151
Natufian 205, 215, 254; carved animal bones 256–258; mortuary/burial practices 259–265
natural cemeteries 119, 125–126, 128, 129
natural selection 49
natural signs 142–148
nature, in Roman antiquity 170–171
Neanderthal reindeer hunting 359–360
Near Oceania 48, 52
necrogeography 124
needs of animals 220
Neo Ireo, Argive Plain 31–34
Neolithic: end of 26–46; faunal assemblages in the Jordan Valley 185, 186, 188, 189–190,

191–192, 193–194; Neolithization of islands 47–64; origins narratives 252–256; role of animals in the transition to 201–213
Neolithic packages: co-evolutionary trajectories in 49–50; as multi-component ecosystems 49–52
Neolithic Revolution 1, 26, 201, 218; impacts on the human microbiome 237–240
networks 252; exchange 334, 343; of social practices 283–285, 288–290; spatial 275–278, 288–290; temporal 279–283, 288–290
Neuville, R. 257–258
Neve David 257, 264
New Mexico 133–153
New York 27
next generation sequencing (NGS) technologies 235–236, 237
niche construction theory (NCT) 3, 202–203, 204–205, 207–208, 316
niche geography 349–351
Nicopolis, Bulgaria 177, 178
northeastern Adriatic 310, 311, 318–327
Northern Channel Islands 65–84
Norway: early Bronze Age human-sheep entanglements 220–225; Eidsbukta beach 85–101
Nugljanska site 310, 311, 318, 320, 322, 323–325, 326

O'ahu 54, 55, 56
Obama, B. 136
object biographies 252
ocean acidification 59, 79
ochre sea stars 70, 78
O'Connor, T. 218
Ohalo II 257, 264
ontological historicism 142
optimal foraging theory 3, 316
orange trees 31–34, 38
organic farming 217
organisms, buildings as 111–114, 115
orthogonality 164
Ostia 175, 176
ostrich: ecology 334–335; eggs 333–346
Otcheredin, A. 20
'otherness' 297, 304–305
out-groups research 233–234
ovens 112, 113
oyster bars 166
oysters: and mound-islands 154–169; symbolical importance 165–166

Pacific Rat (*Rattus exulans*) 48, 52–57; direct impacts on fauna 53–54; direct impacts on flora 54–55; indirect impacts 56–57
Paleo-Agulhas Plain 336, 340–342, 343
paleoethnobotany/archaeobotany 3–4
palm forest 54, 60

Index

Paris Agreement on climate change 47
parks, cemeteries as 126–127
partial migrations 349
Patagonian giants 19–20
pathways: animal tracks and rock art 143–145, 145–147; gathering paths for sheep 280, 281, 282; shell pathways 162
patination 87, 148
Pazyryk culture 296
peat 112, 113
pens, sheep 221–222; *see also* sorting folds
permanent stone construction 187
pestles and mortars 264–265
pets 171, 176–177, 180, 260
pigs 205; community assembly in the Jordan Valley 186–187, 188–193; Roman cities 172, 174–175, 175–176, 179–180; *see also* wild boar
Pinnacle Point, South Africa 333–346
place, and history 134–142
plants 3–4, 258, 315–316; crop domestication 253–254; mortuary practices 264–265; *see also* forest, trees
platform mounds 158, 159–160
plazas 158, 160–161, 164
Pleistocene 357–360
plucking of mussels 78
Poland 118–132
political life 115
politics of the dead body 118
pollution 33, 41
Pompeii 13, 22, 173, 175, 176, 177, 178
population booms 239
postholes 221–222
posthumanism 120
post-processual movement 105–106
poststructuralism 120
preparations for hunting 304
prey species: ostrich 333–346; movements and migrations 347–367
primates 233–234
Pritchardia spp. 54, 55, 56
productivity, marine 67, 75, 76, 77, 79
proteins 4
Protestant cemeteries, abandoned 118–132
Pueblo rock art 139–141
Pupićina site 310, 311, 318, 320–321, 323–325, 326–327
'puppy burial' 260, 263

range size 355
Rapa Nui 54, 56, 60
Raqefet 257, 264, 265
rats 177–178: Pacific Rat 48, 52–57; *Rattus norvegicus* 58; *Rattus rattus* 58
reciprocity 216–217, 290
red deer (*Cervus elaphus*) 312–313, 317, 319–321, 321–323, 326

Red Wine Mountains caribou herd 358
Redding, R.W. 193
reindeer 350, 351, 352; in the late Pleistocene 357–361
relational force 285
religion 123
Remote Oceania 47–64
rhythms 295–309; daily 299–303, 304; environmental 303–305; seasonal 305–306
Rio Grande Gorge, New Mexico 133–153
Rio Puebla de Taos 135
Roberts Island Complex, Florida 154–169
rock art 133–153
roe deer (*Capreolus capreolus*) 313, 319–321, 321–323
Rogaland, Norway 220–224
Roger, J. 19, 20, 21
Roman antiquity 170–182
Rome 171
roundup committee 279
roundups, seasonal 273–294
rupture 38–40
Russell, N. 218

Sagen, G. 86
Sahara, the 215
salinization 33
Sampson, C.P. 160
San Miguel 67–68, 70, 71, 72, 73–75, 76–77, 79
Sangre de Cristo mountains 134, 149
Santa Barbara Channel 67, 68, 77, 78
Santa Cruz 67–68, 70, 71, 73–75, 76–77, 79
Santa Rosa 67–68, 70, 71, 72, 73–75, 76–77, 79
Santarosae 68
scat *see* coprolites
scavengers 171, 177–180
sea level changes 41, 162–163, 166, 204
sea otters 78
Sea Star Wasting Disease (SSWD) 78
sea stars 70, 78
sea surface temperature (SST) 67, 71, 75, 76, 77, 79
seabirds 56–57
seasonal migrations 349
seasonal ranging 349
seasonal rhythms 305–306
seasonal roundup 273–294
seasonality: environmental context and 311–312; herbivore spatial behaviours 347–367; seasonal mobility and multispecies interactions 310–332; of shellfish collection 323–325; and site use 325–326; and terrestrial fauna 321–323
sedentism 205, 259
sediment transport 57
Sha'ar Hagolan 184, 191–192
shamanic practices 145, 263
shamans 255, 263
Shannon's evenness index 188–189

374

Shapiro, J.A. 2
shared flock 224
sheep 215; bighorn sheep 206; community assembly in the Jordan Valley 186–187, 188–193; early Bronze Age human-sheep entanglements in Norway 220–225; Roman cities 171, 172; seasonal roundup in Iceland 273–294
sheep tax 284
shell architecture: in the American Southeast 156; oyster mound-islands 154–169
shell length measurements 67, 70–77
shell middens 66, 67, 68
shell mounds 154–169
shell pathways 162
shellfish: California mussels 65–84; oyster mound-islands 154–169; seasonal mobility and multispecies interactions 314–315, 319–321, 323–325
shifting baseline syndrome 65
Shillourokambos 296
shotgun DNA sequencing 236, 237
sickle hafts 257–258, 261
Skálholt 107, 108–109, 111–113
Skútustaðahreppur, Iceland 273–294
slaughter of sheep 288
Smellie, W. 15
Smith, B. 203
Smith, M.E. 164
snails 53–54, 315, 320, 321, 326
social contracts 216, 224, 225; socio-cultural ramifications 216–217
social force 285
social life 115
social practices, networks of 283–285, 288–290
social zooarchaeology 6, 297
socialization 221–224; power of early socialization 223–224
soil 56, 57, 122
Sorbonne, the 19, 20
sorting folds 282, 284–285, 285–288, 290, 291
South Africa 333–346
South Yachats State Park, Oregon 70
Southwest Asia 251–270
spatial ecology 361
spatial isotope palaeoethology and palaeoecology framework 360–361
spatial networks 275–278, 288–290
species communities 183–197
species memory 20–24
stable isotope analysis 355–356; of oysters 163; strontium isotope analysis *see* strontium isotope analysis
standardization schemes for livestock 172
Stiner, M.C. 316
stone construction, permanent 187
stones as grave markers 125

Streptococcus mutans 238, 242
strontium isotope analysis: ostrich eggshells 336–337, 337–343; prey species movements and migrations 356–361
subsistence systems 50
Suðurafrétt 276–277
sugar 241–242
Summerfield, J.N. 118
swans 296
symbiosis 2, 216; symbiotic architectures 105–117
symmetry 164
synanthropic species 106–110

Taos Pueblo 134, 135–136
taphonomy 236
taskscape 289–290
tattoos of horses 296
tax, sheep 284
teeth: ancient DNA analysis of dental calculus 236–237; intra-tooth strontium isotope analysis 356–361; mammoths 16, 17
Tel Anafa 184, 193
temperature: global temperature oscillations 203–204; sea surface temperature (SST) 67, 71, 75, 76, 77, 79
Temple of Isis at Pompeii 14
temporal networks 279–283, 288–290
Ten Thousand Islands region 161
territorializations 274–275
Texas Cattle City 29, 34–38, 38–39
Thatcham sites, Britain 298–306
Thompson, V.D. 156
tide 90
Tito, R.Y. 236
Tolowa people 78
tortoises 260, 262
traditional lifestyles 234
traditions 164–165
transformation 265; seasonal roundup 285–288
transport 241–242
trapping 302–303, 355
trees 125, 126; citrus trees 31–34, 38; forest in Remote Oceania 54–55, 56, 57, 60
trust 216–217, 221–224
Trzciel cemetery, Poland 122, 127
Tsing, A. 225
tuberculosis (TB) 179, 238, 239
turf buildings 105–117; ecologies 110–113; and symbiosis 113–115; and synanthropic species 106–110

umbo-thickness and width method for mussel shell size 72, 73
upwelling, marine 77
urban herding 29, 34–38, 38–39
urban revolution 1, 26, 27

urbanism: Jordan Valley 183–197; Roman antiquity 170–182
urbanization 177
Ute rock art 141–142
'Uyun al-Hammam 257, 261–262

vaccines 243
varieties, animal 172–173
vegetation 3–4; managing stress on from overgrazing 280; *see also* plants, trees
Vela Špilja 310, 311, 318, 319–320, 321–322, 323–325, 326
Vesuvius 13, 22
virtual cemeteries 127
vitalism 115
volcanism 13, 21, 22, 23

Walker, K.J. 162
Warinner, C. 237
waste management 178
watchdog 13, 22, 23
water: cemeteries' pollution of groundwater 124–125; pollution in the Argive Plain 33; rock art 147, 148; turf building 111–112, 113
water court 158, 161–162

wavy lines rock art 139, 140, 141
weaving 258
Western art 134
whooper swans 296
wild animals: game animals 184, 186–187, 188–191; Roman cities 173–174, 180
wild boar: Mesolithic rhythms 299–301, 301–302, 303–305, 305–306; seasonal mobility and multispecies interactions 314, 319–321, 321–323, 326
wildcats 299–301, 302–303, 304, 305, 306
wildland burning 352–353
within-assemblage diversity 188–189, 193–194
Wolfe, C. 14
wolves 206–208
wood mice 178
woodland cemeteries 119, 125–126, 128, 129
wool 192; textiles 223
Worth, J. 156
wrack zone 88, 92

Yellowstone National Park 357
York 178

zooarchaeology 3; social zooarchaeology 6, 297